Organizational Productivity and Performance Measurements Using Predictive Modeling and Analytics

Madjid Tavana
La Salle University, USA

Kathryn Szabat
La Salle University, USA

Kartikeya Puranam
La Salle University, USA

A volume in the Advances in Business Information Systems and Analytics (ABISA) Book Series

www.igi-global.com

Published in the United States of America by
IGI Global
Business Science Reference (an imprint of IGI Global)
701 E. Chocolate Avenue
Hershey PA, USA 17033
Tel: 717-533-8845
Fax: 717-533-8661
E-mail: cust@igi-global.com
Web site: http://www.igi-global.com

Copyright © 2017 by IGI Global. All rights reserved. No part of this publication may be reproduced, stored or distributed in any form or by any means, electronic or mechanical, including photocopying, without written permission from the publisher. Product or company names used in this set are for identification purposes only. Inclusion of the names of the products or companies does not indicate a claim of ownership by IGI Global of the trademark or registered trademark.

Library of Congress Cataloging-in-Publication Data

Names: Tavana, Madjid, 1957- editor. | Szabat, Kathryn A., editor. | Puranam,
 Kartikeya, 1981- editor.
Title: Organizational productivity and performance measurements using
 predictive modeling and analytics / Madjid Tavana, Kathryn Szabat, and
 Kartikeya Puranam, editors.
Description: Hershey : Business Science Reference, 2016. | Series: Advances
 in business information systems and alanlytics | Includes bibliographical
 references and index.
Identifiers: LCCN 2016023674| ISBN 9781522506546 (hardcover) | ISBN
 9781522506553 (ebook)
Subjects: LCSH: Industrial productivity. | Organizational behavior. |
 Organizational effectiveness.
Classification: LCC HD56 .O73 2016 | DDC 338/.064011--dc23 LC record available at https://lccn.loc.gov/2016023674

This book is published in the IGI Global book series Advances in Business Information Systems and Analytics (ABISA) (ISSN: 2327-3275; eISSN: 2327-3283)

British Cataloguing in Publication Data
A Cataloguing in Publication record for this book is available from the British Library.

All work contributed to this book is new, previously-unpublished material. The views expressed in this book are those of the authors, but not necessarily of the publisher.

For electronic access to this publication, please contact: eresources@igi-global.com.

Advances in Business Information Systems and Analytics (ABISA) Book Series

Madjid Tavana
La Salle University, USA

ISSN: 2327-3275
EISSN: 2327-3283

Mission

The successful development and management of information systems and business analytics is crucial to the success of an organization. New technological developments and methods for data analysis have allowed organizations to not only improve their processes and allow for greater productivity, but have also provided businesses with a venue through which to cut costs, plan for the future, and maintain competitive advantage in the information age.

The **Advances in Business Information Systems and Analytics (ABISA) Book Series** aims to present diverse and timely research in the development, deployment, and management of business information systems and business analytics for continued organizational development and improved business value.

Coverage

- Business Systems Engineering
- Decision Support Systems
- Big Data
- Geo-BIS
- Data Strategy
- Business Intelligence
- Information Logistics
- Performance Metrics
- Business Models
- Algorithms

IGI Global is currently accepting manuscripts for publication within this series. To submit a proposal for a volume in this series, please contact our Acquisition Editors at Acquisitions@igi-global.com or visit: http://www.igi-global.com/publish/.

The Advances in Business Information Systems and Analytics (ABISA) Book Series (ISSN 2327-3275) is published by IGI Global, 701 E. Chocolate Avenue, Hershey, PA 17033-1240, USA, www.igi-global.com. This series is composed of titles available for purchase individually; each title is edited to be contextually exclusive from any other title within the series. For pricing and ordering information please visit http://www.igi-global.com/book-series/advances-business-information-systems-analytics/37155. Postmaster: Send all address changes to above address. Copyright © 2017 IGI Global. All rights, including translation in other languages reserved by the publisher. No part of this series may be reproduced or used in any form or by any means – graphics, electronic, or mechanical, including photocopying, recording, taping, or information and retrieval systems – without written permission from the publisher, except for non commercial, educational use, including classroom teaching purposes. The views expressed in this series are those of the authors, but not necessarily of IGI Global.

Titles in this Series

For a list of additional titles in this series, please visit: www.igi-global.com

Enterprise Big Data Engineering, Analytics, and Management
Martin Atzmueller (University of Kassel, Germany) Samia Oussena (University of West London, UK) and Thomas Roth-Berghofer (University of West London, UK)
Business Science Reference • copyright 2016 • 272pp • H/C (ISBN: 9781522502937) • US $205.00 (our price)

Automated Enterprise Systems for Maximizing Business Performance
Petraq Papajorgji (Canadian Institute of Technology, Albania) François Pinet (National Research Institute of Science and Technology for Environment and Agriculture, France) Alaine Margarete Guimarães (State University of Ponta Grossa, Brazil) and Jason Papathanasiou (University of Macedonia, Greece)
Business Science Reference • copyright 2016 • 312pp • H/C (ISBN: 9781466688414) • US $200.00 (our price)

Improving Organizational Effectiveness with Enterprise Information Systems
João Eduardo Varajão (University of Minho, Portugal) Maria Manuela Cruz-Cunha (Polytechnic Institute of Cávado and Ave, Portugal) and Ricardo Martinho (Polytechnic Institute of Leiria, Portugal & CINTESIS - Center for Research in Health Technologies and Information Systems, Portugal)
Business Science Reference • copyright 2015 • 318pp • H/C (ISBN: 9781466683686) • US $195.00 (our price)

Strategic Utilization of Information Systems in Small Business
M. Gordon Hunter (The University of Lethbridge, Canada)
Business Science Reference • copyright 2015 • 418pp • H/C (ISBN: 9781466687080) • US $195.00 (our price)

Enterprise Management Strategies in the Era of Cloud Computing
N. Raghavendra Rao (FINAIT Consultancy Services, India)
Business Science Reference • copyright 2015 • 359pp • H/C (ISBN: 9781466683396) • US $210.00 (our price)

Handbook of Research on Organizational Transformations through Big Data Analytics
Madjid Tavana (La Salle University, USA) and Kartikeya Puranam (La Salle University, USA)
Business Science Reference • copyright 2015 • 529pp • H/C (ISBN: 9781466672727) • US $245.00 (our price)

Business Technologies in Contemporary Organizations Adoption, Assimilation, and Institutionalization
Abrar Haider (University of South Australia, Australia)
Business Science Reference • copyright 2015 • 388pp • H/C (ISBN: 9781466666238) • US $205.00 (our price)

Business Transformation and Sustainability through Cloud System Implementation
Fawzy Soliman (University of Technology, Sydney, Australia)
Business Science Reference • copyright 2015 • 367pp • H/C (ISBN: 9781466664456) • US $200.00 (our price)

www.igi-global.com

701 E. Chocolate Ave., Hershey, PA 17033
Order online at www.igi-global.com or call 717-533-8845 x100
To place a standing order for titles released in this series, contact: cust@igi-global.com
Mon-Fri 8:00 am - 5:00 pm (est) or fax 24 hours a day 717-533-8661

Editorial Advisory Board

Brian S. Bourgeois, *Naval Research Laboratory – Stennis Space Center, USA*
Debora Di Caprio, *York University, Canada*
Ali Emrouznejad, *Aston University, UK*
Michael N. Katehakis, *Rutgers University, USA*
Briance Mascarenhas, *Rutgers University, USA*
Aidan O'Connor, *France Business School, France*
Mariya Sodenkamp, *University of Bamberg, Germany*
Thomas L. Saaty, *University of Pittsburgh, USA*
Francisco J. Santos-Arteaga, *Universidad Complutense de Madrid, Spain*
Leena Suhl, *University of Paderborn, Germany*

List of Reviewers

Hamid Alinejad-Rokny, *University of Newcastle, Australia*
Mahyar A. Amouzegar, *California State University – Long Beach, USA*
Mostafa K. Ardakani, *State University of New York – Farmingdale, USA*
Hossein Arsham, *University of Baltimore, USA*
Richard Baker, *Adelphi University, USA*
Kakoli Bandyopadhyay, *Lamar University, USA*
Sudip Bhattacharjee, *University of Connecticut, USA*
Indranil Bose, *University of Hong Kong, Hong Kong*
David Brown, *University of Lancaster, UK*
Janice Burn, *Edith Cowan University – Joondalup Campus, Australia*
Timothy E. Busch, *Air Force Research Laboratory, USA*
Christer Carlsson, *Abo Akademi University, Finland*
Byeong-Whan Chang, *Okayama Gakuin University, Japan*
France Cheong, *RMIT University, Australia*
Marco Cococcioni, *University of Pisa, Italy*
Rodger D. Collons, *Drexel University, USA*
John Davies, *Victoria University of Wellington, New Zealand*
John Eatman, *University of North Carolina – Greensboro, USA*

Ali Ebrahimnejad, *Islamic Azad University – Qaemshahr Branch, Iran*
John Erickson, *University of Nebraska – Omaha, USA*
Jerry Fjermestad, *New Jersey Institute of Technology, USA*
Amir H. Ghapanchi, *Griffith University, Australia*
Salvo Greco, *University of Catania, Italy*
Jatinder N.D. Gupta, *University of Alabama – Huntsville, USA*
Rassule Hadidi, *University of Illinois – Springfield, USA*
Payam Hanafizadeh, *Allameh Tabataba'i University, Iran*
Adel Hatami-Marbini, *Universite Catholique de Louvain, Belgium*
Jack C. Hayya, *Pennsylvania State University, USA*
Ira Horowitz, *University of Florida, USA*
Varghese S. Jacob, *University of Texas – Dallas, USA*
Kouroush Jenab, *Embry-Riddle Aeronautical University, USA*
Nathan L. Joseph, *Aston University, UK*
Corinne M. Karuppan, *Missouri State University, USA*
Kaveh Khalili-Damghani, *Islamic Azad University – South-Tehran Branch, Iran*
Ruth King, *University of Illinois – Urbana-Champaign, USA*
Rajiv Kishore, *State University of New York – Buffalo, USA*
Jean-Pierre Kuilboer, *University of Massachusetts – Boston, USA*
Uday Kulkarni, *Arizona State University, USA*
Matthew Kuofie, *Illinois State University, USA*
Gilbert Laporte, *HEC Montreal, Canada*
Kenneth D. Lawrence, *New Jersey Institute of Technology, USA*
Nigel Lockett, *Lancaster University, UK*
Peter Loos, *University of Saarland, Germany*
Christian N. Madu, *Pace University, USA*
Davinder K. Malhotra, *Philadelphia University, USA*
Efrem Mallach, *University of Massachusetts – Dartmouth, USA*
Vicky Manthou, *University of Macedonia, Greece*
Ronald McGaughey, *University of Central Arkansas, USA*
John Militello, *University of St. Thomas, USA*
Deependra Moitra, *Infosys Technologies Limited, India*
Luvai F. Motiwalla, *University of Massachusetts – Lowell, USA*
Karen Neville, *University College, Ireland*
Shan L. Pan, *National University of Singapore, Singapore*
Fariborz Y. Partovi, *Drexel University, USA*
Goran D. Putnik, *University of Minho - Campus of Azurem, Portugal*
Colette Rolland, *Universite Paris 1 Pantheon Sorbonne, France*
Nicholas C. Romano Jr., *Oklahoma State University, USA*
Mohammed Saad, *Bristol Business School – Frenchay Campus, UK*
Mujgan Sagir, *Eskisehir Osmangazi University, Turkey*
Joseph Sarkis, *Clark University, USA*
Vijay Shah, *West Virginia University – Parkersburg, USA*
Bala Shetty, *Texas A&M University, USA*

Phoebe Sharkey, *Loyola College in Maryland, USA*
Sivakumar, *Lehigh University, USA*
Douglas Smith, *University of Missouri – St. Louis, USA*
Sridharan, *Clemson University, USA*
Kathryn E. Stecke, *University of Texas – Dallas, USA*
Glenn Stewart, *Queensland University of Technology, Australia*
Girish Subramanian, *Pennsylvania State University – Harrisburg, USA*
Minghe Sun, *University of Texas – San Antonio, USA*
Sundarraj, *University of Waterloo, Canada*
Srinivas Talluri, *Michigan State University, USA*
Jeffrey E. Teich, *New Mexico State University, USA*
Marvin D. Troutt, *Kent State University, USA*
Gregory Ulferts, *University of Detroit Mercy, USA*
Dirk VandenPoel, *Ghent University, Belgium*
Theo M.M. Verhallen, *Tilburg University, The Netherlands*
Liisa von Hellens, *Griffith University – Nathan Campus, Australia*
Edward Watson, *Louisiana State University, USA*
John G. Wilson, *University of Western Ontario, Canada*
Mohamed A. Youssef, *Norfolk State University, USA*
Peter Zhang, *Georgia State University, USA*

Table of Contents

Preface xviii

Chapter 1
Predictive Analytics for Infrastructure Performance 1
  Sue McNeil, University of Delaware, USA
  Susanne Trimbath, STP Advisory Services, LLC, USA
  Farzana Atique, University of Delaware, USA
  Ryan Burke, U.S. Air Force Academy, USA

Chapter 2
Structural Equation Modeling Algorithm and Its Application in Business Analytics 17
  Shahryar Sorooshian, Universiti Malaysia Pahang, Malaysia

Chapter 3
An Integrated Fuzzy VIKOR Method for Performance Management in Healthcare 40
  Ehsan Shekarian, University of Malaya, Malaysia
  Salwa Hanim Abdul-Rashid, University of Malaya, Malaysia
  Ezutah Udoncy Olugu, UCSI University, Malaysia

Chapter 4
An Analytical Algorithm for Delphi Method for Consensus Building and Organizational
Productivity 62
  Abd Hamid Zahidy, Universiti Malaysia Pahang, Malaysia
  Noor Azlinna Azizan, Universiti Malaysia Pahang, Malaysia
  Shahryar Sorooshian, Universiti Malaysia Pahang, Malaysia

Chapter 5
New Product Development and Manufacturability Techniques and Analytics 80
  Alan D. Smith, Robert Morris University, USA

Chapter 6
Transformation of CRM and Supply Chain Management Techniques in a New Venture 96
  Amber A. Ditizio, Texas Woman's University, USA
  Alan D. Smith, Robert Morris University, USA

Chapter 7
A Hybrid AHP-ELECTRE I Multicriteria Model for Performance Assessment and Team Selection 115
    Ikram Khatrouch, University of Lyon, France & University of Saint Etienne, France
    Lyes Kermad, University of Paris 8, France
    Abderrahman el Mhamedi, University of Paris 8, France
    Younes Boujelbene, University of Sfax, Tunisia

Chapter 8
Predictive Modeling as guide for Health Informatics Deployment 128
    Fabrizio L. Ricci, Italian National Research Council, Italy
    Oscar Tamburis, University of Naples Federico II, Italy

Chapter 9
Analytics Overuse in Advertising and Promotion Budget Forecasting 163
    Burçin Güçlü, Universitat Ramon LLull, Spain
    Miguel-Ángel Canela, University of Navarra, Spain

Chapter 10
Mastering Business Process Management and Business Intelligence in Global Business 192
    Kijpokin Kasemsap, Suan Sunandha Rajabhat University, Thailand

Chapter 11
Information and Communication Technology Impact on Supply Chain Integration, Flexibility, and Performance 213
    Carlos A Talamantes-Padilla, Universidad Autónoma de Ciudad Juárez, Mexico
    Jorge Luis. García-Alcaráz, Universidad Autónoma de Ciudad Juárez, Mexico
    Aide A. Maldonado-Macías, Universidad Autónoma de Ciudad Juárez, Mexico
    Giner Alor-Hernández, Instituto Tecnologico de Orizaba, Mexico
    Cuauhtemoc Sánchéz-Ramírez, Instituto Tecnológico de Orizaba, Mexico
    Juan L Hernández-Arellano, Universidad Autónoma de Ciudad Juárez, Mexico

Chapter 12
A Causal Analytic Model for Labour Productivity Assessment 235
    Manoj Kumar, International Engineering Services, India
    Jyoti Singh, International Engineering Services, India
    Priya Singh, International Engineering Services, India

Chapter 13
Effective Tools for Improving Employee Feedback during Organizational Change 261
    Tanja Sedej, Graduate School of Government and European Studies, Slovenia
    Gorazd Justinek, Graduate School of Government and European Studies, Slovenia

Chapter 14
A Conceptual and Pragmatic Review of Regression Analysis for Predictive Analytics 277
    Sema A. Kalaian, Eastern Michigan University, USA
    Rafa M. Kasim, Indiana Tech University, USA
    Nabeel R. Kasim, University of Michigan, USA

Chapter 15
Student Retention Performance Using Absorbing Markov Chains 293
    Dennis M. Crossen, La Salle University, USA

Chapter 16
An Analytical Employee Performance Evaluation Approach in Office Automation and
Information Systems 324
    Maryam Kalhori, University of Science and Culture, Iran
    Mohammad Javad Kargar, University of Science and Culture, Iran

Compilation of References 344

About the Contributors 388

Index 397

Detailed Table of Contents

Preface xviii

Chapter 1
Predictive Analytics for Infrastructure Performance 1
    Sue McNeil, University of Delaware, USA
    Susanne Trimbath, STP Advisory Services, LLC, USA
    Farzana Atique, University of Delaware, USA
    Ryan Burke, U.S. Air Force Academy, USA

A predictive analysis methodology was designed for application to the Transportation Performance Index, which was first released in September 2010 through the U.S. Chamber of Commerce to benchmark and measure changes in the performance of US infrastructure over time. This article starts with a summary of the development and use of the Index in order to present the performance indicators that were the foundation of the predictive analysis. A new methodology was developed to generate prospective values for the Index by applying elements of the improvement plans from US Metropolitan Planning Organizations (MPOs) that paralleled the performance indicators used in the Index. The results show that over a 24 year period (2011 to 2035) the plans developed by MPOs can slow the decline in infrastructure over a baseline scenario. In addition to forecasting changes in the performance of the infrastructure that undergirds all economic activity, the results serve to further validate the Index as a methodology that captures important performance functions of transportation infrastructure. The original purpose of the Index was to capture trends, making it well-suited to the application of predictive analysis.

Chapter 2
Structural Equation Modeling Algorithm and Its Application in Business Analytics......................... 17
    Shahryar Sorooshian, Universiti Malaysia Pahang, Malaysia

Structural Equation Modeling (SEM) is a statistical-based multivariate modeling methods. Application of SEM is similar but more powerful than regression analysis; and number of scientists using SEM in their research is rapidly increasing. This review article algorithmically discusses the SEM methodology. SEM strategies, SEM steps and SEM stages are introduced in this article; validity tests are presented as well. Novelty of this article is in modified steps of SEM application in modeling strategies, also in its developed practical comprehensive SEM application flowchart. This article is a roadmap for business advisors and those scholars trying to compute SEM for their decision making, complex modeling and data analysis programming.

Chapter 3
An Integrated Fuzzy VIKOR Method for Performance Management in Healthcare 40
Ehsan Shekarian, University of Malaya, Malaysia
Salwa Hanim Abdul-Rashid, University of Malaya, Malaysia
Ezutah Udoncy Olugu, UCSI University, Malaysia

Poor quality control has become a major threat to medical laboratory services, especially in the developing countries. It has become necessary to assess and rank the quality of diagnostic services in medical laboratories using systematic approaches. The main aim of this research is to develop and apply a quantitative method in ranking medical laboratory services. This method is based on a combination of Vlsekriterijumska Optimizacija I Kompromisno Resenje (VIKOR) with fuzzy set theory. VIKOR is a multiple criteria decision making technique which focuses on ranking and selection from a set of alternatives, and determines the compromise solution for a problem with different criteria. This approach aids decision makers to achieve the most acceptable decision amidst numerous alternatives. In the present evaluation method, international standard ISO 15189 (Medical Laboratories Particular Requirements for Quality and Competence) proposed by International Organization for Standardization (ISO) is used as a fundamental source of selected attributes of a medical laboratory. The study compares three medical laboratories to each other and ranks them. This study will be a valuable and effective contribution in enhancing both qualitative and quantitative criteria in the field of medical laboratory services. Finally, some directions for further studies are proposed.

Chapter 4
An Analytical Algorithm for Delphi Method for Consensus Building and Organizational
Productivity.. 62
Abd Hamid Zahidy, Universiti Malaysia Pahang, Malaysia
Noor Azlinna Azizan, Universiti Malaysia Pahang, Malaysia
Shahryar Sorooshian, Universiti Malaysia Pahang, Malaysia

The Delphi technique is being increasingly used in many complex areas where a consensus is to be reached. In such an environment, the Delphi technique allows researchers to acquire high quality, unbiased information from a panel of certified experts. Despite its vast uses, the Delphi method has seen a lack of consistent procedural guidance for its application. A review of literature revealed a significant variation in methodological approach of the method. The purpose of this paper is to develop a practical algorithm for the Delphi study application based on the literature review and the authors' practiced experiences. A few modifications are suggested to make the Delphi study more practical in research and decision making. Using the guidelines provided by this paper, it is expected that the reader may better understand the appropriate application and procedure of the modified Delphi process.

Chapter 5
New Product Development and Manufacturability Techniques and Analytics...................................80
Alan D. Smith, Robert Morris University, USA

The following case study evaluates the New Product Development (NPD) techniques utilized by Forest City Technologies, Incorporated (FCT). Through insight gathered via interviews conducted with the company's product development and materials purchasing management teams, and supported by literature, this study attempts to show how Forest City Technologies, Inc. integrates specific components into its product development process to: 1. Meet its NPD goals, and 2. Achieve better supplier and customer relationships. This study focuses on the components of: NPD models employed by FCT, early customer and supplier involvement, NPD-innovation integration techniques, demand change factors during the NPD process, and risk-mitigation strategies implemented by FCT during the NPD process. The study is segmented into three main sections: Introduction to NPD and FCT, the components of FCTs new product development process, and NPD implications on FCTs supplier and customer relationships.

Chapter 6
Transformation of CRM and Supply Chain Management Techniques in a New Venture 96
    Amber A. Ditizio, Texas Woman's University, USA
    Alan D. Smith, Robert Morris University, USA

The implementations of successful Customer Relationship Management (CRM) and Supply Chain Management (SCM) systems and their associated techniques in order to optimize the analytics available in any organization are daunting task, especially in a new business venture. Upper management must to be committed to focusing these embedded systems in order to enhance supplier integration and customer satisfaction. This chapter focuses on the implementation of CRM systems and analytics as well as SCM considerations in the new startup of the Hard Rock Rocksino at Northfield Park (HRRNP) and the transformation/refinement of their systems over their few years of business. A combination of literature research, interviews of upper management, and personal observations, HRRNP has illustrate their ability to deal with these challenges in a continuous improvement and lean management approach.

Chapter 7
A Hybrid AHP-ELECTRE I Multicriteria Model for Performance Assessment and Team
Selection 115
    Ikram Khatrouch, University of Lyon, France & University of Saint Etienne, France
    Lyes Kermad, University of Paris 8, France
    Abderrahman el Mhamedi, University of Paris 8, France
    Younes Boujelbene, University of Sfax, Tunisia

Human resources management is essential to any health care system. This paper proposes an assessment model to help the decision maker in the selection of an optimal team. In the proposed model, AHP method is applied to identify the weights of each criterion in the decision model. ELECTRE I method is used to obtain the best team that satisfies most of the decision maker preferences. We test the effectiveness of the model on the real data collected from the 'Habib Bourguiba' Hospital in Tunisia.

Chapter 8
Predictive Modeling as guide for Health Informatics Deployment 128
    Fabrizio L. Ricci, Italian National Research Council, Italy
    Oscar Tamburis, University of Naples Federico II, Italy

The present research work shows the main steps conducted towards the exploitation of the LUMIR project, aiming at realizing an EHR framework in the Italian Region of Basilicata (also known as Lucania). It relates to a structure of network–enabled services capable of integrating the ICT solutions used by the operators of the Healthcare System of Basilicata Region. The adoption process of the LuMiR system was meant to address the issues connected to the design features as well as to the EHR diffusion and the acceptance aspects. The mathematical modeling approach introduced aimed at making possible to get to a measure "ex–ante" of both adequacy and significance of the adoption process itself. The final intent is to work out a scalable and exportable model of advanced management of clinical information, towards a stronger cooperation among the provider organizations and a better governance of care processes, as crucial element within the more general path of modernization of the healthcare sector.

Chapter 9
Analytics Overuse in Advertising and Promotion Budget Forecasting 163
    Burçin Güçlü, Universitat Ramon LLull, Spain
    Miguel-Ángel Canela, University of Navarra, Spain

Several studies have recently raised a common concern in the field of management, which is the overspending in marketing activities. In this paper, we propose and empirically test that overspending in marketing investments is an unfortunate outcome of information overload, in a sense that managers who confront too many risk informants in their decision environment tend to overinvest in marketing activities due to the overemphasis on the environmental risk. In a longitudinal experiment, where we manipulated the amount of information through marketing analytics, we demonstrate that firms employing simple marketing analytics are less prone to increase their marketing expenditures due to the fear of losing customers, and have a lower expectancy that their competitors will increase their brand-level advertising and promotional expenditures, compared to firms using a combination of simple and complex marketing analytics. Moreover, we demonstrate that firms employing simple marketing analytics keep their overall marketing spending at a lower level, and spend less in brand-level marketing, especially in promotional activities, compared to when using a combination of simple and complex marketing analytics.

Chapter 10
Mastering Business Process Management and Business Intelligence in Global Business 192
    Kijpokin Kasemsap, Suan Sunandha Rajabhat University, Thailand

This chapter describes the overviews of Business Process Management (BPM) and Business Intelligence (BI); the importance of BPM in global business; and the importance of BI in global business. BPM enables organizations to align business functions with customer needs and helps executives determine how to deploy, monitor, and measure the organizational resources. When properly executed, BPM has the ability to enhance productivity, reduce costs, and minimize risk in global business. BI includes the applications, tools, and best practices that enable the analysis of information to improve organizational performance. Companies use BI to detect the significant events and identify the business trends in order to quickly adapt to their changing business environment. The chapter argues that applying BPM and BI has the potential to enhance organizational performance and reach strategic goals in global business.

Chapter 11
Information and Communication Technology Impact on Supply Chain Integration, Flexibility, and Performance 213
    Carlos A Talamantes-Padilla, Universidad Autónoma de Ciudad Juárez, Mexico
    Jorge Luis. García-Alcaráz, Universidad Autónoma de Ciudad Juárez, Mexico
    Aide A. Maldonado-Macías, Universidad Autónoma de Ciudad Juárez, Mexico
    Giner Alor-Hernández, Instituto Tecnologico de Orizaba, Mexico
    Cuauhtemoc Sánchéz-Ramírez, Instituto Tecnológico de Orizaba, Mexico
    Juan L Hernández-Arellano, Universidad Autónoma de Ciudad Juárez, Mexico

In this chapter, four latent variables will be analyzed to measure the impact of Information and Communications Technology (ICT) on the integration, flexibility and performance of Supply Chain (SC). The aim of the exposition is to provide greater understanding for those responsible of the supply chain, and focus efforts on clear objectives. These clear objectives should help those responsible for the supply chain achieve a better performance within organizations. The information analyzed was obtained from a questionnaire provided to 284 managers in companies located in Ciudad Juarez, Mexico. The results were used to generate a structural equation model in order to learn the relationships between variables. We have postulated six hypotheses regarding the direct, indirect and total effects. The results indicate that there is no direct relationship between ICT integration and SC performance, but an indirect relationship through mediating variables as SC Integration and Flexibility exists.

Chapter 12
A Causal Analytic Model for Labour Productivity Assessment 235
    Manoj Kumar, International Engineering Services, India
    Jyoti Singh, International Engineering Services, India
    Priya Singh, International Engineering Services, India

The Indian government and those of the devolved administrations have adopted a policy framework for boosting regional productivity based on five drivers: Investment, Skills, Innovation, Entrepreneurship, and Competition. We modelled the relationships between the five drivers and labour productivity using a structural equation model that fitted the data well. The main conclusion is that promoting entrepreneurship, spending more on research and development, increasing the capital-worker ratio and the percentage of the workforce with higher qualifications has a significant bearing upon regional labour productivity. In contrast, regulatory barriers to competition do not seem to affect labour productivity at a regional level.

Chapter 13
Effective Tools for Improving Employee Feedback during Organizational Change 261
    Tanja Sedej, Graduate School of Government and European Studies, Slovenia
    Gorazd Justinek, Graduate School of Government and European Studies, Slovenia

Feedback is the fastest and most effective way for organizations to make improvements or get things back on track. Prompt and constructive feedback is strongly linked to employee satisfaction and productivity, and can increase both. During times of change when employees want to be heard and feel involved, it is even more important that the optimal internal communication tools for managing employee feedback are selected. This article tackles these questions and provides fresh empirical data on the selection of internal communication tools in general, with focus then devoted to managing feedback during change from the perspective of a professional communicator. The data evaluated and analyzed was gathered on the basis of research carried out in 2014 among 105 professional communicators of large and medium-sized companies, and was then compared with the results of similar research conducted in 2012.

Chapter 14
A Conceptual and Pragmatic Review of Regression Analysis for Predictive Analytics 277
    Sema A. Kalaian, Eastern Michigan University, USA
    Rafa M. Kasim, Indiana Tech University, USA
    Nabeel R. Kasim, University of Michigan, USA

Regression analysis and modeling are powerful predictive analytical tools for knowledge discovery through examining and capturing the complex hidden relationships and patterns among the quantitative variables. Regression analysis is widely used to: (a) collect massive amounts of organizational performance data such as Web server logs and sales transactions. Such data is referred to as "Big Data"; and (b) improve transformation of massive data into intelligent information (knowledge) by discovering trends and patterns in unknown hidden relationships. The intelligent information can then be used to make informed data-based predictions of future organizational outcomes such as organizational productivity and performance using predictive analytics such as regression analysis methods. The main purpose of this chapter is to present a conceptual and practical overview of simple- and multiple- linear regression analyses.

Chapter 15
Student Retention Performance Using Absorbing Markov Chains.. 293
   Dennis M. Crossen, La Salle University, USA

Performance models are well established in the literature. More specifically, student performance has been of growing concern at all levels. To confront the challenges, researchers have collected data, monitored performance criterion, developed quantitative models, and analyzed patterns to formulate theories and adaptive measures. At the university level, many students' performance deficiencies are keenly noticed and actualized for a variety of reasons. Some reasons may include transition from a home-reporting educational environment to an autonomous setting; lack of a friendly support system; or a host of behavioral circumstances which exacerbate latent academic deficits. One such technique for reviewing student performance can be employed and analyzed using absorbing Markov chains. The use of Markov Chains can provide quantitative information such the characterization potential delays (latency points) within and throughout the system, prediction of probabilistic metrics which define transitions between each stage of a defined state, and adaptability options for enrollment outcomes for use by school administrators. Furthermore, Markov chains can be employed to determine the impact on system resources such as limitations in faculty schedules, classroom assignments, and technology availability. Managers, administrators and advisors may find this information useful when notified of such limitations. This paper is of value to a broad audience such as researchers, managers, and administrators since it augments standard approaches of the Markov model. The blend of stochastic mathematics, applications of stochastic methods and retention theory, as well as the inclusion of adaptive sensitivity analysis are effective performance measures. Therefore, applications in Markov chains and subsequent forecasting models are of contemporary values in educational performance. Each of these concepts and methods contribute to a broader consideration of Markov properties in a branch of mathematics known as Markov Decision Processes (MDP). These types of processes allow researchers the ability to adjust parameters based on rewards, sets of actions, and discount factors. The cases outlined in this paper may be helpful when considering reductions in recidivism rates, improving policies to diminish recidivism, and increasing enrollment options using Markov analysis.

Chapter 16
An Analytical Employee Performance Evaluation Approach in Office Automation and
Information Systems 324
   Maryam Kalhori, University of Science and Culture, Iran
   Mohammad Javad Kargar, University of Science and Culture, Iran

With the extension of information technology, human resource management has experienced fundamental changes. One of the most important issues in human resource management is performance evaluation. Unlike number of studies in employee performance evaluation, there is a lack for systematic and quantitative approaches. Issues such as incomplete information, subjective and qualitative metrics, and also the difficulty of evaluating the performance are the main problems of this field. Hence, the current study exploits the capabilities of information systems and presents an approach for quantitative and automatic evaluation of employee performance in office automation systems. The results reveal the automatic employee performance evaluation system is a discrete dimension for employee performance evaluation systems.

Compilation of References 344

About the Contributors 388

Index 397

Preface

Organizational productivity is determined by a range of factors. Some of these factors can be evaluated quantitatively, while other factors may require a more qualitative, analytical approach. It is critical to understand key drivers that impact productivity when assessing organizational productivity, as well as how to effectively assess those key drivers' contributions to overall productivity. Productivity enhances organizational performance by becoming more efficient in specific areas. Organizational performance refers to how well an organization is doing to reach its vision, mission, and goals. Measuring performance is a vital part of assessing organizational resources and activities. Performance measurement involves collection of data to assess whether correct business processes are being performed and whether desired organizational outcomes are being achieved. Measuring performance can help an organization analyze where and what changes need to be made in order to improve performance. Performance measurement can analyze an individual, a work group, a program or an organization's efforts; the focus can concern maintenance, improvement, and development goals; measures can be quantitative or qualitative.

Businesses are collecting massive amounts of data every day. These data can be used to increase organization productivity and performance. One method of achieving this is by using predictive analytics. Analytics, in general, is the use of skills, technologies, and practices to explore and investigate past performance, gain insight, and drive business decision making; analytics help decision makers determine risk, weigh outcomes, and quantify costs and benefits associated with decisions (Boundless Management, 2015). Predictive analytics is defined as the set of tools, such as predictive modeling, that can be used to predict trends and behavior patterns in data; it can be used to inform and evaluate alternatives during decision making and explain outcomes. Predictive modeling techniques include linear and logistic regression, clustering, association rules, structural equation modeling, decision trees, neural networks, and support vector machines. There are many ways in which organizations can leverage predictive modeling and analytics to improve productivity and performance. It includes collecting appropriate data, measuring productivity and performance on an ongoing basis, learning from the productivity and performance measures and then closing the loop by implementing new ideas.

The quality of information in any organizational productivity or performance decision situation can range from scientifically-derived hard data to subjective interpretations, from certainty about decision outcomes to uncertain outcomes represented by probabilities and fuzzy numbers. This diversity in type and quality of information about a decision problem requires methods and techniques that can assist in information processing and ultimately may lead to better decisions. Multi-criteria decision analysis is a method for decision structuring that permits the use of both quantitative and qualitative data sources with high uncertainty or subjectivity; it improves ad hoc decision criteria and policy alternatives that

Preface

may be chosen by the decision maker. In the multi-criteria decision making context, the selection of a "good choice" from a number of available choices is facilitated by evaluating each choice on a set of criteria. The criteria and their outcomes must be measurable for every decision alternative. Multi-criteria decision making techniques include Analytic Hierarchy Process, Delphi Method, Fuzzy Set Theory, VIKOR, and ELECTRE. Approaches that combine available quantitative data with the more subjective knowledge of experts are desirable; these approaches can provide the decision maker with the ability to look into the future, and to make the best possible decision past on past and present information and future predictions (International Society on Multiple Criteria Decision Making). This book is a collection of 16 chapters on predictive modeling and multi-criteria analytical approaches to organizational productivity and performance measurements.

In their chapter entitled "Predictive Analytics for Infrastructure Performance," McNeil, Trimbath, Atique, and Burke present a methodology to generate prospective values for the Transportation Performance Index (TPI) by applying elements of the improvement plans from US metropolitan organizations (MPOs). It starts with a summary of the development and use of the Transportation Performance Index, which is generated from publicly available data. The Index was designed to bring a rigorous, quantitative, and repeatable methodology to the assessment of infrastructure performance. Transportation performance indicators that serve as the building blocks for the TPI are presented and the technical specifications used to calculate the TPI are given.

In order to demonstrate the role of the TPI in capturing changes in infrastructure performance and influencing transportation policy, a prospective analysis, looking at the impact of investment based on the long range transportation plans (LRTP) of the Metropolitan Planning Organizations (MPOs), is conducted. The analysis provides a better understanding of the impact of specific investments or policies on the TPI and insight into the portfolio of projects that are required to continue to improve the performance of transportation as measured by the TPI. The predictive scenario analysis process applied to a sample of Metropolitan Statistical Areas (MSAs) was outlined in detail and illustrated for the Baltimore- Towson MSA.

The overall results show that over a 24 year period, the plans developed by MPOs can slow the decline in infrastructure over a baseline scenario; the results also serve to further validate the Index that captures important performance functions of transportation infrastructure. The benefit of this chapter is the understanding of the use of a predictive analysis methodology to capture trends and validate a methodology for capturing performance functions.

In his chapter entitled "Structural Equation Modeling Algorithm and its Application in Business Analytics," Sorooshian presents a roadmap for business advisors and scholars using Structural Equation Modeling (SEM) for decision making, complex modeling, and data analysis programming. It starts with an extensive overview of SEM, highlighting three different approaches or modeling strategies: confirmatory modeling strategy, competing model strategy, and model development strategy and two SEM estimation methods: covariance-based SEM (CB-SEM), which is a confirmatory approach, and variance-based partial least squares (PLS-SEM), which is a prediction-oriented approach. The chapter presents a practical flowchart covering all three modeling strategies of CB-SEM, especially model development strategy; in the model development strategy, a model is proposed and empirically tested while gaining insight into its re-specifications. A SEM application flowchart is presented, together with details and justifications of each stage and sub-stage of the SEM process.

The SEM application flowchart presents a modification of five stages (model specification, model identification, model estimation, model testing and evaluation, and model modification or re-specification) common to the conventional SEM process. The modification provided by the chapter adds a data collection stage as a prerequisite for the model identification stage, and a report writing stage to finalize the SEM analysis and practices. This improvement to the SEM process allows for use of analytic devices to analyze causal complex models. The benefit of this chapter is that it provides a roadmap for business advisors in their efforts to use SEM for decision support in which the addition of more complex business analytics can be considered.

In their chapter entitled "An Integrated Fuzzy VIKOR Method for Performance Management in Healthcare," Shekarian, Abdul-Rashid, and Olugu provide a ranking solution for medical laboratories using fuzzy theory. It starts with a literature review, highlighting the application of the MCDM method and fuzzy set theory in health care systems. A brief explanation of fuzzy set theory basic concepts is then presented, followed by an overview of VIKOR method details. Fuzzy set theory is an appropriate tool to quantitatively represent and manipulate imprecision in decision making problems; the multicriteria decision making method, VIKOR, aids the decision maker in ranking a number of alternatives by examining their performance scores in the presence of a set of conflicting criteria.

The proposed method for medical laboratory ranking, which combines fuzzy set theory and VIKOR, is explained as a six-step process. A case study, which aims to choose the best medical laboratory among three candidate laboratories based on the ISO 15189: 2003 medical laboratory requirements for quality and competence, is then illustrated to showcase the effectiveness and efficiency of the proposed model. This case study proposes to be a valuable and effective contribution in enhancing both qualitative and quantitative criteria in the field of medical laboratory services. The benefit of this chapter is that it provides a ranking solution for medical laboratories that ensures redefinition of competition towards offering better clinical laboratory services; this, in turn, will boost the quality of health care services, in general.

In their chapter entitled "An Analytical Algorithm for Delphi Method for Consensus Building and Organizational Productivity," Zahidy, Azizan, and Sorooshian present a practical algorithm for the application of the Delphi method. It starts with a literature review of the Delphi Method, highlighting its origin and use in many complex areas where a consensus is to be reached. The Delphi Method is described as utilizing an iterative feedback technique with a group of experts; several rounds of intensive questionnaires are used to generate a series of qualitative and quantitative data for analysis. The ultimate goal of the Delphi technique is to obtain as many high quality responses and opinions as possible on a given issue from a panel of experts to enhance decision making.

The chapter outlines a general structure of the Delphi process that can be applied in research and decision making. It then presents details of the various Delphi process procedures, suggesting modifications on some of those procedures based on continued literature review and the authors' practiced experiences in conducting a Delphi study. The extensive literature review threaded throughout the chapter identifies a lack of consistency and standard procedures for the Delphi method's application. The benefit of this chapter is its guidelines for better understanding of the philosophy behind the Delphi study, for appropriate application of the modified Delphi process, and for design of Delphi process procedures, namely, the questionnaire, pilot study, instrument reliability and validity, expert panelist selection, panel size, iteration size and consensus size.

In the chapter entitled "New Product Development and Manufacturability Techniques and Analytics," Smith presents a case study that evaluates new product development (NPD) techniques integrated

Preface

into a product development process by a service and manufacturer supplier to meet its NPD goals and achieve better supplier and customer relationships. It begins with an overview of the role of technology and analytical approaches in manufacturing, highlighting websites and scanning equipment, which not only provide a direct contact between the organization and its customers, but also present an opportunity for innovation in both the manufacturability and delivery/sell of products. New product development is then discussed in more detail. Effective new product development strategy is essential for the success of a service or manufacturing company but management techniques used to achieve successful product development results can vary from one company to another. It is for this reason that the author sets out to investigate the most effective set of tools and/or processes to efficiently transition from one product to another.

The author uses a qualitative business case study methodology to evaluate NPD techniques at Forest City Technologies, Incorporated (FCT), an international company involved in production within the R7D environment. The case study sets out to show how FCT integrates specific components into its product development process to meet its NPD goals and achieve better supplier and customer relationships, using insight gathered via interviews conducted with the company's product development and materials purchasing management. The benefit of this chapter is a thorough understanding of one company's NPD process and the strategies, techniques and component integration within its NPD process that lead to the positive outcomes attained by the company due to its success in achieving its new product goals.

In their chapter entitled "Transformation of CRM and Supply Chain Management Techniques in a New Venture," Ditizio and Smith present a case study of a new startup dealing with customer relationship management (CRM) embedded systems requirements and analytics and issues of supply chain management (SCM) performance dealing with issues of integration and collaboration for a new business venture. It starts with an overview of customer relationship management (CRM), highlighting its evolution, implementation, and benefits. CRM as a strategy aims to maintain long-term relationships with customers. An efficient CRM system is comprised of several modules with the analytic and operational CRM modules providing fundamental functions. The analytic module evaluates customer data and patterns of transaction for the improvement of customer relationships. Benefits are achieved through technology-enhanced CRM systems; patterns in consumer behavior can be detected, items can be tracked, customer experience can be enhanced; cross-selling and up-selling can be facilitated; sales forecasting can be improved, and customer loyalty can be strengthened. Technology-based CRM can help a company gain a competitive edge. It is for these reasons that the authors set out to examine the implementation of CRM systems and analytics as well as SCM considerations in the new startup of the Hard Rock Rocksino at Northfield (HRRNP).

The authors use a qualitative business case study approach to guide their exploration of HRRNP using a variety of data sources, namely, literature research, interviews with upper management, and personal observations. The case study starts out by demonstrating the success of management's commitment to full integration of the supply chain and operations management techniques. It then highlights the importance of CRM-related operations and analytics for attracting and creating value for the customer. The benefit of this chapter is a thorough understanding of one company's SCM and CRM strategic initiatives, and its ability to deal with challenges associated with the transformation/refinement of SCM and CRM systems in a continuous improvement and lean management approach.

In their chapter entitled "A Hybrid AHP-ELECTRE I Multicriteria Method for Performance Assessment and Team Selection," Khatrouch, Kermad, Mhamedi, and Boujelbene propose an evaluation model to help decision makers in a team selection problem. The model uses two Multi-criteria Decision Model (MCDM) methods: Analytical Hierarchy Process (AHP) and ELECTRE I. The chapter begins with a detailed description of AHP and ELECTRE I. AHP is a decision approach designed to solve complex multiple criteria problems involving qualitative decisions; the purpose is to determine the relative importance of a set of activities in the multi-criteria decision problem. ELECTRE I aims at reducing the size of the alternatives set in a multi-criteria problem, exploiting the dominance concept. A proposed model for team selection is then presented with a detailed explanation of the four stages of the model. The proposed model combines the two methods of MCDM, (AHP and ELECTRE I), in order to help the decision maker choose the best team. AHP is used to determine weights for each criteria and ELECTRE I is applied to evaluate the alternatives combining all criteria.

To assess the computational tractability and efficiency of the developed model, the model was tested on a set of data collected from the 'Habib Bourguiba' Hospital in Tunisia. The approach led to the determination of the best team with understanding of the outcomes presented in the form of a graph. The benefit of this chapter is the assessment model that it provides decision makers in the selection of an optimal team.

In their chapter entitled "Predictive Modelling and its Role in Effective Health Informatics Deployment," Ricci and Tamburis present the works they did for the LUMIR Project. This chapter introduced Longitudinal Electronic Healthcare Record (L-EHR) handled by the LuMiR system. They also discussed its implementation in the Basilicata Region of Italy. The primary goal of LuMiR is to build a system that can be accessed by all healthcare providers and their support staff including GPs, lab analysts, nurses, pharmacists, social workers, etc. They accomplish this by implementing a timely "infostructure." They also propose a mathematical model that deals with all the possible issues, both technical and political and can give possible optimal solutions.

In their chapter entitled "Analytics Overuse in Advertising and Promotion Budget Forecasting," Güçlü and Canela study the effect of information overload and its effect on marketing spending. They conduct a longitudinal experiment that shows that "firms employing simple marketing analytics are less prone to increase their marketing expenditures due to the fear of losing customers, and have a lower expectancy that their competitors will increase their brand-level advertising and promotional expenditures, compared to firms using a combination of simple and complex marketing analytics."

In the chapter entitled "Mastering Business Process Management and Business Intelligence in Global Business," Kasemsap describes the concepts of Business Process Management (BPM) and Business Intelligence (BI) and how they can be used to detect significant events and trends that a business faces and also to come up with strategies to adapt to them. The author describes how BPM and BI can be used by companies to be competitive in a global business environment.

In their chapter entitled "Information and Communication Technology Impact on Supply Chain Integration, Flexibility and Performance," Talamantes-Padilla, García-Alcaráz, Maldonado-Macías, Alor-Hernandez, Sanchéz-Ramírez, and Hernández-Arellano study the idea of integration and performance analysis in supply chains. They analyse the impact of information and communications technology (ICT) on Supply Chain Integration. They analyz]se four latent variables that can used to test ICT integration, SC integration, SC flexibility and SC performance. A survey of 284 managers in companies located in Cuidad Juarez, Mexico was conducted. The results were used to generate a structural equation model in order to learn the relationships between variables.

Preface

In their chapter entitled "A Causal Analytic Model for Labour Productivity Assessment," Kumar, Singh and Singh, discuss five drivers of labour productivity that were developed by the Indian government and those of the devolved administrations. These five drivers were adopted as a part of a policy framework for boosting regional productivity. They use structural equation modelling to see how the five drivers are related to each other. They show that spending more on research and development and workforce development increases labour productivity. Workforce development includes increasing capital-worker ratio and the percentage of highly qualified workers. They also show that promoting entrepreneurship has a positive relationship on regional labour productivity and regulatory barriers seem to have no effect, positive or negative on regional labour productivity.

In their chapter entitled "Effective Tools for Improving Employee Feedback During Organizational Change," Sedej and Justinek consider the importance of timely and relevant feedback on Organisational change and productivity. Organisations have a wide range of internal communication tools at their disposal in order to effectively realize their goals, strategy and vision. The challenge does not lie in the use of all available internal communication tools, but in the optimal selection that will be the most suitable to solve the organizational problem.

The keystone of organizational change lies in internal communications, and employee communication is a pivotal element in achieving business success. They surveyed 105 employees at various organizations that have direct knowledge of internal communications. They considered 10 key communication tools. Of the 10 key internal communication tools listed, electronic and verbal communication tools dominate.

They show that in order to get the best results in communicating change, it is often necessary to deliver the message several times using different internal communication tools. After each internal communication especially during process of change, it is necessary to ensure a relevant follow up with possibilities for feedback to verify the employee's level of awareness, understanding as well as their emotional reactions and commitment to include it daily work.

In their chapter entitled "A Conceptual and Pragmatic Review of Regression Analysis for Predictive Analytics," Kalaian, Kasim, and Kasim present a conceptual and practical overview of regression analysis which is one of the most commonly used modeling tools used to perform predictive analytics. The conceptual overview provides analysts with the skills necessary to understand and use regression analysis. The methods that are covered in the chapter are: (1) Simple Linear Regression and (2) Multiple Linear Regression. They describe in detail these methods and discuss issues related to them like the correlation coefficient, the coefficient of determination, scatterplots and statistical significance of the coefficients.

In their chapter entitled "Student Retention Performance Using Absorbing Markov Chains," Crossen explores and analyzes student retention within an arbitrary university setting using absorbing Markov chains. The researcher formulates two cases which account for freshman recidivism and increased enrollment of incoming freshman. He develops the research progression by establishing the baseline theory of mathematical modeling using the conceptual and theoretical framework for stochastic processes, discrete random variables, and the memoryless properties of Markovian analysis. In this development, conditional probabilities are reviewed to build toward advancing the concepts of state transition diagrams and retention models, in general. More specifically, the author formulates 6-year transition probabilities in order to analyze the long term probabilities, absorption time, and expectation times within each state classification across the both cases. Three period moving averages and seasonality forecasts are integrated to discover potential linear relationship of the data as it sequences through its life-cycle.

In their chapter entitled "An Analytical Employee Performance Evaluation Approach in Office Automation and Information Systems," Kalhori and Kargar argue that one of the most important issues in human resource management is performance evaluation. They argue that there is a lack for systematic and quantitative approaches for performance evaluation. They focus on issues such as incomplete information, subjective and qualitative metrics, and also the difficulty of evaluating the performance and present an approach for quantitative and automatic evaluation of employee performance using office automation systems. They show that the automatic employee performance evaluation system is a discrete dimension for employee performance evaluation systems.

Madjid Tavana
La Salle University, USA

Kathryn Szabat
La Salle University, USA

Kartikeya Puranam
La Salle University, USA

REFERENCES

Management, B. (2015). Retrieved from: http://boundlessmanagement.com/

Chapter 1
Predictive Analytics for Infrastructure Performance

Sue McNeil
University of Delaware, USA

Susanne Trimbath
STP Advisory Services, LLC, USA

Farzana Atique
University of Delaware, USA

Ryan Burke
U.S. Air Force Academy, USA

ABSTRACT

A predictive analysis methodology was designed for application to the Transportation Performance Index, which was first released in September 2010 through the U.S. Chamber of Commerce to benchmark and measure changes in the performance of US infrastructure over time. This article starts with a summary of the development and use of the Index in order to present the performance indicators that were the foundation of the predictive analysis. A new methodology was developed to generate prospective values for the Index by applying elements of the improvement plans from US Metropolitan Planning Organizations (MPOs) that paralleled the performance indicators used in the Index. The results show that over a 24 year period (2011 to 2035) the plans developed by MPOs can slow the decline in infrastructure over a baseline scenario. In addition to forecasting changes in the performance of the infrastructure that undergirds all economic activity, the results serve to further validate the Index as a methodology that captures important performance functions of transportation infrastructure. The original purpose of the Index was to capture trends, making it well-suited to the application of predictive analysis.

INTRODUCTION

A predictive analysis methodology was designed for the Transportation Performance Index ("TPI" or "Index"), which was first released in September 2010. The Index was developed in a rigorous way, applying standard methods, including taking a representative sample. Because it is impossible to measure every inch of road, bridge, airport, marine terminal, etc. in the nation, a sample of Metropolitan Statistical Areas (MSAs) is selected that is representative of the economic, demographic and geographic configuration of the US. The sampling method is not unlike that applied to the Dow Jones Industrial

DOI: 10.4018/978-1-5225-0654-6.ch001

Average (DJIA) which consists of only 30 stock prices, each selected to be representative of economic activity in the US industrial sectors. One could make predictions for the stock price performance of the individual component companies, apply the DJIA formula to those predictions (which includes price-weighting, scaled averaging, etc.) and arrive at a valid prediction for the DJIA. These results would be interpreted as predictions for the performance of the US economy (or the US stock market). Similarly, our methodology makes informed predictions of changes in the individual components of the TPI to arrive at predictions for changes in the national performance of US transportation infrastructure. We found no similar methodologies for measuring the overall performance of US transportation infrastructure. The application of predictive analytics in the field of transportation is generally limited to predicting traffic flows (e.g., Andrienko, Andrienko & Rinzivillo 2015) or equipment maintenance. Many are offered by private consulting firms; therefore, without transparent methodologies or publically available results.

The Index itself is a rigorous, formula-generated methodology employing measurements made possible by the big data sets routinely generated from observations of the conditions of transportation infrastructure throughout the more than 3 million square miles of the United States. In order to use the Index to forecast changes in the future performance of infrastructure, we add the business-intelligence supplied by individual metropolitan planning organizations that are responsible for selecting improvement projects to be completed in their jurisdictions. Every urbanized area with a population greater than 50,000 is required to form a metropolitan planning organization (MPO) for the purpose of channeling federal transportation funding to projects and programs in their regions. MPOs in the US are required to produce and make publicly available regional transportation plans that cover at least 20 years into the future. Since enactment of the Intermodal Surface Transportation Efficiency Act in 1991, these plans must also meet federal financial constraint requirements, where "federal regulations are explicit that funds must be balanced" to the money provided by the Federal Highway Administration and Federal Transit Administration (Atlanta Regional Commission, 2010). A constrained financial plan is one that includes only projects that can be implemented using current revenue sources while the existing transportation system is adequately operated and maintained. To be most realistic, we limit our predictive analysis to consideration of the fiscally constrained proposals as we take advantage of those published plans for transportation projects to predict the future of infrastructure performance in the United States.

In the next section we provide a summary of the development and use of the Index in order to present the performance indicators that are the subject of the predictive analysis. (Interested readers are referred to the Technical Report (US Chamber of Commerce 2010) which documents the complete development of the Index and includes an analysis of the results for the initial time periods.) The description of the Index and the indicators is followed by a complete presentation of our predictive analysis. We include the methodology, a demonstration of the procedure used to gather and incorporate human intelligence into the statistical analysis and the result of our predictive analysis.

BACKGROUND: THE TRANSPORTATION PERFORMANCE INDEX

By design, the Transportation Performance Index is generated from publicly available data. The transparent process has been reproduced in Brazil and the Netherlands to benchmark and measure changes in the performance of transportation infrastructure over time. The Index was designed to bring a rigorous, quantitative, and repeatable methodology to the assessment of infrastructure performance. In the past, studies that attempted to relate infrastructure to economic growth and prosperity largely had to rely on measuring infrastructure by *expenditures* rather than *performance*. The Index addresses this essential flaw in what we know about how infrastructure supports economic activity. (See Trimbath 2010 for a review of other research on the role of infrastructure in economic prosperity.)

The methodology for constructing a national infrastructure index builds on a broad base of existing research that includes:

- Academic knowledge of indices and decision support tools;
- Methodologically rigorous sampling strategies that ensure representation of all sectors of the economy and regions of the country;
- Integration of expert and user input to capture what is most important about "performance."

The TPI for the United States was developed using a hierarchical structure (represented in Figure 1). Geographic areas are broken down into two groups based on population: large Metropolitan Statistical Areas (MSAs), and other MSAs with population under 1 million. The other MSAs are further broken down into those with a primary airport and those without a primary airport. (All of the large metropolitan areas have primary airports.) Next, we examine the categories of transportation infrastructure – road, rail, transit, air, marine and inter-modal – within each MSA. The next level covers the overarching criteria for assessing performance: supply, quality of service, and utilization (reserve capacity). Within each

Figure 1. Hierarchy of the transportation performance index

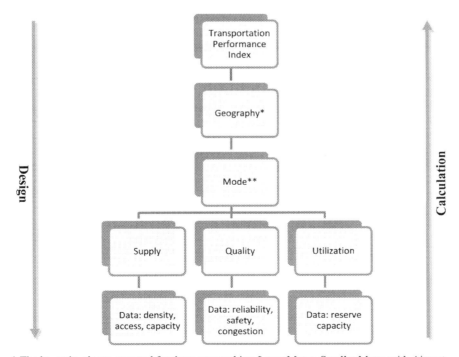

* The lower levels are repeated for three geographies: Large Metro, Smaller Metro with Airport, and Smaller Metro without Airport.
** The lower levels are repeated fro six modes: Highway, Rail, Transit, Air, Marine, and Inter-modal.

criterion, we select measurable indicators of the performance of the system. The final step is to identify the available data that can be used to proxy for the indicators that are critical to measuring performance. The indicators, which are the object of the predictive analysis, are discussed in more detail below.

In order to establish a rigorous methodology for constructing the index, Analytic Hierarchy Process (AHP) (Saaty, 1982) was used as a decision support tool. AHP is used to compare entities that have different units of measure through pairwise comparisons. The results of pairwise comparisons are used to assign weights (contribution to the overall index) to each of the criteria and each of the indicators based on their relative importance to performance. (See Oswald et. al. 2011 for details on the use of surveys to establish weighting factors for performance measures.) The results of the pairwise comparison survey were used to assign weights for each indicator (see Appendix E of U.S. Chamber 2010)

One required adjustment was necessary to account for the fact that the number of indicators is slightly different for the three types of MSAs. For example, where an MSA does not have an airport, the "Air Transportation" indicators are irrelevant. Hence, those weights are re-distributed before the index can be calculated. The second adjustment reflects the contribution of each MSA to the U.S. economy so that a national representative value is obtained. This step assures that several small MSAs or several large MSAs cannot dominate the national values. Each MSA type is weighted by the percent of the U.S. economy that *all* MSAs of that type contribute divided by the contribution of the sampled MSAs. (The calculation and application of the MSA weightings are described in detail in US Chamber 2009.)

Given the impossibility of gathering the data to measure the performance of *every piece of infrastructure in the entire USA*, a sampling strategy was designed. The sample selection criteria ensured a representative sample with attributes that demonstrate sufficient variability to capture all the factors that influence infrastructure usage and performance over time. Some of these attributes interact with each other, and it is important to develop a full design to account for those interactions. For example, the size of the population will be related to the size of the economy in a geographic area both because more people produce more output and because more output requires more people to produce it. The sampling strategy also reflects the diversity of geography as well as the type and intensity of economic activity that makes use of infrastructure. The initial set of geographic areas consisted of the 366 metropolitan statistical areas (MSAs) for which the Department of Commerce's Bureau of Economic Analysis reports industry level economic data (BEA, 2006). Thirty six MSAs were selected based on the 2003 BEA definitions. (The determination of the sample size and the selection of the sample are documented in U.S. Chamber, 2010). The thirty-six MSAs are grouped into three types:

- 23 MSAs with Population over 1 million (all with airports);
- 7 MSAs with Population under 1 million and with a primary airport;
- 6 MSAs with Population under 1 million and without a primary airport.

The sample provides the following coverage: 34.7% of total U.S. population and 34.7% of U.S. MSA economic output based on 2007 data. (Representativeness is further evaluated for Share of GDP by Industry Types, Geographic Distribution and State Coverage in US Chamber, 2010.) The long range transportation plan for every MSA in the sample was examined to identify plans that would impact the indicators (described below). We used a template to extract the relevant information from the plans, an example of which is included below.

Indicators

Transportation performance indicators serve as the building blocks for the TPI. The objective is to identify a set of indicators that reflects the performance of the transportation infrastructure in a way that captures its relationship to economic growth and prosperity. The indicators are selected based on the definitions of transportation infrastructure and performance established through user and expert interviews, discussion and surveys. Interaction with the transportation experts and stakeholders suggested interesting indicators, not all of which can be captured by data. We continue to monitor data releases from a broad array of public sources in an on-going effort to identify data that could be added to the TPI calculation. The current list of indicators is shown in Table 1. For example, the supply of highway infrastructure can be measured by the density of highways in the MSA. The quality of air transportation can be measured by airport congestion. The utilization of rail infrastructure can be measured as the ton-miles per track mile (basically, how many tons of freight are moved over every mile of track).

In all, there are 21 data elements indicating the performance of transportation infrastructure (Table 1). Data for each indicator are initially assembled from 1990 to 2007 and then updated periodically. The

Table 1. Performance indicators used in the index

Criteria	Mode	IND	Description	Measure
Supply	Highway	1	Highway Density	Availability of highways
	Transit	2	Transit Density	Availability of transit
	Air	3	Airport Access	Proximity of airports
		4	Airport Capacity	Availability of airport service
	Rail	5	Rail Density	Availability of railroads
	Maritime	6	Waterway Density	Availability of Inland Waterway maritime
		7	Port Access	Proximity of ports
	Intermodal	8	Intermodal Connectivity	Proximity of intermodal facilities
Quality of Service	Highway	9	Highway Congestion	Variability in travel time due to congestion
		10	Highway Safety	Fatal highway crashes
		11	Road Roughness	Highway ride comfort
		12	Bridge Integrity	Ability of bridges to meet the needs of the users
	Transit	13	Transit Safety	Transit incidents
	Air	14	Air Congestion	Airport congestion
		15	Air Safety	Chances of crashes
	Rail	16	Rail Safety	Railroad incidents
	Maritime	17	Waterway Congestion	Delays on inland waterway
Utilization	Highway	18	Reserve Capacity in Roads	Uncongested lane miles (defined as Level of Service C or better)
	Transit	19	Transit Capacity Utilization	Passenger miles traveled per capacity (standing and seating)
	Air	20	Air Capacity Utilization	Percent of capacity used between 7 am and 9 pm
	Rail	21	Rail Usage for Freight	Ton-miles per track mile

10,440 pieces of data are assembled from approximately 10 Gigabytes of raw data using spreadsheet, database, and Geographic Information System (GIS) tools. (A complete list of the databases explored for this project is available in US Chamber Commerce, 2010.)

Calculating the Index

Utilizing assembled data sets for each MSA, an index is constructed to represent the performance of the transportation infrastructure for benchmarking and measuring change (improvement or decline). Below are the technical specifications used to calculate the Transportation Performance Index.

For each year, the Transportation Index is defined as:

$$\text{Index}_{\text{Tran}} = \sum_{k} \left[\sum_{i=1}^{I_k} \left(\left(\sum_{j=1}^{J} w_{jk} N_{ij} \right) e_{ik} \right) \left(\frac{\sum_{p=1}^{P_k} e_{pk}}{\sum_{i=1}^{I_k} e_{ik}} \right) \right] \quad (1)$$

where

$k = 1....K$ is the MSA type

$p = 1....P_k$ is the MSA in the population of type k

$i = 1....I_k$ is the MSA in the sample of type k

$e_{ik} = $ contribution of MSA i of type k to US economy

$\dfrac{\sum_{p=1}^{P_k} e_{pk}}{\sum_{i=1}^{I_k} e_{ik}} = $ economic expansion factor

$j = 1...J$ is the indicator

$w_{jk} = $ weight for indicator j in type k

$N_{ij} = $ normalized measure of indicator j for MSA i

The report to the U.S. Chamber of Commerce (2010) documents the development of the Transportation Performance Index (and includes an analysis of the results for the initial time periods). This and many other documents related to the Index are available free of charge online at the Chamber's website: https://www.uschamber.com/issue-brief/transportation-performance-index [Accessed January 28, 2016]. See also Oswald, et. al. (2011).

The TPI saw an improvement in 2009 as a result of stimulus money spent on "shovel ready" projects in combination with a decline in usage (resulting from lower economic activity). See Figure 2. Modest improvements in the Index during the recession came from reductions in usage, combined with significant strategic investment focused on state of good repair, intermodal connectivity, mobility and accessibility. Our initial interpretation of these results is that the big drop-off in traffic with the recession of 2007-2008 resulted in an improved TPI for 2009 possibly just from reduced usage. Then, as traffic picked up in 2010, the TPI declined slightly, but, by 2011, the bigger investments (initiated from 2009 onward) offset the increasing pressure from recovering economic activity. Policymakers now need to "maintain the momentum" so that transportation infrastructure in the US lays the path to a new future for US economic prosperity and competitiveness (McNeil et. al. n.d.).

The 2013 update on the TPI added new observations which, when added to the existing economic model, confirmed the original results: a 2.5 point increase in the TPI correlates with a 0.75% increase in the growth of GDP per capita (a measure of prosperity), with the potential to add $120 billion to the economy in the first year after the infrastructure improvements. (Trimbath, 2013).

To assist in interpreting the index, we used scenario analysis with both a retrospective analysis of the impact of past projects and prospective analysis of the impact of proposed or hypothetical projects and policies. The prospective analysis, presented in detail below, is essentially forecasting how we expect the Index to change given the implementation of proposed projects.

Figure 2. Transportation performance index, measured results

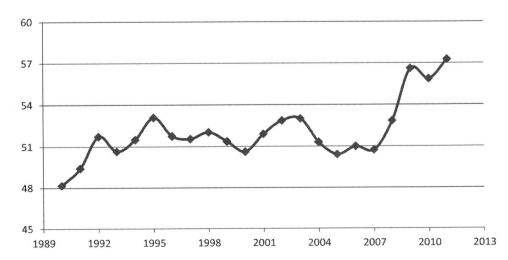

PREDICTIVE SCENARIO ANALYSIS

Our objective is to demonstrate the role of the TPI in capturing changes in infrastructure performance and ultimately to influence transportation policy. We conduct a prospective analysis looking at the impact of investment based on the long range transportation plans (LRTP) of the Metropolitan Planning Organizations (MPOs) for our sample of MSAs. The analysis serve two functions. First the analysis helps us to better understand the impact of specific investments or policies on the TPI. Second, the analysis helps to provide insight into the portfolio of projects and policies that are required to continue to improve the performance of transportation as measured by the TPI.

MPOs in the US are required to produce and make publically available regional transportation plans that cover at least 20 years into the future to assure mobility and access, performance and preservation of the system. For each MSA the appropriate plan was identified and to the extent possible the impact of the proposed investments and policies on the indicators was assessed. We present the template for Baltimore below as an example. An identical analysis was done for the 35 others MSAs in the TPI sample. The average template was 3 pages long where the length varied by the number of effective plans put forward by individual MPOs.

In 2011 (U.S. Chamber of Commerce, 2011), we forecasted to 2020 using a simple, linear trend analysis. To better explore how the TPI might look in the future, we define scenarios, hypothesize how the individual performance indicators in each of the sampled MSAs could be impacted in the future and then recalculate the TPI. To develop realistic scenarios based on local knowledge we extract information from the long-range regional transportation plans for the 36 MSAs in our sample. We begin with a "what if" scenario based on a "do nothing" (baseline) alternative and compare that to the plan-based scenarios.

Methodology

To address the objectives outlined above, we constructed two scenarios:

- **Scenario 1**:
  - **Baseline:** This scenario assumes no new investment, i.e., that the municipality "does nothing" that it is not already doing. Additional capacity is not added and additional investments in maintenance are not made, even in response to aging infrastructure with deteriorating performance.
- **Scenario 2**:
  - **Forecast:** This scenario assumes implementation of LRTP-like investments in all MSAs. Additional capacity and investment in state of good repair are made consistent with the LRTPs.

The baseline scenario, where no improvements are made over basic maintenance, includes a 1% annual population growth. Over the 24 year period (2011 to 2035) the projected changes in each of the indicators of performance used in the TPI are shown in Table 2. For each performance indicator in our MSA sample, we estimated the impact of population growth with no transportation project implementation and then recalculated the TPI. Notice that some indicators are not impacted at the national level, although the values for individual MSAs in the sample may have changed. This point will become clear when we present the full range of statistics on performance indicators for the prospective analysis in Table 6.

Later, for indicators where no data are available (or where no change is indicated by the LRTP), we will assume value to be that of this Baseline scenario.

The LRTP Projects Forecast scenario is based on investments presented in the long-range transportation plans (LRTPs) for the MSAs in the sample. Drawing from the LRTPs for metropolitan planning organizations (MPOs) that correspond to the MSA's used to develop the TPI, the impact of the investment scenario in these plans on the TPI indicators can be estimated. Based on these estimates the value of the TPI can be forecast. For a specific MPO, the steps are as follows:

1. Identify the long range transportation plan for the MPO corresponding to the MSA.
2. Identify the year that the LRTP was published and the forecast year.
3. Identify proposed projects that can change the value of any performance indicators.
4. Compute the change in the indicators as a percentage change between 2011 (the most recent year for which the TPI was calculated from actual data) and 2035 (the most commonly used forecast year).
5. Repeat steps 3 and 4 for each indicator that will be impacted by new investment.
6. Compute the LRTP Projects Forecast TPI.

Table 2. Baseline scenario

Indicator	Description	Change 2011-2035
IND1	Highway Density	-21.2%
IND2	Transit Density	-21.2%
IND3	Airport Access	0.0%
IND4	Airport Capacity	0.0%
IND5	Rail Density	-21.2%
IND6	Waterway Density	-21.2%
IND7	Port Access	0.0%
IND8	Intermodal Freight Access	-21.2%
IND9	Highway Travel Time Reliability	27.0%
IND10	Highway Safety	0.0%
IND11	Road Roughness	27.0%
IND12	Highway Bridge Integrity	27.0%
IND13	Air Congestion	-21.2%
IND14	Air Safety	0.0%
IND15	Transit Safety	0.0%
IND16	Rail Safety	0.0%
IND17	Waterway Congestion	27.0%
IND18	Highway Reserve capacity	-21.2%
IND19	Air Reserve capacity	27.0%
IND20	Transit Reserve capacity	27.0%
IND21	Rail Reserve capacity	27.0%

For indicators where no data are available or where no change is indicated by the LRTP, the future value of the indicator is assumed to be that of the Baseline Scenario. Using a percentage change allowed us to use measures that we believe to be highly correlated with the indicators we have chosen.

For each MSA the appropriate plan was identified and to the extent possible the impact of the proposed investments and policies on the indicators was assessed. A template was used to extract relevant information from the plans and document the sources (see example in Table 3). An appendix documenting the analysis of the Long Range Transportation Plans for MPOs corresponding to each of the 36 MSAs used to compute the TPI is available upon request from the corresponding author.

The application of the procedure to the Baltimore-Towson MSA which is under the jurisdiction of the Baltimore Metropolitan Planning Council, illustrates the process. The Long Range Transportation Plan was published in 2011 with a forecast year of 2035 (Baltimore Metropolitan Planning Council, 2011).

Data was identified to support the estimation of changes in highway density, transit density, travel time reliability, safety, road roughness, and bridge integrity – the relevant TPI indicators that would be impacted by these planned investments. The results are shown in Table 4. The Notes below the table explain the elements in the LRTP that would result in the changed performance.

Table 3. Template demonstration for Baltimore-Townson, Maryland (USA)

Federal Info. Processing Standards Code	Name of MSA	Name of MPO
12060	Baltimore-Towson, MD	Baltimore Metropolitan Planning Council
Year Plan Published	**Forecast Year**	
2011	2035	
Goals	**Performance Measures**	**Performance Data**
Improve Transportation System Safety	Number of fatalities in the region.	238 fatalities in 2009.
Preserve the Existing Infrastructure	Percent of road miles in acceptable condition. Number of structurally deficient bridges. Average age of the transit fleet.	166 structurally deficient bridges in 2009. Average age of transit fleet varies from 3.7 years to 24.3 in 2009.
Improve Accessibility	Proportion of households within ¼ mile of bus route or rail station. % of state owned roads with sidewalks.	In 2010 approximately 45% of households were with ¼ miles of transit. In 2009 32% of state owned roadways had sidewalks.
Increase Mobility	Increase weekday transit ridership. Hours of delay reduced.	In 2010 there were an average of 355,697 weekday transit riders.
Preserve the Environment	Maintain levels of VOC, NOX, PM 2.5, CO emissions.	Values are tabulated in plan.
Improve Transportation System Security	Develop and expand security initiatives.	
Promote Prosperity and Economic Opportunity	Increase investments in freight intermodal connections.	
Foster Participation and Cooperation among All Stakeholder Groups	Increase the number of public private partnerships.	

Source: Baltimore Metropolitan Council. (2011)

Table 4. Forecast scenario indicators input for Baltimore

#	Mode	Description	Change	Note
IND1	Highway	Highway Density (Availability of highways)	-19.0%	1
IND2	Transit	Density (Availability of transit)	-20.8%	2
IND3	Air	Access (Proximity of airports)		
IND4		Capacity (Availability of airport service)		
IND5	Rail	Density (Availability of railroads)		
IND6	Marine	Density (Availability of marine)		
IND7		Port Access (Proximity of ports)		
IND8	Intermodal	Freight Access (Proximity of intermodal facilities)		
IND9	Highway	Travel Time Reliability (Variability in travel time due to congestion)	0.0%	3
IND10		Safety (Fatal highway crashes)	0.0%	4
IND11		Road Roughness (Highway ride comfort)	-1.0%	5
IND12		Bridge Integrity (Ability of bridges to meet the needs of the users)	0.0%	6
IND13	Aviation	Congestion (Airport congestion)		
IND14		Safety (Chances of crashes)		
IND15	Transit	Safety (Transit incidents)		
IND16	Rail	Safety (Railroad incidents)		
IND17	Marine	Congestion (Delays on inland waterway)		
IND18	Highway	Reserve capacity		
IND19	Aviation	Reserve capacity		
IND20	Transit	Reserve capacity		
IND21	Rail	Reserve capacity		

"Change" expressed as a percentage from 2010 to 2035 after normalization such that negative numbers represent declines in *performance*, not necessarily declines in measured data.

Note 1:
New Lane miles by 2035: 32 (p.5-12)
Baltimore MSA Population 2035 = 3,465,000
Highway density = (1158(2011 lane miles) + (32))/ (3,465,000/10,000) = 4.20 lane miles per 10,000 population
Change from 2010: (4.20 − 4.24)/4.24*100 = −19% increase

Note 2: Four new transit projects are described in the plan and the miles of transit are estimated.
- Red line light rail transit (14 miles or 22.4 km).
- Green line extension from Johns Hopkins Hospital to North Avenue (1.5 miles or 2.4 km).
- Yellow line extension from Baltimore Washington International Airport to Dorsey Avenue and Anne Arundel County line to MD 32 (10 miles or 16 km).
- Bus rapid transit from US 29 and Broke Land Parkway to MD 198 (7.3 miles or 11.7 km).
- Assuming a 1% growth in population, the calculation of the value of the transit density indicator used in the TPI for 2035 is shown in Table 5.

Table 5. Computation of the change in transit density

Measure	2011	2035
Miles of Transit	3,566.9	3,599.7
Population	2,729,110	3,465,000
IND2 (Transit Density)	13.07	10.39
% Change		-20.5%

Note 3: Based on the discussion of travel time reliability it was assumed that improvements would net no change.
Note 4: Based on the discussion that safety would hold steady.
Note 5: Based on the discussion of maintaining existing assets so that the condition would not deteriorate.
Note 6: Based on the discussion of maintaining existing assets so that the condition would not deteriorate.

RESULTS

The process outlined above is repeated for all MSAs and all indicators. Only nine indicators of the total of 21 used to calculate the Index show any change (see Table 6). When there is no change in the indicator, the forecast value follows the Baseline scenario using the percentage change shown in Table 2.

Some indicators are not expected to change with the implementation of MPO plans (Transit safety or proximity to airports) for any of the sampled MSAs. Again, we used the values from the Baseline Scenario for those unaffected indicators in the calculation of the predicted Index. Using the methodology outlined above, the forecast values for the Index in 2035 for the two scenarios are shown in Table 7. The results show that over a 24 year period (2011 to 2035) investing in the plans presented in the LRTPs developed by MPOs can result in significant improvement in the TPI over the Baseline scenario.

Table 6. Percent change (2011-2035) in indicators based on long range transportation plans for sample MSAs

	Mode	Description	Mean	Median	Max	Min
IND4	Air	Capacity	56	56	61	51
IND1	Highway	Highway Density	18	10	73	-19
IND9	Highway	Travel Time Reliability	28	4	318	-43
IND10	Highway	Safety	-1	-5	311	-175
IND11	Highway	Road Roughness	-23	-24	0	-51
IND12	Highway	Bridge Integrity	-11	-9	0	-45
IND18	Highway	Reserve capacity	5	5	13	-3
IND8	Intermodal	Freight Access	23	7	150	1
IND5	Rail	Density	15	12	34	3
IND2	Transit	Density	30	19	153	-21

Table 7. Forecast results

Scenario	1991	2008	2011	2035	% Change
Baseline	49.00	52.00	57.26	42.36	-26.03%
LRTP Projects Forecast				46.08	-19.53%

DISCUSSION

There were three major barriers to developing a set of comprehensive, repeatable, measurable indicators of transportation infrastructure performance using publically available data: varying levels of data aggregation, missing and erroneous data, and institutional issues. Each barrier and how that barrier was remediated or managed in the development of the TPI are discussed in Li, et. al. (2011). It was necessary to normalize the data as each indicator has a different scale. For some indicators, larger values are desirable for better performance (e.g., percentage of lane miles uncongested), and for others, smaller values are more desirable (e.g., runway incursions per million operations). The process used to normalize the data is described in detail in the Project Initiation report (U.S. Chamber, 2009). See Oswald and McNeil (2010) for methodology as a way to universalize measuring infrastructure performance using a rating scale.

One obstacle in the predictive analysis was that many long-range transportation plans do not have the required level of specificity to estimate the expected change in an indicator. Other challenges with this method stem from the fact that the Municipal Planning Organization boundaries do not necessarily match the Metropolitan Statistical Area boundaries. For example, the MPO Los Angeles Metro covered two of the MSAs in our sample: Los Angeles and Riverside. It also is not always clear what base year is being presented so that we often had to make assumptions about the data. In other cases, MPOs reported a change in the hours of traffic delay without reporting their method of measurement. We assumed this is correlated with the Travel Time Index that we use for the measure of highway travel time reliability (congestion).

CONCLUSION

This analysis confirms our expectation that the TPI is capturing significant changes in transportation performance. Without investment, the TPI is shown to decline significantly. However, investing in the projects proposed in long range transportation plans shows a marked improvement in the TPI over the baseline scenario where no new projects are undertaken. As these investments reflect strategic investments, and regional priorities and needs, it is encouraging that these investments do in fact result in a significant change. Furthermore, the original intent of using indicators is not to present a comprehensive measure of the infrastructure improvements but to capture trends – this demonstration appears to confirm that the goal was achieved.

Modest improvements in the TPI recently came from reductions in both vehicle miles of travel and ton miles of travel, and significant strategic investment focused on state of good repair, intermodal connectivity, mobility and accessibility. The TPI forecast using predictive analytics that incorporate human intelligence from LRTPs with actual performance data, predicts an almost 20% improvement in 24 years over the "do nothing" baseline scenario. A focus on all modes and all aspects of transportation infrastructure performance will be required on the part of the MPOs to achieve this significant improvement.

Clearly, the long-range plans of the metropolitan planning organizations using only existing revenue sources are not enough to improve the performance of transportation infrastructure throughout the United States. That scenario manages to slow the decline in transportation infrastructure. More needs to be done to reverse the trend. Making the investment to improve transportation performance can result in a measurable return on investment (7%) with a payback period (17 years) that is well short of the life-expectancy of most transportation infrastructure (Trimbath 2013).

The appendices in US Chamber of Commerce (2010) include other methods tested for using the TPI to forecast changes in performance under a variety of "what if" scenarios. Since the 2013 update, several organizations generated estimates of the future needs for infrastructure investments with some breakdowns for transportation (see, for example, McKinsey Global Institute, 2013 and World Economic Forum, 2015). These organizations conclude, as we do, that there needs to be more investment. The consensus for the cost to upgrade the performance of US transportation infrastructure to "first class" comes in at just over $1.2 trillion (Zupan 2013).

A retrospective analysis, using the elimination of actual projects, demonstrates the impact of the magnitude and timing of specific projects. The Retrospective looks at how the performance of infrastructure could have been impacted if nine major projects were not implemented. Using the same Baseline Scenario described in this article – that is, assuming no new investment, additional capacity or additional investments in maintenance. Those results showed that an investment of almost $(US) 23 billion in nine projects changed the TPI by only 0.23%. The analysis also demonstrates the importance of network effects, comprehensive and coherent planning, and the limited impact of isolated regional investments on national infrastructure performance. In addition, it further supports the idea that no one project, nor investment in a single region or a single mode, would significantly change the value of the TPI. Instead, a system or network approach is needed to create considerable change in transportation performance. Our predictive analysis demonstrates this point. Implementing the long-range transportation plans across the board could begin to stem the decline of U.S. transportation infrastructure.

ACKNOWLEDGMENT

This work was partially supported by the National Chamber Foundation of the U.S. Chamber of Commerce, the U.S. Chamber of Commerce, the University of Delaware University Transportation Center, and the University of Delaware. A prospective analysis, using a subset of the data, was originally presented as a conference paper (McNeil et. al., 2014).

REFERENCES

Andrienko, N., Andrienko, G., & Rinzivillo, S. (2015). Exploiting spatial abstraction in predictive analytics of vehicle traffic. *ISPRS International Journal of Geo-Information*, *4*(2), 591–606. doi:10.3390/ijgi4020591

Atlanta Regional Commission. (2010). Retrieved from: http://documents.atlantaregional.com/plan2040/docs/tp_PLAN2040RTP_072711.pdf

Baltimore Metropolitan Council. (2011). *Plan It 2035*. Retrieved 5 October 2013 from: http://www.baltometro.org/plans/plan-it-2035>

Bureau of Economic Analysis (BEA). (2006). *Gross domestic Product by State Estimation Methodology*. U.S. Dept. of Commerce. Retrieved 12 December 2013 from: http://www.bea.gov/regional/pdf/gsp/GDPState.pdf

Li, Q., McNeil, S., Foulke, T.K., Calhoun, J., Oswald, M., Trimbath, S., Kreh, E., & Gallis, M. (2011). *Capturing Transportation Infrastructure Performance: Data Availability, Needs and Challenges*. Transportation Research Record: Journal of the Transportation Research Board, No. 2256. Transportation Research Board of the National Academies.

McKinsey Global Institute. (2013). *Infrastructure Productivity: How to Save $1 Trillion a Year*. McKinsey Infrastructure Practice.

McNeil, S., Atique, F., Burke, R., & Trimbath, S. (2014). Using the Transportation Performance Index to Understand the Impact of Regional Plans. *Proceedings of the ASCE TD&I Congress*. doi:10.1061/9780784413586.061

McNeil, S., Trimbath, S., Atique, F., & Burke, R. (n.d.). *TPI UPDATE 2013: Data for 2010,2011*. Final Report to the US Chamber of Commerce (unpublished).

Oswald, M., Li, Q., McNeil, S., & Trimbath, S. (2011). Measuring Infrastructure Performance: Development of a National Infrastructure Index. *Public Works Management & Policy, 16*(4), 373–394. doi:10.1177/1087724X11410071

Oswald, M., & McNeil, S. (2010). Rating Sustainability: Transportation Investments in Urban Corridors as a Case Study. *Journal of Urban Planning and Development, 136*(3), 177–185. doi:10.1061/(ASCE)UP.1943-5444.0000016

Saaty, T. L. (1982). *Decision making for leaders: The analytical hierarchy process for decisions in a complex world*. Belmont, CA: Lifetime Learning Publications.

Trimbath, S. (2010). *The Economic Importance of Transportation Infrastructure*. STP Advisors Working Paper STP2010_01.

Trimbath, S. (2013). *Calculating the Real Economic Payoff of Infrastructure*. STP Advisory Services Working Paper STP2013_02.

U.S. Chamber of Commerce. (2010). Transportation Performance Index: Complete Technical Report. Washington, DC: McNeil, S., Li, Q., Oswald, M., Foulke, T.K., Calhoun, J. and Trimbath, S.

U.S. Chamber of Commerce. (2011). *Transportation Performance Index:2011Supplement*. McNeil, S., Li, Q., Oswald, M., Foulke, T.K., Calhoun, J. and Trimbath, S.

World Economic Forum. (2015). *Competitiveness Rankings*. Retreived 19 September 2015 from http://www3.weforum.org/docs/WEF_GlobalCompetitivenessReport_2014-15.pdf

Zupan, J. M. (2013). *Upgrading to World Class: The Future of the New York Region's Airports (An Update)*. OECD International Transport Forum, Discussion Paper No. 2013-1.

KEY TERMS AND DEFINITIONS

Analytic Hierarchy Process (AHP): A structured multi-attribute decision-making technique that can be used to weight indicators or indices.

Criteria: Broad classes of infrastructure performance (supply, efficiency, quality of service, and utilization).

Indicator: A specific measure that can be used to quantify infrastructure performance.

Infrastructure: That which is below and contained within all the structures that support economic activity.

Metropolitan Statistical Area (MSA): A geographical area comprising a core urban area of 50,000 or more population for which both infrastructure performance measures and economic data are available.

Performance: A combination of supply, efficiency, quality of service, and utilization specifically measuring the degree to which the infrastructure system serves U.S. economic and multi-level business community objectives.

Transportation Infrastructure: The fixed facilities (roadway segment, railway track, transit terminals, harbors, and airports), flow entities (people, vehicles, container units, railroad cars), and control systems that permit people and goods to transverse geographical space efficiently and in a timely manner in some desired activity. Transportation is provided by modes (highway, rail, air, and waterway).

Transportation Performance Index: A measure used to benchmark the improvement or decline in the performance of transportation infrastructure over time; generated from publicly available data using a transparent process that can be applied to various jurisdictions (states, countries, etc.).

Chapter 2
Structural Equation Modeling Algorithm and Its Application in Business Analytics

Shahryar Sorooshian
Universiti Malaysia Pahang, Malaysia

ABSTRACT

Structural Equation Modeling (SEM) is a statistical-based multivariate modeling methods. Application of SEM is similar but more powerful than regression analysis; and number of scientists using SEM in their research is rapidly increasing. This review article algorithmically discusses the SEM methodology. SEM strategies, SEM steps and SEM stages are introduced in this article; validity tests are presented as well. Novelty of this article is in modified steps of SEM application in modeling strategies, also in its developed practical comprehensive SEM application flowchart. This article is a roadmap for business advisors and those scholars trying to compute SEM for their decision making, complex modeling and data analysis programming.

INTRODUCTION

Structural equation modeling, also known as SEM, is referred to as one of the most effective multivariate statistical tool for analysis. The extent to which SEM's technique is applied to relationship analysis simply ranges from independent and dependent variables to complex analysis of measurement equivalence for first and higher order constructs (Cheung 2008). The framework for developing and analyzing complex relationships among a number of variables is flexible and also permits researchers to test the theory's validity through empirical models. Perhaps its prominent strength is in its capacity to manage errors in measurement, which is among the greatest limitations of most studies. A couple of years back Gonzalez, Boeck and Tuerlinckx (2008), Beran and Violato (2010) and numerous different researchers classified it as a "most of the time" used technique. "With SEM's strength as a statistical tool to analyze complex relationships among variables, and even posit and test causal relationships with non-experimental data, it allows researchers to explain the development of phenomena" (Beran, et al. 2010). The utilization

DOI: 10.4018/978-1-5225-0654-6.ch002

of SEM has now elevated to be the across-the-board, crosswise technique over research domains. The citation recurrence of SEM has consistently increased from 18 in 1980, to 494 in 2000, then to 4269 in 2015, as shown in Figure 1 which is based on Scopus indexed articles (Scopus 2016). A search for SEM in the Scopus database, with "structural equation modeling" in title, abstract and/or keywords of indexed articles, reveals that psychology, social Sciences, engineering, and medicine researchers are among the top users (Scopus 2016). Although SEM is widely used in research, the number of technical note articles showcasing a roadmap or application flowchart are very few. The main purpose of current paper is to introduce a comprehensive programming flowchart for SEM application and computation.

RESEARCH METHODS

Two basic methods of research found in literature are quantitative and qualitative research (Curran & Blackburn, 2001; Trochim, 2005; Gobakhloo, 2009). Qualitative research uses words to describe situations, individuals, or circumstances surrounding a phenomenon, while quantitative research uses numbers and formulas usually in the form of counts or measurement in an attempt to give precision to a set of observations (Remenyi, Williams, Money & Swartz, 1998; Vignali, Gomez, Vignali & Vranesevic, 2001; Gray, Williamson et al. 2007; Gobakhloo, 2009).

These methods complement each other and are therefore mutually supportive. According to Karami (2007), appropriate research in some applied sciences requires the right balance between qualitative and quantitative methods. Figure 2 presents a contingent model development research approach that aims is to identify such a balance. This approach is applicable in both model and theory developments.

There are diverse views on the role and place of theory in the sequence and relationship of the activities involved in research. It has been found by Curran and Blackburn (2001) that there is interwoven play between data collection and analysis. Therefore, data are obtained through quantitative and qualitative

Figure 1. Scopus documents
Source: Scopus (2016)

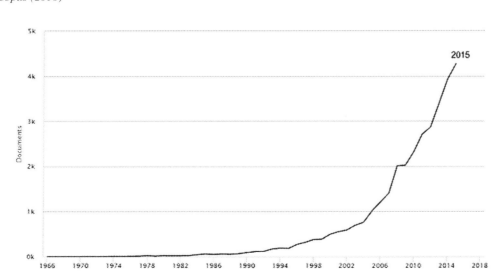

Figure 2. Contingent method approach for modeling studies

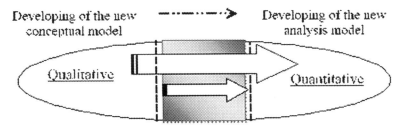

methods or through formal and informal means. Developing an appropriate research process is important when undertaking research, though there is no consensus among researchers on the appropriate research algorithm or flowchart. This article serves to fill this gap in research methodology knowledge by developing a practical research flowchart for modeling complex systems with latent variables.

QUALITATIVE METHODS OF RESEARCH

It is argued that, like secondary data analysis, qualitative research is a major methodology used in exploratory research (Hurley, 1999). Qualitative research methods can be defined as the process of enquiry to understand points. It is basically a way of solving problems by providing the understanding that is needed to identify relevant information in order to interpret them (Malhotra, 2009). According to Prayag (2009), the three major methods used in data gathering in qualitative research include literature review, observation and interview. Table 1 presents some advantages of different qualitative methods.

QUANTITATIVE METHODS OF RESEARCH

Quantitative methods of research aim at finding the relationship between one variable (an independent) and another (a dependent or outcome variable) in a population. Quantitative research designs are either descriptive (subjects usually measured once) or experimental (such as subjects measured before and after a treatment). The benefits of quantitative research methods include ease of making comparisons between variables and capability of standardization of data, which helps in classical survey statistics (Hart, 1987).

Methods of quantitative research are sets of tools that combine deductive logic with precise empirical observation of individual behavior on the side of confirming and/or discovering of causal relations, which helps prediction of activities' patterns (Neuman, 1997). These methods of research help their

Table 1. Methods of qualitative research

Method	Advantage
Literature and document review	Theoretical understanding
Interviews	Understanding experience
Observation	Understanding of subcultures

users establish a quantitative proof of the strength of relationship between dependent and independent variables (2002). These methods show statistical/mathematical results that find direction and paths of relationships/inter-relationships. Quantitative methods are not able to generate theory or provide the in-depth explanation of qualitative enquiry; Cavana, Delahaye, and Sekaran (2001) and Amaratunga, Baldry, Sarshar, and Newton (2002) state that these methods can verify hypotheses and provide validity, as well as reliability.

LATENT VARIABLE METHOD OF DATA ANALYSIS

Among quantitative methods, latent variable methods of analysis recognize that theoretical constructs of interest often are not directly measurable, but rather are represented by the overlapping variance of measured variables and multiple indicator measures (Violato & Hecker, 2007; Sorooshian, Teck, Salimi & How, 2012; Bollen, 2014). According to Hughes, Price and Marrs (1986), there are two strengths in latent variable methods of analysis – one technical, one conceptual. Technically, these models provide researchers with a method for estimating structural relationships among unobservable constructs and for assessing the adequacy with which those constructs have been measured. Conceptually, the use of these models entails a mode of thinking about theory construction, measurement problems, and data analysis that is helpful in stating theory more exactly, testing theory more precisely, and yielding a more thorough understanding of the data (Von der Heidt, 2008; Bollen, 2014). Besides SEM strengths with regards to the latent variable methods of analysis, it has some limitations which need to be acknowledged. In spite of the fact that a latent variable (also called 'factor' (Beran, et al. 2010)) is a closer approximation of a construct than is a measured variable, it may not be an accurate representation of the construct. Its variance may comprise of, in addition to true variance of the measured variables, the error shared between the measured variables (Beran, et al. 2010). The latent variable analysis mentioned in this study is also known as factor analysis (Beran, et al. 2010).

STRUCTURAL EQUATION MODELING (SEM)

According to references (Wright, 1920; Hair Jr, Anderson, Tatham, & William, 1995; Hair, 2006; Beran, et al. 2010), the research model construct has been linked with a number of interdependent variables that are usually represented in a structural equation modeling. Structural equation modeling, generally known as SEM, can be defined as a statistical technique that is used for testing a structural model that is represented as a hypothesis that has a relationship among latent variables measured by multiple items, usually where at least one construct is both a dependent and an independent variable (Hair, 2006). "SEM is a second generation multivariate analysis technique that combines features of the first generation techniques, such as principal component and linear regression analysis" (Hair, Ringle & Sarstedt, 2012). SEM has a number of synonyms and special cases in the literature including covariance structure analysis, causal modeling and path analysis, etc. (Lei & Wu, 2007). It is an extension of general linear model (GLM) that combines different aspect of multiple regression/path analysis as well as latent variable analysis (Hair Jr, et al., 1995; Lei, et al., 2007).

The structural model, which is referred to as the relationships among latent variables, permits the researcher to determine their level of relationship (computed as path coefficients) (Gefen, Straub &

Boudreau, 2000; Jannoo, Yap, Auchoybur & Lazim, 2014). In other words, path coefficients were characterized by Wright (Wright, 1920), as measuring the significance of a given path of impact from cause to impact. Every structural equation coefficient is calculated while every other variances are considered for analysis. Hence, coefficients are calculated simultaneously for every single dependent variable as opposed to consecutively, as calculated in regular multiple regression models.

SEM is now a quasi-standard in research and scientific studies and is particularly use for models and theories development and validation processes (Hair, et al. 2012; Ringle, Sarstedt & Straub, 2012). SEM is considered an appropriate analytical technique for many research endeavors due to the following reason: its ability to estimate a series of separate, but interdependent, multiple regression equations simultaneously by specifying a structural model that allows the modeling of relationships among independent and dependent variables, even when a dependent variable changes to an independent variable in other relationships (Von der Heidt, 2008). This makes SEM an attractive method of estimation techniques to researchers who can only estimate construct values by using observable or manifest variables (Von der Heidt, 2008). A variable in SEM can be exogenous (dependent) or endogenous (independent). A variable that is exogenous has an outwards pointing arrows path which is non-leading to it. Nonetheless, an endogenous variable has no less than one path leading to it and represents the impacts of other variable(s) (Wong, 2013).

SEM can be employed for both exploratory and confirmatory models. An exploratory SEM approach is more traditional in which a detailed model specifying the relationships among variables is not made a priority (Beran, et al., 2010). Every latent variable is assumed to impact every observed variable so that the number of latent variables are not pre-determined, and errors in measurement are not permitted to correlate (Bollen, 2014). Even though exploratory as well as confirmatory factor analyses are a subset of SEM involving the measurement model only, the latter is mostly used to test hypothetical constructs (Beran, et al. 2010). According to Von (2008), the decision on how to access the series of relationship uncovered in the examination of theory depends on the objectives of the research. For example, in a situation where the relationships are strictly specified, the objective will be a confirmation of the relationships. On the other hand, if the relationships are loosely recognized and the objective is on discovering the relationships, there are three different approaches or modeling strategies:

1. **Confirmatory Modeling Strategy:** Usually used for the specification of a single model and SEM to access the significance of the relationship;
2. **Competing Model Strategy:** Involves identifying and testing the competing models that represents different structural relationships (here the research comes a little bit closer to the competing test); and
3. **Model Development Strategy:** Involves modifications of the structural and/or measurement models in order to improve the model.

Having a generalized or best model for other samples and population involves specifying the original model with theoretical support rather than using just an empirical support.

At the point of estimating structural equation models, researchers must pick between two diverse statistical methods: covariance-based SEM (CB-SEM) and variance-based partial least squares (PLS) path modeling, also known as PLS-SEM. There is a significant contrast between these two approaches to SEM in their underlying philosophy and estimation objectives. CB-SEM is a confirmatory approach with spotlight on the model's theoretically established relationships; it seeks to minimize the contrast between the model implied co-variance matrix and the sample co-variance matrix. Conversely, PLS-SEM is a prediction-oriented variance-based approach that centers on endogenous target constructs in the model; seeks to maximize their explained variance (Hair, et al. 2012; Jannoo, et al. 2014). Even though, CB-SEM and PLS-SEM are different, they are complementary statistical methods for SEM. One approach's advantages are the disadvantages of the other and vice versa (Hair, et al., 2012, Astrachan, Patel & Wanzenried, 2014). Furthermore, both methodologies were created at about the same time; as such, their ensuing evolution has been parallel. CB-SEM, which experienced numerous methodological developments, became an extensively utilized methodology (Baumgartner & Homburg, 1996; Hair, et al. 2012; Astrachan, et al. 2014; Jannoo, et al. 2014).

This article develops a practical flowchart covering all three strategies of CB-SEM, especially model development strategy which is more often utilized in soft engineering studies. The distinction between the model development strategy and the other two strategies enumerated earlier is that in the model development strategy, a model is proposed and empirically tested while gaining insight into its re-specifications. By improving the model through aggregations and modifications of the structural and/or the measurement models, the stringency of the test becomes stronger. Our proposed SEM application flowchart is presented in Figure 3, and details and justifications are presented in the following algorithmic sections.

TWO ROUND SEM APPROACH

Anderson and Gerbing (1988); Lei and Wu (Lei, et al. 2007) have demonstrated a two-round approach for SEM which combines statistical tests simultaneously while using the measurement and structured (path) models one after the other as they correct the SEM value; this process is also possible for a single round analysis according to Hair (2006); Anderson and Gerbing (1988).

The latent variables measurement (measurement model) has its root from psychometric theories (Lei, et al. 2007); imperceptibly, measuring unobserved latent variables directly is difficult, yet are shown or inferred by reactions to various observable variables (indicators). An extension of multiple regression is structural or path analysis and this involves diverse models and equations that are simultaneously estimated. Path analysis can be regarded as a unique case of SEM in which structural relations among observed (versus latent) variables are modeled (Lei, et al. 2007).

It is therefore baseless to determine the structural model when the available measurement model is insufficient; model measurement is required for variable relationships as stated by Von der Heidt (2008), Anderson and Gerbing (1988), and Hair (2006). They further show that to maximize the interpretability of structural and measurement models, a two round approach is required to reduce ambiguity in interpretation (Hair, 2006). Firstly, the model measurement is validated by the researcher through confirmatory factor analysis (CFA), and secondly, by the estimate of the structural relationship in latent variables.

Hair (2006) has shown that CFA is the main step in SMEs two round process. He assessed the building block validity theory by estimation of model measurements separately via modifications (Anderson, et al., 1988; Von der Heidt, 2008); this represents the set of endogenous and exogenous structural model variability in conjunction with the direct effects, joining them with the disturbance terms for the varieties.

Figure 3. Proposed SEM application flowchart

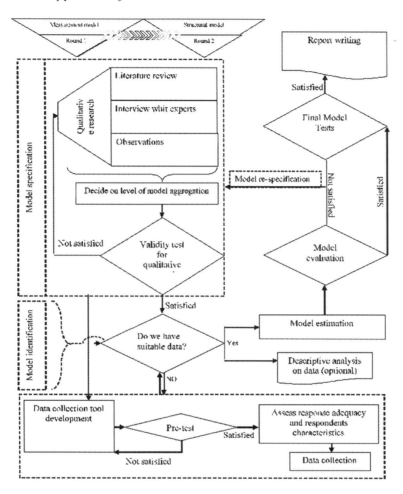

AGGREGATION OF MEASUREMENT MODEL IN STRUCTURAL MODEL

In assessing complicated model structures, three approaches are recommended (Bentler & Wu, 1995). Bagozzi and Heatherton (1994) however, represent these as levels of obstruction in support of the belief that two model assessment extremities exist; these include total disaggregation and aggregation; partial aggregation is sandwiched between them.

1. In total disaggregation, each item utilizes a separate indicator of the construct which gives detailed analysis for testing the model (Bagozzi, et al. 1994) with psychometric characteristics' to report individual items. This approach can result in higher error levels, mainly where there are larger item numbers.
2. Bagozzi and Heartherton (1994) have also shown that a composite variable which is comprised of all items is developed by total aggression whose approach constitutes dimensions and item aggregation. The ability to record the inherent characteristics of the concept and that of the smoothing

of the error is the most important of the total aggregation model as stated by Baumgartner and Homburg (Baumgartner, et al. 1996); Bagozzi and Heartherton (1994).
3. Each indicator dimension of the total construct in a partial aggregation approach retains each separate underlying factor (Bagozzi, et al. 1994).

A composite variable, however, is made out of the items of the separate dimensions of the construct which in this case assumes a single indicator for single factor model as stated by Bentler and Wu (1995). To test all the models of SEM, CFA is then performed. If the model is accepted, it would therefore be suggested that the composite variables would measure a single construct (Bagozzi, et al. 1994). The model assessment approach gives higher substantive content for each variable in smaller matrices, minimal error accumulated problems, and higher reliability (Von der Heidt, 2008). Baumgartner and Homburg (1996) therefore suggest that composite creation be made from scales for the establishment of reliability and unidimensionality. Hair (2006) and Von der Heidt (2008) have demonstrated that the advantages are improved composite applications in managerial and academic research. For complex and higher-order model assessment, it is showed that partial aggregation can be used at regular intervals (Von der Heidt 2008).

THE SEM PROCESS

Conceptualizations of the conventional SEM process somewhat vary with different numbers of stages suggested. Common to these approaches are the following five stages (Von der Heidt, 2008; Beran, et al. 2010):

1. Model specification or the research problem identification.
2. Model identification.
3. Model estimation.
4. Testing and evaluating model's goodness of fit.
5. Model modification or re-specification of the model.

This study modifies the above five stages by adding a data collection stage as a prerequisite for model identification stage and a report writing stage to finalize the SEM analysis and practices. Each stage may have a few sub-stage which are presented in below sections of this article.

SPECIFICATION OF THE MODEL

The exercise of estimation, which formally states the model, is known as model specification, and is as important as the statistical theory for SEM based on the fact that the models should be expressed on the basis of the theory, past empirical discoveries or both (Lei, et al. 2007, Von der Heidt 2008, Wong 2013) before data analysis. This step of SEM is mostly based on qualitative research. Likewise with any technique, SEM has its own limitations. SEM cannot redress the shortcomings inherent in any kind of study. Investigation of relationships among variables without priority specification may bring about statistical importance yet may have minimal theoretical importance. Moreover, poor research planning, unreliable and invalid information, absence of theoretical guidance, and over interpretation of causal relationships can result in deceptive and unreliable conclusions (Beran, et al. 2010).

Specification of the Measurement Models

The expression of the measurement model was discussed after the two round SEM process. Itemized sample pools for each construct were generated according to the qualitative research with its content and validity assessed. The design of the questionnaire was pre-tested before embarking on the target sample, which resulted to the removal of items. The model for measurement was finalized and specified. Model measurement specification involves determining which variable indicators or measures were able to explain each latent factor or construct (Von der Heidt, 2008). A model is explained to be *over-identified* in the event that it contains less parameters to be assessed or estimated than the number of variances and covariances, just-identified when the number of parameters is exactly as the number of variances and covariances, and *under-identified* if the number of variances and covariances is less than the estimated number of parameters (Lei, et al. 2007). However, the model measurement specifies the correspondence of construct indicators where each variable indicates only one construct. A factor is a latent variable which can be explained by loading all the variables. In factor analysis confirmatory mode, the contribution of each item can be assessed and evaluated on how reliable the items measure the concept (Hair, 2006).

Specification of the Structural Model

This explains in detail hypothesized relations within the theoretical constructs or model measurement (Hair, 2006). These relations or connections among variables are represented in models by 'paths', with a 'path' simply the effect or influence (direct or indirect) of one variable on another. Normally, variables in path diagrams are designated as endogenous or exogenous variables (Von der Heidt, 2008). These relationships may also be direct or indirect with interceding variables that may mediate the impact of one variable on another. The researcher should likewise figure out whether the relationships are unidirectional or bidirectional, by utilizing past investigations and theoretical forecasts as a guide (Beran, et al. 2010).

Conceptual Model Test

Model causality, one point of SEM conceptual model test, means that causal interpretation should be based on the available literature and theoretical groundings. The other point is generalizability, which presents the applicability of finding models from one study with a finite, often small sample to a population. Also, confirmation bias should be checked by researchers; this prejudice represents a bias in favor of the models, and qualitative methods of validity tests are suggested (Shah & Goldstein, 2006).

DATA COLLECTION

This section provides details of developing an instrument for the steps of a quantitative study, and the data collection process, that follows the SEM model specification stage.

Question Construction

Questionnaires are one of the main survey data collection tools utilized. (Karami 2007). A questionnaire is a set of questions that are systematically arranged in a formal way for obtaining information from a group of respondents. It is mostly used for information that cannot be easily observed or that is not readily available in written or computerized form. For a questionnaire to be valid, it must be able to translate the research objectives into specific questions whose answers will be used for hypotheses testing. The questions must also provide motivation for the respondents to provide the information being sought (Solomon & Draine, 2009). Since the foundation of all questionnaires is a question, survey questions may be concerned with facts, opinion, attitudes, respondents' motivation as well as their level of familiarity and understanding of the subject matter. Most questions however, can be classified into two major categories; factual questions and questions about subjective experience (Karami, 2005). Factual questions are designed to provoke objective information from the respondents especially responses on their background, environments and habits. Several steps, such as encouraging the respondents to answer the questions or making them feel comfortable when questioned about embarrassing events, are often necessary. In contrast, subjective questions are questions that center on respondents' beliefs, feelings, and opinions (Karami, 2005). Among different methods and scaling of the questions, Likert scales is suggested for SEM data collection.

Pre-Test

Shammout (2007) reports that "there is wide agreement among scholars that pre-testing is an integral part of the questionnaire development process." He pointed out, the researcher needs to ask: "Will the instrument provide data of sufficient quality and quantity to satisfy the objectives of the research?" (Shammout, 2007). According to Zikmund et al (2000), a pre-test can be defined as a trial run with a group of respondents; the aim of the pre-test is to screen out potential problems in the instructions or design of a questionnaire. They also point out that one of the aims of the pre-test is to examine if the questionnaire will be able to provide a sufficient quality and quantity of data that will meet the objectives of the research. There are diverse opinion on the appropriate method of pre-test administration according to Blair and Presser (1992), although the three widely used methods are: planned field survey, personal interviews (face-to-face), and expert panel.

A planned field survey employs a small sample referred to as 'pre-testing' (Zikmund, Carr, Griffin, Babin & Carr, 2003). Personal interview is when the interviewer is required to identify any obstacles, difficulties, or incomprehensible questions blocking respondents' ability to provide accurate answers. An expert panel is when a group of experts are invited to judge the data collection tool to determine errors and problems. Moreover, according to Shammout (2007) and Reynold and Diamantopouls (1998), a planned survey is one of the best choices because it can cover different aspects of the survey and it is less likely to be affected by the possible interaction between interviewers and respondents. However, a considerable problem with planned survey is that respondents who are not the targeted sample might complete the questionnaire. It is therefore suggested by Shammout (2007) and Reynolds and Diamantopoulos (1998) that personal interview is an effective means of conducting a pre-test, due to the completeness and accuracy of the collected data. Personal interview is known to be susceptible to errors resulting from interaction between the interviewer and participants (i.e., bias introduced by interviewers). However, expert panels (the last method) could be used to determine if there are problematic questionnaire items.

Methods of Data Collection

Questionnaires can be administered by several methods such as self-administered, use of postal, telephone, internet or fax. According to Frazer and Lawley (2000), before questionnaires are administered, there is the need to take some factors such as researcher's preference, cost, time constraints, potential response rate and many other important criteria into consideration. Table 2 which is adapted from Zulnaidi's study (2008) presenting the criteria of questionnaire administration.

Survey Sample Size

According to Davis and Cosenza (2000) several factors such as homogeneity of sampling unit, confidence, precision, statistical power, analytical procedure, cost, time and personnel all play a role in determining sample size in a research. Sample size provides the basis for the estimation of sample error and impacts on the ability of the model to be correctly estimated (Hair 2006). A search of literature shows that several method can be used to determine the size of a sample, following the rules of thumb by Roscoe (1975), a sample size larger than 30 and less than 500 are appropriate for most researches. However, the adequacy of sample size should also be determined according to the statistical analysis that was performed.

SEM is a large sample approach (Lei, et al. 2007). Under the normal distribution theory, numerous SEM users adopt the simple technique of the "rule of 5" (a sample size proportional to the number of parameters to be estimated) or the "rule of 10" to acquire suitable significance tests (Jannoo, et al. 2014). Essentially, larger models necessitate larger samples (Lei, et al. 2007). . According to references (Anderson and Gerbing 1984, Medsker Larry and Gina 1994) a minimum sample size of 100 is adequate for CB-SEM analysis. More wide-ranging guidelines are utilized in current research with the recommendation that no less than 100 however ideally 200 cases are expected to obtain stable results (Kline 2006). According to Kelloway (1998) a sample size of at least 200 observations is considered to be an appropriate minimum for survey research. Hair et al. (Hair 2006) proposed 200 as the 'critical sample size.' Boomsma (1983) recommended a sample size of approximately 400 observations for models of moderate complexity. Employing large sample diminishes the probability of irregular variety that can occur in small samples (Bentler and Yuan 1999), however, may be hard to obtain practically. In any case, it is suggested that when there is a small sample size and the data is non-normal, PLS-SEM is a superior technique (Gefen, et al. 2000).

Table 2. Criteria of questionnaire administration

Criteria	Mail questioner	Personal administered questioner	Telephone questioner	Internet questioner
Length of questioner	Long (4-12 pages)	Long (30-60 minutes)	Medium (10-30 minutes)	Long (4-12 pages)
Questionnaire complexity	Simple only	Simple to complex	Simple only	Simple only
Question complexity	Simple to moderate	Simple to complex	Simple only	Simple to moderate
Rapport with respondents	None	High	Moderate	None
Response rate	Low	High	Moderate	Moderate

Sampling

Sampling is the process by which a researcher selects a sample for a study from a large population (Zulnaidi, 2008). A search of literature shows that sampling method can be divided into probability and non-probability sampling. Probability sampling utilizes some form of random sampling. By using probability sampling, every subject in a population has an equal chance to be selected as a sample of the study (Zulnaidi 2008). In next sections, author shows that probability sampling is a choice of SEM practices.

IDENTIFICATION OF THE MODEL

Once the data is collected, the next step is model identification. The correspondence between estimated information and that to be estimated is the main reason for identification, according to Von der Heidt (2008), which therefore suggests guidelines for model identification (Hair 2006, Von der Heidt 2008).

Independent Observations

Bentler and Chou (1987) have demonstrated that responses exhibited by a person will not influence or be influenced by another as observed with interference. Although this believe cannot be tested statistically, care should be taken to ensure that this assumption is met by the researcher (Bentler, et al. 1987); the assumption of probability sampling, that the population should have equal probability of inclusion in the studied samples, is an important consideration here. (Bentler, et al. 1987).

Managing Missing Data

Bentler and Chou (1987) said that only complete data were dealt with in SEMs designed methods due to the fact that direct calculation of data sample covariance is problematic with missing data. In most areas of research, missing observations are part of the order (Kline and Santor 1999) with some occurring beyond the researcher's control, such as failure to respond to questions. The researcher, can remove missing variables, choosing to neglect some missing variables because of randomness of the missing values, or can take measures in missing value estimation, if the problems is far reaching (Hair, 2006).

Two identifiable missing data steps is suggested. In step 1, cases shown to contain high levels of missing data can be deleted. For the remaining data, no pattern in missing data variables should be noticed and it should be concluded that the process of missing data be classified as completely missed at random (Metts, 2004; Hair, 2006). In step 2, the missing values are replaced with the estimated values on other information available in the sample; a mean of the non-missing values can be used to replace the missing data in all subsequent analysis. Metts (2004) has showed similar steps in SEM research; he stated that less than 15% of data replacement will have impact on the outcome of data analysis.

Functional Form

Structural model assumptions are supported from the fact that relations among variables are linear in empirical and in theoretical questions (Bentler, et al. 1987). It further supported the fact that linearity was due to normally distributed multivariate variables or were similar after some approximation and modifications.

Normal Distribution

Hair (2006) has shown that SEM requirements are a function of multivariate normality, as goodness of fit indices and error is influenced by abnormality (Von der Heidt 2008). In normality assessment, care must be taken due to a large number of variables being tested; the complexity of the analysis, relationships and interrelationships may protect the violation of this assumption (Hair, 2006).

ESTIMATION METHOD

After model specification and identification, the process follows with calculation of parameter estimates (Savalei & Bentler, 2007). There are numerous estimation procedures accessible to test models, with three essential ones examined here. As a result of the simplicity of computation, correctness and accuracy of statistical results, the Maximum Likelihood (ML) discrepancy function is most commonly used for model estimation step in CB-SEM and is the default estimate method in most of SEM program packages (Jannoo, et al. 2014). It is an iterative process which estimates the degree to which the model predicts the sample covariance matrix values, with values more closer to zero showing better fit. The maximum likelihood is based on its computation. The estimate maximizes the likelihood that the data were obtain from its population. The estimates require large sample sizes (Beran, et al. 2010), and it is generally preferred when the data to be evaluated is normal as it yields unprejudiced estimates (Jannoo, et al. 2014). Another generally employed estimate is least squares (LS), which minimizes the total of the squares of the residuals in the model. LS is like ML as it also analyzes patterns of relationships, yet does as such by determining the optimal solution by minimizing the total of the squared deviation scores between hypothesized and observed model. It frequently performs better with smaller sample sizes (Hu & Bentler, 1998). The third, asymptotically distribution free (ADF) estimation methods (otherwise called Weighted Least Squares) are less frequently utilized yet may be proper if the information are skewed or peaked. ML, however, has a tendency to be more reliable than ADF (Beran, et al. 2010).

Data Coding

The data coding defines research variables. The creation of a data dictionary was designed to create data matrices, which could be taken care of by software analysis of choice. Different Likert scales can be used in the design of a close-ended questionnaire.

Computer Software for Estimate

With advances in computer programming, such as EQS (Equations implementing Structural Equation Modeling), and LISREL (Linear Structural Relationships), researchers started using SEM techniques in their research (Jöreskog, 1982; Jöreskog & Sörbom, 1993; Bentler, et al. 1995). Today, statistical programs available for SEM include: Mx, LISREL, SAS, AMOS, MPlus, EQS, CALIS, WarpPLS, GeSCA, PLS-Graph, Smart-PLS, LVPLS, among others. Even though WarpPLS, GeSCA, PLS-Graph, Smart-PLS, and LVPLS are more for PLS-SEM users (Hair, et al. 2012; Wong, 2013; Jannoo, et al. 2014), Hair (2006) has shown that the majority of the programs are similarly applied. LISREL, AMOS, and EQS are designed with point and click and graphical interface. A comparison of program features for four programs, AMOS, EQS, LISREL, and SAS CALIS, are reported by Byrne (2006). A more extensive comparison indicates that "The eight packages, Amos, R packages sem, SAS PROC CALIS, lavaan, LISREL, OpenMx, Mplus and EQS can be helpful to users in estimating parameters for a model where the structure is all around indicated. Capacities for dealing with single group, nonnormal variables, multiple group, and missing data are carefully evaluated and a comparison of the eight packages are made across a differing criteria from documentation to parameter estimation. The primary distinction between the packages is the presence of a graphical interface for model specification and presentation of results. Every package varies with regards to the strengths, areas of improvement, and unique elements that may dictate the preference of selection" (Narayanan, 2012). "Analysis of movement structures" software or AMOS is one of the earliest SEMs program for interface simplification and statistically, it is the analysis of choice for many CB-SEM studies due to the fact that it was the most user-friendly and also available in addition to SPSS (Sorooshian & Afshari, 2012).

TESTING AND EVALUATING THE MODEL

Protocols for reliability, validity and unidimensionality check for the models are stated below. The assessment of the model "fit" is linked to the set of tests. These items are separated but are closely related concepts (Shammout, 2007). These estimation methodology decides how well the model fits the data. Fitting the latent variable path model includes minimizing the contrast between the sample covariances and the covariances anticipated by the model (Beran, et al. 2010).

Unidimensionality

Von der Heidt (2008) has defined unidimensionality as the existence of one latent trait where the data underlies. However, an indicator or unidimensional item has only one underlying construct while a unidimensional measure is comprised of unidimensional items or indicators (Anderson, et al. 1988). In this study, unidimensionality was gauged by the use of CFA. The result of CFA for each model measurement, where every item restricted to load is a priority specified factor (Byrne 2006), the pre-specified measurement model should be significantly loaded onto the item (Hair 2006). Evidence of unidimensionality was further made known if measures of goodness-of-fit shows sufficiency of the model fit (Anderson, et al. 1988). A goodness of fit index (GFI) and comparative fit index (CFI) specifically of 0.90 or above for unidimensionality conveys strong evidence for each model (Byrne 2006).

Reliability

Reliability is the extent to which measures are free from random error to produce stable results for repeated measurements made on particular variables (Malhotra, 2009). The extent of scale compliance to stable results is referred to as reliability when repeated measures are made; however, to assess reliability, the alpha coefficient is widely preferred (Von der Heidt 2008). A relationship exist between error and reliability, the larger the reliability, the less the error. The first objective of reliability is to minimize research bias and error (Shammout 2007).

Validity

Reliability and unidimensionality is inadequate for instrument to be considered sufficient (Anderson, et al. 1988; Shammout, 2007). For the validation of this research construct, validity is required. Shammout (2007) has demonstrated that validity is the ability of measurement of the scale to capture the intended measurement. Furthermore, he suggested that two important aspect for valid construct includes: firstly, that the construct be used as a good representation for the area of observable relationship to the construct, and secondly, that the construct should represent alternative measures. Taking these into consideration, validity types including content and construct (discriminant and convergent validity) are suggested for SEM studies, which are related to the respective items and internal validities. In generalizing the research finding models, external validity was investigated which is covered in final model test section.

- **Face or Content Validity:** How the conceptual definitions match with the item (Von der Heidt 2008), as covered in the section for validity in qualitative research.
- **Construct Validity**: Concerned with the instrument and what are measured (Shammout 2007).

Content validity shows how well the result is achieved by employing the theories and measure fitting, around which the test was designed (Sekaran, 2010). It needs to be established qualitatively and prior to quantitative analyses. Validity measurement refers to formation of adequate and correct measures for operation for the concept being tested (Malhotra, 2009).

Construct validity can be examined by analysis on discriminate, convergent validity, and additional nomoligical testing:

- **Convergent Validity:** Determines the level of correlation of a measure with others of similar construct (Sekaran, 2010).
- **Discriminate Validity**: Determines that construct measures have not highly correlated with other constructs (Sekaran, 2010). However, the researcher differentiates empirically, the construct from others which may seem similar (Von der Heidt, 2008).
- **Construct Validity:** Additional criteria is nomological validity. The desired construct should be related to others based on hypothesized ways derived from the theory where the theory is attached to form nomological net for the set of constructs (Von der Heidt, 2008).

Fitness Factors

Model fit measurement, modification and assessment is inextricably related with the unidimensionality assessment, validity and reliability of each construct (Von der Heidt, 2008). Here, sample size is very critical for determining the model's goodness-of-fit, and sufficiently large sample size must be used in order to obtain stable estimates of the parameters (Beran, et al. 2010). Model fit indices are defined in the SEM literature, as new indices are developed (Isik, 2009). SEMs analysis software LISREL and AMOS prints 15 and 25 different goodness of fit measures, respectively. There is confusion among scholars as to which model fit indices should be reported (Metts, 2004; Shammout, 2007). Under certain conditions, some indices performs better than others. Generally, there is recommendation that multiple indices be considered simultaneously during evaluation of overall model fit (Lei, et al. 2007). The choice had been disputed among methodologists who, however, depend on the data properties to determine which indices and values to report (Isik, 2009). Hu and Bentler (Hu & Bentler, 1999) suggest to report at least two indices.

Chi-square ($\chi2$ or CMIN) probably, is one of the most used indices for goodness of fit evaluation; though it is sample size sensitive (Metts, 2004), higher sample size may result in the model rejection. The normal $\chi2$ measure is the ratio of the $\chi2$ value to the degree of freedom ($\chi2/df$), where ratios in the range of 3.0 to 1.0 expresses a good fit between the hypothetical model and the data sample (Byrne, 2006). Shammout (2007); Shumacker and Lomax (2004) have stated an acceptable fit between the range of 1.0 and 5.0, respectively.

The root mean square error of approximation (RMSEA) is an estimate of the approximation error per model degree of freedom if the sample size is to be considered (Isik 2009). The zero value shows the best fit, while worst fit is expressed by higher values. The value for RMSEA up to 0.08 as the rule of thumb, is an indication of good fit while less than 0.1 is acceptable fit (Isik, 2009), RMR measures the average absolute value of the covariance residuals. Perfect model fit is represented by RMR = 0 (less than 0.08 (Shammout, 2007)). RMR values less than 0.10 are widely seen as acceptable (Metts, 2004; Shammout, 2007; Kline, 2011).

Goodness fit index (GFI), comparative fit index (CFI), Relative fit index (RFI), Increment fit index (IFI), Normed fit index (NFI), Tucher lewis index (TLI) and Adjusted goodness of fit (AGFI) indexes are used in this study. They range from 0 – 1 which shows poor fit and perfect fit, respectively (Shammout, 2007). These indexes scores that are in the range of 0.8-0.89 are interpreted by most researchers as reasonable fit and 0.90 or higher as good fit (Metts, 2004).

MODEL MODIFICATION (RE-SPECIFICATION)

The main researcher question is the level at which the hypothesized model agrees with the real model (Von der Heidt 2008). At the point where the hypothesized model is not accepted in light of goodness of-fit statistics, SEM researchers are often keen on discovering an alternative model that fits the data (Lei, et al. 2007). Model examination first attempt results often show non-convergence or poor fit without solution (Anderson, et al. 1988), thus, showing the need for revision of the measurements or structural model. Researchers are cautioned against making unnecessary volume of alterations and against making alterations that are not bolstered by solid substantive hypotheses (Byrne, 2013). To obtain better fit results, the above succession of steps is repeated until the most concise model is derived. A prescribed procedure to enhance the model estimations is through evaluation of the size of the standardized residual values between variables (Beran, et al. 2010).

Von der Heidt (2008) has reported that another useful aid to help in the potential source of model misspecification is the modification index, which is calculated for every non-free parameter. Decreased value of the Chi-square is represented by modification index, when the estimated parameter is a revised model. In support of the guideline, the researcher continues by estimating the associated parameter with the largest modification indices, where the estimated parameter for theoretical rationale is considered (Bentler, et al. 1987; Baumgartner, et al. 1996; Hair, 2006).

Final Model Test

External validity is used to validate the final result, which is in form of a linear model. However, validity which was initially discussed relates to the internal validity for the scales and their perspective items, while external validity takes care of the extent to which the generalization of the study findings was carried out compared to another group (Shammout, 2007). Case studies can be considered, to ensure the external validity as well as predictive validity of the final model, model linearity and/or model accuracy, and model feasibility; and of the final model set.

REPORT WRITING

Two strategies exist to present models in SEM research studies (Nyu, 2011); "one strategy is to present your structured model early on as an organizing device that guides your literature review. The model gives the reader an overview of where you are headed and where you will end up. An alternative strategy is to save the presentation of the model for the end of the introduction. The idea here is that you review all the literature relevant to the model concepts (without ever presenting it) and this review culminates in a synthesized framework that is captured in the model. So, the literature review builds up to the model. Either approach is fine and author's choice of which to pursue depends on what you think will communicate best" (Nyu, 2011).

CONCLUSION

With the improvement of structural equation modeling, scientists now have intense analytic devices to analyze causal complex models. SEM is better over other correlational techniques, as multiple variables are simultaneously analyzed, and latent variables decrease estimation errors. When a confirmatory or exploratory approach is used within good research design, it yields information about the complex nature of disease and health behaviors. It does as such through an examination of both direct and indirect, and unidirectional and bidirectional relationships between latent and measured variables. Notwithstanding the profitable contributions of SEM to research methodology, the researcher must be mindful of a few considerations to build up a stable and legitimate model. These incorporate employing appropriate research design, sufficient measures, and a necessary size of sample. Nonetheless, the theory and application of SEM and their importance to understanding human phenomena are emphasized. In the research context, SEM guarantees the opportunity of examining multiple symptoms and health behaviors that, with advancement in model and refinement, can be used to improve research capacities in sciences.

Business advisors may use advanced methods of structural equation modeling to formulate a prediction model. SEM has the ability to rank facts and decisions variables in any business. It can find moderating and mediation effects of business variables and facts. The modeling strategy of SEM is applicable to measure and/or predict business/decisions failure risks and business decisions success. It is a method to test business hypothesis and to confirm data collection tools for business analytics. SEM is suggested for 21 century business, for decision supports, modeling and complex business analytics.

This article is among few articles presenting bias of SEM application by proving a practical flowchart for SEM users. The flowchart can be used as a foundation for programming and computations of SEM. The main focus of this article is a SEM model development strategy. However, we believe that all SEM practices can fully or partially apply a very similar flowchart. This article argued that CB-SEM practice is a balanced method of qualitative and qualitative research approaches with two potential rounds and seven practical stages. Feasibility of our introduced flowchart has been tested through a few studies and SEM applications. The author believes that still scholars can develop alternative algorithms for SEM applications in different fields, with other SEM strategies.

ACKNOWLEDGMENT

The author would like to thank the anonymous reviewers and the editor for their insightful comments and suggestions.

REFERENCES

Amaratunga, D., Baldry, D., Sarshar, M., & Newton, R. (2002). Quantitative and Qualitative Research in the Built Environment: Application of "Mixed" Research Approach. *Work Study*, *51*(1), 17–31. doi:10.1108/00438020210415488

Anderson, J., & Gerbing, D. (1984). The Effect of Sampling Error on Convergence, Improper Solutions, and Goodness-of-Fit Indices for Maximum Likelihood Confirmatory Factor Analysis. *Psychometrika*, *49*(2), 155–173. doi:10.1007/BF02294170

Anderson, J., & Gerbing, D. (1988). Structural Equation Modeling in Practice: A Review and Recommended Two-Step Approach. *Psychological Bulletin*, *103*(3), 411–423. doi:10.1037/0033-2909.103.3.411

Astrachan, C. B., Patel, V. K., & Wanzenried, G. (2014). A Comparative Study of Cb-Sem and Pls-Sem for Theory Development in Family Firm Research. *Journal of Family Business Strategy*, *5*(1), 116–128. doi:10.1016/j.jfbs.2013.12.002

Bagozzi, R. P., & Heatherton, T. F. (1994). A General Approach to Representingmultifaceted Personality Constructs: Application to State Self-Esteem. *Structural Equation Modeling*, *1*(1), 35–67. doi:10.1080/10705519409539961

Baumgartner, H., & Homburg, C. (1996). Applications of Structural Equation Modeling in Marketing and Consumer Research: A Review. *International Journal of Research in Marketing*, *13*(2), 139–161. doi:10.1016/0167-8116(95)00038-0

Bentler, P. M., & Chou, C. P. (1987). Practical Issues in Structural Modeling. *Sociological Methods & Research*, *16*(1), 78–117. doi:10.1177/0049124187016001004

Bentler, P. M., & Wu, E. (1995). *Eqs for Windows User's Guide*. Encino, CA: Multivariate Software.

Bentler, P. M., & Yuan, K.-H. (1999). Structural Equation Modeling with Small Samples: Test Statistics. *Multivariate Behavioral Research*, *34*(2), 181–197. doi:10.1207/S15327906Mb340203 PMID:26753935

Beran, T. N., & Violato, C. (2010). Structural Equation Modeling in Medical Research: A Primer. *BMC Research Notes*, *3*(1), 267. doi:10.1186/1756-0500-3-267 PMID:20969789

Blair, J., & Presser, S. (1992). An Experimental Comparison of Alternative Pretest Techniques: A Note on Preliminary Findings'. *Journal of Advertising Research*, *32*, 2–5.

Bollen, K. A. (2014). *Structural Equations with Latent Variables*. John Wiley & Sons.

Boomsma, A. (1983). *On the Robustness of Lisrel (Maximum Likelihood Estimation) against Small Sample Size and Non-Normality*. Rijksuniversiteit Groningen.

Byrne, B. (2006). *Structural Equation Modeling with Amos: Basic Concepts, Applications, and Programming* (2nd ed.). Lawrence Erlbaum.

Byrne, B. M. (2013). *Structural Equation Modeling with Lisrel, Prelis, and Simplis: Basic Concepts, Applications, and Programming*. Psychology Press.

Cavana, R., Delahaye, B., & Sekaran, U. (2001). *Applied Business Research*. Wiley.

Cheung, G. W. (2008). Testing Equivalence in the Structure, Means, and Variances of Higher-Order Constructs with Structural Equation Modeling. *Organizational Research Methods*, *11*(3), 593–613. doi:10.1177/1094428106298973

Curran, J., & Blackburn, R. (2001). *Researching the Small Enterprise*. SAGE Publications Ltd.

Davis, D., & Cosenza, R. (2000). *Business Research for Decision Making*. Duxbury Press.

Frazer, L., & Lawley, M. (2000). *Questionnaire Design and Administration: A Practical Guide*. Wiley.

Gefen, D., Straub, D., & Boudreau, M.-C. (2000). Structural Equation Modeling and Regression: Guidelines for Research Practice. *Communications of the Association for Information Systems*, *4*, 7.

Gobakhloo, M. (2009). *It Adobtion in Manufacturing Smes*. University Putra Malaysia, Mechanical and Manufacturing Engineering.

González, J., De Boeck, P., & Tuerlinckx, F. (2008). A Double-Structure Structural Equation Model for Three-Mode Data. *Psychological Methods*, *13*(4), 337–353. doi:10.1037/a0013269 PMID:19071998

Gray, P. S., & Williamson. (2007). *The Research Imagination: An Introduction to Qualitative and Quantitative Methods*. Cambridge University Press.

Hair, B., Babin, Anderson, & Tabtam. (2006). *Multivariate Data Analysis* (6th ed.). Pearson International Edition.

Hair, J., Jr., Anderson, R., Tatham, R., & William, C. (1995). *Multivariate Data Analysis*. Englewood Cliffs, NJ: Prentice Hall.

Hair, J. F., Ringle, C. M., & Sarstedt, M. (2012). Editorial-Partial Least Squares: The Better Approach to Structural Equation Modeling? *Long Range Planning*, *45*(5-6), 312–319. doi:10.1016/j.lrp.2012.09.011

Hart, S. (1987). The Use of the Survey in Industrial Market Research. *Journal of Marketing Management*, *3*(1), 25–38. doi:10.1080/0267257X.1987.9964025

Hu, L.-, & Bentler, P. M. (1998). Fit Indices in Covariance Structure Modeling: Sensitivity to Underparameterized Model Misspecification. *Psychological Methods*, *3*(4), 424–453. doi:10.1037/1082-989X.3.4.424

Hu, L. t., & Bentler, P. M. (1999). Cutoff Criteria for Fit Indexes in Covariance Structure Analysis: Conventional Criteria Versus New Alternatives. *Structural Equation Modeling: A Multidisciplinary Journal*, *6*, 1-55.

Hughes, M., Price, R., & Marrs, D. (1986). Linking Theory Construction and Theory Testing: Models with Multiple Indicators of Latent Variables. *Academy of Management Review*, *11*, 128–144.

Hurley, R. (1999). Qualitative Research and the Profound Grasp of the Obvious. *Health Services Research*, *34*, 1119. PMID:10591276

Isik, Z. (2009). *A Conceptual Performance Measurment Framework for Construction Industry*. Middle East Technical University.

Jannoo, Z., Yap, B., Auchoybur, N., & Lazim, M. (2014). The Effect of Nonnormality on Cb-Sem and Pls-Sem Path Estimates. *International Journal of Mathematical, Computational, Natural and Physical Engineering*, *8*, 6.

Jöreskog, K. G. (1982). The Lisrel Approach to Causal Model-Building in the Social Sciences. *Systems Under Indirect Observation*, *1*, 81-100.

Jöreskog, K. G., & Sörbom, D. (1993). *Lisrel 8: Structural Equation Modeling with the Simplis Command Language*. Scientific Software International.

Karami, A. (2005). *Senior Managers and Strategic Management Process*. University of Bradford, Management School.

Karami, A. (2007). *Strategy Formulation in Entrepreneurial Firms*. Ashgate Pub Co.

Kelloway, E. (1998). *Using Lisrel for Structural Equation Modeling: A Researcher's Guide*. Sage Publications, Inc.

Kline, R. B. (2006). *Structural Equation Modeling*. Concordia University.

Kline, R. B. (2011). *Principles and Practice of Structural Equation Modelling* (3rd ed.). New York: The Guilford Press.

Kline, R. B., & Santor, D. A. (1999). Principles and Practice of Structural Equation Modelling. *Canadian Psychology, 40*(4), 381–383. doi:10.1037/h0092500

Lei, P. W., & Wu, Q. (2007). Introduction to Structural Equation Modeling: Issues and Practical Considerations. *Educational Measurement: Issues and Practice, 26*(3), 33–43. doi:10.1111/j.1745-3992.2007.00099.x

Malhotra, N. (2009). *Marketing Research: An Applied Orientation, 5/E*. Pearson Education India. doi:10.1108/S1548-6435(2009)5

Medsker Larry, J., & Gina, J. (1994). A Review of Current Practices for Evaluating Causal Models in Organizational Behavior and Human Resources Management Research. *Journal of Management, 20*(2), 439–464. doi:10.1177/014920639402000207

Metts, G. (2004). *An Investigation of the Relationship between Strategy Making and Performance*. (PhD Dissertation). University of Toledo.

Narayanan, A. (2012). A Review of Eight Software Packages for Structural Equation Modeling. *The American Statistician, 66*(2), 129–138. doi:10.1080/00031305.2012.708641

Neuman, W. (1997). *Social Research Methods*. Allyn and Bacon London.

Nyu. (2011). *Guidelines for Writing a Proposal That Uses Sem and for Writing the Results Section of a Thesis*. Academic Press.

Prayag, G. (2009). *Visitors to Mauritius - Place Perceptions & Determinants of Repeat Visitation*. University of Waikato, Department of Tourism Management.

Remenyi, D., Williams, B., Money, A., & Swartz, E. (1998). *Doing Research in Business and Management*. Sage London.

Reynolds, N., & Diamantopoulos, A. (1998). The Effect of Pretest Method on Error Detection Rates: Experimental Evidence. *European Journal of Marketing, 32*(5/6), 480–498. doi:10.1108/03090569810216091

Ringle, C. M., Sarstedt, M., & Straub, D. (2012). A Critical Look at the Use of Pls-Sem in Mis Quarterly. *Management Information Systems Quarterly, 36*.

Roscoe, J. (1975). *Fundamental Research Statistics for the Behavioral Sciences*. CBLS.

Savalei, V., & Bentler, P. M. (2007). *Structural Equation Modeling* (4th ed.). New York: Wiley Online Library.

Schumacker, R., & Lomax, R. (2004). *A Beginner's Guide to Structural Equation Modeling*. Lawrence Erlbaum.

Scopus. (2016), Retrieved from: www.scopus.com

Sekaran, U. (2010). Research Methods for Business: A Skill Building Approach (5th ed.). New York: Wiley.

Shah, R., & Goldstein, S. M. (2006). Use of Structural Equation Modeling in Operations Management Research: Looking Back and Forward. *Journal of Operations Management*, *24*(2), 148–169. doi:10.1016/j.jom.2005.05.001

Shammout, A. (2007). *Evaluating an Extended Relationship Marketing Model for Arab Guests of Five-Star Hotels*. (Thesis). Victoria University, Australia. Retrieved from: http://vuir.vu.edu.au/1511/1/Shammout.pdf

Solomon, P., & Draine, J. (2009). An Overview of Quantitative Research Methods. In The Handbook of Social Work Research Methods. Academic Press.

Sorooshian, S., & Afshari, A. (2012). Structural Equation Modeling: Software Comparative Review. In *Proceedings of the 2012 International Conference on Industrial Engineering and Operations Management*.

Sorooshian, S., Teck, T. S., Salimi, M., & How, L. C. (2012). Develops in Latent Variable Methods of Analysis. *International Journal of Soft Computing*, *7*(2).

Trochim, W. (2005). *Research Methods: The Concise Knowledge Base*. Cincinnati, OH: Atomic Dog Publishers.

Vignali, C., Gomez, E., Vignali, M., & Vranesevic, T. (2001). The Influence of Consumer Behaviour within the Spanish Food Retail Industry. *British Food Journal*, *103*(7), 460–478. doi:10.1108/00070700110401595

Violato, C., & Hecker, K. G. (2007). How to Use Structural Equation Modeling in Medical Education Research: A Brief Guide. *Teaching and Learning in Medicine*, *19*(4), 362–371. doi:10.1080/10401330701542685 PMID:17935466

Von der Heidt, T. (2008). *Developing and Testing a Model of Cooperative Interorganisational Relationships (Iors) in Product Innovation in an Australian Manufacturing Context: A Multi-Stakeholder Perspective*. Southern Cross University, School of Commerce and Management.

Wong, K. K.-K. (2013). Partial Least Squares Structural Equation Modeling (Pls-Sem) Techniques Using Smartpls. *Marketing Bulletin*, *24*, 1–32.

Wright, S. (1920). The Relative Importance of Heredity and Environment in Determining the Piebald Pattern of Guinea-Pigs. *Proceedings of the National Academy of Sciences of the United States of America*, *6*(6), 320–332. doi:10.1073/pnas.6.6.320 PMID:16576506

Zikmund, W., Carr, B., Griffin, M., Babin, B., & Carr, J. (2000). *Business Research Methods* (Vol. 6). Dryden Press Fort Worth.

Zikmund, W., Carr, B., Griffin, M., Babin, B., & Carr, J. (2003). Business Research Methods (Vol. 8). Dryden Press.

Zulnaidi, Y. (2008). *A Structural Relationship between Total Quality Management, Strategic Control Systems and Performance of Malaysian Local Governments*. (Thesis). Universiti Utara Malaysia. Retrieved from: http://etd.uum.edu.my/53/2/Zulnaidi_Yaacob(PHD_GRADUATE_SCHOOL_GRADUATE_SCHOOL.pdf

KEY TERMS AND DEFINITIONS

Business Analytics: Modeling and studies to formulate variable relationships in business, industry, and any profession.

Factor Analysis: A mathematical/statistical method to analyses complex interrelations of observed and latent variables.

Modeling: A mathematical/statistical relationship between variables of a study.

Research Method: Any method, qualitative or quantitative, with ability to discover a fact.

SEM Application Algorithm: An step by step roadmap for application of SEM in a study.

Structural Equation Modeling (SEM): An advanced mathematical/statistical method with ability to analyze complex interrelations of dependent, independent and moderator variables.

Variable: Any analyzable condition or factor which can be in different types or amounts.

Chapter 3
An Integrated Fuzzy VIKOR Method for Performance Management in Healthcare

Ehsan Shekarian
University of Malaya, Malaysia

Salwa Hanim Abdul-Rashid
University of Malaya, Malaysia

Ezutah Udoncy Olugu
UCSI University, Malaysia

ABSTRACT

Poor quality control has become a major threat to medical laboratory services, especially in the developing countries. It has become necessary to assess and rank the quality of diagnostic services in medical laboratories using systematic approaches. The main aim of this research is to develop and apply a quantitative method in ranking medical laboratory services. This method is based on a combination of Vlsekriterijumska Optimizacija I Kompromisno Resenje (VIKOR) with fuzzy set theory. VIKOR is a multiple criteria decision making technique which focuses on ranking and selection from a set of alternatives, and determines the compromise solution for a problem with different criteria. This approach aids decision makers to achieve the most acceptable decision amidst numerous alternatives. In the present evaluation method, international standard ISO 15189 (Medical Laboratories Particular Requirements for Quality and Competence) proposed by International Organization for Standardization (ISO) is used as a fundamental source of selected attributes of a medical laboratory. The study compares three medical laboratories to each other and ranks them. This study will be a valuable and effective contribution in enhancing both qualitative and quantitative criteria in the field of medical laboratory services. Finally, some directions for further studies are proposed.

DOI: 10.4018/978-1-5225-0654-6.ch003

An Integrated Fuzzy VIKOR Method for Performance Management in Healthcare

INTRODUCTION

A medical laboratory is an integral part of the health care system in every country, which plays an important role (diagnosis) in the treatment process of patients. It further provides essential public health services, which are required by medical practitioners. Today, medical laboratories are considered as a very important part of the medical diagnosis and treatment process that facilitate the effectiveness and efficiency of physicians. Hence, medical diagnoses provide the fundamentals to medical solutions. Generally, a proper diagnosis is the beginning of a progressive cure, follow up and confirmation of effective treatment is based on regular laboratory testing. However, error rate of 0.1–9.3% in the field of the preanalytical and postanalytical phases of testing has been shown in medical diagnostic laboratories (Kalra, 2004). The quality management systems have partially replaced the requirements for preliminary experiences based on professional self-regulation (Plebani, 2002).

Any error in laboratory results raises the cost of patient care and prolongs the treatment period. Therefore, selecting the best laboratories for patients is a major problem, which may be resolved by ranking the medical laboratories. Thus, the purpose of this study is to provide a suitable ranking solution for medical laboratories using fuzzy set theory. This ranking will ensure redefinition of competition among medical laboratories towards offering better clinical laboratory services. This will in turn boost the quality of health care services in general.

In recent years, the application of multiple criteria decision-making (MCDM) method in the field of health care systems has been gaining a lot of attention. Some of these studies include, groundwater quality assessment (Li et al., 2012), analysis for susceptibility of breast cancer (Xu and Jiang, 2011), and in disease treatment such as chronic plaque psoriasis (Guibal et al., 2009). Other applications are in the areas of improvement of waste reduction (Su et al., 2010), and selection of the appropriate solid waste site (Önüt & Soner, 2008).

Decision making is the process of defining the decision goals, gathering relevant information and selecting the optimal alternative (Hess & Siciliano, 1996). To deal with problems that are characterized by several non-commensurable and competing criteria, MCDM methods are usually employed. In fact, a decision maker (DM) has to choose the best alternative that satisfies the evaluation criteria among a set of possible solutions. According to Tzeng and Huang (2011), MCDM is a technique, which enables multiple criteria consideration at the same time and helps the decision maker to identify the best case by evaluating cases according to the characteristics or criteria of each available case. Since, it is generally difficult to find an alternative that simultaneously meets all the criteria, determining a compromise solution rather than an optimal solution is preferred. In this study, VIKOR method is applied to select the best medical laboratory (alternative) using a compromise solution approach.

In literature, this is the first study that aims to rank the medical laboratories based on the fuzzy-VIKOR method as a powerful operational research method. When a patient who actually is assumed to be a customer for institutional health services seeks among appropriate medical laboratories the level of their quality is a major concern for him. These laboratories are therefore in a competence to satisfy their patients. Medical laboratory managers should enhance their quality to closely meet patients' needs. However, evaluating the service quality of medical laboratories is usually a complicated process. When the ranking of medical laboratories is investigated, it has to be considered many issues such as dealing with many factors, an uncertain environment, and a logical method, just to name a few. In the light of the purpose of this research, we apply MCDM method together with fuzzy set theory in the context of healthcare planning and management. It attempts to bridge the aforementioned gap that exists in the literature. In this regard, the study applied ISO 15189: 2003 (Medical Laboratories particular requirements for quality and competence) to select some critical medical laboratory attributes. Suggested method of current study could help the medical laboratory managers to evaluate their quality and compete.

The VIKOR method was introduced as an applicable technique to implement within MCDM (Opricovic, 1998). It is a helpful tool in multicriteria decision making, particularly in a situation where the decision maker is not able, or does not know to express his/her preference at the beginning of system design (Opricovic & Tzeng, 2004). This method introduces a compromise and feasible solution, which is the closest to the ideal solution. Compromise means an agreement established by mutual concessions (Opricovic & Tzeng, 2007). Furthermore, in order to deal with the uncertainty in decision process, it has been used under a fuzzy environment with fuzzy sets to select the best laboratory. On one hand most of the attributes affecting the decision making process are not certain, complete and specific. On the other hand, the decision maker should rely on this ambiguous information to choose the best options. It is clear that it will complicate the mentioned process. Fuzzy set theory is a tool to capture the uncertainty in the experts' judgments inherits while it combines the knowledge from experts and data to get a better result, and in these circumstances, it is better suited to the process than a crisp one (Shekarian, 2012; Shekarian et al., 2016). We therefore apply it to modify the VIKOR method for handling uncertainty and linguistic interpretability, which is in the form of human language.

Opricovic (1998) developed VIKOR, which is based on the basic concept of the positive-ideal solution (PIS) and negative-ideal solution (NIS). The VIKOR method is widely utilized to determine the best feasible solution in many fields such as prioritizing land-use restraint strategies (Chang and Hsu, 2009), supplier selection (Sanayei et al., 2010), portfolio selection (Jerry et al., 2011), website evaluation (Tsai et al., 2010), evaluation of service quality of airports (Kuo and Liang, 2011), insurance company selection (Yücenur and Demirel, 2012), brand marketing (Wang and Tzeng, 2012), construction project selection (Ebrahimnejad et al., 2012), information security risk control assessment (Ou Yang et al., 2011), financial performance evaluation (Yalcin et al., 2012), and housing economics (Shekarian, 2015).

ISO 15189: 2003 has become a widely accepted standard for the evaluation and accreditation of clinical laboratory in many countries (Bautista-Marín et al., 2012; Theodorou and Anastasakis, 2009; Guzel and Guner, 2009; Sierra-Amor, 2009). Bautista-Marín et al. (2012) showed that implementation of a quality management systems (QMS) ISO 15189 was effective to improve the management of the urine culture unit in Spain. According to the mentioned ISO, Theodorou and Anastasakis (2009) presented a management review checklist which helps laboratories carry out an effective management review. Guzel and Guner (2006) evaluating some leading institutions concluded that every laboratory has to concentrate on patient safety issues related to laboratory testing and should perform quality improvement projects. Sierra-Amor (2009) pointed out the economical support of the government to medical laboratories implementing ISO 15189 in Mexico. This standard allows laboratories to improve their operational procedures effectively in order to fulfill the expectations of clients and improve the services they provide. The ISO 15189:2003 standard is important for evaluating the competence of the medical laboratories in their technical capacity and quality management of professional services and their staff. It is not a certification standard, but an important guide for technical improvement (Unsal et al., 2009).

The remainder of this paper is organized as follows: next Section is devoted to review some recent studies that have been conducted in health care systems dealing with MCDM method and fuzzy set theory. Section 3 looks at material and method of present research. The VIKOR method is briefly demonstrated in Section 4. In Section 5, the proposed MCDM technique for medical laboratories is explained. A case study containing the introduced technique is illustrated to showcase the effectiveness and efficiency of the proposed model in Section 6. Finally, the conclusion is presented in Section 7.

LITERATURE REVIEW

Application of MCDM techniques in health care systems has been discussed in many studies. Besides, application of artificial intelligence methods such as neural network (Kodogiannis, 2014), fuzzy neural network (Mohammed et al., 2014), in healthcare systems significantly increased in recent years. On the other hand, application of fuzzy logic in healthcare has not been well researched, and the topic still remains a niche for dedicated experts (Pagliaro, 2007). In this section, some of the related studies conducted recently in healthcare are being reviewed.

Nobre et al. (1999) applied a MCDM approach known as Tomada de Decisão Interativa Multicritério in Portuguese (TODIM) incorporating fuzzy set approaches to procurement health technology in a University Hospital in Rio de Janeiro, Brazil. Analytic Hierarchy Process (AHP) has been used in an attempt to better define hospital policy in a pilot program at The Hospital for Sick Children, Toronto (Koch and Rowell, 1999). In addition, Bilsel et al. (2006) measured the performance of the Web sites of Turkish hospitals combining the AHP method, fuzzy numbers, and fuzzy Preference Ranking Organization Method for Enrichment Evaluation (PROMETHEE) ranking method. Furthermore, AHP technique was combined with a life cycle management (LCM) in order to establish and optimize health care waste management (HCWM) systems in rural areas of developing countries (Brent et al., 2007). Liberatore and Nydick (2008) reviewed the application of AHP to important problems in medical and health care decision making. Fuzzy TOPSIS to effectively evaluate suitable radio frequency identification (RFID) solution providers in healthcare services has been applied (Wang et al., 2009). Decision-making trial and evaluation laboratory (DEMATEL) method has been applied to the hospital management by evaluating the importance of criteria from patients' or their families' viewpoints at Show Chwan Memorial Hospital in Changhua City, Taiwan (Shieh et al., 2010). A fuzzy MCDM approach with a multilevel hierarchical structure including qualitative as well as quantitative performance attributes has been proposed for evaluating health-care waste disposal alternatives for Istanbul (Dursun et al., 2010). Lee and Kwak (2011) employed a MCDM model based on the Goal programming (GP) and AHP analyzed data obtained from a leading patient-oriented provider of health-care services in Korea to deal with strategic enterprise resource planning (ERP) in a health-care system. A fuzzy multi-criteria group decision making approach, which is based on the principles of fusion of fuzzy information, 2-tuple linguistic representation model has been utilized to order preference by similarity to ideal solution (TOPSIS) to evaluate health-care waste (HCW) treatment alternatives in Istanbul (Dursun et al., 2011). In another study, a new predictive risk assessment model consisting of analytic network process (ANP), reality-design gap evaluation and fuzzy inference system has been developed for a hospital information system (HIS) (Yucel et al., 2012). Dursun et al. (2011) proposed a MCDM technique for conducting an analysis based on multi-level hierarchical structure and fuzzy logic for the evaluation of HCW treatment alternatives. A fuzzy-AHP to evaluate the proposed service quality framework has been proposed in healthcare sector in Turkey in (Büyüközkan et al., 2011). Dursun et al. (2011) presented a fuzzy multi-criteria group decision making framework based on the principles of fuzzy measure and fuzzy integral for evaluating HCW treatment alternatives for Istanbul. Uzoka et al. (2011) extended the fuzzy and AHP techniques to develop a medical diagnosis system. Four experts in health fraternity as decision makers to describe the application of a fuzzy decision making method has been used in ranking indicators of Health-Related Quality of Life (HRQoL) among kidney patients (Abdullah and Jamal, 2011). Rais and Viana (2011) reviewed several applications of operations research in the domain of healthcare. Büyüközkan and Çifçi (2012) determined the key components of electronic service quality (e-sq) using a combined MCDM methodology containing fuzzy AHP and TOPSIS applying a web service performance example of the healthcare sector in Turkey. Besides, the fuzzy AHP to establish an evaluation model of optimal region selection has been applied for joint-venture hospitals in China (Tsai and Lin 2012). A risk determination model according to principles of fuzzy logic and sum fuzzy membership functions to minimize human error has been developed (Ozok, 2012). Recently, an improved VIKOR method has been suggested with enhanced accuracy in the medical field by introducing a new data normalization method (Zeng et al. 2013).

PRELIMINARIES

Fuzzy Preliminaries

In many real life situations, ambiguity and uncertainty always accompany decision-making process. Therefore, it is expected that exact data is insufficient and unsatisfactory for modeling of real-life under these situations. Fuzzy set theory, which was first proposed by Zadeh (1965), is an appropriate tool to represent and manipulate the imprecision in decision-making problems quantitatively. In the ensuing section, some basic concepts are briefly explained (Zadeh, 1975; Zimmermann, 2001).

- **Definition 1:** $\tilde{A}$ is a fuzzy set in a universe of discourse $X = \{x_1, x_2, ..., x_n\}$. It is characterized by a membership function $\mu_{\tilde{A}}(x)$, which is associated with each element x, where x is a real number in the interval $[0,1]$. The function value $\mu_{\tilde{A}}(x)$ is termed as the grade of membership of x in $\tilde{A}$.
- **Definition 2:** The fuzzy set $\tilde{A}$ of the universe discourse X is convex, where:

$$\mu_{\tilde{A}}(\lambda x_1 + (1-\lambda)x_2) \geq \min(\mu_{\tilde{A}}(x_1), \mu_{\tilde{A}}(x_2)) \text{ for all } x_1, x_2 \in X \text{ and for } \lambda \in [0,1].$$

- **Definition 3:** The fuzzy set $\tilde{A}$ of the universe of discourse X is called a normal fuzzy set when. $\exists x_i \in X, \mu_{\tilde{A}}(x_i) = 1$.

- **Definition 4:** A linguistic variable is a variable whose values are linguistic terms. Linguistic terms (such as very poor, poor, fair, good, very good) have been found to be intuitively easy in expressing the viewpoints of a DM as the assessor.

On the basis of definitions 2 and 3, a fuzzy number is a fuzzy subset which is both convex and normal. Among fuzzy numbers, triangular and trapezoidal fuzzy numbers are the most common used. In the present study, trapezoidal fuzzy numbers are preferred for representing the linguistic variables. $\tilde{A}$ is said to be a positive trapezoidal fuzzy number represented by the crisp numbers (a_1, a_2, a_3, a_4), where $a_1 < a_2 < a_3 < a_4$, when its membership function is presented as:

$$\mu_{\tilde{A}}(x) = \begin{cases} 0, & x < a_1, \\ l(x) = (x - a_1)/(a_2 - a_1), & a_1 \leq x \leq a_2, \\ 1, & a_2 \leq x \leq a_3, \\ r(x) = (x - a_4)/(a_3 - a_4), & a_3 \leq x \leq a_4, \\ 0, & x > a_4. \end{cases} \quad (1)$$

When $a_2 = a_3$, the trapezoidal fuzzy number described in Eq. (1) becomes a triangular, which is a special case of the first. Trapezoidal fuzzy numbers have been applied in this research since they have some advantages over other linear and nonlinear membership functions as follow (Bansal, 2011):

1. They form the most generic class of fuzzy numbers with linear membership function.
2. They span entirely the widely discussed class of triangular fuzzy numbers.
3. They have more applicability in modeling linear uncertainty in scientific problems.
4. They have conceptual and computational simplicity.

For the calculations of fuzzy numbers, Function Principle Method is used (Chen, 1985). Now, assume $\tilde{A} = (a_1, a_2, a_3, a_4)$ and $\tilde{B} = (b_1, b_2, b_3, b_4)$ are two positive trapezoidal fuzzy numbers and λ being a real number. Based on the Functional Principle, the operations of the fuzzy numbers $\tilde{A}$ and $\tilde{B}$ are expressed as:

$$\tilde{A} + \tilde{B} = (a_1 + b_1, a_2 + b_2, a_3 + b_3, a_4 + b_4).$$

$$\tilde{A} - \tilde{B} = (a_1 - b_4, a_2 - b_3, a_3 - b_2, a_4 - b_1).$$

$$\tilde{A} \times \tilde{B} = (a_1 b_1, a_2 b_2, a_3 b_3, a_4 b_4).$$

$$\frac{\tilde{A}}{\tilde{B}} = (\frac{a_1}{b_4}, \frac{a_2}{b_3}, \frac{a_3}{b_2}, \frac{a_4}{b_1}).$$

$$\begin{cases} \lambda \times \tilde{B} = (\lambda b_1, \lambda b_2, \lambda b_3, \lambda b_4), & \lambda \geq 0, \\ \lambda \times \tilde{B} = (\lambda b_4, \lambda b_3, \lambda b_2, \lambda b_1), & \lambda < 0. \end{cases}$$

Defuzzification Method

Defuzzification is a concept, which transforms a fuzzy number into a crisp value. In this paper, the Graded Mean Integration Representation (GMIR) method proposed by Chen and Hsieh (1999) for defuzzification is applied.

Suppose $\tilde{A} = (a_1, a_2, a_3, a_4)$ is a trapezoidal fuzzy number, l^{-1} and r^{-1} are respectively inverse functions of l and r (left and right function of trapezoidal fuzzy number), where the graded α-level value of $\tilde{A}$ is $\dfrac{\alpha(l^{-1}(\alpha) + r^{-1}(\alpha))}{2}$ and the GMIR of the fuzzy number $\tilde{A}$ is calculated as:

$$I(\tilde{A}) = \dfrac{\int_0^1 \dfrac{\alpha(l^{-1}(\alpha) + r^{-1}(\alpha))}{2} d\alpha}{\int_0^1 \alpha \, d\alpha} = \int_0^1 \alpha(l^{-1}(\alpha) + r^{-1}(\alpha)) d\alpha, \qquad (2)$$

the values of $l^{-1}(\alpha)$ and $r^{-1}(\alpha)$ are $a_1 + (a_2 - a_1)\alpha$ and $a_4 - (a_4 - a_3)\alpha$, respectively. The solution of Eq. (2) can now be determined by replacing the values of $l^{-1}(\alpha)$ and $r^{-1}(\alpha)$ which yields:

$$I(\tilde{A}) = \dfrac{\int_0^1 \dfrac{\alpha[(a_1 + a_4) + ((a_2 + a_3) - (a_1 + a_4))\alpha]}{2} d\alpha}{\int_0^1 \alpha \, d\alpha} = \dfrac{1}{6}(a_1 + 2a_2 + 2a_3 + a_4) \qquad (3)$$

Final value of Eq. (3) is defuzzified value of trapezoidal fuzzy number $\tilde{A}$.

THE VIKOR METHOD

Opricovic (1998) proposed VIKOR method, which is a technique to solve multi criteria decision making problems. This aids decision-makers rank a number of alternatives by looking at their performance scores in the presence of a set of conflicting criteria. This was further developed by Opricovic and Tzeng (2002, 2003, 2004, 2007).

Let us consider a MCDM problem in matrix format as below:

$$DM = \begin{array}{c} \\ A_1 \\ A_2 \\ \vdots \\ A_m \end{array} \begin{array}{cccc} C_1 & C_2 & \cdots & C_n \end{array} \\ \left[\begin{array}{cccc} x_{11} & x_{12} & \cdots & x_{1n} \\ x_{21} & x_{22} & \cdots & x_{2n} \\ \vdots & \vdots & \ddots & \vdots \\ x_{m1} & x_{m2} & \cdots & x_{mn} \end{array} \right] \qquad (4)$$

where $A_1, A_2, ..., A_m$ denote the m alternatives facing a decision-maker, $C_1, C_2, ..., C_n$ are criteria with which alternative performance are measured and x_{ij} is the rating of alternative $A_i (i = 1, 2, ..., m)$ with respect to criterion $C_j (j = 1, 2, ..., n)$. For such a decision making problem, VIKOR method introduces a compromise solution. In fact, the obtained solution is the closest to the ideal solution, and a compromise means an agreement established by mutual concession. To find the compromise solution, VIKOR uses the following form of LP-metric:

$$L^p_k = \left\{\sum_{j=1}^n \left[w_j\left(\left|f^*_j - f_{kj}\right|\right)/\left(\left|f^*_j - f^-_j\right|\right)\right]^p\right\}^{1/p} \quad (5)$$

where:

$1 \leq p \leq \infty; \; k = 1, 2, \ldots, m$

where f_{kj} is the value of j th criterion function for the alternative A_i and w_j is weight on the j th criterion which expresses the relative importance of that criterion. The VIKOR method utilizes above LP-metric for $p = 1$ (as S_k) and $p = \infty$ (as Q_k) to formulate the ranking measure as below:

$$S_k = L^{p=1}_k = \left\{\sum_{j=1}^n \left[w_j\left(\left|f^*_j - f_{kj}\right|\right)/\left(\left|f^*_j - f^-_j\right|\right)\right]\right\} \quad (6)$$

$$Q_k = L^{p=\infty}_k = \text{Max}_j \left\{w_j\left(\left|f^*_j - f_{kj}\right|\right)/\left(\left|f^*_j - f^-_j\right|\right)\right\} \; j = 1, 2, \ldots, n \quad (7)$$

The solution given by $\min S_k$ is with a maximum group utility (i.e., majority rule), and the solution provided by $\min Q_k$ is with a minimum individual regret of the opponent (Ebrahimnejad et al., 2012). The main procedure of VIKOR technique is described below:

Step 1: Calculate the best f^*_j and the worst f^-_j values of all criterion functions as follow:

$f^*_j = \text{Max}_k f_{kj}$: for benefit criteria (8) $f^*_j = \text{Min}_k f_{kj}$: for cost criteria (9)
$f^-_j = \text{Min}_k f_{kj}$ $f^-_j = \text{Max}_k f_{kj}$

Step 2: Compute the values of S_k and Q_k as Eqs. (6) and (7) and calculate R_k by the below relation:

$$R_k = \upsilon(S_k - S^*)/(S^- - S^*) + (1-\upsilon)(Q_k - Q^*)/(Q^- - Q^*) \quad (10)$$

where S^- is the maximum value of S_k and S^* is the minimum value of S_k; Q^- is the maximum value of Q_k and Q^* is the minimum value of Q_k. Also, υ is presented as the strategy of maximum group utility and $(1-\upsilon)$ is introduced as the weight of individual regret. Although υ can take any value from 0 to 1 but, in the experiment, it is usually taken as 0.5.

Step 3: Order the alternatives decreasingly by the value of S_k, Q_k and R_k. Therefore, there are three ranking lists.

Step 4: Propose the alternative $A^{(1)}$, which is ranked the best by R, as a compromise solution if the following two conditions are satisfied:

C_1: "Acceptable advantage": $R(A^{(2)}) - R(A^{(1)}) \geq 1/(m-1)$, where $A^{(2)}$ is the alternative in second position of the ranking list by R and m is the number of alternatives.

C_2: "Acceptable stability in decision making": The alternative $A^{(1)}$ must also be the best when ranked by S and/or Q.

A set of compromise solutions is proposed if one of the above conditions is not satisfied. The set of compromise solutions consists of:

(α) Alternatives $A^{(1)}$ and $A^{(2)}$, if C_1 is satisfied and C_2 is not satisfied.

(β) Alternatives $A^{(1)}, A^{(2)}, ..., A^{(M)}$, if C_1 is not satisfied. Note that $A^{(M)}$ is determined by the relation

$R(A^{(M)}) - R(A^{(1)}) < 1/(m-1)$ for maximum M (the positions of these alternatives are close).

The compromise-ranking method (VIKOR) is applied to determine the compromise solution and the solution is adoptable for decision-makers in that it offers a maximum group utility of the majority (shown by min S), and a maximal regret of minimum individuals of the opponent (shown by min Q) (Wang and Tzeng, 2012).

PROPOSED METHOD

In this Section, the suggested medical laboratory ranking method is explained.

Step 1. Establishing the Scope and Goal of the Problem: The first step of the algorithm includes specifying the objectives. In this study, the goal is to determine the best medical diagnosis laboratory based on ISO 15189: 2003—medical laboratories particular requirements for quality and competence. It is worthy of note that in the last few years, attempts have been undertaken to strengthen the application of the international standard organization (ISO) 15189 accreditation, to ensure competency and quality of medical laboratories. All countries use ISO 15189 for the accreditation of all their medical laboratories in order to be competitive in a global environment (Sierra-Amor, 2009). It consists of two main parts including:
1. Management requirements and
2. Technical requirements.

Each part contains some subsections evaluating various aspects of a medical laboratory. The ISO 15189 has been used as an effective tool, which is well-known due to its developed teaching system contents, competency in scientific technique and logic purpose (Obayashi et al., 2009). Gathered requirements in this ISO, which is based upon the ISO 17025 and ISO 9001 standards (Guzel and Guner, 2009), provide guidance for laboratory procedures to ensure quality and competence in clinical laboratory examinations. However, not all requirements are easily understandable (Fuentes-Arderiu, 2006). Successful experiences of administrating have been reported in many countries such as Turkey (Unsal, 2009), Spain (Bautista-Marín et al., 2012) and Mexico (Sierra-Amor, 2009).

Step 2. Define a Finite Set of Relevant Attributes and Organizing the Decision Making Group: According to questions of ISO 15189 for medical laboratories, different criteria have been considered. Furthermore, three different laboratories as alternatives and three experts as a group of decision makers have been selected.

Step 3. Identifying the Appropriate Linguistic Variables: The appropriate linguistic variables for the importance weight of criteria, and the fuzzy rating for alternatives with regard to each criterion have been expressed in positive trapezoidal fuzzy numbers, as in Figures 1 and 2.

In these figures, "F", "G", "W", "V", "E", "I", and "U" stands for fair, good, bad, very, extremely, important, and unimportant, respectively.

Step 4. Construct a Fuzzy Decision Matrix: Assume the fuzzy rating and importance weight of the k th decision maker as below:

$$\tilde{x}_{ijk} = (x_{ijk1}, x_{ijk2}, x_{ijk3}, x_{ijk4})$$

Figure 1. Criteria important weight

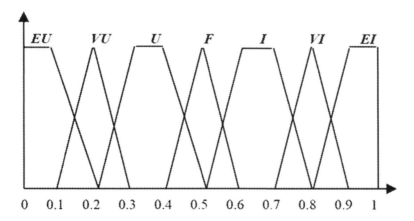

Figure 2. Linguistic variable for performance

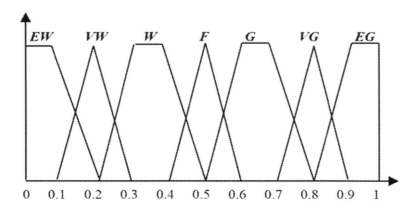

and

$$\tilde{w}_{jk} = (w_{jk1}, w_{jk2}, w_{jk3}, w_{jk4});$$

$i = 1, 2, \ldots, m$, $j = 1, 2, \ldots, n$.

Hence, the aggregated fuzzy rating of the ith alternative with respect to jth criterion can be calculated as below:

$$\tilde{x}_{ij} = (x_{ij1}, x_{ij2}, x_{ij3}, x_{ij4}) \qquad (11)$$

where:

$$x_{ij1} = \min_k \{x_{ijk1}\}, \quad x_{ij2} = \frac{1}{K}\sum_{k=1}^{K} x_{ijk2}, \quad x_{ij3} = \frac{1}{K}\sum_{k=1}^{K} x_{ijk3}, \quad x_{ij4} = \max_k \{x_{ijk4}\}.$$

The aggregated fuzzy weights $(\tilde{w}_j)$ of each criterion can be calculated as:

$$\tilde{w}_j = (w_{j1}, w_{j2}, w_{j3}, w_{j4}) \qquad (12)$$

where:

$$w_{j1} = \min_k \{w_{jk1}\}, \quad w_{j2} = \frac{1}{K}\sum_{k=1}^{K} w_{jk2}, \quad w_{j3} = \frac{1}{K}\sum_{k=1}^{K} x_{jk3}, \quad w_{j4} = \max_k \{w_{jk4}\}.$$

Therefore, problem of selection of the best medical laboratory can be concisely expressed in matrix format as follows:

$$\tilde{D} = \begin{bmatrix} \tilde{x}_{11} & \tilde{x}_{12} & \cdots & \tilde{x}_{1n} \\ \tilde{x}_{21} & \tilde{x}_{22} & \cdots & \tilde{x}_{2n} \\ \vdots & \vdots & \cdots & \vdots \\ \tilde{x}_{m1} & \tilde{x}_{m2} & \cdots & \tilde{x}_{mn} \end{bmatrix} \qquad \tilde{W} = [\tilde{w}_1 \quad \tilde{w}_2 \quad \cdots \quad \tilde{w}_n]$$

where $\tilde{x}_{ij}$ th rating of alternative A_i with respect to C_j, $\tilde{w}_j$ the importance weight of the jth criterion $j = 1, 2, \ldots, n$ holds, $\tilde{x}_{ij} = (x_{ij1}, x_{ij2}, x_{ij3}, x_{ij4})$ and $\tilde{w}_j = (w_{j1}, w_{j2}, w_{j3}, w_{j4})$; $i = 1, 2, \ldots, m$ and $j = 1, 2, \ldots, n$ are linguistic variables can be approximated by positive trapezoidal fuzzy numbers.

Step 5. Defuzzification: This step includes defuzzyfing of the fuzzy decision matrix and fuzzy weight into crisp values. GMIR method for defuzzyfing is applied as described previously in Section 3.2.

Step 6. Now the problem is ready to be solved using VIKOR method and to identify the best alternative.

A CASE STUDY

In this Section, the best medical laboratory is selected using the proposed model in the following steps:

Step 1: The aim is to choose the best laboratory among three candidate laboratories (L_1, L_2, L_3) based on the ISO 15189: 2003 for Medical Laboratory.

Step 2: Considering different functional areas of a laboratory, three decision makers (DM_1, DM_2, DM_3) in the fields of virology, bacteriology, and immunology have been contacted to select the most suitable laboratory. In order to avoid excessively long calculations, ten criteria have been considered in consultation with experts as depicted in Figure 3. In fact, to derive these criteria and the gathered data in Tables 1 and 2, we used a semi-structure interview in which permits interviewees to illustrate and describe their work in their own words (human linguistic). First, we asked them to study the protocol of ISO 15189. Then, a 50-to 60 min interview with each expert was conducted. Finally, analyzing the audio recordings, these criteria that were highlighted by the experts were identified by the research team. They are explained as below:

- **Monitoring:** Check up on all work performed in the laboratory to determine that reliable data are being generated.
- **Training:** Assessing the competency of the staff undergoing training.
- **Furnishing:** All the items of equipment required for medical laboratory services (including primary sample collection, and sample preparation and processing, examination and storage).
- **Software:** Documentation and validation of computer software as adequate for the use of the facility.
- **Storing:** Samples storing for a specified time under conditions ensuring stability of sample properties, to enable repetition of the examination after reporting of the result or for additional examinations.
- **Evaluation:** Evaluation of methods and procedures for satisfactory results before implementation.

Figure 3. Model selection

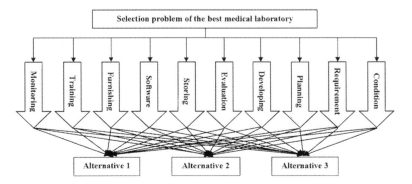

- **Developing:** Developing a mechanism for deciding the acceptability of procedures not otherwise evaluated.
- **Planning:** An organizational plan, personnel policies and job descriptions for all personnel which are done by laboratory management.
- **Requirement:** The requirements, including the pre-examination and post-examination procedures which are adequately defined, documented and understood.
- **Condition:** Laboratory resources maintained in a functional and reliable condition.

Step 3: Utilizing linguistic weighting variables shown in Figure 1, three decision makers assess the importance of the criteria. Also the decision makers use the linguistic rating variables shown in Figure 2 to evaluate the ratings of candidates with respect to each criterion. The results of this step are shown in Tables 1 and 2 respectively.

Step 4: The linguistic evaluations shown in Tables 1 and 2 are converted into trapezoidal fuzzy numbers. Then the aggregated weight of criteria and aggregated fuzzy rating of alternatives are calculated to construct the fuzzy decision matrix and determine the fuzzy weight of each criterion, as in Tables 3 and 4.

Step 5: The crisp values for decision matrix and weight of each criterion are calculated as presented in Table 5. As mentioned earlier, GMIR method has been used for defuzzyfying.

Table 1. The importance of criteria from the perspective of decision makers

Decision Maker	Criteria									
	Monitor	Train	Furnish	Software	Store	Evaluation	Develop	Plan	Requirement	Condition
DM_1	EI	I	EI	I	EI	VI	VI	VI	EI	VI
DM_2	VI	I	VI	VI	VI	VI	VI	I	VI	VI
DM_3	EI	I	EI	VI	I	VI	I	F	F	VI

Table 2. Criteria rating of alternatives from the perspective of decision makers

Decision Maker		Criteria									
		Monitor	Train	Furnish	Software	Store	Evaluation	Develop	Plan	Requirement	Condition
		Laboratory									
DM_1	L_1	G	EG	VG	G	VG	VG	G	G	VG	G
	L_2	VG	F	VG	VG	EG	G	F	VG	G	VG
	L_3	G	VG	VG	G	F	G	G	W	F	G
DM_2	L_1	VG	F	G	G	VG	EG	F	G	G	VG
	L_2	VG	G	F	EG	G	F	W	VG	F	EG
	L_3	W	G	VG	G	G	F	G	VG	G	VG
DM_3	L_1	F	G	W	G	G	G	F	G	F	G
	L_2	G	F	VG	EG	VG	G	F	G	G	VG
	L_3	F	G	G	F	VG	W	G	VG	VG	EG

An Integrated Fuzzy VIKOR Method for Performance Management in Healthcare

Step 6: Finally, the decision problem can be solved using VIKOR method.

The continuation of problem corresponding to algorithm of VIKOR method can be solved as follows:

Step 1: The best and worst values of all criterion ratings are determined as presented in Table 6.
Step 2, 3: The values of S, Q and R are calculated for all laboratories as Table 7. Also, the ranking of the alternatives by S, Q and R in decreasing order is shown in Table 7.
Step 4: L_2 is the best medical laboratory since it is the best ranked by R and satisfies conditions C_1 and C_2 of VIKOR method. Thereafter, L_1 is in second place according to R value.

According to the Table 7, medical laboratory 2 has a better service quality performance based on the mentioned criteria of ISO 15189. From Table 5, it is clear that Monitoring and Furnishing are the most important criteria in experts' views and medical laboratories 1 and 3 should pay more attention to them and other important criteria such as condition and evaluation. Furthermore, laboratory 2 should

Table 3. Aggregated fuzzy rating of alternatives and aggregated fuzzy weight of criteria

	Criteria				
	Monitor	Train	Furnish	Software	Store
L_1	(0.40,0.63,0.67,0.90)	(0.40,0.67,0.73,1.00)	(0.20,0.57,0.63,0.90)	(0.50,0.60,0.70,0.80)	(0.50,0.73,0.77,0.90)
L_2	(0.50,0.73,0.77,0.90)	(0.40,0.53,0.57,0.80)	(0.40,0.70,0.70,0.90)	(0.70,0.87,0.93,1.00)	(0.50,0.77,0.83,1.00)
L_3	(0.20,0.47,0.53,0.80)	(0.50,0.67,0.73,0.90)	(0.50,0.73,0.77,0.90)	(0.40,0.57,0.63,0.80)	(0.40,0.63,0.67,0.90)
Weight	(0.70,0.87,0.93,1.00)	(0.50,0.60,0.70,0.80)	(0.70,0.87,0.93,1.00)	(0.50,0.73,0.77,0.90)	(0.50,0.77,0.83,1.00)

Table 4. Aggregated fuzzy rating of alternatives and aggregated fuzzy weight of criteria

	Criteria				
	Evaluation	Develop	Plan	Requirement	Condition
L_1	(0.50,0.77,0.83,1.00)	(0.40,0.53,0.57,0.80)	(0.50,0.60,0.70,0.80)	(0.40,0.63,0.67,0.90)	(0.50,0.67,0.73,0.90)
L_2	(0.40,0.57,0.63,0.80)	(0.20,0.43,0.47,0.60)	(0.50,0.73,0.77,0.90)	(0.40,0.57,0.63,0.80)	(0.70,0.83,0.87,1.00)
L_3	(0.20,0.47,0.53,0.80)	(0.50,0.60,0.70,0.80)	(0.20,0.63,0.67,0.90)	(0.40,0.63,0.67,0.90)	(0.50,0.77,0.83,1.00)
Weight	(0.70,0.80,0.80,0.90)	(0.50,0.73,0.77,0.90)	(0.40,0.63,0.67,0.90)	(0.40,0.73,0.76,1.00)	(0.70,0.80,0.80,0.90)

Table 5. Crisp values for decision matrix and weight of each criterion

	Criteria									
	Monitor	Train	Furnish	Software	Store	Evaluation	Develop	Plan	Requirement	Condition
L_1	0.65	0.70	0.58	0.65	0.73	0.78	0.57	0.65	0.65	0.70
L_2	0.73	0.57	0.68	0.88	0.78	0.60	0.43	0.73	0.60	0.85
L_3	0.50	0.70	0.73	0.60	0.65	0.50	0.65	0.62	0.65	0.78
Weight	0.88	0.65	0.88	0.73	0.78	0.80	0.73	0.65	0.73	0.80

Table 6. The best and the worst values of all criterion

Criteria	Monitor	Train	Furnish	Software	Store	Evaluation	Develop	Plan	Requirement	Condition
f_i^*	0.73	0.70	0.73	0.88	0.78	0.78	0.65	0.73	0.65	0.85
f_i^-	0.50	0.57	0.58	0.60	0.65	0.50	0.43	0.62	0.60	0.70

Table 7. The values of S, R and Q for all alternatives and the ranking of them in decreasing order

	Laboratory				Ranking		
	L_1	L_2	L_3		By S	By Q	By R
S	3.62	2.92	4.21	1	L_2	L_2	L_2
Q	0.88	0.73	0.88	2	L_1	L_1	L_1
R	0.73	0.00	1.00	3	L_3	L_3	L_3

improve its service quality in those criteria which have weak performance to continue to be the best medical laboratory. Although it is assumed that all three laboratories are able to improve their service qualities, the managers' viewpoints about each criterion are still a vital issue. None of the criteria should be neglected in three medical laboratories. The key to being the best laboratory is pay more attention to those criteria which are most important in order of preference as it is viewable in Table 5. A strategic recommendation is that to improve the quality it is necessary to focus on the criteria in which have the more weight and at the same time enhance the performance of the other criteria. Increasing the quality of an especial part does not affect all the system; and it is better to have a balance among all parts of the laboratory in a long time.

CONCLUSION AND RECOMMENDATIONS

Laboratory results influence 70% of medical diagnoses. The quality of laboratory service is the major factor which directly affects the quality of health care. In this study, a real and applicable method to demonstrate how MCDM model can be applied to evaluate the medical laboratory services was presented. This was achieved by building an effective model for evaluating the medical laboratories using fuzzy set theory and extended VIKOR method. In order to determine related attributes of a medical laboratory, ISO 15189: 2003—Medical Laboratories, particular requirements for quality and competence was used. The findings proved the application of extended VIKOR and fuzzy set theory techniques can help to assess and evaluate the quality of medical laboratories in the presence of multitudes of criteria. This may be used in scoring the laboratories which helps to manage the laboratory system in covering and meeting the requirement of the standard in quality management system. Furthermore, this study will be a valuable and effective contribution for enhancing both qualitative and quantitative criteria selection in the field of medical laboratories. The study presents a new and unique approach on the assessment, development and advancement in the application of ISO 15189 as an effective tool to medical laboratories.

Unlike developed countries, access to the micro-data in developing countries is a major challenge due to the lack of free flow of information. This could be assumed as another limitation of this paper. Future research could apply the proposed method for experimental example.

Although there are many factors in the ISO 15189, we considered some important criteria in order to ignore some unnecessary calculations. This was one of the limitations that was encountered in the current study. Another limitation of the current study was an inadequate number of research on the topic of laboratory errors (Foubister, 2000) and ranking.

For future research, other MCDM methods such as multi attribute utility theory (MAUT), outranking methods, analytical hierarchy process (AHP), analytical network process (ANP), and techniques for order performance by similarity to ideal solution (TOPSIS) along with artificial intelligence methods such as Adaptive Network Based Fuzzy Inference System (ANFIS) (Shekarian & Gholizadeh, 2013), and Gene Expression Programming (GEP) (Shekarian & Fallahpour, 2013) may be applied in this field. Besides, considering different linguistic rating variables for different types of criteria can be investigated. Building and developing a decision making software that is able to rank the medical laboratories based on a plat form that works with the suggested method of this paper applying more attributes of ISO 15189 is another future direction.

ACKNOWLEDGMENT

The author would like to thank the anonymous reviewers and the editor for their insightful comments and suggestions.

The first author wishes to express his gratitude to University of Malaya for funding his research (Grant no. RP018b-13aet).

REFERENCES

Abdullah, L., & Jamal, N. J. (2011). Determination of Weights for Health Related Quality of Life Indicators among Kidney Patients: A Fuzzy Decision Making Method. *Applied Research in Quality of Life*, *6*(4), 349–361. doi:10.1007/s11482-010-9133-3

Bansal, A. (2011). Trapezoidal fuzzy numbers (a, b, c, d): Arith-metic Behavior. *International Journal of Physical and Mathemat-ical Sciences*, *2*(1), 39–44.

Bautista-Marín, M.-F., Rojo-Martín, M.-D., Pérez-Ruiz, M., Miranda-Casas, C., Martínez-Muñoz, P., & Navarro-Marí, J.-M. (2012). Implementation and monitoring of a quality management system based on the standard UNE-EN-ISO 15189 in a urine culture unit. *Clinical Biochemistry*, *45*(4), 374–377. doi:10.1016/j.clinbiochem.2011.12.016 PMID:22240066

Bilsel, R. U., Büyüközkan, G., & Ruan, D. (2006). A fuzzy preference-ranking model for a quality evaluation of hospital web sites. *International Journal of Intelligent Systems*, *21*(11), 1181–1197. doi:10.1002/int.20177

Brent, A. C., Rogers, D. E., Ramabitsa-Siimane, T. S., & Rohwer, M. B. (2007). Application of the analytical hierarchy process to establish health care waste management systems that minimise infection risks in developing countries. *European Journal of Operational Research, 181*(1), 403–424. doi:10.1016/j.ejor.2006.06.015

Büyüközkan, G., & Çifçi, G. (2012). A combined fuzzy AHP and fuzzy TOPSIS based strategic analysis of electronic service quality in healthcare industry. *Expert Systems with Applications, 39*(3), 2341–2354. doi:10.1016/j.eswa.2011.08.061

Büyüközkan, G., Çifçi, G., & Güleryüz, S. (2011). Strategic analysis of healthcare service quality using fuzzy AHP methodology. *Expert Systems with Applications, 38*(8), 9407–9424. doi:10.1016/j.eswa.2011.01.103

Chang, C.-L., & Hsu, C.-H. (2009). Multi-criteria analysis via the VIKOR method for prioritizing land-use restraint strategies in the Tseng-Wen reservoir watershed. *Journal of Environmental Management, 90*(11), 3226–3230. doi:10.1016/j.jenvman.2009.04.020 PMID:19482411

Chen, S.-H. (1985). Operations on fuzzy numbers with function principle. *Tamkang Journal of Management Sciences, 6*(1), 13–26.

Chen, S. H., & Hsieh, C. H. (1999). Graded mean integration representation of generalized fuzzy number. *Journal of Chinese Fuzzy Systems, 5*(2), 1–7.

Dursun, M., Karsak, E. E., & Karadayi, M. A. (2010). Fuzzy Group Decision Making for the Assessment of Health-Care Waste Disposal Alternatives in Istanbul. World Academy of Science. *Engineering and Technology, 42*, 850–854.

Dursun, M., Karsak, E. E., & Karadayi, M. A. (2011). A fuzzy multi-criteria group decision making framework for evaluating health-care waste disposal alternatives. *Expert Systems with Applications, 38*(9), 11453–11462. doi:10.1016/j.eswa.2011.03.019

Dursun, M., Karsak, E. E., & Karadayi, M. A. (2011). A Fuzzy MCDM Approach for Health-Care Waste Management. World Academy of Science. *Engineering and Technology, 49*, 720–726.

Dursun, M., Karsak, E. E., & Karadayi, M. A. (2011). Assessment of health-care waste treatment alternatives using fuzzy multi-criteria decision making approaches. *Resources, Conservation and Recycling, 57*, 98–107. doi:10.1016/j.resconrec.2011.09.012

Ebrahimnejad, S., Mousavi, S., Tavakkoli-Moghaddam, R., Hashemi, H., & Vahdani, B. (2012). A novel two-phase group decision making approach for construction project selection in a fuzzy environment. *Applied Mathematical Modelling, 36*(9), 4197–4217. doi:10.1016/j.apm.2011.11.050

Foubister, V. (2000). Bench press: The technologist/technicians shortfall is putting the squeeze on laboratories nationwide. *CAP Today*, 84.

Fuentes-Arderiu, X. (2006). Biological reference intervals and ISO 15189. *Clinica Chimica Acta, 364*(1), 365–366. doi:10.1016/j.cca.2005.07.014 PMID:16139260

Gholizadeh, A.A., & Shekarian, E. (2012). A new approach on housing choice using fuzzy logic. *Tahghighat- E- Eghtesadi (University of Tehran), 47*(3), 65-84

Guibal, F., Iversen, L., Puig, L., Strohal, R., & Williams, P. (2009). Identifying the biologic closest to the ideal to treat chronic plaque psoriasis in different clinical scenarios: Using a pilot multi-attribute decision model as a decision-support aid. *Current Medical Research and Opinion, 25*(12), 2835–2843. doi:10.1185/03007990903320576 PMID:19916728

Guzel, O., & Guner, E. I. (2009). ISO 15189 Accreditation: Requirements for quality and competence of medical laboratories, experience of a laboratory I. *Clinical Biochemistry, 42*(4), 274–278. doi:10.1016/j.clinbiochem.2008.09.011 PMID:19863920

Hess, P. W., & Siciliano, J. (1996). *Management: Responsibility for performance*. New York: McGraw-Hill.

Jerry Ho, W.-R., Tsai, C.-L., Tzeng, G.-H., & Fang, S.-K. (2011). Combined DEMATEL technique with a novel MCDM model for exploring portfolio selection based on CAPM. *Expert Systems with Applications, 38*(1), 16–25. doi:10.1016/j.eswa.2010.05.058

Kalra, J. (2004). Medical errors: Impact on clinical laboratories and other critical areas. *Clinical Biochemistry, 37*(12), 1052–1062. doi:10.1016/j.clinbiochem.2004.08.009 PMID:15589810

Koch, T., & Rowell, M. (1999). The dream of consensus: Finding common ground in a bioethical context. *Theoretical Medicine and Bioethics, 20*(3), 261–273. doi:10.1023/A:1009995919835 PMID:10474312

Kodogiannis, V. S. (2014). Point-of-care diagnosis of bacterial pathogens in vitro, utilising an electronic nose and wavelet neural networks. *Neural Computing & Applications, 25*(2), 353–366. doi:10.1007/s00521-013-1494-8

Kuo, M.-S., & Liang, G.-S. (2011). Combining VIKOR with GRA techniques to evaluate service quality of airports under fuzzy environment. *Expert Systems with Applications, 38*(3), 1304–1312. doi:10.1016/j.eswa.2010.07.003

Lee, C. W., & Kwak, N. (2011). Strategic enterprise resource planning in a health-care system using a multicriteria decision-making model. *Journal of Medical Systems, 35*(2), 265–275. doi:10.1007/s10916-009-9362-x PMID:20703564

Li, P., Wu, J., & Qian, H. (2012). Groundwater quality assessment based on rough sets attribute reduction and TOPSIS method in a semi-arid area, China. *Environmental Monitoring and Assessment, 184*(8), 4841–4854. doi:10.1007/s10661-011-2306-1 PMID:21894505

Liberatore, M. J., & Nydick, R. L. (2008). The analytic hierarchy process in medical and health care decision making: A literature review. *European Journal of Operational Research, 189*(1), 194–207. doi:10.1016/j.ejor.2007.05.001

Mohammed, M. F., Lim, C. P., & Quteishat, A. (2014). A novel trust measurement method based on certified belief in strength for a multi-agent classifier system. *Neural Computing & Applications, 24*(2), 421–429. doi:10.1007/s00521-012-1245-2

Nobre, F. F., Trotta, L. T. F., & Gomes, L. F. A. M. (1999). Multi-criteria decision making– an approach to setting priorities in health care. *Statistics in Medicine, 18*(23), 3345–3354. doi:10.1002/(SICI)1097-0258(19991215)18:23<3345::AID-SIM321>3.0.CO;2-7 PMID:10602156

Obayashi, K., Teramoto, K., Yamamoto, K., Ikeda, K., & Ando, Y. (2009) Accreditation of ISO 15189 in the Department of Laboratory Medicine, Kumamoto University Hospital: successful cases. Rinsho Byori: The Japanese Journal of Clinical Pathology, 57(2), 156-160.

Önüt, S., & Soner, S. (2008). Transshipment site selection using the AHP and TOPSIS approaches under fuzzy environment. *Waste Management (New York, N.Y.), 28*(9), 1552–1559. doi:10.1016/j.wasman.2007.05.019 PMID:17768038

Opricovic, S. (1998). *Multi-criteria optimization of civil engineering systems.* Belgrade: Faculty of Civil Engineering.

Opricovic, S., & Tzeng, G. H. (2002). Multicriteria Planning of Post-Earthquake Sustainable Reconstruction. *Computer-Aided Civil and Infrastructure Engineering, 17*(3), 211–220. doi:10.1111/1467-8667.00269

Opricovic, S., & Tzeng, G.-H. (2003). Fuzzy multicriteria model for post-earthquake land use planning. *Natural Hazards Review, 4*(2), 59–64. doi:10.1061/(ASCE)1527-6988(2003)4:2(59)

Opricovic, S., & Tzeng, G.-H. (2004). Compromise solution by MCDM methods: A comparative analysis of VIKOR and TOPSIS. *European Journal of Operational Research, 156*(2), 445–455. doi:10.1016/S0377-2217(03)00020-1

Opricovic, S., & Tzeng, G.-H. (2007). Extended VIKOR method in comparison with outranking methods. *European Journal of Operational Research, 178*(2), 514–529. doi:10.1016/j.ejor.2006.01.020

Ou Yang, Y.-P., Shieh, H.-M., & Tzeng, G.-H. (2011). A VIKOR technique based on DEMATEL and ANP for information security risk control assessment. *Information Sciences.*

Ozok, A. F. (2012). Fuzzy modelling and efficiency in health care systems. *Work (Reading, Mass.), 41,* 1797–1800. PMID:22316974

Pagliaro, L. (2007). Probabilistic and fuzzy logic in the clinical diagnosis. *Internal and Emergency Medicine, 2*(2), 75–75. doi:10.1007/s11739-007-0039-5 PMID:17622493

Plebani, M. (2002). Continuing medical education: A challenge to the Italian Scientific Societies of Laboratory Medicine. *Clinica Chimica Acta, 319*(2), 161–167. doi:10.1016/S0009-8981(02)00038-4 PMID:11955494

Rais, A., & Viana, A. (2011). Operations Research in Healthcare: A survey. *International Transactions in Operational Research, 18*(1), 1–31. doi:10.1111/j.1475-3995.2010.00767.x

Sanayei, A., Farid Mousavi, S., & Yazdankhah, A. (2010). Group decision making process for supplier selection with VIKOR under fuzzy environment. *Expert Systems with Applications, 37*(1), 24–30. doi:10.1016/j.eswa.2009.04.063

Shekarian, E. (2015). A novel application of the VIKOR method for investigating the effect of education on housing choice. *International Journal of Operational Research, 24*(2), 161–183. doi:10.1504/IJOR.2015.071493

Shekarian, E., & Fallahpour, A. (2013). Predicting house price via gene expression programming. *International Journal of Housing Markets and Analysis, 6*(3), 250–268. doi:10.1108/IJHMA-08-2012-0039

Shekarian, E., & Gholizadeh, A. A. (2013). Application of adaptive network based fuzzy inference system method in economic welfare. *Knowledge-Based Systems*, *39*, 151–158. doi:10.1016/j.knosys.2012.10.013

Shekarian, E., Olugu, E. U., Abdul-Rashid, S. H., & Kazemi, N. (2016). An economic order quantity model considering different holding costs for imperfect quality items subject to fuzziness and learning. *Journal of Intelligent & Fuzzy Systems*, *30*(5), 2985–2997. doi:10.3233/IFS-151907

Shieh, J.-I., Wu, H.-H., & Huang, K.-K. (2010). A DEMATEL method in identifying key success factors of hospital service quality. *Knowledge-Based Systems*, *23*(3), 277–282. doi:10.1016/j.knosys.2010.01.013

Sierra-Amor, R. I. (2009). Mexican experience on laboratory accreditation according to ISO 15189: 2003. *Clinical Biochemistry*, *42*(4), 318. doi:10.1016/j.clinbiochem.2008.09.095 PMID:19863944

Su, J.-P., Hung, M.-L., Chao, C.-W., & Ma, H.-. (2010). Applying multi-criteria decision-making to improve the waste reduction policy in Taiwan. *Waste Management & Research*, *28*(1), 20–28. doi:10.1177/0734242X09103839 PMID:19710114

Theodorou, D. G., & Anastasakis, P. C. (2009). Management review checklist for ISO/IEC 17025 and ISO 15189 quality-management systems. *Accreditation and Quality Assurance*, *14*(2), 107–110. doi:10.1007/s00769-008-0466-7

Tsai, M.-C., & Lin, C.-T. (2012). Selecting an optimal region by fuzzy group decision making: Empirical evidence from medical investors. *Group Decision and Negotiation*, *21*(3), 399–416. doi:10.1007/s10726-010-9214-6

Tsai, W.-H., Chou, W.-C., & Lai, C.-W. (2010). An effective evaluation model and improvement analysis for national park websites: A case study of Taiwan. *Tourism Management*, *31*(6), 936–952. doi:10.1016/j.tourman.2010.01.016

Tzeng, G. H., & Huang, J.-J. (2011). *Multiple attribute decision making: Methods and applications*. CRC Press.

Unsal, I., Fraterman, A., Kayihan, I., Akyar, I., & Serteser, M. (2009). ISO 15189 accreditation in medical laboratories: An institutional experience from Turkey. *Clinical Biochemistry*, *42*(4), 304–305. doi:10.1016/j.clinbiochem.2008.09.022 PMID:19863932

Uzoka, F.-M. E., Obot, O., Barker, K., & Osuji, J. (2011). An experimental comparison of fuzzy logic and analytic hierarchy process for medical decision support systems. *Computer Methods and Programs in Biomedicine*, *103*(1), 10–27. doi:10.1016/j.cmpb.2010.06.003 PMID:20633949

Wang, T.-C., Lee, H.-D., & Cheng, P.-H. (2009). Applying fuzzy TOPSIS approach for evaluating RFID system suppliers in healthcare industry. In *New Advances in Intelligent Decision Technologies* (pp. 519–526). Springer. doi:10.1007/978-3-642-00909-9_49

Wang, Y.-L., & Tzeng, G.-H. (2012). Brand marketing for creating brand value based on a MCDM model combining DEMATEL with ANP and VIKOR methods. *Expert Systems with Applications*, *39*(5), 5600–5615. doi:10.1016/j.eswa.2011.11.057

Xu, C., & Jiang, Y. (2011). Analysis for susceptibility of breast cancer due to gene SMC4L1 based on a multi-criteria evaluation model. *Journal of Biomedical Engineering*, *28*(3), 582.

Yalcin, N., Bayrakdaroglu, A., & Kahraman, C. (2012). Application of fuzzy multi-criteria decision making methods for financial performance evaluation of Turkish manufacturing industries. *Expert Systems with Applications*, *39*(1), 350–364. doi:10.1016/j.eswa.2011.07.024

Yucel, G., Cebi, S., Hoege, B., & Ozok, A. F. (2012). A fuzzy risk assessment model for hospital information system implementation. *Expert Systems with Applications*, *39*(1), 1211–1218. doi:10.1016/j.eswa.2011.07.129

Yücenur, G. N., & Demirel, N. Ç. (2012). Group decision making process for insurance company selection problem with extended VIKOR method under fuzzy environment. *Expert Systems with Applications*, *39*(3), 3702–3707. doi:10.1016/j.eswa.2011.09.065

Zadeh, L. A. (1965). Fuzzy sets. *Information and Control*, *8*(3), 338–353. doi:10.1016/S0019-9958(65)90241-X

Zadeh, L. A. (1975). The concept of a linguistic variable and its application to approximate reasoning—I. *Information Sciences*, *8*(3), 199–249. doi:10.1016/0020-0255(75)90036-5

Zeng, Q.-L., Li, D.-D., & Yang, Y.-B. (2013). VIKOR Method with Enhanced Accuracy for Multiple Criteria Decision Making in Healthcare Management. *Journal of Medical Systems*, *37*(2), 1–9. doi:10.1007/s10916-012-9908-1 PMID:23377778

Zimmermann, H. J. (2001). *Fuzzy set theory-and its applications* (4th ed.). Springer. doi:10.1007/978-94-010-0646-0

KEY TERMS AND DEFINITIONS

Fuzzy Set Theory: An essential theory introduced by Lotfi A. Zadeh to deal with the uncertainty and impreciseness in real world. In this theory, an element can be a member of a set with a degree of membership function. It can be useful when there is a lack of historical data or the previous experience of decision maker is helpful.

ISO 15189: A particular kind of ISO that is related to assessment of Medical Laboratories regarding their quality and competence.

MCDM: Letters stand for multiple criteria decision making method when a decision should be made among some alternatives with some special criteria.

Medical Laboratory: A laboratory where tests are usually done on clinical samples.

Trapezoidal Fuzzy Number: It is a special case of fuzzy numbers that are quantities whose values are imprecise, rather than exact.

VIKOR: A multiple criteria decision making method stands for Vlsekriterijumska Optimizacija I Kompromisno Resenje which focuses on ranking and selection from a set of alternatives, and determines the compromise solution for a problem with different criteria.

An Integrated Fuzzy VIKOR Method for Performance Management in Healthcare

Chapter 4
An Analytical Algorithm for Delphi Method for Consensus Building and Organizational Productivity

Abd Hamid Zahidy
Universiti Malaysia Pahang, Malaysia

Noor Azlinna Azizan
Universiti Malaysia Pahang, Malaysia

Shahryar Sorooshian
Universiti Malaysia Pahang, Malaysia

ABSTRACT

The Delphi technique is being increasingly used in many complex areas where a consensus is to be reached. In such an environment, the Delphi technique allows researchers to acquire high quality, unbiased information from a panel of certified experts. Despite its vast uses, the Delphi method has seen a lack of consistent procedural guidance for its application. A review of literature revealed a significant variation in methodological approach of the method. The purpose of this paper is to develop a practical algorithm for the Delphi study application based on the literature review and the authors' practiced experiences. A few modifications are suggested to make the Delphi study more practical in research and decision making. Using the guidelines provided by this paper, it is expected that the reader may better understand the appropriate application and procedure of the modified Delphi process.

DOI: 10.4018/978-1-5225-0654-6.ch004

An Analytical Algorithm for Delphi Method for Consensus Building and Organizational Productivity

INTRODUCTION

The Delphi technique is being increasingly used in many complex areas where a consensus is to be reached (Chan, 2002). Norman Dalkey of the RAND Corporation developed the original Delphi concept in the 1950's for a United States Air Force sponsored project. The goal of the project was to solicit expert opinions, from the view point of a Soviet strategic planner, of an optimal USA industrial target system and to the estimation of the number of A-bombs required to reduce the munitions output by a prescribed amount (Dalkey & Helmer, 1963). In academic research, the Delphi concept is particularly useful for highly controversial or multi-dimensional subjects such as technological, economic, sociological or medical (Derian & Morize, 1973). In other words, the Delphi study is well suited as a research instrument when there is incomplete knowledge about a problem or phenomenon where there are no 'correct' answers (Skulmosti et al., 2007; Paliwoda, 1983). Hanafin et al. (2007) and Linstone (1978) viewed that the method is particularly well suited to highly complex problems in which:

1. Ethical, political, legal, or social dilemmas dominate economic or technical ones;
2. Face-to-face contact is not possible or desirable, due to prohibitive financial, geographical or temporal constraints and/or concerns regarding democratic participation;
3. Precise analytical techniques and exact knowledge are absent and the gathering of subjective opinion, moderated through group consensus, is the only approach available; and
4. Relevant experts are in different fields and/or occupations and not in direct communication.

The Delphi method uses an iterative feedback technique with a group of experts and is based on qualitative research methods. It relies on the opinions of individuals who are believed to be experts on the subject under consideration (Schmidt, 1997). The Delphi method is a highly formalized method of communication that is designed to extract the maximum amount of unbiased information from a panel of experts (Chan, 2002). Moreover, as compared to the traditional surveys and interviews, the Delphi method requires participants to have expert certification before the survey process begins. It allows the expert to interact anonymously to achieve consensus (Tran et al., 2014). The research data, i.e. expert opinions, are typically collected using several rounds of intensive questionnaires, which generate a series of qualitative and quantitative data for analysis. The analysis findings then determine the form and content of subsequent questionnaires, and so on, until group opinion is formed and declared stable (Gupta & Clarke, 1996). Rowe and Wright (1999) characterized the classical Delphi method into four key attributes:

1. **Anonymity:** Allows the panellists the opportunity to express their opinions and judgments freely without undue social pressures from dominant or dogmatic others members in the group, and is achieved through the use of questionnaires.
2. **Iteration**: Allows the panellists the opportunity to refine their opinions and judgments without fear of losing face in the eyes of the (anonymous) others in the group, and are achieved through a number of rounds of questionnaires distribution.
3. **Controlled Feedback:** Informs the panellists of the opinions of their anonymous colleagues, and is presented as a simple statistical summary in terms of a mean or median value.
4. **Group Judgment**: Allows for statistical analysis and interpretation of data.

Therefore, the Delphi technique is useful for situations where individual judgement is to be captured in order to address lack of agreement on an incomplete state of knowledge (Delbecq et al., 1975; Skulmoski et al., 2007). The technique is particularly valued due to its ability to structure and organize group communication. The structure of the Delphi technique is intended to allow access to the positive attributes of interacting groups. It includes knowledge from a variety of sources and creative synthesis of literature while pre-empting negative aspects attributable to social, personal and political conflicts. From a practical perspective, the method allows input from a larger number of participations than could feasibly be included in a group or committee meeting (Rowe & Wright, 1999). The ultimate goal of the Delphi technique is not only to elicit a single answer or to arrive at consensus, but to obtain as many high quality responses and opinions as possible on a given issue from a panel of experts to enhance decision-making (Gupta & Clarke, 1996). This process enhances the success, credibility, and validity of the technique used (Clayton, 1997).

DELPHI PROCESS

Theoretically, the Delphi process can be continuously iterated until reaching a predetermined level of consensus, or until no new information can be gained from further rounds of the Delphi processes (Linstone & Turoff, 1975). Brockhaus and Mickelsen (1977) reported that most of the Delphi studies utilise three or fewer iterations. Christie and Barela (2005), and Mullen (2003) asserted that a minimum of two rounds is required to allow feedback and revision of responses. However, to benefit from the Delphi's purported advantages, a clear understanding is necessary to enable methodological application and adaptation (Ayton et al., 1999). Hallowell and Gambatese (2010) outlined a general structure of Delphi process that could be applied in research and decision making activities, as illustrated in Figure 1.

Figure 1. Delphi procedure
(Source: Hallowell & Gambatese, 2010)

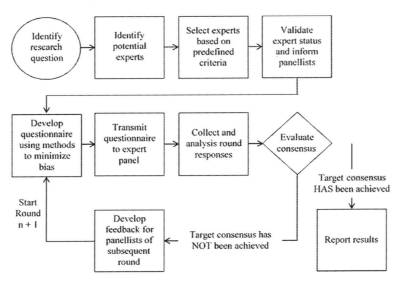

DELPHI QUESTIONNAIRE

In the first round of a Delphi study, researchers have the choice to use either an open-ended questionnaire as in the traditional Delphi process or a structured questionnaire or both structured and open-ended questionnaire as in the modified Delphi process. It should be noted that the utilization of both approaches is an acceptable and a common practice that is frequently found in academic research (Hsu & Sandford, 2007; Kalaian & Kasim, 2012). Open-ended questions are recognised as beneficial for increasing the richness of data collected (Powell, 2003; Okoli & Pawlowski, 2004). However, it could lead to a high attrition of experts (Hsu and Sandford, 2007). In the case of a structured questionnaire, the questions could also result from issues identified during the literature reviewed (Nworie, 2011).

The use of a modified Delphi process will make sense under two conditions. First, the basic information concerning the target issue is available and usable (Kerlinger, 1973). Second, an extensive literature review has been conducted prior to the use of a modified Delphi (Hsu & Sandford, 2007; Nworie, 2011).

To guide participants toward the research objectives of our *practiced* Delphi study, we employed a modified Delphi process with the use of a structured questionnaire in the first round. Open-ended questions are also provided at the end of each perspective. This approach was consistent with the study of Smith et al. (2011), Vatalis et al. (2011), Afshari and Yusuff (2012), and Zou and Moon (2014). The first round of the Delphi questionnaire was developed from an extensive literature review and our prior experience in the related field under study. This instrument consisted of demographic information, experience, qualifications and other information that would able to confirm the invited participants to be experts in the field of study, and the questions to be evaluated by experts. The content of each section of the questionnaire was explained clearly including the brief description of each of the items in all the Delphi rounds. The participants were instructed to rate the importance of the items using the importance scale based on a five-point Likert-scale: 1 = no judgment, 2 = very unimportant, 3 = unimportant, 4 = important, and 5 = very important. Participants may also be asked to list and describe any other additional items or decision alternatives that they think should be included in the evaluation process in the provided column at the end of every perspectives asked.

PILOT STUDY

Leedy and Ormrod (2010) viewed that a pilot test of the initial Delphi questionnaire is optional, but noted that it may help to identify ambiguities and improve the feasibility of administration of the main survey. Skulmoski et al. (2007) highlighted the need to pilot a Delphi questionnaire as to improve its comprehension, and to rectify any procedural problems. In a similar vein, Mead and Moseley (2001) noted that pilot studies could offer a means to ensure greater rigour, particularly in light of criticisms about the design of first-round questions. Linstone and Turoff (1975) stressed the importance to test each questionnaire on individuals who meet the participant selection criteria but not involved in the actual study. However, Keeney et al. (2001) found only a few Delphi studies reported undertaking pilot studies. A literature search revealed no clear guidelines about whether to pilot the whole process, each round, or just the initial round. It led to individual variations and lack of reporting of the pilot processes used. Quinn and Sulivan (2000), and Meskell et al. (2014), for example, piloted all the five and three rounds of their Delphi questionnaires, respectively. In other studies, Cramer et al., 2008; Hung et al., 2008; and Valdez, 2009 piloted only the first round of their Delphi studies to increase the validity of the questions.

To establish the 'best' approach to conducting a Delphi pilot study, Clibbens et al. (2012) reviewed twenty-five Delphi research papers in healthcare published between 2000 and 2011. The authors found two approaches had been used by researchers in piloting the Delphi research. First, the most common approach was to pilot the first round of the Delphi study to increase the validity of its questions because question design is difficult, and the first round questions are the basis for subsequent rounds. However, the authors argued that limiting the pilot study to the first round would lead to failure to test the complex processes of analysis and measurement later in the Delphi process. The second approach was to pilot all stages of the Delphi processes to make the phrasing of the questions, instructions, and information clearly understood. In light of the second approach, Clibbens et al. (2012) considered and tested two options: first, piloted each round of the Delphi process immediately before conducting each round of the full study, and second, piloted all the rounds of the Delphi process in advance of recruiting to the full Delphi study. Table 1 shows the findings of the study.

Following the suggestion and recommendation by Clibbens et al. (2012), we employed a pilot study of all rounds of the Delphi study in advance of recruiting to the full Delphi study. The process of the pilot study for our practiced research is shown in the following Figure 2.

RELIABILITY AND VALIDITY

Failure to assess the worth of a study, in terms of the soundness of its method, the accuracy of its findings, and the integrity of assumptions conclusions made, could have dire consequences which may result in

Table 1. Benefits and disadvantages of different approaches to piloting Delphi surveys

	Pilot of the Whole Study	**Pilot Round by Round**
Benefits	• Full review of all aspects of the study gives a stronger sense of the whole. • Review of all complex processes improves rigour. • Avoids the complexity of managing two samples at the same time. • Avoids unnecessary delays between rounds.	• Full study begins sooner. • Gives contemporaneous and round-specific feedback.
Disadvantages	• Significantly delays the start of the full study.	• Causes delays between rounds, potentially increasing sample attrition. • Causes added complexity by managing two samples. • Danger of finding methodological problems in round two or three that should have been dealt with earlier.

Source: Clibbens et al. (2012)

Figure 2. Flowchart of the pilot study process

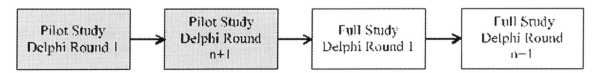

wasted time and effort (Long & Johnson, 2000). In the worst case, such wrong findings could result in the adoption of dangerous or harmful practices. For that reason, the evaluation of studies is an essential pre-requisite for the application of findings. Traditionally, such evaluation has centred on assessment of reliability and validity.

Reliability

Reliability refers the extent to which data collection technique(s) yielded consistent findings. Thus, similar observations would lead to same conclusions reached by other researchers or there is transparency in how sense was made from the raw data (Saunders et al., 2014). There is no evidence in the literature indicating the reliability of the Delphi study. Hasson *et al.* (2000) suggested that criteria for qualitative methods could be used in the Delphi study to produce credible interpretations of the findings. In the case of the traditional Delphi method, attributes make it impossible to conduct a reliability test as is done in quantitative research. This is true because the questionnaire in the initial round of the Delphi method is normally in the form of open-ended questions and the reliability test would not be possible to apply. Nevertheless, the question arises: how, if in the initial round, the Delphi study uses a structured questionnaire, can reliability be measured?

To this end, we argue that the reliability test may be possible to apply in the modified Delphi study where the structured questionnaire is used, especially with the use of Likert scales. Therefore, we used the Cronbach's alpha coefficient analysis to test the reliability and internal consistency of each item used in the questionnaire. According to Santos (1999), Cronbach's alpha correlation coefficient is the most widely accepted and commonly used statistical tool to assess internal reliability, and, therefore, could be used to gauge data reliability.

Validity

Hasson *et al.* (2000) pointed out that the basis of the Delphi process is the assumption of safety in numbers, in the sense that several people are less likely to arrive at a wrong decision than a single individual. Then, decisions will strengthened by reasonable arguments that challenge the assumptions, thus help in enhancing validity. Goodman (1987) added that the use of participants who have the knowledge and interest on the topic under study may help to increase the content validity of the Delphi questionnaire. Hasson et al. (2000) asserted that the use of successive rounds of the questionnaire may also help to increase the concurrent validity. In our practiced study, the experts were examined based on the pre-determined criteria, and only those who were qualified were selected and invited to be the expert panellists. Furthermore, the Delphi study was conducted in two subsequent rounds, thus complying with the validation criteria proposed by Goodman (1987) and Hasson et al. (2000).

In addition to the above, three more measures of external validity were applied. First, the supervisors were consulted to validate the readability, content, ease of answering, and the rating scale used. Second, the expert validation of content was used to address validity issues of the questionnaire. A group of two experts from an academician's group was selected to review the first round questionnaire. It aimed to ensure that all statements were valid, understandable and practical. All of them had proven research expertise in the Delphi methodology, and in the field under study. This expert group did not participate in any aspect of the full study except in this content validity exercise. Third, a pilot study of eight experts who complied with the pre-determined criteria was conducted to test the effectiveness of the survey instrument, establishing the face validity of the developed instrument. Therefore, the instrument is considered to have achieved the content validity. Moreover, the use of importance scales for consensus building ensured that the measures achieved internal consistency.

PANEL COMPOSITION

The success of a Delphi study clearly rests on the combined expertise of the participants in the relevant field that make up the expert panel (Powell, 2003). According to Nworie (2011), expert panelists must be experienced professionals who can provide an informed view or expert opinion on issues in their given field. They are selected because of their knowledge of their field or the issue being investigated. In other words, knowledge in a field, or subject matter area, or expertise of the issue being investigated is an essential requirement for participation of an expert panellist.

To understand the expert panel, one must first recognize what an expert is. Merriam-Webster (2005) defined an expert as 'a person with a high level of knowledge or skill in a field'. From this definition, it could be understood that an expert is restricted to those with specialized training such as an engineer, technologist, or scientist. This definition excludes an individual who derives expertise from real experience. Cantrill et al. (1996) opposed such a definition, arguing that the definition should include an individual with relevant knowledge and experience of a particular field. Needham and de Loë (1990) introduced the concept of 'closeness' to give more recognition to a variety of experts as shown in Figure 3. According to this concept, experts can be identified in terms of their 'closeness' to a problem or issue, and that exists along a 'closeness' continuum.

As explained by Needham and de Loë (1990), within the 'closeness' continuum, an expert population comprises of individuals with subjective, mandated, and objective 'closeness'. It can be found through individuals' profession, occupation, training, education, experience, and other explanatory variables. Individuals (such as industry practitioners) who possess deep experiential knowledge or hands-on experience in the particular fields are classified as subjective 'closeness' and refer to subjective experts. On the other hand, individuals (such as academic researchers) who did research in the particular fields are classified as objective 'closeness' and refer as objective experts. Individuals (such as professional) who possess job responsibility in the particular fields are categorized as mandated 'closeness' and refer to mandated experts. 'Closeness', therefore, ensures that the participants bring a wide range of direct knowledge and experience to the decision-making process (Powell, 2003).

Accordingly, Andranovoch (1995), Delbecq et al. (1975), Gordon (1994), Linstone (2002), and Rowe and Wright (1999) asserted that to achieve meaningful, legitimate and quality Delphi results, the research problem and survey questions must be congruent with the interests, knowledge, and skills of participant

Figure 3. The 'closeness' continuum
(Source: Needham and de Loë, 1990)

experts. Moreover, experts should represent different perspectives on the issue (Kaynak et al., 1994), all of which represent to the 'closeness' to the subject under study.

PANEL SIZE

The optimal size of participants in Delphi technique has not been established. As a consequence, there was a varied opinion on the prerequisite panel size. The impact of the panel size on the accuracy and effectiveness of the Delphi process has been studied by Brockhoff (1975) and Boje et al. (1982). Nevertheless, none of the studies found a significant correlation between the panel size and effectiveness. In a summary by Rowe and Wright (1999), the size of a Delphi panel in peer-reviewed studies ranged from a low of three members to a high of eighty. Some researchers related the panel size with the group characteristics. Skulmoski et al. (2007), for example, noted that in the homogenous group, small panels of ten experts to fifteen experts are sufficient to obtain reasonable results. Paliwoda (1983), on the other hand, asserted that if the group is heterogeneous, it would be practical to solicit up to four panels from ten to eighteen members. Powell (2003) clarified that representativeness in Delphi study is assessed on the qualities of the expert panel rather than its size because the method does not need a representative sample for statistical purposes.

Needham and de Loë (1990) warned that larger populations may result in cost-inefficiencies related to time, product, and iteration process, while smaller populations may result in idea-generation paucity. In a similar vein, Skulmoski et al. (2007) noted that larger populations may greatly increase the complexity and difficulty in collecting data, reaching consensus, conducting analysis, and verifying results as well. In contrast, the larger the populations, the more convincingly the results can be said to be verified. Thus, the researcher must appropriately design the panel size as it may affect results quality. The decision must be based on several factors that have been suggested in the literature. Among the considered factors are the purpose of the study (Cantrill et al., 1996), the scope of the problem (Delbecq et al., 1975; Powell, 2003), the availability of resources (Delbecq et al., 1975; Powell, 2003), the desired balance of expertise (Delbecq et al., 1975; Powell, 2003), if the sample is a heterogeneous or homogeneous sample (Skulmoski et al., 2007; Paliwoda, 1983), decision quality or Delphi manageability trade-off (Skulmoski et al., 2007), and internal and external verification (Skulmoski et al., 2007).

The Delphi technique traditionally has been identified as best suited for objective 'closeness' (Donohoe & Needham, 2009). However, according to Delbecq et al. (1975), to produce higher quality results, heterogeneous groups characterised by experts with varied 'closeness' and different perspectives on the problem at hand, are much better than homogeneous groups. Based on the evidence from literature and personal judgment, we formed a heterogeneous group of four independent panels of eight to fifteen members each. The basis of this decision is that the panel size is congruent with established methodological norms, and allows for potential drop-out (Briedenhann & Butts, 2006). It is also small enough to ensure the respondents are all experts in their fields (Pan et al., 1995). The four independent panels were:

1. Contractors/developers,
2. Professional engineering consultants (architects, engineers, and quantity surveyors),
3. Government technical officers, and
4. Academicians.

In addition, the selection of panel size is based on purposive sampling on the basis of 'closeness' to the topic under study (Donohoe & Needham, 2009). According to Polit and Hungler (2013), purposive sampling is a non-probability sampling technique where participants are not randomly selected, but instead are deliberately selected to capture a range of group characteristics. This form of sampling based on the assumption that the researcher's knowledge of the population can be used to select individuals carefully to include in the sample. Therefore, this size was deemed to be sufficient for the composition of highly qualified expert panelists.

PANEL MEMBER QUALIFICATION

A Delphi study does not depend on a statistical sample that attempts to be representative of any population. It is a group decision mechanism requiring qualified experts who have deep understanding of the issues. Therefore, one of the most critical requirements is the selection of qualified experts. As previously indicated, the characteristics required to define an individual as an expert is equivocal. Needham and de Loë (1990) provided one of the more interesting insights on the expert selection found in the literature. They asserted that two fundamental principles should guide the expert selection. First, experts must be representative of the industry or sectoral experience that relates to the subject under study. This criterion is measured in terms of demonstrated education and training (natural, social, and engineering sciences), profession and occupation (commerce, education, government, industry), and regional and sectoral affiliation. In the context of the current research study, firstly, the experts must be representative of the Malaysian construction industry. Secondly, the experts must also exhibit recognised authority or sufficient expertise. It is measured in terms of standing within disciplines connected to the subject under study (academicians), standing within professions sensitive to the subject under study (professional engineering consultants), and experience with applied management and research (government technical officers).

Needham and de Loë (1990) emphasized the important of procedural openness in the expert selection process. Literature related to the Delphi research is rife with examples of expert opinion being consulted and used as an expert panel. Nevertheless, the same literature fails to demonstrate the procedural openness for selection of the most appropriate experts. Most of them only mentioned the criteria that the potential participants must have to meet. Hallowell and Gambatese (2010) provided one of the few examples of procedural openness. They offered a relative point system that allows one to select specific expert qualities more appropriate. The point system based on the relative time commitment required to complete successfully each of the achievements or experiences. It refers to the best judgment of the writers and practices of professional licensing agencies. To meet a minimum level of qualification, the panellists' score should be at least one point in four different achievement or experience categories and a minimum of eleven total points in order to qualify for participation.

In the case of the published Delphi studies in the construction engineering management research, experts were identified along the 'closeness' continuum, and various expert group combinations had been consulted. For example, in a study to identify competencies needed for the working environment of construction projects, Sabet et al. (2014) established a homogeneous panel of mandated experts as represented by the site engineers, project managers, construction managers, and site supervisors. The external validation of their expertise was having over seven years of experiences in construction projects. In their assessment of the effectiveness of risk management of road construction project, Parera et al. (2014) established a heterogeneous panel comprised of mandated experts (consultants, project managers), and subjective experts (client, contractors). Zou and Moon (2014) in their development of an evaluation framework for measuring the environmental performance of a construction operation, also established a heterogeneous panel. But, in addition to mandated and subjective experts as represented by government officers, owners, and contractors, they included objective experts as represented by academicians. According to Donohoe and Needham (2009), the measure of expert 'closeness' and the balance of expertise in Delphi study is dictated by research purpose and objectives. On the basis of the expert continuum and the participant requirements for a successful Delphi study, a description of the selection criteria for each expert panel must be clearly defined (Briedenhann & Butts, 2006). Wright (2006) suggested that it should based purposively on their strong interest and knowledge in areas under study (Wright, 2006). In addition, Hollowell (2009) noted that the method of selecting expert panels should be strategic and unbiased.

In our practiced Delphi study, the fundamental objective was to identify the predictors of success and survival for entrepreneurs in the construction industry. It focused on the perspectives of an entrepreneurship phenomenon, all of which gleaned from the experiences of construction industry practitioners. Participants should be selected to reflect a wide range of opinions. According to Meskell et al. (2014), the panellists are experts, assumed to have some special insights that allow them to predict the future better than lay people. In addition, the findings of Vick (2002) and Simonton (2014) on the development of engineering expertise, indicated that engineering experts reach the height of their expertise between career ages of ten and thirty three. It corresponds to chronological ages of thirty five and fifty three. Therefore, we set the mandatory requirement for all panels to be that the individuals must have at least ten years of professional experience in the construction industry.

To make the study more interesting, beside the mandatory requirement, we set up different requirements for each panel as indicated in Table 2. For example, to qualify as an expert of the contractors/developers panel, an individual must meet at least one of the listed three requirements. It considers that registration as a certified professional or committee member of construction association is not the mandatory requirement to become a contractor or developer. Holding an advanced degree is also not the mandatory requirement to become a contractor or developer. However, this requirement was included in the current study, because the nature of the study investigates a new aspect in literature and this requires advanced knowledge and experience. In the professional engineering consultants' panel, the individual must meet all the two requirements. In the government technical officers' panel, an individual must meet at least two of the listed three requirements. It takes into account that not all of the government technical officers are registered as professional or have presented a paper at conference. Finally, in the academicians' panel, an individual must meet at least four of the listed five requirements. It includes a minimum of a masters degree in the fields directly related to the construction industry, assuming that a masters degree is a minimum requirement to become a lecturer.

DELPHI ROUND

The objectives of rounds in a Delphi study are to reach consensus by reducing variance in responses and improve precision. These objectives can be achieved through the use of controlled feedback and iteration (Hallowell & Gambatese, 2010). However, literature provides very little guidance for the acceptable number of iteration rounds. According to Mullen (2003), if the sample is small, in most cases, no more than one round may be needed. However, to allow feedback and revision of responses, a minimum of

Table 2. Requirement for selection of qualified expert

Panel	Criteria/Requirement	Minimum Requirement
Contractors/Developers	1. A minimum of a bachelor degree in the fields directly related to the construction industry, from an accredited institution of higher learning. 2. At least five (5) years registered as certified professional engineer, professional architect, professional quantity surveyor, or project management professional. 3. Committee member of a construction or developer associations.	One requirement
Professional Engineering Consultants	4. A minimum of bachelor degree in the fields directly related to the construction industry, from an accredited institution of higher learning. 5. At least five years registered as certified professional engineer, professional architect, professional quantity surveyor, or project management professional.	All two requirements
Government Technical Officers	6. A minimum of bachelor degree in the engineering fields, from an accredited institution of higher learning. 7. At least five (5) years registered as certified professional engineer, professional architect, professional quantity surveyor, or project management professional. 8. Invited to present at a conference focused on the topic of CEM.	One requirement
Academicians	9. A minimum of a master degree in the engineering or other fields related to the construction industry, from an accredited institution of higher learning. 10. Primary or secondary author of at least three (3) peer-reviewed journal articles on the topic of CEM. 11. Invited to present at a conference focused on the topic of CEM. 12. Author and editor of a book or book chapter on the topic of CEM, or infrastructure management. 13. At least five (5) years registered as certified professional engineer, professional architect, professional quantity surveyor, or project management professional.	Three requirements

two rounds are required (Christie & Barela, 2005; Mullen, 2003). Brockhaus and Mickelsen (1977) reported that most studies utilise three or fewer iterations. Dietz (1987) contended that most changes in Delphi responses would occur in the first two rounds. Giannarou and Zervas (2014) suggested that the Delphi rounds are open to the choices of the researcher. The researcher may prefer to sacrifice rounds to guarantee panel participation and continuity (Landeta, 2006). Indeed, according to Mitchell (1991), the number of rounds needs to be as few as possible as to eliminate fatigue and time pressure that result in high panel attrition. In fact, a highly suggestive is from the outcome of Dalkey's et al. (1972) experiment that the answers were most accurate on round two and became less accurate on subsequent rounds. Therefore, in our practiced Delphi study, the study was limited to two iterative rounds which the aimed to allow feedback and revision of responses.

CRITERIA FOR ATTAINING CONSENSUS

One of the aims of using Delphi is to achieve greater consensus amongst panellists (Rowe & Wright, 1999). Consensus simply means general agreement on the subjects under investigation (Gunhan & Arditi, 2005). According to Rowe and Wright (1999), consensus can be determined by measuring the variance in responses of Delphi panellists over rounds. A greater consensus is achieved when reduction in variance occurs. Although the principal aim of Delphi study is to reach consensus among the experts, a common practice to measure consensus does not exist (Holey et al., 2007). Hence, many studies have used different measurements. Normally, two methods were used to determine when to stop a Delphi process, namely stability and consensus (Dajani et al., 1979; Holey et al., 2007). Stability refers to the percentage of change in variables between two subsequent rounds, whereas, consensus is measured by averaging the chosen percentage values of each factor (von der Gracht, 2012; Dajani et al., 1979). Meanwhile, Miller (2006) suggested that consensus can be decided if a certain percentage of votes fall within a prescribed range. Therefore, for our practiced Delphi study, we had pre-determined as the criteria to reach: a consensus of a *median 4 to 5, and 80% or more of respondents rating the indicators within 4 to 5* on the importance scale. These criteria are consistent with the works of Smith et al. (2011) and Hollander et al. (2013).

CONCLUSION

The Delphi study is well suited as a research instrument particularly in the complete areas when there is incomplete knowledge on the matter under study. Despite its vast uses in many research fields, the Delphi method has seen a lack of consistency and standard procedures for its application. This is likely due to variation procedures among studies found in literature associated with the method. This paper suggests a few modifications on the Delphi procedures based on the literature review and the authors' practiced experiences in conducting the Delphi study. Using the guidelines provided by this paper, it is expected that the reader may better understand:

1. The philosophy behind the Delphi study,
2. Appropriate application of the modified Delphi process, and
3. Procedures in designing the Delphi process, such as questionnaire design, pilot study, reliability and validity of the instrument, selection of expert panellists, panel size, iteration rounds, and criteria for attaining consensus.

ACKNOWLEDGMENT

The authors would like to thank the anonymous reviewers and the editor for their insightful comments and suggestions.

REFERENCES

Afshari, A. R., & Yusuff, R. M. (2012). Developing a structural method for eliciting criteria in project manager selection. *Proceedings of the 2012 International Conference on Industrial Engineering and Operations Management*.

Andranovoch, G. (1995). *Developing community participation and consensus: The Delphi technique.* Los Angeles: Western Regional Extension.

Ayton, P., Ferrel, W. R., & Stewart, T. R. (1999). Commentaries on 'The Delphi technique as a forecasting tool: Issues and analysis' by Rowe and Wright. *International Journal of Forecasting, 15*(4), 377–381. doi:10.1016/S0169-2070(99)00013-8

Boje, D. M., Fedor, D. B., & Rowland, K. M. (1982). Myth making: A qualitative step in OD interventions. *The Journal of Applied Behavioral Science, 18*(1), 17–28. doi:10.1177/002188638201800104

Briedenhann, J., & Butts, S. (2006). The application of the Delphi technique to rural tourism project evaluation. *Current Issues in Tourism, 9*(2), 171–190. doi:10.1080/13683500608668246

Brockhaus, W. L., & Mickelsen, J. F. (1977). An analysis of prior Delphi applications and some observations on its future applicability. *Technological Forecasting and Social Change, 10*(1), 103–110. doi:10.1016/0040-1625(77)90010-5

Brockhoff, K. (1975). The performance of forecasting groups in computer dialogue and face to face discussions. In H. Linstone & M. Turoff (Eds.), *The Delphi method: Techniques and applications.* London: Addison-Wesley.

Cantrill, J. A., Sibbald, B., & Buetow, S. (1996). The Delphi and nominal group techniques in health sciences research. *International Journal of Pharmacy Practice, 4*(2), 67–74. doi:10.1111/j.2042-7174.1996.tb00844.x

Chan, A. P. C. (2002). Developing an expert system for project procurement. *Advances in Building Technology, 2,* 1681–1688. doi:10.1016/B978-008044100-9/50207-2

Christie, C. A., & Barela, E. (2005). The Delphi technique as a method for increasing inclusion in the evaluation process. *The Canadian Journal of Program Evaluation, 20*(1), 105–122.

Clayton, M. J. (1997). Delphi: A technique to harness expert opinion for critical decision-making tasks in education. *Educational Psychology: An International Journal of Experimental Educational Psychology, 17*(4), 373–386. doi:10.1080/0144341970170401

Clibbens, N., Walters, S., & Baird, W. (2012). Delphi research: Issues raised by a pilot study. *Nurse Researcher, 19*(2), 37–44. doi:10.7748/nr2012.01.19.2.37.c8907

Cramer, C. K., Klasser, K. D., Epstein, J. B., & Sheps, S. B. (2008). The Delphi process in dental research. *The Journal of Evidence-Based Dental Practice, 8*(4), 211–220. doi:10.1016/j.jebdp.2008.09.002

Dajani, J. S., Sincoff, M. Z., & Talley, W. K. (1979). Stability and agreement criteria for the termination of Delphi studies. *Technological Forecasting and Social Change, 13*(1), 83–90. doi:10.1016/0040-1625(79)90007-6

Dalkey, N. C., & Helmer, O. (1963). An experimental application of the Delphi method to the use of experts. *Management Science, 9*(3), 458–467. doi:10.1287/mnsc.9.3.458

Dalkey, N. C., Rourke, D. L., Lewis, R., & Synder, D. (1972). *Studies in the quality of life: Delphi and decision making.* Lexington: Lexington Books.

Delbecq, A. L., Gustafson, D. H., & de Ven, V. (1975). *Group techniques for program planning: A guide to nominal group and Delphi processes*. Glenview: Scott, Foresman and Company.

Derian, J.-C., & Morize, F. (1973). Delphi in the assessment of research and development projects. *Futures*, *5*(5), 469–483. doi:10.1016/0016-3287(73)90038-4

Dietz, T. (1987). Methods for analyzing data from Delphi panels: Some evidence from a forecasting study. *Technological Forecasting and Social Change*, *31*(1), 79–85. doi:10.1016/0040-1625(87)90024-2

Donohoe, H. M., & Needham, R. D. (2009). Moving best practice forward: Delphi characteristics, advantages, potential problems, and solutions. *International Journal of Tourism Research*, *11*(5), 415–437. doi:10.1002/jtr.709

Giannarou, L., & Zervas, E. (2014). Using Delphi technique to build consensus in practice. *International Journal of Business Science and Applied Management*, *9*(2), 1–18.

Goodman, C. M. (1987). The Delphi technique: A critique. *Journal of Advanced Nursing*, *12*(6), 729–734. doi:10.1111/j.1365-2648.1987.tb01376.x

Gordon, T. J. (1994). *The Delphi method: Future research methodology*. Washington: AC/UNU Millennium Project.

Gunhan, S., & Arditi, D. (2005). Factors affecting international construction. *Journal of Construction Engineering and Management*, *131*(3), 273–282. doi:10.1061/(ASCE)0733-9364(2005)131:3(273)

Gupta, U. G., & Clarke, R. E. (1996). Theory and applications of the Delphi Technique: A bibliography (1975-1994). *Technological Forecasting and Social Change*, *53*(2), 185–211. doi:10.1016/S0040-1625(96)00094-7

Hallowell, M. (2009). Techniques to minimize bias when using the Delphi method to quantify construction safety and health risks. *Proceedings of the Construction Research Congress 2009: Building a Sustainable Future*. doi:10.1061/41020(339)151

Hallowell, M., & Gambatese, J. (2010). Qualitative research: Application of the Delphi method to CEM research. *Journal of Construction Engineering and Management*, *136*, 99–107.

Hanafin, S., Brooks, A.-M., Carroll, E., Fitzgerald, E., Gabhainn, S. N., & Sixsmith, J. (2007). Achieving consensus in developing a national set of child well-being indicators. *Social Indicators Research*, *80*(1), 79–104. doi:10.1007/s11205-006-9022-1

Hasson, F., Keeney, S., & McKenna, H. (2000). Research guidelines for the Delphi survey technique. *Journal of Advanced Nursing*, *33*(4), 1008–1015.

Holey, A. H., Feeley, J. L., Dixon, J., & Whittaker, V. J. (2007). An exploration of the use of simple statistics to measure consensus and stability in Delphi studies. *BMC Medical Research Methodology*, *7*(1), 52. doi:10.1186/1471-2288-7-52

Hollander, M. C., Sage, J. M., Greenler, A. J., Pendl, J., Avcin, T., Espada, G., & Brunner, H. I. et al. (2013). International consensus for provisions of quality-driven care in childhood-onset systemic lupus erythematosus. *Arthritis Care and Research*, *65*(9), 1416–1423. doi:10.1002/acr.21998

Hsu, C.-C., & Sandford, A. B. (2007). Minimizing non-response in the Delphi process: How to respond to non-response. *Practical Assessment, Research & Evaluation, 12*(17), 62–78.

Hung, H.-L., Altschuld, J. W., & Lee, Y.-F. (2008). Methodological and conceptual issues confronting a cross-country Delphi study of education program evaluation. *Evaluation and Program Planning, 31*(2), 191–198. doi:10.1016/j.evalprogplan.2008.02.005

Kalaian, S. A., & Kasim, R. M. (2012). Terminating sequential Delphi survey data collection. *Practical Assessment, Research & Evaluation, 17*(5), 1–9.

Kaynak, E., Bloom, J., & Leibold, M. (1994). Using the Delphi technique to predict future tourism potential. *Marketing Intelligence & Planning, 12*(7), 18–29. doi:10.1108/02634509410065537

Keeney, S., Hasson, F., & McKenna, H. P. (2001). A critical review of the Delphi technique as a research methodology for nursing. *International Journal of Nursing Studies, 38*(2), 195–200. doi:10.1016/S0020-7489(00)00044-4

Kerlinger, F. N. (1973). Foundations of behavioral research. Holt, Reinhart, and Winston.

Landeta, J. (2006). Current validity of the Delphi method in social sciences. *Technological Forecasting and Social Change, 73*(5), 467–482. doi:10.1016/j.techfore.2005.09.002

Leedy, D. P., & Ormrod, E. J. (2010). *Practical research: Planning and designing* (9th ed.). Pearson Education.

Linstone, H. A. (1978). The Delphi technique. In J. Fowles (Ed.), *Handbook of future research*. London: Greenwood Press.

Linstone, H. A. (2002). Eight basic pitfalls: A checklist. In M. Turoff & H. A. Linstone (Eds.), *The Delphi approach: Techniques and applications*. Reading: Addison-Wesley.

Linstone, H. A., & Turoff, M. (1975). *The Delphi method: Techniques and applications*. London: Addison-Wesley.

Long, T., & Johnson, M. (2000). Rigour, reliability and validity research. *Clinical Effectiveness in Nursing, 4*(1), 30–37. doi:10.1054/cein.2000.0106

Mead, D., & Moseley, L. (2001). The use of Delphi as a research approach. *Nurse Researcher, 8*(4), 4–23. doi:10.7748/nr2001.07.8.4.4.c6162

Merriam-Webster. (2005). *The Merriam-Webster Thesaurus*. Springfield: Merriam-Webster.

Meskell, P., Murphy, K., Shaw, D. G., & Casey, D. (2014). Insights into the used and complexities of the policy Delphi technique. *Nurse Researcher, 21*(3), 32–39. doi:10.7748/nr2014.01.21.3.32.e342

Miller, L. E. (2006). *Determining what could/should be: The Delphi technique and its application*. Paper presented at the meeting of the 2006 Annual Meeting of the Mid-Western Educational Research Association, Columbus, OH.

Mitchell, V. W. (1991). The Delphi technique: An exposition and application. *Technology Analysis and Strategic Management, 3*(4), 333–358. doi:10.1080/09537329108524065

Mullen, P. M. (2003). Delphi myths and reality. *Journal of Health Organization and Management, 17*(1), 37–52. doi:10.1108/14777260310469319

Needham, R. D., & de Loë, R. (1990). The policy Delphi: Purpose, structure, and application. *The Canadian Geographer, 34*(2), 133–142. doi:10.1111/j.1541-0064.1990.tb01258.x

Nworie, J. (2011). Using the Delphi technique in educational technology research. *TechTrends: Linking Research and Practice to Improve Learning, 55*(5), 24–30. doi:10.1007/s11528-011-0524-6

Okali, C., & Pawlowski, S. D. (2004). The Delphi method as a research tool: An example, design considerations and applications. *Information & Management, 42*(1), 15–29. doi:10.1016/j.im.2003.11.002

Paliwoda, S. J. (1983). Predicting the future using Delphi. *Management Decision, 21*(1), 31–38. doi:10.1108/eb001309

Pan, S. Q., Vega, M., Vella, A. J., Archer, B. H., & Parlett, G. R. (1995). Mini-Delphi approach: An improvement on single round technique. *Progress in Tourism and Hospitality Research, 2*(1), 27–39. doi:10.1002/(SICI)1099-1603(199603)2:1<27::AID-PTH29>3.0.CO;2-P

Parera, B. A. K. S., Rameezdeen, R., Chileshe, N., & Hosseini, M. R. (2014). Enhancing the effectiveness of risk management practices in Sri Lankan road construction projects: A Delphi approach. *International Journal of Construction Management, 14*(1), 1–14. doi:10.1080/15623599.2013.875271

Polit, D. F., & Hungler, B. P. (2013). *Essentials of nursing research: Methods, appraisal and utilisation.* New York: Lippincott Williams & Wilkins.

Powell, C. (2003). The Delphi technique: Myths and realities. *Journal of Advanced Nursing, 41*(4), 376–382. doi:10.1046/j.1365-2648.2003.02537.x

Quinn, B., & Sulivan, S. J. (2000). The identification by physiotherapists of the physical problems resulting from a mild traumatic brain injury. *Brain Injury: [BI], 14*(12), 1063–1076. doi:10.1080/026990050050203568

Rowe, G., & Wright, G. (1999). The Delphi technique as a forecasting tool: Issues and analysis. *International Journal of Forecasting, 15*(4), 353–375. doi:10.1016/S0169-2070(99)00018-7

Sabet, P. G. P., Ansari, R., Fard, A. B., Aadal, H., & Raad, K. G. (2014). Necessary competencies of construction managers in Iran as a developing country. *Research Journal of Applied Sciences, Engineering and Technology, 7*(10), 2161–2171.

Santos, J. R. A. (1999). Cronbach's alpha: A tool for assessing the reliability of scales. *Journal of Extension, 37*(2), 1–5.

Saunders, M., Lewis, P., & Thornhill, A. (2014). *Research methods for business students* (5th ed.). New Delhi: Dorling Kindersley.

Schmidt, R. C. (1997). Managing Delphi surveys using nonparametric statistical techniques. *Decision Sciences, 28*(3), 763–774. doi:10.1111/j.1540-5915.1997.tb01330.x

Simonton, D. K. (2014). Creative expertise: A lifespan developmental perspective. In K. A. Ericsson (Ed.), *The road to excellence: The acquisition of expert performance in the arts and sciences, sports and games.* East Sussex, UK: Psychology Press.

Skulmoski, J. G., Hartman, T. F., & Krahn, J. (2007). The Delphi method for graduate research. *Journal of Information Technology Education, 6,* 1–21.

Smith, J. P., Miller, K., Christofferson, J., & Hutchings, M. (2011). Best practices for dealing with price volatility in Utah's residential construction market. *International Journal of Construction Education and Research, 7*(3), 210–225. doi:10.1080/15578771.2011.552935

Tran, D., Lester, H., & Sobin, N. 2014. Toward Statistics on Construction Engineering and Management Research.*Proceedings of the Construction Research Congress 2014: Construction in a Global Network.* doi:10.1061/9780784413517.117

Valdez, A. M. (2009). So much to learn, so little time: Educational priorities for the future of emergency nursing. *Advanced Emergency Nursing Journal, 31*(4), 337–353. doi:10.1097/TME.0b013e3181bcb571

Vatalis, K. I., Manoliadis, O. G., & Charalampides, G. (2011). Assessment of the economic benefits from sustainable construction in Greece. *International Journal of Sustainable Development and World Ecology, 18*(5), 377–383. doi:10.1080/13504509.2011.561003

Vick, S. G. (2002). *Degrees of belief – subjective probability and engineering judgement.* Danvers: ASCE Press.

von der Gracht, H. (2012). Consensus measurement in Delphi studies: Re-opinion and implications for future quality assurance. *Technological Forecasting and Social Change, 79*(8), 1525–1536. doi:10.1016/j.techfore.2012.04.013

Wright, T. S. A. (2006). Giving "teeth" to an environmental policy: A Delphi Study at Dalhousie University. *Journal of Cleaner Production, 14*(9), 761–768. doi:10.1016/j.jclepro.2005.12.007

Zou, X., & Moon, S. (2014). Hierarchical evaluation of on-site environmental performance to enhance a green construction operation. *Civil Engineering and Environmental Systems, 31*(1), 5–23. doi:10.1080/10286608.2012.749871

KEY TERMS AND DEFINITIONS

Data Collection: Collection the needed information to solve a problem.
Data Reliability: The trust of decision maker on the reliability of collected data for decision making.
Decision Making: The process of finding a way to solve a problem.
Delphi: A research technique to make decision with help of expert panels.
Experts: A group of people who are well experienced in the area of chosen research.
Qualitative Research: Type of research dealing with opinions and ideas.

Result Validity: Ability of the results of research process to solve the problem.

Chapter 5
New Product Development and Manufacturability Techniques and Analytics

Alan D. Smith
Robert Morris University, USA

ABSTRACT

The following case study evaluates the New Product Development (NPD) techniques utilized by Forest City Technologies, Incorporated (FCT). Through insight gathered via interviews conducted with the company's product development and materials purchasing management teams, and supported by literature, this study attempts to show how Forest City Technologies, Inc. integrates specific components into its product development process to: 1. Meet its NPD goals, and 2. Achieve better supplier and customer relationships. This study focuses on the components of: NPD models employed by FCT, early customer and supplier involvement, NPD-innovation integration techniques, demand change factors during the NPD process, and risk-mitigation strategies implemented by FCT during the NPD process. The study is segmented into three main sections: Introduction to NPD and FCT, the components of FCTs new product development process, and NPD implications on FCTs supplier and customer relationships.

INTRODUCTION

Role of Technology and Analytical Approaches in Manufacturing

The achievement of innovation through the development and marketing of products and services has been a key source of competitive advantage for many large and small manufacturing firms in order to improve upon operations efficiency. Numerous process modifications, modeling and simulation techniques, and design for manufacturability projects can be found through the academic and practitioner's literature. Managers typically spend much time and resources in prototyping and putting new products on the market, constantly weighing the factors that they feel as though will make the products ultimately sell or fail (Smith & Rupp, 2015; Wee, Peng, & Wee, 2010; Whitten, 2004; Yao & Carlson, 1999; Zang

DOI: 10.4018/978-1-5225-0654-6.ch005

& Fan, 2007). Essentially, new product manufacturability (NPM) is a strategic fit between the product design specifications from the new product development (NPD) team and the actual capabilities of the manufacturing/production processes (Fumi, Scarabotti, & Schiraldi, 2013; Helo, Anussornnitisarn, & Phusavat, 2008; Hu, Wang, Fetch, & Bidanda, 2008; Ifinedo & Nahar, 2009; Johansson & Sudzina, 2008). There are many dynamic factors associated with successful global NPD/NPM strategic ventures that are not related to performance factors alone (Baxter & Hirschhauser, 2004; Bhat, 2008; Park & Min, 2013).

As suggested by Durham (2002), manufacturability and related manufacturing research into processing technologies and systems analysis must include evaluation of the environmental and energy impacts, as well as the economic considerations. The entire process of manufacturability is complex and requires the ability to assess process or systems modifications in terms of their impacts on resource use, at both the global as well as the local evaluation. "The need to conduct this assessment on several levels induces system complexity. Current models and methods either simplify, provide bulk assessment of events, or serve in a reductionist fashion, providing decision-makers with limited information" (p. 37). Poor manufacturability due to poor NPD and team integration processes can enact significant costs and loss of market share. Managerial integration issues associated with the ability of a firm to accelerate NPD activities may have significant impacts on generating initial production start-up problems, increased employee morale problems, cost over-runs, increased complexity, delays in quality assurance programs, and increased customer dissatisfaction from increased in products' defects and resultant failures.

Websites and scanning equipment provide not only a direct contact between the organization and its customers, but also present an opportunity for innovation in both the manufacturability and delivery/sell of products. One factor determining whether the organization will use its website for the electronic delivery of its products may be the firm's pre-existing distribution structure and channel relationships. Hence, "Some innovative organizations are attempting to provide customers greater value by using this technology within their value chain" (Palmer & Griffith, 1998, p.47). Companies can gain significant advantage by utilizing the Web and the associated IT technologies of automatic identification and data capture (AIDC), especially smart cards, for communication and product management purposes. Information sharing within a technical project environment can make use of these tools, such as shared-secret symmetry cryptography together with smart-card technology. The access key of a person is carefully encoded and stored on a smart card, which can also be used for many other purposes. Thus, for example, access records are kept on these smart cards in a distributive fashion and with duplication.

The information intensity of the product/service is a key element, which is greatly aided by the timeliness and accuracy of the associated AIDC-related systems. Highly information-intensive products and services require a higher frequency of contact with customers to achieve effective communication that may be achieved through the use of RFID and related technologies (Aldaihani & Darwish, 2013; Azadeh, Gholizadeh, & Jeihoonian, 2013; Bhamu, Khandelwal, & Sangwan, 2013; Chen, Wu, Su, & Yang, 2008; Dutta, Lee, & Whang, 2007; Fisher & Monahan, 2008). "The more information-intense the product, the more likely the website will utilize promotional activities to stimulate repeat consumer patronage of the site" (Palmer & Griffith, 1998, p. 47). Therefore, the Internet coupled with AIDC systems integration offers a method of distribution and project managerial control of information to a vast host of potential users. In addition, this union of IT systems can provide accurate and timely information as well. These methods of information management strategies are allowing manufacturers leverage and streamline the tremendous volume of data flows. As Keller (2002) noted:

No doubt obstacles abound, but the good news is that Web-based software is now coming to market to automate the paper-based processes that make-up strategic sourcing, enabling manufacturers to capture data, analyze their spend history and categories, streamline negotiations, and better monitor supplier performance and contract compliance. (p. 19)

AIDC-related technologies and strategic management of innovative product design and manufacturability through project team integration, coupled with better monitoring of supplier performance and contract compliance results directly into better product and service quality. The ability to foster these trends within a project-team management environment should lead to improvement in both processes and products.

As for both manufacturing and service quality, for example, issues of delivery reliability and short response/cycle times are frequently cited. In terms of product quality, combinations of product design elements with durability and maintainability are common. As suggested by Finch (1999), the definition that captures the essence of quality embodies those characteristics that precisely match customer desires.

This occurs through a combination of product design efforts and attention to conformance to specifications, both linked to customer needs. The need for customer-based information has prompted a variety of collection approaches that have evolved into what has become known as customer involvement. (p. 535)

This producer/customer involvement is evident in B2B as well as B2C transactions, as these markets have formal dialogue between customer and suppliers through the management of the supply chain. This is evident in the business partnering that has been commonplace in most businesses. For example, communication and information systems integration is a vital element of successful Customer Relationship Management (CRM) and the Internet allows companies to easily reach millions of customers around the world at a very low cost (Rao, Salam, & DosSantos, 1998).

Documentation of the team integration processes coupled with the project management characteristics as defined in Figure 1 should provide a baseline for comparisons with other manufacturing and service concerns. This study should provide the needed baseline in order to formally contrast the more traditional, non-AIDC-related industries frequently cited in the project and manufacturing management literature for discussion and comparative purposes.

New Product Development (NPD)

Companies need to learn to manage the complex product transitions to sustain their competitive advantage. Coordinating supply and demand between two product generations can be a difficult and costly problem. The alignment of actions and decisions across different internal groups and across organizations helps ensure proper information is being passed. Doing this has the potential to greatly improve the company's ability to anticipate and react to market changes. The field studies conducted at Intel Corp. show that while numerous factors affect the rate and success of product transitions, inadequate information sharing and coordination among groups is one of the more important challenges to successful transitions. Lack of information can prevent managers from adequately assessing the state of the transition and impair the effective design and implementation.

Effective new product development strategy is essential for the success of a service or manufacturing company. Many companies will utilize scholarly management techniques to achieve successful product

New Product Development and Manufacturability Techniques and Analytics

Figure 1. Conceptualization of related performance metrics and related components associated with the processes of NPD/NPM

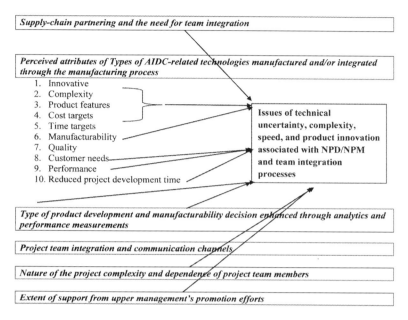

development results. These techniques can include Quality Function Deployment (QFD), or the Booz, Allen and Hamilton (BAH) model which, according to Bhuiyan (2011) is probably one of the best known models that have been developed over the years. However, while companies may share similar aspects of new product development strategies, their product development techniques can also be uniquely tailored to meet their needs and the individual needs of their customers.

Although new product development is not the beginning of customer-supplier interaction, it is an initial introduction of processing capabilities and standards directly related to the customer's order. Therefore, factors that must be considered within new product development can have long-lasting effects on the future of the customer-supplier relationship, company growth, and competitive advantage. These dynamics can include techniques such as innovation integration into new product development, early supplier/customer involvement, capabilities and demand change probabilities, and risk-mitigation, which are all embedded within various product development stages.

METHODS

With the information gathered from the interviews and analysis, the present author set out to investigate the most effective set of tools and/or processes to efficiently transition from one product to another. Forest City Technologies, Inc. (FCT) was selected because of its international presence and ever increasingly product line in the high R7D environment and its constant need to innovate in its processes and product lines in order to remain competitive. A qualitative business case study methodology was employed for this chapter (Baxter & Jack, 2008). The current research effort inspects multiple generations of products and service and suggests numerous factors that affect the adoption rate and success of a new product and its manufacturability. The major factors general fall into the categories of risks/drivers and demand/supply. Eventually, through trial and error as well as predictive analytics, both supply risks and demand risks can cause a product failure, while successful product introductions depend on a balance of both.

In this chapter, the author first set out to assess the key factors in developing and implementing new products effectively. To do so, key players in selected functional groups involved in planning NPD/NPM were interviewed at FCT. Basic discussion of baselines from past products was discussed. Managers and other professional employees were asked to identify the weak and strong points in the firm's knowledge of the product.

CASE STUDY

Forest City Technologies (FCT), Inc.

Overview and Manufacturing Description

Forest City Technologies, Inc. (FCT), founded in 1956, functions as both a service- and manufacturing-supplier. The company is predominately a second-tier supplier, though also aids as a third- and fourth-tier supplier. They 100s of customers in more than 20 countries and have an extensive product base that includes over 20 product lines for areas such as aerospace, automotive, and electronic devices. As a manufacturing-supplier, FCT stocks many items for sale in bulk. As a service-supplier, they utilize just-in-time (JIT) manufacturing techniques and advanced technology for the efficient processing of their customers' products. Essentially, FCT employs a two-way, bi-directional interaction technique in which they encourage customer communications to flow back and forth in the order of supplier succession, which acts to enhance the supply chain's functionality and processing flow. The reputation of the company and its relationships are quite diverse, serving an equally diverse global environment, with many complex arrangements of partnerships, technologies, and materials. Several comprehensive product/service lines deal with a variety of industries (i.e., aerospace, automotive, consumer goods, electronics and safety devices, industrial transportation and equipment, lighting and secondary optics, motorsports, structural bonding and assembly). The company currently holds certificates in ISO 9001 and 14001.

New Product Development Techniques/Models Employed

While there are many product development models, as well as, new techniques that can augment the effectiveness of a company's NPD strategy, FCT employs a blend of techniques unique to their services along with failure mode and effects analysis (FMEA) according to Fran Stack, Vice President of Product Development (Stark, 2015). Through the use of failure mode and effects analysis, FCT can not only locate root causes in product development failures and solve them, but also assess the likelihood a failure will occur later in the developmental process (Lago, Bizzarri, Scalzotto, Parpaiola, & Amigoni, 2012). Their customized techniques are created within the confines of industry standards and allow them to successfully navigate product development stages and challenges that are relative to their services.

They extensively leverage predictive models that use analytics that help valid the models' usefulness through several years' worth of prior research and performance data. The goal is to seek patterns via data mining techniques to seek out relevant critical success factors. Obviously, the accuracy of such predictive

New Product Development and Manufacturability Techniques and Analytics

models is extremely important and must be based on other external factors than just in-house predictive analytics and capacity. Management takes several steps to continually monitor the dynamic changes in industrial standards and competitive improvements and efficiency gains for foreign companies.

Early Supplier/Customer Involvement within NPD

Customer and supplier involvement is of great importance to the management of FCT, especially in its formulation of product development strategy. Early supplier involvement is a well-known technique wherein a more efficient design process can be achieved through the use of the supplier's experience (Biswas & Sarker, 2008; Carvalho, Cruz-Machado, & Tavares, 2012; Chan & Kumar, 2009; Drejer & Riis, 2000; Grewal, 2008). How and when the customer involves the supplier is the strategic focus (Browning & Heath, 2009; Cabral & Cruz-Machado, 2012; Cavaleri, 2008). Yet, as a service supplier, Forest City Technologies has a distinct relationship with its customers. According to Sampson and Spring (2012), this need to have a direct and compelling relationship can be studied in part to the Unified Service Theory, which basically postulates that the major distinguishing characteristic of services is that they possess bidirectional supply chain relationships, based on treating customers as suppliers as well. It is then reasonable to assume, that from the service supplier's perspective, early customer involvement can, in its own right, be considered an effective and purposeful technique, and is, in this case, the same as early supplier involvement.

Teece and Pisano (1994) offered some additional types of routines in manufacturing that directly impact on coordination problems frequently found in manufacturing environments (i.e., gathering and processing information, linking customer experiences with product and organizational design choices, coordinating factories and component suppliers, and bringing new products to market). As found in this chapter, the traditional forces of technological and product complexity, product newness, technological uncertainty, design outsourcing, and intentional project acceleration are not the only major forces that should be sharing strategic manufacturing management. These forces are not generally cost effective to become manageable in the foreseeable future, but project team and technical team integration are certainly under more control of management and deserve to be treated with dignity and respect. As evident in this and Swink's (1999, 2000) studies, team member integration and technical project management are the critical roles that should be leveraged for sustainable competitive advantage.

As a primarily service-based supplier, FCT's products are driven by the customer's needs, and are birthed from the customer's expertise as a supplier and management's experience in customizable service applications. The customer's participation in FCT product development can range from the simple submission of prints and specifications, a quote request, or the active participation and communication throughout the entire design process. "In some cases, the customer can have a great impact on product development, such as changing their specifications many times during the initial design stage, looking for a solution!" according to Lemke, Product Administrator at FCT, Inc.

Early raw materials supplier involvement is of lesser concern for FCT due to FCTs solid material base and supplier relationships. The company has a wide range of raw materials that are commonly used in their applications. These materials are kept to an inventory standard and the proper material for the customer's proposed application is frequently delegated by the service request team, or requested by current customers based on their past interactions with FCT. There are times though, that a new or current customer requests a material that FCT does not stock, or material specifications that the inventoried material does not currently meet. In these rare cases, according to Jack Nunney, Purchasing Manager, FCT relies on its suppliers' expertise to assist FCT product development professionals in material acquisition or material "tweaks". Material "tweaks" generates a common make or buy decision in which FCT, like all companies, makes their decision based on the traditional factors of cost, capabilities, advantage, and cultural strategies.

Supplier-Customer Relationship Considerations within NPD

Customer relationship management (CRM) begins with the initial contact between the supplier and customer and is cultivated during the product's life cycle. The ability for a supplier "to adequately meet the needs of supply chain customers is paramount for the success of the supply chains" (Wisner, Chan, & Keong. 2012, p. 348). This basic goal is of clear focus to FCT management. Fran Stack sums it up by stating, "The customer's needs will dictate the product development." Though the customer's needs are the main factor in the customer relationship component of product development, management FCT does incorporate smaller factors that work in conjunction with this main element to achieve customer satisfaction. One such factor is that of feasibility. FCT professionals consider what the customer is trying to accomplish, how FCT can help achieve this goal, and the possible impacts of the proposed techniques. "In the long-term", states Lemke (2015), "the feasibility factor can help to cultivate FCTs customer relationships."

Some of the many the factors that FCT must consider for the materials supply component of product development are much more specific, though common among manufacturing and service suppliers. FCT must match the qualifications required by the customer to the materials supplier. These qualifications can include whether the supplier is QS or ISO certified, the quality management system utilized by the supplier, as well as delivery performance of the supplier. Delivery performance is a supplier aspect that must be made clear to FCT as it can have serious implications for the company's performance baselines of JIT-based lead-times and customer satisfaction.

Innovation Integration into FCT Product Development

FCTs decision to integrate new products and innovative techniques or new manufacturing technology is accomplished on a case-by-case basis. According to Fran Stack, the decision is cost-driven. FCTs integration strategy is based on what techniques and technologies best serve the customers' needs and provides the greatest return. A second variable in the decision to integrate NPD and innovation is that of customer demand. For instance, generally, if the projected quantity per year is relatively small, FCT strategy dictates there will be little advantage to "break-in" situations of an innovative process, while it is being used for large quantity jobs. This is very much, a simple common-sense approach that provides large benefits for the company. Other times, FCT will use innovations to expand their customer base by offering new product manufacturing capabilities, increased quality, or decreased product manufacturing cost, essentially creating opportunities for new product development, and therefore new sales.

Although knowing when and how to integrate innovative techniques into NPD, can be cumbersome. Some research claims there are other challenges service suppliers, like FCT, must overcome, beyond those of manufacturing suppliers. According to Sampson and Spring (2012), one challenge presented by service suppliers, per the Unified Service Theory, is that of customer stifling on innovation. It is a combination supply chain collaboration and innovation that may also lead to opportunities for innovation. Collaboration and supply chain management (SCM) are synonymous aspects of each other because they

New Product Development and Manufacturability Techniques and Analytics

both include communication and teamwork to reach an end goal. A firm's collaborations with suppliers, customers, and their own staff can often improve quality and business practices that fuel growth.

Kohli and Jensen (2012) empirically studied how effective collaborative efforts are within a supply chain as it compares to companies demographics, current collaborations, and independent variables that had to do with operational techniques. They found that joint planning is another important aspect of SCM and its collaboration because it is a direct conversation between buyer and supplier about future actions and forecasts. In their studies, the two types of planning are operational and sales/business planning. These often coincide with each other because once the sales department has sold a number of units, the production department has to fulfill the order in an efficient and timely manner. This information is then shared with the various suppliers and planned out over the course of the lead time. This situation allows for goal congruence to form among all parties involved and allows for a firm to develop performance measures, joint goals and objectives, IT standardization, defining roles and responsibilities of each partner, formalizing the nature of information shared, as well as alignment of collaborative schedules. The ultimate result is the joint development of an implementation plan (Kohli & Jensen, 2012). Once each firm is on the same page and knows each other's goals/expectations, there is a smooth transition into completing tasks and objectives over time.

In the case of FCT, product development team members agree that there is little to no external dampening of innovation. In fact, Stack (2015) suggested that there can be more internal inhibiting of innovation, than external; which results from pre-conceived notions. Overall, FCT's NPD innovation integration strategy is one of optimization of the factors of cost, productivity, and customer satisfaction in a simultaneous fashion through scoring analytics and performance baseline comparisons.

Planning for Production Demand Changes within the NPD Process

FCT' product development personnel agree that it is very difficult to plan for over- or under-estimated quantities. In the product development stage, there are few customer guarantees regarding volume. Nonetheless, it is possible to reduce the strain fluctuating volumes may have on the company once the product enters its launch phase. FCT uses two particular methods to reduce the impact of capacity instabilities; flexibility and a combination of qualitative and quantitative measures.

During product development, FCT personnel determine the processing parameters such as quality specs, processing technique, and product characteristics, which enable them to gain insight into full production feasibility. Understanding how smooth a product will most likely be processed, FCT can then make an educated decision regarding the amount of flexibility the process will offer. FCT also utilizes qualitative methods during this phase. They incorporate flexibility into their daily operations as well, via scheduling techniques, temp sources, or capabilities changes, so they can better manage process and quantity oscillation.

FCTs' forecasting methods are similar to, and a mixture of, the jury of executive opinion qualitative model, and, both time-series, and cause-and-effect quantitative models. Through collaboration, based on the product development team's combined experience, data collection, and factual evidence, FCT creates a solid platform to make the best possible decisions regarding processing techniques and related quality and cost parameters, relevant to the product. Once the product development begins, the team then compares the results to their predictions in order to check the accuracy of their forecast.

During the commercialization phase (BAH model), or product launch phase, the transition from conceptual to full-production can be particularly sensitive to fluxes in volume. FCT navigates this period via 'first-process' tooling and set-up lead-times. According to Lemke (2015, "FCT-customer communication is very important during this evolution". Supplier relationships and supply management are also critical in this stage.

FCT New Product Development Risk-Mitigation Strategies

Risk-mitigation is of high-importance to a company's bottom-line, public relations, and the safety of personnel and the environment. According to Jerrard, Barnes, & Reid (2008, p. 22), "the environment in which the conception and development of new products takes place is complex and involves creativity and risk at a number of levels in a wide range of situations." During its NPD projects, FCT utilizes a few different strategies to ensure these high-risk areas are properly managed. Their varying approaches include ISO-14001 environmental management system, FMEA, raw material evaluation, and internal and external communication. Their earned ISO-14001 certificate combined with their policies regarding materials that contain harmful ingredients, though environmentally ethical, have very little effect on many of their product development endeavors. However, their use of failure mode and effects analysis, along with strong communication policies have a much larger impact on managing risk during this phase.

As previously mentioned, FMEA allows FCT to evaluate the chances of a failure occurring upon, or after, product launch. Their use of FMEA also means that they can evaluate the "severity, likelihood, and feasibility of detecting and intercepting" a failure (Lago et. al, 2012). FCTs product development process gives them information they can use to determine these FMEA attributes, which can then be analyzed, if needed, to create quotes, troubleshoot processes, or meet the customer's specifications. Clear communication is also used to reduce errors and ensure team members' and customers' expectations are understood. FCT encourages these communications through empowerment policies, team meetings, and customer service techniques.

NPD and Its Implications on FCT's Supplier and Customer Relationships

Information sharing is a critical part of SCM because it can determine order size, specifications of design, and even production aspects among employees. It also has a critical role in collaboration because it is the actual transference of information from one party to another, allowing them to correctly make a decision/fulfill a request by the other. There are three aspects of information sharing including operations, marketing, and information systems. The operations aspect allows for the buying department to collaborate with a supplier based on their own min/max system in order to keep production on time and efficient. Marketing collaboration includes "new product introductions, promotional planning, market trends data, and customer preferences. "FCTs goal in new product development is first and foremost to make a product that meets the customer's needs" according to Stack (2015). He also suggested that "other goals could be to secure the source of supply for a material, try to oust a competitor, and ultimately… make more money for the company. After all, it all flows from this; a better community, the ability to help employees, and making a positive impact on the bigger picture." The strategies and components involved in FCT' NPD process are professional, ethical, and effective. Each of the NPD component techniques so far discussed has clear benefits for the company, their customers, and their suppliers, which helps to achieve their goals.

In particular, the company's use of FMEA combined with unique product development techniques, enables them to provide quality assurance, meet or exceed the customers' needs/expectations, and maximize resource management; even as early as the product development stage. Overall, this allows them, and the customer, to achieve competitive pricing, customer satisfaction, and an overall market advantage.

As a predominately service-supplier, they embrace customer involvement in product development. This collaboration can lead to improvements in both processing techniques and material formulas which benefits FCT, their customers, and their suppliers. Trust can also be nurtured through the supplier-customer interaction, strengthening the supply chain. Their early material supplier involvement strategy has many benefits as well. With the expertise of the material vendor, FCT product quality increases, cost can decrease, and the supplier can acquire additional marketing.

Management at FCT demonstrated strategically leverages qualitative determination techniques regarding innovation and product development integration that helps ensures the proper process will be used to meet each customer's individual needs while optimizing the technology available. From a long-term perspective, this equates to lower costs, higher outputs, increased options, increased customer retention, and easier entry. Hence, risk-mitigation strategies used by FCT effectively help to protect their community, employees, capabilities, and processes; thus reducing any risk that could flow from them through the supply chain.

CONCLUSION

What have been well-documented in the operation management literature that the essential concepts of incremental innovation (e.g., improvement of pre-existing products) and radical product innovation (e.g., involving new technologies or ideas) processes in general terms are much in demand in any predictive modelling exercise in organizational performance. Much of the strategic manufacturing literature suggests that these successful processes are largely supported by reliable information technologies and good people (McDermott, 1999; Smith, 2010). These innovations or experiments may provide the foundation upon which the next generation of manufactured products may be made. According to McDermott (1999), firms that have large shares in one product generation may not be able to take advantage of the new wave of technologies and innovations and, thus, their existence may be threatened. Clearly, the benefits achieved by FCT, for them, their customers, and their suppliers, help to solidify their supply chain relationships. The strategies, techniques, and component integration within their NPD process are incredibly effective and professional. Through successfully achieving their new product development goals, they are able to create customer satisfaction and trust. They strive to be a strong link within their respective supply chain and undoubtedly have great impact on the success of that supply chain.

FURTURE RESEARCH DIRECTIONS

Companies must learn to manage the complex product transitions to sustain their competitive advantage. Coordinating supply and demand between two product generations can be a difficult and costly problem. The alignment of actions and decisions across different internal groups and across organizations helps ensure proper information is being passed. Doing this greatly improves the company's ability to anticipate and react to market changes. Ultimately, individual companies need to conduct field studies that illustrate the numerous interacting factors such as the rate and success of product transitions, inadequate information sharing and coordination among groups is one of the more important challenges to successful transitions. Lack of information can prevent managers from adequately assessing the state of the transition and impair the effective design and implementation. More research needs to be completed on the many nontechnology factors (e.g., accounting on operational processes, inventory forecasting accuracy, actual demand, case size, available shelf and warehouse spaces), that aid management in balancing the costs/benefits in any NPD/NPM strategic venture.

ACKNOWLEDGMENT

The author wishes to thank most heartedly for the valuable contributions by the reviewers for their input into the final paper. Peer reviewing and editing are commonly tedious and thankless tasks.

REFERENCES

Aldaihani, M. M., & Darwish, M. A. (2013). Optimal production and inventory decisions for supply chains with one producer and multiple newsvendors. *International Journal of Services and Operations Management.*, *15*(4), 430–448. doi:10.1504/IJSOM.2013.054884

Azadeh, A., Gholizadeh, H., & Jeihoonian, M. (2013). A multi-objective optimisation model for university course timetabling problem using a mixed integer dynamic non-linear programming. *International Journal of Services and Operations Management.*, *15*(4), 467–481. doi:10.1504/IJSOM.2013.054886

Baxter, L. F., & Hirschhauser, C. (2004). Reification and representation in the implementation of quality improvement programmes. *International Journal of Operations & Production Management*, *24*(2), 207–224. doi:10.1108/01443570410514894

Baxter, P., & Jack, S. (2008). Qualitative case study methodology: Study design and implementation for novice researchers. *Qualitative Report*, *13*(4), 544–559.

Bhamu, J., Khandelwal, A., & Sangwan, K. S. (2013). Lean manufacturing implementation in an automated production line: A case study. *International Journal of Services and Operations Management.*, *15*(4), 411–429. doi:10.1504/IJSOM.2013.054883

Bhat, S. (2008). The effect of ordering policies for a manufacturing cell changing to lean production. *Proceedings - Institution of Mechanical Engineers*, *222*(11), 1551–1560. doi:10.1243/09544054JEM1216

Bhuiyan, N. A. (2011). Framework for successful new product development. *Journal of Industrial Engineering and Management*, *4*(4), 746–770. doi:10.3926/jiem.334

Biswas, P., & Sarker, B. R. (2008). Optimal batch quantity models for a lean production system with in-cycle rework and scrap. *International Journal of Production Research*, *46*(23), 6585–6610. doi:10.1080/00207540802230330

Browning, T. R., & Heath, R. D. (2009). Reconceptualizing the effects of lean on production costs with evidence from the F-22 program. *Journal of Operations Management*, *27*(1), 23–35. doi:10.1016/j.jom.2008.03.009

Cabral, I. G. A., & Cruz-Machado, V. (2012). A decision-making model for Lean, Agile, Resilient and Green supply chain management. *International Journal of Production Research, 50*(17), 4830–4845. doi:10.1080/00207543.2012.657970

Carvalho, H., Cruz-Machado, V., & Tavares, J. G. (2012). A mapping framework for assessing supply chain resilience. *International Journal of Logistics Systems and Management, 12*(3), 354–373. doi:10.1504/IJLSM.2012.047606

Cavaleri, S. A. (2008). Are learning organizations pragmatic? *The Learning Organization, 15*(6), 474–481. doi:10.1108/09696470810907383

Chan, F. T. S., & Kumar, V. (2009). Performance optimization of a legality inspired supply chain model: A CFGTSA algorithm based approach. *International Journal of Production Research, 47*(3), 777–791. doi:10.1080/00207540600844068

Chen, C. C., Wu, J., Su, Y. S., & Yang, S. C. (2008). Key drivers for the continued use of RFID technology in the emergency room. *Management Research News, 31*(4), 273–288. doi:10.1108/01409170810851348

Drejer, A., & Riis, J. O. (2000). New dimensions of competence development in industrial enterprises. *International Journal of Manufacturing Technology and Management, 2*(1/7), 660-882.

Durham, D. R. (2002). Environmentally benign manufacturing: Current practice and future trends. *Journal of Operations and Manufacturing, 54*(5), 34–38.

Dutta, A., Lee, H. L., & Whang, S. (2007). RFID and operations management: Technology, value and incentives. *Production and Operations Management, 16*(5), 646–655. doi:10.1111/j.1937-5956.2007.tb00286.x

Finch, B. J. (1999). Internet discussions as a source for consumer product involvement and quality information: An exploratory study. *Journal of Operations Management, 17*(5), 535–556. doi:10.1016/S0272-6963(99)00005-4

Fisher, J. A., & Monahan, T. (2008). Tracking the social dimensions of RFID systems in hospitals. *International Journal of Medical Informatics, 77*(3), 176–183. doi:10.1016/j.ijmedinf.2007.04.010 PMID:17544841

Fumi, A., Scarabotti, L., & Schiraldi, M. M. (2013). The effect of slot-code optimisation on travel times in common unit-load warehouses. *International Journal of Services and Operations Management., 15*(4), 507–527. doi:10.1504/IJSOM.2013.054925

Grewal, C. (2008). An initiative to implement lean manufacturing using value stream mapping in a small company. *International Journal of Manufacturing Technology and Management, 15*(3/4), 404–421. doi:10.1504/IJMTM.2008.020176

Helo, P., Anussornnitisarn, P., & Phusavat, K. (2008). Expectation and reality in ERP implementation: Consultant and solution provider perspective. *Industrial Management & Data Systems, 108*(8), 1045–1158. doi:10.1108/02635570810904604

Hu, G., Wang, L., Fetch, S., & Bidanda, B. (2008). A multi-objective model for project portfolio selection to implement lean and Six Sigma concepts. *International Journal of Production Research, 46*(23), 6611–6648. doi:10.1080/00207540802230363

Hu, G., Wang, L., Fetch, S., & Bidanda, B. (2008). A multi-objective model for project portfolio selection to implement lean and Six Sigma concepts. *International Journal of Production Research, 46*(23), 6611–6648. doi:10.1080/00207540802230363

Ifinedo, P., & Nahar, N. (2009). Interactions between contingency, organizational IT factors, and ERP success. *Industrial Management & Data Systems, 109*(1), 118–126. doi:10.1108/02635570910926627

Jerrard, R. N., Barnes, N., & Reid, A. (2008). Design, risk and new product development in five small creative companies. *International Journal of Design, 2*(1), 21–30.

Johansson, B., & Sudzina, F. (2008). ERP systems and open source: An initial review and some implications for SMEs. *Journal of Enterprise Information Management, 21*(6), 649–659. doi:10.1108/17410390810911230

Kohli, A. S., & Jensen, B. J. (2010). Assessing effectiveness of supply chain collaboration: an empirical study. *Supply Chain Forum, 11*(2), 1-16.

Kwok, S., & Wu, K. W. (2009). RFID-based intra-supply chain in textile industry. *Industrial Management & Data Systems, 109*(9), 1166–1178. doi:10.1108/02635570911002252

Lago, P., Bizzarri, G., Scalzotto, F., Parpaiola, A., Amigoni, A., Putoto, G., & Perilongo, G. (2012). Use of FMEA analysis to reduce risk of errors in prescribing and administering drugs in pediatric wards: A quality improvement report. *BMJ Open, 2*(6), 1–31. doi:10.1136/bmjopen-2012-001249 PMID:23253870

McDermott, C. M. (1999). Managing radical product development in large manufacturing firms: A longitudinal study. *Journal of Operations Management, 17*(6), 631–644. doi:10.1016/S0272-6963(99)00018-2

Park, B.-N., & Min, H. (2013). Global supply chain barriers of foreign subsidiaries: The case of Korean expatriate manufacturers in China. *International Journal of Services and Operations Management, 15*(1), 67–78. doi:10.1504/IJSOM.2013.050562

Rao, H., Raghay, S. A. F., & DosSantos, B. (1998). Marketing and the Internet. *Association for Computing Machinery. Communications of the ACM, 41*(3), 32–34. doi:10.1145/272287.272294

Sampson, S. E., & Spring, M. (2012). Customer Roles in Service Supply Chains and Opportunities for Innovation. *Journal of Supply Chain Management, 48*(4), 30–50. doi:10.1111/j.1745-493X.2012.03282.x

Smith, A. D. (2010). Balancing internal supply chain logistics: A comparative analysis of manufacturing and service firm operations. *International Journal of Logistics Systems and Supply Management, 3*(2), 145–166.

Smith, A. D., & Rupp, W. T. (2015). Supply chain integration and innovation in a global environment: Case studies of best business practices. *International Journal of Logistics Systems and Chain Management, 22*(8), 313–330. doi:10.1504/IJLSM.2015.072284

Swink, M. (1999). Threats to new product manufacturability and the effects of development team integration processes. *Journal of Operations Management, 17*(6), 691–709. doi:10.1016/S0272-6963(99)00027-3

Swink, M. (2000). Technological innovativeness as a moderator of new product design integration and top management support. *Journal of Product Innovation Management, 17*(3), 208–220. doi:10.1016/S0737-6782(00)00040-0

Wee, H.-M., Peng, S.-Y., & Wee, P. K. (2010). Modelling of outsourcing decisions in global supply chains: An empirical study on supplier management performance with different outsourcing strategies. *International Journal of Production Research, 48*(7), 2081–2094. doi:10.1080/00207540802644852

Whitten, D. (2004). User Information satisfaction scale reduction: Application in an IT outsourcing environment. *Journal of Computer Information Systems, 45*(2), 17–26.

Wisner, J. D., Chan, K.-C., & Keong, L. G. (2012). *Principles of Supply Chain Management: A Balanced Approach* (3rd ed.). Mason, OH: Southwestern.

Yao, A., & Carlson, J. (1999). The impact of real-time data communication on inventory management. *International Journal of Production Economics, 59*(1), 213–219. doi:10.1016/S0925-5273(98)00234-5

Zang, C., & Fan, Y. (2007). Complex event processing in enterprise information systems based on RFID. *Enterprise Information Systems, 1*(1), 3–23. doi:10.1080/17517570601092127

ADDITIONAL READING

Ha, O., Park, M., Lee, K., & Park, D. (2013). RFID application in the food-beverage industry: Identifying decision making factors and evaluating SCM efficiency. *KSCE Journal of Civil Engineering, 17*(7), 1773–1781. doi:10.1007/s12205-013-0297-x

Hall, J. A., & Liedtka, S. L. (2005). Financial performance, CEO compensation, and large scale information technology outsourcing decisions. *Journal of Management Information Systems, 22*(1), 193–221.

Jain, V., Benyoucef, L., & Deshmukh, S. G. (2008). What's the buzz about moving from 'lean' to 'agile' integrated supply chains? A fuzzy intelligent agent-based approach. *International Journal of Production Research, 46*(23), 6649–6678. doi:10.1080/00207540802230462

Jones, E., Riley, M., Franca, R., & Reigle, S. (2007). Case study: The engineering economics of RFID in specialized manufacturing. *The Engineering Economist, 52*(3), 285–303. doi:10.1080/00137910701503951

Kamhawi, E. M. (2008). System characteristics, perceived benefits, individual differences and use intentions: A survey of decision support tools of ERP systems. *Information Resources Management Journal, 21*(4), 66–83. doi:10.4018/irmj.2008100104

Kennedy, F. A., & Widener, S. K. (2008). A control framework: Insights from evidence on lean accounting. *Management Accounting Research, 19*(4), 301–319. doi:10.1016/j.mar.2008.01.001

Koong, L., & Lin, C. (2007). Evaluating the decision to adopt RFID systems using analytic hierarchy process. *Journal of American Academy of Business, 11*(1), 72–77.

Mateen, A., & More, D. (2013). Applying TOC thinking process tools in managing challenges of supply chain finance: A case study. *International Journal of Services and Operations Management*, *15*(4), 389–410. doi:10.1504/IJSOM.2013.054882

Pacciarelli, D., D'Ariano, A., & Scotto, M. (2011). Applying RFID in warehouse operations of an Italian courier express company. *NETNOMICS: Economic Research and Electronic Networking*, *12*(3), 209–222. doi:10.1007/s11066-011-9059-4

Smith, A. A., Smith, A. D., & Baker, D. J. (2011). Inventory management shrinkage and employee anti-theft approaches. *International Journal of Electronic Finance*, *5*(3), 209–234. doi:10.1504/IJEF.2011.041337

Smith, A. D. (2011). Component part quality assurance concerns and standards: Comparison of world-class manufacturers. *Benchmarking: An International Journal*, *18*(1), 128–148. doi:10.1108/14635771111109850

Smith, A. D., & Minutolo, M. C. (2014). Green supply chain acceptability and internal stakeholder concerns. *International Journal of Logistics Systems and Management*, *19*(4), 464–490. doi:10.1504/IJLSM.2014.065666

Smith, A. D., & Offodile, O. F. (2007). Exploring forecasting and project management characteristics of supply chain management. *International Journal of Logistics and Supply Management*, *3*(2), 174–214.

Smith, A. D., & Rupp, W. T. (2013). Data quality and knowledge/information management in service operations management: Regional supermarket case study. *International Journal of Knowledge-Based Organizations*, *3*(3), 35–52. doi:10.4018/ijkbo.2013070103

Ustundag, A. (2010). Evaluating RFID investment on a supply chain using tagging cost sharing factor. *International Journal of Production Research*, *48*(9), 2549–2562. doi:10.1080/00207540903564926

Visich, J. K., Li, S., Khumawala, B. M., & Reyes, P. M. (2009). Empirical evidence of RFID impacts on supply chain performance. *International Journal of Operations & Production Management*, *29*(12), 1290–1315. doi:10.1108/01443570911006009

Wyld, D. C. (2006). RFID 101: The next big thing for management. *Management Research News*, *29*(4), 154–173. doi:10.1108/01409170610665022

KEY TERMS AND DEFINITIONS

Automatic Identification and Data Capture Technologies (AIDC): Types of AIDC-related technologies to leave the human element out of the data collection and storage functions of information derived from manufacturing, integrated through the manufacturing process, types of authentication concerns and/or e-security strategies, and relationship links to customer profiles. Typical types of AIDC include, bar-coding, RFID, magnetic strips, touch memory, and smart cards.

Customer Relationship Management (CRM): CRM is software-driven processes that allow companies to find solutions to customize their products and service offerings for their customers via social listening, enhanced sales, marketing, and customer services.

Lean Management: Lean management refers to high quality, low costs business environments. Companies need to operate in the most efficient and effective means possible to maintain a competitive advantage on their competitors. As they strive to make every penny count towards maintaining margins on their products, more and more companies are finding the need to implement lean manufacturing techniques. However, simply implementing just one technique may not be the leanest strategy for these at-risk companies.

New Product Development (NPD): NPD is a universal term to the designing and testing of new product ventures. The achievement of innovation through the development and marketing of products and services has been a key source of competitive advantage for many large and small manufacturing firms. Numerous process modifications, modeling and simulation techniques, and design for manufacturability projects can be found through the academic and practitioner's literature. Essentially, new product manufacturability (NPM) is a strategic fit between the product design specifications from the new product development (NPD) team and the actual capabilities of the manufacturing/production processes.

New Product Manufacturing (NPM): NPM is a universal term referring to the inherent complexity of manufacturing a new product. In general, manufacturability and related manufacturing research into processing technologies and systems analysis must include evaluation of the environmental and energy impacts, as well as the economic considerations. The entire process of manufacturability is complex and requires the ability to assess process or systems modifications in terms of their impacts on resource use, at both the global as well as the local evaluation..

Operations Efficiency: Improving efficiency and reducing waste is a major challenge for hospitals and other patient care facilities looking to lower the cost of providing healthcare services. Far and away the largest contributor to operational costs in this industry is patient care activities. Since most clinical decisions involve managing products and medical supplies, finding ways to more efficiently manage supply chain activities can have a big impact on overall operational performance.

RFID-Embedded Technologies: RFID technologies are types of automatic data capture techniques that uses a combination of active and passive senders and receivers to collect and store codified information for further uses. The implementation of such technologies should lead to improved managerial and/or supply chain performance. On the surface, there appears to be few drawbacks to implementing such technology into a production process, assuming it enhances performance and improves output of the product. The main issues surrounding the RFID applications are whether the initial costs and labor required to utilize this technology are worth it, and will result in a positive outcome of revenues.

Supply Chain Management (SCM): In basic terms, supply chain is the system of organizations, people, activities, information and resources involved in moving a product or service from supplier to customer. The configuration and management of supply chain operations is a key way companies obtain and maintain a competitive advantage. The typical manufacturing supply chain begins with raw material suppliers, or inputs. The next link in the chain is the manufacturing, or transformation step; followed the distribution, or localization step. Finally, the finished product or service is purchased by customers as outputs. Service and Manufacturing managers need to know the impact of supply on their organization's purchasing and logistics processes. However, supply chain performance and its metrics are difficult to develop and actually measure.

Chapter 6
Transformation of CRM and Supply Chain Management Techniques in a New Venture

Amber A. Ditizio
Texas Woman's University, USA

Alan D. Smith
Robert Morris University, USA

ABSTRACT

The implementations of successful Customer Relationship Management (CRM) and Supply Chain Management (SCM) systems and their associated techniques in order to optimize the analytics available in any organization are daunting task, especially in a new business venture. Upper management must to be committed to focusing these embedded systems in order to enhance supplier integration and customer satisfaction. This chapter focuses on the implementation of CRM systems and analytics as well as SCM considerations in the new startup of the Hard Rock Rocksino at Northfield Park (HRRNP) and the transformation/refinement of their systems over their few years of business. A combination of literature research, interviews of upper management, and personal observations, HRRNP has illustrate their ability to deal with these challenges in a continuous improvement and lean management approach.

INTRODUCTION

Foundations of Customer Relationship Management and Performance Metrics

The evolution of the concept of Customer Relationship Management (CRM) has vital implications on organizations in the 21st century. The basic aim of this strategy is the maintenance of long-term relationships with customers (Smith, 2010; Smith & Clinton, 2015; Smith & Motley, 2010; Tsai, Huang, Jaw, & Chen, 2006; Warden, Wu, & Tsai, 2006). For business success, a healthy long-term relationship with the customer is vital for long survival and prosperity. Relationship building and management are leading approaches in marketing, with customer relationship management (CRM) strategies are increas-

DOI: 10.4018/978-1-5225-0654-6.ch006

ingly necessary in the improvement of the customer lifetime value (Patel & Hackney, 2010; Rigby & Ledingham, 2004; Sarkar, et al., 2010; Smith & Smith, 2012). Understanding customer needs and offering value-added services are essential factors that set the difference between successful and non-successful companies (Urbanskienė, Žostautienė, & Chreptavičienė, 2008). Equally, the importance of electronic customer relationship management (eCRM), in considering the customer's needs in all business aspects ensures customers' satisfaction.

Providing information on customer profiles, data, and history facilitates the strengthening of core processes of companies, specifically in service, sales, and marketing (Mishra & Mishra, 2009). CRM operating systems typically focus on optimizing profitability and ensuring control over the customer by making them feel included in the business operations (Kamakura, et al., 2005). A successful CRM system integrates the management of customers groups, enhances loyalty and raises the switching costs (Rigby & Ledingham, 2004). The basic concept is that knowledge and basic information concerning consumer preferences provides the organization with a competitive advantage. The system benefits both customers and enterprises' employees through needs fulfillment and mutual value creation activities.

Evolutions of Customer Relationship Management

The interest of researchers and organizations in relationship marketing probably emerged in the second half of the 20th century with the needs for global competitiveness. The dynamic state of the market and the changing service market sector provided significant challenges to the traditional marketing concept. These trends have lead businesses to develop software-based optimizing and analytics to better define customers' needs and reduction in costs (Long, 2010; Mohanty, Ravi, & Patra, 2010; Pahlavani, 2010). Probably the major disadvantage of traditional concepts is that it did not focus on sustaining long-term relationships with market partners and customers (Beldona & Tsatsoulis, 2010; Guo, 2010; Hilmola, 2010). Changing market conditions necessitate new forms of competitiveness, individual random interaction with competitors, suppliers and customer needs satisfaction (Kamakura, et al., 2005). The focus on marketing continually shifted towards maintaining long-term relationships from a focus on the business activity system. The shift in marketing from setting prices, creation of goods and services, and distribution, to including the marketing mix. Current marketing systems also focus on supporting, maintaining and strengthening relationships with other vital market participants. Marketing systems' shift further led to the uprising of eCRM that improves customer management (Smith & Smith, 2012; Smith, 2011). These systems are essential in increasing the productivity of companies and maximizing customer satisfaction. CRM systems also increase the income earned by companies.

Implementation of CRM

The complete implementation of a CRM-related system per se is not assurance for a change in the activity process of an enterprise and the investment on software intelligent systems does not guarantee a return on investment (Mohanty, Ravi, & Patra, 2010; O'cass & Fenech, 2003; Oetega, Martinez, & Hoyos, 2006). Becoming customer oriented is not automatic for an enterprise, and it does not necessarily mean an assurance of the loyalty of a customer or benefits to the enterprise (Sarkar, et al., 2010; Urbanskienė, et al., 2008). An efficient CRM system comprises of several modules (e.g., sales and service activities; customer focused marketing business processes and analytical CRM) (Kamakura, et al., 2005). The analytical module evaluates customer data and patterns of transaction for the improvement of customer relationships. The analytical and operational CRM modules provide the fundamental functions of an efficient CRM system (Mishra, et al., 2009). Successful implementation of CRM involves significant transformation of an organization since managing customer relationships is complex and involves several operations (Patel & Hackney, 2010; Rigby & Ledingham, 2004). The implementation of a CRM system is only a component of the overall transformation process. To ensure full transformation, an organization has to adopt new methods of interacting with its customers. Moreover, other important organizational aspects of the business, such as strategies, employee training, business processes and top management support, need to align with the implemented CRM system (Baran, et al., 2008).

There are at least 6 iterative processes essential in the implementation of a CRM system (Mishra & Mishra, 2009). These iterative processes include exploration and analysis, visioning, building the business case, planning and design of an efficient solution, implementing and integrating the solution, and realizing the value, to ensure further successful implementation of a CRM system of the application. The complexity of the project deeply influences the success of its implementation (Swink, 1999, 2000). According to recent literature research, an efficient project has a reduced project scope, reduced complexity and a tailored application (Baran, et al., 2008). It is, therefore, imperative for project designers to ensure that the system scope is small and reasonable. This can occur through phasing the functionality of the software through a series of systematic implementation phases (Urbanskienė et al., 2008). In the same way, to lower the risk of the project, the designers need to reduce the customization of the CRM application system's functionality. The business operations need to be the determinant of the scope of functions that the CRM application implements (Baran, et al., 2008). To ensure the initial and long-term success of a CRM initiative, organizations need to begin with fast, specific and profitable attempts.

Another strategy vital in the implementation of an efficient CRM system is to understand customer requirements; fulfilling those requirements in a manner that exceeds their expectations to retain customers and attracting new customers by the use of marketing approaches that are customer specific (Mishra & Mishra, 2009). The total commitment of the whole organization is essential for this system. Conventional CRM systems use information technology to track the interactions of a company with its customers. An analysis of these interactions is necessary for the maximization of the lifetime value of the customers and maximizing customer satisfaction (Aeron, Kumar, & Janakiraman, 2010; Cao, Kambayashi, Wang, & Zhang, 2004; Castaneda, Rodriguez, & Luque, 2009; Chan, 2005). The system is popular with large companies with a massive customer base, but with low business value for each customer (Blake, Neuendorf, & Valdiserri, 2005; Bourlakis, Papagiannidis, & Fox, 2008). The system helps the companies in the identification of customers with significant revenues for every marketing dollar spent. These customers typically require very little cost to attract (Baran, et al., 2008). In an analysis of a company's customer base, this customer usually contributes to about 85% of the total profits of the company, and yet comprise of only 15% of the customer base (Kamakura, et al., 2005).

Benefits of a CRM System

It is imperative for an organization to select a CRM system that increases its business value. There are a number of analytical methods in which the value of a business promotes cost reduction, ultimately, enhances incremental improvement of income per customer. Specially, CRM analytics is a type of online analytical processing that serves very similar functions that the more traditional field of data mining techniques perform. In a world of increased memory and speed, via better connectivity of websites, much of the transactional data associated with purchases can be combined with other databases to detect patterns in consumer behavior. Therefore, there is true value perceived by companies to engage software developers to deliver products that perform such pattern analysis.

Automatic identification and data capture/collection (AIDC) and associated information technologies are more than just bar codes. They are a variety of technologies that offer both strengths and limitations based on the jobs they are required to perform, and include magnetic stripe, radio frequency identification, biotechnology, and voice data entry. AIDC technologies are the terms used to describe the direct entry of data into a computer system, programmable logic controller (PLC) or other microprocessor-controlled device without using a keyboard via direct human input. In addition, AIDC technologies provide a reliable means to both identify and track items – characteristics that are the hallmarks of modern e-commerce. Through AIDC, it is possible to encode a wide range of information -- from basic item/person identification to comprehensive details about the item/person in a read/write format. For example, a MIT Auto-ID project was recently spearheaded by some of the world's largest consumer packaged goods, retail and computer companies -- International Paper, Procter & Gamble, Sun Microsystems, Unilever and Wal-Mart -- and supported by the Uniform Code Council (UCC), a standards-generating body that represents companies in 23+ industries (Smith, 2011). The management of information technology (IT) as well as business is greatly concerned about promoting linking and connectivity in organizational structures. In its simplest form, management must link products to orders and orders to shipments and shipments to payments.

Cost-reduction results from an automated sales process decreased customer management costs and automated process that improve total effectiveness. An increase in income is due to high sales ratios, improved management of customer information and improved quality of sales. Traditional systems store customer information in potential disparate applications (Mishra & Mishra, 2009). It is essential to consolidate the customer information, analyze, clean, and distribute it to various customer access points within the organization (Baran, et al., 2008). This ensures that all organization stakeholders have access to a single version of the customer information (Kamakura, et al., 2005). Once the organization has a single source for the customer information, reducing the churn-rate and enhancing the customer experience is a possibility (Blake, et al., 2005; Bourlakis, et al., 2008; Smith, 2010; Urbanskienė, et al., 2008). The churn rate measures the proportion of customers who stop using the products of the company. This information is applicable in sales, marketing and customer service departments. Previously stored information is essential for future customized selling or personal recommendations to customers. This information also facilitates cross selling and up selling. Such systems are essential in facilitating an organizations understanding of the market demand for design of products and thus facilitates decision making (Smith, 2011; Smith & Clinton, 2015; Smith & Motley, 2010). Such systems improve sales forecasting, standardization of sales and marketing operations and team selling. It should also improve the marketing operations such as campaigns (Urbanskienė, et al., 2008). The recorded data on product information, customer data, prospective customer preferences and information on marketing, scheduling and tracking direct communication on marketing are essential (Baran, et al., 2008; Smith & Clinton, 2015;).

Identification of profitable customers and affording them preferential treatment to enhance customer loyalty is also possible with an efficient CRM system. For employees of organizations, the CRM systems help to facilitate carrying out his responsibilities (Smith, 2011; Smith & Clinton, 2015; Smith & Motley, 2010). As a direct result of improved productivity, the employee earns a higher salary. The formation of the CRM process typically comprises of three fundamental items: setting the goal of CRM, choosing partners or a team, and choosing or creating the CRM-embedded program. An organization's profitability relies heavily on customer retention has a significant impact on firm profitability (Mishra et al., 2009). Research shows that improving customer retention by one percent results in a five percent improvement on the value of a firm (Baran, et al., 2008). Ultimately, organizations prioritizing the maximization of life term value generally focus on client retention.

Toma, Mihoreanu, and Ionescu (2014) discussed the need for innovation for the CRM sector of businesses. Through an empirically based research, they investigated the roles of CRM and innovation capability. In general, as previously stated, many companies are not using the right amount of technological advancements as they could to improve the innovation of their CRM departments (Patel & Hackney, 2010; Rigby & Ledingham, 2004). This situation may cause a serious problem for companies to optimize their operations and maximize profit since customers are not being satisfied in the best way possible as well as market shares not being as high as possible. Toma, et al. (2014) used methods studied by previous researchers in order to measure success. These include methods to measure marketing innovation, administrative innovation, and service innovation. Their experiment focused on improving a company by focusing their development on innovation. They suggested 5 major areas where innovation can be used to improve customer relationships; the first area dealt with the need for information sharing. In a previous study, Verhoef (2003) and Lagrosen (2005) found that manufacturers can launch more new products and services by using information from clients gained through CRM. This incitation supports their hypothesis that innovation is a necessity to improve CRM.

Another example that Toma, et al. (2014) explored is the fact that information sharing between manufacturers and clients enables manufacturers to adopt technologies that can improve CRM even more. The second major area researched was customer involvement. Customer involvement in the new product development stage has been recognized as a key component of the new products success. They found that customer involvement has had a positive effect on product innovation for CRM. The third area that was discussed is long-term partnerships in CRM. This concept involves having strategic alliances and joint-ventures in order to successfully form a long-term sustainable relationship. This supports their research since having a long-term partner; companies are able to use the innovative process between the companies to support their goals. This is helpful in maintaining a competitive advantage over other firms.

The fourth section that Toma, et al. (2014) discussed was joint-problem solving. It is inherently easier for manufacturers to improve product quality and technical process ability when customers voluntarily provide assistance to solve product design or technical process problems. Perhaps having a CRM-embedded system that involves customers in their problem solving will improve their chances at development. This is an innovative analytic to improve CRM, which will higher their competitive advantage. Ultimately, managers utilize innovation to improve CRM and their completive advantage is through technology-based CRM. By having innovation applied to technologically advanced method for customers to complain, complement, and ask for assistance, and so forth, a company will gain a competitive edge. By being technologically advanced, managers will be able to provide real-time responses' that will improve the relationships between customers and employees.

METHODS

Case Study: Hard Rock Rocksino at Northfield Park (HRRNP)

Company Background

The Hard Rock Rocksino broke ground in late December 2012. It is located at Northfield Park, Northfield, OH, near Cleveland, OH. This was a joint venture between Brock Milstein, owner of the Northfield Park Race Track, Hard Rock International, and The Seminole Tribe of Florida. The US$268,000,000, 220,000 square-foot facility, took just under one year to build (Barker, 2014). Since it was such a new company there is not much to their background; they are building their background as I-type. Routine decision-making in their operations management decisions, changes, and improvements are an ongoing state of flux as they normalize their operations within a 5-10 years range.

This facility contains a 1,822-capacity concert venue, a 302-capacity comedy club that may be used for banquets, trade shows, and other special events, 4 restaurants, a traditional Hard Rock retail shop, and 3 bars. However, these amenities are pale in comparison to what makes the Hard Rock Rocksino at Northfield Park (HRRNP) successful. The revenue generated by HRRNP is generated by the 2,279 video lottery terminals (VLTs) on the Rocksino floor. Although the money is made through the VLTs, the operations management techniques of HRRNP are mostly focused on the non-gaming aspects previously mentioned. Upper management of HRRNP generally understands that getting people to come gamble is easy, but the mission of Hard Rock International and HRRNP is "To spread the spirit of rock 'n' roll by creating authentic experiences that rock!"

Qualitative Business Case Study

The qualitative business case study is an approach to research that helps the exploration of a study of interest within its context using a variety of data sources. This ensures that the issue is not explored through one lens, but rather a variety of many possible viewpoints to help to reveal and understand the concepts associated with the study. According to Baxter and Jack (2008), one of the common problems associated with a case study is that there is a tendency for researchers to attempt to answer too broad questions or topics with too many objectives. To avoid this problem, Yin (2003) and Stake (1995) have suggested that placing boundaries on a case can prevent this explosion from occurring. This case is bounded both by time and place and by definition and context; namely, only one company, dealing with CRM-embedded systems requirements and analytics and issues of SCM performance, especially in dealing with issues of integration/collaboration for a new business venture.

CASE DISCUSSION

SCM Techniques

The SCM techniques strategically focused by HRRNP embody that mission statement and employ common techniques such as vendor-managed inventory systems (VMI) and supplier integration. The numbers posted for March by the Ohio Lottery Commission show that HRRNP has 44% of the regional market share ("The Ohio Lottery," 2015). Senior VP of Finance and Operations at HRRNP, Jeff Michie, predicts that when the numbers are out for April, he expects to see that they now have 48% of the market share (Michie, 2015). This would not be possible without management commitment to full integration of the supply chain and operations management techniques most focused on by HRRNP.

Problem Definitions

In essence, as evident in the previous research and discussion, CRM has as its centerpiece goal to enhance customer loyalty; hence, how to gain customers and keep them loyal? (Sarkar, et al., 2010; Smith & Smith, 2012; Smith, 2010, 2011). In order to accomplish this task, a business must know the value of each customer. Naturally, a business cannot retain all of its customers, but they can try to retain the loyal ones; namely the customers with the highest customer lifetime value. With this being said, the problem that was concluded by Rigby and Ledingham (2004) was that the generally accepted CRM model was not being fully used properly. Both employees and customers are not satisfied with their service, and this leads to high-job turnover. Thus, hoteliers are reluctant to invest. According to research conducted WIPRO Consulting Services, Inc., the primary three reasons supply chain transformations fail are falling into the "leading practices" trap, relying on the "Big Bang of Technology" as the main driver, and failing to address organizational issues ("WIPRO Consulting Services," 2011). Perhaps the biggest SCM problem faced by HRRNP is simply that they are new. A new venture company that has recently opened its operations to the public cannot expect to be perfect in understanding and satisfying its client base. Management needs to concentrate on continuous improvement in every aspect of its SCM partners and customers as true stakeholders in its operations.

As suggested by Senior Vice President of Finance and Operations at HRRNP, Jeff Michie, says that with 44% of the market share, it would be easy to get complacent but that would ultimately turn in to getting stagnant, and that's never good for business (Michie, 2015). When asked how difficult it was for upper management to stay focused on their core management values during the hectic time of planning, construction, and their first year, Michie stated it was not as difficult as one might imagine. Initially, there was a relatively small group of about 40 people involved in the planning and pre-opening process that were very close and committed to the management techniques laid out for them by former President Jon Lucas (currently Executive Vice President of Hotel and Casino Operations for Hard Rock International). The problem that HRRNP needs to focus on, as suggested by Michie, is ensuring the principles of continuous improvement are adhered to. Their core SCM values are embedded in the various aspects of continuous improvement and becoming leaner in their operations over time.

SCM Techniques Focused on by HRRNP

Although one might think that supply management in a company that does not manufacture or even actually sell tangible products would not be a major concern, to the management team at HRRNP, it is a major concern in strategic planning and operations. The company operates 4 restaurants, 3 bars, a retail shop, and 2 entertainment venues within HRRNP. It is important to keep in mind that while the company does not sell a tangible product, they sell an experience; hence, the various nongaming outlets within HRRNP are part of that experience and, if management is successful, promotes customer retention and value. Although the various nongaming revenue accounts for less than 2% of total revenue for

HRRNP, a nongaming outlet running out of a product or serving a poor quality product can tarnish the entire customer experience.

Director of Purchasing at HRRNP, Karen Roush, has a very distinct philosophy when it comes to supply management, "garbage in, garbage out" Roush (2015). When asked what it was like developing a supply chain from the group up for the new venture, Roush stated that it was quite a challenge. Corporate only mandated that they use 2 vendors, US Foods and Office Depot; everything else was up to her. Management at HRRNP made a strong effort in the beginning, and still makes an effort today to source from local vendors, minority vendors, and small businesses, while still trying to find the best product at the best price. According to Roush, creating and maintaining good relationships with suppliers is the most important aspect of what her purchasing team does. Although using a vendor that is not as cooperative, but has the lowest price may occur, it would be due to special circumstances that the company would deal with such a vendor without establishment of good working relationships. The purchasing teams at HRRNP focus on sourcing from vendors that are willing to cooperate and collaborate to make sure both companies are mutually benefiting. Since HRRNP does not have an onsite warehouse, they receive 6 days a week and about 75% of buys are based on the JIT model. Roush stated that she is currently working on a proposal for an onsite warehouse. Based on her calculations, the cost savings of being able to make bigger purchases would outweigh the overhead costs of a warehouse. This would allow them to be leaner in operations, especially concerning supply management considerations.

HRRNP uses the Stratton Warren System (SWS) for their purchasing and inventory system. Applications of SWS allow users to leverage the power of aggregate procurement across all departments and locations (Agilysys, 2016). SWS is a popular technology-based solution that helps manage the entire process from requisition to invoice, allowing automation to reduce tedious and time-consuming, error-prone paperwork and record keeping activities. To get an opinion of the benefits of SWS, an interview with a full-time employee that routinely uses the system was completed with Food and Beverage Buyer for HRRNP, Shellie Lovell. When asked on a scale from one to ten, how productive would the purchasing department be without SWS, she responded with the answer, "-2" (Lovell, 2015). Lovell went on to explain that, "Because of the little amount of revenue we make off of our food and beverage outlets, the cost of purchasing on an old paper system wouldn't even make it worth it to have restaurants here."

While managing the supply efficiently is important, it is not what generates revenue for HRRNP. Obviously, it is the gaming activities that attracts and creates value for the customer. The value proposition at HRRNP needs to be significantly attractive in order for consumers to choose to spend their discretionary income at HRRNP instead of at a competitor or even at the movies. CRM-related operations are absolutely important operations management techniques and analytics at HRRNP in order to "To create authentic experiences that ROCK!" Michie, 2015). That is the mission of Hard Rock International and Michie explained that they strive to fulfil this mission by focusing on CRM on two fronts, "front of house" and "back of house" operations that are totally seamless and transparent in the firm's customers.

"Back of house" responsibilities typically dwell within a massive customer database, with a single employee managing the database and 3 people that analyze the information and applications derived from its operations. HRRNP uses CRM-related software called Casino Market Place (CMP). According to HRRNP's CMP Database Manager, Vincent Green, "CRM in any casino would be impossible without CMP or a product like it" (Green, 2015). Listed in Table 1 are some of the primary benefits associated with implementing CMP ("Bally Technologies," 2015).

Green (2015) gave me his own opinion of the primary benefits of CMP. Green's response after reading the list in Table 1 suggested that their system's application of CMP was that it was relatively easy to use.

Table 1. The major benefits of CRM software enablers (i.e., Casino Market Place or CMP). Adapted from Bally Technologies (2015)

Primary Five Benefits of CMP according to the Bally Technologies Website
CMP's array of products operates in a Windows® PC environment and provides player-tracking, bonusing, promotions, and cage and pit accounting
CMP was developed by a team of gaming-industry experts experienced gaming. The software applications are relatively simple as CMP is an easy-to-use tool that helps improve the company's operation.
CMP's Bally Power Rewards™ software gives managers the tools to create an array of exciting slot promotions that can be fully automated from PCs or mobile devices.
CMP fully supports **Bally Power Bonusing**™, an award-winning suite of superior cashless gaming products, as well as the **Elite Bonusing Suite**™ of player-centric solutions that drive coin-in.
CMP allow credit and collections needs to be met.

"Our Players Club reps don't have to be computer geniuses to input tags on player accounts, but the real primary benefit of CMP is being able to extract the information in the CMP database for analysis." Green further explained that Players Club representatives can "tag" players with keywords based on location or related interests, to name a few examples of keywords. Then, in utilizing the Back of House application, Green would be able to extrapolate all players' data (i.e., age, birthday, gender, location, frequency of visits, amount bet/won per visit and other tags and use that information to segment players for marketing purposes). With a database of almost 350,000 customers, the ability to segment these consumers and target market them is priceless. The analysis of the database allows for evaluating a promotion or a mailer to find out return on investment and is used to calculate customer value determination.

CRM-related in the Front of House applications are quite different in access and use. Through HRRNP's Rockin' Service™ training program, team members who interact face-to-face with guests are trained to give every guest that little something extra that sets them apart from other businesses. President of HRRNP, Mark Birth, "attributes The Rocksino's tremendous success and multiple awards won in 2014 to the ability of the team members to take their Rockin' Service™ training and make sure every guest leaves feeling like a rock star" (Birtha, 2015) This aspect of HRRNP's CRM does more than help provide good guest service though. HRRNP's Learning and Development Manager, Bonnie Garlock, is currently working on developing an even more detailed Rockin' Service™ training program that is tailored to each department (Garlock, 2015)

Working simultaneous with CRM-embedded system is HRRNP's service response logistics. Although perfection is strived for, not every experience can be perfect. At HRRNP every guest survey is input into a system, analyzed, and feedback is provided to department managers so they can continue to know what works and focus on areas that need improvement. During peak business times, Rocksino Hosts will interact with guests in line at the buffet, the cage, or guests waiting on jackpot payouts to manage that service issue so that it doesn't turn into a guest complaint. Although The Rocksino does have special queues for their "high roller" players, they are clearly marked to alleviate the irritation it may cause for other guests. HRRNP also uses cross-training and information sharing techniques among its employees to manage service capacity. Specifically, team members in "The Café" have been cross-trained to work in "The Rock Shop" when necessary and security officers have been cross-trained to help valet duties during peak times. When a guest complaint is received, it ends up on the desk of HRRNP's Guest Service

Specialist, who reaches out to the guest and does whatever she reasonably can to resolve the complaint to the guest's satisfaction.

Important in the SCM systems at HRRNP was the development of lean management strategic initiatives. Michie (2015) explained that this initiative was gaining more momentum as their operations techniques and management mature. With more experience, every department has been able to see where they can cut costs without cutting quality and that will only improve over time. Roush (2015) suggested that her purchasing department has not made as much progress in that area as she would like but there has been some significant milestones reached. To resolve this she is putting a special staff training emphasis on sourcing more bids, negotiating lower prices, and finding discounts that vendors don't openly offer unless they are asked for (Roush, 2015). The two most significant areas that the Rocksino has been able to become more lean in are workforce empowerment, the cross-training of team members to help avoid overstaffing, and cost savings at the executive level. HRRNP opened its doors with a President, a General Manager and 4 Vice Presidents of various departments. Michie (2015) explained that that is how essentially all casinos operate. The collective experience and knowledge base is necessary in the planning, development, and initial implementation of management strategies, but after time it's not, and people move on and go open other casinos (Michie, 2015). HRRNP now has a President, a Senior VP of Finance and Operations, and currently looking for a VP of marketing at the time of the interviews.

Areas of Improvement

For a business that has only been operating to the public since December 2013, every area could be considered an area for improvement but as discovered throughout the various discussions with upper management, they already put an emphasis on continuous improvement. The one area that may need addressing is in the area of knowledge management systems and the need to retain valuable knowledge workers. From the supervisory level and up, gaming industry employees generally do not stay at one casino for more than a few years. When they leave they are taking a vast amount of knowledge with them and at HRRNP, that knowledge and experience is not as well documented in any easy access database or, in some instances, there may not be a simple training guide for certain tasks. These issues were brought to the attention of Michie and he acknowledged that there is still much work to be in done in those areas to improve organizational abilities to properly train and retain knowledge workers.

CONCLUSION

CRM systems integrate customer groups' management and relationship marketing. Understanding relationship management is essential in the implementation of CRM systems. These systems integrate new communication strategies among customer groups and create a communication platform with the customers. CRM is fundamentally a business strategy that develops customer relationships and results in optimal productivity, increased income and meeting customer needs. It incorporates multimedia use and integration of technological resources and activities of a company. The aim of CRM systems is to maximize customer satisfaction. From the analysis of the different systems at KeyCorp and Progressive Corporation, it is obvious that CRM systems are essential for increased income and productivity. Though the companies use different strategies, the outcomes are similar, maximized customer satisfaction.

After interviews, personal observations and experiences, it is fairly clear that there is an aspect of continuous improvement in every SCM and CRM strategic initiative and associated supports techniques at HRRNP; from supplier relationships to organizational changes to analytics to face-to-face customer service. As noted by Michie (2015), "The worst thing a successful business can do is become complacent, and as people come and go here, I hope that never happens." I wouldn't be surprised at all if the OLC numbers that are posted for April reflect the 48% regional market shares that Mr. Michie predicts."

FURTURE RESEARCH DIRECTIONS

As McDermott (1999) commented, "Across all the projects, there was a persistence among team believers that simply would not let the projects die" (p. 638). There appeared to be both a strong champion as well as a strong sponsor, usually a director through the CEO that provided the encouragement and/or financial backing to the projects when traditional sources were eliminated. This trend was especially true in projects requiring long payback periods. Unfortunately, many projects that are viable and possibly essential for the long-term survival of the firm may be denied due to the need for short-term high rate of return mentality exhibited by the "Wall Street" mentality found in many service firms.

Rather than based on promises of specific economic payback hurdles, sponsors commonly cited continued investment on a gut feel that the project could have significant impact on the long-term success of the firm. Without a sponsor, many of the projects would have "fallen between the cracks" of the existing businesses of their corporations. The sponsor of each of these projects worked to keep them alive (even unofficially), and encourage business units to adopt them. (p. 638-639)

Hence, much of the research by McDermott (1999) that it is critical, regardless of all the other factors, someone within the firm with a position of power must be willing to identify and promote high-risk, high-potential projects.

Quinn, Anderson, and Finkelstein (1996) suggested "the success of a corporation lies more in its intellectual and systems capabilities than in its physical assets" (p. 71). The traditional method of management of human capital, creativity, innovation, and the learning culture within an organization has long over-shadowed the management of the professional intellect. As with the Resource Based View of the Firm (Michalisin, Smith, & Kline, 1997, 2000), the intangible strategic intelligence creates most of professional intellect of an organization, and operates on the following four levels (in increasing importance): Cognitive Knowledge or basic mastery of a professional discipline; Advanced Skills or the ability to translate theory into effective execution or practice; Systems Understanding or the deep knowledge of the cause and effect relationships underlying the professional discipline, and; Self-motivated creativity or the motivation and adaptability for success. The interaction of these factors allow nurturing organizations the ability to "simultaneously thrive in the face of today's rapid changes and renew their cognitive knowledge, advanced skills, and systems understanding in order to compete in the next wave of advances" (p. 72).

Quinn, et al. (1996) also noted that the professional intellect within an organization frequently becomes isolated inside the organization (again any attempts to isolate project teams from the rest of the organization were viewed very negatively in terms of impacts on achieving the firms' service goals in the present study). It is a fact that the existence of a large organizational culture creates conflict with other groups, such as marketing or service conflicting with research and development departments. Thus, at the heart of an effective professional organization, managing and developing the professional intellect is critical for sustained competitive advantage. Quinn, et al. (1996) suggested the following successful "coaching" practices to ensure the development and growth of the professional intellect: Recruit the best, force intensive early development, constantly increase professional challenges, and evaluate and weed. As the authors point out, "heavy internal competition and frequent performance appraisal and feedback are common in outstanding organizations" (p. 74). Organizations constantly need to leverage their professional intellect for sustainable competitive advantage. This leveraging of professional intelligence can be accomplished by capturing knowledge in systems and software, overcoming reluctance to share information, and organize about reinvestment in intellectual capital. Unfortunately, to accomplish these important characteristics, organizations may have to abandon their familiar hierarchical structures and reorganizing in patterns that best suit their professional intellect to create value within the organization. Hence, by creating intellectual webs and connectivity within the organization, networking and culture, and incentives for sharing are the keys to success with these outstanding organizations. Just as important, how the various professional intellectual groups interact and communicate within the organization is as critical as the actual knowledge that is created and transferred.

Business decision support systems within service environments must take advantage of the professional intellect that are found in technical project teams and leverage the power of interactive computer-based systems directed toward the complex and dependent decision problems found in strategic service management. CRM, SCM, and project team integration should be included in any system that is designed to help domestic service firms to formulate generic competitiveness strategies, to test them, and to establish when and how to make a specific plan or a combination of actions. Hence, it is becoming increasingly apparent that an organization should be a catalyst for such networking, instead of creating barriers for its development. Only through sincere sharing of information and the development of the professional intellect within the organizations' project team culture can sustainable strategic advantage be created in a meaningful way. Through this formulation of project team culture that supports the achievement of long-term directions and mission, key strategic and financial objectives, overall business strategies, specific functional strategies, and tactical decision-making sincere sharing of information and the development of a collaborative environment may be created. Future directions in research may reap the benefits of such collaboration.

ACKNOWLEDGMENT

The authors would like to thank the reviewers for their valuable contributions that served as input into the final chapter. Peer reviewing and editing are essentially tedious and thankless tasks.

REFERENCES

Aeron, H., Kumar, A., & Janakiraman, M. (2010). Application of data mining techniques for customer lifetime value parameters: A review. *International Journal of Business Information Systems*, 6(4), 530–546. doi:10.1504/IJBIS.2010.035744

Agilysys. (2015). *Stratton Warren System at Agilysys*. Retrieved February 12, 2016 from http://www.agilysys.com/solutions/by-products/inventory-procurement

Bally Technologies. (2015). Retrieved February 9, 2016 from https://www.ballytech.com/Systems/Player-Tracking/CMS/CMP

Baran, R., Zerres, C., & Zerres, M. (2008). Customer Relationship Management. *OSR Journal of Business and Management, 16*(1), 51-57. Retrieved February 9, 2016 from http://iosrjournals.org/iosr-jbm/papers/Vol16-issue1/Version-6/F016165157.pdf

Barker, B. (2014). *The News Leader*. Retrieved February 9, 2016 from http://the-news-leader.com/news%20local/2014/12/31/hard-rock-rocksino-northfield-park-celebrates-first-anniversary

Beldona, S., & Tsatsoulis, C. (2010). Identifying buyers with similar seller rating models and using their opinions to choose sellers in electronic markets. *International Journal of Information and Decision Sciences, 29*(1), 1–16. doi:10.1504/IJIDS.2010.029901

Blake, B. F., Neuendorf, K. A., & Valdiserri, C. M. (2005). Tailoring new websites to appeal to those most likely to shop online. *Technovation, 25*(10), 1205–1215. doi:10.1016/j.technovation.2004.03.009

Bourlakis, M., Papagiannidis, P., & Fox, H. (2008). E-consumer behaviour: Past, present and future trajectories of an evolving retail revolution. *International Journal of E-Business Research, 4*(3), 64–75. doi:10.4018/jebr.2008070104

Cao, J., Kambayashi, Y., Wang, H., & Zhang, Y. (2004). A global ticket-based access scheme for mobile users. *Information Systems Frontiers, 6*(1), 35–46. doi:10.1023/B:ISFI.0000015873.35795.5e

Castaneda, J. A., Rodriguez, M. A., & Luque, T. (2009). Attitudes' hierarchy of effects in online user behavior. *Online Information Review, 33*(1), 7–21. doi:10.1108/14684520910944364

Chan, J. O. (2005). Toward a unified view of customer relationship management. *Journal of American Academy of Business, 6*(1), 32–39.

Chen, L., Gillenson, M. L., & Sherrell, D. L. (2002). Enticing online consumers: An extended technology acceptance perspective. *Information & Management, 39*(8), 705–719. doi:10.1016/S0378-7206(01)00127-6

Cho, V. (2006). A study of the roles of trusts and risks in information-oriented online legal services using an integrated model. *Information & Management, 43*(4), 502–520. doi:10.1016/j.im.2005.12.002

Guo, P. (2010). One-shot decision approach and its application to duopoly market. *International Journal of Information and Decision Sciences, 2*(3), 213–232. doi:10.1504/IJIDS.2010.033449

Hilmola, O.-P. (2010). Analysing global railway passenger transport through two-staged efficiency model. *International Journal of Information and Decision Sciences, 2*(3), 273–284. doi:10.1504/IJIDS.2010.033451

Kamakura, W., Mela, C. F., Ansari, A., Bodapati, A., Fader, P., Iyengar, R., & Wilcox, R. et al. (2005). Choice models and customer relationship management. *Marketing Letters, 16*(4), 279–291. doi:10.1007/s11002-005-5892-2

Long, J. (2010). Do what yourself: Reevaluation of the value created by online and traditional intermediary. *International Journal of Information and Decision Sciences, 2*(3), 304–317. doi:10.1504/IJIDS.2010.033453

McDermott, C. M. (1999). Managing radical product development in large manufacturing firms: A longitudinal study. *Journal of Operations Management, 17*(6), 631–644. doi:10.1016/S0272-6963(99)00018-2

Michalisin, M. D., Kline, D. M., & Smith, R. F. (2000). Intangible strategic assets and firm performance: A multi-industry study of the resource-based view. *The Journal of Business Strategy, 17*(2), 91–117.

Michalisin, M. D., Smith, R. F., & Kline, D. M. (1997). In search of strategic assets. *The International Journal of Organizational Analysis, 5*(4), 360–387. doi:10.1108/eb028874

Mishra, A., & Mishra, D. (2009). Customer relationship management: Implementation process perspective. *Acta Polytechnica Hungarica, 6*(4), 83–99.

Mohanty, R., Ravi, V., & Patra, M. R. (2010). The application of intelligent and soft-computing techniques to software engineering problems: A review. *International Journal of Information and Decision Sciences, 2*(3), 233–272. doi:10.1504/IJIDS.2010.033450

O'cass, A., & Fenech, T. (2003). Web retailing adoption: Exploring the nature of Internet users Web retailing behaviour. *Journal of Retailing and Consumer Services, 10*(2), 81–94. doi:10.1016/S0969-6989(02)00004-8

Oetega, B. H., Martinez, J. J., & Hoyos, M. J. M. (2006). Analysis of the moderating effect of industry on online behaviour. *Online Information Review, 30*(6), 681–698. doi:10.1108/14684520610716162

Pahlavani, A. (2010). A hybrid algorithm of improved case-based reasoning and multi-attribute decision making in fuzzy environment for investment loan evaluation. *International Journal of Information and Decision Sciences, 2*(1), 17–49. doi:10.1504/IJIDS.2010.029902

Patel, N. V., & Hackney, R. (2010). Designing information systems requirements in context: Insights from the theory of deferred action. *International Journal of Business Information Systems, 6*(1), 44–57. doi:10.1504/IJBIS.2010.034004

Rigby, D., & Ledingham, D. (2004). CRM done right. *Harvard Business Review, 82*(11), 119–129. PMID:15559450

Sarkar, B. K., Sana, S. S., & Chaudhuri, K. (2010). Accuracy-based learning classification system. *International Journal of Information and Decision Sciences, 2*(1), 68–86. doi:10.1504/IJIDS.2010.029904

Smith, A. A., & Smith, A. D. (2012). CRM and identity theft issues associated with e-ticketing of sports and entertainment. *Electronic Government: An International Journal, 9*(1), 1–26. doi:10.1504/EG.2012.044776

Smith, A. D. (2010). Customer relationships, information technology, and concerns for violence in videogaming materials. *International Journal of Management in Education, 4*(1-2), 233–250. doi:10.1504/IJMIE.2010.033460

Smith, A. D. (2011). Strategic leveraging total quality and CRM initiatives: Case study of service-orientated firms. *Services Marketing Quarterly, 32*(1), 1–16. doi:10.1080/15332969.2011.533088

Smith, A. D., & Clinton, S. R. (2015). E-commerce and its impact on expectations of customer service and quality control. In W. D. Nelson (Ed.), *Advances in Business and Management* (Vol. 7). Hauppauge, NY: NOVA Science Publishers, Inc.

Smith, A. D., & Motley, D. (2010). Operational and customer relationship management considerations of electronic prescribing among pharmacists. *International Journal of Electronic Healthcare, 5*(3), 245–272. doi:10.1504/IJEH.2010.034175 PMID:20643640

Stake, R. E. (1995). *The art of case study research*. Thousand Oaks, CA: Sage Publications.

Swink, M. (1999). Threats to new product manufacturability and the effects of development team integration processes. *Journal of Operations Management, 17*(6), 691–709. doi:10.1016/S0272-6963(99)00027-3

Swink, M. (2000). Technological innovativeness as a moderator of new product design integration and top management support. *Journal of Product Innovation Management, 17*(3), 208–220. doi:10.1016/S0737-6782(00)00040-0

The Ohio Lottery. (2015). *Ohio Lottery*. Retrieved February 9, 2016 from https://www.ohiolottery.com/About/Financial/VLT-Revenue

Toma, M., Mihoreanu, L., & Ionescu, A. (2014). Innovation capability and customer relationship management: A review. *Economics, Management, and Financial Market, 9*(4), 323–331.

Tsai, H. D., Huang, H. C., Jaw, Y. L., & Chen, W. K. (2006). Why on-line customers remain with a particular e-retailer: An integrative model and empirical evidence. *Psychology and Marketing, 23*(5), 447–464. doi:10.1002/mar.20121

Urbanskienė, R., Žostautienė, D., & Chreptavičienė, V. (2008). The economic conditions of enterprise functioning: The model of creation of customer relationship management (CRM) system. *Engineering Economics, 3*(58). Retrieved February 10, 2016 from http://faculty.mu.edu.sa/public/uploads/1361952698.7644customer%20relationship54.pdf

Warden, C. A., Wu, W. Y., & Tsai, D. (2006). Online shopping interface components: Relative importance as peripheral and central cues. *Cyberpsychology & Behavior, 9*(3), 285–294. doi:10.1089/cpb.2006.9.285 PMID:16780396

WIPRO Consulting Services. (2011). *WIPRO Consulting Services*. Retrieved February 9, 2016 from https://www.wipro.com/.../SupplyChainTransformations_Final.pdf

Yin, R. K. (2003). *Case study research: Design and methods* (3rd ed.). Thousand Oaks, CA: Sage Publications.

ADDITIONAL READING

Adams, D. A., Nelson, R. R., & Todd, P. (1992). Perceived usefulness, ease of use, and usage of information technology: A replication. *Management Information Systems Quarterly*, *16*(2), 227–247. doi:10.2307/249577

Al-Karaghouli, W., & Fadare, E. B. (2010). The impact of information lifecycle management process in the Nigerian financial sector. *International Journal of Business Information Systems*, *6*(1), 111–132. doi:10.1504/IJBIS.2010.034008

Alderete, M. V., & Gutiérrez, L. H. (2014). Drivers of information and communication technologies adoption in Colombian services firms. *International Journal of Business Information Systems*, *17*(4), 373–397. doi:10.1504/IJBIS.2014.065553

Alexopoulou, N., Nikolaidou, M., Kanellis, P., Mantzana, V., Anagnostopoulos, D., & Martakos, D. (2010). Infusing agility in business processes through an event-centric approach. *International Journal of Business Information Systems*, *6*(1), 58–78. doi:10.1504/IJBIS.2010.034005

Ali, M., El-Haddadeh, R., Eldabi, T., & Mansour, E. (2010). Simulation discounted cash flow valuation for Internet companies. *International Journal of Business Information Systems*, *6*(1), 18–33. doi:10.1504/IJBIS.2010.034002

Althonayan, A., & Sharif, A. M. (2010). Aligning business and technology strategy within the airline industry. *International Journal of Business Information Systems*, *6*(1), 79–94. doi:10.1504/IJBIS.2010.034006

Badii, A., & Thiemert, D. (2010). A framework towards a multi-modal fingerprinting scheme for multimedia assets. *International Journal of Business Information Systems*, *6*(1), 133–149. doi:10.1504/IJBIS.2010.034009

Barra, R. A., Savage, A., & Tsay, J. J. (2010). Equational zero vector databases, non-equational databases, and inherent internal control. *International Journal of Business Information Systems*, *6*(3), 354–377. doi:10.1504/IJBIS.2010.035050

Burton-Jones, A., & Hubona, G. S. (2005). Individual differences and usage behavior: Revisiting a technology acceptance model assumption. *The Data Base for Advances in Information Systems*, *36*(2), 58–77. doi:10.1145/1066149.1066155

Chahal, K., & Eldabi, T. (2010). A multi-perspective comparison for selection between system dynamics and discrete event simulation. *International Journal of Business Information Systems*, *6*(1), 4–17. doi:10.1504/IJBIS.2010.034001

Chand, M., Raj, T., & Shankar, R. (2015). A comparative study of multi criteria decision making approaches for risks assessment in supply chain. *International Journal of Business Information Systems*, *18*(1), 67–84. doi:10.1504/IJBIS.2015.066128

Dabholkar, P. A., & Bagozzi, R. P. (2002). An attitudinal model of technology-based self-service: Moderating effects of consumer traits and situational factors. *Journal of the Academy of Marketing Science*, *30*(3), 184–201. doi:10.1177/0092070302303001

Daim, T., Basoglu, N., & Tanoglu, I. (2010). A critical assessment of information technology adoption: Technical, organisational and personal perspectives. *International Journal of Business Information Systems, 6*(3), 315–335. doi:10.1504/IJBIS.2010.035048

Daramola, J. O., Oladipupo, O. O., & Musa, A. G. (2010). A fuzzy expert system (FES) tool for on-line personnel recruitments. *International Journal of Business Information Systems, 6*(4), 444–462. doi:10.1504/IJBIS.2010.035741

Dharni, K. (2014). Exploring information system evaluation in Indian manufacturing sector. *International Journal of Business Information Systems, 17*(4), 453–468. doi:10.1504/IJBIS.2014.065564

Dominic, P. D. D., Goh, K. N., Wong, D., & Chen, Y. Y. (2010). The importance of service quality for competitive advantage – with special reference to industrial product. *International Journal of Business Information Systems, 6*(3), 378–397. doi:10.1504/IJBIS.2010.035051

Elysee, G. (2015). An empirical examination of a mediated model of strategic information systems planning success. *International Journal of Business Information Systems, 18*(1), 44–66. doi:10.1504/IJBIS.2015.066126

Gefen, D., Elena, K., & Straub, D. W. (2003). Trust and tam in online shopping: An integrated model. *Management Information Systems Quarterly, 27*(1), 51–90.

Han, W., Ada, S., Sharman, R., Gray, R. H., & Simha, A. (2015). Factors impacting the adoption of social network sites for emergency notification purposes in universities. *International Journal of Business Information Systems, 18*(1), 85–106. doi:10.1504/IJBIS.2015.066129

Igbaria, M., Schiffman, S. J., & Wieckowski, T. J. (1994). The respective roles of perceived usefulness and perceived fun in the acceptance of microcomputer technology. *Behaviour & Information Technology, 13*(6), 349–361. doi:10.1080/01449299408914616

Jones, T. M. (1991). Ethical decision making by individuals in organizations: An issue-contingent model. *Academy of Management Journal, 16*(2), 366–394.

Kapur, P. K., Gupta, A., Jha, P. C., & Goyal, S. K. (2010). Software quality assurance using software reliability growth modelling: State of the art. *International Journal of Business Information Systems, 6*(4), 463–496. doi:10.1504/IJBIS.2010.035742

Keramati, A., & Behmanesh, I. (2010). Assessing the impact of information technology on firm performance using canonical correlation analysis. *International Journal of Business Information Systems, 6*(4), 497–513. doi:10.1504/IJBIS.2010.035743

Kim, E., & Tadisina, S. (2010). A model of customers' initial trust in unknown online retailers: An empirical study. *International Journal of Business Information Systems, 6*(4), 419–443. doi:10.1504/IJBIS.2010.035740

Latha, T. J., & Suganthi, L. (2015). An empirical study on creating software product value in India - an analytic hierarchy process approach. *International Journal of Business Information Systems, 18*(1), 26–43. doi:10.1504/IJBIS.2015.066125

Maad, S., & Coghlan, B. (2010). The next generation Grid: An infrastructure for global business systems. *International Journal of Business Information Systems*, 6(1), 95–110. doi:10.1504/IJBIS.2010.034007

Marthandan, G., & Tang, C. M. (2010). Information systems evaluation: An ongoing measure. *International Journal of Business Information Systems*, 6(3), 336–353. doi:10.1504/IJBIS.2010.035049

Patel, N. V., & Hackney, R. (2010). Designing information systems requirements in context: Insights from the theory of deferred action. *International Journal of Business Information Systems*, 6(1), 44–57. doi:10.1504/IJBIS.2010.034004

Shukai, L., Chaudhari, N. S., & Dash, M. (2010). Selecting useful features for personal credit risk analysis. *International Journal of Business Information Systems*, 6(4), 419–443. doi:10.1504/IJBIS.2010.035745

Smith, A. D., & Offodile, O. F. (2007). Exploring forecasting and project management characteristics of supply chain management. *International Journal of Logistics and Supply Management*, 3(2), 174–214.

Smith, A. D., & Rupp, W. T. (2013). Data quality and knowledge/information management in service operations management: Regional supermarket case study. *International Journal of Knowledge-Based Organizations*, 3(3), 35–52. doi:10.4018/ijkbo.2013070103

Soon, J. N. P., Mahmood, A. K., Yin, C.-P., Wan, W.-S., Yuen, P.-K., & Heng, L.-E. (2015). Barebone cloud IaaS: Revitalisation disruptive technology. *International Journal of Business Information Systems*, 18(1), 26–43. doi:10.1504/IJBIS.2015.066130

Sundarambal, M., Dhivya, M., & Anbalagan, P. (2010). Performance evaluation of bandwidth allocation in ATM networks. *International Journal of Business Information Systems*, 6(3), 398–417. doi:10.1504/IJBIS.2010.035052

Venkatesh, V., & Davis, F. D. (2000). A theoretical extension of the technology acceptance model: Four longitudinal field studies. *Management Science*, 46(2), 186–204. doi:10.1287/mnsc.46.2.186.11926

Vijayasarathy, L. R. (2004). Predicting consumer intentions to use on-line shopping: The case for an augmented technology acceptance model. *Information & Management*, 41(6), 747–762. doi:10.1016/j.im.2003.08.011

Wu, J. H., & Wang, S. C. (2005). What drives mobile commerce? An empirical evaluation of the revised technology acceptance model. *Information & Management*, 42(5), 719–729. doi:10.1016/j.im.2004.07.001

KEY TERMS AND DEFINITIONS

Automatic Identification and Data Capture Technologies (AIDC): Types of AIDC-related technologies to leave the human element out of the data collection and storage functions of information derived from manufacturing, integrated through the manufacturing process, types of authentication concerns and/or e-security strategies, and relationship links to customer profiles. Typical types of AIDC include, bar-coding, RFID, magnetic strips, touch memory, and smart cards.

Customer Relationship Management (CRM): CRM is software-driven processes that allow companies to find solutions to customize their products and service offerings for their customers via social listening, enhanced sales, marketing, and customer services.

Lean Management: Lean management refers to high quality, low costs business environments. Companies need to operate in the most efficient and effective means possible to maintain a competitive advantage on their competitors. As they strive to make every penny count towards maintaining margins on their products, more and more companies are finding the need to implement lean manufacturing techniques. However, simply implementing just one technique may not be the leanest strategy for these at-risk companies.

Stratton Warren System (SWS): SWS is popular software, technology-based solutions that help manages the entire process from requisition to invoice, allowing automation to reduce tedious and time-consuming, error-prone paperwork and record keeping activities.

Supply Chain Management/Performance: In basic terms, supply chain is the system of organizations, people, activities, information and resources involved in moving a product or service from supplier to customer. The configuration and management of supply chain operations is a key way companies obtain and maintain a competitive advantage. The typical manufacturing supply chain begins with raw material suppliers, or inputs. The next link in the chain is the manufacturing, or transformation step; followed the distribution, or localization step. Finally, the finished product or service is purchased by customers as outputs. Service and Manufacturing managers need to know the impact of supply on their organization's purchasing and logistics processes. However, supply chain performance and its metrics are difficult to develop and actually measure.

Vendor-Managed Inventory Systems (VMI): VMI-based systems are designed to transfer the control of inventory and its planning activities to a manufacturer or distributor in order to provide a beneficial relationship to promote a more transparent and seamless flow of goods and services at lower costs. As in many recent retailer applications, the supplier/vendor assumes responsible for replenishing and stocking inventory at appropriate levels to minimize inconvenience to the ultimate customer.

Chapter 7
A Hybrid AHP–ELECTRE I Multicriteria Model for Performance Assessment and Team Selection

Ikram Khatrouch
University of Lyon, France & University of Saint Etienne, France

Lyes Kermad
University of Paris 8, France

Abderrahman el Mhamedi
University of Paris 8, France

Younes Boujelbene
University of Sfax, Tunisia

ABSTRACT

Human resources management is essential to any health care system. This paper proposes an assessment model to help the decision maker in the selection of an optimal team. In the proposed model, AHP method is applied to identify the weights of each criterion in the decision model. ELECTRE I method is used to obtain the best team that satisfies most of the decision maker preferences. We test the effectiveness of the model on the real data collected from the 'Habib Bourguiba' Hospital in Tunisia.

INTRODUCTION

Operating theater is a deeply human place where the individual works on an individual and with an individual. These individuals have personalities, logic, interests and specific different viewpoints and sometimes conflicting. They constitute a surgical team where performance and outcomes depend on the degree of coordination the efforts made by everyone; that is, teamwork. Selection teams ensure that the right team is in place and that it will have a capable leader in place.

Successful selection teams are still an open problem in various fields of social, business, and hospital studies. To solve this problem, several methods were proposed such as AHP (Chen et al., 2004), fuzzy-genetic algorithm (Strnad et al., 2010), multi-objective optimization (Ahmed, 2013), and fuzzy logic (Shipley et al., 2013). The main objective of this paper is to propose an evaluation model to help

DOI: 10.4018/978-1-5225-0654-6.ch007

the decision maker in the selection of an optimal team among a set of available alternatives. The team selection problem can be assimilated as a MCDM problem where many criteria should be considered in decision-making. Therefore, this model uses two MCDM methods: AHP to determine the importance weights of evaluation criteria and ELECTRE I to obtain the best team that satisfies the decision maker preferences.

The remainder of this paper is organized as follows: Section 1 describes the AHP and the ELECTRE I method. In Section 2, the proposed model for team selection is presented and the stages of the proposed approach are explained in detail. How the proposed model is used on a real world example is explained in Section 3. In Section 4, experimental results and data analysis are discussed. Finally, conclusions of this study are made in section 5.

A DETAILED DESCRIPTION OF AHP

The AHP is a decision approach created to solve complex multiple criteria problems involving qualitative decisions (Saaty, 1994). The purpose of the method is to determine the relative importance of a set of activities in a multi-criteria decision problem. AHP is easy, comprehensive and logical. It can be used in both quantitative and qualitative multi-criteria decision making problems and it is widely accepted by the decision making community, be they the academics or the practitioners (Mamat et al., 2007). AHP permits collection of all relevant elements of a decision problem into one model to work out their interdependencies and their perceived consequences interactively. Its use of pairwise comparisons forces AHP users to articulate the relative importance of criteria and then to decide the relative contributions of the alternatives to the criteria (Carlsson et al., 1995).

The AHP method has been used in various fields to solve complex decision problems. It has widely applied in industrial engineering (Calabrese et al., 2013), the business domain (Kumar & Parashar, 2009), the medical domain (Vidal, Sahin, Matelli, Berhoune, & Bonan, 2010), and other fields.

The AHP is a powerful decision-making methodology in order to determine the priorities among different criteria. It encompasses three main stages (Bouhana et al., 2011):

1. Decomposing the decision problem into hierarchical decision elements.
2. Collection of data to be entered by pairwise comparisons of the decision elements using the chart proposed by Saaty (1982). This allows us to represent the relative importance of criterion compared with the other one by assigning a number between 1 and 9. From the pair-pair comparisons between elements (A1 ... An), a comparison matrix is established. The comparison is always made of the elements of each row to the elements of each column. The comparisons obtained from the matrix A, is designated by a_{ij}, the degree of importance of element i relative to the element j (also $a_{ji} = 1/a_{ij}$).

$$A = \begin{bmatrix} a_{11} & a_{12} & \cdots & a_{1n} \\ a_{21} & a_{22} & \cdots & a_{2n} \\ \cdots & \cdots & \cdots & \cdots \\ a_{n1} & a_{n2} & \cdots & a_{nn} \end{bmatrix}$$

3. Evaluating the decision alternatives taking into account the weights of decision criteria. In order to find the weight relating to decision elements, we calculate the specific values λ according to Equation (1) and the clean vector X for each matrix according to Equation (2).

$$\text{Det } (A - \lambda I) = 0 \tag{1}$$

$$AX = \lambda X \tag{2}$$

Once all criteria weight are calculated, we evaluate the judgment by calculating the Coherence ratio, CR, which should not exceed 0.10, using Equation (3).

$$RC = \frac{IC}{IR} \tag{3}$$

IC is the consistency index given by the following equation:

$$IC = \frac{\lambda_{max} - n}{n - 1} \tag{4}$$

With λ_{max} = Maximum own value.
IR is given by a scale of Saaty (see Table 1).

A BRIEF OVERVIEW OF ELECTRE I

The ELECTRE I method, developed by Bernard Roy in 1986, solves the problem of multi-criteria choice. It identifies a subset of alternatives with the best compromise and the criteria taken into account. The ELECTRE I method basically aims at reducing the size of the alternatives set, exploiting the dominance concept. So, a concordance index, C(a, b), is applied to measure the relative advantage of each alternative over the others. Similarly, a discordance index, D(a, b), evaluates the relative disadvantage.

The concordance index takes its values between 0 and 1, and can be seen as measuring the arguments in favor of the statement 'a outranks b' (denoted by aSb). This index identifies the strength of affirmation: F = 'alternative a is at least as good as alternative b'. The concordance index C represents the higher of the arguments that support the affirmation F. The concordance index is estimated as follows:

Table 1. Scale random Saaty (1982)

n	1	2	4	5	6	7	8	9	...
IR	0.00	0.00	0.58	0.9	1.12	1.24	1.32	1.41	...

$$C(a,b) = \frac{1}{w} \sum_{j:g_j(a) \geq g_j(b)} w_j \tag{5}$$

where

$$w = \sum_{j=1}^{n} w_j$$

$g_j(a)$ is the value or performance of alternative a in relation to criterion j (j=1, ..., n).
n = number of criteria considered.
w_j = weight of the criteria j.
C(a, b) = the sum of the weights associated to the criteria whose value of $g_j(a) \geq g_j(b)$, which represents the strength of the arguments that support the affirmation aSb.

The discordance index also takes its values between 0 and 1 and evaluates the strength of the arguments against the affirmation F. The higher the discordance index (d) is, the more significant the opposition of criteria that opposes F. Therefore, among the criteria in favour of b, some may shed some doubt upon the statement 'a outranks b', and this phenomenon is represented by a discordance index. The discordance index is estimated as follows:

$$D(a,b) = \begin{cases} 0 \text{ if } g_j(a) \geq g_j(b), \forall j. \\ \frac{1}{\delta} \max_{j:g_j(a) < g_j(b)} [g_j(a) \geq g_j(b)] \end{cases} \tag{6}$$

where:
D(a, b) is the maximum difference between g(b) and g(a) for all criteria (j),
g(b)>g(a) divided by the interval of scale of the criterion considered.

Thus, this index increases if the preference of b over a becomes very large for at least one criterion.
Once the concordance and discordance indexes are established, their results are combined to construct the final outranking relationship. To interpret the information contained in concordance and discordance matrices, threshold values (p and q) are defined by the decision makers to specify the amount of desired concordance and tolerated discordance. The technique comprises the establishment of concordance and discordance levels stating that a dominance hypothesis is justified. This combination is performed as follows:

$$aSb \rightarrow C(a,b) \geq p$$

$$D(a,b) \leq q$$

where:
p is the concordance threshold
q is the discordance threshold

A Hybrid AHP-ELECTRE I Multicriteria Model for Performance Assessment and Team Selection

Solutions with values above the concordance threshold p, and below the discordance threshold q, are subjected to pair-wise comparisons. Solutions with intermediate concordance and discordance index are said to be not comparable. The actors involved in the process decide the values for p and q.

THE MODEL DESCRIPTION

For selecting teams, the model in Figure 1 will help the decision maker to find the best team and the relation with other teams. In the proposed model, we combine two methods of multi-criteria decision support, AHP and ELECTRE I, in order to offer the best team (see Figure 1).

The proposed model is presented in four main phases which are explained below.

Figure 1. The structure of team selection system

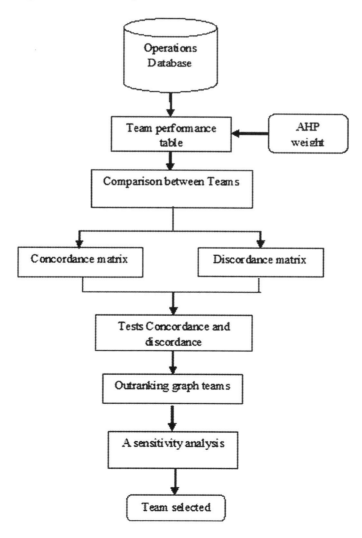

Step 1: Building of Team Performance Table

The performance table (Table 2.) is the starting point of the ELECTRE I method. This table is defined as lines which represent the alternatives and column criteria. The boxes contain performance alternatives for each criterion.

Then these values are transferred into notes based on their own scale for each criterion in order to end with a table called "the performance table" with:

- **M**: The number of alternatives
- **N**: The number of criterion
- **W_j**: The weight of criterion j, j = 1,..,n.
- **A**: $\{a_1, a_2, ..., a_m\}$ represents the set of alternatives
- **G**: $\{g_1, g_2, ..., g_n\}$ represents the set of evaluation criteria
- **$g_j(a_i)$**: Represents the alternative evaluation of a_i according to the criterion g_j.

In our work, the criteria characterizing the team choice are shown in Table 3.

The solution is represented by the best team that satisfies most closely the needs and the preferences of the decision maker. This is defined by a set of criteria. For calculating the weight of each criterion, we use the analytic hierarchy process (AHP) based on its importance. The first step is to compose our problem in three hierarchical levels presented by Figure 2.

Table 2. Table of decision matrix

Criteria	g_1	g_2	...	g_j	...	g_n
Weight	w_1	w_2	...	w_j	...	w_n
Alternatives						
a_1	$g_1(a_1)$	$g_2(a_1)$	...	$g_j(a_1)$	...	$g_n(a_1)$
a_2	$g_1(a_2)$	$g_2(a_2)$	...	$g_j(a_2)$	...	$g_n(a_2)$
.	.	.	...	.	...	.
.	.	.	...	.	...	.
a_i	$g_1(a_i)$	$g_2(a_i)$	...	$g_j(a_i)$	...	$g_n(a_i)$
.						
a_m	$g_1(a_m)$	$g_2(a_m)$	...	$g_j(a_m)$	...	$g_n(a_m)$

Table 3. Criteria and sub criteria

Criteria	Sub Criteria	Description
Operation criteria	The time (T)	The duration of operation
	Risk criticality (R)	The criticality degree of risk
Team criteria	Competence (Ct)	The technical competence of the team
	Communication (Co)	The communication between team members

Figure 2. An AHP structure for team selection

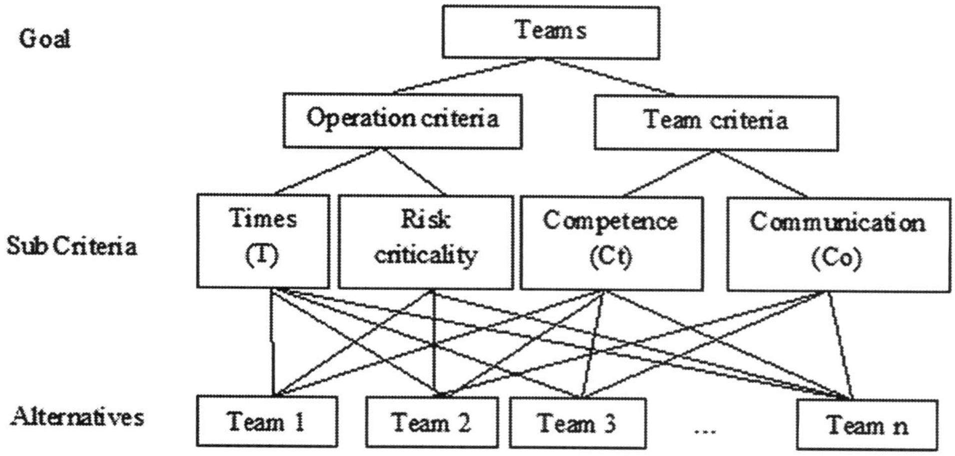

```
Goal                              Teams
                          /                  \
                 Operation criteria      Team criteria
                    /        \           /          \
Sub Criteria    Times      Risk      Competence   Communication
                 (T)    criticality     (Ct)          (Co)
                         
Alternatives   Team 1    Team 2    Team 3   ...    Team n
```

The next step is to conduct a survey via questionnaire distributed to each member. The value assigned is based on the scale of 1–9. These preferences are presented in the form of a square matrix.

$$\begin{array}{c} T \\ CT \\ Co \\ R \end{array} \begin{bmatrix} 1 & 0.333 & 0.5 & 0.25 \\ 3 & 1 & 2 & 0.5 \\ 2 & 0.5 & 1 & 0.333 \\ 4 & 2 & 3 & 1 \end{bmatrix}$$

Then, we calculate the relative weights to decision criteria:

$(W_T, W_{Ct}, W_{Co}, W_R) = (0.095, 0.276, 0.160, 0.465)$

Each team will be assessed against the criteria using a qualitative scale, if we would have qualitative data. Preference scales of indicators should be increasing (all values are to maximize). The table also contains the weight of each criteria W_i.

Table 6. Performance table for the team selection problem

Teams	Criteria			
	T (Min)	CT (Max)	CO (Max)	R (Max)
	0.095	0.276	0.160	0.465
Team 1	160	5	4	3
Team 2	130	6	4	2
Team 3	150	4	5	4
Team 4	115	3	6	2
Team 5	110	5	4	5
Team 6	85	5	4	3

A Hybrid AHP-ELECTRE I Multicriteria Model for Performance Assessment and Team Selection

We get a table of team performance as indicated in Table 6.

Once the performance table is filled, we move to calculate the concordance matrix and the discordance matrix, which we explain below.

Step 2: Building of the Concordance and Discordance Matrix

Concordance indexes are calculated for each criterion, then, aggregated into an overall concordance index, calculated for each pair of alternatives. The corresponding matrix is composed of C_{ik} overall concordance indexes; it is based on specific c_j concordance index (a_i, a_k) and weight, W_j, criteria,

where
$c_j(a_i, a_k) = 1$ if $g_j(a_i) \geq g_j(a_k)$
$c_j(a_i, a_k) = 0$ otherwise

The value of a C_{ik} overall concordance index is thus determined as:

$$C_{ik} = \frac{\sum_{j=1}^{n} c_j(a_i, a_k)}{\sum_{j=1}^{n} w_j} \tag{7}$$

Table 4 shows the results found by calculating overall concordance indexes.

The discordance index, noted $D_j(a_i, a_k)$, is also calculated for criteria whose role is to weaken the match. A discordance index justifies to what extent the alternative scenario can outclass a_k because the assessment that presents the deficit for criterion j is considered too important.

$D_j(a_i, a_k) = 0$ if $g_j(a_i) \geq g_j(a_k)$
$D(a_i, a_k) = (1/\mu) \max_j [g_j(a_k)-g_j(a_i)]$ otherwise

where μ as the maximum difference between the same criterion for two given alternatives.

Table 5 shows the results found by calculating discordance indexes.

Once we have calculated the index of concordance and discordance, we check the outranking assumption setting two thresholds upgrade:

Table 4. Calculation of overall concordance indexes

	Team 1	Team 2	Team 3	Team 4	Team 5	Team 6
Team 1		0.63	0.28	0.74	0.44	0.90
Team 2	0.53		0.37	0.74	0.44	0.44
Team 3	0.72	0.63		0.74	0.16	0.63
Team 4	0.26	0.72	0.26		0.16	0.16
Team 5	1	0.72	0.84	0.84		0.90
Team 6	1	0.72	0.37	0.84	0.53	

A Hybrid AHP-ELECTRE I Multicriteria Model for Performance Assessment and Team Selection

Table 5. Calculation of discordance index values

	Team 1	Team 2	Team 3	Team 4	Team 5	Team 6
Team 1		0.4	0.133	0.6	0.666	1
Team 2	0.013		0.026	0.2	0.266	06
Team 3	0.013	0.266		0.466	0.533	0.013
Team 4	0.026	0.04	0.026		0.026	0.4
Team 5	0.013	0.013	0.013	0.026		0.333
Team 6	0.013	0.013	0.013	0.026	0.026	

- A concordance threshold S_c which presents the minimum of required concordance.
- A discordance threshold S_d which represents the maximum tolerated unconformity.

We then analyze the relations between the different alternatives. If the two following tests are satisfied, that is to say, if:

- Test of concordance: $C_{ik} \geq S_c$
- Test of non-discordance: $D_{ik} \leq S_d$

then, we can say that a_i have a_k (the alternative a_i has outclassed alternative a_k).

We take for our example a match threshold of $S_c = 0.80$ and discordance threshold of $S_d = 0.30$, and demonstrate the building of an upgrade graph in the next step.

Step 3: Building of the Upgrade Graph

The upgrade relations for the set of pairs (a_i, a_j) are presented by the upgrade graph. According to graph theory, each alternative is represented by a vertex (a circle). An arrow goes from the apex a_i to the top a_k if the alternative a_i have outclassed the alternative a_k.

When no arrow exists between two vertices then there is no outranking relation between the two peaks. The kernel of the graph does not contain the best alternatives but the alternatives that are most difficult to compare between them; and among them we find the best team.

The decision support process stops when we dispose of an answer. A good process of decision support, generally, should investigate the sensitivity of parameters which have led us to this answer (Mouine and al. 2011).

Step 4: A Sensitivity Analysis

The role of sensitivity analysis is to vary the parameters to see at which level the results are sensitive. The aim is to find a gap in which each parameter may fluctuate without impacting the ranking of the alternatives supplied by ELECTRE I.

According to Mouine and al. (2011) there are two different methods for this analysis. The first consists in varying the parameters until obtaining the intervals in which pre-orders do not change. We will base sensitivity analysis on this approach. A second form of sensitivity analysis is to make a change in pre-orders and determine the minimum and maximum values of the parameters resulting in this change.

COMPUTATIONAL STUDY AND DATA ANALYSIS

To assess the computational tractability and efficiency of the developed model, we tested the operation of our model on an operating theatre in 'Habib Bourguiba' hospital in Tunisia. We have 36 employees with three disciplines (10 surgeons, 11 anesthetists, and 15 instrumentalists) and we have to select teams for each surgical case. The framework proposed can help to choose the best team that satisfies the preferences of the decision maker and the surgical need. Our main objective here is to determine the best team for a new case arising, using the case base, described in Table 6.

Using this performance table, we obtained the following upgrade graph

In Figure 3, the kernel of the graph consists of vertices of the alternatives 5 and 6, which means that the Teams 5 and 6 are the best; Team 6, however, is outclassed by Team 5.

SENSITIVITY ANALYSIS

In this part, we rely on the method of Vetschera (1986), which was applied for ELECTRE I, and whose aim is to find the interval (min and max) settings where the choice is always the same. It is reasonable to consider the variation of the thresholds as set and shown in Figure 4.

Figure 3. Upgrade graph

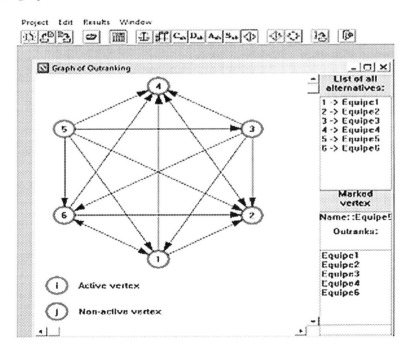

A Hybrid AHP-ELECTRE I Multicriteria Model for Performance Assessment and Team Selection

Figure 4. Scale of concordance and discordance

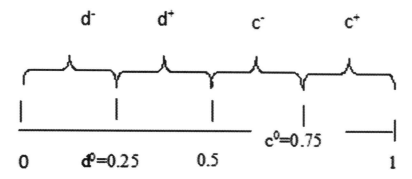

$d_0 = 0.25$ and $c_0 = 0.75$ are fixed and we varied d^-, d^+ and c^-, c^+.

Results of concordance thresholds variation are depicted in upgrade graphs (see Figure 5 a-g).

The sensitivity analysis regarding the thresholds in Figure 5 a and c shows that the Team 5 presents the kernel with Team 2. Team 3 is dominated by Team 5. For graph g, Teams 5 and 6 are the core of the graph. In graphs e and f, Team 3 is dominated only by the team 5.

Figure 5. Representation of results of concordance thresholds variation

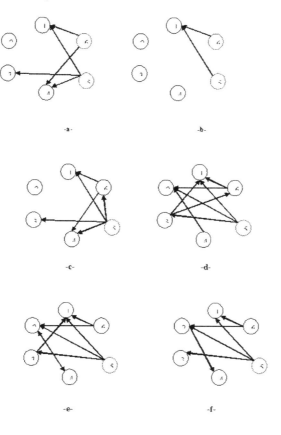

We can say that, following this sensitivity analysis based on the variation of discordance and concordance thresholds, Team 5 is the best team and Team 6 is the poorest.

This approach helps us to extract the best team and the relation with other teams. It presents a strength support to the decision maker to make the best choice. It's also easier to understand the outcomes which are in the form of a graph. This approach provides a very detailed sensitivity analysis to the decision maker, which enables the decision maker to determine the concordance and discordance thresholds depending on the operation complexity level.

CONCLUSION

In this paper, a multicriteria decision model is presented integrating two different approaches: the AHP and the ELECTRE I methods. The AHP method is applied to determinate the weights for each criterion. The ELECTRE I method is applied in order to evaluate the alternatives combining all criteria. The proposed approach was tested on data collected from the 'Habib Bourguiba' Hospital in Tunisia. We are also planning to imbed this model in a general, project management system, currently under development. Future considerations for model improvement include consideration of additional attributes, such as experience and leadership.

ACKNOWLEDGMENT

The authors would like to thank the anonymous reviewers and the editor for their insightful comments and suggestions.

REFERENCES

Ahmed, F., Deb, K., & Jindal, A. (2013). Multi-objective optimization and decision making approaches to cricket team selection. *Journal of Applied Soft Computing, 13*(201), 402-414.

Bouhana, A., Abed, M., & Chabchoub, H. (2011). *An integrated Case_Based Reasoning and AHP method for personalized itinerary search.* LOGISTIQUA.

Calabrese, A., Costa, R., & Menichini, T. (2013). Using Fuzzy AHP to manage Intellectual Capital assests: An application. *Journal of Expert Systems with Applications,* (40), 3747–3755.

Carlsson, C., & Walden, P. (1995). AHP in political group decisions: A study in the art of possibilities. *Interfaces, 25*(4), 14–29. doi:10.1287/inte.25.4.14

Chen, S. J., & Lin, L. (2004). Modeling team member characteristics for the formation of multifunctional team in concurrent engineering. *IEEE Transactions on Engineering Management, 51*(2), 111–124. doi:10.1109/TEM.2004.826011

Kumar, S., & Parashar, N. (2009). Analytical Hierarchy Process Applied to Vendor Selection Problem, Small Scale, Me-dium Scale and Large Scale Industries. *Business Intelligence Journal, 2*(2), 245-257.

Mamat, N. J. Z., & Danil, J. K. (2007). Statistical analyses on time complexity and rank consictency between singular value decomposition and the duality approach in AHP: A case study of faculty member selection. *Mathematical and Computer Modelling, 46*(7-8), 1099–1106. doi:10.1016/j.mcm.2007.03.025

Mouine, M. (2011). *Combinaison de deux d'analyse de sensibilité*. Mémoire à l'université Laval.

Saaty, T. L. (1982). *Decision Making for Leaders*. Belmont, CA: Lifetime Learning Publications.

Saaty, T. L. (1994). *The analytic hierarchy process*. New York: Mac Gray-Hill.

Shipley, M. F., & Johnson, M. (2009). A fuzzy approach for selecting project membership to achieve. *European Journal of Operational Research*, (192), 918-928.

Strnad, D., & Guid, N. (2010). A fuzzy-genetic decision support system for project team formation. *Applied Soft Computing, 10*(10), 1178–1187. doi:10.1016/j.asoc.2009.08.032

Vetschera, R. (1986). Sensitivity Analysis for the ELECTRE Multicriteria Method. *Z. Oper. Res.*, (30), 99-117.

Vidal, L.A., Sahin, E., Matelli, N., Berhoune, M., & Bonan, B. (2010). Applying AHP to select drugs to be produced by anticipation in a chemotherapy compounding unit. *Journal of Expert Systems with Applications*, (37), 1528-1534.

KEY TERMS AND DEFINITIONS

Analytic Hierarchy: A structured technique for analyzing complex decisions, based on mathematics and psychology. It was developed by Thomas L. Saaty in the 1970s.

ELECTRE I: A multi-criteria analysis method developed in the late 1960s. It means Elimination and Choice Reflecting Reality.

Operating Theatre: A room in which surgical operations are performed.

Selection Teams: Choose the right team the right in place and that it will have a capable leader in place.

Surgical Team: A unit providing the continuum of care composed by surgeon, anesthesiologist or nurse, instrumentalist.

Chapter 8
Predictive Modeling as guide for Health Informatics Deployment

Fabrizio L. Ricci
Italian National Research Council, Italy

Oscar Tamburis
University of Naples Federico II, Italy

ABSTRACT

The present research work shows the main steps conducted towards the exploitation of the LUMIR project, aiming at realizing an EHR framework in the Italian Region of Basilicata (also known as Lucania). It relates to a structure of network–enabled services capable of integrating the ICT solutions used by the operators of the Healthcare System of Basilicata Region. The adoption process of the LuMiR system was meant to address the issues connected to the design features as well as to the EHR diffusion and the acceptance aspects. The mathematical modeling approach introduced aimed at making possible to get to a measure "ex–ante" of both adequacy and significance of the adoption process itself. The final intent is to work out a scalable and exportable model of advanced management of clinical information, towards a stronger cooperation among the provider organizations and a better governance of care processes, as crucial element within the more general path of modernization of the healthcare sector.

1. INTRODUCTION

The LUMIR project (Italian acronym for: network of physicians in Lucania Region), run from 2008 to 2013 under the direction of the Institute of Biomedical Technologies of the Italian National Research Council (ITB-CNR), aimed at the realization of a network–enabled services (the LuMiR system) that integrates all the local information systems deployed in the Healthcare System of the Basilicata Region (also known as Lucania). The scope was to support the integrated management of the care paths as well as to share useful information concerning patients in the territorial assistance dynamics [Contenti *et al.*, 2010a]. A participative approach was adopted for both the planning and realization phases of the project: many end-users of the LuMiR system were directly involved and a cyclic process was performed, meaning that the final objective was reached through the continuous verification of end-users' exigiencies and

DOI: 10.4018/978-1-5225-0654-6.ch008

needs. A first prototype of the LuMiR system (called LuMiR p0) was then tested for healthcare operators to gather all the available information allocated so far inside a number of local information systems. The support structure for the system implementation was tested too (help-desk, Lumir group, etc.).

The experimentation of the LuMiR p0 system allowed moreover to highligh all the issues related its diffusion and reception among the users: the systems showed in fact new ways of care delivery, based on the models of continuity of care [e.g. Larma e Basil, 2003; Morosini, 2004], disease management [e.g. WHO, 1978, Wagner, 2004] and patient empowerment [e.g. Maceratini e Ricci, 2000; Pinna Pintor, 2005]. This made necessary to design a specific plan for GPs recruitment for the trial stage period, so that a more succesful diffusion of the system could be guaranteed for the next future among healthcare operators and citizens as well.

The chapter is structured as follows: the LuMir system is introduced in Section 2; in the Section 3 the issues connected to the adoption of the system are described; Section 4 deals with the enrollment plan (for GPs and citizens) during the trial stage period; in Sections 5 and 6 the set up and implementation of a mathematical model of the system are described and discussed. Some conclusions and future prospects are described in Section 7.

2. THE LUMIR SYSTEM

The LuMiR system is a network-based systems infrastructure that allows healthcare operators (GPs, specialists, lab analysts, nurses, social operators, pharmacists, etc.) to exchange via an electronic support both clinical and administrative information about citizens. In particular, the LuMiR system:

- Gathers socio-sanitary information concerning the entire citizen's life from all the healthcare organizations the citizen deals with;
- Facilitates the information exchange between information systems and healthcare operators, and can be accessed anytime from anywhere;
- Supports the security management policies as to the access control. The citizens who make use of the LuMiR system can actively control the status of their information. More in detail, every citizen can decide which information can be accessed, by whom, and in what circumstances;
- Guarantees the respect of transparency policies, since every user can visualize who provided his/her information to whom, where the information come from, and who requested them.

The service infrastructure of the LuMiR system allows the connection between organizations via the connection of their local information systems, by means of specific algorithms of information sharing and access control. Figure 1 shows the entire architecture of the LuMiR system.

The LuMiR system also includes:

- A specific module for the management of the clinical events (infoBroker);
- A set of universal wrappers to oversee that the information generated in the local organizations (hospitals, GPs' offices, etc.) are correctly delivered to the central system;
- The LumirWeb system (web navigator) to get access to the information concerning citizen's health events and related documents, according to the existing privacy policies.

Figure 1. LuMiR system architecture

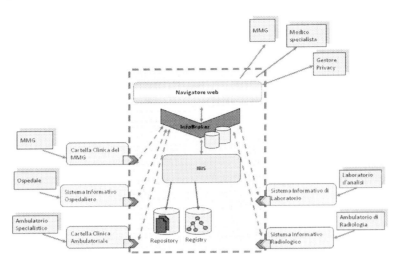

The wrappers guarantee the interoperability between all the different information systems connected to the LuMiR system, since it allows a semi-automatic upload of contents and documents and sends notifications to all the single systems after each information/document has been delivered. In this way, the single healthcare operator is aware of the entire set of information exchanges inside the system, and can easily trace and extract information about his/her patients' care paths.

The experimentation of the LuMiR p0 system made it possible a strong improvement of the information exchange thanks to the analysis of the ways through which the different operators use the system to ease their collaboration for designing the patient's care path. This allowed on the one hand to figure out the real information needs for the future users, meaning: the basic clinical context to be delivered for an effective patients' data and information exchange, their structural organization in data, metadata and document, as well as the most timely communication patterns to be performed [Berry, 2003; Atun, 2004]. On the other hand, it was possible to find out many possible bottlenecks for the phases of massive diffusion of the system, making so easier the definition of a specific adoption roadmap. The main issues were related to the scarce experience of GPs in using ICT solutions, not to mention the lack of a solid technical assistance service. The problems to be worked out concerned therefore:

- The installation of the universal wrapper in the offices of the GPs involved;
- Teaching the GPs how to use the Longitudinal Electronic Healthcare Record (L-EHR) handled by the LuMiR system by means of the LumirWeb navigator;
- Making the use of the LumirWeb navigator an essential part of their daily work.

This implied as consequence:

- The organization of training courses about the use of the LuMiR system, as a first step toward a "full knowledge" of the system;

- The creation of a so-called "Lumir Group", featuring some among GPs and specialists already familiar with healthcare informatics, aimed at leading their colleagues as to the diffusion of the system and the creation of a first consensus base among the future operators;
- The creation of a help-desk service, capable of providing technical assistance to the system's users.

The Lumir Group was meant to convey the users' feedbacks in order to induce the eventual re-engineering of existing services delivering process and the designing of new ones [Coiera et al., 2007; Petroni, 2010]. Moreover, the group was supposed to interact with the help-desk in order to improve the quality of the services provided.

3. ISSUES CONNECTED TO THE ADOPTION OF THE LUMIR SYSTEM

The process of adoption and implementation of the LuMiR system was performed as a series of steps, based on the specific issues to be worked out [Geroski, 2000]:

- The adoption arrangement, that is dealing with privacy policies, enabling support services (e.g. help-desk), providing healthcare organization with the necessary hardware and software;
- Conducting the first trial stage of both the LuMiR system and the support services among the healthcare organizations involved;
- Extension of the entire architecture to all the organizations of the Healthcare System of the Basilicata Region;
- Full covering of the regional territory by including also the non-public organizations that are part of the state run health care.

3.1 Technological and Organizational Arrangement for the System Adoption

This phase was articulated as follows:

1. Identification of a supervisor for the adoption process for each healthcare organization involved;
2. Analysis of the state-of-the-art of hardware and software solutions in use for each healthcare organization involved;
3. Identification of a supervisor for the privacy policies for each healthcare organization involved;
4. Identification, inside the Italian National Research Council, of the temporary responsible for the use of personal data;
5. Identification of the first field site for the LuMiR system adoption;
6. Performing automation of the healthcare organization within the chosen field site;
7. Creation of the help-desk;
8. First presentation of the LuMiR system to the GPs and following recruitment activity;
9. First presentation of the LuMiR system to the specialists;
10. Identification of a set of chronic diseases to focus on for the experimentation scopes;
11. Softwarehouses involvement for the supplying of the software adaptors;
12. Identification of the GPs to be enrolled;

13. Identification of the specialists to be enrolled;
14. Software adaptors delivery;
15. Analysis and identification of the necessary data and information to upload in the system;
16. Vocational training for the help-desk personnel;
17. First enrollment of the healthcare operators (GPs and specialists) and creation of the work group;
18. Launch of the help-desk service;
19. Issue of the access credentials for the autentifications of the operators enrolled;
20. Installation of the software adaptors in the information systems of the healthcare organizations involved;
21. Installation of the software adaptors in the computer systems of the GPs involved;
22. Training of the operators involved;
23. Patients enrollment;
24. L-EHR activation for the enrolled patients;
25. Upload of the patients' healthcare data and information in their personal L-EHR.

Figure 2 describes the logical sequence of the mentioned activities: the green activities deal with the predisposition of the organizational model, while the red ones deal with the phase of software testing. In particular, the latter requested a higher investment in terms of time and resources, since they directly impacted on the success of the L-EHR implementation.

Figure 2. sequence of the activities performed for the arrangement of the LuMiR system adoption

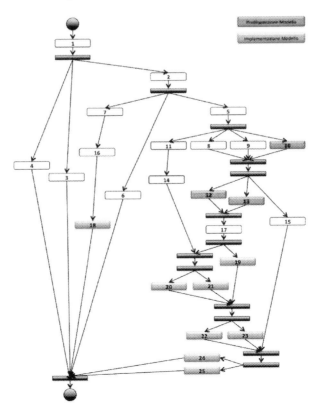

Predictive Modeling as guide for Health Informatics Deployment

In the first phase of adoption the doctors were the "main players" of the system, since they acted both as providers of the clinical information concerning their patients' care events and episodes (and related electronic documents), and as end-users of the contents of the L-EHR.

A trial stage period was deemed as necessary in order to support the users to become familiar with the new technology [Petroni, 2010], also given the paucity of similar experiences performed in Italy or abroad. A limited area and a limited period of time were then considered for the experimentation, also for testing the help-desk and arrange a first draft for the roadmap. It was eventually chosen not to include the specialists in the trial stage.

4. THE ENROLLMENT PLAN FOR THE TRIAL STAGE PERIOD

For the adoption phase, the GPs that were eventually chosen had to meet specific requirements:

- Already using routinarily a EHR solution (e.g. BASMED);
- An high speed data line (ADSL) already available in their workplace;
- A specific number of patients to enroll, lower anyway than the average number of patients per GP (calculated on regional basis), comprising a good percentage of chronic patients consistent with the chronic diseases chosen for the experimentation scopes;

The enrollment plan for the trial stage period worked as follows. In the first (*absolute*) month of adoption of the LuMiR system were identified:

- A very low number of GPs (m_0) to help set up the work for the help-desk;
- A very low number of patients (p_0) for each one of the m_0 GPs, in order to allow them to become gradually familiar with the system.

The second (*absolute*) month of adoption of the system, due to the foreseen increase of the population involved, featured:

- A higher number of new GPs enrolled ($m_1 > m_0$);
- A higher number of patients ($p_1 > p_0$) enrolled for each one of the m_0 and m_1 GPs considered.

The m_0 and m_1 values were chosen depending on the number of universal wrappers that the help-desk managed to install in a single day on GPs' computers.

In the following months, the increase of the patients was translated in a higher number of patients ($p_2 > p_1$) enrolled every month for each one of the m_0 and m_1 GPs. In other words, p_2 means the number of patients per month enrolled by every m_1 GP from the second month of full operativity (the third month for m_0).

The adoption phase was expected to be in full-swing from the third (*absolute*) month: this meant the enrollment of m_1 new GPs every month. The enrollment of the patients for each one of the m_1 GPs occurred in two consecutive moments:

- In the first (*relative*) month of adoption of the system by the single GP, p_1 patients from each GP were chosen in order to allow the GP to become even more familiar with the system;
- From the second (*relative*) month onward of adoption of the system by the single GP, p_2 patients from each GP were chosen for the experimentation.

According to the resources provided by the Healthcare System of the Basilicata Region, given a sample a M=100 GPs involved in the experimentation, the adoption plan for the trial stage period was supposed to works as follows:

- 5 GPs are enrolled in the first (*absolute*) month. Each GP involves 5 patients;
- 23 GPs are enrolled in the second (absolute) month. Each GP (old and new) involves 5 patients;
- The system is in full-swing from the third (absolute) month: every month 23 GPs are enrolled. Each GP (old and new) involves 100 patients.

The values introduced are depicted in Table 1.

Table 2. shows instead the overall distribution of GPs and patients enrolled under the initial condition of M=100 GPs involved. This implies that, since at the end of the fifth month the GPs enrolled are 97, in the next month the last group of GPs enrolled is: $m_{rest} = 100 - 97 = 3$ GPs.

5. THE MATHEMATICAL MODEL OF ADOPTION IN THE TRIAL STAGE PERIOD

In order to evaluate the capacity for an EHR solution to provide a specific set of high-quality, effective and timely services it was necessary to figure out a structured number of strictly intertwined context

Table 1. Adoption plan for the trial stage period

Month 1 (absolute)	GPs enrolled	m_0	5
	Patents enrolled	p_0	4
Month 2 (absolute), or Month 1 (relative)	GPs enrolled	m_1	23
	Patients enrolled by m_0 and m_1	p_1	5
Regime: from Month 3 (absolute), or Month 2 (relative)	GPs enrolled	m_1	23
	Patients enrolled per month	p_2	100

Table 2. Distribution of GPs and patients

Months	Total GPs	Total Patients
1	5	20
2	28	160
3	51	3.075
4	74	8.290
5	97	15.805

Predictive Modeling as guide for Health Informatics Deployment

variables. The development of a mathematical model, as quantitative methodological approach, emerged as the most fitting option to the project and planning of the mentioned roadmap for the adoption of the LuMiR system in the Basilicata Region. As seen, all the healthcare professionals involved were called to be part of the planning process, since the system would become integral part of their ordinary working activities. Similarly, the testing phase was aimed at identifying possible threats as to the reception and the diffusion of the system, as innovative way for healthcare services delivering on a regional scale.

A vast and consolidated scientific literature exists as to the use of mathematical models in the healthcare sector, especially for what concerns the evaluation on the population of the potential impacts originated from decision-making policies, or particular intervention strategies [e.g. McKendrick, 1926; Star et al., 2010]. In the present work, the evaluation of the impact originated from the adoption of the LuMiR system was based on the use of discrete functions that depend on the months (duration) of the experimentation. In particular, the functions point out the total number of GPs enrolled every month, and the total number of patients enrolled from the single GP every month.

After the first month, the model shows an overall linear progressive increase, while the trend of the patients enrolled by the single GP becomes linear from the second month of enrollment of the same GP. Moreover, for each month the trend of the total number of patients enrolled has to be intended as the sum of the trends of the patients enrolled by the single GPs. The choices made to set up the model take also into account that the upper limit only depends on the total number of citizens/patients enrolled by the single GP for the experimentation. This means that they cannot overcome the total number of citizens/patient that can normally be assigned to the single GP (in Italy, a single GP is usually assigned max 1500 patients). All the functions considered for the model are infinite divergent monotonic series, since the number of both GPs and patients always increases; it is also licit to hypothesize that for every month of the trial stage there are always GPs and patients available to be enrolled. It is clear that, at a given moment, both GPs and patients will tend to saturate: the specific aspect will be described in Section 6, whilst in the present moment the set up of the model is not taking into account the phenomenon.

In order to make the model as close to the reality as possible, is has to be considered that both GPs and patients enrolled at the beginning of a certain month will not actually be operative at the beginning of that month, but rather by the end of it: this means that their involvement shows a non-discrete trend. In order to translate such dynamic into the model, the *generic month n* (meaning the n-th month after the beginning of the experimentation) was splitted in two connected parameters:

- n_{adp} (**n Adoption**): The month in which GPs and/or patients are "officially" involved in the experimentation. As said, the enrollment process spans the entire n_{adp}, so that the subjects will be considered as "operative" only by the end of it;
- n_{rdn} (**n Readiness**) = $n_{adp} + 1$: The month in which GPs and/or patients enrolled during the previous month are actually "operative".

All the variables introduced belong to N, i.e. the set of the natural numbers $\{0,1, 2, 3. \ldots\}$.

5.1 Distribution of GPs Enrolled

At the *generic month* $n \geq 1$ (meaning the n-th month after the beginning of the experimentation), the distribution of the number of GPs involved is expressed by the (5.1). Based on what previously introduced, the month has to be considered as the one in which GPs are completely "operative", i.e. M = Med(n) = Med(n_rdn):

$$Med(n) = m_0 + (n-1) * m_1 \qquad (5.1)$$

5.2 Distribution of Total Patients Enrolled

At the *generic month* $n \geq 1$ (meaning the n-th month after the beginning of the experimentation), the distribution of the total number of patients involved is expressed by the (5.2). Based on what previously introduced, the month has to be considered as the one in which the patients are completely "operative", i.e $Paz^a(n) = Paz^a(n_{rdn})$:

$$Paz^a(n) = \begin{cases} m_0 * p_0 & (n=1) \\ (m_0 * p_0) + (m_0 + m_1) * p_1 & (n=2) \\ (m_0 * p_0) + [m_0 + m_1 * (n-1)] * p_1 + \left[m_0 * (n-2) + m_1 * \sum_{j=1}^{n-2} j\right] * p_2 = \\ = (m_0 * p_0) + Med(n) * p_1 + \left[(n-2) * m_0 + m_1 * \frac{(n-1)*(n-2)}{2}\right] * p_2 & (n>2) \end{cases}$$

(5.2)

5.3 Distribution of the Patients Enrolled Per Single GP

The model was introduced as divergent, meaning that the number of both GPs and patients continuously increases. Of course this is not possible, so the model features a range of validity: the number of patients enrolled per single GP cannot exceed the *average numer* of patients of the single GP. To this purpose, Table 3. shows the overall distribution of GPs and patients in the Basilicata Region for the two Provincial Healthcare Trusts that form the Regional Healthcare System.

It was decided to split the population in two ranges (under 18 years old: Paz I; over 18 years old: Paz II), in order to understand whether a different set up for the model had to be performed. The Table shows that Paz II is far greater than Paz I. This result, coupled with the need to focus also on patients with chronic diseases, brought to include in the experimentation only the Paz II category.

Table 3. Overall distribution of GPs and patients in Basilicata Region

		ASP (Potenza Province Healthcare Trust)	ASM (Matera Province Healthcare Trust)	TOTAL
	Total Population	388.000	203.000	**591.000**
Paz I	Population under 18 years old	54.000	30.000	**54.000**
Paz II	Population over 18 years old	334.000	173.000	**507.000**
	GPs	342	175	**517**
p_{avg}	Average number = Paz.II / GPs	976	988	**980**

Predictive Modeling as guide for Health Informatics Deployment

One relatively strong condition imposed to the model was to consider that the maximum number of patients enrollable by the single GPs during the experimentation (P_{real}) is equal to the average number of patients per single GP (p_{avg}) introduced in Table 3. Since $p_{avg} \approx 980$, it was set $P_{real} = 900$ patients enrollable per single GP. The condition $P_{real} \leq p_{avg}$ depends on the need to attain to relistic data, in order to get to as more realistic results as possible.

At the *generic month* $n \geq 1$ (meaning the n-th month after the beginning of the experimentation), the number of patients enrolled per single GP is expressed by the following distribution functions:

- **Case I:** GP enrolled in the first month of the trial stage period (m_0). On the basis of what stated before, the month considered is the one in which the patients are actually "operative", i.e. $Paz^{MMG}(n) = Paz^{MMG}(n_{rdn})$:

$$Paz^{MMG}(n) = \begin{cases} p_0 + p_1 * (n-1) & (1 \leq n_{rdn} \leq 2) \\ p_0 + p_1 + p_2 * (n-2) & (n_{rdn} \geq 2) \end{cases} \quad (5.3)$$

- **Case II:** GP enrolled from the second month of the trial stage period (m_1). The enrollment month is $n_{arr} = n_{adp}$:

$$Paz^{MMG}(n) = \begin{cases} 0 & (n \leq n_{adp}) \\ p_1 + p_2 * (n - n_{adp} - 1) & (n > n_{adp}) \end{cases} \quad (5.4)$$

with the constraint: $n_{arr} = n_{adp} \geq 2$.

It has to be noticed that, should all GPs feature the same number of patients, in any month the maximum number of patients enrolled belongs to one of the GPs enrolled in the very first month of the experimentation ("most enroller" GP). Such value, called $Paz^{MAX}(n)$ is expressed as well by means of a distribution function corresponding to the (5.3), for $n \geq 1$.

It has also to be set forth that, with reference to the (5.3) and for $n \geq 2$, the minimum value of patients enrolled per month during the experimentation is equal to p_1: this means that, for the generic month $n_{rdn} > 2$ the following inequality is valid for the number of patients enrolled by the single GP involved in the experimentation:

$$p_1 \leq Paz^{MMG}(n) \leq p_0 + p_1 + p_2 * (n-2) = Paz^{MAX}(n) \quad (5.5)$$

Accordingly, from now on the concept of maximum number of patients enrolled by the single GP will always be referred to one of the m_0 GPs, since they are active from the beginning of the eperimentation. The formulas introduced in the Section can be expressed in an iterative form, as depicted in Table 4.

6. DISCUSSION

The main aspects to be considered are the following:

Predictive Modeling as guide for Health Informatics Deployment

Table 4. Iterative form of the formulas implemented

Month (n_{rdn})	GP	Patients	Max. number of patients per single GP
1	m_0	$m_0 * p_0$	p_0
2	$m_0 + m_1$	$m_0 * (p_0 + p_1) + m_1 * p_1$	$p_0 + p_1$
...			
n - 1	Med_{n-1}	$Paz^a(n-1)$	$Paz^{MMG}(n-1)$
n (for n ≥ 3)	$m_1 + Med_{n-1}$	$m_0 * p_2 + m_1 * p_1 + m_1 * p_2 * (n-2) + Paz^a(n-1)$	$p_2 + Paz^{MMG}(n-1)$

1. The equations as connection between *variables*, dependent and independent, and *parameters* inside the adoption model;
2. The compliance of the model, to be intended as the correspondence between the dynamics of the real world and the equations performed to figure out such dynamics;
3. The statistical significance of the population (GPs and patients involved) set up for the trial stage.

6.1 Description and Evaluation of the Model

The equations described in (5.1) and (5.2) deal with both variables and parameters. In particular, p_2 is the only parameter that features a wide range of admissible values, and whose choice is not influenced from technical constraints: conversely, the values of the parameters m_0 and m_1 strictly depend on the work capacity of the help-desk, while p_0 and p_1 depend on the capacity of the GPs to learn how to use the LuMiR system. Therefore, the variables to be accounted on are:

- **n:** Duration of the adoption plan (expressed in months);
- **p** = p_2;
- **M** = Med(n): number of GPs enrolled in n months;
- **P** = $Paz^a(n)$: number of patients enrolled in n months.

6.1.1 Evaluation of the GPs Enrolled

As for the GPs enrolled, the variables have to be related to the total number of GPs enrolled (M) and the necessary amount of months to perform their enrollment (n): the equation, valid for n ≥ 1, is described in (5.1); if we consider M = Med(n) = Med(n_{rdn}) as a fixed value, the value of n is expressed with the following:

$$n = INT\left(\frac{M - m_0 + m_1}{m_1}\right) + 1 \tag{6.1a}$$

The (6.1a) sets forth that n is the littlest integer that includes [(M−m0+m1)/m1], whereas INT means the integer part of a real number. The "+1" addend has then to be considered a sort of "security ap-

Predictive Modeling as guide for Health Informatics Deployment

proximation" to balance the previous condition. It has also to be remembered that it is highly likely that all the GPs involved are "operative" only by the end of the month (n_{adp}).

Should the quantity $[(M-m_0+m_1)/m_1]$ be integer, the (6.1a) simplifies as follows:

$$n = \frac{M - m_0 + m_1}{m_1} = \frac{M - m_0}{m_1} + 1 \qquad (6.1b)$$

In the end, being $M \gg m_1 > m_0$, there follows: $n > 2$.

6.1.2 Evaluation of the Patients Enrolled

As for the patients enrolled, the variables have to be identified between: the total number of patients enrolled [$Paz^a(n) = P$]; the necessary number of month to enroll them (n); the number of patients per month enrolled by the single GP from the second month of the experimentation ($p_2 = p$). The equation, valid for $n > 2$, is described in (5.2); if we consider n and P as fixed values, the value of p for $n > 2$ is expressed as follows:

$$p = \frac{\left[P - (m_0 * p_0) - (m_0 * p_1) - (m_1 * p_1) * (n-1)\right]}{\left[2m_0 * (n-2) + m_1 * (n-1) * (n-2)\right]} \qquad (6.2)$$

The sum described in (5.2) indicates an arithmetic progression of reason 1, with 1 as the first element, and comprising (n-2) elemens. The inverse of the (6.2) with p and P as fixed values allows instead to calculate n, for $n > 2$:

$$\begin{aligned}&\left(n^2 * m_1 * p\right) + n * \left(2m_1 * p_1 + 2m_0 * p - 3m_1 * p\right) + \\ &+ 2 * \left(m_0 * p_0 + m_0 * p_1 - m_1 * p_1 - 2m_0 * p + m_1 * p - P\right) = 0\end{aligned} \qquad (6.3)$$

6.1.3 Identification of the Unknown Variables

The model introduces some initial conditions:

1. The value of *n*, considering (5.2) as valid, is comprised in the range: $n_{inf} < n \leq n_{sup}$, where n_{inf} and n_{sup} mean respectively the minimum and the maximum duration of the trial stage period. More specifically, n_{inf} depends on different contingent factors: in particular, the trial stage cannot start unless all the issues related to the adoption of the new system are worked out (see Section 3). Moreover, the validity itself of the model can be evaluated only after the necessary amount of time (expressed in months) for the model to get to be in full-swing. For these reasons, the condition introduced is better specified as: $n_{inf} > 2$.
2. The value of *p* is comprised in the range: $0 < p_0 < p_1 < p \leq p_{sup}$, where p_{sup} means the maximum number of patients that the single GP can enroll for each month.

3. The strong condition introduced in the paragraph 5.3, according to which $P_{real} = 900$, is part of a more general scenario. The variant of the (5.3) introduced for $Paz^{MAX}(n)$ leads for n > 2 to the following condition: $Paz^{MAX}(n) < P_{real}$. Replacing therefore the first part of the equation the result is:

$p_0 + p_1 + p_2 *(n - 2) < P_{real}$

If we consider the term $a' = P_{real} - (p_0 + p_1) > 0$, the previous inequality can be written as:

$(p*n) - (2*p) - a' \leq 0$

Besides these conditions, it has also to be considered that: the choice of n_{sup} depends on the dynamics of saturation performed from the GPs involved; p_{sup} depends instead on the capacity shown by the single GP to enrol patients. Moreover, it can be stated that $p_{sup} < P_{real}$, meaning that the maximum number of patients per month enrolled by the sinle GP cannot overcome the total number of patients assisted by the GP him/herself during the experimentation: in other words, p_{sup} is generally lower than the average number of patients assisted by the single GP. For these reasons it was decided to use for the model set up n_{sup} and p_{sup}, instead n_{max} and p_{max}. Eventually, the choice of M and P is based on empirical evidences as well, since it depends on the objectives defined from the institution of the Basilicata Region for the trial stage period.

Having identified n and p as the main variables of the model, their functional relation has to be studied within a specific domain on the XY plane (for our study, the np plane). The domain is defined by the conditions introduced in the previous paragraphs and summarized as follows:

$$\begin{cases} n > 2 \\ (p*n) - (2*p) - a' \leq 0 \\ 2 < n_{inf} < n < n_{sup} \\ 0 < p_0 < p_1 < p \leq p_{sup} \end{cases} \quad (6.4)$$

Figure 3 depicts the EDCBA domain composed by four segments and an arc of hyperbole. Inside the domain an "objective function" is defined that marks the connection between the variables n and p by means of the parameter $P = Paz^a(n)$, considered as an external element for the model. The objective function was introduced with the (6.3), and can be expressed in the following symbolic form:

$$a*p*n^2 + b*p*n + c*n + d*p + e = 0 \quad (6.5a)$$

The (6.5a) can be then changed into a p = p(n) form, that represents a conic curve:

$$p = -\frac{e + c*n}{a*n^2 + b*n + d} \quad (6.5b)$$

Figure 3: Domain on the np plane

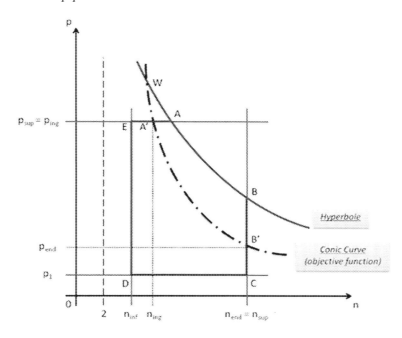

Here following the steps performed to get to the coefficients and their properties (assuming P >> 1.000) are described:

- $a = m_1 > 0$
- $b = (2 * m_0) - (3 * m_1) < 0$ $\Rightarrow m_0 < \frac{3}{2} * m_1 \searrow$
- $c = 2 * m_1 * p_1 > 0$ $m_0 < \frac{m_1}{2}$
- $d = (2 * m_1) - (4 * m_0) > 0$ $\Rightarrow m_1 < 2 * m_0 \nearrow$
- $e = (2 * m_0 * p_0) + (2 * m_0 * p_1) - (2 * m_1 * p_1) - 2 * P < 0$

The conic curve that represents the objective function of the model intersects the domain in A' (n_{ing}; p_{ing}) (way in) and in B' (n_{end}; p_{end}) (way out). Outside the domain, the objective function intersects the hyperbole in W. The main scope of the objective function is to *maximize the feasibility of the model*, that is the time period within which both suitability and viability of the adoption process of the LuMiR system in the Basilicata region can be evaluated.

The (n_{ing}, n_{end}) interval depicted in Figure 3 is introduced through the following:

Theorem 6.1

HP: On the y-coordinate of the np plane the following condition is verified:

$$\left(p_{end}, p_{ing}\right) \subseteq \left(p_1, p_{sup}\right)$$

TH: On the x-coordinate of the np plane the following interval is recognized:

$$\left(n_{ing}, n_{end}\right) \subseteq \left(n_{inf}, n_{sup}\right)$$

Demonstration: The case $2 < n_{ing} < n_{inf}$ is trivial; n_{ing} is by definition the x-coordinate of A', that is the intersection point between conic curve and domain. Given the slope of the conic curve, A' can be found on the segments AE or ED: this means that n_{ing} ranges in the interval $n_{inf} < n < n_{sup}$ (see 6.4), so the condition $n_{ing} < n_{inf}$ is not acceptable and the condition $n_{inf} \leq n_{ing} \leq n_{sup}$ is verified. For the same reason, A' also features the y-coordinate $p_1 < p_{ing} \leq p_{sup}$ (in Figure 3 $p_{ing} = p_{sup}$).

As for B', given the slope of the conic curve the point can be found on the arc of hyperbole AB (standing the obvious condition B' ≠ A), or on the segments BD or DC (standing the obvious condition B' ≠ D). This means that the x-coordinate of B' may match with the x-coordinate of B or C, i.e. $n_{inf} < n_{end} \leq n_{sup}$. Similarly, the y-coordinate of B' may match with the y-coordinate of the points of the segment DC, i.e.: $p_1 \leq p_{end} < p_{sup}$.

The value of p_{sup} is the upper limit of the range of admissible values for p_2, as described in the following:

Theorem 6.2

HP: on the x-coordinate of the np plane the following condition is verified:

$n_{inf} < n < n_{sup}$

TH: on the y-coordinate of the np plane the following condition is recognized:

$p_1 \leq p_2 \leq p_{sup}$

Demonstration: The hypothesis belongs to the set of formulas of the (6.4) that circumscribe the dominion in the np plane. In particular, it highlights the time ranging between the lower and the upper limits of the trial stage period. Similarly, the condition $p_1 < p \leq p_{sup}$ belongs to (6.4). For $n > 2$, during the experimentation the m_1 GPs enroll at least p_1 patients, and p_{sup} means the maximum number of patients per month that each GP con enroll when the system is in full-swing. This implies that p_2 necessarily stands between the two mentioned values.

Predictive Modeling as guide for Health Informatics Deployment

6.1.4 Recognition of the Optimal Solutions

Both the domain EDCBA and the conic curve introduced in (6.5b) are described in the np plane as functions of the elements figured out in the adoption plan: M, P, m_0, m_1, n_{inf}, n_{sup}, p_0, p_1, p_{sup}. The np plan describes effectively the model dynamics only if at least one couple of values (n, p) is recognized within the domain after the definition of the parameters and the choice of the variables. This means in other words that, in those circumstances, there has to be at least one optimal solution for the problem described through the model. Such assumption is verified in the following:

Theorem 6.3

Necessary and sufficient condition for the resolution of the problem concerning the definition of an adoption plan, is that at least one of the following statemements is verified:

- [ABS(E) < ABS(A')] ∧ [ABS(A') < ABS(A)] = TRUE *(Input)*
- [ORD(B') < ORD(B)] ∧ [ORD(C) < ORD(B')] = TRUE *(Output)*
- [ABS(D) < ABS(B')] ∧ [ABS(B') < ABS(C)] = TRUE *(Input)*
- [ORD(D) < ORD(A')] ∧ [ORD(A') < ORD(E)] = TRUE *(Output)*

where ORD means the y-coordinate and ABS means the x-coordinate of the specific point.

- **Demonstration of the Necessary Condition:** The possible intersections between domain and conic curve are depicted in Figure 4.

Figure 4. Graph of the intersections between dominion and conic curve

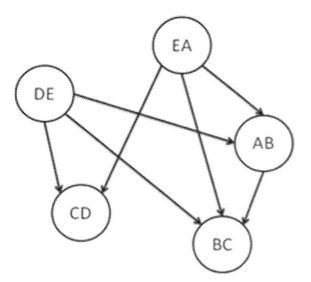

- Given the slope of the curve, the graph shows two "sources" (the conic curve only enters the domain through the segments ED or EA), two "wells" (the conic curve only leaves the domain through the segments DC or CB) and an "intermediate node" (the conic curve can as enter as leave the domain through the segment AB). The straight lines and the hyperbole that form the domain intersect the conic curve in just one point at most. If at least one of the given statements is fulfilled, is trivial that conic curve and domain are secant: this means the the conic curve crosses the domain in at least one point, or in other words that exists at least one couple of values (n, p) within the domain that allows to verify the feasibility of the objective function (via the parameter P). The problem of the definition of adoption plan can be therefore solved.
- **Demonstration of the Sufficient Condition**: Using a demonstration by the absurd, we state that the problem of the adoption plan cannot be solved. This implies that the conic curve and the domain cannot be secant, but at most tangential. The graph in Figure 4 makes clear that the only node that can fulfill at the same time the mandatory requirements of tangency and input/output is the arc AB: this means that at least one point of the arc should fulfill both the conditions. In analytical language, this means that there is one point of the arc AB in which the derivative functions in respect to n of both conic curve and hyperbole must match. The result is an equation of fourth grade, with four different roots: this implies that there should be four tangency points on AB between hypebole and conic curve. The two curves should therefore match in four different points, that is to say that the two curves completely match with each other. Given the characteristics of the (6.4) on which the domain is defined, the results obtained clearly contradicts the demonstration by the absurd, so the problem can actually be solved.

The set up of the mathematical model was refined thanks to the data gathered "on the field" for the technological and organizational arrangement of the system adoption from 2010 to 2013. The main scope was to get to an as more effective as possible "*ex-ante*" evaluation of the feasibility of the entire adoption plan of the LuMiR system in the Basilicata Region, in order to:

1. Redefine and adapt the adoption plan depending on the actual available resources (human, organizational and financial); or
2. Pushing where possible towards a better definition of the resources to be implemented, to fulfill the results displayed after a correct implementation of the mathematical model.

6.2 Compliance of the Model

The correct positioning of the domain as well as the slope of the objective function in the np plane depend on a further series of constraints, related to the actual time available for both GPs and patients that can be enrolled in the experimentation. Up to this moment, the model had been set up according to the hypothesis that every month there are always GPs and patients to be enrolled. Actually, their number is not unlimited. More specifically, the distribution of the patients enrolled reachs the saturation in:

- **n^i_{sat}**: The "saturation month", when all the expected patients (P_{real}) of the GP involved in the i-th month ($n^i = n_{rdn}$) have been enrolled;
- **n_{med}**: The month in which all the GPs involved (M_{med}) have been enrolled;

Predictive Modeling as guide for Health Informatics Deployment

- $n^{last}_{sat} = n_{last}$: The month when the experimentation ends, since all the citizens involved have been enrolled (P_{pop}). It is also the month in which the enrollment of all the patients (P_{real}) related to the last group of m_1 GPs involved ends.

6.2.1 Saturation of the Patients Enrolled by the Single GP

Consider the month in which the total satutarion of the patients enrolled by the m_0 GPs is reached $[Paz^{MMG}(n) = P_{real}]$. The (5.3) for $n_{rdn} > 2$ changes in:

$$n_{sat} = n^I_{sat} = INT\left(\frac{P_{real} - p_0 - p_1 + 2*p_2}{p_2}\right) + 1 = INT\left(\frac{P_{real} - p_0 - p_1}{p_2}\right) + 3 \quad (6.6a)$$

That being valid, for $n \geq n_{sat}$ there is the need to discard all the next patients, that cannot be enrolled anymore, calling them "virtual". Such virtual patients $Paz^s(n)$ can be calculated by means of an appropriate "corrective" function, starting from the hypothesis that $n_{sat} \geq 2$, since under this condition $P_{real} \geq p_0 + p_1$, with $p_0 + p_1$ meaning the number of patients enrolled by the "most enroller" m_0 GP for $n = 2$.

Under the same initial conditions, the same procedure can be performed to calculate the saturation month (n^{II}_{sat}) for the patients enrolled by the first group of m_1 GPs involved in the second month (and that become "operative" from the third month onward of the experimentation).

In this case the (5.3) for $n_{rdn} > 2$ changes in:

$$n^{II}_{sat} = INT\left(\frac{P_{real} - p_1 + 2*p_2}{p_2}\right) + 1 = INT\left(\frac{P_{real} - p_1}{p_2}\right) + 3 \quad (6.6b)$$

The comparison between (6.6a) and (6.6b) makes clear that $n_{sat} = n^I_{sat} \approx n^{II}_{sat}$, since the factor $p_0/p_2 \approx 0$: this means that the patients of the m_0 GPs enrolled in the first month of the experimentation, and the patients of the first group of m_1 GPs enrolled in the second month of the experimentation reach the saturation about at the same time.

The function $Paz^s(n)$ describes the trend of the "virtual" patients for all the GP s, as follows:

$$Paz^s(n_{rdn}) = \begin{cases} 0 & (n \leq n_{sat}) \\ \left[(m_0 * p_0) + \left[p_1 + (n_{sat} - 2)*p_2 - P_{real}\right]*(m_0 + m_1) + m_1 * p_2 * \sum_{j=1}^{n-n_{sat}-1} j\right] & (n \geq n_{sat}) \end{cases}$$
(6.7)

6.2.2 Saturation of the Enrollable GPs

Consider the month n_{med} in which the saturation M_{med} of the GPs is reached. The (6.1a) changes in:

$$n_{med} = INT\left(\frac{M_{med} - m_0 + m_1}{m_1}\right) + 1 = INT\left(\frac{M_{med} - m_0}{m_1}\right) + 2 \quad (6.8)$$

Similarly to what seen before for the patients, for $n \geq n_{med}$ there is the need to discard all the next patients, that cannot be enrolled anymore since no more GPs are enrolled in turn.

Such patients $Paz^m(n)$ can be calculated as well by means of a "corrective" function, starting from the hypothesis that $2 \leq n_{med} \leq n_{sat}$: under this condition, in fact, on the one hand $M >> m_0 + m_1$; on the other hand the concept of $m_{rest} \leq m_1$ is introduced, meaning the number of GPs enrolled as the last group, and expressed as follows:

$$m_{rest} = M_{med} - \left[m_0 + \left(n_{med} - 2 \right) * m_1 \right] \qquad (6.9a)$$

For $n = n_{med} + 1$, the first group of "virtual" GPs is somehow called to "complete" the last group of GPs enrolled in the previous month; if $m_{rest} = m_1$, the first group of "virtual" GPs will be equal to m_1.
The function $Paz^m(n)$, describes the trend of the "virtual" patients for all the GPs, as follows:

$$Paz^m\left(n_{rdn}\right) = \begin{cases} 0 & (n \leq n_{med}) \\ \left(m_1 - m_{rest}\right) * p_1 & (n = n_{med}) \\ \left\{\left(m_1 - m_{rest}\right) * \left[p_1 + \left(n - n_{med}\right) * p_2\right]\right\} + \\ + \left\{\left[\left(n - n_{med}\right) * p_1 + p_2 * \sum_{j=1}^{n-n_{med}-1} j\right]\right\} & (n \geq n_{med}+1) \end{cases} \qquad (6.9b)$$

6.2.3 Saturation of All the Patients Enrolled

Consider the month $n_{rdn} = n_{last}$ in which the total saturation of the patients (P_{pop}) is reached. The distribution of $Paz(n_{rdn})$, that means the patients effectively enrolled, is expressed as follows:

$$Paz\left(n_{last}\right) = P_{real} * M_{med} = P_{pop} \qquad (6.10)$$

The maximum value for n is n_{last}. The function $Paz(n_{last})$ therefore becomes:

$$Paz\left(n_{rdn}\right) = \begin{cases} Paz^a\left(n_{rdn}\right) - Paz^m\left(n_{rdn}\right) - Paz^s\left(n_{rdn}\right) & (1 \leq n < n_{last}) \\ P_{pop} & (n \geq n_{last}) \end{cases} \qquad (6.11)$$

where:

- **$Paz^a(n_{rdn})$**: The total number of patients assisted by the GPs involved in the experimentation, without taking into account saturation phenomena (see 5.2);
- **$Paz^m(n_{rdn})$**: The "virtual" patients after the saturation of the GPs (see 6.9b);
- **$Paz^s(n_{rdn})$**: The "virtual" patients after the saturation of the patients for a given GP (see 6.7).

Predictive Modeling as guide for Health Informatics Deployment

As a result of the discussion, it is possible to figure out under a new perspective the already mentioned distribution functions for both GPs enrolled and patients enrolled per single GP.

The new function Med(n), related to the GPs enrolled, is the combination of (5.1), (6.8), (6.9a) and (6.9b) and can be expressed as follows:

$$Med(n) = \begin{cases} m_0 + (n-1)*m_1 & (1 \leq n < n_{med}) \\ M_{med} & (n \geq n_{med}) \end{cases} \quad (6.12)$$

The new function $Paz^{max}(n)$, related to the maximum number of patients enrolled by the "most enroller" GP, is the combination of (5.3), (5.4), (6.6a) and (6.6b) and can be expressed as follows:

$$Paz^{max}(n) = \begin{cases} p_0 & (n=1) \\ p_0 + p_1 + (n-2)*p_2 & (2 \leq n < n_{last}) \\ P_{real} & (n \geq n_{last}) \end{cases} \quad (6.13)$$

It becomes now possible to compare the trend of the functions related to the enrolment of the patients per single GP, with the trend of the function Paz(n) described in (6.11) (see Figures 5 and 6). Based on the data introduced in Tables 1 and 2, it emerges in particular that: $n_{med} < n_{sat} = n^I_{sat} = n^{II}_{sat}$.

As already said, the trend of the patients enrolled by the single GP becomes linear from the second month of enrollment of the GPs. The trend of Paz(n) has instead to be intended, point by point, as the sum of the functions related to the patients enrolled by the single GPs.

Joining these results from those emerging from the analysis of the saturation phenomena, it can be noticed that:

1. Once reached the value $P_{real} = 900$, the trend of the patients enrolled per single GP does not increase anymore;
2. The trend of the function $Paz(n_{rdn})$, that includes also the "virtual" increase of the patients, features a decreasing slope [Paz'(n) > 0; Paz''(n) < 0] until it settles as well on a given value ($P_{pop} = 90.000$).

6.3 Description of the Real Model

Once made clear the real dynamics of enrollment and saturation of the subjects involved in the experimentation, the original formulation of the model introduced in the paragraph 6.1.3 undergoes some modifications. The introduction of the formulas (6.6a), (6.6b), (6.8) and (6.13) does not affect directly the definition of the domain, but rather the conic curve introduced with the formulas (6.5a) and (6.5b), starting from the (5.2), as objective function.

For $n < n_{last}$, the saturation phenomena have to be taken into account for both the number of GPs (M_{med}) and the number of patients per single GP (P_{real}): this means that, for each month in which episodes of saturation occur (related to GPs and/or patients), the function will feature points of removable discontinuity. As an example:

Figure 5. Comparison between the function Paz(n) and the functions related to the enrolment of patient per single GP,

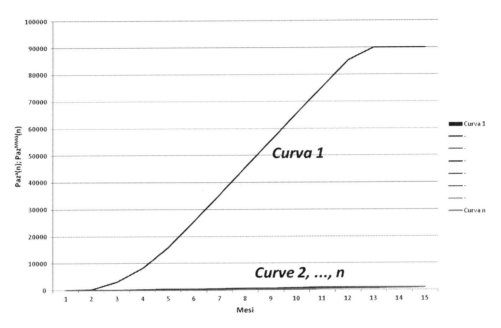

Figure 6. Particular of Figure 5 on a more limited range of values

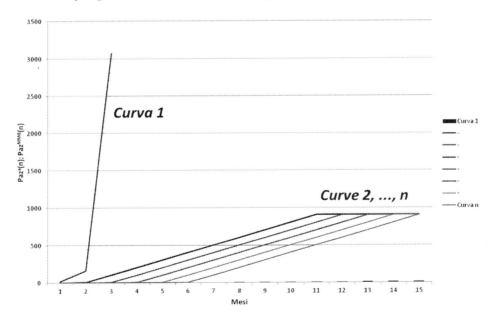

Predictive Modeling as guide for Health Informatics Deployment

$$f\left(n_{med}^{-}\right) = f\left(n_{med}^{+}\right) \neq f\left(n_{med}\right)$$

It becomes so clear that the overall function for the calculation of the total number of patients enrolled is actually formed by different functions. In Figure 7. a more realistic trend of the objective function, as the implementation of the (6.11) for $1 \leq n < n_{last}$, is described.

6.3.1 The Lumir Zone

As a completion to the results described in the previous paragraphs, it is important to compare to each other the saturation dynamics of GPs and patients involved in the adoption of the LuMiR system. The scope is to get to an as more precise as possible recognition of the time interval (called *Lumir Zone*) that marks the feasibility of the model studied in the present work (see Figure 8).

Starting from (6.10), it is possible to write the formulas (6.6a), (6.6b) and (6.8) as a function of P_{pop}. Skipping the intermediate passages, The final result is the following:

Figure 7. The real objctive function within the domain (discontinuities exist also for the months next to n_{sat}, until n_{last})

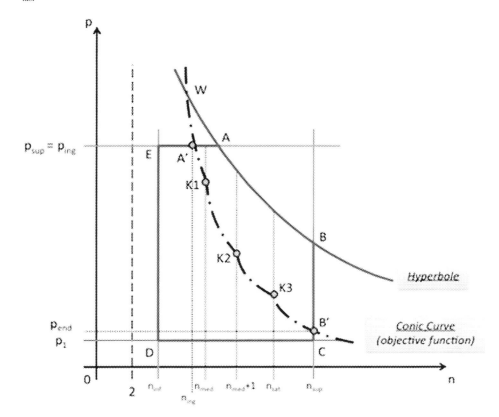

Predictive Modeling as guide for Health Informatics Deployment

$$n_{sat} = INT\left[\frac{P_{pop} - M_{med} * (p_0 + p_1)}{M_{med} * p_2}\right] + 3 \qquad (6.14a)$$

$$n_{med} = INT\left[\frac{P_{pop} - m_0 * P_{real}}{m_1 * P_{real}}\right] + 2 \qquad (6.14b)$$

The *Lumir Zone* makes possible an almost effective comparison of the evolution dynamics of both the populations of GPs and patients involved in the experimentation. This is also why the two timelines of GPs and patients are depicted separately. The only limitation concerns the already mentioned peculiar nature of $n_{sat} = n^I_{sat}$ and n_{med}, that makes these elements not directly comparable with each other.

The choice to report the saturation of the patients before the saturation of the GPs was arbitrary, and origins from the analysis of the data reported in Tables 1 and 2, as well as from the formulas (6.6a) and (6.6b), according to which: **$n_{med} < n_{sat} = n^I_{sat} = n^{II}_{sat}$**.

- **Patients:** Once the experimentation has began, the "Running Field" points out that in the first (absolute) month of adoption n_1 a number of p_0 patients for the m_0 GPs is defined, while in the second (absolute) month of adoption n_2, a number of p_1 patients is enrolled for both m0 and m1 GPs. In the "Saturation Field" the mentioned (6.6a) and (6.6b) set forth that $n^I_{sat} = n^{II}_{sat}$.

The time interval ranging between n_1 and $n^I_{sat} = n^{II}_{sat}$ is called **β**, corresponding in paticular to (6.6b); to follow, every month the patient enrolled by the m_1 GPs saturate. More in general, the (5.4) describes

Figure 8. Description of the Lumir Zone

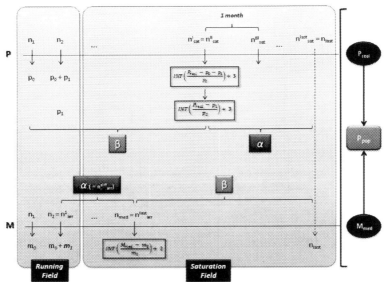

Predictive Modeling as guide for Health Informatics Deployment

the distribution of the patients for the GP enrolled in the i-th month; considering $i = n_{rdn} = n_{adp} + 1$, with $i = \{1, 2, 3, \ldots\}$, there follows:

$$Paz^{MMG}(n) = p_1 + p_2 * (n - i) \qquad (n > i) \qquad (6.15a)$$

Applying the mentioned saturation logic to the (6.15a), the month of saturation (n^i_{sat}) for the GP enrolled in the i-th month is:

$$n^i_{sat} = INT\left(\frac{P_{real} - p_1}{p_2}\right) - i + 1 \qquad (6.15b)$$

where "i" means the order of enrollment of the groups of GPs. The last group of patients will be completed at $n^{last}_{sat} = n_{last}$, and the time interval ranging between n^1_{sat} and n^{last}_{sat} is called α. The entire period of validity of the model (from the first absolute month of adoption of the system, to the total saturation of the population involved) is therefore the sum of the time periods $\alpha + \beta$.

- **GPs:** in the "Running Field", m_0 GPs are involved in the first (absolute) month of adoption ($n_{adp} = 1$), and become "operative" in $n_{rdn} = 2 = n_{adp} + 1$. In the second (absolute) month of adoption $n_{adp} = 2 = n^1_{arr}$, a group of $m_0 + m_1$ GPs are involved, and become "operative" in $n = n_{rdn} = 3$. In the "Saturation Field", $n_{med} = n^{last}_{arr}$ means the month in which the last of the m_1 GPs involved is enrolled. A time interval called n^{diff}_{arr} is then defined, and ranges between the enrollment of the first and the last group of m_1 GPs: such interval is most likely matching with the necessary time for the saturation of all the m_1 GPs involved, and is called α, since the first group of m_1 GPs enrolled is likely to be the first one to saturate, and so on. It is so possible to express the value of α by means of the following:

$$\alpha = n^{diff}_{arr} = n_{med} - n^1_{arr} = n^{last}_{arr} - n^1_{arr} \qquad (6.16)$$

As $\alpha + \beta$ represents the total duration of the experimentation, there follows that for the GPs the value of β means the remaining time interval ranging between n_{med} (the saturation of the GPs) and n_{last} (the saturation of the patients). More specifically, β means the number of months during which the saturation of the patients enrolled by the GPs of the generic m_1 group occurs.

Accordingly, the adoption of the LuMiR system on the whole becomes:

$$n_{last} = n_{med} + \beta + 1 = INT\left[\left(\frac{M_{med} - m_0}{m_1}\right) + 1 + \left(\frac{P_{real} - p_1}{p_2}\right) + 2\right] + 1 \qquad (6.17)$$

The last addend indicates a margin of error of about a month: a sort of "tolerance" preventively accounted because of the unavoidable uncertainty of the saturation dynamics, that may slightly differ from what resulted after the deployment of the model.

6.4 Model Implementation

6.4.1 Initial and Surrounding Conditions

The field data gathered between 2010 and 2013 among actors and institutions involved in the LuMiR project made possible to verify for the trial stage period the feasibility of the model, according to the resources provided by the Healthcare System of the Basilicata Region. Table 5. shows the input data, compliant to those reported in Table 1.

In particular:

- 5 m_0 GPs (3 from the Potenza Province Healthcare Trust, and 2 from the Matera Province Healthcare Trust) were enrolled as volunteers in the first absolute month ($n_{adp} = 1$). Each GP was supposed to enroll at least 4 p_0 patients in the same month.
- 23 m_1 GPs (15 from the Potenza Province Healthcare Trust, and 8 from the Matera Province Healthcare Trust) were enrolled as volunteers in the second absolute month ($n_{adp} = 2$). Each m_0 and m_1 GP was supposed to enroll at least 5 p_1 patients in the same month.
- The system got to be in full-swing from the third month onward. Every month other 23 m_1 GPs (15 from the Potenza Province Healthcare Trust, and 8 from the Matera Province Healthcare Trust) were enrolled, obliged to involve 5 patients (p_1) in their first month, and 100 (p_2) for the next months.

The value for m_1 mainly depended on the capacity of the help-desk to support not more that two GPs per day in the installation of the universal wrapper. During the trial stage period, the GPs were called to focus on specific chronic diseases among the patients involved: in the Potenza Province Healthcare Trust it was chosen to focus on the cardiovascular diseases, in the Matera Province Healthcare Trust it was instead chosen to focus on the diabetes mellitus type 2.

Under the hypothesis that each GP involved featured at least 900 patients (P_{real}), Figure 9. shows the total distribution of the patients enrolled for a period of about 15 months, comparing the ideal trend

Table 5. Input data for the experimentation

m_0	5
m_1	23
P_{real}	900
p_0	4
p_1	5
p_2	100
p_{sup}	200
M	100 (total number of GPs in the Basilicata Region: 500)
P	90.000 (total number of inhabitants of the Basilicata Region: about 500.000)
n_{sup}	11
M_{med}	100

Predictive Modeling as guide for Health Informatics Deployment

of the Paz^a(n) function from the (5.2) with the actual one from the (6.11). While the former increases indefinitely, the latter settles on $P_{pop} = 90.000$ patients.

Similarly, Table 6. shows the comparison between "ideal" and "actual" patients, along with their percentage variation. It has to be noticed that the increase of the percentage variation expresses the increasing "weight" of the virtual patients, as the saturation dynamics take place.

6.4.2 Model Sizing

The minimum duration of the trial stage for the experimentation was set equal to $n_{inf} = n_{med} = 6$ months, according to what stated in the (6.4) – $n_{inf} > 2$ – and to the amount of available resources provided from the Basilicata Region: this meant that the most motivated GPs would be enrolled in the first groups. The real model set up is depicted in Figure 10. The solution of the equations for the hyperbole and the objective function (conic curve) highlighted that: the hyperbole intersects the value of p_{sup} for $n \approx 6$ (point A); the intersection between the two curves occurs outside the domain, for $n \approx 12,5$ (point W); $p_{ing} = p_{sup} = 200$. The model showed that $n_{sup} = 11$, meaning that during the trial stage period the objective function does not cross the domain, so that neither A' (n_{ing}; p_{ing}) nor B' (n_{end}; p_{end}) can be formally defined as introduced in the paragraph 6.1.3: the intersection between objective function and p_{sup} is in fact located outside the domain for $n_{ing} \approx 7,6$. This implies that:

- The real time interval for the evaluation of the feasibility of the adoption process of the LuMiR system, according to the available resources, was narrowed down to the period: $8 \approx n_{ing} < n \leq n_{sup} = 11$;
- According to what demonstrated in the theorem 6.2, the range of admissible values for p_2 is comprised between 0 and 200: under this conditions, the hypothesis $p_2 = 100$ showed in Table 5 is acceptable.

Figure 9. Comparison between ideal and actual trend of the patients enrolled

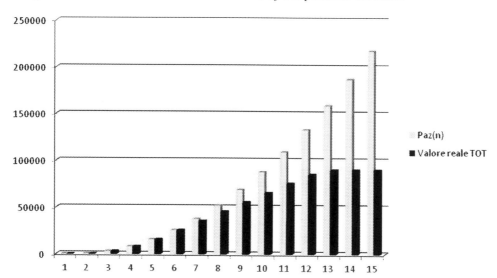

153

Table 6. Distribution of GPs and patents during the experimentation

Month	GPs	"Ideal" patients – $Paz(n_{rdn})$	"Actual" patients – $Paz^a(n)$	% Variation
1	5	20	20	0,00%
2	28	160	160	0,00%
3	51	3075	3075	0,00%
4	74	8290	8290	0,00%
5	97	15805	15805	0,00%
6	120	25620	25520	0,39%
7	143	37735	35520	6,24%
8	166	52150	45520	14,57%
9	189	68865	55520	24,04%
10	212	87880	65520	34,13%
11	235	109195	75360	44,90%
12	258	132810	85360	55,59%
13	281	158725	90000	76,36%
14	304	186940	90000	107,71%
15	327	217455	90000	141,62%

Figure 10. the real domain of the adoption model, according to the resources provided from the Basilicata Region

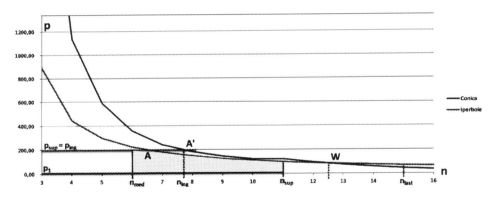

Focusing on the saturation dynamics, the application of the (6.8) implied that the "M" GPs enrollable were supposed to saturate in 6 months; as for the patients, the application of the (6.6a) and (6.6b) implied that the patients enrolled by both m_0 and m_1 GPs were supposed to saturate for $n^1_{sat} = n^2_{sat} = 11$. Moreover, the study of the *Lumir Zone* highlighted that $\alpha = n^{diff}_{arr} = 5 - 1 = 4$, and $\beta = 11$. The application of the (6.17) showed eventually that $n_{last} = 16$, that is the month in which all the population was supposed to saturate ($P_{pop} = 90.000$ foreseen patients involved).

All the results are summarized in Table 7.

Predictive Modeling as guide for Health Informatics Deployment

6.5 Interpretation of the Results and Limitations of the Study

The analysis of the data reported in Tables 5 and 6 made possible, as first result, to foresee that once started the experimentation about the 45% of the GPs and about the 21% of the inhabitants of the Basilicata Region would have been involved in the trial stage period, comprised between $n_{inf} = 6$ and $n_{sup} = 11$. In particular, the enrollment of about the 20% of the total GPs would have been reached by the end of the fifth month ($97 \approx 100$), therefore saturating the number of GPs made available from the Basilicata Region.

Nonetheless, it clearly emerged that as such the model was undersized if compared to the actual needs set forth from the study. In the first place, the upper limit calculated for the trial stage period ($n_{sup} = 11$), at the light of what stated in the Tables 1 and 5, was unsuitable for two main reasons:

- The lenght of the experimentation was calculated in a first moment without taking into appropriate account the saturation dynamics for both GPs and patients, that highly affect the trend of the total patients enrolled: the actual trend of the function $Paz(n)$ is in fact described by the (6.11) and not by the (5.2). This was moreover highlighted from the fact that the patients were supposed to start to saturate for $n = 11$, that marked instead the end of the experimentation;
- The actual time for the model to work in full-swing was narrowed down to only four months.

In the second place, an as important (though opposite) result emerged from the analysis of p_2. The strong condition introduced in the paragraph 6.1.3 asked for the sum of patients per month enrolled by the GPs to remain under the value of $P_{real} = 900 \leq p_{avg}$. Choosing $p_2 = 100$ made this condition fulfilled all along the experimentation period – in particular, for $n = 11$ the "most enroller" GPs would have reached a value of $P_{real} = 909 \approx 900$. Setting $p_2 = 200$ (all the other conditions unchanged) in the model, the objective function would have "entered" the domain intersecting the hyperbole by the half of the seventh month: this would made possible to calculate the coordinates for A' ($n_{ing} \approx 9{,}3$; $p_{ing} \approx 121$) and B' ($n_{end} = n_{sup} = 11$; $p_{end} \approx 105$). The patients would have started to saturate from the seventh month, and $n_{last} = 11$. This scenario features two main issues:

1. The new value of p_2, defined "a priori", was actually a particular case inside the admissible range of values recognized for the model;
2. It is nearly impossible to figure out the enrollment of 200 patients per month for the single GP, even when the system is in full-swing.

Table 7. Values from the real adoption model

p_1	p_{sup}	p_{ing}	n_{ing}	p_{end}	n_{end}	n_{inf}	n_{sup}	n_{med}	n^1_{sat}	n^2_{sat}	n_{last}
5	200	200	7,6	-	-	6	11	6	11	11	15

These results made clear the overall unsuitability of the resources made available from the Region for an effective implementation of the adoption strategy for the LuMiR system, in spite of the significant dimension of the sample population. More in general, the following conclusions can be drawn:

- The limited time interval of the experimentation, though considered as suitable from the Region's institutions, actually did not allow an effective planning of the actors' involvement dynamics. If on the one hand the process of model-setting was based on a series of linear conditions (e.g. choice of motivated GPs, same number of patients enrolled per month, same velocity of enrollment performed by each GP), on the other hand the design of the saturation dynamics was carefully performed. Nonetheless, the mentioned unsuitability of the resources available made the saturation phenomena very difficult to be evaluated, and therefore for the great part ineffective;
- The possibility, as seen, to modify the value of p_2 before the experimentation, whilst made apparently possible to follow the condition set for n_{sup}, actually altered the perception as to the suitability of the resources made available: a higher value of p_2 allows in fact to somehow "mask" ex-post the eventual limitations intrinsic with the initial and surrounding conditions, on which the very steadiness of the domain is actually founded.

6.5.1 Sensitivity Analysis

After the main results described above, it was as well important to evaluate the modifications that can affect the model due to the variation of some among the main variables introduced. In particular, given their importance for the model set up, the analysis concerned M_{med}, P_{real}, p_2.

$\mathbf{M_{med}}$) consider to double the number of GPs involved (M = 200): with all the other conditions unchanged, this implies the increase of the total population involved in the experimentation ($P_{real}*M_{med}=P_{pop}$), and accordingly the increase of the necessary time for both GPs and patients to saturate, as described:

$$\frac{\Delta n_{med}}{\Delta M_{med}} = \frac{10-6}{200-100} = +4\% \qquad (6.18a)$$

$$\frac{\Delta n_{last}}{\Delta M_{med}} = \frac{19-15}{200-100} = +4\% \qquad (6.18b)$$

$\mathbf{P_{real}}$) consider to increase as much as possible the number of patients that the single GP can enroll during the experimentation, so to have the condition $P_{real} = p_{avg} = 980$ verified (see paragraph 5.3): with all the other conditions unchanged, this implies the increase of the total population involved in the experimentation ($P_{real}*M_{med}=P_{pop}$), and accordingly the increase of the necessary time for both GPs and patients to saturate, as described:

$$\frac{\Delta n_{sat}^l}{\Delta P_{real}} = \frac{12-11}{980-900} = +1,25\% \qquad (6.19a)$$

Predictive Modeling as guide for Health Informatics Deployment

$$\frac{\Delta n_{last}}{\Delta P_{real}} = \frac{17-15}{980-900} = +2,5\% \qquad (6.19b)$$

p$_2$) consider to double the value of p$_2$, as already seen: with all the other conditions unchanged (especially P$_{pop}$), this implies a shortening of the necessary time for both GPs and patients to saturate, as described:

$$\frac{\Delta n^I_{sat}}{\Delta p_2} = \frac{7-11}{200-100} = -4\% \qquad (6.20a)$$

$$\frac{\Delta n_{last}}{\Delta p_2} = \frac{11-15}{200-100} = -4\% \qquad (6.20b)$$

The extent of the modifications suggested for the three variables was set to test the robustness of the model, providing at the same time realistic values and taking into account the amount of resources made available from the Basilicata Region. This is the reason why non-negligible alterations of the input lead anyway to trajectories very similar to the original ones. In the first two cases the alteration of P$_{pop}$ induces a general – though not much substantial – increase of the adoption process timings. As for p$_2$, instead, once P$_{pop}$ is defined the workload for the GPs must increase, causing the shortening of the scheduled timings for both adoption and saturation dynamics.

Being the model a linear system, it was also possible to deploy the superimposition principle, thanks to which the overall modification of a parameter depending on more variables is equal to the sum of the modifications of the single variables. Considering the three variables studied, it was possible to deploy the principle for n$_{last}$ and n$^I_{sat}$.

n$^I_{sat}$) the simultaneous variation of P$_{real}$ and p$_2$ seen before causes: $\Delta n^I_{sat} = -2,75\%$. The extent of the variations for the other two combinations is negligible.

n$_{last}$) the simultaneous variation of P$_{real}$ and M$_{med}$ seen before causes: $\Delta n_{last} = +6,5\%$. The simultaneous variation of the opposed (and equal in absolute value) forces related to M$_{med}$ and p$_2$ does not bring changes ($\Delta = 0$). The simultaneous variation of P$_{real}$ and p$_2$ causes instead: $\Delta n_{last} = -1,5\%$.

This last analysis clearly shows that the modification of p$_2$ has a more remarkable impact on the model than M$_{med}$ and P$_{real}$ for different reasons:

- $\Delta n^I_{sat} < 0$ means an earlier saturation of the patients. The increase of p$_2$ influences the result more deeply than the increase of the patients enrollable during the experimentation (P$_{real}$), since the former gives a "boost" to the system dynamics from the very beginning, and not gradually;
- $\Delta n_{last} < 0$ means a shorter time for the population to get to the final value P$_{pop}$. Also in this case, if the systems' inputs are set on higher values, it is highly likely that the experimentation timings will generally turn out as faster.

The sensitivity analysis on the inputs of the model was conducted in order to figure out preventively as many future changes of the scenario as possible [see e.g. Taguchi and Clausing, 1990; Dehnad, 2012]. As already mentioned, the population involved had to feature a good percentage of chronic patients consistent with the chronic disease chosen by the Local Healthcare Trusts for future stages of the experimentation. It is therefore likely to expect that modification to the original model will be implemented, and a new round of collaboration with GPs, specialists and patients will have to be performed.

7. CONCLUSION

The systemic development of the eHealth dynamics means the deployment of web-based ICT solutions to improve or enable the creation and the supply of high level services in the healthcare sector [e.g. Berwick & Nolan, 1998; Eng, 2004; Monteagudo & Moreno, 2006, 2007]. This is seen not only as an opportunity to work out potential solutions to unsolved problems or to overcome old and new contradictions, but also as the mean to achieve high relevant "political" targets, such as equity, quality and governance in the health management [Campbell *et al.*, 2000; Berkman *et al.*, 2002].

To this end, the introduction of the Longitudinal Electronic Healthcare Record (L-EHR) handled by the LuMiR system in the Basilicata Region pursued the main scope of figuring out a system accessible by all the subjects involved in the territorial assistance (GPs, lab analysts, nurses, pharmacists, social workers, etc.) via the implementation of a timely information infrastructure (or infostructure) for a better definition of paths of coordination and integration as well as new organizational dynamics [Rossi Mori, 2010; Tamburis *et al.*, 2012]. A proper planning of all the phases concerning the adoption plan of the LuMiR system was therefore needed, in order to deal with all the possible issues, both technical and political: this has led to the choice of a mathematical model to be set up, as optimal way to figure out all the possible feasible solutions.

The implementation of a mathematical model in the Public Health field, despite its undeniable potentialities, has to cope with a number of limitations, mostly due to the initial conditions to be defined and the data input accuracy. Other limitations may relate to the intrinsic structure of the model designed, called to provide a balance between the requested level of "predictive capacity" and the consequent level of complexity needed to achieve it. Such balance depends in great part on the issues that its implementation is called to work out [Fries, 1976, 1979; Brailsford *et al.*, 2009; Tamburis *et al.*, 2014]. Many decisions then have to be taken in terms of variables and parameters to be included during the set up of the model, based on their relative importance as well as the ways through which they could affect the accuracy of the results. The inclusion of very specific data input (e.g. peculiarities of the population analysed, demographic variables, risk factors connected to the age of the subjects studied, etc.) may imply on the one hand an increased accuracy as to the definition of possible future scenarios; on the other hand, it may generate a very complex model to be handled.

The study conducted in the Basilicata Region for the implementation of the LuMiR system tried to address all these matters, and a clear evidence raised that the shift towards innovative eHealth services requires great amounts of time and resources to be invested: this is why the unsuitability of the resources provided for the experimentation hindered its succesful deployment. The study highlighted moreover that a great gap still to be overcome is the common lack of "technology readiness" among the healthcare operators – to be intended as people's propensity to recognize and implement new technologies to achieve concrete results in both the social and working environment [Parasuraman, 2000].

Predictive Modeling as guide for Health Informatics Deployment

Similarly, especially for what concerns the first steps in the process of adoption of a new technology, the Healthcare Organizations involved are requested to acquire an as "care-driven" as "technology-driven" attitude, as first and most important requisite to cope with all the necessary efforts to bring actual innovation from the local to the national level.

Table 8. Table of variables

Variable	Description
m_0	Number of GPs enrolled per month in the first month
m_1	Number of GPs enrolled per month from the second month onward
$Med(n) = M$	Number of GPs enrolled at the n-th month
M_{med}	Total number of GPs enrolled
n_{adp}	Means the month during which the enrolment of GPs and/or patients occurs (the "nominal" enrolment is set at the beginning of n_{adp}, whilst it actually is distributed over the entire month, so that at the end of n_{adp} all GPs and/or patients are effectively "operative")
$n_{rdn} = n_{adp} + 1$	The month next to n_{adp}, where all GPs and/or patients enrolled the previous month are actually "operative"
m_{rest}	Total number of GPs enrolled in the last group
n	Generic month
n^i_{arr}	Month in which the i-th group of GPs m_1 is enrolled (with $i \geq 2$, $n^i_{arr} = i-1$)
n_{inf}	Lower limit of the of the trial stage period
n^i_{sat}	Month in which is reached the full saturation of the patients (P_{real}) enrollable from those GPs m_1 that joined the experimentation at the i-th month (with $i \geq 2$)
$n_{last} (= n^{last}_{sat})$	Month in which the total saturation of the patients (P_{pop}) is reached. Alternatively: month in which is reached the full saturation of the patients (P_{real}) enrollable from the last GPs m_1 that joined the experimentation
$n_{med} (= n^{last}_{arr})$	Month in which the total saturation of the GPs is reached. Alternatively: month in which the last group of GPs m_1 is enrolled
$n_{sat} (= n^1_{sat})$	Month in which is reached the full saturation of the patients (P_{real}) enrollable from GPs m_0
n_{sup}	Upper limit of the of the trial stage period
p_0	Number of patients enrolled per month in the first month
p_1	Number of patients enrolled per month in the second month
$p_2 = p$	Number of patients enrolled per month in the months next to the second one
$Paz(n)$	Total number of patients enrolled at the n-th month
$Paz^a(n) = P$	Number of patients enrolled at the n-th month in the running zone (saturation dynamics not considered)
$Paz^m(n)$	"Virtual" patients to be considered after the saturation of the GPs enrollers
$Paz^{MAX}(n)$	Max number of patients enrolled by the "most enrollers" GPs at the n-th month
$Paz^{MMG}(n)$	Number of patients enrolled at the n-th month by the single GP
$Paz^{rs}(n)$	"Real" patients to be considered after the saturation of the patients
$Paz^s(n)$	"Virtual" patients to be considered after the saturation of the patients
P_{pop}	Total number of citizens the joined the experimentation
P_{avg}	Average number of patients per GP in the Basilicata Region
P_{real}	Number of patients enrolled per GP during the experimentation
p_{sup}	Max number of patients that the sinle GP manages to enrol every month

continued on following page

Table 8. Continued

Variable	Description
n_{ing}	X-coordinate of the entrance intersection point between conic and admissibility domain
n_{end}	X-coordinate of the exit intersection point between conic and admissibility domain
p_{ing}	Y-coordinate of the entrance intersection point between conic and admissibility domain
p_{end}	Y-coordinate of the exit intersection point between conic and admissibility domain

N.B: all the variables introduced $\in N$, i.e. the set of the natural numbers {0,1, 2, 3. ...}

REFERENCES

Atun, R. (2004). *What are the advantages and disadvantages of restructuring a health care system to be more focused on primary care services? Health Evidence Network (HEN)*. Copenhagen: Who Regional Office for Europe.

Berkman, T., Wagner, E. H., & Grumbach, K. (2002). Improving primary care for patients with chronic illness. *Journal of the American Medical Association*.

Berry, L. L., & Seiders, K. (2003). Innovations in access to care: A patient-centered approach. *Annals of Internal Medicine, 139*(7), 568. doi:10.7326/0003-4819-139-7-200310070-00009 PMID:14530228

Berwick, D. M., & Nolan, T. W. (1998). Physicians as Leaders in Improving Health Care: A New Series in Annals of Internal Medicine. *Annals of Internal Medicine, 128*(4), 289–292. doi:10.7326/0003-4819-128-4-199802150-00008 PMID:9471932

Brailsford, S. C., Harper, P. R., Patel, B., & Pitt, M. (2009). An analysis of the academic literature on simulation and modelling in health care. *Journal of Simulation, 3*(3), 130–140. doi:10.1057/jos.2009.10

Campbell, S. M., Roland, M. O., & Buetow, S. A. (2000). Defining quality of care. *Social Science & Medicine*, 51. PMID:11072882

E. Coiera, J. I. Westbrook, J. L. Callen, & J. Aarts (Eds.). (2007) Information Technology in Health Care 2007.*Proceedings of the 3rd International Conference on Information Technology in Health Care: Socio-technical Approaches*. IOS Press.

Contenti, M., Mercurio, G., Ricci, F. L., & Serbanati, L. D. (2008). LuMIR: A Region-wide Virtual Longitudinal EHR.Proceedings of 9th International HL7 Interoperability Conference.

Contenti M., Mercurio G., Ricci F.L. & Serbanati L.D. (2010a). *Il processo di adozione del sistema LuMiR*. Deliverable progetto PreURT, n. PREURT31b_100.

Contenti, M., Mercurio, G., Ricci, F. L., & Serbanati, L. D. (2010b). LuMiR: The Region-wide EHR-S in Basilicata. *Proceedings of 13th International Congress on Medical Informatics, Medinfo 2010*. IOS Press.

Dehnad, K. (2012). *Quality control, robust design, and the Taguchi method*. Springer Science & Business Media.

Eng, T. R. (2004). Population health technologies: Emerging innovations for the health of the public. *American Journal of Preventive Medicine, 26*(3), 237–242. doi:10.1016/j.amepre.2003.12.004 PMID:15026105

Fries, B. E. (1976). Bibliography of operations research in health-care systems. *Opns Res*, *24*(5), 801–814. doi:10.1287/opre.24.5.801

Fries, B. E. (1979). Bibliography of operations research in health-care systems: An update. *Opns Res*, *27*(2), 408–419. doi:10.1287/opre.27.2.408 PMID:10297447

Geroski, P. A. (2000). Models of technology diffusion. *Research Policy*, *29*(4-5), 603–625. doi:10.1016/S0048-7333(99)00092-X

Il Progetto, L. U. M. I. R. (n.d.). Retrieved on 01/07/2015 at: http://www.sanitaelettronica.cnr.it/lumir/

Larma, C., & Basil, V. R. (2003). Iterative and Incremental Development: A Brief. *History & Computing*, *36*(6).

Maceratini, R., & Ricci, F. L. (2000). *Il medico on-line. Manuale di informatica medica*. Verduci, Editore.

McKendrick, A. G. (1926). Applications of mathematics to medical problems. *Proceedings of the Edinburgh Mathematical Society*, *14*, 98–130.

Monteagudo, J. L. (2006). *eHealth ERA. Priority Cluster Topic 2, focus on eHealth for Patient Empowerment*. Retrieved on 02/07/2015 at: http://www.ehealth-era.org/documents/

Monteagudo, J. L., & Moreno, O. (2007). *Report on Priority Topic Cluster two and recommendations - Patient Empowerment*. Deliverable D2.5, Project eHealth ERA - Towards the Establishment of a European Research Area. Retrieved on 01/07/2015 at: http://www.ehealth-era.org/documents/eH-ERA_D2.5_Patient_Empowerment_Final_31-03-2007_revised.pdf

Morosini, P. (2004). *Indicatori in valutazione e miglioramento della qualità professionale*. Istituto Superiore di Sanità.

Parasuraman, A. (2000). Technology Readiness Index (TRI): A Multiple Item Scale to Measure Readiness to Embrace New Technologies. *Journal of Service Research*, *2*(4), 307–320. doi:10.1177/109467050024001

Petroni, G. (2010). *Il trasferimento tecnologico*. Egea.

Pinna Pintor P. (2005). La qualità delle cure vista dal paziente. *QA*, *16*(3).

Rossi Mori, A. (2010). La gestione elettronica della documentazione clinica. In F. Di Resta & B. Ferraris Di Celle (Eds.), *Il Fascicolo Sanitario Elettronico*. Roma: Edisef.

Star L., & Moghadas S.M. (2010). *The Role of Mathematical Modelling in Public Health Planning and Decision Making*. Purple Paper. National Collaborative Center for Infectious Diseases. Issue n.22.

Taguchi, G., & Clausing, D. (1990). Robust quality. *Harvard Business Review*, *68*(1), 65–75.

Tamburis, O., Mangia, M., Contenti, M., Mercurio, G., & Rossi Mori, A. (2012). The LITIS Conceptual Framework: Measuring eHealth Readiness and Adoption Dynamics across the Healthcare Organizations. [Springer]. *Health Technology*, *2*(2), 97–112. doi:10.1007/s12553-012-0024-5

Tamburis, O., Ricci, F. L., & Pecoraro, F. (2014). A Mathematical Model to Plan the Adoption of EHR Systems. In J. Wang (Ed.), *EBAO – Encyclopedia of Business Analytics and Optimization*, (pp. 14-29). IGI-Global. doi:10.4018/978-1-4666-5202-6.ch002

TSE, Tavolo di sanità Elettronica. (2006). *La strategia architetturale per l'eHealth*. Author.

TSE, Tavolo di sanità Elettronica. (2010). *Specifiche tecniche per la creazione del "Documento di Referto" secondo lo standard HL7-CDA*. Author.

Wagner, E. H. (2004). Chronic disease care. *BMJ (Clinical Research Ed.)*, 328. PMID:14739164

WHO. (1978). *Alma-Ata 1978: primary health care*. Geneva: World Health Organisation.

Chapter 9
Analytics Overuse in Advertising and Promotion Budget Forecasting

Burçin Güçlü
Universitat Ramon LLull, Spain

Miguel-Ángel Canela
University of Navarra, Spain

ABSTRACT

Several studies have recently raised a common concern in the field of management, which is the overspending in marketing activities. In this paper, we propose and empirically test that overspending in marketing investments is an unfortunate outcome of information overload, in a sense that managers who confront too many risk informants in their decision environment tend to overinvest in marketing activities due to the overemphasis on the environmental risk. In a longitudinal experiment, where we manipulated the amount of information through marketing analytics, we demonstrate that firms employing simple marketing analytics are less prone to increase their marketing expenditures due to the fear of losing customers, and have a lower expectancy that their competitors will increase their brand-level advertising and promotional expenditures, compared to firms using a combination of simple and complex marketing analytics. Moreover, we demonstrate that firms employing simple marketing analytics keep their overall marketing spending at a lower level, and spend less in brand-level marketing, especially in promotional activities, compared to when using a combination of simple and complex marketing analytics.

Procter & Gamble is the biggest advertiser in the US, the world's biggest advertising market, and its decisions influence those of other big spenders. In 2010, P&G spent $3.2bn in America, almost half as much again as second placed General Motors. (Financial Times, March 7th 2012)

Efficient market theory suggests that marketing behavior, on average, will be pushed toward optimal behavior or the enterprise will fail. (Lilien 1979)

DOI: 10.4018/978-1-5225-0654-6.ch009

INTRODUCTION

A widely recognized phenomenon is that firms overspend in marketing activities (Hanssens et al., 2001; Sethuraman et al., 2011), meaning that their actual marketing expenditures overpass their forecasted budget driven by normative models (Dekimpe et al., 2007). Although several advances have been made to address potential drivers of suboptimal investment decisions in the context of marketing strategy (Joseph and Richardson, 2002; Lilien, 2011; Mintz, 2012; Mintz & Currim, 2013), there is little understanding of what drives, specifically, overspending in marketing investments.

To the best of our knowledge, formal models of overspending in the literature overemphasize economic effectiveness (Srinivasan et al., 2011), in a sense that they integrate econometric concepts of synergy, carryover and time effects in assessing the effectiveness of marketing investments (Shankar, 2008). In order to explain why firms cannot sustain economic effectiveness in marketing expenditures, scholars from diverse disciplines mainly follow a rational approach by attributing the persistence of suboptimal investment decisions to managers' strategic considerations (Rapoport & Chammah, 1965; Thisse & Vives, 1988), lack of financial accountability (Mintz, 2012; Mintz & Currim, 2013), exposure to rigid incentive systems (Jensen & Meckling, 1976).

Although the prior literature provides crucial guidelines to take an initial step for this research, it is subject to several shortcomings. First of all, overspending does not perish when strategic considerations die out with decreased market concentration (Naik & Raman, 2003). Second, the level of analysis is not consistent among studies. For instance, many studies take into account the suboptimal decisions of one individual, mainly of the CEO, in order to associate a manager's suboptimal decisions with organizational outcomes (Hirshleifer et al., 2012; Malmendier & Tate, 2005). On the other hand, there are also studies that argue that the impact of an individual's suboptimal decision can be observed at the organizational level, regardless of the level of the individual (Dutton & Jackson, 1987). The lack of significant work on the topic, from our perspective, pertains to this divergence on the level of analysis.

The primary objective of the current study is to empirically test a behavioral model of overspending in marketing activities in a competitive context stripped off from incentive motives, where the information necessary to assess the economic effectiveness of investment decisions is revealed through the market research tools. To be more specific, controlling for competitive dynamics and lack of financial metrics, our goal is to show that overspending in marketing investments is an unfortunate outcome of the information overload, in a sense that managers who confront too many risk informants in their decision environment tend to overinvest in marketing activities because they overestimate the environmental risk on the demand side.

We conducted a longitudinal market experiment using StratSim (Deighan et al., 2006), a management simulation game, in which we manipulated the availability of market research tools in order to observe how market information disclosed in different levels of restrictions alters investments in marketing mix activities. We demonstrated that firms employing simple marketing analytics are less prone to increase their marketing expenditures due to the fear of losing customers, and have a lower expectancy that their competitors will increase their brand-level advertising and promotional expenditures, compared to firms using a combination of simple and complex marketing analytics. We also demonstrated that firms employing simple marketing analytics keep their overall marketing spending at a lower level, and spend less in brand-level marketing, especially in promotional activities, compared to when using a combination of simple and complex marketing analytics.

Our findings, overall, suggest that the use of simpler market research tools results in less perceived risk from the demand side of the market and less competitive rivalry in marketing expenditures, and efficient use of marketing resources. The use of all market research tools available, in contrast, leads to an alarmist action against the competitive rivalry, due to high degree of perceived risk of losing customers, in which firms respond by substantially increasing their marketing expenditures. Our research contributes to the literature on overspending by revealing new insights and fostering further research on the matter. We believe that these findings offer important implications for practitioners, as well as for researchers in the field of strategic management, decision analysis and cognitive science. Thus, we emphasize that greater sensitivity to these insights is needed for the sake of employing marketing analytics optimally in order to improve resource allocation decisions.

LITERATURE OVERVIEW

This section provides a review of the existing literature on suboptimal spending decisions. There are three streams of research that address suboptimal spending decisions, each one of them attributing suboptimal spending decisions to a) strategic considerations, b) lack of financial accountability and c) incentive system, adopting a rational perspective. We now discuss these streams in greater detail:

Strategic Interactions

This stream of research argues that the most important driver of marketing overspending is managers' strategic considerations. According to this view, managers are aware of the fact that they are investing a suboptimal (i.e. not profit-maximizing) amount in marketing, but fear from being the first ones to be hurt by their competitors if they reduce their spending to the optimal amount, following customers steering to competitors. This behavior is captured by the well-known prisoner's dilemma game, which predicts that managers rationally equilibrate at a high level of spending, which would not maximize their profits, because they expect that they will be harmed by their competitors if they reduce their spending to a profit maximizing level (Axelrod, 1984). Consequently, they result in higher level of spending with lower payoffs. In the marketing literature, this type of behavior has been studied within different topics, such as advertising budgeting (Pruyn & Riezebos, 2001), multichannel customer management (Neslin & Shankar, 2009) and brand equity (Rusetski, 2012). The overall finding of these aforementioned studies confirms the prisoner's dilemma argument, indicating that managers' failure to cooperate on the optimal level of spending due to the fear of competition gravitate them to spending levels with suboptimal payoff.

Lack of Financial Accountability

This stream of research claims suggests that managers make suboptimal marketing decisions because they do not possess adequate marketing tools and/or metrics that quantify the optimal allocation of resources (for a recent review, see Mintz & Currim, 2013). Marketing accountability has been of interest to many academicians and practitioners over the last decades, not only because it is a crucial matter for resource allocation decisions, but also a vital one for the reputation of marketing as an academic discipline, as well as for marketing department's role in practice (Rust et al., 2004). For instance, anecdotal evidence suggests that practitioners mostly blame marketing managers for the lack of financial accountability, criticizing their ongoing belief that marketing simply works well without the need to quantify (Financial Times, January 26th 2009). From this standpoint, marketing managers would be able to make optimal investment in marketing if they had adequate analytics to calculate the optimal amount of investment. Thus, the decision making process is rational.

Cash Flow Behavior

This stream of research argues that managers overspend in marketing efforts for the sake of boosting the operational expenses associated with their incentive system. Jensen [Jensen, (1986), p. 323] defines free cash flow as "cash flow in excess of that required funding all projects that have positive net present value when discounted at the relevant cost of capital." When free cash flow is present and the compensation system fails to align managers' interests with shareholders', the typical manager-shareholder agency problem arises (Vogt, 1994), such that managers have a tendency to commonly overinvest in operations in order to capture the benefits of increased firm size through reinvestment (Jensen & Meckling, 1976), while shareholders prefer dividends over reinvestment in order to clear out free cash flow (Lang & Litzenberger, 1989). Several factors can trigger this behavior, such as a metric-based compensation system which incentives marketing executives with respect to the budget invested into marketing activities (Jensen, 1986), degree of managerial ownership (Joseph & Richardson, 2002), and abundance of free cash flow in late stages of the product cycle (Thorelli & Burnett, 1981). Consequently, overspending is described as an unfortunate outcome of managers' rational choice to overstate their contribution to firm size.

THEORY

In our theory, we propose that overspending in marketing efforts is the outcome of an alarmist action triggered by the use of too many informants (i.e. business analytics) in risky managerial decisions. To be more specific, in our theory, the environmental risk triggered by the competitive rivalry is perceived as more gradual when the market information is disclosed through too many business analytics, and managers become more risk-averse when considering the welfare costs if they fail to respond to the competitive rivalry by exceeding competitors' marketing spending. In this section, we explain our conceptual framework in detail.

A major driver of advertising intensity is the advertising elasticity of demand (Cabral, 2000). The literature on the effectiveness of advertising has long acknowledged that a firm which can influence the demand for its product by advertising will, by any means, allocate an advertising budget, such that the increase in gross revenue resulting from a one dollar increase in advertising expenditure will match the regular elasticity of demand for the firm's product (Dorfman & Steiner, 1954). The advertising elasticity for demand is subject to gradual changes across consumer segments and product categories (Steenkamp et al., 2005), as well as over the product life cycle (Tellis & Fornell, 1988). Consequently, in order to achieve good financial performance, managers are expected to monitor changes on the demand side, initiate necessary marketing activities on time to accommodate to these changes, and to estimate the optimal allocation of marketing resources with given information.

The competitive rivalry is embedded in the allocation of marketing resources because of the significance of reaching the demand side of the market. Steenkamp and his colleagues (2005) suggest that the effectiveness of advertising is crucial for the financial performance, to the extent that any competitive threat to the advertising effectiveness can motivate managers to react to competitors' advertising attacks in order to avoid the welfare cost due to the loss of customers on the demand side. In fact, an evident issue in advertising attacks is that managers' response to this competitive rivalry by intuitively increasing their own spending is perceived as a common practice (Keil et al. 2001). Consequently, the allocation of marketing resources is very responsive to the competitive rivalry in order not to run the risk of losing customers.

The optimal allocation of resources in marketing is not only plagued by the competitive rivalry, but also embeds high risks. To be more specific, the optimal allocation of resources in marketing is a context of decision making under information competencies, where the decision maker knows the probabilities and outcomes of each alternative action with respect to the available information. Taking into consideration the basic tenet in the Neo-classical economics, that more information is better (Alchian & Demsetz, 1972), it is feasible to calculate the only optimal response and to minimize the environmental risk through the acquisition of more information.

The risk perception is proven to vary with respect to the amount of informants in the decision environment, contrary to the conventional economic theory that would predict greater reassurance. To be more specific, Viscusi (1997) demonstrated that the receipt of risk information through multiple sources causes differences in risk information, generates alarmist actions that are disproportionate to the magnitude of the actual risk, and often leads managers to have quite different risk perceptions than others. When considering the famous quotation by Little (1970), that managers hardly benefit from decision support systems, what drives suboptimal investment decisions might not be the failure of these tools per se, but managers' failure to benefit from these tools when there are too many of them.

Recent studies concerned with experts' risk perceptions demonstrated that the external representations of risk that are adapted to the human cognitive system improved risk communication in diverse fields and are privileged for shared decision making (for a recent review, see Gigerenzer, 2008). For this reason, experts in the field emphasize simple decision making mechanisms in harmony with their specific decision environments, which enable fast and frugal decision making yielding better outcomes (Goldstein & Gigerenzer, 2002; Little, 1970). This issue of adaptability is in accordance with bounded rationality (Simon, 1955; Simon, 1979), which emphasizes that managers lack economic rationality because their cognitive shortcuts do not allow them to process all the information available in their decision context. Consequently, they enroll into a "satisficing" behavior, where they selectively use the cues in their decision environment to come up with an "acceptably optimal" solution.

As a result of the argumentation of our theory, we expect that the restricted access to simple management tools, which help marketing managers conduct market research, will reduce the problem of overspending in brand-level marketing activities. To be more specific, the simplicity will help them perceive the environmental risk more efficiently, and the use of limited number of management tools will prevent them from overestimating the environmental risk. Thus, they will not fall prey to the alarmist behavior by overspending in marketing activities.

METHOD AND MATERIALS

Method

We examined how the use of market research tools impacts on individuals' risk perception and their beliefs about their competitors' actions within StratSim (Deighan et al., 2006), a management simulation game, in order to replicate the nature of managerial decision making in marketing. Bearing in mind that studying managers' beliefs as they occur in the field would hardly be feasible, StratSim provided a real setting, where participants (i.e. managers) enroll in management team debates, and make strategic decisions in the face of risk.

In particular, StratSim by Interpretive Software, Inc. is a simulation game, specifically based on marketing decisions in the automotive industry. The participants are assigned to teams representing different companies, and the team performance is evaluated with respect to three dimensions - team, their competitors and the industry evolution - at each round corresponding to a yearly decision. Through the game, teams make decisions concerning product development, marketing, manufacturing, distribution and financing using tools provided by the simulation. Input into the game is industry reports and market analyses to provide information for decision makers.

In StratSim, aggregate marketing expenditures comprise of brand level and corporate marketing expenditures. Brand-level marketing expenditures include product advertising and promotion. Product advertising, for instance, plays an important role in establishing vehicle awareness and shaping consumers' perceptions of products. In the simulation, firms are responsible for setting an advertising budget and theme for the focal product(s). The majority of the budget is spent on media buys, while the remainder on the creative is spent on input and theme. The theme emphasizes one of the primary characteristics of the vehicle (i.e. performance, interior, styling, safety, or quality). Brand-level promotional budgets, on the other hand, include special incentive programs and general promotional activities. The purpose of special incentive programs is to move product during slower periods of demand. The last but not the least, corporate advertising budgets are set on a regional basis. These funds are spent on generating a corporate identity in support of the product advertising. A public relations budget is also set to support publicity events for the firm, corporate, and investor relations.

Sample

Our empirical study took place in the Erasmus School of Economics, Erasmus University of Rotterdam, the Netherlands, where StratSim is used as a significant part of FEM11028 Seminar in Marketing Strategy, which is a key seminar in their Master in Marketing program accounting for 12 ECTS out of 60. 114 full-time master students, who have already completed a credible amount of courses in marketing, were candidates to participate in our study. Among 114 full-time master students, 75 participants were randomly assigned to 10 teams of 6-8 people, with each 5 teams comprising a StratSim (automotive) industry, which develops uniquely based on how the competitors interact, which products are introduced, and how these products are supported.

Experimental Conditions

We modified the normal procedure of the game by altering the availability of market research tools across rounds, such that firms could either access a) simple market research tools alone, or b) a combination of simple and complex market research tools in a given round. Consequently, two experimental conditions were created, and each experimental condition was assigned to a StratSim industry. Table 1 presents the experimental conditions.

Market Research Tools

The market research tools employed during the experiment were conjoint analysis, perceptual maps, focus groups and concept test, the former two corresponding to complex ones, and the latter two corresponding to simple ones. The participants basically had the following information extracted from the simulation game manual (Deighan et al., 2006) for each tool:

- **Conjoint Analysis:** Conjoint analysis estimates a consumer's underlying choice structure, and provides important insights about what is most important to consumers and what particular attributes they prefer. Data for estimating consumers' underlying choice structures is gathered from surveys where consumers are asked to make trade-offs among various attributes.
- **Perceptual Maps:** The perceptual mapping tool uses a multi-dimensional scaling technique to position vehicle brands in a two-dimensional space, an in a cluster analysis, based on how similar the products are in consumers' perception, and delivers an understanding of competition from customers' point of view.
- **Focus Group:** A focus group is a form of qualitative research, where six to ten people gather and enroll into a moderated discussion on how they feel about particular product/service attributes, how they make purchase decisions, or anything else that may be valuable for the company from marketing perspective. This tool gathers descriptive measurements about the attractiveness of various initiatives to be employed by marketing experts.

Table 1. Experimental manipulations

Round	Industry 1	Industry 2
R1	SIMPLE TOOLS ONLY	ALL TOOLS
R2	SIMPLE TOOLS ONLY	ALL TOOLS
R3	SIMPLE TOOLS ONLY	ALL TOOLS
R4	SIMPLE TOOLS ONLY	ALL TOOLS
R5	ALL TOOLS	SIMPLE TOOLS ONLY
R6	ALL TOOLS	SIMPLE TOOLS ONLY
R7	ALL TOOLS	SIMPLE TOOLS ONLY
R8	ALL TOOLS	SIMPLE TOOLS ONLY

- **Concept Tests:** Concept testing is and exploratory method which grants early feedback on a potential product before the development cycle begins, and data for this tool comes from surveys and/or interviews with consumers on how they feel about a new concept.

STUDY 1

In Study 1, conducted in the beginning of the experiment, we observe beliefs and expectancies regarding the perceived risk on the demand side and expectations about competitors' expenditures. The purpose of this study is to demonstrate that the behavioral processes that lead to overspending in brand-level marketing activities are grounded in individual-level.

Hypotheses

In line with our theory, we provide our hypotheses as follows. First, we expect that firms employing simple market research tools will have less tendency to increase their spending due to the fear of losing customers, compared to those using all market research tools available, since firms employing simple market research tools alone will downgrade the risk of losing customers if they do not keep their brand-level advertising and promotional expenditures high, compared to firms employing all market research tools available.

H1: Firms employing simple market research tools will be less prone to increase their marketing expenditures due to the fear of losing customers, compared to those using all market research tools available.

Second, we expect that firms employing simple market research tools only will downgrade their competitors' increase in their brand-level advertising and promotional expenditures, compared to firms employing all market research tools available because they will expect lower competitive rivalry due to lower perception of risk regarding the market dynamics (i.e. demand side).

H2: Firms employing simple market research tools only will downgrade their competitors' increase in their brand-level advertising and promotional expenditures, compared to firms employing all market research tools available.

Procedure

We conducted surveys among the participants at the end of each seven actual round of the game (i.e. excluding the practice round and the last round). The purpose of these surveys was to measure participants' perceived degree of risk and beliefs about their competitors' actions. Each survey was delivered once the participants submitted their decisions to the simulation, and collected after they have completed. There was no time restriction to fill out the surveys, but the students completed them in a reasonable time interval, which is around ten minutes.

Although we measured participants' perceived degree of risk and beliefs about their competitors' actions at each round, we mainly focused on data collected from the first round of the game in Study 1. The first round of the game was the first real round, where participants made managerial decisions using market research tools for the first time. Thus, this initial round is supposed to reveal the impact of information overload on their alarmist action, and the differences in their perceived degree of risk and beliefs about their competitors' actions with respect to their alarmist tendencies. In addition to that, the survey conducted in this round was the first time that the participants encountered the survey questions. Consequently, the participants were expected to report their perceived degree of risk and beliefs about their competitors' actions with highest accuracy:

- **Pretesting:** We followed a conventional pretesting procedure: An initial draft of the survey was prepared one week prior to the experimental sessions, and the teaching team (i.e. the course instructor and three teaching assistants) revised this draft over the week. We eliminated unnecessary questions, added clarification sentences and changed the wording of some questions in order to avoid confusion.
- **Data Gathering:** As we desired that each participant reported his/her own proper belief about what their competitors will do, we did not allow the participants to communicate among each other while filling out the questionnaire. Only the aforementioned research team was allowed to resolve participants' doubts. The surveys circulated in print, and the answers are recorded to an Excel sheet after the first round.
- **Response:** Four participants were missing in this round, which yielded us 71 participants for the survey. We achieved high response rate from these participants for each question: 70 participants out of 71 answered the question regarding the tendency to increase marketing spending due to the fear of losing customers, and 71 participants out of 71 answered the question regarding the expected increase in competitors' brand-level advertising and promotional spending. The students were fairly incentivized to complete the surveys because the surveys constituted 10% of their overall grade. The surveys were not graded in terms of content (as there was no correct answer for any question), but were graded based on completeness.

For the sake of our theory, we were mainly interested in participants' tendency to increase their marketing spending if they were to confront the risk of losing customers. To be more specific, participants were expected to believe that they had to have high marketing expenditures in order for their products to be perceived good quality by their customers, yet their belief on to what extent they would increase their expenditures to satisfy this could vary with respect to the experimental conditions. Thus, in the first round of the survey, participants were asked "Please indicate, on a scale of -2 *(I would significantly decrease my spending)* to 2 *(I would significantly increase my spending)*, to what extent would you increase or decrease your spending level due to each of the following factors," and "Reputational Concerns (If we spend less, consumers may perceive us poorly)" was listed.

We were also interested in participants' beliefs about their competitors' spending in brand-level advertising and promotional activities. To be more specific, based upon the anecdotal evidence, participants were expected to believe that competitors will increase their brand-level advertising and promotional expenditures by round, yet their belief on to what extent their competitors would increase their expenditures could vary with respect to the experimental conditions. Thus, in the first round of the survey, participants were asked "Regarding your beliefs about your competitors, on a scale of -2 *(They will spend much less)* to 2 *(They will spend much more)*, rate how you think your competitors will behave in the next round, compared to the current round," and were listed below the spending decisions of interest, "Advertising" and "Promotion."

Modeling

Group Means

In each condition, we mainly looked at the differences in group means regarding the tendency to increase marketing spending due to the fear of losing customers, and expected increase in competitors' their brand-level advertising and promotional expenditures.

- **MEAN_SIMPLE_H1:** Mean value of the tendency to increase marketing spending due to the fear of losing customers in simple tools availability condition,
- **MEAN_ALL_H1:** Mean value of the tendency to increase marketing spending due to the fear of losing customers in all tools availability condition,
- **MEAN_SIMPLE_H2a:** Mean value of the expected increase in competitors' brand-level advertising expenditures in simple tools availability condition,
- **MEAN_ALL_H2a:** Mean value of the expected increase in competitors' brand-level advertising expenditures in all tools availability condition.
- **MEAN_SIMPLE_H2b:** Mean value of the expected increase in competitors' brand-level promotional expenditures in simple tools availability condition,
- **MEAN_ALL_H2b:** Mean value of the expected increase in competitors' brand-level promotional expenditures in all tools availability condition.

Estimation

We tested the significance of the differences in group means using two-sample, one-sided parametric t-tests with unequal variances. So, the null hypotheses were:

- MEAN_SIMPLE_H1 < MEAN_ALL_H1
- MEAN_SIMPLE_H2a < MEAN_ALL_H2a
- MEAN_SIMPLE_H2b < MEAN_ALL_H2b

RESULTS

Table 2 summarizes the results of our survey study. In the first round of the game, we measured their tendency to increase their marketing spending taking into account their firm might be perceived poorly otherwise. The mean response from 70 participants was 0.700, indicating a tendency to increase their marketing spending taking into account their firm might be perceived poorly otherwise. The mean response from 34 participants in simple tools only condition was 0.529, while the mean response from 36 participants in all tools availability condition was 0.861, indicating differences in tendencies to increase their marketing spending taking into account their firm might be perceived poorly otherwise. The corresponding t-test indicated that the difference in group means was significant (one-sided p=0.047).

In addition to that, we also measured their beliefs about how their competitors will behave in the next round compared to the current round. The mean response from 71 participants was 0.761 for brand-level advertising and 0.662 for promotions, indicating an expected increase in competitors' brand-level

Table 2. Survey results

Sample	H1	H2a	H2b
Mean	0.700	0.761	0.662
Standard Deviation	0.823	0.948	1.041
Observations	70	71	71
Condition	**H1**	**H2a**	**H2b**
Simple Tools Only (SIMPLE)			
Mean	0.529	0.486	0.171
Standard Deviation	0.896	0.818	0.923
Observations	34	35	35
All Tools (ALL)			
Mean	0.861	1.028	1.139
Standard Deviation	0.723	1.000	0.931
Observations	36	36	36
Difference in means	**-0.332**	**-0.542**	**-0.967**
T	**-1.699**	**-2.504**	**-4.398**
P (two-sided)	**0.094**	**0.015**	**0.000**
P (one-sided)	**0.047**	**0.008**	**0.000**

advertising and promotional expenditures. The mean response from 35 participants in simple tools only condition was 0.486 for brand-level advertising and 0.171 for promotions, while the mean response from 36 participants in all tools availability condition was 1.028 for brand-level advertising and 1.139 for promotions, indicating gradual differences in expected increases in competitors' brand-level advertising and promotional expenditures. The corresponding t-tests indicated that the differences in group means were significant for both brand-level advertising expenditure (one-sided p=0.008) and brand-level promotional expenditure (one-sided p=0.000).

STUDY 2

In Study 2 that we conducted over the simulation game, we look at the spending decisions concerning the aggregate marketing, brand-level marketing, brand-level advertising and brand-level promotions. As we have demonstrated in the previous study that the behavioral processes that lead to overspending in brand-level marketing activities are grounded in individual-level, the purpose of the current study is to demonstrate that these behavioral tendencies have firm-level consequences in the long-run.

Hypotheses

First, we expect that firms employing simple market research tools only will have lower aggregate marketing expenditure compared to when they have all market research tools available because, when using simple market research tools alone, firms will be less likely to enroll into an alarmist behavior against competitive threats and aggressive marketing rivalry through increasing their marketing expenditures.

H3: Firms employing simple market research tools only will have lower aggregate marketing expenditure compared to when they have all market research tools available.

Second, we expect that firms employing simple market research tools only will have lower brand-level marketing expenditure compared to when they have all market research tools available because, when using simple market research tools alone, firms will be less likely to enroll into an alarmist behavior against competitive threats and aggressive marketing rivalry through increasing their brand-level marketing expenditures. To be more specific, we expect the aforementioned alarmist action will be valid especially for brand-level marketing efforts, but not for marketing at corporate level because brand-level marketing efforts aim customers and thus the demand side of the market while marketing efforts at corporate level aim investors.

H4: Firms employing simple market research tools only will have lower brand-level marketing expenditure compared to when they have all market research tools available.

Third, we expect that firms employing simple market research tools only will have lower brand-level advertising expenditure and brand-level promotional expenditure compared to when they have all market research tools available because, when using simple market research tools alone, firms will be less likely to enroll into an alarmist behavior against competitive threats and aggressive marketing rivalry through increasing their brand-level advertising and promotional expenditures separately. To be more specific, we expect the aforementioned alarmist action will be valid especially for brand-level marketing efforts, but also for brand-level advertising and brand-level promotional expenditures separately because both activities aim customers, and thus the demand side of the market.

H5a: Firms employing simple market research tools only will have lower brand-level advertising expenditure compared to when they have all market research tools available.
H5b: Firms employing simple market research tools only will have lower brand-level promotional expenditure compared to when they have all market research tools available.

Procedures

In this section, we first introduce the game procedure, which is a standard, computerized setting created by Interpretive Simulations, Inc. for groups to compete against each other. For the purpose of conducting a rigorous study, we followed up with several additional procedures to improve participants' knowledge about the game, and to enhance further data collection.

- **Game Procedure:** The two StratSim industries shared the same parameter setting, were thus identical at the start of the simulation, and were run independently in different sessions. The game was played over nine rounds, and the team decisions were made after analyzing the previous period's results, as well as using market research tools in the current period. Firms are managed by participants in a marketing strategy course whose grades depend on their firms' profit at the end of nine rounds. For the sake of good performance, each firm needed to collect market information using available market research tools (see Market Research Tools), and make key marketing (e.g. pricing and advertising spending) and innovation (new product launching, upgrading, entering into new categories) decisions based upon the market information gathered.

- **Additional Procedures:** In order to guarantee that participants were sufficiently knowledgeable about the game, they attended two compulsory 3-hour class sessions and played one practice round before the actual game started. The two compulsory 3-hour sessions, for instance, debriefed students about the purpose of the game, which is to expose participants to the vital importance of marketing intelligence in strategic marketing decisions. Following the two compulsory three-hour sessions, the practice round helped participants get used to the simulation procedure and software. To be more specific, participants were told that the practice round was designed exactly the same as their first real round, meaning that all firms had access to the exact same market research tools they would have in the first real round, and that they were free to use the same information in the first real round. During the practice round, the course instructor repeatedly alerted participants for the value of making evidence-based strategic marketing decisions.

For the sake of ensuring that participants were proficient enough to make use of the market research tools, they were required to deliver one short essay per each tool, once every two weeks, where they specified how they define the focal market research tool, what advantages/disadvantages are identified by practitioners, and most importantly, they had to report an experience when they employed it in the simulation. These essays were regularly examined and graded in order to ensure that participants are comfortable with the tools.

Modeling

In this section, we provide how we measure explanatory and response variables and control factors, and estimate models.

Variables

In this section, we explain how we measured explanatory and response variables and control factors.

- Dependent Variables
  - We observed firms' decisions concerning aggregate spending in marketing activities (sum of brand-level and corporate marketing expenditures), aggregate spending at brand level, and spending in brand advertising and promotion separately. At each round, the participants make product decisions (i.e. launch, upgrade, etc.) and then set their marketing budget corresponding to their product strategy. These decisions involve products from different vehicle classes (Economy, Family, Luxury, Sports, Minivan, Truck and Utility), and consumers from different segments (Value Seekers, Families, Singles, High Income and Enterprisers), and grant firms diverse portfolios. We model decisions concerning marketing expenditures using the following variables:
    - **SPMARKETING$_{i,t}$:** Sum of brand-level and corporate marketing expenditures of firm i at time t, in million dollars;

- **SPBRANDMKTG$_{i,t}$**: Sum of brand-level marketing expenditure of firm *i* at time *t*, in million dollars;
        - **SPBRANDADV$_{i,t}$**: Brand-level advertising expenditure of firm *i* at time *t*, in million dollars;
        - **SPBRANDPROM$_{i,t}$**: Brand-level promotional expenditure of firm *i* at time *t*, in million dollars.
- Independent Variables
    - We explain the dependent variable using tool manipulation, which are our main interest:
        - **SIMPLE$_{i,t}$**: Dummy variable equal to 1 if firm *i* employed simple market research tools at time *t* and 0 otherwise;
- Control Variables
    - In the analyses, we control for time, as well as for firm (product strategy) and industry characteristics (competition) bearing in mind that these factors are available to the participants in the simulation. An important aspect of control variables is the temporal consistency because decisions for the next round are made in the current round. For this reason, we lagged industry characteristics in order to capture the conditions that prevailed at the time firms made their decisions regarding marketing expenditures.

First of all, we expect that there are linear and quadratic time trends because firms tend to invest more in marketing activities by time (Joshi and Hanssens, 2010), but they reduce the inertia of their marketing spending once they notice that the marginal effect of marketing spending wears out (Parsons, 1975; Tellis, 2007). Thus, we include a time trend term ROUND, which corresponds to a one-year period in the simulation game, and a quadratic-in-ROUND (ROUNDSQ) term, which captures non-linear time trend. Overall, the inclusion of these variables is common in the literature because it provides a parsimonious way to capture temporal effects (Manchanda et al., 2008).

Second, we include one-lagged spending variables for each spending model because spending decisions can be based upon reference points. For instance, Ludvigson (2004) one-lagged dependent variables as controls in modeling consumer spending because he proposes that one-lagged dependent variables are baseline indicators to predict current period's spending. For this reason, we include SPMARKETINGi,t-1, SPBRANDMKTGi,t-1, SPBRANDADVi,t-1 and SPBRANDPROMi,t-1 as baseline indicators for the corresponding decision models.

Third, we expect that the competition will be an important factor affecting marketing expenditures. Strict emphasis on competition fosters overspending in marketing efforts, in a sense that managers asymmetrically increase their level of marketing spending in order to generate more profits in case their competitors keep their level of spending constantly low (Armstrong & Collopy, 1996; Kalra & Soberman, 2008). The participants were aware of the competitive pressure because the simulation output disclosed spending decisions at industry-level prior to the current simulation period, as well as values of and changes in market shares corresponding to their products at each round. For this reason, we initially included COMPETITION$_{i,t-1}$ variable driven by Herfindahl index in our models to control for industry-specific competition effects (Lee & Grewal, 2004), yet the change of scale in this variable did not allow us to control for competitive dynamics in spending models. Danaher, Bonfer and Dhar (2008) propose that competitive "clutter" is dependent on the number of competitors and total amount of advertising by the competing firms, and Montgomery and Wernerfelt (1988) suggest that a firm's spending per market tries to match with industry competitive spending. Thus, we justify the use of an industry-level spending to account for the competition. As a result, we introduced industry-level variables of competitive spending, computed by the highest spending of each industry for the corresponding decision as the competitive baseline variable upon which firms will set their spending levels with respect to the perceived degree of competition. A similar control for the same purpose has also been used in Christen and Sarvary (2007). Thus, we included the highest spending within industries for each decision, $COMPSPMARKETING_{i,t-1}$, $COMPSPBRANDMKTG_{i,t-1}$, $COMPSPBRANDADV_{i,t-1}$ and $COMPSPBRANDPROM_{i,t-1}$ as controls.

The last but not the least, we expect that number of product launches will increase marketing expenditures at brand level. To be more specific, once firms make the decision to launch products, they determine the marketing budget associated with these products in order to communicate the properties of the new product to consumers. Thus, we include $LAUNCH_{i,t}$ in spending models as control:

- **ROUND:** Time variable to capture the linear time trend;
- **ROUNDSQ:** Time variable to capture the quadratic time trend;
- **$SPMARKETING_{i,t-1}$:** Sum of brand-level and corporate marketing expenditures of firm i at time $t-1$, in million dollars;
- **$SPBRANDMKTG_{i,t-1}$:** Sum of brand-level marketing expenditure of firm i at time $t-1$, in million dollars;
- **$SPBRANDADV_{i,t-1}$:** Brand-level advertising expenditure of firm i at time t, in million dollars;
- **$SPBRANDPROM_{i,t-1}$:** Brand-level promotional expenditure of firm i at time t, in million dollars;
- **$COMPSPMARKETING_{i,t-1}$:** Highest brand-level and corporate marketing expenditure in firm i's industry at time t, in million dollars;
- **$COMPSPBRANDMKTG_{i,t-1}$:** Highest brand-level marketing expenditure in firm i's industry at time t, in million dollars;
- **$COMPSPBRANDADV_{i,t-1}$:** Highest brand-level advertising expenditure in firm i's industry at time t, in million dollars;
- **$COMPSPBRANDPROM_{i,t-1}$:** Highest brand-level promotional expenditure in firm i's industry at time t, in million dollars;
- **$LAUNCH_{i,t}$:** Number of product launches by firm i at time t.

Table 3. provides the descriptive statistics overall.

For the sake of the experiment, we also present the descriptive statistics concerning the dependent variables within each experimental condition in Table 4.

- **Estimation:** We fitted the following equations in order to measure the impact of market research tools on spending in marketing activities. We set all-tools availability as our baseline condition. All models were estimated using fixed-effects Ordinary Least Squares (OLS) because the dependent variables are metric. Within-subjects effects represent the variability of the dependent variables of interest for each firm. To be more specific, they are a measure of how firms tend to change over time, controlling for unobserved heterogeneity.

    - $SPMARKETING_{i,t} = \delta_0 + \delta_1 * SIMPLE_{i,t} + \delta_2 * ROUND + \delta_3 * ROUNDSQ + \delta_4 * SPMARKETING_{i,t-1} + \delta_5 * COMPSPMARKETING_{i,t-1} + \delta_6 * LAUNCH_{i,t} + FE_i + \varepsilon_{i,t}$
    - $SPBRANDMKTG_{i,t} = \beta_0 + \beta_1 * SIMPLE_{i,t} + \beta_2 * ROUND + \beta_3 * ROUNDSQ + \beta_4 * SPBRANDMKTG_{i,t-1} + \beta_5 * COMPSPBRANDMKTG_{i,t-1} + \beta_6 * LAUNCH_{i,t} + FE_i + \varepsilon_{i,t}$

Table 3. Descriptive statistics

Dependent Variables	Variable Type	Mean	Std. Dev.
SPMARKETIN$G_{i,t}$	Metric	847.73	288.29
SPBRANDMKT$G_{i,t}$	Metric	675.50	263.81
SPBRANDAD$V_{i,t}$	Metric	402.01	152.39
SPBRANDPRO$M_{i,t}$	Metric	273.49	193.66
Independent Variables	**Variable Type**	**Mean**	**Std. Dev.**
SIMPL$E_{i,t}$	Dummy	0.50	0.50
Control Variables	**Variable Type**	**Mean**	**Std. Dev.**
ROUND	Metric	4.50	2.31
ROUNDSQ	Metric	25.50	21.26
SPMARKETIN$G_{i,t-1}$	Metric	775.10	318.99
SPBRANDMKT$G_{i,t-1}$	Metric	615.63	290.01
SPBRANDAD$V_{i,t-1}$	Metric	370.58	165.91
SPBRANDPRO$M_{i,t-1}$	Metric	245.05	193.09
COMPSPMARKETIN$G_{i,t-1}$	Metric	1016.75	426.10
COMPSPBRANDMKT$G_{i,t-1}$	Metric	848.81	388.07
COMPSPBRANDAD$V_{i,t-1}$	Metric	504.13	202.26
COMPSPBRANDPRO$M_{i,t-1}$	Metric	459.63	272.49
LAUNC$H_{i,t}$	Count	0.31	0.50

Table 4. Descriptive statistics with experimental conditions

SIMPLE TOOLS ONLY			
Dependent Variables	**Variable Type**	**Mean**	**Std. Dev.**
SPMARKETIN$G_{i,t}$	Metric	803.73	326.30
SPBRANDMKT$G_{i,t}$	Metric	631.05	292.40
SPBRANDAD$V_{i,t}$	Metric	397.93	169.30
SPBRANDPRO$M_{i,t}$	Metric	233.13	168.46
ALL TOOLS AVAILABILITY			
Dependent Variables		**Mean**	**Std. Dev.**
SPMARKETIN$G_{i,t}$	Metric	891.73	240.64
SPBRANDMKT$G_{i,t}$	Metric	719.95	226.76
SPBRANDAD$V_{i,t}$	Metric	406.10	135.45
SPBRANDPRO$M_{i,t}$	Metric	313.85	210.34

Analytics Overuse in Advertising and Promotion Budget Forecasting

- $SPBRANDADV_{i,T} = \varphi_0 + \varphi_1 * SIMPLE_{i,t} + \varphi_2 * ROUND + \varphi_3 * ROUNDSQ + \varphi_4 * SPBRANDADV_{i,t-1} + \varphi_5 * COMPSPBRANDADV_{i,t-1} + \varphi_6 * LAUNCH_{i,t} + FE_i + \varepsilon_{i,t}$
- $SPBRANDPROM_{i,t} = \gamma_0 + \gamma_1 * SIMPLE_{i,t} + \gamma_2 * ROUND + \gamma_3 * ROUNDSQ + \gamma_4 * SPBRANDPROM_{i,t-1} + \gamma_5 * COMPSPBRANDPROM_{i,t-1} + \gamma_6 * LAUNCH_{i,t} + FE_i + \varepsilon_{i,t}$

RESULTS

Table 5 summarizes the results of our study on firm panel. In Model (1), we found strong evidence that firms that employ simple market research tools alone have lower marketing expenditures (p=0.001) compared to when they have all-tools availability. That is, controlling for other factors, firms tend to spend 97.983 million dollars less in overall marketing activities when they employ simple market research tools alone, compared to when they have all market research tools availability.

In Model (2), we found strong evidence that firms that employ simple market research tools alone have lower brand-level marketing expenditures (p=0.003) compared to when they have all-tools availability. That is, controlling for other factors, firms tend to spend 97.936 million dollars less in brand level marketing when they employ simple market research tools alone, compared to when they have all market research tools availability.

In Model (3), we failed to find evidence that firms that employ simple market research tools alone have lower brand-level advertising expenditures (p=0.411) compared to when they have all-tools availability. To be more specific, although the direction and magnitude of the impact of simple market research tools were in line with our prediction, we failed to reject the null hypothesis that such an impact does not exist in the context of brand-level advertising expenditure.

In Model (4), we found strong evidence that firms that employ simple market research tools alone have lower brand-level promotional expenditures (p=0.010) compared to when they have all-tools availability. That is, controlling for other factors, firms tend to spend 66.974 million dollars less in brand-level promotions when they employ simple market research tools alone, compared to when they have all market research tools availability.

SENSITIVITY ANALYSES

We conducted additional analyses in order to validate the experimental manipulations employed in this paper. A very commonly raised concern in experimental studies is the adherence to the experimental manipulations. Consequently, we needed to control for to what extent firms used market research tools in case their set of tools was unrestricted. Using this study, we observed whether firms had preference for simple/complex tools in the condition of unrestricted set of tools, and inferred about firms' perceived risk profiles over the experiment. For this reason, we needed to know a) the perceived complexity of market research tools, b) the perceived usefulness of market research tools in the context of advertising and promotional activities, and c) the employment of market research tools by each firm at each round.

This section is organized as follows: First, using questionnaires gathered from 75 participants over seven rounds during the experimental sessions, we provide some descriptive statistics on the perceived complexity and usefulness of market research tools in advertising and promotional expenditures. Second,

Table 5. Panel data results

Independent Variables	SPMARKETINGi,t (1) Coefficient	SPBRANDMKTGi,t (2) Coefficient	SPBRANDADVi,t (3) Coefficient	SPBRANDPROMi,t (4) Coefficient
Constant	335.619***	291.080***	142.028***	128.652**
	(61.748)	(65.952)	(35.924)	(51.566)
SIMPLEi,t	**-97.983***	**-97.936***	-14.360	**-66.974***
	(29.165)	(32.027)	(17.364)	(25.164)
ROUND	51.724	50.093	48.402	19.774
	(40.546)	(43.064)	(30.368)	(29.535)
ROUNDSQ	-3.051	-2.702	-3.494	-0.616
	(3.724)	(4.086)	(2.838)	(3.036)
SPMARKETINGi,t-1	0.199*			
	(0.104)			
SPBRANDMKTGi,t -1		0.110		
		(0.112)		
SPBRANDADVi,t-1			0.304**	
			(0.115)	
SPBRANDPROMi,t-1				0.189*
				(0.120)
COMPSPMARKETINGi,t-1	0.194**			
	(0.084)			
COMPSPBRANDMKTGi,t-1		0.188**		
		(0.093)		
COMPSPBRANDADVi,t-1			0.003	
			(0.106)	
COMPSPBRANDPROMi,t-1				0.074
				(0.084)
LAUNCHi,t	174.177***	158.928***	88.541***	78.782***
	(32.558)	(35.732)	(19.940)	(28.671)
Number of observations	80	80	80	80
Number of groups	10	10	10	10
Observations per group	8	8	8	8
F(6,64)	36.59	21.84	19.85	9.45
***$\alpha<0.01$				
***$\alpha<0.05$				
***$\alpha<0.10$				

Standard errors are in parentheses.

we present the adherence to the experimental conditions at each round, and per industry, looking at the data on purchase of market research tools.

Perceived Complexity and Usefulness of Market Research Tools

Participants

We conducted questionnaires among 75 participants over seven rounds at the end of every experimental session to explore participants' perceptions about the usefulness and complexity of the market research tools. Each questionnaire was delivered once the participants submitted their decisions to the simulation, and collected after they have completed. There was no time restriction to fill out the questionnaires, but the students completed them in a reasonable time interval, which is around ten minutes.

Pretesting

We followed a conventional pretesting procedure: An initial draft of the questionnaire was prepared one week prior to the experimental sessions, and the teaching team (comprising of the course instructor and three teaching assistants) revised this draft over the week. We eliminated unnecessary questions, added clarification sentences and changed the wording of some questions in order to avoid confusion.

Data Gathering

As we desired that each participant reported his/her own proper belief about how complex or useful the market research tools are, we did not allow the participants to communicate among each other while filling out the questionnaire. Only the aforementioned teaching team was allowed to resolve participants' doubts. The surveys circulated in print, and the answers were recorded to an Excel sheet after each round.

Measurement

In order to assess the perceived complexity of the market research tools available in the experimental conditions, the participants were asked to rate the complexity of each tool available for the corresponding round on a 5-points scale, from 1 *(very easy)* to 5 *(very complex)*. In order to assess the perceived usefulness of market research tools in the corresponding decision contexts, on the other hand, the participants were asked to respond whether they agreed on the statements concerning the usefulness of market research tools on a 5-points scale, from 1 *(I strongly disagree that the tool was useful)* to 5 *(I strongly agree that the tool was useful)*.

Results

Table 6 presents the results. The participants rated Conjoint Analysis as the most, and Focus Groups as the least complex market research tools. In addition to that, Perceptual Maps ranked the second and Concept Tests ranked the third most complex market research tools.

CONCLUSION

This finding justifies the binding of Conjoint Analysis and Perceptual Maps in the condition of complex tools availability, as well as the binding of Focus Groups and Concept Tests in the condition of simple tools availability.

Moreover, the participants reported that they considered Focus Groups and Concept Tests to be more useful than Perceptual Maps and Conjoint Analysis. This finding indicates that the use of simple market research tools is more beneficial in the context of decisions concerning advertising and promotional spending, and goes in parallel with our argument that managers benefit from simplicity in the context of decision making using business analytics. Table 7 presents the results.

On the other hand, it also raises a concern that managers' preference for simple market research tools can alter the use of market research tools in all-tools availability condition. For this reason, we followed up with the adherence test described below.

Adherence to the Experimental Conditions

Definition

We define firms' adherence to the experimental conditions as their tendency to purchase at least one market research tool from their given set of tools. To be more specific, any firm that has purchased at least one simple tool in a round with simple tools availability is labeled as having adhered to the simple tools availability condition, and any firm that has purchased at least one simple and one complex tool in a round with all tools availability is labeled as having adhered to all tools availability condition.

Table 6. Perceived complexity of market research tools

Tool		Mean	95% CI	Std. Dev.	Observations
Conjoint Analysis	Overall	3.23	[3.10, 3.36]	1.07	N=276
	between			0.86	n=75
	Within			0.64	T=3.68
Perceptual Maps	Overall	2.95	[2.82, 3.08]	1.10	N=284
	between			0.82	n=75
	Within			0.74	T=3.79
Focus Groups	Overall	2.13	[2.05, 2.21]	0.89	N=497
	between			0.58	n=75
	Within			0.69	T=6.6
Concept Tests	Overall	2.28	[2.19, 2.36]	0.94	N=495
	between			0.65	n=75
	within			0.68	T=6.6

Table 7. Evaluation of tool usefulness in advertising and promotions

Tool	Decision Context		Mean	95% C.I.	Std.Dev.	Observations
Conjoint Analysis	Advertising and Promotions	Overall	2.99	[2.87,3.10]	0.97	N=274
		Between			0.71	n=75
		Within			0.67	T=3.65
Perceptual Maps	Advertising and Promotions	Overall	3.10	[2.99,3.20]	0.93	N=283
		Between			0.59	n=75
		Within			0.71	T=3.77
Focus Groups	Advertising and Promotions	Overall	3.34	[3.26,3.43]	0.92	N=497
		Between			0.59	n=75
		Within			0.71	T=6.63
Concept Tests	Advertising and Promotions	Overall	3.20	[3.11,3.29]	1.03	N=495
		Between			0.71	n=75
		Within			0.75	T=6.6

Data Gathering

We extracted firms' records on market research tool purchase (Conjoint Analysis, Perceptual Maps, Focus Group and Concept Tests only) over seven rounds stored in the simulation.

Measurement

We measured a firm's adherence to the experimental condition for each round as a binary variable that equals one if the firm has purchased at least one of the market research tools corresponding to its experimental condition, 0 if otherwise.

Results

Table 8 presents the results. We achieved high degree of adherence to the experimental conditions corresponding to simple research tools alone, as well as to all tools availability. Nevertheless, we also perceived tendency to choose simple market research tools alone in the condition corresponding to all market research tools available. Thus, only in the last round, we observed a decline in the adherence to the all tools availability condition, and attributed it to the impact of fatigue.

DISCUSSION

The goal of the current paper was to empirically test a behavioral model of overspending in marketing activities, in a competitive context stripped off from incentive motives, where the information necessary to assess the economic effectiveness of investment decisions is revealed through the market research tools. This model advanced a central hypothesis that managers tend to overinvest in marketing efforts

Table 8. Number of firms adhering to experimental conditions

ACTUAL			
Period	ALL	FGCT	Total
1	5	5	10
2	4	5	10
3	4	6	10
4	5	5	10
5	5	5	10
6	5	5	10
7	3	7	10
8	3	7	10

for the sake of avoiding losses due to competitive interactions. To be more specific, the existing theory predicted that managers play safer bets by investing a risk premium on top of the optimal amount of marketing expenditures in order to avoid being perceived poorly by customers, and that the stronger the perceived risk, the larger the losses are in managers' perspective due to such competitive interactions. Instead, we proposed and tested the alarmist action theory, where managers who build different risk profiles with respect to the amount and characteristics of informants (i.e. market research tools) in their decision environment. In general, our results from the longitudinal experiment confirmed "less is better than more effect." As we demonstrated, firms employing simple marketing analytics have less tendency to increase their marketing expenditures due to the fear of losing customers, and a lower expectancy that their competitors will increase their brand-level advertising and promotional expenditures, compared to firms using a combination of simple and complex marketing analytics. In addition that, we also demonstrated that firms employing simple marketing analytics keep their overall marketing spending at a lower level, and spend less in brand-level marketing, especially in promotional activities, compared to when using a combination of simple and complex marketing analytics.

A key aspect of our experiment was that we observed the decision making process within the firm through the survey study by following managers' expectancies and risk perceptions. From that perspective, Study 1 has an impactful contribution to the studies on managerial decision making because it enlightens how participants' early beliefs about their competitors have continuity over the simulation game. Specifically, in Study 1, we found that participants' risk perceptions and beliefs about their competitors shape from the very beginning of the simulation game, as their risk perceptions and beliefs about their competitors' brand-level marketing expenditures reflect what happens over the simulation: The participants in the simple tools availability condition underestimated the risk of being perceived poorly by customers, and downgraded increases in competitors' brand-level advertising and promotional spending, while those in all-tools availability condition overestimated the risk of being perceived poorly by customers, and increases in competitors' brand-level advertising and promotional spending.

The results from Study 2 further substantiated our theoretical predictions. To be more specific, we found evidence that firms that employ simple market research tools alone have higher aggregate marketing expenditures, and spend more in brand-level marketing efforts, especially in brand-level promotional activities, compared to when they have all-tools availability. As we suggested, the use of simpler market research tools results in less perceived risk from the demand side of the market and less competitive rivalry in marketing expenditures, and efficient use of marketing resources. The use of all market research tools available, in contrast, led to an alarmist action against the competitive rivalry, due to high degree of perceived risk of losing customers, where firms responded by substantially increasing their marketing expenditures. The alarmist behavior was more evident in brand-level marketing decisions than in corporate marketing decisions because the risk behavior is initiated through customers, rather than through stakeholders. In addition to that, brand-level promotional activities are subject to overspending because slower periods of demand can trigger more volatile spending habits in order to overcome the risk of loss.

In this paper, we adhered to the concept of economic rationality, which implies that every decision context is structured differently and might require different analytical tools. Previously, some researchers argued that sticking to the "satisficing" argument may result in accepting behavioral deficiencies as given and legitimizing cognitive shortcuts that lead to merely erroneous decisions, and warn about the perils of the overuse of simplifying mechanisms (Tversky & Kahneman, 1974). For this reason, we did not emphasize that the use of numerous business analytics is always wrong, but we raised our concern about its negative consequences for the nature of human cognition. Thus, we emphasized our contribution to, and empirically demonstrated the need to integrate the organizational consequences to behavioral outcomes in the context of planning (Krantz & Kunreuther, 2007). From our perspective, the empirics employed in two separate studies conducted at individual- and group-level respectively, overall, strengthened the link between cognitive biases and organizational outcomes in the context of planning decisions

We positioned our study as an example of decision making under risk, rather than uncertainty, taking into account the information structure of the simulation. Risk, according to Knight (1921), refers to situation of perfect knowledge, where the decisions are made by subjects, who are well informed about the probabilities of all outcomes for all alternatives. Thus, complete information regarding the decision environment makes the optimality of resource allocation decisions feasible. Uncertainty, in contrast, refers to situations where the probabilities cannot be expressed with any mathematical precision (Volz & Gigerenzer, 2012). As we presented, StratSim simulation game provided a great deal of information for the sake of the optimality of the resource allocation decisions. However, what we observed was that managers steered to different allocations due to their risk attitude. To be more specific, subjects perceived the environmental risk different across the experimental conditions and made their resource allocation decisions with respect to their risk preferences. Consequently, the perceived environmental risk and the risk attitude towards resource allocation decisions were the key elements of this paper, while the uncertainty was beyond our scope.

Our study has impactful contributions to several disciplines. First, we address a general concern in the field of management, which is overspending in marketing activities, and propose that the root of this problem potentially lies in the way market information is presented. Academicians in the field of management should further integrate behavioral consequences of employing decision support systems in solving complex, ill-structured problems in decision environments.

Second, we also address a common issue in the practitioners' world, which is the consequence of using management tools that destroy firm value. We conclude that management tools per se do not destroy firm value, but the overuse of the tools that fosters too much risk-aversion is a suitable candidate to blame. Thus, we propose practitioners to revise their decision making protocols, especially those that require employment of management tools.

Third, in the field of cognitive science, we encourage further work on "less is better than more" effect in the context of decision support systems. We acknowledge that the last decade has been very promising on this matter, but we believe that the impact of information overload on managers' perceived environmental risk requires further excavation.

LIMITATIONS

This research was subject to some limitations because there were several issues that contradicted with real-life competitive scenario. First of all, a general concern was that participants knew in advance that the setting was artificial, and that their adherence to the simulation game itself as if in a real market was hard to achieve. We addressed the first limitation as follows: Initially, we inventoried testimonies regarding StratSim simulation game played in Erasmus School of Economics in Fall 2012 from social media. For instance, we found testimonies on how much they enjoyed StratSim, and sharing their StratSim task (i.e. CEO, brand manager, etc.) on their professional profile, from Twitter and LinkedIn respectively. Moreover, a participant reported in Erasmus Marketing Association review that participants had the general perception that they felt intense competition in the simulation more than ever compared to their prior experience. These findings from social media indicated that participants have gradually complied with the experimental setting as if in a real business environment and that participants had indeed adhered to the simulation game.

The final limitation of this research was that the longitudinal field experiment was run in a learning environment where the main purpose was to get familiar with all market research tools, which did not permit over-restrictive experimental manipulations. We addressed the final limitation by considering the positive side of having conducted the longitudinal field experiment in a learning environment, suggesting that this learning environment encouraged participants to employ the market research tools prudently and more often than in another setting.

CONCLUSION

The motivation of this paper is to empirically test a behavioral model of overspending in marketing activities in a competitive context stripped off from incentive motives, where the market information is revealed through the market research tools. We show that overspending in marketing investments is an unfortunate outcome of information overload, in a sense that managers who confront too many risk informants in their decision environment tend to overinvest in marketing activities due to overemphasis on the environmental risk inherent in the demand side.

We acknowledge the contribution of prior works on suboptimal resource allocations, but believe that, to the best of our knowledge, we grant a broader understanding of overspending and crucial guidelines to identify drivers of overspending. First of all, as we demonstrated, overspending in marketing investments is not only about an unfortunate outcome of lack of financial accountability, misuse of financial information, and cash flow behavior, but it is quite relevant to the use of market research tools.

Second, we propose that a suitable level-of-analysis to study overspending is group-level, like in StratSim simulation game, which is the brain of an organization. To be more specific, we rationalize that linking top management team decisions to organizational outcomes is as legitimate as linking human behavior to the cognitive style of the human being.

We encourage further work in the field, mainly because overspending in marketing investments is a very relevant issue considering the impact of global financial crises plaguing or threatening firms with bankruptcy.

REFERENCES

Alchian, A. A., & Demsetz, H. (1972). Production, information costs and economic organization. *The American Economic Review*, *62*(5), 777–795.

Armstrong, J. S., & Collopy, F. (1996). Competitor orientation: Effects of objectives and information on managerial decisions and profitability. *JMR, Journal of Marketing Research*, *33*(2), 188–199. doi:10.2307/3152146

Axelrod, R. (1984). *The Evolution of Cooperation*. Basic Books.

Cabral, L. M. B. (2000). *Introduction to Industrial Organization*. Cambridge, MA: MIT Press.

Christen, M., & Sarvary, M. (2007). Competitive pricing of information: A longitudinal experiment. *JMR, Journal of Marketing Research*, *44*(February), 42–56. doi:10.1509/jmkr.44.1.42

Danaher, P. J., Bonfrer, A., & Dhar, S. (2008). The effect of competitive advertising interference on sales for packaged goods. *JMR, Journal of Marketing Research*, *45*(April), 211–225. doi:10.1509/jmkr.45.2.211

Deighan, M., James, S. W., & Kinnear, T. C. (2006). *StratSim Marketing: The Marketing Strategy Simulation*. Charlottesville, VA: Interpretive Software, Inc.

Dekimpe, M. G., Franses, P. H., Hanssens, D. M., & Naik, P. A. (2007). Time series models in marketing. In Handbook of Marketing Decision Models. New York, NY: Springer Science + Business Media.

Dorfman, R., & Steiner, P. O. (1954). Optimal advertising and optimal quality. *The American Economic Review*, *44*(5), 826–836.

Dutton, J. E., & Jackson, S. E. (1987). Categorizing strategic issues: Links to organizational action. *Academy of Management Review*, *12*(1), 76–90.

Gigerenzer, G. (2008). Why heuristics work. *Perspectives on Psychological Science*, *3*(: 1), 20–29. doi:10.1111/j.1745-6916.2008.00058.x PMID:26158666

Goldstein, D. G., & Gigerenzer, G. (2002). Models of ecological rationality: The recognition heuristic. *Psychological Review*, *109*(1), 75–90. doi:10.1037/0033-295X.109.1.75 PMID:11863042

Hanssens, D. M., Parsons, L. J., & Schultz, R. L. (2001). *Market Response Models and Econometric Time Series Analysis*. Boston, MA: Kluwer Academic Publishers.

Hirshleifer, D., Low, A., & Teoh, S. H. (2012). Are overconfident CEOs better innovators? *The Journal of Finance*, *67*(4), 1457–1498. doi:10.1111/j.1540-6261.2012.01753.x

Jensen, M. C. (1986). Agency costs of free cash flow, corporate finance, and takeovers. *The American Economic Review*, *76*(2), 323–339.

Jensen, M. C., & Meckling, W. H. (1976). Theory of the firm: Managerial behavior, agency costs and ownership structure. *Journal of Financial Economics*, *3*(4), 305–360. doi:10.1016/0304-405X(76)90026-X

Joseph, K., & Richardson, V. J. (2002). Free cash flow, agency costs, and the affordability method of advertising budgeting. *Journal of Marketing*, *66*(1), 94–107. doi:10.1509/jmkg.66.1.94.18453

Joshi, A., & Hanssens, D. M. (2010). The direct and indirect effects of advertising spending on firm value. *Journal of Marketing*, *74*(January), 20–33. doi:10.1509/jmkg.74.1.20

Kalra, A., & Soberman, D. A. (2008). The curse of competitiveness: How advice from experienced colleagues and training can hurt marketing. *Journal of Marketing*, *72*(3), 32–47. doi:10.1509/jmkg.72.3.32

Keil, S. K., Reibstein, D., & Wittink, D. R. (2001). The impact of business objectives and time horizon of performance evaluation on pricing behavior. *International Journal of Research in Marketing*, *18*(1-2), 67–81. doi:10.1016/S0167-8116(01)00027-1

Knight, F. (1921). *Risk, Uncertainty and Profit*. New York: Houghton Mifflin.

Krantz, D. H., & Kunreuther, H. C. (2007). Goals and plans in decision making. *Judgment and Decision Making*, *2*(3), 137–168.

Lang, L. H. P., & Litzenberger, R. H. (1989). Dividend announcements: Cash flow signaling vs. free cash flow hypothesis. *Journal of Financial Economics*, *24*(1), 181–191. doi:10.1016/0304-405X(89)90077-9

Lee, R. P., & Grewal, R. (2004). Strategic responses to new technologies and their impact on firm performance. *Journal of Marketing*, *68*(4), 157–171. doi:10.1509/jmkg.68.4.157.42730

Lex team. (2012). Advertising: Valuations don't ad up. *Financial Times*. Retrieved 17 September 2013 from: http://www.ft.com/intl/cms/s/3/0d9b6450-66fe-11e1-9d4e-00144feabdc0.html#axzz2Vv5NhUM7

Lilien, G. L. (1979). Advisor 2: Modeling the marketing mix decision for industrial products. *Management Science*, *25*(2), 191–204. doi:10.1287/mnsc.25.2.191

Lilien, G. L. (2011). Bridging the academic-practitioner divide in marketing decision models. *Journal of Marketing*, *75*(July), 196–210. doi:10.1509/jmkg.75.4.196

Little, J. D. (1970). Models and managers: The concept of a decision calculus. *Management Science*, *16*(4), B466–B486. doi:10.1287/mnsc.16.8.B466

Ludvigson, S. C. (2004). Consumer confidence and consumer pricing. *The Journal of Economic Perspectives*, *18*(2), 29–50. doi:10.1257/0895330041371222

Malmendier, U., & Tate, G. (2005). CEO overconfidence and corporate investment. *The Journal of Finance*, *60*(6), 2661–2700. doi:10.1111/j.1540-6261.2005.00813.x

Manchanda, P., Xie, Y., & Youn, N. (2008). The role of targeted communication and contagion in product adoption. *Marketing Science*, *27*(6), 961–976. doi:10.1287/mksc.1070.0354

Mintz, O. (2012). *What drives metric use? Evidence from 30 Countries*. Retrieved 25 Septebmer 2015 from: https://webfiles.uci.edu/omintz/www/MC%20Intl%20Metric%20Use.pdf

Mintz, O., & Currim, I. (2013). What drives the use of marketing and financial metrics and does metric use impact performance of marketing mix activities? *Journal of Marketing, 77*(March), 17–40. doi:10.1509/jm.11.0463

Montgomery, C. A., & Wernerfelt, B. (1988). 'Diversification, Ricardian rents, and Tobin's q'. *The Rand Journal of Economics, 19*(4), 623–632. doi:10.2307/2555461

Morton-Clark, S. (2009). Peter Fader: How marketing works best with big messy maths. *Financial Times*. Retrieved 17 September 2013 from: http://www.ft.com/intl/cms/s/0/87fb6c82-e8de-11dd-a4d00000779fd2ac.html#axzz2Vv5NhUM7

Naik, P. A., & Raman, K. (2003). Understanding the impact of synergy in multimedia communications. *JMR, Journal of Marketing Research, 40*(4), 375–388. doi:10.1509/jmkr.40.4.375.19385

Neslin, S. A., & Shankar, V. (2009). Key issues in multichannel customer management: Current knowledge and future directions. *Journal of Interactive Marketing, 23*(1), 70–81. doi:10.1016/j.intmar.2008.10.005

Parsons, L. J. (1975). The product life cycle and time-varying advertising elasticities. *JMR, Journal of Marketing Research, 12*(4), 476–480. doi:10.2307/3151101

Pruyn, A., & Riezebos, R. (2001). Effects of the awareness of social dilemmas on advertising budget-setting: A scenario setting. *Journal of Economic Psychology, 22*(1), 43–60. doi:10.1016/S0167-4870(00)00036-2

Rapoport, A., & Chammah, A. M. (1965). *Prisoner's Dilemma: A Study in Conflict and Cooperation*. Ann Arbor, MI: Univ. of Michigan Press.

Rusetski, A. (2012). Brand equity: Can there be too much of a good thing? *International Business & Economics Research Journal, 11*(3), 357–368.

Rust, R. T., Ambler, T., Carpanter, G. S., Kumar, V., & Srivastava, R. (2004). Measuring marketing productivity: Current knowledge and future directions. *Journal of Marketing, 68*(4), 76–89. doi:10.1509/jmkg.68.4.76.42721

Sethuraman, R., Tellis, G. J., & Briesch, R. (2011). How well does advertising work? Generalizations from a meta-analysis of brand advertising elasticity. *JMR, Journal of Marketing Research, 48*(3), 457–471. doi:10.1509/jmkr.48.3.457

Shankar, V. (2008). *Strategic allocation of marketing resources: Methods and managerial insights*. Marketing Science Institute Special Report, 08-207.

Simon, H. A. (1955). A behavioral model of rational choice. *The Quarterly Journal of Economics, 69*(1), 99–118. doi:10.2307/1884852

Simon, H. A. (1979). Information processing models of cognition. *Annual Review of Psychology, 30*(February), 363–396. doi:10.1146/annurev.ps.30.020179.002051 PMID:18331186

Srinivasan, R., Lilien, G. L., & Sridhar, S. (2011). Should firms spend more on research and development and advertising during recessions? *Journal of Marketing, 75*(3), 49–65. doi:10.1509/jmkg.75.3.49

Steenkamp, J. B. E. M., Nijs, V. R., Hanssens, D. M., & Dekimpe, M. G. (2005). Competitive reactions to advertising and promotion attacks. *Marketing Science, 24*(1), 35–54. doi:10.1287/mksc.1040.0069

Tellis, G. J. (2007). Advertising effectiveness in contemporary markets. In G. J. Tellis & T. Ambler (Eds.), *The SAGE Handbook of Advertising*. Thousand Oaks, CA: Sage Publications. doi:10.4135/9781848607897.n17

Tellis, G. J., & Fornell, C. (1988). The relationship between advertising and product quality over the product life cycle: A contingency approach. *JMR, Journal of Marketing Research*, 25(February), 64–71. doi:10.2307/3172925

Thisse, J. F., & Vives, X. (1988). On the strategic choice of spatial price policy. *The American Economic Review*, 78(1), 122–137.

Thorelli, H. B., & Burnett, S. C. (1981). The nature of product life cycles for industrial goods businesses. *Journal of Marketing*, 45(4), 97–108. doi:10.2307/1251477

Tversky, A., & Kahneman, D. (1974). Judgment under uncertainty: Heuristics and biases. *Science*, 185(4157), 1124–1131. doi:10.1126/science.185.4157.1124 PMID:17835457

Viscusi, W. K. (1997). Alarmist decisions with divergent risk information. *The Economic Journal*, 107(445), 1657–1670. doi:10.1111/j.1468-0297.1997.tb00073.x

Vogt, S. C. (1994). The cash flow/investment relationship: Evidence from U.S. manufacturing firms. *Financial Management*, 23(2), 3–20. doi:10.2307/3665735

Volz, K. G., & Gigerenzer, G. (2012). Cognitive processes in decisions under risk are not same as in decisions under uncertainty. *Frontiers in Neuroscience*, 6(July), 1–6. PMID:22807893

KEY TERMS AND DEFINITIONS

Field Experiment: A field experiment applies the scientific method to experimentally examine an intervention in a naturally occurring environment rather than in the laboratory. Field experiments, like lab experiments, generally randomize sampling units into treatment and control groups and compare outcomes between these groups, but in settings which do not enforce scientific control.

Information Overload: Information overload refers to the difficulty a person can have understanding an issue and making decisions that can be caused by the presence of too much information. Data expansion and overuse of analytical tools are seen as primary reasons for information overload due to their ability to produce more information more quickly and to communicate to large audiences.

Marketing Strategy: Marketing strategy is an organization's strategy that combines all of its marketing goals into one comprehensive plan. A good marketing strategy should be drawn from market research and focus on the right product mix in order to achieve the maximum profit potential and sustain the business. The marketing strategy is the foundation of a marketing plan.

Overspending: Overspending is the act of spending more than is allowed in the budget or indicated by the formal models of budget forecasting.

Risk Behavior: Risk behavior is characterized by decision maker's reaction to degree of risk associated with the decisions, with respect to the uncertainty of the outcomes, difficulty of the decision goals, and extremeness of the consequences as gains and losses.

Analytics Overuse in Advertising and Promotion Budget Forecasting

Simulation Game: A simulation game is a computer or video game designed to closely simulate aspects of a real or fictional reality. A simulation game attempts to copy various activities from real life in the form of a game for various purposes such as training, analysis, or prediction. Usually there are no strictly defined goals in the game, with players instead allowed to freely control a character.

Chapter 10
Mastering Business Process Management and Business Intelligence in Global Business

Kijpokin Kasemsap
Suan Sunandha Rajabhat University, Thailand

ABSTRACT

This chapter describes the overviews of Business Process Management (BPM) and Business Intelligence (BI); the importance of BPM in global business; and the importance of BI in global business. BPM enables organizations to align business functions with customer needs and helps executives determine how to deploy, monitor, and measure the organizational resources. When properly executed, BPM has the ability to enhance productivity, reduce costs, and minimize risk in global business. BI includes the applications, tools, and best practices that enable the analysis of information to improve organizational performance. Companies use BI to detect the significant events and identify the business trends in order to quickly adapt to their changing business environment. The chapter argues that applying BPM and BI has the potential to enhance organizational performance and reach strategic goals in global business.

INTRODUCTION

Business process management (BPM) is a paradigm for enterprise computing that uses information technology (IT) to support the business processes and to improve these processes to effectively achieve business objectives (Decreus, Poels, Kharbili, & Pulvermueller, 2010). BPM is an important concept that enables the efficient adaptation in the business environment conditions (Bitkowska, 2015). BPM is a management practice which encompasses all activities of the identification, definition, analysis, design, execution, measurement, and continuous improvement of business processes (Rohloff, 2011). With the emergence of BPM and of service-oriented architecture, the focus has shifted to the development of electronic services that integrate the business processes and that diversify the functionalities available to customers (Chou & Seng, 2012). The discipline of BPM requires both business and IT organizational

DOI: 10.4018/978-1-5225-0654-6.ch010

perspectives, in order to adopt a common set of practices, and obtain a holistic view of managing the organizational business processes (Antonucci & Goeke, 2011).

Business intelligence (BI) is the process of gathering the correct information in the correct format at the correct time and delivering the results for decision-making purposes toward gaining the positive impact on business operations, tactics, and strategy in the business enterprises (Zeng, Li, & Duan, 2012). BI has become the top priority for many organizations who have implemented BI solutions to improve their decision-making process (Isik, Jones, & Sidorova, 2011). BI promises to turn data into knowledge and to help managers succeed in decision making (Niu, Lu, Zhang, & Wu, 2013). BI can improve the organizational performance as a result of improvement on business decision making (Chen, Chiang, & Storey, 2012). The strength of this chapter is on the thorough literature consolidation of BPM and BI. The extant literature of BPM and BI provides a contribution to practitioners and researchers by describing the multifaceted applications of BPM and BI to appeal to the different segments of BPM and BI in order to maximize the business impact of BPM and BI in global business.

BACKGROUND

Business process is defined as the specific ordering of work activities across time and place, with a beginning, an end, and identified input and output (Davenport, 1993). Business process is a sequence of executions in a business context based on the purpose of creating products and services (Scheer, 1999). Business process involves people from the different functional units in the same organization and go across organizational boundaries for the reasons of business partnership, thus increasing the complexity of managing the process (Stohr & Zhao, 2001). Shaw et al. (2007) stated that an organization's current performance depends upon its business processes' collective ability to achieve its fundamental objectives. Organizations implement business processes in order to produce the value for customers (Earl, Sampler, & Short, 1995).

BPM has been an intensely discussed topic in the information system (IS) research field as well as in practice since the late 1980s (Houy, Fettke, & Loos, 2010). BPM is a methodology that allows companies a faster organizational adaptation to the continuously changing requirements of customers (Neubauer, 2009). The operations of BPM practices have evolved from the functional division of work (Taylor, 1911) and business process reengineering (BPR) (Davenport & Short, 1990) to the complex practices of the holistic end-to-end business processes involving the integration of business and IT (Smith & Fingar, 2007). BPM includes the components of total quality management (TQM), the value chain, Six Sigma, Lean, and enterprise resource planning (ERP) (Paim, Cauliraux, & Cardoso, 2008). By integrating IT and business practices, BPM broadens the scope of BPR, focusing on achieving performance improvement by eliminating the non-value added process steps (Khalil, 1997).

BI is a very popular topic in the field of data mining and knowledge discovery from databases (Niu et al., 2013). BI remains a topic of interest in the practitioner's research (Ramakrishnan, Jones, & Sidorova, 2012). BI encompasses a broad category of methodologies, applications, and technologies for collecting, storing, manipulating, analyzing, and providing the access to data to help enterprise users make the better and faster business decisions (Chaudhuri, Dayal, & Narasayya, 2011). Khan et al. (2014) stated that BI is one of the most important concepts that have lived to the expectations. BI has evolved to become a foundational cornerstone of enterprise decision support (Côrte-Real, Ruivo, & Oliveira, 2014).

BI technology includes several software applications for extraction, transformation, and loading (ETL), data warehousing, database query and reporting, online analytical processing, data analysis, data mining, and visualization (Sahay & Ranjan, 2008). The four major components of BI constitute data warehouse, data sources, data mart, and the reporting tools (Brannon, 2010). BI tools are broadly recognized as middleware between transactional applications and decision support applications (Sahay & Ranjan, 2008). BI technology is important because it provides the applicable technologies to organize the data warehouses, thus providing the strategic intelligence to support the decision-making process of modern organizations (Niu et al., 2013).

MASTERING BUSINESS PROCESS MANAGEMENT AND BUSINESS INTELLIGENCE IN GLOBAL BUSINESS

This section describes the overviews of BPM and BI; the importance of BPM in global business; and the importance of BI in global business.

Overview of Business Process Management

Although organizations have worked on improving their business processes for many years as they implemented ERP systems (Reich & Nelson, 2003), BPR remains one of the top five management perspectives (Luftman, Kempaiah, & Nash, 2006). BPR is a systematic approach to helping an organization analyze and improve its business processes in the digital age (Kasemsap, 2015a). Evolutionary improvement of business processes as a continuous transformation with several phases is of higher relevance for BPM efforts (Weske, 2007). Although BPM has roots in some of the earliest industrial management techniques, the meaning and content of BPM (Antonucci & Goeke, 2011). Kasemsap (2015b) recognized ERP as the major approach to the improved productivity and performance in the manufacturing industries and in the small and medium-sized enterprises (SMEs).

BPM is a management principle which companies apply in order to sustain their competitive advantage (Hung, 2006). BPM is a comprehensive set of activities that must be performed to fulfill the organizational strategic goals to customers (Strnadl, 2006). Emerging technologies evolving from workflow automation and enterprise application integration effectively support BPM (Scott, 2007). BPM is informed by complexity theory and that business processes can evolve and adapt to changing business circumstances (Vidgen & Wang, 2006). Since business process owners need to collaborate with the IS organization to optimize the business processes, IT, and business alignment (Hirshheim, Schwarz, & Todd, 2006) are required for BPM. Success in BPM requires that traditional IT roles become more process-focused, and that traditional business roles become IT savvy (McDonald, 2007).

BPM enables the execution of services as opposed to the hard-coded workflows in the off-the-shelf software (Schulte, Janiesch, Venugopa, Weber, & Hoenisch, 2015). BPM is considered as one of the important success factors in business process improvement initiatives (Bhatt & Saad, 2005). Jeston and Nelis (2008) viewed BPM as the achievement of organization's objectives through the improvement, management, and control of essential business processes. BPM encompasses not only the analysis and modeling of business processes but also the organizational implementation leadership and performance controlling (Becker, Kugeler, & Rosemann, 2003). The business process provision of the technical business infrastructure and the redesign of local business processes in using business process model-

Mastering Business Process Management and Business Intelligence in Global Business

ing and BPR have been identified as the major elements determining the success of business process (Kasemsap, 2016a).

Karim et al. (2007) indicated that IT will have a positive impact on organizational performance if it matches the business processes. Organizations should establish which business processes are the key processes and contribute to the competitive advantage (Trkman, 2010). Ensuring that organizational IT is in alignment with and provides support for organization's business strategy is critical to the business success (Bleistein, Cox, Verner, & Phalp, 2006). Organizations aiming to increase business performance and achieve business goals should focus on developing IT, technical alignment, and IS effectiveness (Kasemsap, 2015c).

Project-based organizations should develop an effective working culture in utilizing IT and knowledge management to reach the project goals (Kasemsap, 2015d). Information about project types of BPM is substantive for the design of situational methods in support of BPM (Bucher & Winter, 2009). The progress toward organizational excellence through process-oriented management takes place in the different stages and every organization has developed its own approach to BPM (Balzarova, Bamber, McCambridge, & Sharp, 2004). Bucher and Winter (2006) stated that four phases of BPM involve process identification, design, and modeling; process implementation and execution; process monitoring and controlling; and process enhancements.

BPM requires a holistic view of planning for leading, and managing the end-to-end business processes that are sensitive to the organization-specific dimensions, such as culture, governance, change management issues, process, measurement, and technology (Hammer, 2007). The managerial perspectives needed for successful BPM activities require both BPM knowledge and firm-specific business expertise, combined with the extensive IT skills (Antonucci & Goeke, 2011). Successful BPM requires a well-organized team in order to analyze, design, implement, and optimize the business processes along with the business strategy (Neubauer, 2009). A well-defined strategy is the basis for the optimal alignment with the associated-business processes and enables the implementation of the well-integrated business processes.

Regarding BPM implementation, effective communication is an important factor when considering the changes and it is required through the whole business process and on all levels, although employees are not directly connected with BPM (Harmon, 2007). Employees are less sensitive to the possible destructive impacts from the business environment (Umble & Umble, 2002). Even if organizations manage to form a productive environment, including top management support, readiness to change, and the required technological competence, the project would lead to a failure if the employees lack the eligible skills and knowledge about the new process, or if they are not properly educated (Grover, Jeong, Kettinger, & Teng, 1995).

The rapid adoption of BPM has resulted in a shortage of qualified BPM professionals, and firms are expressing difficulty hiring the individuals skilled in BPM. Change management in human resources includes the activities (e.g., the training of employees affected by the business process change) toward developing new skills needed by the new business processes (Zabjek, Kovacic, & Stemberger, 2009). The features of human capital that are crucial to an organization's business performance are the flexibility and creativity of individuals, their ability to develop the employees' skills in an effective manner (Armstrong, 2006).

Business process management system (BPMS) is the platform for the integration of the business architecture, business processes model, the management system for business flows and information infrastructure as support to the execution of business processes (Khan, 2004). To be successful in BPMS, the IS employees need to become more business-centric, improve their data modeling skills (Reich &

Nelson, 2003) and analytical capabilities (Davenport, 2006). The IS organization will become involved with developing and maintaining the BPMS that present metrics for process improvement (Shim, Varshney, & Dekleva, 2006).

Significant features of BPMS are the metrics, business activity monitoring (BAM), and the facilitation of organizational ability (Scott, 2007). Metrics generated from the radio frequency identification (RFID), such as tracking patient services in hospitals (Janz, Pitts, & Otondo, 2005) and BAM for real-time inventory tracking (Houghton, El Sawy, Gray, Donegan, & Joshi, 2004), can help improve processes. RFID solutions can be utilized to reduce the operating costs through decreasing labor costs, enhancing automation, improving tracking and tracing, and preventing the loss of materials (Kasemsap, 2015e). Business analytics can be utilized to validate the causal relationships within traditional input, process, output, and outcome categories toward business success (Kasemsap, 2015f). Companies that compete on business analytics effectively utilize the BI tools to enhance the decision making (Davenport, 2006).

Among the various approaches that support business BPM, maturity models receive increasing attention (de Bruin, Rosemann, Freeze, & Kulkarni, 2005). This is in line with the popularity of maturity models across a wide range of application domains (de Bruin et al., 2005), the expected increase in adoption by industry (Scott, 2007), and the growing academic interest in maturity models (Becker, Niehaves, Poppelbuß, & Simons, 2010). Based on the assumption of predictable patterns of organizational evolution and change, maturity models represent theories about how organization's capabilities evolve in a stage-by-stage manner (Gottschalk, 2009). Maturity models are termed stages-of-growth models, stage models, or stage theories (Prananto, Mckay, & Marshall, 2003). Early examples of maturity models refer to a hierarchy of human needs (Maslow, 1954), economic growth (Kuznets, 1965), and the development of IT in organizations (Nolan, 1979).

Maturity model is a prospering approach to improving a company's processes and BPM capabilities (Roglinger, Poppelbuß, & Becker, 2012). Maturity models include a sequence of levels establishing a logical path from an initial state to maturity (Becker, Knackstedt, & Poppelbuß, 2009). An organization's current maturity level represents its capabilities as regards a specific class of objects and application domain (Rosemann & de Bruin, 2005). Maturity models are used to evaluate the as-is situations, to guide improvement initiatives, and to control progress (Iversen, Nielsen, & Norbjerg, 1999). Regarding BPM, two types of maturity models include process maturity models and BPM maturity models. Process maturity models refer to the condition of processes in general or distinct process types. BPM maturity models address a company's BPM capabilities (Rosemann & de Bruin, 2005).

Overview of Business Intelligence

BI has become an important product in the IT industry because of lack of efficient data mining tools to support unstructured datasets (Niu et al., 2013). BI is a concept of using IT as an effective tool for achieving the competitiveness of businesses, the perception of risk that occurs in the environment within the firm, and the possibility of business action (Habul & Pilav-Velic, 2010). BI is defined as system which collects, transforms, and presents the structured data from multiple sources (Negash, 2004). BI systems are accounted for the potential to shorten the time to obtain the relevant information and enable the efficient utilization (den Hamer, 2005).

The traditional data mining tools are easily applicable to the structured datasets, but have limitations with the unstructured datasets (Baars & Kemper, 2008). BI works very well with both structured and unstructured datasets (Lamont, 2006). BI systems are regularly referred to as the successor to the

Mastering Business Process Management and Business Intelligence in Global Business

decision-support systems and facilitate the various kinds of enterprise reporting tools (Brannon, 2010). BI transforms information into knowledge and has the capability of putting the right information into the hands of the right user at the right time to support the decision-making process (Reinschmidt & Françoise, 2000).

BI contributes to the increased business performance, thus leading to the higher levels of business efficiency, higher and better quality outputs, better marketing decisions, and lessened risk of business failure in order to gain a competitive advantage in the global business environments (Kasemsap, 2015g). Applying data mining for BI in the knowledge management environments will improve organizational performance and reach business goals in modern business (Kasemsap, 2015h). BI competency is characterized by skills related to the commercial products of large software vendors (Debortoli, Muller, & vom Brocke, 2014).

BI success is associated with the positive value an organization obtains from its BI investment (Sabherwal & Becerra-Fernandez, 2010). Watson et al. (2006) indicated that a lack of fit between an organization's BI and its goals and characteristics is the main reason for a lack of BI success. BI plays an important role in enhancing this agility with the BI capabilities (Chen & Siau, 2011). With the right capabilities, BI can help an organization predict the changes in product demand and detect an increase in a competitor's new product market share and respond by introducing a competing product (Watson & Wixom, 2007). BI capabilities have been examined by practitioner-oriented research, especially from the BI maturity model perspective (Eckerson, 2006).

BI capabilities can be examined from both organizational and technological perspectives (Isik, Jones, & Sidorova, 2013). Technological BI capabilities are the sharable technical platforms and databases that ideally include a well-defined technology architecture and data standards, while organizational BI capabilities are the essential assets that support the effective application of BI in the organization, such as flexibility and shared risks and responsibilities (Ross, Beath, & Goodhue, 1996). Organizational and technological capabilities impact the way that an organization processes information and the performance of the organization (Zhang & Tansuhaj, 2007).

Azvine et al. (2007) explained that BI systems suffer from a number of obstacles that prevent the realization of their potential. Firstly, the transition from data into information is obstructed by the shortage of analysts who are required to run the analytical software. The second issue is the bottle neck in the transition from information into action, which has been of a manual nature because of the lack of automatic links back into the business process layer that promotes the rapid adaptation of process parameters to improve the performance. The third issue is associated with the ability to merge a huge amount of data from the different sources into a practical source of information, including the ability to validate the data and deal with the quality issues.

Importance of Business Process Management in Global Business

BPM is the discipline that encompasses the analysis, modeling, implementation, execution, control, and continuous improvement of business processes (Minonne & Turner, 2012). BPM is used as a tool for intellectual capital management (Kujansivu & Lönnqvist, 2008). BPM gains the business process improvements through the integration of business processes, organizational units, products, and IS (Mansar & Reijers, 2005) with data being the foundation of the integration effort (Scheer, 1992). BPM enables the continuous improvement of corporate strategies and allows companies to concentrate on business processes (Neubauer, 2009).

Practitioner and researchers have promoted BPM practices by focusing on agility (Wang & Wang, 2006), strategy (Grefen, Mehandjiev, Kouvas, Weichhart, & Eshuis, 2009), knowledge management (Jung, Choi, & Song, 2007), and performance measurement (Trkman, 2010). Lifelong learning and knowledge management become a valuable origin of competitive advantage in the information age (Kasemsap, 2016b). Organizations utilize entrepreneurship education and knowledge management as the major assets and organizational resources for producing the high-technology goods and services in order to obtain sustainable competitive advantage in modern organizations (Kasemsap, 2016c).

BPM has gained much attention by management and IT department in organizations as a method to increase flexibility and agility (Ravesteyn, 2009). To realize this goal, it is important to have a flexible information system in support of processes. The most promising approach to achieve this perspective is service-oriented architecture (Lippert & Govindarajulu, 2006). BPM effectively supports the business processes using methods, techniques, and software to design, enact, control, and analyze the operational processes involving humans, organizations, applications, documents, and other sources of information (van der Aalst, Dumas, & ter Hofstede, 2003). While technical approaches to BPM emphasize the support of business processes through IT, holistic approaches are much wider, integrating further organizational, human-centric, and cultural aspects (von Brocke & Sinnl, 2011).

BPM efforts involve aligning the processes with the organization's strategic goals, implementing process architectures, establishing process measurement systems aligned with organizational goals, and organizing managers to manage processes (Chaffey & Wood, 2005). Mergers and acquisitions necessitate choosing between two organizations' business process or integrating both (Scott, 2007). Modeling these business processes is the first step in making an optimal decision on what aspects to keep or discard. In order to survive in a highly competitive business environment, modern organizations are subject to the continuous change of their business processes (Bosilj-Vuksic & Spremic, 2004). Most organizations lack the process owners or they are defined to a minor extent, which is a consequence of a traditional organization of people and their thinking, which is not process-oriented (Hammer & Champy, 2003).

One of the most important challenges in BPM is the coordination and management of outsourced business processes with internal business processes and integrating information between them (Mahmoodzadeh, Jalalinia, & Yazdi, 2009). Processes are the essence of many methods, such as Six Sigma, reengineering, and activity-based costing (Smith & Fingar, 2007). For many companies, BPM becomes the basis for realizing the different technologies (e.g., balanced scorecard, workflow management, and business monitoring) (Neubauer, 2009). Balanced scorecard requires a process approach (Kaplan & Norton, 1996). Workflow systems have become a standard solution for managing complex processes in business domains, such as supply chain management, customer relationship management, and knowledge management (Kumar & Zhao, 2002).

Successful BPM depends on effective workflow design, modeling, and analysis. Workflow models can be used to represent a business process from five dimensions: functional, behavioral, informational, operational, and organizational perspectives (Curtis, Kellner, & Over, 1992). The behavioral perspective indicates the conditions for tasks to be executed. The information perspective considers what data are consumed and produced associated with each activity in a business process. The operational perspective identifies what tools and applications are utilized to execute a specified task. The organizational perspective explains the relationships among individuals that are qualified to manage the job functions.

Concerning workflow design in BPM, workflow modeling paradigms mainly focus on the activity sequencing and coordination, including Petri nets (van der Aalst, 1998) and the activity-based workflow modeling (Bi & Zhao, 2004). The dataflow perspective is important in workflow management because relationships among data elements enhance the operational constraints that practically control the activity sequencing (Kwan & Balasubramanian, 1998). Workflow management systems enable the discovery of dataflow errors only through simulation, which is inefficient and inaccurate. The traditional approach to workflow design, referred to as the participative approach (Herrmann & Walter, 1998), is logical for confirming the business requirements about the workflow but it does not offer any formalism for developing the workflow model in an effective manner.

Regarding BPM, data quality is an important factor for gaining the strategic business goals (Ofner, Otto, & Osterle, 2012), such as the improved decision making (Price & Shanks, 2005), the efficient customer relationship management (Reid & Catterall, 2005), the compliance with the regulatory requirements (Friedman, 2006), and supply chain management excellence (Kagermann, Osterle, & Jordan, 2010). Data are used across the boundaries of business processes and business units in an uncoordinated way, which has the negative effects on the quality of data and produces the high costs (Redman, 2004).

Importance of Business Intelligence in Global Business

The benefits of the BI technology can be recognized in the perspective of the increased autonomy and flexibility of users, thus creating the reports, simple analyses, improved decision support, and operational efficiency, as well as a range of new analytical functions (Hocevar & Jaklic, 2010). Flexibility is the organizational capability of BI to provide the decision support when variations exist in business processes (Gebauer & Schober, 2006). BI technologies are used to shorten the time lag between data acquisition and decision making (Chaudhuri et al., 2011). BI is a technique and solution that helps managers understand the business situation (Nofal & Yusof, 2013). Due to its ability to generate the reporting, BI allows the dynamic enterprise data search, retrieval, analysis, and explanation of the needs of managerial decisions (Nofal & Yusof, 2013).

BI has largely relied on structured and numerical data, which can be measured on a numerical scale and analyzed with the statistical methods and computing equipment (Sukumaran & Sureka, 2006). However, in an increasing number of BI application areas, the collection and analysis of qualitative and/or unstructured data are critical (Baars & Kemper, 2008). This type of data cannot be used in mathematical calculations; it refers to data in the text, image, and sound formats that require the interpretation (Isik et al., 2013). BI helps in consolidating, analyzing, and providing the amount of data for decision making (Phan & Vogel, 2010). BI systems support the decision making and information sharing in the complex organizational environments (Rubin & Rubin, 2013). Under BI, information can be accessed in a timelier manner, decisions become data-driven, and reports become more informative (Rubin & Rubin, 2013).

The decision environment is defined as the combination of different types of decisions made and the information-processing requirements of the decision maker when making those decisions (Munro & Davis, 1977). The decision environment affects the relationship between BI success and capabilities, such as the extent to which BI supports flexibility and risk in decision making (Isik et al., 2013). The suitable match between the decision environment and the support that the business system provides is key to the organization's ability to leverage that system to achieve the BI success (Arnott, 2004). The complexity of the decisions being made impacts the level of this match (Clark, Jones, & Armstrong, 2007). The decision maker's information needs are part of the decision environment because decision making involves applying the gathered information (Zack, 2007). Because appropriate information depends on the characteristics of the decision-making context, it is difficult to separate the information processing needs from decision making (Zack, 2007).

Although BI capabilities have been studied from the organizational and technological perspectives (Manglik & Mehra, 2005), some organizations fail to achieve the BI success (Jourdan, Rainer, & Marshall, 2008). This may be because the relationship between the decision environment and BI capabilities has remained largely unexamined (Isik et al., 2013). Examining the relationship between the decision environment and BI capabilities is important, however, because the primary purpose of BI is to support decision making in organizations (Buchanan & O'Connell, 2006). BI, which is used within an organization, must suit the problem space, or decision environment, within which it is utilized and this match is key to BI success (Clark et al., 2007).

Because organizations have multiple purposes for user groups within BI, they need to employ the different BI applications with the different access methods. Some organizations deploy a BI that provides unlimited access to data analysis and reporting tools to all its users, while others offer relatively restricted access. Although most web-centric applications are relatively easy to use, especially for the non-technical users, desktop applications are dedicated to the specific users and provide the specialized functionalities for more effective analysis (Inmon, Imhoff, & Sousa, 2001).

Risk management support refers to the organizational BI ability to support decisions under the conditions of uncertainty when not all the facts are known (Harding, 2003). Risk management is crucial to organizational success, and risk management support by BI applications is important, especially for organizations operating in the high-risk environments (Isik et al., 2013). Innovative organizations, which are recognized risk-tolerant, rely on BI to make the entrepreneurial decisions motivated by the exploration and discovery of new opportunities and new risks (Davenport, 2006).

Baars et al. (2014) indicated that major trends with a potential impact on BI include an ongoing increase of process complexity in the volatile global markets, a more informed consumer base interconnected by social networks, or the requirement to include the sustainability rationales into the product and supply chain strategies. Hopken et al. (2015) stated that various methods of BI have been applied in the field since the early stages of information and communication technology (ICT) adoption in tourism. Most ICT systems used in the tourism industry offer the BI functionalities, such as reporting and online analytical processing.

BI applications have been gradually ported to the web in search of a global platform for the consumption and publication of data and services. BI web applications need interfaces with a high level of interoperability (similar to the traditional desktop interfaces) for the visualization of data (Hermida, Melia, Montoyo, & Gomez, 2013). Regarding BI, analyzing data to predict the market trends of products and services and to improve the performances of enterprise business systems has always been part of running a competitive business (Azvine, Cui, & Nauck, 2005). The management of trust among the interacting parties are the significant parts of the overall BI strategy for modern organizations (Raza, Hussain, Hussain, & Chang, 2011).

Since ERP systems were not originally designed to provide the real-time reports to the users, the entire ERP systems could not facilitate the decision-support function (Chou, Tripuramallu, & Chou, 2005). Within the context of ERP, BI is the process of leveraging the detailed customer behavior information to effectively manage the relationships for increasing customer satisfaction, loyalty, retention, and profitability (Hall, 2004). The key component of BI strategy is a data management infrastructure that allows companies to acknowledge the changes of customer behavior (Gessner & Volonino, 2005). ERP with the collaboration of BI is expected to be more competitive in order to share the data for decision making and control (Umble, Haft, & Umble, 2003). For success in the ERP, the organization must have and shared knowledge on many manifestations around the process of BI since the relationship between BI and ERP has been recognized.

FUTURE RESEARCH DIRECTIONS

The strength of this chapter is on the thorough literature consolidation of BPM and BI. The extant literature of BPM and BI provides a contribution to practitioners and researchers by describing the multifaceted applications of BPM and BI to appeal to the different segments of BPM and BI in order to maximize the business impact of BPM and BI in global business. The classification of the extant literature in the domains of BPM and BI will provide the potential opportunities for future research. Future research direction should broaden the perspectives in the implementation of BPM and BI to be utilized in the knowledge-based organizations.

Practitioners and researchers should acknowledge the applicability of a more multidisciplinary approach toward research activities in implementing BPM and BI in terms of knowledge management-related variables (e.g., knowledge-sharing behavior, knowledge creation, organizational learning, learning orientation, and motivation to learn). It will be useful to bring the additional disciplines together (e.g., strategic management, marketing, finance, and human resources) to support a more holistic examination of BPM and BI in order to transfer the existing theories and approaches to the inquiry in this area.

CONCLUSION

This chapter aimed to master BPM and BI in global business, thus describing the overviews of BPM and BI; the importance of BPM in global business; and the importance of BI in global business. Effective management of business processes is essential for driving business agility in an enterprise. BPM enables organizations to align business functions with customer needs and helps executives determine how to deploy, monitor, and measure the organizational resources. When properly executed, BPM has the ability to enhance productivity, reduce costs, and minimize risk in global business.

BPM approach helps a business innovate and transform its approach to achieving more business value. Effective BPM ensures the great returns in terms of process automation and use of technology to enable the business user's experience; business agility to be able to identify and change as per changing business needs; ability to create the obvious understanding of the business process flow across the organization; ability to indicate business as a service for non-core business processes; and ability to better control and comply with audits and regulatory needs. Implementing best practices in BPM contributes to the improved financial management and provides the visibility into how well an organization is succeeding in meeting its strategic goals in global business.

BI represents the systems and tools that are important in the strategic planning processes of organization. BI is a perspective that typically involves the delivery and integration of relevant and useful business information in an organization. The purpose of BI is to support the business-related decision making via the interactive access, and the analysis of important corporate information. A proper BI system helps with obtaining the right information, at the right time, in the right format bridging the gaps between information silos of an organization. BI includes the applications, tools, and best practices that enable the analysis of information to improve organizational performance. Companies use BI to detect the significant events and identify the business trends in order to quickly adapt to their changing business environment. BI empowers decision making at all levels of management. BI provides the quick notification of business exceptions, advanced reporting, and the ability to compare data to improve the strategic management in global business.

The achievement of BPM and BI is significant for modern organizations that seek to serve suppliers and customers, increase business performance, strengthen competitiveness, and achieve continuous success in global business. Therefore, it is urgent for modern organizations to investigate their BPM and BI and develop a strategic plan to regularly check their practical advancements toward satisfying customer requirements. Applying BPM and BI has the potential to enhance organizational performance and gain sustainable competitive advantage in global business.

REFERENCES

Antonucci, Y. L., & Goeke, R. J. (2011). Identification of appropriate responsibilities and positions for business process management success: Seeking a valid and reliable framework. *Business Process Management Journal*, *17*(1), 127–146. doi:10.1108/14637151111105616

Armstrong, M. (2006). *A handbook of human resource management practice*. London, UK: Kogan Page.

Arnott, D. (2004). Decision support systems evolution: Framework, case study and research agenda. *European Journal of Information Systems*, *13*(4), 247–259. doi:10.1057/palgrave.ejis.3000509

Azvine, B., Cui, Z., Majeed, B., & Spott, M. (2007). Operational risk management with real-time business intelligence. *BT Technology Journal*, *25*(1), 154–167. doi:10.1007/s10550-007-0017-5

Azvine, B., Cui, Z., & Nauck, D. D. (2005). Towards real-time business intelligence. *BT Technology Journal*, *23*(3), 214–225. doi:10.1007/s10550-005-0043-0

Baars, H., Felden, C., Gluchowski, P., Hilbert, A., Kemper, H. G., & Olbrich, S. (2014). Shaping the next incarnation of business intelligence. *Business & Information Systems Engineering*, *6*(1), 11–16. doi:10.1007/s12599-013-0307-z

Baars, H., & Kemper, H. (2008). Management support with structured and unstructured data: An integrated business intelligence framework. *Information Systems Management*, *25*(2), 132–148. doi:10.1080/10580530801941058

Balzarova, M. A., Bamber, C. J., McCambridge, S., & Sharp, J. M. (2004). Key success factors in implementation of process-based management: A UK housing association experience. *Business Process Management Journal*, *10*(4), 387–399. doi:10.1108/14637150410548065

Becker, J., Knackstedt, R., & Poppelbuß, J. (2009). Developing maturity models for IT management: A procedure model and its application. *Business and Information Systems Engineering*, *1*(3), 213–222. doi:10.1007/s12599-009-0044-5

Becker, J., Kugeler, M., & Rosemann, M. (2003). *Process management: A guide for the design of business processes*. Berlin, Germany: Springer–Verlag. doi:10.1007/978-3-540-24798-2

Becker, J., Niehaves, B., Poppelbuß, J., & Simons, A. (2010). *Maturity models in IS research*. Paper presented at the European Conference on Information Systems (ECIS 2010), Pretoria, South Africa.

Bhatt, G. D., & Saad, G. H. (2005). Examining the relationship between business process improvement initiatives, information systems integration and customer focus: An empirical study. *Business Process Management Journal, 11*(5), 532–558. doi:10.1108/14637150510619876

Bi, H. H., & Zhao, J. L. (2004). Applying propositional logic to workflow verification. *Information Technology Management, 5*(3/4), 293–318. doi:10.1023/B:ITEM.0000031583.16306.0f

Bitkowska, A. (2015). The orientation of business process management toward the creation of knowledge in enterprises. *Human Factors and Ergonomics in Manufacturing & Service Industries, 25*(1), 43–57. doi:10.1002/hfm.20533

Bleistein, S. J., Cox, K., Verner, J., & Phalp, K. T. (2006). B-SCP: A requirements analysis framework for validating strategic alignment of organizational IT based on strategy, context, and process. *Information and Software Technology, 48*(9), 846–868. doi:10.1016/j.infsof.2005.12.001

Bonney, W. (2013). Applicability of business intelligence in electronic health record. *Procedia: Social and Behavioral Sciences, 73*, 257–262. doi:10.1016/j.sbspro.2013.02.050

Bosilj Vuksic, V., & Spremic, M. (2004). *Case study of PLIVA Pharmaceuticals Inc. – Aligning ERP system implementation with business process change*. Paper presented at the 26th International Conference on Information Technology Interfaces (ITI 2004), Cavtat, Croatia.

Brannon, N. (2010). Business intelligence and E-discovery. *Intellectual Property & Technology Law Journal, 22*(7), 1–5.

Buchanan, L., & O'Connell, A. (2006). A brief history of decision making. *Harvard Business Review, 84*(1), 32–40. PMID:16447367

Bucher, T., & Winter, R. (2006). Classification of business process management approaches: An exploratory analysis. *BIT – Banking and Information Technology, 7*(3), 9–20.

Bucher, T., & Winter, R. (2009). Project types of business process management: Towards a scenario structure to enable situational method engineering for business process management. *Business Process Management Journal, 15*(4), 548–568. doi:10.1108/14637150910975534

Chaffey, D., & Wood, S. (2005). *Business information management: Improving performance using information systems*. Englewood Cliffs, NJ: Prentice Hall.

Chaudhuri, S., Dayal, U., & Narasayya, V. (2011). An overview of business intelligence technology. *Communications of the ACM, 54*(8), 88–98. doi:10.1145/1978542.1978562

Chen, H., Chiang, R., & Storey, V. (2012). Business intelligence and analytics: From big data to big impact. *Management Information Systems Quarterly, 36*(4), 1165–1188.

Chen, X., & Siau, K. (2011). *Impact of business intelligence and IT infrastructure flexibility on competitive performance: An organizational agility perspective*. Paper presented at the International Conference on Information Systems (ICIS 2011), Shanghai, China.

Chou, D. C., Tripuramallu, H. B., & Chou, A. Y. (2005). BI and ERP integration. *Information Management & Computer Security*, *13*(5), 340–349. doi:10.1108/09685220510627241

Chou, T. H., & Seng, J. L. (2012). Telecommunication e-services orchestration enabling business process management. *Transactions on Emerging Telecommunications Technologies*, *23*(7), 646–659. doi:10.1002/ett.2520

Clark, T. D., Jones, M. C., & Armstrong, C. P. (2007). The dynamic structure of management support systems: Theory development, research focus, and direction. *Management Information Systems Quarterly*, *31*(3), 579–615.

Côrte-Real, N., Ruivo, P., & Oliveira, T. (2014). The diffusion stages of business intelligence & analytics (BI&A): A systematic mapping study. *Procedia Technology*, *16*, 172–179. doi:10.1016/j.protcy.2014.10.080

Curtis, B., Kellner, M. I., & Over, J. (1992). Process modeling. *Communications of the ACM*, *35*(9), 75–90. doi:10.1145/130994.130998

Davenport, T. H. (1993). *Process innovation*. Cambridge, MA: Harvard Business School Press.

Davenport, T. H. (2006). Competing on analytics. *Harvard Business Review*, *84*(1), 99–107. PMID:16447373

Davenport, T. H., & Short, J. (1990). The new industrial engineering: Information technology and business process redesign. *MIT Sloan Management Review*, *31*(4), 11–27.

de Bruin, T., Rosemann, M., Freeze, R., & Kulkarni, U. (2005). *Understanding the main phases of developing a maturity assessment model*. Paper presented at the Australasian Conference on Information Systems (ACIS 2005), Sydney, Australia.

Debortoli, S., Muller, O., & vom Brocke, J. (2014). Comparing business intelligence and big data skills. *Business & Information Systems Engineering*, *6*(5), 289–300. doi:10.1007/s12599-014-0344-2

Decreus, K., Poels, G., Kharbili, M. E., & Pulvermueller, E. (2010). Policy-enabled goal-oriented requirements engineering for semantic business process management. *International Journal of Intelligent Systems*, *25*(8), 784–812. doi:10.1002/int.20431

den Hamer, P. (2005). *The organisation of business intelligence*. The Hague, The Netherlands: SDU Publishers.

Earl, M. J., Sampler, J. L., & Short, J. E. (1995). Strategies for business process reengineering: Evidence from field studies. *Journal of Management Information Systems*, *12*(1), 31–56. doi:10.1080/07421222.1995.11518069

Eckerson, W. W. (2006). *Performance dashboards: Measuring, monitoring, and managing your business*. Hoboken, NJ: John Wiley & Sons.

Friedman, T. (2006). *Gartner study on data quality shows that IT still bears the burden*. Stamford, CT: Gartner.

Gebauer, J., & Schober, F. (2006). Information system flexibility and the cost efficiency of business processes. *Journal of the Association for Information Systems*, *7*(3), 122–145.

Gessner, G. H., & Volonino, L. (2005). Quick response improves returns on business intelligence investments. *Information Systems Management*, *22*(3), 66–74. doi:10.1201/1078/45317.22.3.20050601/88746.8

Gottschalk, P. (2009). Maturity levels for interoperability in digital government. *Government Information Quarterly*, *26*(1), 75–81. doi:10.1016/j.giq.2008.03.003

Grefen, P., Mehandjiev, N., Kouvas, G., Weichhart, G., & Eshuis, R. (2009). Dynamic business network process management in instant virtual enterprises. *Computers in Industry*, *60*(2), 86–103. doi:10.1016/j.compind.2008.06.006

Grover, V., Jeong, S. R., Kettinger, W. J., & Teng, J. T. C. (1995). The implementation of business process reengineering. *Journal of Management Information Systems*, *12*(1), 109–144. doi:10.1080/07421222.1995.11518072

Habul, A., & Pilav-Velic, A. (2010). *Business intelligence and customer relationship management*. Paper presented at the 32nd International Conference on Information Technology Interfaces (ITI 2010), Cavtat, Croatia.

Hall, J. (2004). Business intelligence: The missing link in your CRM strategy. *DM REVIEW*, *14*, 36–40.

Hammer, M. (2007). The process audit. *Harvard Business Review*, *85*(4), 111–123. PMID:17432158

Hammer, M., & Champy, J. (2003). *Reengineering the corporation: A manifesto for business revolution*. New York, NY: Harper Business.

Harding, W. (2003). BI crucial to making the right decision. *Financial Executive*, *19*(2), 49–50.

Harmon, P. (2007). *Business process change: A guide for business managers and BMP and Six Sigma professionals*. Amsterdam, The Netherlands: Elsevier/Morgan Kaufmann Publishers.

Hermida, J. M., Melia, S., Montoyo, A., & Gomez, J. (2013). Applying model-driven engineering to the development of rich Internet applications for business intelligence. *Information Systems Frontiers*, *15*(3), 411–431. doi:10.1007/s10796-012-9402-9

Herrmann, T., & Walter, T. (1998). *The relevance of showcases for the participative improvement of business processes and workflow management*. Paper presented at the Participatory Design Conference (PDC 1998), Seattle, WA.

Hirschheim, R., Schwarz, A., & Todd, P. (2006). A marketing maturity model for IT: Building a customer-centric IT organization. *IBM Systems Journal*, *45*(1), 181–199. doi:10.1147/sj.451.0181

Hocevar, B., & Jaklic, J. (2010). Assessing benefits of business intelligence systems: A case study. *Management: Journal of Contemporary Management Issues*, *15*(1), 87–119.

Hopken, W., Fuchs, M., Keil, D., & Lexhagen, M. (2015). Business intelligence for cross-process knowledge extraction at tourism destinations. *Information Technology & Tourism*, *15*(2), 101–130. doi:10.1007/s40558-015-0023-2

Houghton, R., El Sawy, O. A., Gray, P., Donegan, C., & Joshi, A. (2004). Vigilant information systems for managing enterprises in dynamic supply chains: Real-time dashboards at western digital. *MIS Quarterly Executive*, *3*(1), 19–35.

Houy, C., Fettke, P., & Loos, P. (2010). Empirical research in business process management: Analysis of an emerging field of research. *Business Process Management Journal, 16*(4), 619–661. doi:10.1108/14637151011065946

Hung, R. Y. (2006). Business process management as competitive advantage: A review and empirical study. *Total Quality Management, 17*(1), 21–40. doi:10.1080/14783360500249836

Inmon, W. H., Imhoff, C., & Sousa, R. (2001). *Corporate information factory*. New York, NY: John Wiley & Sons.

Isik, O., Jones, M. C., & Sidorova, A. (2011). Business intelligence (BI) success and the role of BI capabilities. *Intelligent Systems in Accounting, Finance & Management, 18*(4), 161–176. doi:10.1002/isaf.329

Isik, O., Jones, M. C., & Sidorova, A. (2013). Business intelligence success: The roles of BI capabilities and decision environments. *Information & Management, 50*(1), 13–23. doi:10.1016/j.im.2012.12.001

Iversen, J., Nielsen, P. A., & Norbjerg, J. (1999). Situated assessment of problems in software development. *The Data Base for Advances in Information Systems, 30*(2), 66–81. doi:10.1145/383371.383376

Janz, B. D., Pitts, M. G., & Otondo, R. F. (2005). Information systems and health care II: Back to the future with RFID: Lessons learned–some old, some new. *Communications of the Association for Information Systems, 15*(1), 132–148.

Jeston, J., & Nelis, J. (2008). *Business process management: Practical guidelines to successful Implementations*. Amsterdam, The Netherlands: Elsevier.

Jourdan, Z., Rainer, R. K., & Marshall, T. E. (2008). Business intelligence: An analysis of the literature. *Information Systems Management, 25*(2), 121–131. doi:10.1080/10580530801941512

Jung, J., Choi, I., & Song, M. (2007). An integration architecture for knowledge management systems and business process management systems. *Computers in Industry, 58*(1), 21–34. doi:10.1016/j.compind.2006.03.001

Kagermann, H., Osterle, H., & Jordan, J. M. (2010). *IT-driven business models*. Hoboken, NJ: John Wiley & Sons.

Kaplan, R. S., & Norton, D. P. (1996). *The balanced scorecard*. Boston, MA: Harvard Business School Press.

Karim, J., Sommers, T. M., & Bhattacherjee, A. (2007). The impact of ERP implementation on business process outcomes: A factor-based study. *Journal of Management Information Systems, 24*(1), 101–134. doi:10.2753/MIS0742-1222240103

Kasemsap, K. (2015a). The role of business process reengineering in the modern business world. In A. Singh (Ed.), *Achieving enterprise agility through innovative software development* (pp. 87–114). Hershey, PA: IGI Global. doi:10.4018/978-1-4666-8510-9.ch005

Kasemsap, K. (2015b). Implementing enterprise resource planning. In M. Khosrow-Pour (Ed.), *Encyclopedia of information science and technology* (3rd ed., pp. 798–807). Hershey, PA: IGI Global. doi:10.4018/978-1-4666-5888-2.ch076

Kasemsap, K. (2015c). The role of information system within enterprise architecture and their impact on business performance. In M. Wadhwa & A. Harper (Eds.), *Technology, innovation, and enterprise transformation* (pp. 262–284). Hershey, PA: IGI Global. doi:10.4018/978-1-4666-6473-9.ch012

Kasemsap, K. (2015d). The roles of information technology and knowledge management in project management metrics. In G. Jamil, S. Lopes, A. Malheiro da Silva, & F. Ribeiro (Eds.), *Handbook of research on effective project management through the integration of knowledge and innovation* (pp. 332–361). Hershey, PA: IGI Global. doi:10.4018/978-1-4666-7536-0.ch018

Kasemsap, K. (2015e). The role of radio frequency identification in modern libraries. In S. Thanuskodi (Ed.), *Handbook of research on inventive digital tools for collection management and development in modern libraries* (pp. 361–385). Hershey, PA: IGI Global. doi:10.4018/978-1-4666-8178-1.ch021

Kasemsap, K. (2015f). The role of business analytics in performance management. In M. Tavana & K. Puranam (Eds.), *Handbook of research on organizational transformations through big data analytics* (pp. 126–145). Hershey, PA: IGI Global. doi:10.4018/978-1-4666-7272-7.ch010

Kasemsap, K. (2015g). Implementing business intelligence in contemporary organizations. In A. Haider (Ed.), *Business technologies in contemporary organizations: Adoption, assimilation, and institutionalization* (pp. 177–192). Hershey, PA: IGI Global. doi:10.4018/978-1-4666-6623-8.ch008

Kasemsap, K. (2015h). The role of data mining for business intelligence in knowledge management. In A. Azevedo & M. Santos (Eds.), *Integration of data mining in business intelligence systems* (pp. 12–33). Hershey, PA: IGI Global. doi:10.4018/978-1-4666-6477-7.ch002

Kasemsap, K. (2016a). The roles of business process modeling and business process reengineering in e-government. In J. Martins & A. Molnar (Eds.), *Handbook of research on innovations in information retrieval, analysis, and management* (pp. 401–430). Hershey, PA: IGI Global. doi:10.4018/978-1-4666-8833-9.ch015

Kasemsap, K. (2016b). The roles of lifelong learning and knowledge management in global higher education. In P. Ordóñez de Pablos & R. Tennyson (Eds.), *Impact of economic crisis on education and the next-generation workforce* (pp. 71–100). Hershey, PA: IGI Global. doi:10.4018/978-1-4666-9455-2.ch004

Kasemsap, K. (2016c). Advocating entrepreneurship education and knowledge management in global business. In N. Baporikar (Ed.), *Handbook of research on entrepreneurship in the contemporary knowledge-based global economy* (pp. 313–339). Hershey, PA: IGI Global. doi:10.4018/978-1-4666-8798-1.ch014

Khalil, O. (1997). Implications for the role of information systems in a business process reengineering environment. *Information Resources Management Journal*, *10*(1), 36–43. doi:10.4018/irmj.1997010103

Khan, M. K., Sohail, M., Aamir, M., Chowdhry, B. S., & Hyder, S. I. (2014). Web support system for business intelligence in small and medium enterprises. *Wireless Personal Communications*, *76*(3), 535–548. doi:10.1007/s11277-014-1723-1

Khan, R. N. (2004). *Business process management: A practical guide*. Tampa, FL: Meghan–Kiffer Press.

Kujansivu, P., & Lönnqvist, A. (2008). Business process management as a tool for intellectual capital management. *Knowledge and Process Management*, *15*(3), 159–169. doi:10.1002/kpm.307

Kumar, A., & Zhao, J. L. (2002). Workflow support for electronic commerce applications. *Decision Support Systems, 32*(3), 265–278. doi:10.1016/S0167-9236(01)00114-2

Kuznets, S. (1965). *Economic growth and structure*. London, UK: Heinemann Educational Books.

Kwan, M. M., & Balasubramanian, P. R. (1998). Adding workflow analysis techniques to the IS development toolkit. Paper presented at the 31st Hawaii International Conference on System Sciences (HICSS-31), Honolulu, HI. doi:10.1109/HICSS.1998.655287

Lamont, J. (2006). Business intelligence: The text analysis strategy. *KM World, 15*(10), 8–10.

Lippert, S. K., & Govindarajulu, C. (2006). Technological, organizational, and environmental antecedents to web services adoption. *Communications of the IIMA, 6*(1), 146–158.

Luftman, J., Kempaiah, R., & Nash, E. (2006). Key issues for IT executives 2005. *MIS Quarterly Executive, 5*(2), 81–99.

Mahmoodzadeh, E., Jalalinia, S., & Yazdi, F. N. (2009). A business process outsourcing framework based on business process management and knowledge management. *Business Process Management Journal, 15*(6), 845–864. doi:10.1108/14637150911003748

Manglik, A., & Mehra, V. (2005). Extending enterprise BI capabilities: New patterns for data integration. *Business Intelligence Journal, 10*(1), 10–17.

Mansar, S. L., & Reijers, H. A. (2005). Best practices in business process redesign: Validation of a redesign framework. *Computers in Industry, 56*(5), 457–471. doi:10.1016/j.compind.2005.01.001

Maslow, A. (1954). *Motivation and personality*. New York, NY: Harper Business.

McDonald, M. P. (2007). The enterprise capability organization: A future for IT. *MIS Quarterly Executive, 6*(3), 179–192.

Minonne, C., & Turner, G. (2012). Business process management: Are you ready for the future? *Knowledge and Process Management, 19*(3), 111–120. doi:10.1002/kpm.1388

Munro, M. C., & Davis, G. B. (1977). Determining management information needs: A comparison of methods. *Management Information Systems Quarterly, 1*(2), 55–67. doi:10.2307/249168

Negash, S. (2004). Business intelligence. *Communications of the Association for Information Systems, 13*(1), 177–195.

Neubauer, T. (2009). An empirical study about the status of business process management. *Business Process Management Journal, 15*(2), 166–183. doi:10.1108/14637150910949434

Niu, L., Lu, J., Zhang, G., & Wu, D. (2013). FACETS: A cognitive business intelligence system. *Information Systems, 38*(6), 835–862. doi:10.1016/j.is.2013.02.002

Nofal, M. I., & Yusof, Z. M. (2013). Integration of business intelligence and enterprise resource planning within organizations. *Procedia Technology, 11*, 658–665. doi:10.1016/j.protcy.2013.12.242

Nolan, R. L. (1979). Managing the crisis in data processing. *Harvard Business Review, 57*(2), 115–126.

Ofner, M. H., Otto, B., & Osterle, H. (2012). Integrating a data quality perspective into business process management. *Business Process Management Journal, 18*(6), 1036–1067. doi:10.1108/14637151211283401

Paim, R., Cauliraux, H. M., & Cardoso, R. (2008). Process management tasks: A conceptual and practical view. *Business Process Management Journal, 14*(5), 694–723. doi:10.1108/14637150810903066

Phan, D. D., & Vogel, D. R. (2010). A model of customer relationship management and business intelligence systems for catalogue and online retailers. *Information & Management, 47*(2), 69–77. doi:10.1016/j.im.2009.09.001

Prananto, A., Mckay, J., & Marshall, P. (2003). *A study of the progression of e-business maturity in Australian SMEs: Some evidence of the applicability of the stages of growth for e-business model.* Paper presented at Pacific Asia Conference on Information Systems (PACIS 2003), Adelaide, Australia.

Price, R., & Shanks, G. G. (2005). A semiotic information quality framework: Development and comparative analysis. *Journal of Information Technology, 20*(2), 88–102. doi:10.1057/palgrave.jit.2000038

Ramakrishnan, T., Jones, M. C., & Sidorova, A. (2012). Factors influencing business intelligence (BI) data collection strategies: An empirical investigation. *Decision Support Systems, 52*(2), 486–496. doi:10.1016/j.dss.2011.10.009

Ravesteyn, P. (2009). A context dependent implementation method for business process management systems. *Communications of the IIMA, 9*(1), 31–45.

Raza, M., Hussain, O. K., Hussain, F. K., & Chang, E. (2011). Maturity, distance and density (MD^2) metrics for optimizing trust prediction for business intelligence. *Journal of Global Optimization, 51*(2), 285–300. doi:10.1007/s10898-010-9598-5

Redman, T. C. (2004). Barriers to successful data quality management. *Studies in Communication Sciences, 4*(2), 53–68.

Reich, B. H., & Nelson, K. M. (2003). In their own words: CIO visions about the future of in-house IT organizations. *ACM SIGMIS Database, 34*(4), 28–44. doi:10.1145/957758.957763

Reid, A., & Catterall, M. (2005). Invisible data quality issues in a CRM implementation. *Journal of Database Marketing & Customer Strategy Management, 12*(4), 305–314. doi:10.1057/palgrave.dbm.3240267

Reinschmidt, J., & Françoise, A. (2000). *Business intelligence certification guide.* San Jose, CA: IBM, International Technical Support Organization.

Roglinger, M., Poppelbuß, J., & Becker, J. (2012). Maturity models in business process management. *Business Process Management Journal, 18*(2), 328–346. doi:10.1108/14637151211225225

Rohloff, M. (2011). Advances in business process management implementation based on a maturity assessment and best practice exchange. *Information Systems* and *e-Business Management, 9*(3), 383–403. doi:10.1007/s10257-010-0137-1

Rosemann, M., & de Bruin, T. (2005). *Towards a business process management maturity model.* Paper presented at the European Conference on Information Systems (ECIS 2005), Regensburg, Germany.

Ross, J. W., Beath, C. M., & Goodhue, D. L. (1996). Develop long-term competitiveness through IT assets. *MIT Sloan Management Review*, *38*(1), 31–44.

Rubin, E., & Rubin, A. (2013). The impact of business intelligence systems on stock return volatility. *Information & Management*, *50*(2-3), 67–75. doi:10.1016/j.im.2013.01.002

Sabherwal, R., & Becerra-Fernandez, I. (2010). *Business intelligence: Practices, technologies, and management*. Hoboken, NJ: John Wiley & Sons.

Sahay, B. S., & Ranjan, J. (2008). Real time business intelligence in supply chain analytics. *Information Management & Computer Security*, *16*(1), 28–48. doi:10.1108/09685220810862733

Scheer, A. W. (1992). *Architecture of integrated information systems: Foundations of enterprise modelling*. Berlin, Germany: Springer–Verlag. doi:10.1007/978-3-642-97389-5

Scheer, A. W. (1999). *ARIS – business process frameworks*. Berlin, Germany: Springer–Verlag. doi:10.1007/978-3-642-58529-6

Schulte, S., Janiesch, C., Venugopa, S., Weber, I., & Hoenisch, P. (2015). Elastic business process management: State of the art and open challenges for BPM in the cloud. *Future Generation Computer Systems*, *46*, 36–50. doi:10.1016/j.future.2014.09.005

Scott, J. E. (2007). Mobility, business process management, software sourcing, and maturity model trends: Propositions for the IS organization of the future. *Information Systems Management*, *24*(2), 139–145. doi:10.1080/10580530701221031

Shaw, D. R., Holland, C. P., Kawalek, P., Snowdon, B., & Warboys, B. (2007). Elements of a business process management system: Theory and practice. *Business Process Management Journal*, *13*(1), 91–107. doi:10.1108/14637150710721140

Shim, J. P., Varshney, U., & Dekleva, S. (2006). Wireless evolution 2006: Cellular TV, wearable computing, and RFID. *Communications of the Association for Information Systems*, *18*(1), 497–518.

Smith, H., & Fingar, P. (2007). *Business process management: The third wave*. Tampa, FL: Meghan-Kiffer Press.

Stohr, E. A., & Zhao, J. L. (2001). Workflow automation: Overview and research issues. *Information Systems Frontiers*, *3*(3), 281–296. doi:10.1023/A:1011457324641

Strnadl, C. F. (2006). Aligning business and it: The process-driven architecture model. *Information Systems Management*, *23*(4), 67–77. doi:10.1201/1078.10580530/46352.23.4.20060901/95115.9

Sukumaran, A., & Sureka, A. (2006). Integrating structured and unstructured using text tagging and annotation. *Business Intelligence Journal*, *11*(2), 8–17.

Taylor, F. W. (1911). *The principles of scientific management*. New York, NY: Harper Business.

Trkman, P. (2010). The critical success factors of business process management. *International Journal of Information Management*, *30*(2), 125–134. doi:10.1016/j.ijinfomgt.2009.07.003

Umble, E. J., Haft, R. R., & Umble, M. M. (2003). Enterprise resource planning: Implementation procedures and critical success factors. *European Journal of Operational Research, 146*(2), 241–257. doi:10.1016/S0377-2217(02)00547-7

Umble, E. J., & Umble, M. M. (2002). Avoiding ERP implementation failure. *Industrial Management (Des Plaines), 44*(1), 25–33.

van der Aalst, W. M. P. (1998). The application of Petri nets to workflow management. *Journal of Circuits, Systems, and Computers, 8*(1), 21–66. doi:10.1142/S0218126698000043

van der Aalst, W. M. P., Dumas, M., & ter Hofstede, A. H. (2003). *Web service composition languages: Old wine in new bottles?* Paper presented at the 29th Conference on EUROMICRO (EUROMICRO 2003), Washington, DC. doi:10.1109/EURMIC.2003.1231605

Vidgen, R., & Wang, X. (2006). From business process management to business process ecosystem. *Journal of Information Technology, 21*(4), 262–271. doi:10.1057/palgrave.jit.2000076

von Brocke, J., & Sinnl, T. (2011). Culture in business process management: A literature review. *Business Process Management Journal, 17*(2), 357–377. doi:10.1108/14637151111122383

Wang, M., & Wang, H. (2006). From process logic to business logic: A cognitive approach to business process management. *Information & Management, 43*(2), 179–193. doi:10.1016/j.im.2005.06.001

Watson, H. J., & Wixom, B. H. (2007). Enterprise agility and mature BI capabilities. *Business Intelligence Journal, 12*(3), 13–28.

Watson, H. J., Wixom, B. H., Hoffer, J. A., Anderson-Lehman, R., & Reynolds, A. M. (2006). Real-time business intelligence: Best practices at Continental Airlines. *Information Systems Management, 23*(1), 7–18. doi:10.1201/1078.10580530/45769.23.1.20061201/91768.2

Weske, M. (2007). *Business process management: Concepts, languages, architectures*. Berlin, Germany: Springer–Verlag.

Zabjek, D., Kovacic, A., & Stemberger, M. I. (2009). The influence of business process management and some other CSFs on successful ERP implementation. *Business Process Management Journal, 15*(4), 588–608. doi:10.1108/14637150910975552

Zack, M. H. (2007). The role of decision support systems in an indeterminate world. *Decision Support Systems, 43*(4), 1664–1674. doi:10.1016/j.dss.2006.09.003

Zeng, L., Li, L., & Duan, L. (2012). Business intelligence in enterprise computing environment. *Information Technology Management, 13*(4), 297–310. doi:10.1007/s10799-012-0123-z

Zhang, M., & Tansuhaj, P. (2007). Organizational culture, information technology capability, and performance: The case of born global firms. *Multinational Business Review, 15*(3), 43–77. doi:10.1108/1525383X200700012

KEY TERMS AND DEFINITIONS

Business: An organization or economic system where products and services are exchanged for one another or for money.

Business Intelligence: The computer-based techniques used in spotting and analyzing business data, such as sales revenue by products or associated costs and incomes.

Business Process Management: The development and control of processes used in a company, department, and project to ensure they are effective.

Data: The information collected to be examined and used to help decision making.

Data Mining: The examination of large amounts of information stored in a computer in order to look for patterns and changes.

Enterprise Resource Planning: A system of software which is designed to manage all the information and activities of a company by using shared data.

Information System: A combination of hardware, software, infrastructure, and trained personnel organized to facilitate the planning, control, coordination, and decision making in an organization.

Information Technology: The set of tools, processes, and associated equipment employed to collect, process, and present the information.

Chapter 11
Information and Communication Technology Impact on Supply Chain Integration, Flexibility, and Performance

Carlos A Talamantes-Padilla
Universidad Autónoma de Ciudad Juárez, Mexico

Jorge Luis. García-Alcaráz
Universidad Autónoma de Ciudad Juárez, Mexico

Aide A. Maldonado-Macías
Universidad Autónoma de Ciudad Juárez, Mexico

Giner Alor-Hernández
Instituto Tecnologico de Orizaba, Mexico

Cuauhtemoc Sánchéz-Ramírez
Instituto Tecnológico de Orizaba, Mexico

Juan L Hernández-Arellano
Universidad Autónoma de Ciudad Juárez, Mexico

ABSTRACT

In this chapter, four latent variables will be analyzed to measure the impact of Information and Communications Technology (ICT) on the integration, flexibility and performance of Supply Chain (SC). The aim of the exposition is to provide greater understanding for those responsible of the supply chain, and focus efforts on clear objectives. These clear objectives should help those responsible for the supply chain achieve a better performance within organizations. The information analyzed was obtained from a questionnaire provided to 284 managers in companies located in Ciudad Juarez, Mexico. The results were used to generate a structural equation model in order to learn the relationships between variables. We have postulated six hypotheses regarding the direct, indirect and total effects. The results indicate that there is no direct relationship between ICT integration and SC performance, but an indirect relationship through mediating variables as SC Integration and Flexibility exists.

DOI: 10.4018/978-1-5225-0654-6.ch011

INTRODUCTION

Supply Chains

The Supply Chain study has taken an important role within companies, because it is formed by all the institutions and processes that are involved in meeting the customer needs; starting from the extraction of raw materials to finished product and delivery to the end costumer. Efficient administration of supply chains can provide significant competitive advantage and increase organizational performance.

Supply Chain management is defined as the integration of key business processes from end customer until original suppliers that provide products, services and information, which add value for customers and stakeholders of the company (Lambert, Cooper, & Pagh, 1998; Themistocleous, Irani, & Love, 2004; Yu, Suojapelto, Hallikas, & Tang, 2008).

The main elements of a supply chain are: customers, retailers, distributors, manufacturers and suppliers and along this chain there is a two-way flow of materials, products, services, payment and information. In Figure 1, these elements are shown linearly; however in practice it is a network of companies connected.

In supply chain management, some factors can affect performance, including working capital, proximity to suppliers and customers, stability of government policies, structure of the supply chain, among others (Acar & Uzunlar, 2014; Capaldo & Giannoccaro, 2015; C. Marinagi, Trivellas, & Reklitis, 2015; Vlachos, 2014). Another critical factor is region infrastructure, both physical and technological, in this sense, ICTs have proven to be an important support in the Supply Chain performance (Acar & Uzunlar, 2014; Catherine Marinagi, Trivellas, & Sakas, 2014; Singh & Teng, 2016).

ICTs and Its Integration into Supply Chains

The term information and communications technology (ICT) includes the set of techniques and devices used for the processing and transmission of data. The ICT concept encompasses all information exchange services, telecommunications networks that support the data exchange and terminals used to access to services (Altés, 2013).

The integration of information and communications technology has proved been indispensable not only in the modern world, but also in the business environment, due to companies established offices and branches in any location regardless of distance, focusing on the benefits that site represents, maintaining trade relations with partners in these points and speeding the material flow. Thus, it is important to maintain communication between departments and branches around the world, this can be achieved by integrating information and communication technology, as well as keeping in touch in an effective and virtual way to all of the different functions and partners in the supply chain (Li, Lin, Wang, & Yan, 2006; Ngai, Chau, & Chan, 2011).

Figure 1. Components of supply chain

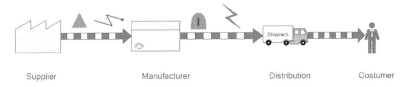

Information and Communication Technology Impact

ICT provides organizations with elements to collect, store, enter, share, and analyze data (Swafford, Ghosh, & Murthy, 2008), and as a result, they have become into essential tools for companies. Besides other benefits of maintaining an integrated structure of ICT between companies and their SC are mentioned, such as reducing costs and achieve competitive advantages through real-time response (Themistocleous et al., 2004). It also helps the organization through the efficient information flow, tracking market needs and allowing to move resources in a quick way (Ngai et al., 2011).

Focusing on the ICTs impact on the supply chain integration, it is important to maintain a good structure to promote it, providing business information to the appropriate group in an efficient way, timely and transparent, in addition, it reduces the time needed to share knowledge and information (Pearcy & Giunipero, 2008). Therefore, the following hypothesis is proposed:

Supply Chain Integration

The supply chain integration has been considered one of the most important competences in the supply chain management (Pearcy & Giunipero, 2008) and is defined as the formation of a network in which, outside members manage in collaboration with intra- and inter-organizational processes, in order to achieve mutually acceptable results (D. Kim & Cavusgil, 2009; Ngai et al., 2011).

Some benefits associated with the integration of supply chain systems include the acquisition of competitive advantage, reducing operating costs and achieving better collaboration and coordination between partners, which sounds appealing to any administrator (Themistocleous et al., 2004). The integration of intra-and inter-organizational processes is imperative, due to it can increase performance of individual companies as well as the global supply chain, and the internal integration is achieved when a firm effectively coordinates multiple processes throughout a company. In order to achieve integration through different companies (external integration), companies must recognize the importance of suppliers as an integral part in the supply chain and engage in collaborative efforts with them. Some potential benefits of effective integration of the supply chain, include efficiency and interaction through the members, increasing visibility and operational efficiency (Pearcy & Giunipero, 2008). Nowadays, the external integration is achieved through efficiency by information and communications technology.

According to last paragraphs, the following hypothesis is proposed:

H$_1$: *ICT integration* has a direct and positive impact on the *SC Integration*.

Supply Chain Flexibility

The flexibility of the supply chain represents the inner workings of a company such as development, purchasing, manufacturing and distribution, as well as reducing product development time, ensuring production capacity and providing different products and at the same time meet to the customer expectations, and it is classified into strategic flexibility and manufacturing flexibility (Swafford, Ghosh, & Murthy, 2008).

Strategic flexibility is competition to identify changes in the environment, commit resources quickly to new courses of action in response to change, recognize and act immediately to stop and reverse the commitment of that resource. Manufacturing flexibility is competition to manage manufacturing resources in order to meet customer requirements (Ngai et al., 2011). Based on this, strategic flexibility is related to fast decision making and commitment to the answer, while manufacturing flexibility is related to the operational ability to implement strategic decisions (Ngai et al., 2011), so flexibility is given to the supply chain, by making decisions, the resources needed to perform appropriate actions and the ability to process these resources. The flexibility of the supply chain can also be defined as the different states that a manufacturing system can take, the ability to shift production from one product to another, and the ability to perform satisfactorily by manufacturing good quality products within a specific range (Ngai et al., 2011; Stevenson & Spring, 2007).

According to last information, the following hypotheses are proposed:

H$_2$: The *ICT Integration* has a direct and positive impact on the *SC Flexibility*.
H$_3$: The *SC Integration* has a direct and positive impact on the *SC Flexibility*.

Supply Chain Performance

The supply chain performance is measured based on different attributes, which are considered metrics used to determine the ability to deliver products and services of good quality, on time, quantity and lower cost (Böhm, Leone, & Henning, 2007). In order to get a better idea of the SC state, it is recommended to generate metrics associated with marketing, policies and regulations, technologies available to aid in the movement of materials, product development, production process capability, procurement and operations, transportation and logistics (Hassini, Surti, & Searcy, 2012).

Some authors consider that the taxonomy of metrics should include economic aspects (Clemens, 2006; Vachon & Klassen, 2008; Zhu & Sarkis, 2004), environmental factors (Clemens, 2006; Hervani, Helms, & Sarkis, 2005; Sarkis, 2006; Searcy, McCartney, & Karapetrovic, 2007; Vachon & Klassen, 2008; Vachon & Mao, 2008; Zhu & Sarkis, 2004), as well as social elements (Searcy et al., 2007; Zhu & Sarkis, 2004).

However, the generation of financial resources has always been the main objective for industrial enterprises, thus, economic metrics in the SC are traditionally used (Chen & Paulraj, 2004; Mansoornejad, Pistikopoulos, & Stuart, 2013), which help to measure the growth in sales, profitability and return on inventory (Gunasekaran, Patel, & McGaughey, 2004).

Thus, all companies must measure the SC Economic Performance, which will allow them to know their actual status and generate continuous improvement procedures (Popova & Sharpanskykh, 2010; Wlendahl, von Cleminskf, & Begemann, 2003). These metrics obtained in the SC performance, are based on several aspects, such as the SC Flexibility, thus, the following hypothesis is proposed:

H$_4$: The *SC Flexibility* of a company has a direct and positive impact on the *SC Economic Performance*.

However, the SC Performance has several sources, one is the integration level that achieve companies that conform it, although, studies realized warn of the risks and dangers when those integration levels and interdependence are high (Wiengarten, Humphreys, Gimenez, & McIvor, 2015), then there may be bullwhip effects in the material flow (Świerczek, 2014) therefore, the supply chain managers face a number of challenges to achieve this integration (Mohammad, Shukor, Mahbub, & Halil, 2014). Even, some authors question whether these integration levels are beneficial from a financial view to the supply chain members (Zhao, Feng, & Wang, 2015). In order to contribute to this research topic, the following hypothesis is proposed.

H₅: The *SC Integration* has a direct and positive effect on the *SC Performance*

Another source of *SC Performance* is the technology level along it, due to they are different enterprises, information and communications technology is great to keep the members of the SC in communication in real time (Acar & Uzunlar, 2014) and currently its application is an industrial trend (El Kadiri et al., 2015). At the present, it is recommended considering the use of ICT as an essential part in the formulation of strategies that can generate a competitive advantage (Mensah, Merkuryev, & Longo, 2015), as they help to achieve better SC visibility and therefore streamline the decision-making process. (Lee, Kim, & Kim, 2014). The following hypothesis is proposed in order to contribute to this research topic.

H₆: The *ICT Integration* has a direct and positive impact on the *SC Performance*

Graphical representation of the hypotheses are illustrated in Figure 2 as a sequential flow and indicating the hypotheses as relationships with arrows from a latent variable to another.

METHODOLOGY

The methodology that is used in this research involves the design of a data collection instrument (questionnaire) and identification of benefits that are obtained after a successful ICTs implementation process. Then the survey has been applied to active managers in manufacturing industries in logistics related areas to collect information, do some statistical analysis and get a conclusion based on findings, so the work is executed on different stages described below.

Figure 2. Proposed hypotheses

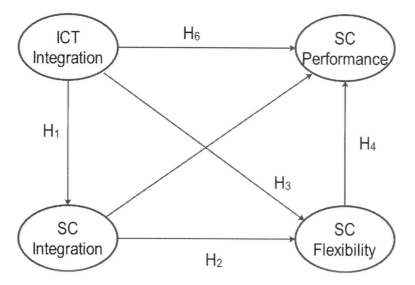

Survey Development

This stage is focused on the design of a survey and a literature review is conducted. Four latent variables are analyzed in this research, but each one is integrated by another observable variables or items. In Table 1 appears the distribution for every latent variable: *ICT Integration* with 13 items, *SC Integration* with 15 items, *SC Flexibility* with 11 items, and finally, *SC performance* with 6 items, but also appears some authors that are supporting the item integration in that latent variable.

Table 1. Latent variables and items

ICTs Integration
The company has a network of ICT systems (ERP, CRM, SCM, Intranet, etc.) integrated with key suppliers (Burt, Dobler, & Starling, 2003; Cook, 2001; Gunasekaran & Ngai, 2004; S. W. Kim, 2009; Moon, Yi, & Ngai, 2012; Swafford et al., 2008; Themistocleous et al., 2004)
The company shares information in real time through ICT with key suppliers (Ballou, 2004; Cook, 2001; Geissbauer, Roussel, Schrauf, & Strom, 2013; Moon et al., 2012; Themistocleous et al., 2004)
The company allows access and share sensitive information through ICT with key suppliers. (Burt et al., 2003; S. W. Kim, 2009; Themistocleous et al., 2004)
The company works to get a better ICT alignment with key suppliers (Burt et al., 2003; Moon et al., 2012; Themistocleous et al., 2004)
The company shares information in real-time through ICT within the organization. (Ballou, 2004; Burt et al., 2003; S. W. Kim, 2009; Moon et al., 2012; Themistocleous et al., 2004)
The company allows access and share sensitive information through ICT within the organization (Ballou, 2004; Burt et al., 2003; S. W. Kim, 2009; Moon et al., 2012; Themistocleous et al., 2004)
The company has a network of ICT systems (ERP, CRM, SCM, Intranet, etc.) integrated with key customers (Burt et al., 2003; Gunasekaran & Ngai, 2004; S. W. Kim, 2009; Moon et al., 2012; Swafford et al., 2008; Themistocleous et al., 2004)
The company shares information in real time through ICT with key customers (Burt et al., 2003; Geissbauer et al., 2013; S. W. Kim, 2009; Moon et al., 2012; Themistocleous et al., 2004)
The company allows access and share sensitive information through ICT with key costumers (Ballou, 2004; Burt et al., 2003; S. W. Kim, 2009; Themistocleous et al., 2004)
The company works to get a better ICT alignment with key costumers (Burt et al., 2003; Themistocleous et al., 2004)
The company has a high degree of feedback through ICT (Alfalla-Luque, Marin-Garcia, & Medina-Lopez, 2015)
The company shares demand forecasts and production planning with suppliers (Cook, 2001; Geissbauer et al., 2013)
The company receives demand forecasts and production planning from their customers (Cook, 2001; Geissbauer et al., 2013)
SC Integration
The company develops strategic plans and forecasts in collaboration with key suppliers (Alfalla-Luque et al., 2015; Burt et al., 2003; Hoejmose, Brammer, & Millington, 2012; S. W. Kim, 2009)
The company has a small number of key suppliers (Burt et al., 2003)
The company shares information about purchasing, inventory levels and forecasts with key suppliers (Alfalla-Luque et al., 2015; Burt et al., 2003; Geissbauer et al., 2013; S. W. Kim, 2009)
The company expects a long-term relationship with key suppliers (Alfalla-Luque et al., 2015; Burt et al., 2003)
The company expects a long-term relationship with costumers (Burt et al., 2003)
The company provides services and support to its customers. (Alfalla-Luque et al., 2015; Burt et al., 2003)
The company measures customer satisfaction (Alfalla-Luque et al., 2015; S. W. Kim, 2009)
In the company exist cross-functional working groups which discuss issues about material and design (Burt et al., 2003; S. W. Kim, 2009)

continued on following page

Information and Communication Technology Impact

Table 1. Continued

Customers are part of the product design process (Alfalla-Luque et al., 2015; Burt et al., 2003; S. W. Kim, 2009)
The company measures the performance of its suppliers in CS. (Cook, 2001)
The company measures the performance of its customers in CS. (Cook, 2001)
The company has a high-level of internal integration (Alfalla-Luque et al., 2015)
The company has a lot of information about the state of CS (Alfalla-Luque et al., 2015; Ballou, 2004; Burt et al., 2003; Geissbauer et al., 2013; S. W. Kim, 2009)
The company maintains a high-level of interdepartmental communication (Alfalla-Luque et al., 2015; Burt et al., 2003)
The company keeps strategic relationships with key suppliers based on loyalty and trust (Burt et al., 2003; Hoejmose et al., 2012)
SC Flexibility
Regarding competitors, exist processes that can adjust to changes in mass and mix of products. (Alfalla-Luque et al., 2015; Cook, 2001; Geissbauer et al., 2013; S. W. Kim, 2009; Moon et al., 2012; Swafford et al., 2008; Thomé, Scavarda, Pires, Ceryno, & Klingebiel, 2014)
Regarding competitors, the CS of company responds faster to quotes (Ngai et al., 2011)
Regarding competitors, the CS of the company responds quickly and effectively to changes and customer needs. (Geissbauer et al., 2013; S. W. Kim, 2009; Moon et al., 2012; Swafford et al., 2008; Thomé et al., 2014)
Regarding competitors, the company develops and markets new products more quickly and efficiently. (S. W. Kim, 2009; Moon et al., 2012; Swafford et al., 2008; Thomé et al., 2014)
The company has the capacity to ensure the material availability in case of changes (Geissbauer et al., 2013; S. W. Kim, 2009; Moon et al., 2012; Swafford et al., 2008; Thomé et al., 2014)
The company has the ability to adjust to delivery schedules and to meet customer requirements (Geissbauer et al., 2013; S. W. Kim, 2009; Moon et al., 2012; Swafford et al., 2008; Thomé et al., 2014)
The company has different SC configurations for multiple customer segments (Ballou, 2004; Cook, 2001; Geissbauer et al., 2013)
The company is based on inventories to meet demand (Ballou, 2004)
The company differentiates its products in relation to the life cycle in which they are. (Ballou, 2004)
The company keeps various channels of CS regarding to product differentiation (product, channel, costumer) (Ballou, 2004; Cook, 2001; Geissbauer et al., 2013)
The company implements structural changes in the organization in an effective way. (Ngai et al., 2011)
SC Performance
The company can modify its products quickly in order to meet customer requirements (Burt et al., 2003; Geissbauer et al., 2013; S. W. Kim, 2009; Swafford et al., 2008)
The company can quickly introduce new products on the market. (Burt et al., 2003; Geissbauer et al., 2013; S. W. Kim, 2009; Swafford et al., 2008)
The company responds quickly to changes in market demand. (Geissbauer et al., 2013; S. W. Kim, 2009; Swafford et al., 2008)
The company meets delivery times and amounts pledged. (Geissbauer et al., 2013; Swafford et al., 2008)
The cycle time to meet customer orders is short. (Ballou, 2004; Burt et al., 2003; S. W. Kim, 2009)
The company provides a high-level customer service (Ballou, 2004; Geissbauer et al., 2013; S. W. Kim, 2009)

The questionnaire is answered on a Likert-based-scale on subjective assessments, where the lower value (1) indicated that the task never is done, and the highest value (6) represents that the task or operative index is always obtained. But also in the judge's validation, the first draft questionnaire contains blank spaces where the respondents could incorporate some other specific task or items that are not included in the initial questionnaire.

Data Collection

For data collection, the sample is stratified and focused on maquiladora industries that have a mature supply chain in Chihuahua, Mexico. Two hundred and eighty-four (284) managers are contacted via email.

For the survey application, three strategies are applied. The first one consists in face to face interviews with managers who work in supply chain departments or relate to material flow in industries established in Ciudad Juarez, Chihuahua, Mexico.

The second strategy consists of e-mails sent to some company managers to survey and answer within two weeks. After that time, a reminder is send and after three unsuccessful attempts, the case is abandoned. The third strategy consists in sending to every manager a link to answer the survey in a specialized web page for surveys application.

Capturing Information and Questionnaire Validation

At this stage the information is captured and analyzed using SPSS 21® software. Internal consistency or reliability of the questionnaire for each latent variable is performed using the Cronbach coefficient and composite reliability index (Cronbach, 1951; Liu, Ke, Wei, & Hua, 2013), considering a minimum cutoff values of 0.7 (Fornell & Larcker, 1981; Nunnaly, 1978; Nunnaly & Bernstein, 1994; Rexhausen, Pibernik, & Kaiser, 2012). Additionally, some tests are also performed at this stage to improve the quality of the questionnaire and the reliability in analyzed dimensions, since analyzing the elimination of some items, often the reliability in latent variable can increases (Nunnaly & Bernstein, 1994) and the procedure is used by (Blome, Schoenherr, & Eckstein, 2014; Lin, Chow, Madu, Kuei, & Pei, 2005; Ramanathan & Gunasekaran, 2014; Zailani, Jeyaraman, Vengadasan, & Premkumar, 2012) in supply chain surveys.

Also, this stage included a data screening process in order to detect missing values, which are then replaced using the median, because data is obtained by using an ordinal scale (Likert-based scale), although it is always kept in mind that there should be a maximum of 10% missing values for every item (Hair, Anderson, & Tatham, 1987; Hair, Black, Babin, & Anderson, 2009). Also, the values in the database are analyzed for outliers or extreme values and for this, a standardization process is executed for every item considering a standardized value as an outlier if its absolute value is bigger than 5 (Giaquinta, 2009; Hair et al., 2009; Kaiser, 2010; Rosenthal & Rosnow, 1991; Wold, Trygg, Berglund, & Antti, 2001).

Also, considering that the survey is answered on an ordinal scale using only assessments and not measurements, then the Q-squared coefficient is used since it is a nonparametric measure traditionally calculated via blindfolding. Q-squared coefficient is also used for the assessment of the predictive validity (or relevance) associated to each latent variable in the model. Acceptable predictive validity in connection with an endogenous latent variable is suggested by a Q-squared coefficient greater than zero (Kock, 2013) and preferably, must be similar to R-Squared values.

Descriptive Analysis

This stage focuses on a univariate analysis for identifying the central tendency and deviation measures in items collected in latent variables. As a central tendency measure, the median or percentile 50th is obtained; where high values indicate that the task is always done; lower values indicate that those tasks are not done or the operative index is not obtained. Also, as deviation measure, the interquartile range (IR) is obtained (difference between percentile 75th and percentile 25th). High values in IR indicate that the task listed does not present agreement or consensus among respondents, while lower values represent little dispersion in those items (Tastle & Wierman, 2007) and therefore, a greater consensus among respondents.

Structural Equation Model

In order to prove the hypotheses stated in Figure 1, the model is evaluated using the Structural Equation Modelling (SEM) technique, due to its widely and recent use in causal relations validations and specifically in the supply chain. For example, the impact of JIT in supply chain performance (Green Jr, Inman, Birou, & Whitten, 2014), the flexibility, uncertainty and firm performance in supply chain (Merschmann & Thonemann, 2011) and the effect of green supply chain management on green performance and firm competitiveness (Yang, Albert, & Carlo, 2013).

The SEM model is executed in WarpPls 5.0® software because its main algorithms are based on Partial Least Squared (PLS), widely recommended for low sample size (Kock, 2013). The model here presented is specifically executed using the WarpPls5 PLS algorithm, with a bootstrapping resampling method for a better coefficients values convergence and diminish the effect of possible outliers.

Six model fit indices are analyzed: average path coefficient (APC), the average R-squared (ARS), average adjusted R-squared (AARS), average block VIF (AVIF), average full collinearity VIF (AFVIF) and Tenenhaus goodness of fit (GoF), that are recommended by (Kock, 2013) and used by (Ketkar & Vaidya, 2012) in the supply chain environment. For the APC, ARS and AARS, the p-values are analyzed in determining the model efficiency, establishing a maximum cutoff p-value of 0.05, which mean that statistical inferences are made with 95% of confidence level, testing the null hypotheses that APCs, ARSs and AARSs are equal to 0, versus the alternative hypotheses that APCs, ARSs and AARSs are different to zero; while for AVIF and AFVIF, values low than 5 are desirable. For Tenenhaus goodness fit index, values high than 0.36 are desirables for a stable model.

Three different effects are measured in the structural equation model: (1) direct effect (that appears in Figure 1 as arrows from a latent variable to another), (2) indirect effect (given for paths with two or more segments), and (3) total effects (the sum of direct and indirect effects), and with the aim to determine their significance, the P values are analyzed, considering the null hypothesis: $\beta i = 0$, versus the alternative: hypothesis $\beta i \neq 0$.

RESULTS

The results are presented for a better understanding and are carried out in different stages, according to the information being presented.

Descriptive Analysis of the Sample

The descriptive analysis of the sample was made in which it can be observed a total of 284 valid surveys in companies located at Ciudad Juarez, Mexico. Table 2 refers to industrial sectors that were surveyed, which are listed in descending order according to the frequency, which shows that the automotive sector was the most participatory in this study with 128 participants, followed by electrical/electronic industry

Table 2. Industrial sectors analyzed

Industrial Sector	Frequency	Accumulated Frequency
Automotive	128	128
Electric/Electronic	80	208
Medical	19	227
Metal Mechanics	16	243
Plastics	12	255
Communications	8	263
Services	5	268
Textile	5	273
Undeclared	11	284

with 80 surveys. It is noteworthy that these two sectors account for 73.23% of the entire sample. The remaining percentage is represented by the medical, metalworking, plastics, among others industry sectors.

Table 3. refers to the years of experience in the position against gender of each of the respondents, which are listed according to first variable. It is noted that the composition of the sample is 184 male participants, 84 female and 14 undeclared, which is why the sum is only 268 respondents. It is observed that 68.64% representing to 184 males is bigger than 31.34% representing 84 male. According to the information in Table 3, shows that the most representative category is displayed in 2 to 5 years, followed by category 1 to 2 years.

Questionnaire Validation and its Variables

Before any analysis of the information, we proceeded to perform data validation. The information associated with such tests is illustrated in Table 4, where according to the R-square values and adjusted R-square, the overall model has predictive validity from a parametric point of view, since all values are greater than 0.2 on the dependent latent variables. Similarly, according to indexes of composite validity and Cronbach's alpha, it has internal validity, since all the values obtained are higher than 0.7, minimum value allowed.

Table 3. Years of experience against gender

Years of Experience	Gender		Total
	Male	Female	
Less than 1 year	23	24	47
1 to 2 years	48	20	68
2 a 5 years	69	22	91
5 a 10 years	29	12	41
Greater than 10 years	15	6	21
Total	184	84	268

Table 4. Data validation

	ICT Integration	SC Integration	SC Flexibility	SC Performance
R-squared		0.54	0.633	0.572
Adjusted R-squared		0.539	0.631	0.569
Composite reliability	0.941	0.873	0.873	0.908
Cronbach's Alpha	0.93	0.825	0.781	0.878
AVE	0.591	0.535	0.696	0.623
Full VIF	2.351	3.206	3.273	2.346
Q-squared		0.541	0.633	0.571
Initial items	13	15	11	6
Final items	11	6	3	6

Regarding convergent validity, it is observed that all the latent variables analyzed have values greater than 0.5, so it is concluded that this requirement is met. Also, regarding the collinearity for final model reported in Table 4, it is observed that none of the values of the VIFs are greater than 3.3, so it is considered that the latent variables are clear of collinearity problems.

It is important to note that in the last two rows is illustrated the number of items with that the model was initiated, and which were described in Table 1; however, to solve the problems of collinearity that are existed, it was necessary to remove some items on the latent variables, so the row labeled as *final items*, denotes the number of items that keeps the latent variable, due to the elimination some of these items. For example, the latent variable *SC Integration* initially had 13 items, but 2 items were eliminated due to collinearity problems and evaluated the final model has only 11 items. Here is important to note that latent variable named *SC Flexibility* initially had 11 items but the final model is reporting only 3 dur to collinearity problems.

Finally, the values of Q-square are very similar to R-square and adjusted R-square, and they are above zero, so it is concluded that the model has predictive validity from a nonparametric point of view too.

Descriptive Analysis

Following is show the descriptive analysis of the variables remaining in the model, the percentiles; 25th (Q_1), 50th or median (Q_2), 75th (Q_3) and interquartile range (IR) are shown, as described above in the methodology section. Table 5 illustrates this descriptive analysis and the items are sorted in descending order in each of the analyzed latent variables.

As shown in Table 5, the median, which is represented by the 50th percentile, the variable with the highest value in the category *ICT Integration* is corresponding to the availability of a system of information technologies that find integrated with suppliers who supply raw materials. Note that the other variables in this category remain medians above 4, meaning that the *ICT integration* is present in most scenarios and which is considered of great importance by the managers surveyed. In the category of *SC Integration*, the variable with the highest median is referred to service and support granted by the company to its customers, so it comes as a landmark for people in charge of supply chain administration. As can be seen the other variables have medians greater than 4 in the same manner as in the first category

Table 5. Percentiles of variables in final evaluated model

Latent Variable	Items	Q_1	Q_2	Q_3	IR
ICTs Integration	The company has a network of ICT systems (ERP, CRM, SCM, Intranet, etc.) integrated with key suppliers.	3.67	4.78	5.64	1.97
	The company receives demand forecasts and production planning from their customers.	3.68	4.74	5.6	1.92
	The company has a network of ICT systems (ERP, CRM, SCM, Intranet, etc.) integrated with key customers.	3.52	4.6	5.52	2
	The company works to get a better ICT alignment with key customers.	3.43	4.48	5.39	1.96
	The company shares information in real-time through ICT within the organization.	3.41	4.46	5.36	1.95
	The company shares demand forecasts and production planning with suppliers.	3.32	4.46	5.42	2.1
	The company has a high degree of feedback through ICT.	3.34	4.39	5.32	1.98
	The company works to get a better ICT alignment with key suppliers.	3.27	4.36	5.28	2.01
	The company allows access and share sensitive information through ICT within the organization.	3.12	4.27	5.24	2.12
	The company allows access and share sensitive information through ICT with key customers.	3.16	4.27	5.19	2.03
	The company shares information in real-time through ICT within the organization.	2.89	4.02	4.97	2.08
SC Integration	The company provides services and support to its customers.	3.89	4.83	5.63	1.74
	In the company exist cross-functional working groups which discuss issues about material and design.	3.78	4.73	5.57	1.79
	Customers are part of the product design process.	3.7	4.73	5.6	1.9
	The company has a high-level of internal integration.	3.38	4.41	5.31	1.93
	The company shares information about purchasing, inventory levels and forecasts with key suppliers.	3.04	4.15	5.09	2.05
	The company has a small number of key suppliers.	3.09	4.14	5.08	1.99
SC Flexibility	The company is based on inventories to meet demand.	3.59	4.66	5.57	1.98
	The company implements structural changes in the organization in an effective way.	3.76	4.66	5.48	1.72
	Regarding competitors, exist processes that can adjust to changes in mass and mix of products.	3.44	4.41	5.29	1.85
SC Performance	The company can modify its products quickly in order to meet customer requirements.	3.54	4.58	5.44	1.9
	The company meets delivery times and amounts pledged.	3.67	4.58	5.43	1.76
	The company considers the SC management is vital in business activities.	3.59	4.53	5.41	1.82
	The company can quickly introduce new products on the market.	3.36	4.43	5.36	2
	The cycle time to meet customer orders is short.	3.39	4.4	5.32	1.93
	The company offers incentives for performance in SC.	2.75	4.05	5.09	2.34

Information and Communication Technology Impact

or latent variable. It is noteworthy that this same item has the smaller IR in the category, which indicates that there is consensus on the value that it has, since it reports a lowest dispersion.

As for category *SC Flexibility*, two variables are observed with the same highest value of 4.66, and refer to the use of inventories to satisfy demand in the supply chain and the implementation of structural changes in the company quickly and effectively. This means that logistics managers consider of great importance these skills of supply chain. The remaining variable maintains a median greater than 4 and the second variable having the lowest IR, indicating consensus regarding the value of that item.

Finally, the last category or latent variable named *SC performance*, for the item with the highest median value it is has again a tie, and these relate to the ability to quickly make changes to products to meet changing customer needs, and the ability of the company to comply with the agreed delivery dates and quantities. However, the smaller of the IR is in the second variable with the highest median value.

Structural Equation Model

The structural equation model was evaluated according to the methodology described above, where some items have been removed due to collinearity problems. Following appears the efficiency indices for the final model and Figure 3 presents such model:

- Average path coefficient (APC)=0.474, P<0.001
- Average R-squared (ARS)=0.582, P<0.001
- Average adjusted R-squared (AARS)=0.579, P<0.001
- Average block VIF (AVIF)=2.394, acceptable if <= 5, ideally <= 3.3
- Average full collinearity VIF (AFVIF)=2.794, acceptable if <= 5, ideally <= 3.3
- Tenenhaus GoF (GoF)=0.596, small >= 0.1, medium >= 0.25, large >= 0.3

Figure 3. Final model- direct effects validation

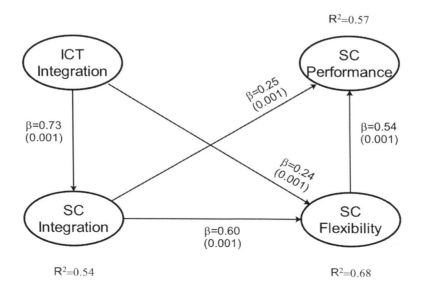

For the first three indexes, which have a P value measure, it is observed that have values lower than 0.05, so it can make statistical inferences in the model in general terms, and that mean that in average the final model has sufficient predictive validity and that the values assigned to betas or parameters that measure the relationship between latent variables are statistically significant. Similarly, regarding the two indices that measure the collinearity in the model (VIF and AVIF), since there are values lower that 3.3, this lets to conclude again that the model in general terms is efficient and predictive.

Also note that the arrow representing to H_6, relationship between *ICT Integration* and *Performance SC*, does not appear and it is because it was not statistically significant. The other five hypotheses were statistically significant.

Direct Effects

The direct effects helped to validate the hypotheses made above in Figure 1, which according to the values shown in Figure 2, the conclusions are:

H_1: There is sufficient statistical evidence to declare that the *ICT integration* has a positive and direct effect on *SC Integration*, since when the first latent variable increases its standard deviation in one unit, the second one goes up by 0.73 units.

H_2: There is sufficient statistical evidence to declare that *ICT Integration* has a direct and positive effect on *SC Flexibility*, since when the first latent variable increases its standard deviation in one unit, the second one goes up by 0.24 units.

H_3: There is sufficient statistical evidence to declare that the *SC Integration* has a direct and positive effect on *SC Flexibility*, since when the first latent variable increases its standard deviation in one unit, the second one goes up by 0.60 units.

H_4: There is sufficient statistical evidence to declare that *SC Flexibility* in a company have a direct and positive effect on the *SC Economic Performance*, because when the first latent increases its standard deviation in one unit, the second goes up by 0.54 units..

H_5: There is sufficient statistical evidence to declare that *SC Integration* has a direct and positive effect on *SC Performance*, since when the first latent variable increases its standard deviation in one unit, the second one goes up by 0.25 units.

H_6: There is not enough statistical evidence to declare that the *ICT Integration* has a direct and positive impact on *SC Performance*, since the P value obtained in statistical significance test results exceed 0.05, maximum value allowed for inferences made at a 95% confidence level.

Direct Effect Size

The model evaluated in Figure 2 shows that the latent variables that refers to *SC Performance* and *SC Flexibility* receive effects from more than one independent latent variable, so it is necessary to decompose the percentage of variance in which are explained:

1. In the case of latent dependent variable called *SC Performance*, it is explained by 57%, due to $R^2 = 0.57$ from the latent independent variables *SC Flexibility* and *SC Integration*. However, 0.173 is due to the first variable and 0.399 is due to the second one, so based on the sizes of these effects,

those values let's to conclude that the *SC Flexibility* is the variable that best helps to explain *SC Performance*.

2. In the case of latent dependent variable called *SC Flexibility*, it is explained by 63% due to $R^2 = 0.63$ from the latent independent variables *SC Integration* and *ICT Integration*. However, 0.467 is due to the first variable and 0.166 is due to the second one, so based on the sizes of these effects, it is concluded that the *SC Integration* is the variable that best helps to explain *SC Flexibility*.

Sum of Indirect Effects

The analysis of indirect effects between latent variables analyzed is important because it helps to understand certain phenomena, such as those found in the conclusion about H_6, in which it was determined that there is no direct relationship between *ICT Integration* and *SC Performance*, but indirect effects occur through other variables which are called mediators.

Table 6 summarizes the indirect effects between the variables analyzed, the P value of the statistic test of the estimated parameters, in addition, the effect size (ES) or percentage of variance. It is important to remember that H_6 referred to the relationship between *ICT Integration* and *SC Performance*, and it was statistically rejected because the direct effect was not significant, but indirectly have a very high relation, which is 0.556 (highest indirect effect on the Table 6) and it means that when *ICT integration* incremented by one unit its standard deviation, the *SC Performance* goes up by 0.556 units, which is given through the mediating variables called *ICT Integration* and *SC Flexibility*, but is also able to account for up to 32.9%, because the effect size is 0.329.

Likewise, it is observed that the indirect effect of *ICT Integration* on *SC Flexibility* is higher, 0.441, which indicates that each time the first latent variable incremented by one unit its standard deviation, the second one goes up by 0.441 units, and it is responsible for explaining 30.2% of variability, since the effect size is 0.302. This indirect effect is given through *SC Integration*.

A similar interpretation can be made for indirect effect between *SC Integration* and *SC Performance*, which is given by the mediator variable called *SC Flexibility*.

Total Effects

The total effects are represented by the sum of direct effects and indirect effects. Table 7 illustrates the total effects, the P value for statistical significance test and the effect size.

According to the values of total effects shown in Table 7, the highest value corresponds to the relationship between the latent variables *SC Integration* with *ICT Integration*, its value is 0.73, which

Table 6. Sum of indirect effects

To	From	
	ICT Integration	SC Integration
SC Flexibility	0.441 P(<0.001) ES= 0.302	
SC Performance	0.556 P(<0.001) ES= 0.329	0.324 P(<0.001) ES= 0.219

Table 7. Total effects

To	From		
	ICT Integration	CS Integration	SC Flexibility
SC Integration	0.73 P(<0.001) ES= 0.540		
SC Flexibility	0.684 P(<0.001) ES= 0.468	0.6 P(<0.001) ES= 0.467	
SC Performance	0.556 P(<0.001) ES= 0.329	0.578 P(<0.001) ES= 0.392	0.54 P(<0.001) ES= 0.399

belongs to the H_1 hypothesis that has already been explained in the section of direct effects. However, the relationship between *ICT Integration* with *SC Flexibility*, the total effect is 0.684, a high value, but only 0.25 corresponds to the direct effect established by H_3 and the rest is due to the indirect effect, the which is the higher than the previous one.

Also, it is important the relationship between *SC Integration* with *SC Performance*, here the direct effect is only 0.25, but the total effect is 0.578, which indicates that the indirect effect is higher than the direct effect, which is given through *SC Flexibility*.

CONCLUSION

Based on the results shown above, the following conclusions are derived:

1. The relationship between *ICT Integration* and *SC Performance* in a chain supply is indirect and occurs by mediator variables, such as *SC Integration* and *SC Flexibility*.
2. The *SC Integration* has a positive and direct effect on the *SC Performance*, but the indirect effect is achieved through the mediator variable denominated *SC Flexibility*, and is higher than the direct effect.
3. The role of *SC Integration* and *SC Flexibility* as mediator variables in the *SC Performance* is important, due to some of the indirect effects occurring through these variables are higher than the direct effects, indicating that managers should take efforts to achieve these characteristics in the supply chains.
4. Supply chain managers should pay attention in determining the type of ICT to be implemented, since from it depends integration levels and flexibility that are achieved, which directly impact on SC performance.

FUTURE RESEARCH DIRECTIONS

The main limitation of this research is that it has completed in the maquiladora industry located at Mexico, thus inferences are valid only in that environment. Furthermore, when analyzing the final model in Figure 3, it is shown that the values of R^2 in the latent dependent variables are higher than 0.5, an acceptable value in this type of models, but does suggest that there are other variables that help to explain the *SC Integration, SC Flexibility* and *SC Performance*, so it means that in future research there must include the knowledge levels and skills that ICT operators have in supply chain, that maybe helps to increase that R^2 values.

REFERENCES

Acar, A. Z., & Uzunlar, M. B. (2014). The Effects of Process Development and Information Technology on Time-based Supply Chain Performance. *Procedia: Social and Behavioral Sciences, 150*, 744–753. doi:10.1016/j.sbspro.2014.09.044

Alfalla-Luque, R., Marin-Garcia, J. A., & Medina-Lopez, C. (2015). An analysis of the direct and mediated effects of employee commitment and supply chain integration on organisational performance. *International Journal of Production Economics, 162*(0), 242–257. doi:10.1016/j.ijpe.2014.07.004

Altés, J. (2013). Papel de las tecnologías de la información y la comunicación en la medicina actual. *Seminarios de la Fundación Española de Reumatología, 14*(2), 31–35. doi:10.1016/j.semreu.2013.01.005

Ballou, R. H. (2004). Logistica Administracion de la Cadena de Suministro (E. Q. Duarte Ed. 5 ed.). Pearson Education

Blome, C., Schoenherr, T., & Eckstein, D. (2014). The impact of knowledge transfer and complexity on supply chain flexibility: A knowledge-based view. *International Journal of Production Economics, 147*, 307-316. doi:10.1016/j.ijpe.2013.02.028

Böhm, C. A., Leone, H., & Henning, G. (2007). Industrial supply chains: Performance measures, metrics and benchmarks. In P. Valentin & A. Paul Şerban (Eds.), Computer Aided Chemical Engineering (Vol. 24, pp. 757-762). Elsevier.

Burt, D. N., Dobler, D. W., & Starling, S. L. (2003). World Class Supply Management (7th ed.). McGraw-Hill.

Capaldo, A., & Giannoccaro, I. (2015). How does trust affect performance in the supply chain? The moderating role of interdependence. *International Journal of Production Economics, 166*, 36–49. doi:10.1016/j.ijpe.2015.04.008

Chen, I. J., & Paulraj, A. (2004). Towards a theory of supply chain management: The constructs and measurements. *Journal of Operations Management, 22*(2), 119–150. doi:10.1016/j.jom.2003.12.007

Clemens, B. (2006). Economic incentives and small firms: Does it pay to be green? *Journal of Business Research, 59*(4), 492–500. doi:10.1016/j.jbusres.2005.08.006

Cook, M. (2001). *Supply-Chain Survey*. Bain & Company. Retrieved from: http://www.bain.com/Images/BB_Supply-chain_survey.pdf

Cronbach, L. (1951). Coefficient alpha and the internal structure of tests. *Psychometrika, 16*(3), 297–334. doi:10.1007/BF02310555

El Kadiri, S., Grabot, B., Thoben, K.-D., Hribernik, K., Emmanouilidis, C., von Cieminski, G., & Kiritsis, D. (2015). Current trends on ICT technologies for enterprise information systems. *Computers in Industry*. doi:10.1016/j.compind.2015.06.008

Fornell, C., & Larcker, D. (1981). Evaluating structural equation models with unobservable variables and measurement error. *JMR, Journal of Marketing Research, 18*(1), 39–50. doi:10.2307/3151312

Geissbauer, R., Roussel, J., Schrauf, S., & Strom, M. A. (2013). *Next Generation Supply Chains- Global Supply Chain Survey 2013*. Academic Press.

Giaquinta, M. (2009). *Mathematical analysis: An introduction to functions of several variables*. New York, NY: Springer. doi:10.1007/978-0-8176-4612-7

Green Jr, K. W., Inman, R. A., Birou, L. M., & Whitten, D. (2014). Total JIT (T-JIT) and its impact on supply chain competency and organizational performance. *International Journal of Production Economics, 147,* 125-135. doi:10.1016/j.ijpe.2013.08.026

Gunasekaran, A., & Ngai, E. W. T. (2004). Information systems in supply chain integration and management. *European Journal of Operational Research, 159*(2), 269–295. doi:10.1016/j.ejor.2003.08.016

Gunasekaran, A., Patel, C., & McGaughey, R. E. (2004). A framework for supply chain performance measurement. *International Journal of Production Economics, 87*(3), 333–347. doi:10.1016/j.ijpe.2003.08.003

Hair, J., Anderson, R., & Tatham, R. (1987). *Multivariate data analysis*. New York, NY: Macmillan.

Hair, J., Black, W., Babin, B., & Anderson, R. (2009). *Multivariate data analysis*. Upper Saddle River, NJ: Prentice Hall.

Hassini, E., Surti, C., & Searcy, C. (2012). A literature review and a case study of sustainable supply chains with a focus on metrics. *International Journal of Production Economics, 140*(1), 69–82. doi:10.1016/j.ijpe.2012.01.042

Hervani, A. A., Helms, M. M., & Sarkis, J. (2005). Performance measurement for green supply chain management. *Benchmarking: An International Journal, 12*(4), 330–353. doi:10.1108/14635770510609015

Hoejmose, S., Brammer, S., & Millington, A. (2012). "Green" supply chain management: The role of trust and top management in B2B and B2C markets. *Industrial Marketing Management, 41*(4), 609–620. doi:10.1016/j.indmarman.2012.04.008

Kaiser, H. (2010). *Mathematical programming for agricultural, environmental, and resource economics*. Hoboken, NJ: Wiley.

Ketkar, M., & Vaidya, O. S. (2012). Study of Emerging Issues in Supply Risk Management in India. *Procedia: Social and Behavioral Sciences, 37*(0), 57–66. doi:10.1016/j.sbspro.2012.03.275

Kim, D., & Cavusgil, E. (2009). The impact of supply chain integration on brand equity. *Journal of Business and Industrial Marketing, 24*(7), 496–505. doi:10.1108/08858620910986730

Kim, S. W. (2009). An investigation on the direct and indirect effect of supply chain integration on firm performance. *International Journal of Production Economics, 119*(2), 328–346. doi:10.1016/j.ijpe.2009.03.007

Kock, N. (2013). Using WarpPLS in e-collaboration studies: What if I have only one group and one condition. *International Journal of e-Collaboration, 9*(3), 12. doi:10.4018/jec.2013070101

Lambert, D. M., Cooper, M. C., & Pagh, J. D. (1998). Supply Chain Management: Implementation Issues and Research Opportunities. *The International Journal of Logistics Management, 9*(2), 1–20. doi:10.1108/09574099810805807

Lee, H., Kim, M. S., & Kim, K. K. (2014). Interorganizational information systems visibility and supply chain performance. *International Journal of Information Management, 34*(2), 285–295. doi:10.1016/j.ijinfomgt.2013.10.003

Li, G., Lin, Y., Wang, S., & Yan, H. (2006). Enhancing agility by timely sharing of supply information. *Supply Chain Management: An International Journal, 11*(5), 425–435. doi:10.1108/13598540610682444

Lin, C., Chow, W., Madu, C., Kuei, C., & Pei, Y. (2005). A structural equation model of supply chain quality management and organizational performance. *International Journal of Production Economics, 96*(3), 355–365. doi:10.1016/j.ijpe.2004.05.009

Liu, H., Ke, W., Wei, K. K., & Hua, Z. (2013). The impact of IT capabilities on firm performance: The mediating roles of absorptive capacity and supply chain agility. *Decision Support Systems, 54*(3), 1452–1462. doi:10.1016/j.dss.2012.12.016

Mansoornejad, B., Pistikopoulos, E. N., & Stuart, P. (2013). Metrics for evaluating the forest biorefinery supply chain performance. *Computers & Chemical Engineering, 54*(0), 125–139. doi:10.1016/j.compchemeng.2013.03.031

Marinagi, C., Trivellas, P., & Reklitis, P. (2015). Information Quality and Supply Chain Performance: The Mediating Role of Information Sharing. *Procedia: Social and Behavioral Sciences, 175*, 473–479. doi:10.1016/j.sbspro.2015.01.1225

Marinagi, C., Trivellas, P., & Sakas, D. P. (2014). The Impact of Information Technology on the Development of Supply Chain Competitive Advantage. *Procedia: Social and Behavioral Sciences, 147*, 586–591. doi:10.1016/j.sbspro.2014.07.161

Mensah, P., Merkuryev, Y., & Longo, F. (2015). Using ICT in Developing a Resilient Supply Chain Strategy. *Procedia Computer Science, 43*, 101–108. doi:10.1016/j.procs.2014.12.014

Merschmann, U., & Thonemann, U. W. (2011). Supply chain flexibility, uncertainty and firm performance: An empirical analysis of German manufacturing firms. *International Journal of Production Economics, 130*(1), 43–53. doi:10.1016/j.ijpe.2010.10.013

Mohammad, M. F., Shukor, A. S. A., Mahbub, R., & Halil, F. M. (2014). Challenges in the Integration of Supply Chains in IBS Project Environment in Malaysia. *Procedia: Social and Behavioral Sciences, 153*, 44–54. doi:10.1016/j.sbspro.2014.10.039

Moon, K. K.-L., Yi, C. Y., & Ngai, E. W. T. (2012). An instrument for measuring supply chain flexibility for the textile and clothing companies. *European Journal of Operational Research, 222*(2), 191–203. doi:10.1016/j.ejor.2012.04.027

Ngai, E. W. T., Chau, D. C. K., & Chan, T. L. A. (2011). Information technology, operational, and management competencies for supply chain agility: Findings from case studies. *The Journal of Strategic Information Systems, 20*(3), 232–249. doi:10.1016/j.jsis.2010.11.002

Nunnaly, J. (1978). *Psychometric theory*. New York, NY: Mc Graw Hill.

Nunnaly, J., & Bernstein, I. (1994). *Psychometric theory*. New York, NY: Mc Graw Hill.

Pearcy, D. H., & Giunipero, L. C. (2008). Using e-procurement applications to achieve integration: What role does firm size play? *Supply Chain Management: An International Journal, 13*(1), 26–34. doi:10.1108/13598540810850292

Popova, V., & Sharpanskykh, A. (2010). Modeling organizational performance indicators. *Information Systems, 35*(4), 505–527. doi:10.1016/j.is.2009.12.001

Ramanathan, U., & Gunasekaran, A. (2014). Supply chain collaboration: Impact of success in long-term partnerships. *International Journal of Production Economics, 147*, 252-259. doi:10.1016/j.ijpe.2012.06.002

Rexhausen, D., Pibernik, R., & Kaiser, G. (2012). Customer-facing supply chain practices—The impact of demand and distribution management on supply chain success. *Journal of Operations Management, 30*(4), 269–281. doi:10.1016/j.jom.2012.02.001

Rosenthal, R., & Rosnow, R. (1991). *Essentials of behavioral research: Methods and data analysis*. Boston, MA: Mc Graw Hill.

Sarkis, J. (2006). The adoption of environmental and risk management practices: Relationships to environmental performance. *Annals of Operations Research, 145*(1), 367–381. doi:10.1007/s10479-006-0040-9

Searcy, C., McCartney, D., & Karapetrovic, S. (2007). Sustainable development indicators for the transmission system of an electric utility. *Corporate Social Responsibility and Environmental Management, 14*(3), 135–151. doi:10.1002/csr.124

Singh, A., & Teng, J. T. C. (2016). Enhancing supply chain outcomes through Information Technology and Trust. *Computers in Human Behavior, 54*, 290–300. doi:10.1016/j.chb.2015.07.051

Stevenson, M., & Spring, M. (2007). Flexibility from a supply chain perspective: Definition and review. *International Journal of Operations & Production Management, 27*(7), 685–713. doi:10.1108/01443570710756956

Swafford, P. M., Ghosh, S., & Murthy, N. (2008). Achieving supply chain agility through IT integration and flexibility. *International Journal of Production Economics, 116*(2), 288–297. doi:10.1016/j.ijpe.2008.09.002

Świerczek, A. (2014). The impact of supply chain integration on the "snowball effect" in the transmission of disruptions: An empirical evaluation of the model. *International Journal of Production Economics, 157*, 89–104. doi:10.1016/j.ijpe.2013.08.010

Tastle, W. J., & Wierman, M. J. (2007). Consensus and dissention: A measure of ordinal dispersion. *International Journal of Approximate Reasoning, 45*(3), 531–545. doi:10.1016/j.ijar.2006.06.024

Themistocleous, M., Irani, Z., & Love, P. E. D. (2004). Evaluating the integration of supply chain information systems: A case study. *European Journal of Operational Research, 159*(2), 393–405. doi:10.1016/j.ejor.2003.08.023

Thomé, A. M. T., Scavarda, L. F., Pires, S. R. I., Ceryno, P., & Klingebiel, K. (2014). A multi-tier study on supply chain flexibility in the automotive industry. *International Journal of Production Economics, 158*(0), 91–105. doi:10.1016/j.ijpe.2014.07.024

Vachon, S., & Klassen, R. D. (2008). Environmental management and manufacturing performance: The role of collaboration in the supply chain. *International Journal of Production Economics, 111*(2), 299–315. doi:10.1016/j.ijpe.2006.11.030

Vachon, S., & Mao, Z. (2008). Linking supply chain strength to sustainable development: A country-level analysis. *Journal of Cleaner Production, 16*(15), 1552–1560. doi:10.1016/j.jclepro.2008.04.012

Vlachos, I. P. (2014). A hierarchical model of the impact of RFID practices on retail supply chain performance. *Expert Systems with Applications, 41*(1), 5–15. doi:10.1016/j.eswa.2013.07.006

Wiengarten, F., Humphreys, P., Gimenez, C., & McIvor, R. (2015). Risk, risk management practices, and the success of supply chain integration. *International Journal of Production Economics*. doi:10.1016/j.ijpe.2015.03.020

Wlendahl, H.-P., von Cleminskf, G., & Begemann, C. (2003). A Systematic Approach for Ensuring the Logistic Process Reliability of Supply Chains. *CIRP Annals - Manufacturing Technology, 52*(1), 375-380. doi:10.1016/S0007-8506(07)60605-2

Wold, S., Trygg, J., Berglund, A., & Antti, H. (2001). Some recent developments in PLS modeling. *Chemometrics and Intelligent Laboratory Systems, 58*(2), 131–150. doi:10.1016/S0169-7439(01)00156-3

Yang, S., Albert, R., & Carlo, T. A. (2013). Transience and constancy of interactions in a plant-frugivore network. *Ecosphere, 4*(12), art147. doi:10.1890/ES13-00222.1

Yu, L., Suojapelto, K., Hallikas, J., & Tang, O. (2008). Chinese ICT industry from supply chain perspective—A case study of the major Chinese ICT players. *International Journal of Production Economics, 115*(2), 374–387. doi:10.1016/j.ijpe.2008.03.011

Zailani, S., Jeyaraman, K., Vengadasan, G., & Premkumar, R. (2012). Sustainable supply chain management (SSCM) in Malaysia: A survey. *International Journal of Production Economics, 140*(1), 330–340. doi:10.1016/j.ijpe.2012.02.008

Zhao, G., Feng, T., & Wang, D. (2015). Is more supply chain integration always beneficial to financial performance? *Industrial Marketing Management, 45*, 162–172. doi:10.1016/j.indmarman.2015.02.015

Zhu, Q., & Sarkis, J. (2004). Relationships between operational practices and performance among early adopters of green supply chain management practices in Chinese manufacturing enterprises. *Journal of Operations Management, 22*(3), 265–289. doi:10.1016/j.jom.2004.01.005

KEY TERMS AND DEFINITIONS

Customer: A person or an organization who purchases goods or services from another person or organization.

Data: A single piece a body or collection of facts, statistics or information.

Distributor: A person a firm or a company that distributes a line of merchandise generally or within a given territory.

Infrastructure: The facilities or basic structure supporting a system or organization such as transportation, buildings and communication systems.

Integration: To bring together or incorporate into a whole or a larger unit.

Manufacturer: A person, group, or organization that make or produce goods by hand or machinery on a large scale.

Network: An association of individuals having a common interest or any system or group of interrelated or interconnected elements.

Performance: The efficiency with which something reacts or fulfills its purpose.

Retailer: Person or an organization that sells goods to ultimate consumers, usually in small quantities.

Supplier: A person or an organization that provide things necessary for maintaining an army, business or other enterprise.

Chapter 12
A Causal Analytic Model for Labour Productivity Assessment

Manoj Kumar
International Engineering Services, India

Jyoti Singh
International Engineering Services, India

Priya Singh
International Engineering Services, India

ABSTRACT

The Indian government and those of the devolved administrations have adopted a policy framework for boosting regional productivity based on five drivers: Investment, Skills, Innovation, Entrepreneurship, and Competition. We modelled the relationships between the five drivers and labour productivity using a structural equation model that fitted the data well. The main conclusion is that promoting entrepreneurship, spending more on research and development, increasing the capital-worker ratio and the percentage of the workforce with higher qualifications has a significant bearing upon regional labour productivity. In contrast, regulatory barriers to competition do not seem to affect labour productivity at a regional level.

1. INTRODUCTION

The Productivity Council have identified five drivers of productivity, which account for the five priority areas for policy action to promote productivity levels and growth: Investment, Skills, Innovation, Entrepreneurship, and Competition. However, there is no published model explaining how these five drivers affect labour productivity. Furthermore, no empirical analyses have been published, which provide estimates the relative importance of each driver to total labour productivity. In other words, the contention that investment, skills, innovation, entrepreneurship and competition are the main drivers of productivity was been neither theoretically formulated nor empirically tested.

Nevertheless, regional development policy has very much influenced by this set of indicators – by way of illustration, the Department of Enterprise, Trade and Industry's Economic Research Agenda has

DOI: 10.4018/978-1-5225-0654-6.ch012

structured along these drivers. Similarly, Indian government have designed the strategic economic policy for rural development, based on the five drivers of productivity. Given the central role the five drivers play in policy design and delivery, it should be apparent that it is of crucial importance to estimate the relative contribution of each driver to labour productivity bearing in mind their interrelationships –and this is the aim of this chapter. This chapter investigates whether these variables affect labour productivity and, if so, to what extent. In order to do so, we use "structural equation modelling" (SEM) -a statistical method of defining, identifying, and estimating total, direct and indirect causal influences and effects.

To illustrate, the model presented in this chapter estimates the direct effects of, for example, Entrepreneurship, Skills and Innovation on Labour Productivity. Besides, it estimates any indirect effects of Entrepreneurship on Labour Productivity via the impact that Entrepreneurship has on other drivers –for example, through Innovation –as the more entrepreneurial are the firms in a region, the more intense are the region's innovative activities. Furthermore, we could assume that the higher the educational levels of the resident population in a region, the higher are both the regional entrepreneurial and research and development activities. The model also captures these additional effects amongst drivers. Consequently, with SEM we can simultaneously estimate the effects of Skills on Entrepreneurship and Innovation, the indirect effects of Skills on Labour Productivity through Innovation and Entrepreneurship as well as the direct effect of Skills on Labour Productivity as shown in Figure 1.

This chapter does not attempt to provide an alternative set of indicators or a fully-fledged theoretical model of labour productivity. For this reason, we have not included other variables that have reported to have a bearing upon productivity –such as social capital, agglomeration, industrial structure, or distance to a major economic hub- although we briefly discuss these issues in Subsection 2.6. Instead, as we said above, this chapter sets out a model to estimate the direct effects of each of the five drivers that inform regional economic policy in the India on labour productivity, their interrelationships and their indirect effects on labour productivity.

The structure of the chapter is as follows. Section 2 briefly discusses the rationale behind each driver. Section 3 describes the data. Section 4 presents the model. Section 5 presents on the results. Section 6 comments on the Delhi-NCR's case. Section 7 concludes.

Figure 1.

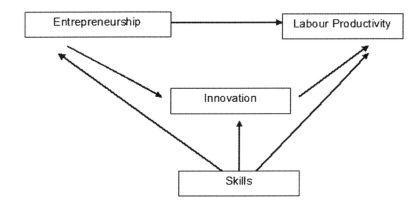

2. THE FIVE DRIVERS OF PRODUCTIVITY

Productivity Council set out a framework to develop the Indian Government's policy agenda on productivity by establishing five priority areas assumed to correspond to the five drivers of productivity growth: Investment, Skills, Innovation, Entrepreneurship, and Competition. The agenda rests upon research that looks on the relationship between productivity and one or more drivers but not between productivity, the five drivers, and the relationships between the latter at the same time. Furthermore, no explanation is given as to why other variables that the literature also highlights as being relevant to productivity were omitted -such as social capital, firms' restructuring, innovation absorptive capacity, industrial structure, agglomeration, firm exit or churning, or distance to main economic hub, to mention a few. Nor do we explore the relative importance of the variables not included within the productivity policy framework, however, we will briefly comment upon their relationships with labour productivity in subsection 2.6; before that, we will discuss the links between the five drivers and labour productivity.

2.1. Investment

Investment in physical capital (i.e. in tangible assets such as public infrastructure, consumers' and government durables, land, machinery and equipment) as a key input for economic growth. In turn, investment can also affect economic growth via increased productivity, if the added capital raises the marginal product of the capital stock. Investment may positively influence economic performance either by expanding the production possibility frontier without changing marginal products or by increasing the marginal contribution of capital. In other words, the economy can grow because there is a bigger stock of capital of a given quality, or due to the introduction of new capital of higher productivity. The fact that investment in physical capital may have a bearing upon economic growth without affecting productivity reflects that investment is one of the components of aggregate demand (i.e. total expenditure in an economy) so that net capital formation necessarily implies (all else constant) an increase in Gross Domestic Product (GDP) / Gross Value Added (GVA).

Moreover, physical capital is also a factor of production that defines the level of productive capacity. Consequently, investment in physical capital has a direct impact upon aggregate supply and thus is positively related to economic growth. Jorgenson (2005) found that capital accumulation explains over 50 per cent of total economic growth in the United States between 1948 and 2002 and over 57 per cent of all GDP growth between 1995 and 2001 in Canada, the UK, France, Germany, Italy and Japan. A recent study for France, Italy and Germany (Bassanetti *et al.*, 2006) estimated that capital deepening has been decreasing in these three countries since the mid 1990s; however, it has contributed by about 40 per cent to labour productivity growth since then. Bradford DeLong and Summers (1991) studied the relationship between investment in machinery and equipment (M&E) and economic growth in selected developed countries for a period of over 100 years and found that increasing investment in M&E by one percent would increase GDP per capita by 0.7 per cent. Similarly, Abdi (2004) analysed data for 20 industries in Canada between 1961 and 2000 and obtained an elasticity coefficient of output to M&E investment of 0.67. Furthermore, Schiffbauer (2006) looked on the relationship between infrastructure (telecommunication) capital and economic growth in selected OECD countries between 1975 and 2002. The findings support the hypothesis that infrastructure capital enhances economic growth mostly because it reduces transportation and coordination costs. Other authors (for example, Carroll & Weil, 1994 or Blomström *et al.*, 1996) contended that any positive association between investment in physical capital and economic growth actually reflects causal mechanisms from growth to investment: rapid growth would foster capital formation. In turn, Mankiw, Romer and Weil (1992) studied both M&E and structures and claimed that investment has no long-run impact on economic growth. Furthermore, even a negative causal relationship between investment and economic growth has been reported (Podrecca & Carmeci, 2001): increasing investment ratios might negatively affect future economic growth. This last result is not without some theoretical backing: it is in line with the so-called neoclassical growth model (Solow, 1956). On the other hand, a positive relationship between investment in physical capital and productivity rests on the assumption that tangible assets are more productive because of the embodiment of technological progress in successive vintages of capital. The embodiment hypothesis assumes that innovations incorporated into the production process only as part of material, tangible capital goods. Therefore, technical progress improves the quality of capital and, hence, its marginal product. As Greenwood and Jovanovic (2000, pp.2-3) assert: "there can be no technological progress without investment". Figure 2 presents the relationship between levels in labour productivity (GVA per worker) and physical investment (gross fixed capital formation by worker) for India in 2014. There is a strong positive correlation ($R^2=0.77$) between regional levels of investment and productivity.

Figure 3 shows the relationship between changes in investment and changes in productivity between 2008 and 2014. The correlation is lower ($R^2=0.30$) than between levels for 2014. (It is worth noting that due to data unavailability Figure 3 uses the Net Capital Expenditure per Worker as indicator of Investment, rather than Gross Fixed Capital Formation by Worker, and that over the period 2008 - 2014, NCE per Worker has decreased in all India).

2.2. Skills

Investing in human capital may positively contribute to productivity inasmuch as a more skilled workforce is likely to be more productive. As explained in Iparraguirre (2005a), there are two main strands of thought about the relationship between human capital and economic growth and productivity:

Figure 2. Labor productivity and investment: India 2014

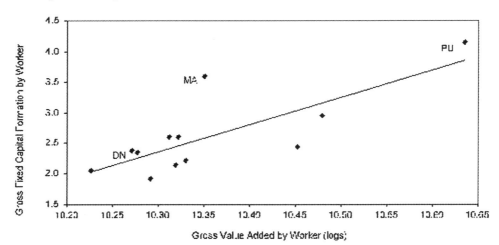

A Causal Analytic Model for Labour Productivity Assessment

Figure 3. Changes in labor productivity and investment: India 2008-2014

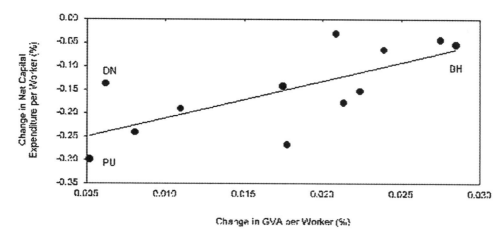

- Growth and productivity depend on the rate of accumulation of human capital (Lucas, 1988); and
- Growth and productivity depend on the stock of human capital (Nelson & Phelps, 1966).

The Lucas model implies that an increase in human capital has a one-off effect on the level of GDP/GVA, whereas the Nelson and Phelps approach assumes that an increase in human capital results in a permanent increase in economic growth. The empirical evidence tends to support the latter view, which suggests that education increases labour productivity. Nelson and Phelps's view is that: "a major role for education is to increase the individual's capacity, first, to *innovate* (i.e., to create new activities, new products, new technologies) and, second, to *adapt* to new technologies, thereby speeding up technological *diffusion* throughout the economy (Aghion & Howitt, 1998, p.338 – italics in the original)". Figures 4 and 5 present relationships between skills levels and GVA per worker for the India for 2013. Figure 4 shows the percentage of economically-active adults qualified to NVQ Level 4 or above, whereas Figure 5 presents those qualified to NVQ 1 and those without qualification. It is apparent that the higher the education levels of the workforce in a region, the higher the level of productivity and vice versa. The correlation coefficient for the relationship in Figure 4 is 0.66 and for that in Figure 5 is -0.31.

2.3. Innovation

The OECD Oslo Manual defines an innovation as "the implementation of a new or significantly improved product (good or service), or process, a new marketing method, or a new organisational method in business practices, workplace organisation or external relations." (OECD, 2005, para. 146, p. 46). The Manual adds that: "Innovation activities are all scientific, technological, organisational, financial and commercial steps which actually, or are intended to, lead to the implementation of innovations. Some innovation activities are themselves innovative; others are not novel activities but are necessary for the implementation of innovations. Innovation activities also include R&D that is not directly related to the development of a specific innovation. (OECD, 2005, para. 149, p. 47)". The Oslo Manual distinguishes four types of innovation activities: product innovations, process innovations, marketing innovations and organisational innovations. The link between innovations, productivity and economic growth is usually

Figure 4. Labor productivity and skills – India 2014

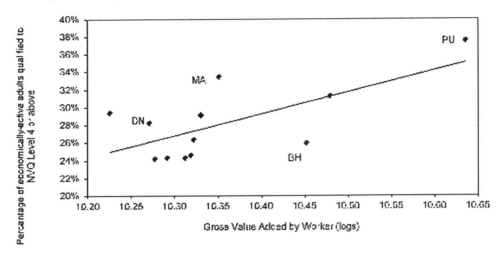

Figure 5. Labor productivity and low skills: India 2014

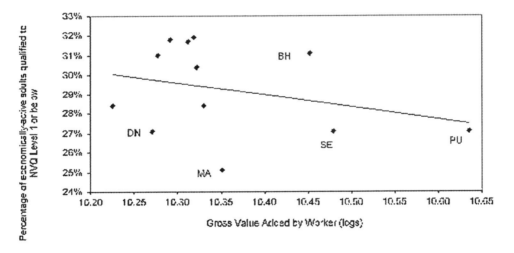

associated with Schumpeter (1934, 1942). Schumpeter argued that innovative activities drive economic growth through a process in which new technologies creatively destruct old ones. This description corresponds to the vintage capital model already mentioned. Innovation brings about dynamic technical efficiency gains, which positively affect productivity levels and growth in the long run. However, as Nickell and Van Reenen (2001) point out, innovation can only impact productivity if it is spread around the economy – somehow reflecting the approach introduced by Romer (1990) in which technology is neither a conventional good nor a public good but a non-rival, partially excludable good. Furthermore, Nickell and Van Reenen (2001) argue that the UK presents a strong basic science sector but a weak commercial absorption of basic innovations. These authors explain that this discrepancy is due to low levels of investment in R&D combined with low product market competition, high regulation levels, financial

A Causal Analytic Model for Labour Productivity Assessment

constraints, insufficient number of workers with intermediate technical and general management skills, and a lack of exposure to best-practice methods.

Finally, Nichel and Van Reenen, several analyses at firm level have emphasised the importance of firm characteristics in explaining the link between innovation and productivity. For example, Griffith *et al.* (2003) found that productivity growth largely explained by R&D- innovation, technology transfer, and R&D-based absorptive capacity. Finally, Lokshin *et al.* (2006) found some complementarily between internal and external R&D, with a positive impact of external R&D on productivity only in case of sufficient internal R&D. These authors conclude that in-house research and development activity stimulates innovation and productivity and enhances the suppliers' absorptive capacity needed to derive benefits from the externally acquired R&D. Figure 6 presents the relationship between Gross Expenditure in Research and Development and Labour Productivity of India for 2014. There is a moderate positive relationship ($R^2=0.56$).

2.4. Entrepreneurship

Indian firms are traditionally included as the fourth factor of production, alongside natural resources, capital and labour. Audretsch and Keilbach (2003, 9.2) define 'entrepreneurship capital' as "the capacity for economic agents to generate new firms". The importance of enterprises for production activity is that they organise the other factors. Carree and Thurik (2005) identify three entrepreneurial roles: the innovator, the opportunity seeker, and the risk taker. Two different approaches usually ascribed to Schumpeter (1950): the creative destruction processes by which new inventions turn existing technologies obsolete (so-called Schumpeter Mark I regime) and the positive feedback loop between innovation and R&D that makes larger firms outperform their smaller counterparts (i.e. the Schumpeter Mark II regime).

The opportunity-seeking entrepreneur was emphasised by Kirzner, who defined as the main feature of entrepreneurial behaviour the ""alertness to possibly newly worthwhile goals and to possibly newly available resources" (Kirzner, 1973, p. 35).

Figure 6. Labor productivity and innovation: India 2014

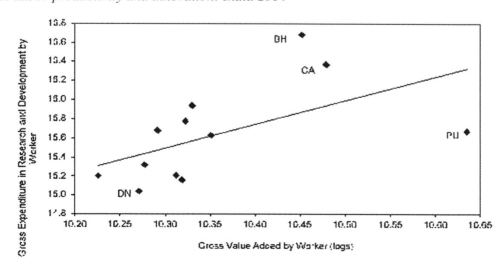

Finally, the risk-taking entrepreneur is associated with Knight, for whom apart from workers on routine and mental operations and managers, the organisation of economic activity depends upon those who have "confidence in their judgment and powers and in disposition to act on their opinions, to 'venture'. This fact is responsible for the most fundamental change of all in the form of organization, the system under which the confident and venturesome 'assume the risk' or 'insure' the doubtful and timid by guaranteeing to the latter a specified income in return for an assignment of the actual results" (Knight, 1921, III.IX.10).

Combining these three approaches, the OECD defines entrepreneurs as "agents of change and growth in a market economy and they can act to accelerate the generation, dissemination and application of innovative ideas... Entrepreneurs not only seek out and identify potentially profitable economic opportunities but are also willing to take risks to see if their hunches are right" (OECD, 1998, p.11). Consequently, the more entrepreneurial is a region, the more likely it will contain people willing to take risks in uncertain economic ventures and ready to grab commercial opportunities -and who therefore will introduce new products and processes in the market. These activities would result in higher productivity and growth. In this respect, Audretsch and Keilbach (2003) looked on the importance of entrepreneurship to explain output across 327 regions in Germany and found a positive and statistically significant relation. Furthermore, Van Stel *et al.* (2005) studied whether total entrepreneurial activity influenced GDP growth between 1999 and 2003 in a sample of 36 countries and found that the relationship is not linear: it is negative for poorer countries and positive for relatively rich ones. These findings support the view that larger firms dominate R&D and innovative activities (Mark II regime) and that, therefore, regions or countries with a dearth of large companies fail to exploit economies of scale and scope even in the presence of relative high levels of entrepreneurial activity.

Figure 7. presents the relationship between entrepreneurship (measured as the number of VAT registrations per capita) and labour productivity of India for 2014. The relationship is positive and very strong ($R^2=0.91$).

Figure 7. Labor productivity and entrepreneurship: India 2014

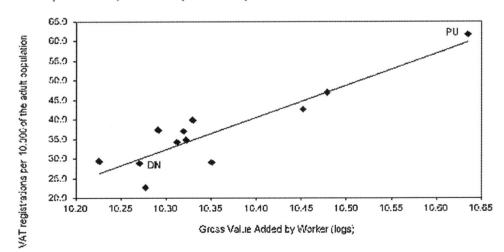

A Causal Analytic Model for Labour Productivity Assessment

2.5. Competition

Scarpetta and Tressel (2002) explain that competition forces prices to converge to marginal costs and thus raise static efficiency and that it makes firms continually improve their performance bringing about, thus, dynamic efficiency as well. More competitive markets encourage cost-reducing improvements because their higher price elasticity of demand means that there is more room for firms to increase profit than in less competitive markets. Furthermore, the higher is the competitive environment of a market, the less likely is that inefficient firms may operate in it. However, competition may also have adverse consequences for productivity. The Schumpeterian approach contends that innovation and creative destruction thrive in highly concentrated markets, because monopoly rents quickly eroded in competitive ones. Aghion and Howitt (1998) attempted to reconcile both views on the relationship between product market competition and productivity growth. They argued that the relationship should be positive in industries:

1. Characterised by weak control of managers by shareholders,
2. Where tacit knowledge is the main limiting barrier to imitation relative to patent protection,
3. With low density of technologic-specific fixed investments.

A number of empirical studies have confirmed this conjecture. Furthermore, firm-level studies in India have reported positive effects of competition on productivity. However, Aghion *et al.* (2004) detected an inverted-U relationship between product market competition and innovation, which would indicate that "some kind of an 'escape competition' effect should dominate at lower levels of PMC as measured by the Lerner index, whereas the 'Schumpeterian effect' should dominate at high initial levels of PMC. The inverted-U relationship means that as competition decreases, the equilibrium profit level of neck-and-neck firms increases, resulting eventually in a fall in the economy-wide rate of growth." Therefore, the expected sign of the relationship between competition and productivity is not as clear-cut as that between the other drivers and productivity. Competition has a regional dimension: as HM Treasury (2001, p. 31) states: "Markets can have an important regional and local dimension as they are segmented by transportation costs and consumer tastes. Ensuring that markets are competitive in every region and locality is essential in ensuring firms face incentives to innovate, keep prices down and minimise their costs of production." Figure 8 presents the relationship between an indicator of regional competition levels (the percentage of firms that responded that Competition was the main barrier to success) and productivity for 2013. The result –an almost non-existent correlation ($R^2=0.05$)- suggests that either there is no relationship between (this indicator of) competition and labour productivity or that contrasting forces might be affecting this relationship.

2.6. Drivers that Have Been Left Behind

As mentioned above, the specialised literature has proposed other factors influencing productivity than the five drivers. This subsection will briefly comment on the following variables missing from the framework: social capital, firms' restructuring, innovation absorptive capacity, industrial structure, population and job density, firm churning, and distance to main economic hub.

Figure 8. Labor productivity and competition: India 2014

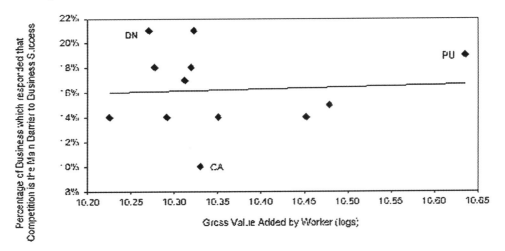

2.6.1. Social Capital

The OECD defines social capital as "networks together with shared norms, values and understandings that facilitate co-operation within or among groups" (OECD, 2001, p.41). Social capital may influence productivity by reducing transaction costs and employee turnover and by increasing risk-taking (i.e. Knightian entrepreneurship –see subsection 2.5 above) and the sharing of knowledge (See Aspin, 2004). Social capital presents both a horizontal and a vertical dimension. At a horizontal level, social capital helps in 'bonding' and 'bridging' communities. The vertical dimension refers to its capacity for 'linking' people in different economic, social or political strata. These three dimensions of social capital may not have the same effect on labour productivity: Sabatini (2006a, 2006b) found that bonding and bridging social capital presented a negative effect on labour productivity but that linking social capital of voluntary organizations exerted a positive influence. Also, Ichniowski *et al.* (2003) found a positive influence of networks among workers within an organisation upon labour productivity.

2.6.2. Restructuring

There are two kinds of restructuring processes: internal or external. Internal restructuring is the process by which firms introduce technological and management changes to make better use of existing inputs; external restructuring is the process by which successful manufacturing plants grow at the same time that less efficient plants exit the markets. Thus, internal restructuring occurs within firms whereas external restructuring takes place between firms. External restructuring is partially and indirectly captured within the five drivers' framework by innovation – the start-ups indicator measures the proportion of new entrants. However, the framework fails to count for any processes of internal restructuring and, although Disney *et al.* (2003) and Roberts and Thompson (2005) failed to find any significant effects of internal restructuring on productivity, Carreira (2006), Hakkala (2004), Falvey *et al.* (2004), Balsvik and Haller (2006) and Bartelsman *et al.* (2004) did find that internal restructuring has a significant effect on productivity.

A Causal Analytic Model for Labour Productivity Assessment

2.6.3. Absorptive Capacity

Absorptive capacity is "the ability of a firm to recognise the value of new, external information, assimilate it, and apply it to commercial ends" Cohen and Levinthal (1990, p. 128). The relative inability to absorb the most efficient technology available would determine how far away from the production frontier a firm (region, country, etc) would be –in other words, its degree of technical inefficiency. However, the five drivers' framework does not allow for any differences in absorptive capacity across regions and sectors. Kneller and Stevens (2006), Girma (2005) and Girma and Görg (2005) report some positive relations between absorptive capacity and productivity.

2.6.4. Industrial Structure

Industries differ in terms of productivity levels and growth. Consequently, the industrial mix within regions may explain to some extent differences in regional productivity levels. Iparraguirre (2005b) found that sectoral specialisation in GVA, sectoral concentration of GVA and employment and sectoral re-allocation of labour have a significant effect on labour productivity across the India. In particular, the Delhi-NCR's industry mix compared to the India average negatively contributed to the region's labour productivity growth between 2007 and 2014: Labour productivity would have grown 3.6 per cent more over this period had Delhi-NCR's industry had the same industrial structure as the India as a whole. Sectoral composition is also relevant for differences in the intensity of the five drivers across regions. Demand for skills and technology in a region varies, among other things, according to the industrial structure. For example, a study by DTI found that differences in the industrial structure explain almost all the gap in R&D intensity levels between firms in India and other countries. Furthermore, ERU (2006) reports that industrial structure provides a significant explanation for differences in VAT registration rates between Mumbai and India.

2.6.5. Agglomeration and Distance to Main Economic Hub

Agglomeration economies implies that the concentration of productive activities creates externalities and spillovers mostly bounded to the geographic area in which they occur, which reinforces the process of spatial concentration of economic activity (Marshall, 1890). Jacobs (1969) presented an alternative view: the more diversified the productive structure within a certain geographic area is, the higher are the increasing returns derived from agglomeration: knowledge would be better spread across complementary industries than similar ones. Thus, two main types of externalities derive from the agglomeration of economic activity: pecuniary and technological externalities. The Pune Authority has recently found a strong and non-linear effect of agglomeration across the India on economic activity: output per head initially rises linearly with employment density, but beyond a threshold, the gradient of this relationship increases (GLA Economics, 2006). Similarly, Anastassova (2006), Rice and Venables (2004) and Boddy *et al.* (2005) report the importance of agglomeration and distance to economic hub on productivity.

2.6.6. Regulation

As HM Treasury (2006, p. 63) explains: "Regulations can restrict the efficient running of firms, slowing innovation; restrict good management practice and therefore reduce productivity. However, appropriate regulation can benefit firms and consumers by providing certainty on product quality and giving consumers confidence to try the products of new entrants." A Better Regulation Task Force report (BRTF, 2005) estimated that the India GDP could be increased by £16 billion per annum if the administrative burden of regulation is reduced and that the total cost of regulation represents about 10 per cent of GDP (see also Crafts, 2006). HM Treasury (2004) includes product market regulation as an indicator for competition when it benchmarks the India's productivity performance against the other countries; however, regulation not considered as one of the five drivers of productivity growth.

3. DATA

We have used the following indicators for India for 2014:

- **Labour Productivity:** Gross Value Added per Person in Employment (source: ONS). We have also run the different models with Gross Value Added per Hour Worked as indicator of labour productivity, but we obtained a much lower statistical significance.
- **Entrepreneurship:** Total Entrepreneurial Activity (source: GEM) and VAT registrations per 10,000 of adult population (Start-ups) (source: Inter-Departmental Business Register, ONS, and Small Business Service, DTI).
    - We included both indicators and included a co-variation between them, under the assumption that they may respond to a set of common causes apart from those explicitly included in the model (i.e. Regulation and Skills –including Training).
- **Innovation:** Gross Expenditure on Research and Development (GERD) per Person in Employment and as a per cent of Gross Value Added (source: Office for National Statistics, Regional Trends 38). GERD per Person in Employment rendered a better fit than GERD as a per cent of GVA.
    - Distinguishing between Business Expenditure on R&D and Government Expenditure on R&D did not improve the results.
- **Investment**: Total Net Capital Expenditure (NCE) per Person in Employment and as a per cent of Gross Value Added (source: RBI). We obtained better results using NCE per Person in Employment than NCE as a per cent of GVA.
- **Skills**: Percentage of economically active adults qualified to NVQ Level 4 or above and Percentage of employees receiving job-related training within the last 4 weeks (source: LFS).
    - We have used other indicators (namely the percentage of economically active adults with no qualification; that of those qualified to NVQ Level 2 or below; that of those with NVQ 2 and NVQ 3) but they were not statistically significant or render a lower significance than the indicators reported.
- **Competition**: Percentage of businesses with employees responding that Competition is the main barrier to business success (source: Annual Survey of Small Businesses: India 2013/14 - Small Business Service - Table 10.3 - p. 204).

A Causal Analytic Model for Labour Productivity Assessment

- We have not used 'Exports' as an indicator of competition (included by DTI and the HM Treasury as a benchmark for the competition driver), because most studies suggest that export performance is a result of firm or regional productivity rather than one of its drivers.

Furthermore, we have included an additional variable, Regulation, albeit neither it has been chosen as one of the five drivers nor included as an indicator within the regional framework. However, there are two reasons for its inclusion. Firstly, regulation and market competition are interlinked features of economic life and, secondly, the indicator of competition has not proved to be significant whereas the indicator of regulation has. As an indicator of regulation, we used the percentage of businesses with employees responding that regulation is the main barrier to business success (source: Annual Survey of Small Businesses: India 2013/14 - Small Business Service - Table 10.3 - p. 204).

4. A MODEL OF REGIONAL PRODUCTIVITY DRIVERS

Figure 9 presents the model as a path diagram. We only present the best-fit model –i.e. the one that fits best the data according to several statistical tests- out of several specifications. Arrows show the direction of the causal relationships (for example, Competition influences Investment and not vice versa). For expositional simplicity, the chart does not show co-variances between indicators. The actual model includes co-variances when we assumed that two variables relate to each other due to common causes beyond those explicitly modelled. For example, the percentage of economically-active adults qualified to NVQ Level 4 or above and the percentage of employees receiving job-related training within the last 4 weeks could respond to some variables outside those included in the model –hence, the model included a co-variance component between these variables.

We used data for 2014 because there are no regional data about barriers to business success (or about any alternative indicators of regulation) for any previous years -the Omnibus Survey, which preceded the Annual Survey of Small Businesses, did not cover Delhi-NCR, Mumbai and Madras. The model in Figure 9 is the one that provided the best results. SEM assumes that the researcher knows the model (i.e. which variables to include and which relate to which) and, given this assumption, it provides a test of whether the model fits the data well or not. Therefore, SEM does not produce models; these have to create by the researcher. There are many contending theories providing alternative hypothesis that relate either each driver to productivity or to other drivers. Consequently, we could have tested an almost endless list of models. In order to reduce the array of contending specifications, we have chosen those relationships between drivers that have been widely reported in the literature as econometrically robust. In other words, our choice has been empirically driven rather than theoretically driven. The model presented in Figure 9 assumes the following interrelationships between the drivers, apart from their direct effects on labour productivity:

- Regulatory barriers, competitive pressures, influence the level of Investment effort in a region and skills level of the workforce in the region.
- The proportion of highly skilled people in the workforce affects the level of investment, of expenditure on research and development, of entrepreneurial activity and start-ups.

Figure 9.

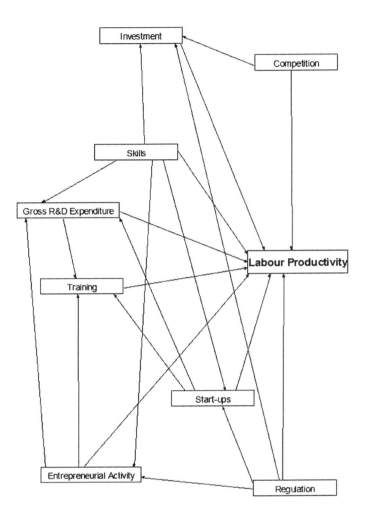

- The proportion of highly skilled workers in the workforce influences regional innovation and by how much entrepreneurial the population in the region is. Furthermore, the level of research and development activity affects the level of in-company training.
- In-company training depends upon innovation and entrepreneurship.
- Entrepreneurship influences in-company training activity and gross expenditure on research and development.
- Regulation affects entrepreneurship and investment.

In addition, not included in Figure 9, the model assumes that some drivers respond to common causes not explicitly included in the model (i.e. co-vary). In particular,

- Competition and Regulation.
- Start Ups and Total Entrepreneurial Activity.
- Skills and Training.

A Causal Analytic Model for Labour Productivity Assessment

- R&D, Start Ups and Total Entrepreneurial Activity.

5. RESULTS

SEM allows distinguishing between direct and indirect effects of endogenous and intermediate (i.e. intervening or mediating) variables upon a response (i.e. outcome or dependent) variable. The following tables present standardised coefficients only. There is a preference in SEM literature, mostly for theoretical reasons, to work with un-standardised variables and therefore to present un-standardised results. However, standardised estimates are easier to interpret, where the variables are transformed so that their mean is set to 0 and their standard deviation is set to 1. In all cases, we calculated the statistical significance of the coefficients for direct and indirect effects by bootstrapping the original sample of 12 observations (i.e. regions) per variable one thousand times.

In the tables below, the directionality goes from left to right: that is, the variables in the left-hand column affect those in the right-hand column (e.g. in Table 1, the first row indicates that Skills influence Start Ups). The coefficients show the changes in the variables to the right as the variables to the left change, irrespective of their initial measurement units given the standardisation. The coefficients express a change in the variables to the right in standard deviations due to a change of one standard deviation in the variables to the left. For example, according to the first row in Table 1, a one standard deviation change in the percentage of economically-active adults qualified to NVQ Level 4 or above (i.e. Skills) would increase the number of VAT registrations per 10,000 of adult population (i.e. Start-ups) by 0.574 standard deviations. Another way to express this is that a 1-point difference on the Skills indicator would increase the indicator of Start-ups by 0.574 points. Another useful feature of standardised coefficients is that they provide a snapshot of the relative importance of the effect of each variable on the right onto those on the left. For example, according to Table 1, changes in Skills seem to have a higher effect on Entrepreneurial Activity than on Start Ups (i.e. 0.749 against 0.574).

Tables 1 to 3 show standardised direct, indirect and total effects as resulting from the model presented in Figure 9 for the India using data for 2014. As mentioned above, Figure 9 presents the best-fit model out of several alternative specifications we have worked with. The Annex includes the estimates for an array of fit measures. Table 1 shows that Investment, Entrepreneurship, Start Ups, and R&D Expenditure have positive and significant effects on Labour Productivity. Competition and Training are the only drivers with non-significant direct effects on Labour Productivity. Furthermore, Skills (i.e. NVQ4 or above) would have a negative direct impact on Labour Productivity. However, Skills presents positive and significant effects on Start Ups, Entrepreneurship and Investment, which also impact positively on Labour Productivity, as a result of which the indirect effect of Skills on Labour Productivity is significant and positive (Table 2).

Table 2 presents the standardised indirect effects of each driver on the rest and on labour productivity.

Apart from skills, also entrepreneurship has a net positive indirect effect on labour productivity. it is worth noting that start-ups present a positive indirect effect and entrepreneurial activity presents a negative indirect effect, and that both coefficients are statistically significant. however, as the coefficient of start-ups is higher than that of entrepreneurial activity, and both measure the same driver, namely Entrepreneurship, this driver has a net indirect positive effect on Labour Productivity. Finally, Table 3 presents the standardised the total effects of one variable onto the other and onto labour productivity according to the causal influences assumed in the model in Figure 9.

Table 1. Standardized direct effects India, 2014

Skills	-->	Start Ups	0.574	
Skills	-->	Entrepreneurial Activity	0.749	
Regulation	-->	Start Ups	0.144	ns
Regulation	-->	Entrepreneurial Activity	0.156	ns
Start Ups	-->	R&D	4.092	ns
Entrepreneurial Activity	-->	R&D	-0.637	ns
Skills	-->	R&D	-1.680	ns
Regulation	-->	Investment	-0.104	ns
Skills	-->	Investment	0.841	
R&D	-->	Training	-0.161	ns
Start Ups	-->	Training	-0.333	ns
Entrepreneurial Activity	-->	Training	0.553	ns
Competition	-->	Investment	0.131	ns
Investment	-->	Labour Productivity	0.742	
Entrepreneurial Activity	-->	Labour Productivity	0.523	
Start Ups	-->	Labour Productivity	0.263	
R&D	-->	Labour Productivity	0.353	
Regulation	-->	Labour Productivity	-0.178	
Skills	-->	Labour Productivity	-0.531	
Training	-->	Labour Productivity	-0.033	ns
Competition	-->	Labour Productivity	-0.023	ns

NS = not significant (at 10 per cent)

Table 2. Standardized Indirect effects India, 2014

regulation	-->	r&d	0.489	
skills	-->	r&d	1.871	ns
regulation	-->	training	-0.041	ns
skills	-->	training	0.192	ns
start ups	-->	training	-0.661	ns
entrepreneurial activity	-->	training	0.103	ns
regulation	-->	labour productivity	0.216	ns
skills	-->	labour productivity	1.227	
start ups	-->	labour productivity	1.479	
entrepreneurial activity	-->	labour productivity	-0.247	
competition	-->	labour productivity	0.097	ns
r&d	-->	labour productivity	0.005	ns

ns = not significant (at 10 per cent)

A Causal Analytic Model for Labour Productivity Assessment

Table 3. Standardised total effects India, 2014

Skills	-->	Start Ups	0.574	NS
Competition	-->	Investment	0.131	NS
Entrepreneurial Activity	-->	R&D	-0.637	
Entrepreneurial Activity	-->	Training	0.656	NS
R&D	-->	Training	-0.161	NS
Regulation	-->	Start Ups	0.144	
Regulation	-->	Entrepreneurial Activity	0.156	
Regulation	-->	Investment	-0.104	NS
Regulation	-->	R&D	0.489	
Regulation	-->	Training	-0.041	NS
Skills	-->	Entrepreneurial Activity	0.749	
Skills	-->	R&D	0.191	NS
Skills	-->	Investment	0.841	
Skills	-->	Training	0.192	NS
Start Ups	-->	R&D	4.092	
Start Ups	-->	Training	-0.993	
Investment	-->	Labour Productivity	0.742	
Start Ups	-->	Labour Productivity	1.742	
R&D	-->	Labour Productivity	0.359	
Skills	-->	Labour Productivity	0.696	
Entrepreneurial Activity	-->	Labour Productivity	0.276	NS
Regulation	-->	Labour Productivity	0.038	NS
Training	-->	Labour Productivity	-0.033	NS
Competition	-->	Labour Productivity	0.075	NS

NS = not significant (at 10 per cent)

Increasing the density of VAT registrations, the investment per worker, the number of people with high qualifications, and the expenditure on R&D would have a positive and significant impact on Labour Productivity. In contrast, increasing the level of entrepreneurial activity (not translated into new VAT registrations) or the intensity of training activities within firms would not have any significant effects. The same applies to reducing barriers to doing business resulting from the levels of Competition and Regulation: they would not have any significant impacts on regional labour productivity.

6. THE CASE OF DELHI: NCR

Labour productivity in Delhi - NCR grew by 6.3 per cent since 2008. Productivity changes in a region may come as a result of changes in the country as a whole (national share), in sectors across the country with a significant presence within that region (industry mix), or in variables specific to the region (regional shift). Changes in labour productivity in the India as a whole pushed forward labour productivity in Delhi-NCR by almost 14 per cent; however, the region's industrial structure (with its mix of high and low performing sectors) and other factors specific to the region had an adverse impact on productivity growth. Therefore, labour productivity only grew by less than half that otherwise would have been the case if only the national share had operated. Even more worrying is the fact that labour productivity in Delhi-NCR has been lagging behind other regions in the India in the recent years, as Figure 10 shows.

In 2014, Delhi-NCR presented the second lowest labour productivity level of all India regions (after Wales) and, not shown, the lowest hourly productivity level. These results should come as no surprise once we consider Delhi-NCR's relative performance in the different productivity drivers.

6.1 Investment

This is the only driver for which Delhi-NCR exhibits a satisfactory ranking amongst the India, along with Regulation. There are published data on gross fixed capital formation by region for 2014 –the latest available data is for 2010. Therefore, we used data for Net Capital Expenditure (NCE) for 2014. However, in terms of regional rankings, both indicators present a similar picture: Delhi-NCR has one of the highest investment ratios (i.e. in terms of GVA). In terms of the amount invested per person in employment in 2014, the situation is not as favourable: Delhi-NCR ranks seventh out of twelve regions.

It is worth noting, though, that NCE, both as a percentage of total GVA or per worker, has been diminishing across the India since 2010.

Figure 10. India regional labor productivity 2007-2014

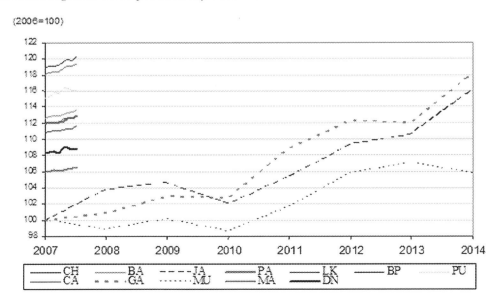

For a more accurate representation of this figure, please see the electronic version.

A Causal Analytic Model for Labour Productivity Assessment

6.2. Skills

Considering the economically active population with high qualifications, Delhi-NCR ranked 7th in 2014. Since 2008, the region's relative position has been changing; although, Pune, the Calcutta and Madras has led the regional rankings throughout the period.

On the other hand, Delhi - NCR presents the highest proportion of people with intermediate qualifications and with no qualifications to its population of working age. Furthermore, Delhi - NCR has consistently presented the lowest percentage of employees receiving job-related training of all India regions since 2008.

6.3 Innovation

We used four alternative indicators to measure innovation: Business or Government Expenditure on R&D as a percentage of GVA and per person in employment. In the four indicators, Delhi - NCR comes up with the worst percentages. In contrast, the Bhopal and Calcutta have presented the highest measures of innovation since 2008.

6.4 Entrepreneurship

There are two overall measures of entrepreneurship available at the regional level: the number of VAT registrations per 10,000 population and the Total Entrepreneurial Activity as a percentage of total adult population (although for the latter, data are only available since 2012). The number of VAT registrations per 10,000 population –an indicator of start-ups or business formation- shows Delhi - NCR has one of the two or three worst regions in India since 2008. The TEA indicator presents a similar picture, with Delhi - NCR ranking between 11th and 9th over the period 2013-2014.

6.5 Competition and Regulation

According to the Annual Survey of Small Business 2013/14, 21 per cent of businesses with employees in Delhi - NCR responded that Competition was the main barrier to success. This was the highest percentage along with that of the Banglore. In contrast, Regulation presents a more favourable situation: the percentage of respondents in Delhi - NCR stating that this was the main barrier to their success was 38 per cent, which ranked the region in the 3rd best place for 2013/14. That is, it is the region with the third lowest percentage of respondents affirming that regulations were hampering their success.

Figure 11 summarises Delhi - NCR relative ranking amongst the India regions for different indicators of the drivers of labour productivity.

As the model introduced in section 3 and tested in section 4 makes evident, it is not just this or that variable, but rather the combination of relatively poor performances in most of the drivers which is conspiring against Delhi – NCR's labour productivity performance. In addition, and returning to the initial contention in this chapter, this would be affecting the economic prospect of the region in the end.

Figure 11. Delhi: NCR: regional rankings by productivity driver

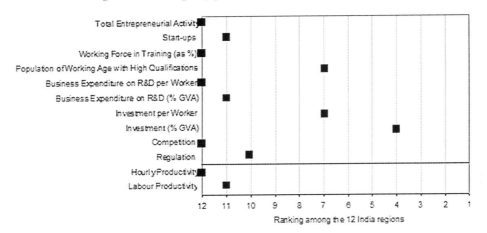

7. CONCLUSION

The Indian government and those of the devolved administrations have adopted a policy framework for boosting regional productivity based on five drivers: Investment, Skills, Innovation, Entrepreneurship, and Competition. However, there are no published estimates of a "five drivers" model. This chapter aims to fill that gap: to present a formal test of the claim that those five variables are driving productivity at a regional level. We modelled the relationships between the five drivers and labour productivity using a structural equation model that fitted the data well. However, due to data unavailability, we could only run the model with data for 2013; this represents a relevant limitation, for we could only test the hypotheses on levels of labour productivity rather than on both levels and changes. The main conclusion is that promoting entrepreneurship (in particular, increasing the density of VAT registrations), spending more on research and development, increasing the capital-worker ratio and the percentage of the workforce with higher qualifications have a significant bearing upon regional labour productivity. In contrast, regulatory barriers to competition do not seem to affect labour productivity at a regional level.

REFERENCES

Aghion, P., & Howitt, P. (1998). *Endogenous Economic Growth*. Cambridge, MA: The MIT Press.

Arrow, K. (1969). Classificatory notes on the production and transmission of technical knowledge. *The American Economic Review, 59*, 29–35.

Bernard, A., & Jensen, J. (1999). Exceptional exporter performance: Cause, effect, or both? *Journal of International Economics, 47*(1), 1–25. doi:10.1016/S0022-1996(98)00027-0

Blomström, M., Lipsey, R., & Zejan, M. (1996). Is fixed investment the key to economic growth? *The Quarterly Journal of Economics, 111*(1), 269–276. doi:10.2307/2946665

Bradford DeLong, J., & Summers, L. (1991). Equipment Investment and Economic Growth. *The Quarterly Journal of Economics*, *106*(2), 445–502. doi:10.2307/2937944

Broersma, L., & van Dijk, J. (2005). Regional Differences in Labour Productivity in the Netherlands. *Tijdschrift voor Economische en Sociale Geografie*, *96*(3), 334–343. doi:10.1111/j.1467-9663.2005.00464.x

BRTF. (2005). *Regulation – Less is More. Reducing Burdens, Improving Outcomes. A BRTF Report to the Prime Minister*. London: Better Regulation Task Force.

Carreira, C. (2006). *Firms' learning and selection and productivity growth over the economic cycle. Seminário GEMF*. Coimbra, Portugal: Grupo de Estudos Monetários e Financieros. Facultade de Economia. Universidade de Coimbra.

Carroll, C., & Weil, D. (1994). Carnegie-Rochester Conference Series on Public Policy: Vol. 40. *Savings and growth: a reinterpretation* (pp. 133–192).

Ciccone, A. (2002). Agglomeration-Effects in Europe. *European Economic Review*, *46*(2), 213–228. doi:10.1016/S0014-2921(00)00099-4

Ciccone, A., & Hall, R. (1996). Productivity and the Density of Economic Activity. *The American Economic Review*, *86*(1), 54–70.

Cingano, F., & Schivardi, F. (2004). Identifying the Sources of Local Productivity Growth. *Journal of the European Economic Association*, *2*(4), 720–742. doi:10.1162/1542476041423322

Cohen, W., & Levinthal, D. (1990). Absorptive Capacity: A New Perspective on Learning and Innovation. Administrative Science Quarterly, 35(1), 128-152. doi:10.2307/2393553

Disney, R., Haskel, J., & Heden, I. (2003). Restructuring and Productivity Growth in UK Manufacturing. *The Economic Journal*, *113*(489), 666–694. doi:10.1111/1468-0297.t01-1-00145

Economics, G. L. A. (2006). *Why distance doesn't die: Agglomeration and its benefits*. London: Greater London Authority.

Engelbrecht, H. (2003). Human Capital and Economic Growth: Cross-Section Evidence for OECD Countries. *The Economic Record*, *79*(Special Issue), S40–S51. doi:10.1111/1475-4932.00090

EU. (1995). *Green Paper on Innovation. Com (95) 688*. Brussels, Belgium: European Commission.

Girma, S. (2005). Absorptive Capacity and Productivity Spillovers from FDI: A Threshold Regression Analysis. *Oxford Bulletin of Economics and Statistics*, *67*(3), 281–306. doi:10.1111/j.1468-0084.2005.00120.x

Girma, S., Greenaway, D., & Kneller, R. (2004). Does Exporting Increase Productivity? A Microeconometric Analysis of Matched Firms. *Review of International Economics*, *12*(5), 855–866. doi:10.1111/j.1467-9396.2004.00486.x

Glaeser, E. L., Kallal, H. D., Scheinkman, J. A., & Shleifer, A. (1992). Growth in Cities. *Journal of Political Economy*, *66*, 1125–1152.

Greenaway, D., & Kneller, R. (2004). Exporting and Productivity in the United Kingdom. *Oxford Review of Economic Policy, 20*(3), 358–371. doi:10.1093/oxrep/grh021

Griffith, R., Redding, S., & Van Reenen, J. (2003). R&D and absorptive capacity: From theory to data. *The Scandinavian Journal of Economics, 105*(1), 99–118. doi:10.1111/1467-9442.00007

Griliches, Z., & Regev, H. (1995). Firm Productivity in Israeli Industry: 1979-1988. *Journal of Econometrics, 65*(1), 175–203. doi:10.1016/0304-4076(94)01601-U

Jacobs, J. (1969). *The economy of cities*. New York: Random House.

Jorgenson, D. (2005). Accounting for Growth in the Information Age. In P. Aghion & S. Durlauf (Eds.), *Handbook of Economic Growth* (vol. 1, pp. 743–815). Amsterdam: North-Holland. doi:10.1016/S1574-0684(05)01010-5

Kirzner, I. (1973). *Competition and Entrepreneurship*. University of Chicago Press.

Kline, R. (2005). *Principles and Practice of Structural Equation Modeling* (2nd ed.). New York: The Guildford Press.

Knack, S., & Keefer, P. (1997). Does Social Capital have an economic payoff? A cross-country Investigation. *The Quarterly Journal of Economics, 112*(November), 1251–1288. doi:10.1162/003355300555475

Kneller, R., & Stevens, P. (2006). Frontier Technology and Absorptive Capacity: Evidence from OECD Manufacturing Industries. Oxford Bulletin of Economics and Statistics, 68(1). doi:10.1111/j.1468-0084.2006.00150.x

Lucas, R. Jr. (1988). On the mechanics of economic development. *Journal of Monetary Economics, 22*(1), 3–24. doi:10.1016/0304-3932(88)90168-7

Mankiw, N., Romer, P., & Weil, D. (1992). A Contribution to the Empirics of Economic Growth. *The Quarterly Journal of Economics, 107*(2), 407–437. doi:10.2307/2118477

Marshall, A. (1890). *Principles of Economics*. London: Macmillan and Co., Ltd.

Morris, B. (2001, Summer). Can differences in industrial structure explain divergences in regional economic growth?. Bank of England Quarterly Bulletin, 195-202.

Nelson, R., & Phelps, E. (1966). Investment in humans, technological diffusion, and economic growth. *The American Economic Review, 56*(1/2), 65–75.

Nickell, S. (1996). Competition and Corporate Performance. *Journal of Political Economy, 104*(4), 724–746. doi:10.1086/262040

Nickell, S., Nicolitsas, D., & Dryden, N. (1997). What makes firms perform well?. European Economic Review, 41. doi:10.1016/S0014-2921(97)00037-8

Olley, G., & Pakes, A. (1996). The Dynamics of Productivity in the Telecommunications Equipment Industry. *Econometrica, 64*(4), 1263–1297. doi:10.2307/2171831

Podrecca, E., & Carmeci, G. (2001). Fixed investment and economic growth: New results on causality. *Applied Economics*, *33*(2), 177–182. doi:10.1080/00036840122890

Romer, P. (1986). Increasing returns and long-run growth. *Journal of Political Economy*, *94*(5), 1002–1037. doi:10.1086/261420

Romer, P. (1990). Endogenous technological change. *Journal of Political Economy*, *98*(2), 71–102. doi:10.1086/261725

Schumpeter, J. (1934). Theory of Economic Development. Harvard University Press.

Solow, R. (1956). A Contribution to the Theory of Economic Growth. *The Quarterly Journal of Economics*, *70*(1), 65–94. doi:10.2307/1884513

Tinbergen, J. (1942). On the Theory of Trend Movements. In Jan Tinbergen, Selected Papers. Amsterdam: North-Holland.

Tolentino, A. (2004). *New Concepts of Productivity and its Improvement*. Paper presented at the European Productivity Network Seminar, Budapest, Hungary.

WEF. (2004). *Global Competitiveness Report 2003/2004*. World Economic Forum, Geneva, Switzerland.

KEY TERMS AND DEFINITIONS

Competition: Competition is also a major tenet of market economies and business is often associated with competition as most companies are in competition with at least one other firm over the same group of customers, and also competition inside a company is usually stimulated for meeting and reaching higher quality of services or products that the company produces or develop. Competition forces prices to converge to marginal costs and thus raise static efficiency and that it makes firms continually improve their performance bringing about, thus, dynamic efficiency as well. More competitive markets encourage cost-reducing improvements because their higher price elasticity of demand means that there is more room for firms to increase profit than in less competitive markets.

Entrepreneurship: Entrepreneurship is the process of designing, launching and running a new business, i.e. a startup company offering a product, process or service. It has been defined as the "... capacity and willingness to develop, organize and manage a business venture along with any of its risks in order to make a profit."

Innovation: Innovation is a new idea, or more-effective device or process. Innovation can be viewed as the application of better solutions that meet new requirements, unarticulated needs, or existing market needs. This is accomplished through more-effective products, processes, services, technologies, or business models that are readily available to markets, governments and society. The term "innovation" can be defined as something original and more effective and, as a consequence, new, that "breaks into" the market or society. Innovation as the implementation of a new or significantly improved product (good or service), or process, a new marketing method, or a new organizational method in business practices, workplace organization or external relations. Innovation activities are all scientific, technological, organizational, financial and commercial steps which actually, or are intended to, lead to the implementation of innovations.

Investment: Investment generally results in acquiring an, also called an investment. If the asset is available at a price worth investing, it is normally expected either to generate income, or to appreciate in value, so that it can be sold at a higher price (or both). Investment in physical capital (i.e. in tangible assets such as public infrastructure, consumers' and government durables, land, machinery and equipment) as a key input for economic growth.

Skills: A skill is the learned ability to carry out a task with pre-determined results often within a given amount of time, energy, or both. In other words, the abilities that one possesses. Investing in human capital may positively contribute to productivity inasmuch as a more skilled workforce is likely to be more productive.

APPENDIX

We also run a Bollen-Stine bootstrap test which rejected the hypothesis that the data significantly departed from the model (p=0.845).

Table 4. Fit measures - Model in Figure 9

Fit Measure	Default Model	Saturated	Independence
Discrepancy	3.069	0.000	121.576
Degrees of freedom	9	0	36
P	0.962		0.000
Discrepancy / df	0.341		3.377
GFI	0.946	1.000	0.383
Adjusted GFI	0.728		0.229
Tucker-Lewis index	1.277		0.000
RMSEA	0.000		0.465
P for test of close fit	0.965		0.000
Akaike information criterion (AIC)	75.069	90.000	139.576
Browne-Cudeck criterion	795.069	990.000	319.576
Bayes information criterion	171.625	210.696	163.715
Consistent AIC	128.525	156.821	152.940
Expected cross validation index	6.824	8.182	12.689
ECVI lower bound	7.364	8.182	9.984
ECVI upper bound	7.364	8.182	16.085
MECVI	72.279	90.000	29.052

(India Regions, 2014)

Table 5. Fit measures – Model in Figure 1

Fit Measure	Default Model	Saturated	Independence
Discrepancy	42.685	0.000	632.423
Degrees of freedom	10	0	36
P	0.000		0.000
Discrepancy / df	4.269		17.567
GFI	0.913	1.000	0.283
Adjusted GFI	0.606		0.104
Tucker-Lewis index	0.803		0.000
RMSEA	0.200		0.449
P for test of close fit	0.000		0.000
Akaike information criterion (AIC)	112.685	90.000	650.423
Browne-Cudeck criterion	122.407	102.500	652.923
Bayes information criterion	274.247	297.723	691.968
Consistent AIC	232.345	243.848	681.193
Expected cross validation index	1.374	1.098	7.932
ECVI lower bound	1.172	1.098	6.982
ECVI upper bound	1.668	1.098	8.972
MECVI	1.493	1.250	7.962

(Data, 2014)

Chapter 13
Effective Tools for Improving Employee Feedback during Organizational Change

Tanja Sedej
Graduate School of Government and European Studies, Slovenia

Gorazd Justinek
Graduate School of Government and European Studies, Slovenia

ABSTRACT

Feedback is the fastest and most effective way for organizations to make improvements or get things back on track. Prompt and constructive feedback is strongly linked to employee satisfaction and productivity, and can increase both. During times of change when employees want to be heard and feel involved, it is even more important that the optimal internal communication tools for managing employee feedback are selected. This article tackles these questions and provides fresh empirical data on the selection of internal communication tools in general, with focus then devoted to managing feedback during change from the perspective of a professional communicator. The data evaluated and analyzed was gathered on the basis of research carried out in 2014 among 105 professional communicators of large and medium-sized companies, and was then compared with the results of similar research conducted in 2012.

INTRODUCTION

The general consensus is that organizational changes are becoming increasingly frequent, and so must be planned and managed with great care (Barrett, 2002; D'Aprix, 2008; Kitchen, 2002; Kotter, 1996; Luecke, 2003; Sedej & Mumel, 2013). Sedej and Mumel (2013, p. 25) argue that implementing change often takes longer than planned, whereas Balogun and Hope Hailey (2004) report that approximately 70 percent of changes implemented within organizations fail to achieve their set objectives.

Therefore, a critical factor to be taken into account during an organizational change is internal communications. It is widely accepted that internal communications play a key role in the successful implementation of change (Goodman & Truss, 2004; Kalla, 2005; Kotter, 1996; Proctor & Doukakis,

DOI: 10.4018/978-1-5225-0654-6.ch013

2003; Young & Post, 1993). Communicating effectively within organization is not something that is nice to have. Indeed, internal communication is essential for the smooth running of every organization. Justinek and Sedej (2011) argue that internal communications represent a key performance and productivity issue, especially for international companies. It is therefore vital to ensure that employees have an optimal range of internal communication tools in general and for giving and receiving feedback. Rapidly changing circumstances require internal communication tools to be continuously improved and revised.

Particularly, when change has a significant impact on employees, organizations need to provide a broad range of options for employees to communicate, ask questions, vent anxieties and express opinions. Working without feedback during a change process is akin to setting off on an important journey without a map. Relying only on sense of direction is not sufficient and of itself to make improvements or keep things on the right track.

The number of ways to communicate in organizations has rapidly increased over the last two decades (Lengel & Daft, 1998; Lydon, 2005; Richardson & Denton, 1996; Wojtecki & Peters, 2000). It is therefore crucial that this area is comprehensively understood in order to achieve best results for setting a feedback system using internal communication tools.

There is a lack of understanding about the link between the effectiveness of internal communications, internal communication tools and feedback during change. Each internal communication tool has features that make it suitable and appropriate in certain situations, but entirely inadequate in others. This chapter therefore explores which internal communication tools are the most appropriate during change generally, as well as in terms of achieving overall business success and facilitating feedback.

The purpose of this chapter is therefore to present not only a critical review of the theories and approaches currently presented regarding internal communications and the facilitation of feedback through internal communication tools, but also the results of an empirical study that will encourage further research into the nature of organizational change, change communications, and internal communication tools and setting feedback system in order to create a more pragmatic framework in which to operate.

This chapter begins with a conceptual analysis of the meaning of organizational change and change management, internal communications and the internal communication tools which are used in this regard. It then concludes with an investigation of the understanding of feedback and its power to enhance the change process.

The results of research conducted on the selection of tools for improving employee feedback in internal communication during change are also presented. The topic was first researched in 2012, but was repeated in 2014. The analysis however reveals that there has been a gradual shift in the use of internal communication tools generally and, more specifically, for exchanging feedback.

THEORETICAL BACKGROUND

Change Management and Internal Communications

Technological development, fierce competition and globalization are just some of the critical elements that force organizations to transform or adjust to new business conditions. Organizational changes are a fact of everyday life and vital for survival. They must therefore be successfully planned and managed (Balogun & Hope Hailey, 2004; Beshtawi & Jaaron, 2014; Ćirić & Raković, 2010; D'Aprix, 2008; Koonce, 1991; Kitchen & Daly, 2002; Kotter, 1996; Luecke, 2003). Kitchen and Daly (2002, p. 46) argue that twenty-first century organizations are preoccupied with the concept of change. Ćirić and Raković (2010, p. 24) explain that changes are difficult to predict, and tend to occur with growing frequency. Therefore, change management is becoming an increasingly significant issue in the business world.

As change management garners increasing attention, many definitions of the concept have emerged. For example, Moran and Brightman (2000, p. 66) define change management as the process of continually renewing an organization's direction, structure, and ability to serve the ever-changing needs of its external and internal customers. Kitchen (2002, p. 48) explains that change management implies an attempt to understand the dynamics in the business environment, as well as the organization's own internal dynamics. Beshtawi and Jaaron (2014, p. 128) argue that the main intention behind a change management framework is to help all employees, even managers, to move successfully from the current state to a future state while achieving the business results desired.

The keystone of organizational change lies in internal communications, and employee communication is a pivotal element in achieving business success (Elving, 2005; Frahm & Brown, 2007; Goodman & Truss, 2004; Kitchen & Daly, 2002; Koivula, 2009; Lydon, 2006; Richardson & Denton, 1996). Goodman and Truss (2004, p. 217) believe that appropriate communication helps employees understand the need for change and its direct impact. Sande (2008, p. 29) considers communication to be real only when it is two-way. Elving (2005, p. 131) states that one of the main purposes of change communication can be to prevent, or at least reduce, resistance to change. Goodman and Truss (2004, p. 226) listed some examples of potential purposes for internal communication: getting buy-in, securing commitment to change, minimizing resistance, reducing personal anxiety, ensuring clarity of objectives, sharing information, setting out the vision, challenging the status quo, increasing clarity and mitigating uncertainty.

Organizational change can be both invigorating and intimidating (Sedej & Mumel, 2013, p. 23). Once employees are encouraged to carry out their jobs differently, the whole organization begins to change. Effective internal communication is therefore essential for addressing organizational concerns. Goodman and Truss (2004, p. 226) listed some examples of potential purposes for internal communication: getting buy-in, securing commitment to change, minimizing resistance, reducing personal anxiety, ensuring clarity of objectives, sharing information, setting out the vision, challenging the status quo, increasing clarity and mitigating uncertainty.

Despite the growing attention of the presented field, numerous errors in change management are directly linked to the collapse of internal communications (Elving, 2005; Gilsdorf, 1998; Kotter, 1996). Newton (2007, p. 186) also believes that it is necessary to take into account how much damage is sustained through too little or too much communication when considering the level of communication intensity in the context of change management. Sedej and Mumel (2015, p. 9) explain that employees always want to be kept abreast of what is happening in an organization and how the changes implemented will affect their work life.

The above observations highlight the huge importance of internal communications during the change process. It draws attention in particular to the importance of careful planning and change management. Justinek and Sedej (2011, p. 230) emphasize that internal communications must be sufficiently flexible to adapt smoothly to business needs.

Internal Communication Tools during Change

The immense significance of internal communications during change is therefore noted, but there remain some specific areas which have not been adequately investigated in this regard. Few studies have investigated internal communication tools in detail. The results of those studies usually highlight the importance of giving sufficient thought to tool selection (Goodman & Truss, 2004; Merrell, 2012; Richardson & Denton, 1996; Young & Post, 1993).

Indeed, internal communication tools need to be chosen carefully, especially during times of change. Appropriate tool selection helps employees adapt more smoothly to organizational changes and new business needs. Austin and Currie (2003, p. 236) believe that managers should use a variety of the tools available to them, find innovative ways to strengthen employee relations, and disseminate information as soon as it is known. Lydon (2006) agrees that organizations need to use communication tools that have been proven to work.

Buckingham (2008) argues that if the internal communication tools used do not fit the true culture of the organization, then only few individuals will truly take heed of the internal information flows. Sedej and Mumel (2013, p. 23) believe that unsuitable internal communication approaches are frequently employed during change; mistakes occur as unclear goals are set, inappropriate messages are relayed and inappropriate communication tools and channels are selected, which all too often result in poor communication results. It is therefore clear that the selection of appropriate internal communication tools represents a challenge.

It is crucial that internal communication tools, which should include both personal and impersonal modes of internal communications, are selected with due thought and consideration (Mumel, 2008; Ranken, 2007; Richardson & Denton, 1996). Barrett (2002, p. 221) states that effective employee communication uses all the tools available in order to reach its audience, but relies more on direct communication (verbal or face-to-face) than indirect communication (written and electronic tools).

Face-to-face communication is generally considered more efficient than other forms (Holtz, 2004; Mumel, 2008; Richardson & Denton, 1996), but is time-consuming and costly for widely dispersed organizations. Richardson and Denton (1996, p. 215) add that if personal (verbal) communication is limited, it is necessary to consider interactive tools, particularly video and telephone conferencing. Holtz (2005, p. 22) underlines that innovations in web-based technology have generated a wide range of exciting new tools in internal communications.

Handling change electronically is sometimes more convenient and efficient, but can be counterproductive when dealing with complex issues. Wojtecki and Peters (2000, p. 1) believe that many managers use e-mail, intranets, and other innovative technological tools to communicate and see them as effective internal communication solutions that meet the high demand for communicating during times of change.

Many authors divide internal communication tools according to the mode of transmission (Bratton & Gold, 1994; Klein, 1996; Mumel, 2008). In this context, organizations have a wide range of written (printed), verbal (oral), and electronic internal communication tools available.

Sedej and Mumel (2005, p. 12) explain and clarify verbal, written and electronic internal communication tools as mode of transmission. In general, verbal (personal face-to-face) communication ranges from informal conversations between two employees to formal large meetings with directors. The key feature of this mode of communications is that the information is sent from the sender directly; the information is also expressed through tone of voice and non-verbal communication such as hand gestures and facial expressions, which enrich the interpretation and contribute to a better understanding of the message. Written communications vary from monthly reports to annual reports and corporate brochures. Electronic communications encompass the commonly used e-mails up to modern video content.

In Table 1, the internal communication tools are divided as mentioned above into three categories (verbal, written and electronic). Some of the tools in the table are classified into several subcategories.

Effective Tools for Improving Employee Feedback during Organizational Change

Table 1. *Internal communication tools according to mode of transmission*

	Internal Communication Tools	Verbal	Written	Electronic
Direct	Working breakfast	✓		
	Internal events	✓		
	Annual performance interview	✓		
	Leader walkabouts	✓		
	Meetings	✓		
Indirect	Brochures		✓	
	Internal magazines		✓	
	Flyers, posters		✓	
	Suggestion box		✓	
	Bulletin board		✓	
	Reports		✓	
	Corporate guides		✓	
	Questionnaires		✓	
	CD/DVD/USB		✓	✓
	Social media	✓	✓	✓
	Electronic bulletin board		✓	✓
	E-mails		✓	✓
	Electronic newsletter		✓	✓
	Internal radio	✓		✓
	Internal research		✓	✓
	Intranet		✓	✓
	Telefax		✓	✓
	Telephone	✓		✓
	Teleconference	✓		✓
	Videoconference	✓		✓
	Video clips	✓	✓	✓
	Virtual world (3D)	✓	✓	✓

Source: Sedej and Mumel (2005, p. 12)

If the information is transmitted via electronic equipment, this equipment will hereinafter be regarded only as electronic internal communication tools.

Feedback Tools in Internal Communication during Change

Especially during process of change internal communications and the tools represent an underutilized way to get closer to employees' expectations and opinions by simply listening and responding to them. The systematic gathering of feedback within any organization is crucial for its smooth and normal functioning.

Many authors (Kreps, 1990; Theaker, 2004; Russ, 2007; Parker, 2009; Sande, 2009) underline the significance of feedback in internal communications. Hattie and Timperley (2007, p. 81) define feedback as information that is provided by an agent regarding aspects of one's performance or understanding. Kotter and Cohen (2003, p. 101), on the other hand, define feedback as one of the most important forms of information required to achieve success in an organization.

It is vital to have a clear understanding of the concept throughout the organization. As feedback is a critical business component Hattie and Timperley (2007, p. 81) describe it as a consequence of performance.

Indeed, all good communications consist of not only effectively delivering information, but also actively listening. Even Sande (2009, p. 29) emphasizes that internal communications require an active sender, active receiver and a healthy feedback loop.

It is a mistake to expect that only increasing the frequency of messages through different internal communication tools and the introduction of new tools will be sufficient to encourage feedback information flows. The methods for obtaining feedback are becoming increasingly diverse and innovative (Holtz, 2005; Sedej & Mumel, 2005). In addition to the most commonly used questionnaires and suggestion boxes, the use of quizzes, games, forums and blog are establishing a foothold in internal communications. Russ (2007, p. 8) clarifies that feedback can be obtained using multiple internal communication tools, verbal (within large or small groups and interpersonal communication) and nonverbal (written) feedback.

Especially in a process of change it is important to regularly facilitate and acquire feedback. Organizations need to clarify ambiguities through internal communications and gain the support and cooperation of their employees. Parker (2009, p. 25) firmly believes that if employees have the opportunity to express their personal fears, only then can progress in the process of change be made.

In order for organizations to promote open communication with all their employees, i.e. from those who are more vocal to those less willing to speak up, it is vital that there are several ways to obtain feedback. As a result, organizations often offer employees the option to provide feedback anonymously through research projects or suggestion boxes, through which employees and executives exchange opinions. Harris (2007, p. 12) argues that it is important to provide an opportunity for personal feedback communication, but it is also important to provide some channels that allow adequate anonymity because employees are often wary of expressing their real opinion, but this is largely dependent on the culture of the organization.

RESEARCH

There is no longer any doubt that employees are the most important part of the success of any organization. The employee communication process, together with internal communication tools for an effective feedback system, has undergone fundamental change, as technology has become an important part of the business world. It is imperative to have a comprehensive overview of what resonates with employees in internal communications as well as a solid understanding of the most appropriate internal communication tools for giving and receiving feedback.

Therefore, a question that addresses this chapter is in place: What are the most appropriate internal communication tools to facilitate communication and consequently employee feedback?

Methods

To begin, theoretical and background information was gathered on the concepts of change management in internal communications generally and more detailed internal communication tools for facilitating employee feedback. The existing research and literature on change processes and internal communications were used to construct the research framework.

The theoretical framework was then verified empirically with a structured questionnaire on internal communications during organizational change, in which the main focus was on internal communication tools in general and in detail for facilitating feedback during process of change.

Similar research was first conducted in 2012, with a follow-up project conducted two years later in 2014, thereby allowing the two sets of data to be compared.

Design of Research

The questionnaires were designed solely for internal communication experts who have adequate knowledge and appropriate access to this kind of information. The focus was on experts who operate in large and medium-sized companies, where the high number of employees requires not only systematically planned and thoughtful internal communications but also a carefully managed system for feedback. The questionnaire was available to communication experts to complete for approximately three months in 2012 and again in 2014.

In 2012 a total of 71 internal communication experts participated in the research, of whom 48 (68%) represented large companies and 23 (32%) medium-sized companies.[1] The youngest company participating in the research was only 2 years old, with the oldest having been established for 137 years; the average duration of incorporation for all the participating companies was 21.5 years. The key share represents companies that have been established for 2 to 30 years (87%). In terms of NACE,[2] the structure of the participating companies reveals that most operate in the manufacturing sector (15%), with second and third place shared by information and communication (14%) and financial and insurance activities (14%). The following activities are also well represented: other services activities, wholesale and retail trade, repair of motor vehicles and motorcycles, administrative and support service activities, and education.

In 2014, a total of 105 internal communication experts participated in the research, of whom 63 (60%) represented large companies and 42 (40%) medium-sized companies. The youngest company participating in the research was only 3 years old, the oldest 139; the average of all participating companies in terms of number of years of existence was 20.5 years. The key share represents companies that have operated from 3 to 30 years (89%). The structure of the participating companies in terms of NACE shows that most operate in the manufacturing sector (17%); the second place belongs to information and communication sector (16%) and the third place to financial and insurance activities sector (13%). The following activities also have an essential share: wholesale and retail trade, other services activities, repair of motor vehicles and motorcycles, education, administrative and support service activities.

The Results

As presented earlier in the chapter, the organizations today have a wide range of internal communication tools at their disposal and thereby numerous of possibilities to receive and give feedback to their employees. Especially during the process of change it is important to communicate openly and frequently to prevent or at least reduce employee resistance. Their concerns should be discovered in the early phase and addressed as soon as possible. In this manner all internal communications have to be cautiously planned and managed. Bellow results of the research tackle comprehensively the mentioned issues.

Frequency and Types of Organizational Change

Organizations face changes relatively often; this was also verified by the research conducted in both 2012 and 2014.

In 2012 the experts estimated that an average of 4 major organizational changes had occurred in the previous three years. After more detailed analysis, the types of changes were also established (Figure 1). In the last three years, the organizations had to deal most frequently with the introduction of new products and services (79%) and reorganization (72%), followed by expansion into new markets and changes to the management and organizational culture. The last three listed changes were identified by approximately every second organization that participated in the research.

Two years later, in 2014 the experts estimated that in the last three years on average 4.5 major organizational changes had occurred (Figure 2). Analysis also shows that in the last three years, the organizations had to deal most frequently with the introduction of new products and services (81%) and reorganization (75%), followed by change in organizational culture, expansion into new markets and change of management (approx. 50–60%).

Internal Communication Tools Used during Change in General

The right frequency and combination of internal communication tools are also vital, especially during change processes, a time when employee anxiety increases. Consequently, a series of questions related to internal communication tools was established.

In the research carried out in 2012 and 2014, the experts were required to choose exactly three key internal communication tools that are used most often in times of change in general. They could choose from among the 25 most commonly used internal communication tools. Also, three options to record alternative internal communication tools were available. Based on the experts' selection, a list of the 10 most frequently used internal communication tools during times of change was conceived.

Figure 1. Type of organizational changes 2009-2011 (as a percentage)

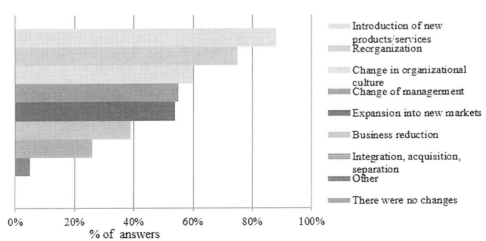

For a more accurate representation of this figure, please see the electronic version.

Figure 2. Type of organizational changes 2011-2013 (as a percentage)

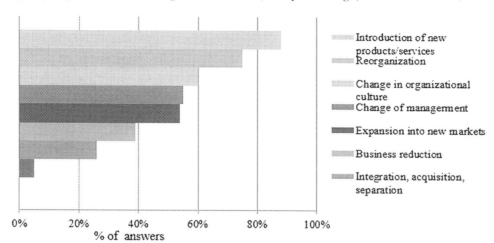

For a more accurate representation of this figure, please see the electronic version.

In 2012 the first place on the list of internal communication tools was taken by meetings, which was partially expected as personal internal communication during change is usually the most preferred mode of communication within organizations (Figure 3). Other internal communication tools ranked as follows in terms of being the most appropriate: e-mails, internal events, intranet, internal magazines, leader's walkabout, reports, telephone, bulletin boards, and electronic bulletin boards.

Of the 10 key internal communication tools listed, electronic and verbal communication tools dominate. Written tools are also well represented, but are mainly ranked in the lower half of the top ten list.

Among the verbal communication tools available, the most important are meetings, closely followed by internal events and management walkabouts. Of the electronic communication tools available, the most important are e-mails, which ranked the second most important tool on the list. The next most important

Figure 3. Key internal communication tools used during change in general 2012 (as a percentage)

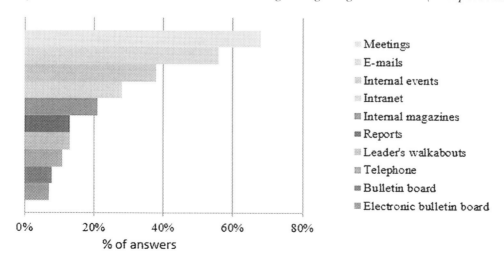

For a more accurate representation of this figure, please see the electronic version.

electronic tool is the intranet, placing third among all the tools listed. Telephone communication and electronic news also feature. Reports, bulletin boards and internal magazines feature among the written communication tools, which are all ranked in the lower half of the list of all tools.

In 2014, meetings and e-mails remained in first and second place respectively on the list of internal communication tools (Figure 4). Interestingly, the intranet placed third on this occasion. Other internal communication tools ranked as follows in terms of being the most appropriate: internal events, electronic internal magazines, reports, leader's walkabout, telephone and internal research.

Of the 10 key internal communication tools listed, electronic and verbal communication tools dominate. The share of written tools is the smallest and ranked in the lower half of the list.

Among verbal communication tools, the most important are meetings, followed by internal events and management walkabouts. Of the electronic communication tools available, the most important are e-mails, which ranked the second most important tool on the list. The next most important electronic tool is the intranet, placing third among all the tools listed. Telephone communication and e-news also feature. Reports and internal research as the written communication tools are all ranked in the lower half of the list of all tools.

Internal Communication Tools Used during Change for Facilitating Feedback

In the research carried out in 2012 and 2014, the experts were required to choose the three key internal communication tools for facilitating feedback that are used most often in times of change.

In 2012, internal research ranked first on the list of internal communication tools for facilitating feedback (Figure 5), with meetings placing second. Other internal communication tools ranked as follows in terms of being the most appropriate: suggestion box, annual interviews, e-mails, internal events, intranet, telephone, breakfast briefings and reports.

Figure 4. Key internal communication tools used during change in general 2014 (as a percentage)

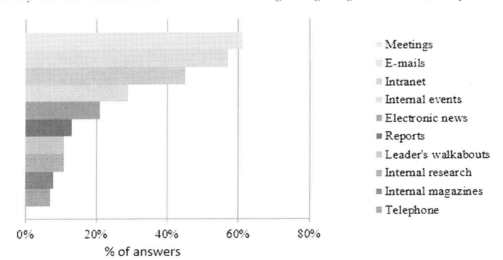

For a more accurate representation of this figure, please see the electronic version.

Effective Tools for Improving Employee Feedback during Organizational Change

Figure 5. Key internal communication tools used during change for feedback 2012 (as a percentage)

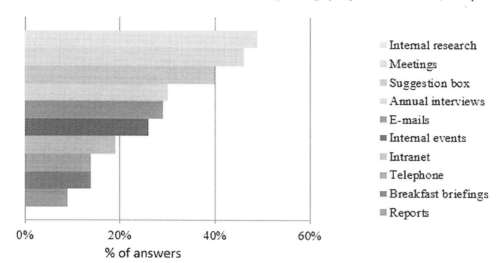

*For a more accurate representation of this figure, please see the electronic version.

The list of ten key internal communication tools shows the importance of all types of internal communication tools, whether they are written, verbal or electronic. Written tools are considered the most important, however, since they ranked first and third on the top ten list.

Among the various written communication tools available, the most important is internal research. A suggestion box also ranks highly in third place on the list, with reports placing last. Among verbal communication tools meetings are in the foreground, followed by the annual interviews, internal events and breakfast briefings. Despite e-mails being the most important electronic tool, they nevertheless ranked only in fifth place, followed by intranet and telephone.

In 2014, internal research once again took first place on the list of the most popular internal communication tools (Figure 6), with meetings ranking second. Other internal communication tools ranked as follows in terms of being the most appropriate: e-mails, intranet, suggestion box, reports, telephone, internal events, annual interviews and breakfast briefings.

The list of ten key internal communication tools shows the importance of all types of internal communication tools, whether they are written, verbal or electronic.

Among the various written communication tools available, the most important is internal research. A suggestion box and reports also have a significant role, ranking fifth and sixth on the list respectively. Among the verbal communication tools, meetings placed first, followed by internal events, annual interviews and breakfast briefings. Despite e-mail being the most important electronic tool, it nevertheless ranked only third, followed by intranet and telephone.

DISCUSSION

The business environment within which organizations operate has undergone rapid development, and organizations are required to cope with change more frequently than ever. Internal communications represent a key element in the success of organizational change (Goodman & Truss, 2004; Kalla, 2005;

Figure 6. Key internal communication tools used during change for feedback 2014 (as a percentage)

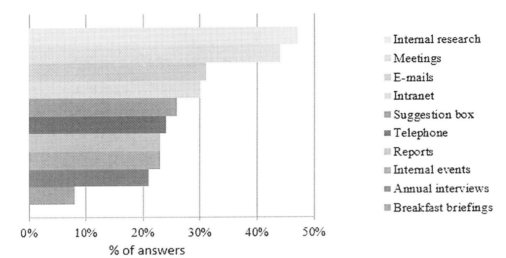

For a more accurate representation of this figure, please see the electronic version.

Kotter, 1996; Proctor & Doukakis, 2003; Young & Post, 1993) and this is the main reason why organizations must give more thought to internal communication tools (Merrell, 2012; Richardson & Denton, 1996; Wojtecki & Peters, 2000; Young & Post, 1993).

The research we have conducted in past years shows that the pace of change has not slowed down. Analysis conducted on research data gathered in 2012 and 2014 suggests that it has even slightly increased.

In the process of change, internal communications should not be underestimated or even neglected. Just because a message is delivered, this does not mean that it was delivered successfully. The mission of internal change communications is complete only when the receiver has understood and successfully integrated the message relayed.

In order to get the best results in communicating change, it is often necessary to deliver the message several times using different internal communication tools. The adequate combination of verbal, electronic and written internal communication tools is therefore essential in order to ensure that the communication process is being carried out effectively.

After each internal communication especially during process of change, it is necessary to ensure a relevant follow up with possibilities for feedback to verify the employee's level of awareness, understanding as well as their emotional reactions and commitment to include it daily work. In fact, our research proves that in order to communicate change effectively in general meetings and e-mails are still the most important tools, although the difference between them is getting smaller. It can be noted that the position of electronic tools in internal communications is growing even stronger, when comparing the data for 2014 and 2012. Three electronic tools in fact rank among the first five places. In line with expectations, the role of written tools is less prominent in 2014 than was the case in 2012, as they are all ranked only in the lower half of the top ten list.

A comprehensive picture for facilitating feedback with internal communication tools during change shows another perspective. When experts have in their mind facilitating feedback, they ranked the importance of the internal communication tools entirely differently. At the top of the scale for the research conducted in 2012 and 2014 is internal research that represents written internal communication tools, while second place belongs to meetings. In addition to verbal and electronic internal communication tools, written tools have a significant role to play during change in this regard.

CONCLUSION

All organizations, regardless of their size, are required to change significantly in order to develop or survive in a new business environment. The way in which employees are kept informed and engaged in the workplace is also changing radically.

The research conducted confirms that the number of changes faced by organizations is increasing every year. The foundation of organizational success therefore lies in planning all the phases in the change process well, especially the ability to communicate change properly and provide the best and most appropriate range of internal communication tools.

When planning internal communications during change, it is important for experts to bear in mind how the feedback is exchanged. Previous research demonstrates that written internal communication tools should not be neglected, especially during periods of change. Despite the new media and tools at our disposal, it is vital to remember that change communications are not effective when a message is simply delivered; only when the message has been heard, understood and applied in practice can it be deemed a success.

Research shows that a healthy feedback system which comprises written, electronic and verbal internal communication tools is a viable approach for communicating change in organizations. It suggests that sensible planning and managing internal communication tools for facilitating feedback can improve the implementation of changes in organizations.

ACKNOWLEDGMENT

The authors would like to thank the anonymous reviewers and the editor for their insightful comments and suggestions.

REFERENCES

Austin, J., & Currie, B. (2003). Changing organisations for a knowledge economy: The theory and practice of change management. *Journal of Facilities Management*, *3*(2), 229–243. doi:10.1108/14725960410808221

Balogun, J., & Hope Hailey, V. (2003). *Exploring Strategic Change*. London: Prentice Hall.

Barrett, D. J. (2002). Change communication: Using strategic employee communication to facilitate major change. *Corporate Communications*, *7*(4), 219–231. doi:10.1108/13563280210449804

Beshtawi, M., & Jaaron, A. (2014). Change Management in Telecommunication Sector: A Managerial Framework. *Review of Contemporary Business Research, 3*(1), 127–141.

Bratton, J., & Gold, J. (1994). *Human Resource Management – Theory and Practice*. Houndmills, UK: The Macmillan Press Ltd.

Buckingham, I. (2008). Communicating in a recession: Employee must engage with the brand during tough times. *Strategic Communication Management, 12*(3), 7.

Ćirić, Z., & Raković, L. (2010). Change Management in Information System Development and Implementation Projects. *Management Information Systems, 5*(2), 23–28.

D'Aprix, R. (2008). Providing a frame of references is key during times of change. In G. Ginsberg (Ed.), *Mecum's Top 50 Internal Communication Case Studies: An Anthology of Best-selling Research to Tackle Key Communication Issues* (pp. 123–127). London: Melcrum Publishing Limited.

Elving, W. J. L. (2005). 'The role of communication in organisational change. *Corporate Communications, 10*(2), 129–138. doi:10.1108/13563280510596943

Frahm, J., & Brown, K. (2007). First steps: Linking change communication to change receptivity. *Journal of Organizational Change Management, 20*(3), 370–387. doi:10.1108/09534810710740191

Gilsdorf, J. W. (1998). Organizational rules on communicating: How employees are and are not learning the ropes. *Journal of Business Communication, 35*(2), 173–201. doi:10.1177/002194369803500201

Goodman, J., & Truss, C. (2004). The medium and the message: Communicating effectively during a major change initiative. *Journal of Change Management, 4*(3), 217–228. doi:10.1080/1469701042000255392

Harris, S. (2007). Supporting leaders through change. *Strategic Communication Management, 11*(4), 12.

Hattie, J., & Timperley, H. (2007). The Power of Feedback. *The Journal of Educational Research, 77*(1), 81–112.

Holtz, S. (2004). *Corporate Conversations: A Guide to Crafting Effective and Appropriate Internal Communications*. New York: AMACOM.

Holtz, S. (2005). The impact of new technologies on internal communications. *Strategic Communication Management, 10*(1), 22–25.

Justinek, G., & Sedej, T. (2011). Knowledge sharing as a part of internal communication within internationalized companies. In *Knowledge as Business Opportunity: Proceedings of the Management, Knowledge and Learning International Conference 2011*. International School for Social and Business Studies.

Kalla, H. (2005). *Integrated internal communications: a multidisciplinary perspective*. Corporate.

Kitchen, J. P., & Daly, F. (2002). Internal communication during the change management. *Corporate Communications:International Journal (Toronto, Ont.), 7*(1), 46–53.

Klein, S. M. (1996). A management strategic communication for change. *Journal of Organizational Change Management, 9*(2), 32–46. doi:10.1108/09534819610113720

Koivula, J. (2009). *Succeeding in Project Communication – Effective Tools for the Purposes of Change Management Case Company: VR Ltd. – Passenger Services.* Retrieved 18 October 2010 from: http://enable06.myenable.com/fusion/apps/doc/public/130/Productivity%20Study/2008%20Proudfoot%20Global%20Productivity%20Study.pdf

Koonce, R. (1991). The people side of organizational change. *Credit, 17*(6), 22–25.

Kotter, J. P. (1996). *Leading Change.* Boston: Harvard Business School Press.

Kotter, J. P., & Cohen, D. S. (2003). *Srce sprememb: resnične zgodbe o tem, kako ljudje spreminjajo svoje organizacije.* Ljubljana: GV Založba.

Kreps, G. L. (1990). *Organizational Communication: Theory and Practice* (2nd ed.). New York: Longman.

Lengel, R., & Daft, R. L. (1988). The selection of communication media as an executive skill. *The Academy of Management Executive, 11*(3), 225–232. doi:10.5465/AME.1988.4277259

Luecke, R. (2003). *Managing Change and Transition.* Boston: Harvard Business School Press.

Lydon, S. (2006). *Common Sense in a Changing world: Ipsos MORI Employee Relationship Management.* Retrieved 20 January 2009 from: http://www.ipsos-mori.com/_assets/erm/common-sense-in-a-changingworld.pdf

Merrell, P. (2012). Effective change management: The simple truth. *Management Services, 56*(2), 20–23.

Moran, J. W., & Brightman, B. K. (2000). Leading organizational change. *Journal of Workplace Learning: Employee Counselling Today, 12*(2), 66–74. doi:10.1108/13665620010316226

Mumel, D. (2008). *Komuniciranje v poslovnem okolju.* Maribor: De Vesta.

Newton, R. (2007). *Managing Change Step by Step: All You Need to Build a Plan and Make It Happen.* Harlow: Pearson Prentice Hall Business.

Parker, J. (2009). Using informal networks to encourage change at BP. *Strategic Communication Management, 13*(1), 24–27.

Proctor, T., & Doukakis, I. (2003). Change management: The role of internal communication and employee development. *Corporate Communications:International Journal (Toronto, Ont.), 8*(4), 268–277.

Ranken, N. (2007). Communicating an IT system change: Eight tips for success. *Strategic Communication Management, 11*(4), 16–19.

Richardson, P., & Denton, K. (1996). Communicating change. *Human Resource Management, 35*(2), 203–216. doi:10.1002/(SICI)1099-050X(199622)35:2<203::AID-HRM4>3.0.CO;2-1

Russ, T. L. (2007). Communication Strategies for Implementing Organizational Change. *Proceedings of the 2007 Association for Business Communication Annual Convention.*

Sande, T. (2009). Taking charge of change with confidence. *Strategic Communication Management, 13*(1), 28–31.

Sedej, T., & Mumel, D. (2013). How C-level views selection of internal communication tools in times of change. *Akademija MM. Slovenian Scientific Journal of Marketing, 21*, 23–36.

Sedej, T. & Mumel, D. (2015). The optimal selection of internal communication tools during change in organisations. *International Journal of Globalisation and Small Business, 7*(1), 6-25.

Theaker, A. (2004). *Priročnik za odnose z javnostmi*. Ljubljana: GV Založba.

Wojtecki, J.G. & Peters, R.G. (2000). Communicating organizational change: information technology meets the carbon-based employee unit. *The 2000 Annual, 2*, 1–16.

Young, M., & Post, J. E. (1993). Managing to communicate, communicating to manage: How leading companies communicate with employees. *Organizational Dynamics, 22*(1), 31–43. doi:10.1016/0090-2616(93)90080-K

KEY TERMS AND DEFINITIONS

Change Management: A process, approach or method that increases the likelihood that employees will successfully manage through a change process.

Internal Communications: Represent a function responsible for effective communications among employees within organizations.

Internal Communication Tools: Through internal communication tools with informing, creating dialogue and relationship among employee's communication objectives can be achieved.

Feedback in Internal Communications: Feedback in internal communications is a system where the reaction or response of the receiver after he has interpreted the message reaches the sender through one or more internal communication tools.

Organisational Change: An organizational transition from its current state to a desired future state.

ENDNOTES

[1] **European Commission criteria determining company size**: **micro companies** are defined as companies that employ fewer than 10 persons and whose annual turnover or annual balance sheet total does not exceed EUR 2 million; **small companies** are defined as companies that employ fewer than 50 persons and whose annual turnover or annual balance sheet total does not exceed EUR 10 million; **medium-sized companies** are defined as companies that employ fewer than 250 persons and whose annual turnover or annual balance sheet total does not exceed EUR 43 million; **large companies** are defined as companies that employ more than 250 persons and whose annual turnover or annual balance sheet total does exceed EUR 43 million.

[2] The statistical classification of economic activities in the European Community, abbreviated as NACE, is the nomenclature for economic activities in the European Union.

Chapter 14
A Conceptual and Pragmatic Review of Regression Analysis for Predictive Analytics

Sema A. Kalaian
Eastern Michigan University, USA

Rafa M. Kasim
Indiana Tech University, USA

Nabeel R. Kasim
University of Michigan, USA

ABSTRACT

Regression analysis and modeling are powerful predictive analytical tools for knowledge discovery through examining and capturing the complex hidden relationships and patterns among the quantitative variables. Regression analysis is widely used to: (a) collect massive amounts of organizational performance data such as Web server logs and sales transactions. Such data is referred to as "Big Data"; and (b) improve transformation of massive data into intelligent information (knowledge) by discovering trends and patterns in unknown hidden relationships. The intelligent information can then be used to make informed data-based predictions of future organizational outcomes such as organizational productivity and performance using predictive analytics such as regression analysis methods. The main purpose of this chapter is to present a conceptual and practical overview of simple- and multiple- linear regression analyses.

DOI: 10.4018/978-1-5225-0654-6.ch014

INTRODUCTION

Regression analysis methods are powerful predictive analytics and modeling techniques that are used most often to develop predictive models and make future predictions of organizational productivity and performances (e.g., profits, sales) using past and current data in efforts to make informed and strategic organizational decisions. Their uses become more common and significant as predictive analytical tools due largely to:

1. Collecting massive amount of data such as internet traffic data (e.g., Web server logs, transaction data, and social media activities), which is referred to as "Big Data." It is called Big Data because the volume, velocity, and variety of the data exceed the processing, computing and/or storage capacities of the available computers, and
2. The increased need to transform the collected large volume of data into intelligent information (knowledge) and insights such as trends and patterns of hidden associations and relationships between variables (Hair, 2007; Kalaian & Kasim, 2015; Kuhns & Johnson, 2013; Siegel, 2014).

Consequently, the intelligent information can be used to create a holistic and a comprehensive view of a business enterprise to make smart and informed data-based competitive decisions, strategic planning, strategic organizational performance improvements, and predictions of future organizational performance to gain competitive advantage.

Methods of predictive analytics for quantitative data sets, including Big Data sets, are significant and relevant for executives and leaders across public (e.g., government, nonprofit organizations) and private sectors (e.g., companies, for-profit organizations) to improve organizational performance and increase the productivity of their organizations. Also, predictive analytics help firm leaders and executives to make informed data-based decisions and future predictions of organizational productivity and performance outcomes based on current and past data (Kuhns & Johnson, 2013; Maisel & Cokins, 2014).

Organizational Performance measurement is one of the most important and widely used constructs for evaluating organizational success. Organizational performance is an abstract construct that is presented by measurable indicators and factors that have direct and indirect effects on performance. Reviewing the literature of organizational performance reveals that studies defining organizational performance are divergent in how the organizational performance construct is conceptualized, measured, and defined as well as the factors that are included in the measurement model of organizational performance. Richard, et al. (2009) and Kasemsap (2014) defined organizational performance as an analysis of company's performance as compared to goals and objectives. Within corporate organizations, there are three primary outcomes analyzed: financial performance such as profits and return on investments (ROI), market performance such as sales and market share, and shareholder value performance such as total shareholder return.

In this chapter, organizational performance is defined as being a multidimensional construct that includes both financial and non-financial performance indicators to measure the organizational outcomes and quality of processes and practices within an organization to achieve the organizational strategic goals (e.g., increasing profits, reducing costs) and operational goals (e.g., optimizing operational efficiency, enhancing human capital). Organizational success, enhancement, improvement, and growth are the main objectives of any organization and it depends on its continuous performance. Examples of organizational performance indicators and factors are: productivity, profitability, leadership style, company

A Conceptual and Pragmatic Review of Regression Analysis for Predictive Analytics

size, information technology (IT), organization's strategy, research and development, human resources, innovations, and organizational climate.

However, the use of appropriate data analytical methods for Big Data to explore the characteristics of the data and predict future organizational performance is becoming increasingly important to large, medium and small organizations. In such predictive-oriented research studies, organizational productivity and performance outcomes are treated as dependent variables in the predictive models. Specifically, the main objectives of various regression modeling methods, as predictive analytics tools, are to:

1. Explore the relationships between the dependent variable (e.g., organizational performance construct, organizational productivity measure) and one or more independent variables (e.g., organizational climate, the use of information technology (IT), employees' satisfaction and motivation) to build accurate and valid predictive models, and
2. Use the prediction models to predict an unknown value of a dependent (outcome) variable from known values of a set of exploratory independent (predictor) variables by analyzing and capturing the relationships between the dependent and independent variables in a massive amount of quantitative (numerical) data (Field, 2009; Kalaian & Kasim, 2015).

In other words, the results and the findings of the exploratory regression analysis and model building are often used to make future predictions such as predicting specific future trends, risks, and behavior patterns of organizational productivity and performances.

Although *business data analytics (BDA)* covers three major analytic perspectives (descriptive, predictive, and prescriptive), the main purpose of this chapter is to present a conceptual and practical overview of few of the analytical methods that are most commonly used as tools to perform predictive analytics and modeling in organizational research to predict future organizational productivity and performance. The conceptual and methodological overview provides data analysts with the necessary skills to understand and conduct accurate and valid predictive analytics and interpret the reported findings and conclusions to technical and nontechnical audiences based on the use of the most appropriate regression analysis methods. The regression analysis and modeling methods that are covered in this chapter are:

1. Simple (bivariate) linear regression analysis; and
2. Multiple linear regression analysis.

(I) SIMPLE (BIVARIATE) REGRESSION ANALYSIS

Simple regression analysis is one of the most basic predictive analytics tools for analyzing and modeling the relationship between a single continuous dependent (outcome) variable and a single continuous or categorical independent (predictor) variable to build a predictive model that can be used for making future predictions. It is the simplest and the most basic regression analysis method in the predictive analytics toolbox because it includes only a single independent (predictor) variable and a single dependent variable. Simple regression analysis can be used to answer the following research question: What is the effect of the independent variable (e.g., organizational climate) on the dependent variable (e.g., organizational productivity or performance)?

The main goals of the simple linear regression analysis are to:

1. Examine the relationships between the variables to build and explain the best predictive model that represents the linear relationship between a single quantitative dependent variable and a single quantitative continuous or categorical independent variable; and
2. Predict the value of a dependent (outcome) variable such as organizational performance given the specific values of a single independent (predictor) variable based on the best specified predictive regression model (Field, 2009; Kalaian & Kasim, 2015; Kalaian & Kasim, 2016).

Examples of such independent variables (predictors) that have effects on organizational productivity and performance, which had been explored and studied in previously conducted organizational research studies are: Organizational climate (Patterson, et al., 2005); Organization's IT use (Mahmood & Mann, 2005; Weill, 1992); Human capital and Resources (Felicio, Couto, & Caiado, 2014; Okoye & Ezejiofor, 2013); Employee satisfaction measure (Imran, Majeed, & Ayub (2015).

In simple linear regression analysis, the linear relationship between a single dependent (outcome) variable and a single known independent (predictor) variable for n individuals (cases) is represented by the following simple linear regression model:

$$Y_i = \alpha + B X_i + e_i \qquad (1)$$

where:

Y_i: Is the value of the dependent (outcome) variable for the ith individual (e.g., employee, manger, executive, or leader in a company) and i = 1, 2, …, n individuals. Organizational performance and productivity are examples of such commonly used dependent variable in organizational research;

α: Which is known as Y-intercept, is a constant that represents the intercept of the regression line with the Y-axis. That is, it is the value of the outcome (dependent) variable (Y_i) when the value of the independent (predictor) variable (X_i) is equal to zero. For example, the intercept is the value of organizational productivity, which is the dependent variable, when the amount of investment in new organizational IT is zero dollars (i.e., the company haven't invested in any new technology), which is the independent variable;

B: is the regression coefficient of the independent variable (X) in the regression model and it represents the slope of the regression line, which can be interpreted as the amount of change in the dependent (outcome) variable for one unit change (e.g., one point, one year, one dollar) in the independent (predictor) variable (X). For example, the amount of change in company's productivity, which is the dependent variable, when the amount of company's investment in IT is changed by one unit, for example, $1000;

X_i: Is the value of the independent (predictor) variable for the ith individual (i = 1, 2, …, n). Organizational climate, technology use, and human resources are examples of such independent (predictor) variables; and

e_i: Which is the error or residual of the regression equation, represents the amount by which the observed value of the dependent variable, Y_i deviates from its predicted value ($\hat{Y}_i$) for individual (case), i, in the estimated simple regression model. It is represented as follows:

$$e_i = Y_i - \hat{Y}_i \qquad (2)$$

A Conceptual and Pragmatic Review of Regression Analysis for Predictive Analytics

One method for estimating the regression coefficients and the errors is the ordinary *least squares (OLS)* method, which minimizes the *sum of squared errors (SSE)* of the regression model. The total (sum) of the errors or residuals, which are randomly scattered around the regression line, is equal to zero and this is the main reason that we square the errors (e_i^2) before summing them in the OLS estimation method. SSE is calculated and represented as follows:

$$SSE = \sum e_i^2 \tag{3}$$

Where, $\sum e_i^2$ is the sum of squared errors. The intercept (α) and the slope (B) are estimated as follows:

$$b = S_{XY} / S^2_X \tag{4}$$

And,

$$a = \overline{Y} - b\overline{X} \tag{5}$$

Where, S_{XY} in equation 4 is the covariance between the independent variable (X) and the dependent variable (Y). The value of the covariance is used for calculating the correlation between (X) and (Y); (b) is the estimated regression coefficient (slope) of the regression parameter (B). The value of the slope is positive when the numerical values of the independent (predictor) variable increase as the numerical values of the dependent (outcome) variable increase. Conversely, the value of the slope is negative when the numerical values of the independent variable increase as the numerical values of the dependent variable decrease; and S^2_X is the variance of (X) values. In equation 5, $\overline{X}$ and $\overline{Y}$ are the means (averages) of the independent variable (X) and the dependent variable (Y) respectively; and "a" is the estimated value of the intercept of the regression line parameter (α).

Correlation Coefficient (r)

The *correlation coefficient* is a measure of the degree of the relationship between the numerical values of a pair of quantitative variables in a data set. It is referred to in the literature as the *Pearson product-moment correlation coefficient* and represented in a lower case (*r*). The correlation coefficient is the most widely used measure of correlation or relationship between a pair of quantitative variables (e.g., organizational performance and organizational climate). It is important to note that before analyzing the data using regression analysis, the data analyst should take the following descriptive analytics steps:

1. Examine the distribution of each of the dependent and independent variables to ensure the normality assumptions of the variables have been met,
2. Examine the relationships between pairs of variables in a data set to examine and assess the relationships, and
3. Graphically portray the relationships among the dependent and each of the independent variables in a data set using a scatterplots (scatter charts).

The values of the correlation coefficients range from -1.00 to +1.00. Positive values of *r* indicate that as the numerical values of one variable increase the numerical values of the other variable also increase. For example, do the employees who are highly satisfied with their working environment are more productive and conversely do the employees who are not satisfied with their work environment are less productive? Such a relationship with a perfect correlation coefficient of +1.0 is referred to as a high positive correlation between employees' satisfaction and employees' productivity and performance. The relationship between organizational performance or productivity and other organizational and human factors are explored and studied in previous research studies such as the relationship between organizational climate and the performance of the firm (Patterson, et al., 2005); the relationship between employee satisfaction and organizational productivity (Imran, Majeed, & Ayub (2015).

Negative values of *r* indicate that as the numerical values of one variable increase the numerical values of the other variable decrease (Field, 2009; Kalaian & Kasim, 2015; Sprinthall, 2011). For example, do the employees who work longer hours are less productive? Such a relationship with a perfect correlation coefficient of -1.0 is referred to as a high negative correlation between satisfaction and organizational productivity. It is important to note that the larger the absolute numerical value of the correlation coefficient (e.g., close to absolute 1), the greater the relationship between the two variables (either positive or negative relationship). A correlation coefficient of zero indicates no relationship between a pair of the quantitative variables in a data set (Field, 2009; Kalaian & Kasim, 2015; Kalaian & Kasim, 2016).

The correlation coefficient is calculated by dividing the covariance between the two variables by the standard deviation of the two variables. The formula for calculating the correlation coefficient is represented as follows:

$$r = S_{XY} / S_X S_Y \qquad (6)$$

Where, S_{XY} is the covariance between the dependent variable (X) and the dependent variable (Y); S_X is the standard deviation of the values of the independent variable (X); and S_Y is the standard deviation of the values of the dependent variable (Y).

Scatterplots (Scatter Charts)

A *scatterplot (scatter chart)* of the data points of pairs of quantitative variables is often used to graphically portray the relationships between any pairs of variables (for example, the relationship between employees' workplace satisfaction and the organizational productivity) and it is referred to as a *bivariate scatterplot*. The graphical display of a bivariate scatterplot has two axes (e.g., x-axis and y-axis): in cor-

Figure 1. Scatterplots (scatter charts) of bivariate data for different types of relationships

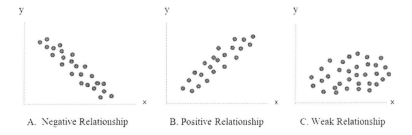

A Conceptual and Pragmatic Review of Regression Analysis for Predictive Analytics

relation, one axis for each of the two variables. In the scatterplot each individual's (subject's) numerical measurement (e.g., achievement score, weight, height) on both variables is represented by a dot. Figure 1, shows three bivariate scatterplots for three different types of relationships. Scatterplot "A" represents a strong negative relationship between the two quantitative variables (for example, employees' high level of satisfaction and high level of organizational performance). Scatterplot "B" shows a strong positive relationship between the two variables. Scatterplot "C" shows a weak or no relationship between the two quantitative variables (Kalaian & Kasim, in press).

Linear Regression Line

In simple linear regression, the bivariate scatterplot is often used to graphically portray the linear relationship between the predictor variable (X) and the dependent variable (Y). Organizational climate and organizational performance are examples of such independent and dependent variables, respectively. Viewing the bivariate scatterplots in Figure 1, we can envision many possible straight lines that can be drawn through the data points. But, only one of these straight lines would be the best-fitting regression line (Field, 2009; Mertler & Vannatta, 2013; Sprinthall, 2011). A straight regression line that represents the best fit of the regression model is usually drawn through many scatterplot data points that lies closest to all the points and minimizes the sum of squared errors (that is, $\sum e_i^2$ is minimized). Therefore, identifying the best-fitted regression line depends on three important factors that serves as the basis for the calculating the regression equations (Mertler & Vannatta, 2013; Sprinthall, 2011). These factors are: (1) The regression coefficient (slope) of the linear regression line; (2) The intercept of the linear regression line, which is the point at which the line intercepts (crosses) the Y-axis; and (3) The extent to which the bivariate points in the scatterplot are scattered around the regression line, which is measured by the correlation coefficient.

The regression line portrays the direction and the extent of the deviations of the actual data values (e.g., values of the organizational performance construct) from their predictive values ($\hat{Y}_j$), which are located on the regression line (Kalaian & Kasim, 2015). In Figure 2, graph "A" represents a linear regression line with a high and negative slope (B) value. An example of negative regression line might be that firm's hiring and firing practices have a negative effect on organizational productivity and performance. Graph "B" in Figure 2, represents a regression line with a high and positive slope (B) value. An example of positive regression line might be that organizational climate has a positive effect on organizational

Figure 2. Regression lines fitted to bivariate data displaying different types of regression lines

A. Negative Regression Line   B. Positive Regression Line

productivity and performance. The regression line will be horizontally flat when the value of the slope is zero, which indicates that there is no relationship between the dependent and the independent variables.

Assumptions of Simple Linear Regression Analysis

Simple linear regression analysis is based on specific assumptions about the quantitative data (Kalaian & Kasim, in press). Meeting these assumptions is necessary in order to achieve the best linear estimation of the parameters of the regression model such as the intercept and slope. These assumptions are:

1. The distribution of the numerical values of the dependent variable is normal.
2. The error terms (e_i) are independent and identically normally distributed with mean equal to zero.
3. The relationship between the dependent and the single independent variable is linear.
4. The errors of fitting the regression model are not correlated with the independent (predictor) variable.
5. The distribution of the errors of the regression model for each value of the independent variable (X) has an approximately normal distribution with constant variance across all values of the independent (predictor) variable X. This assumption is referred to as "homoscedasticity" or "equality of variances.

As a result of testing the assumptions, if the relationship between the dependent and the independent variable appears to be nonlinear (curvilinear) then nonlinear regression methods should be used to analyze the data instead of the linear regression. However, if there is sufficient number of cases and no violations of the assumptions are evident, then it is safe to interpret the linear regression analysis results (Field, 2009; Kalaian & Kasim, 2015; Tabachnik & Fidell, 2012).

Statistical Significance of the Regression Coefficient in Simple Regression

A *t-test* can be used to test whether or not the associated population parameter of the regression coefficient is equal to zero. In other words, it tests the null hypothesis that the slope of the regression is equal to zero (i.e., H_0: B = 0). The t-test is computed by dividing the estimated regression coefficient, *b*, by the standard error (S.E.) of the estimated regression coefficient, *b*. Therefore, the t-statistic formula is represented as follows:

$$t = b / S.E._{(b)} \tag{7}$$

Predictive Simple Linear Regression Models

Predictive regression models are used to:

1. Predict the values of the dependent variable given known values of an independent (predictor) variable (X), and
2. Evaluate the accuracy of predicting the unknown values of the dependent variable from known values of the independent variable.

The regression model fitting process is achieved by using the *Ordinary Least Squares (OLS)* method that minimizes the sum of squared errors (SSE). Practically, in using real data, the best fitted regression line will not pass through all the pairs of X and Y values of a dataset, but definitely will pass through the intersection of the mean (average) of the X values and the mean of the Y values. Therefore, the value of the slope is determined by the best fit (least squares) criterion, which is typically chosen so that the *sum of squared differences* ($\sum e_i^2$) between the values on the best fitted-line (predicted values) and the observed data values is minimized using the ordinary least squared method (Mertler & Vannatta, 2013; Kalaian & Kasim, 2015). The predicted value ($\hat{Y}$) of the dependent variable (Y) in simple linear regression is represented as follows:

$$\hat{Y}_i = a + b X_i \tag{8}$$

Where, "a" is the estimated intercept of the population parameter, α. "b" is the estimated regression coefficient of the population's regression coefficient parameter for the independent variable. B.

The accuracy of the predicted value of the dependent variable, Y, is calculated by subtracting the corresponding predicted value of the dependent variable, $\hat{Y}$, from the original observed value of the dependent variable, Y. The closer the value of the difference to zero the more accurate and better fit is the predictive model. This difference is called the error of prediction (Y_e) and represented as:

$$Y_e = Y - \hat{Y} \tag{9}$$

Coefficient of Determination (R^2)

One of the goals of simple regression is to measure the contribution of a single independent variable to the overall fit of the simple regression equation. The *coefficient of determination* (R^2) is such commonly used measure and it is a descriptive measure of goodness-of-fit of the regression model. It is a measure of the proportion (percentage) of the total variance in the dependent variable (Y) that is accounted for and explained by the variation of a single independent variable in the simple regression model. The unexplained variance in the dependent variable is assumed to result from other factors not included in the specified regression model or from random error. Having high R^2 indicates that the specified regression model explains the variation in the dependent variable well, suggesting that the regression model can be used for predictive purposes.

R^2 represents the squared correlation between the actual values of the dependent variable, Y, and the predicted values of the dependent variable that are obtained from the regression model. Its numeric value ranges from 0 to 1.0 and the closer the value of the R^2 statistic is to the value of 1.0, the better the fit of the estimated regression line to the bivariate data with a single independent (predictor) variable (Kalaian & Kasim, 2015; Kalaian & Kasim, 2016; Nathans, Oswald, & Nimon, 2012).

(II) MULTIPLE LINEAR REGRESSION ANALYSIS

The main goals of the multiple linear regression analyses where the researcher or analyst have two or more independent variables in the regression model are to: (a) Explore and understand the relationships between the dependent variable (e.g., organizational performance or productivity) and the multiple independent (predictor) variables (e.g., organizational climate, leadership style, technology use); (b) Identify and explain the best model that captures and represents the linear relationships between a quantitative dependent variable and two or more quantitative independent variables; (c) Predict the value of the dependent variable given the specific values of the multiple independent variables based on the best fitted model; and (d) Examine the relative importance of the independent (predictor) variables by comparing the regression coefficients in the specified regression model.

In multiple linear regression analysis, which is an extension of the simple linear regression, the linear relationship between a dependent variable and two or more known independent (predictor) variables (X_1, X_2, ..., X_k) in the population is represented by the following linear regression model:

$$Y_i = \alpha + B_1 X_{i1} + B_2 X_{i2} + \ldots\ldots + B_k X_{ik} + e_i \tag{10}$$

Where, Y_i is the value of the dependent (outcome) variable for individual i (i = 1, 2, …,n); α, is the intercept of the regression model, which is the value of the dependent variable (Y) when all the predictors in the regression model have values equal to zero; B_1, B_2, ..., B_k are the regression coefficients for the k independent (predictor) variables X_{i1}, X_{i2}, ..., and X_{ik} respectively. Each of these coefficients (regression weights) represents the effects of its associated predictor (X_j) on the dependent variable (Y) while holding the other predictors in the model constant. Similar to the simple regression model, the errors (e_i) represents the amount by which the observed value of the dependent variable deviates from the predicted value for an individual, i, from the estimated multiple regression model. The errors represent the "noise" term reflecting the other factors (variables) that influence the dependent (outcome) variable and are not accounted in the regression model (Kalaian & Kasim, 2015; Kalaian & Kasim, 2016; Tabachnik & Fidell, 2012). However, if all the error terms are randomly scattered around the regression line, their total sum will be 0.

The regression weights are called "*Beta Weights*" when each of the numerical values the dependent variable and each of the independent variables are standardized by converting them to *z-scores*. For each of the independent (predictor) variables, $z = (X_i - \bar{X})/S_X$, where $\bar{X}$ and S_X are the mean and standard deviation of the independent variable; and for the dependent (outcome) variable, $z = (Y_i - \bar{Y})/S_Y$, where $\bar{Y}$ and S_Y are the mean and standard deviation of the dependent variable. A Beta weight for an independent variable indicates the expected change (increase or decrease) in the dependent variable, in standard deviation units, given a one standard deviation change in a particular independent variable with all other independent variables in the regression model held constant.

Beta weights provide a measure of the importance of each of the independent (predictor) variable holding the other independent variables constant in the regression model. Beta weights are easily computed and provided by using any of the available statistical software packages. If there are no relationships (associations) between the independent variables in the specified regression equation, the Beta weights can provide an initial assessment of the contributions of each of the independent variables to the regression model. In practical cases where there are associations between the independent variables (that is, the predictors are correlated) in the specified regression model, researchers should employ other methods to determine the contributions of each of the independent variables to the regression model such as "*Product Measure*", which is presented later in this chapter.

Assumptions of Multiple Linear Regression Analysis

Multiple linear regression analysis is based on specific assumptions about the data. Meeting these assumptions is necessary in order to achieve the best linear estimation of the parameters of the regression model such as the intercept and the multiple slopes (Kalaian & Kasim, 2016). These assumptions are:

1. The distribution of the numerical values of the dependent variable is normal.
2. The relationship between the dependent variable and each of the multiple independent variables is linear.
3. The multiple independent (predictor) variables in the regression model are not correlated with each other. The existence of strong relationships among the predictors is one of the most significant problems when using multiple regression analysis. The phenomenon is referred to as "*multicollinearity problem*" when the correlations between any pairs of predictors are high, which indicate strong relationships.
4. The errors are not correlated with each of the independent (predictor) variables. The existence of relationships between the errors of prediction and one or more of the predictors is referred to in the literature as "Incidental Endogeneity" phenomena.
5. The error terms (e_i) of the regression model are independent and identically normally distributed with mean equal to zero and a constant variance. The later requirement of equal variances (constant variance) is referred to as "homoscedasticity" or "equality of variances" assumption.

Statistical Significance of the Regression Coefficients in Multiple Regression

Similar to simple regression analysis, in multiple-regression analysis, we are interested in testing whether each of the multiple regression coefficients (B_i) is statistically significant. A t-test can be used to test whether or not the associated population parameter of each of the multiple regression coefficients, which is adjusted (controlled) for all the other independent (predictor) variables in the regression model, is equal to zero ($H_0: B_i = 0$). For example, the regression model with two independent variables (e.g., organizational climate and leadership style), the value of the regression coefficient for organizational climate variable is controlled (or held constant) for the leadership style variable. The t-statistic is computed by dividing each of the multiple estimated regression coefficients, b_i, by the standard error (S.E.) of the estimated regression coefficient, b_i. The formula for testing each of the regression coefficients is represented as follows:

$$t = b_i / S.E._{(bi)} \qquad (11)$$

With a large sample size such as a sample size of 100 or more, a t-test value of 2.0 or greater for any of the regression coefficients in the regression model is statistically significant at a significance level of .05. This significant result leads to rejecting the null hypothesis of the specific regression coefficient ($H_0: B_i = 0$), which is adjusted (controlled) for the other variables included in the regression model. In multiple regression analysis, a significant regression coefficient indicates that the particular independent (predictor) variable has an effect on the dependent (outcome) variable controlling for the effects of the other predictors in the regression model.

Omnibus F-statistic tests can also be used to test the collective multiple regression coefficients in the regression model. It tests whether or not all of the regression coefficients, B_i for all of the variables in the regression model are simultaneously equal to zero (H_0: $B_1 = B_2 = ... = 0$)

Predictive Multiple Linear Regression Model

As in simple linear regression, predictive regression models are used to (a) predict the values of the dependent variable given known values of the independent (predictor) variables, and (b) evaluate the degree of accuracy in prediction of the unknown numerical values of a dependent variable from multiple known numerical values of the multiple independent variables (George & Mallery, 2010; Kalaian & Kasim, 2016). In multiple linear regression, the predicted value ($\hat{Y}$) of the dependent variable (Y) is represented as follows:

$$\hat{Y}_i = a + b_1 X_{i1} + b_2 X_{i2} + ... + b_k X_{ik} \tag{12}$$

Where, "a" is the estimated intercept of the population parameter, α; and $b_1, b_2, ..., b_k$ are the estimated regression coefficients of the regression coefficient parameters, $B_1, B_2, ..., B_k$ for the independent variables $X_{i1}, X_{i2}, ..., X_{ik}$ respectively.

As in simple regression, the accuracy of the predicted values of any Y value can be found by subtracting the predicted value of the dependent variable ($\hat{Y}$) from its corresponding original numerical value of the dependent variable (Y). This difference is called the error of prediction (Y_e) and represented as

$$Y_e = Y - \hat{Y} \tag{13}$$

Evaluating the Adequacy of the Fitted Regression Model

Once the regression model is specified and built, it is necessary to evaluate the goodness of fit of the model and test the statistical significance of the estimated regression parameters (Kalaian and Kasim, 2015). As it is presented earlier, a t-test is used to test each of the individual parameters of the regression model (the intercept and each of the multiple slopes). F-statistic tests whether or not all of the regression coefficients, B_i for all of the variables in the regression model are simultaneously equal to zero (H_0: $B_1 = B_2 = ... = 0$). The t-tests and the F-tests are the initial statistical tests for assessing the significance of each of the individual independent (predictor) variables. Beta weights (standardized regression coefficients) are also used as the initial statistical tests to examine the contribution of each individual independent (predictor) variable to the regression equation. These initial significance tests and contribution assessments are often followed by examining the overall fit of the regression model to the quantitative data with two or more independent (predictor) variables.

The key goals of model fitting in multiple-regression is to examine: (a) The overall contribution of all the independent variables in the regression model; and (b) The differential contribution of each independent variable to the overall fit of the best multiple regression model, while accounting for the contributions of the remaining independent variables in the regression equation. One such measure to examine the overall model fitting and the differential contribution of each of the individual independent variable to the regression model is the *coefficient of determination, R^2*.

R^2 is a descriptive measure of goodness-of-fit. It is a measure of the proportion of the total variance in the dependent variable (Y) that is accounted for and explained by the linear combination of the independent (predictor) variables in the regression model. The unexplained variance in the dependent variable is assumed to result from other independent variables not included in the model or from random error. R^2 represents the squared correlation between the actual values of the dependent variable (Y) and its predicted values ($\hat{Y}$) obtained from the fitted regression equation. Its numeric value ranges from 0 to 1.0 and the closer R^2 statistic is to the value 1.0, the better the fit of the estimated regression line to the data with multiple independent (predictor) variables (Kalaian & Kasim, 2016). A high value of R^2 indicates that the specified regression model with multiple (two or more) independent variables explains the variation in the dependent (outcome) variable well, suggesting that the regression model can be used for predictive purposes.

Product Measure is one of the available methods to determine the contributions of each of the independent variables to the regression model. It is calculated by multiplying the independent variable's slope by its correlation coefficient with the dependent variable holding the other independent variables in the multiple regression model constants. Therefore, the product measure partitions the R^2 across the independent variables in the regression model and its sum equals R^2 (Nathans, Oswald, & Nimon, K., 2012; Pratt, 1987; Tonidandel & LeBreton, 2011).

CONCLUSION

Since the regression analysis methods, which are predictive analytics tools, cover a wide-range of basic and advanced regression analytical techniques, all the different regression methods (e.g., simple linear regression, multiple linear regression, polynomial regression, nonlinear regression, logistic regression, structural equation modeling, and multilevel regression) are impossible to be covered in detail in a single chapter. Therefore, this chapter focuses on covering only the simple linear regression and multiple linear regression methods, which are the most important and commonly used as predictive analytics tools by data analysts and researchers across a wide spectrum of disciplines and fields of study.

The main purpose of this chapter has been to present a conceptual and practical overview of some of the widely used regression analysis methods for analyzing quantitative data sets including Big Data sets. These regression analytical methods can be used by data analysts and researchers to accurately analyze their quantitative data to explore the relationships in the data and make accurate and valid predictions of future organizational productivity and performance (Kalaian & Kasim, in press). The conceptual overview also provides students, researchers, and analysts in various disciplines and fields of study with the skills necessary to interpret the scientific reports that employed simple- and multiple- regression analysis methods.

It is important to note that organizational researchers and data analysts should be informed that the greatest challenge in using regression analysis methods is not simply having the right software and the knowledge of the analytical methodology, but also making sure that the numerical data in the Big Data set is:

1. Error-free from outliers and data-entry errors, and
2. Meets the assumptions of the regression analysis methods.

Despite the overview of each of the simple- and multiple- linear regression analysis methods for analyzing quantitative data, it is important to note that these methods can be expanded to include more information about these linear regression methods such as *"residual analysis"* and the analytical software that can be used to analyze the data. Thus, the reader is recommended to use other statistical textbooks (e.g., Carlberg, 2013; Field, 2009; Tabachnick & Fidell, 2012) to seek additional advanced information about regression analysis such as residual analysis and how to use computer software packages (e.g., Excel, Minitab, SPSS, R, or SAS) to analyze quantitative data sets including Big Data sets and interpret the results of the linear regression analysis.

REFERENCES

Carlberg, C. (2013). *Predictive analytics: Microsoft excel*. Pearson Education, Inc.

Felicio, J. A., Couto, E., & Caiado, J. (2014). Human capital, social capital and organizational performance. *Management Decision*, *52*(2), 350–364. doi:10.1108/MD-04-2013-0260

Field, A. (2009). *Discovering statistics using SPSS* (3rd ed.). Thousand Oaks, CA: Sage Publications.

George, D., & Mallery, P. (2014). *IBM SPSS statistics 21 step by step: A simple guide and reference* (13th ed.). Boston, MA: Allyn and Bacon.

Hair, J. F. Jr. (2007). Knowledge creation in marketing: The role of predictive analytics. *European Business Review*, *19*(4), 303–315. doi:10.1108/09555340710760134

Imran, R., Majeed, M., & Ayub, A. (2015). Impact of organizational justice, job security and job satisfaction on organizational productivity. *Journal of Economics. Business and Management*, *3*(9), 840–845. doi:10.7763/JOEBM.2015.V3.295

Kalaian, S. A., & Kasim, R. M. (2015). Predictive analytics. In M. Tavana, S. B. Zhou, & S. K. Puranam (Eds.), *Handbook of research on organizational transformations through big data analytics* (pp. 12–29). Hershey, PA: IGI Global.

Kalaian, S. A., & Kasim, R. M. (2016). Analyzing quantitative data. In J. E. Jones & M. L. Baran (Eds.), *Mixed methods research for improved scientific study*. Hershey, PA: IGI Global. doi:10.4018/978-1-5225-0007-0.ch008

Kasemsap, K. (2014). The role of business analytics in performance management. In M. Tavana, S. B. Zhou, & S. K. Puranam (Eds.), *Handbook of research on organizational transformations through big data analytics* (pp. 126–145). Hershey, PA: IGI Global.

Kuhns, M., & Johnson, K. (2013). *Applied predictive modeling*. New York: Springer. doi:10.1007/978-1-4614-6849-3

Mahmood, M. A., & Mann, G. J. (2005). Information technology investments and organizational productivity and performance: An empirical investigation. *Journal of Organizational Computing and Electronic Commerce*, *15*(3), 185–202. doi:10.1207/s15327744joce1503_1

Maisel, L. S., & Cokins, G. (2014). *Predictive business analytics: Forward looking capabilities to improve business performance.* Hoboken, NJ: John Wiley & Sons, Inc.

Mertler, C. A., & Vannatta, R. A. (2013). *Advanced and multivariate statistical methods* (5th ed.). Glendale, CA: Pyrczak Publishing.

Nathans, L. L., Oswald, F. L., & Nimon, K. (2012). Interpreting multiple linear regression: A guidebook of variable importance. *Practical Assessment, Research & Evaluation, 17*(9). Available online http://pareonline.net/getvn.asp?v=17&n=9

Okoye, P. V. C., & Ezejiofor, R. A. (2013). The effect of human resources development on organizational productivity. *International Journal of Academic Research in Business and Social Sciences, 3*(10), 250–268. doi:10.6007/IJARBSS/v3-i10/295

Patterson, M. G., Michael, A., West, M. A., Shackleton, V. J., Dawson, J. F., Lathom, R., & Wallace, A. M. et al. (2005). Validating the organizational climate measure: Links to managerial practices, productivity and innovation. *Journal of Organizational Behavior, 26*(4), 379–408. doi:10.1002/job.312

Pratt, J. W. (1987). Dividing the indivisible: Using simple symmetry to partition variance explained. In T. Pukkila, & S. Puntanen (Eds.), *Proceedings of the second international Tampere conference in statistics* (pp. 245-260). Tampere, Finland: University of Tampere.

Richard, P. J., Devinney, T. M., Yip, G. S., & Johnson, G. (2009). Measuring organizational performance: Towards methodological best practice. *Journal of Management, 35*(3), 718–804. doi:10.1177/0149206308330560

Siegel, E. (2014). *Predictive Analysis: The power to predict who will click, buy, lie, or die.* Indianapolis, IN: John Wiley & Sons, Inc.

Sprinthall, R. C. (2011). *Basic statistical analysis* (9th ed.). Boston, MA: Allyn & Bacon.

Tabachnick, B. G., & Fidell, L. S. (2012). *Using multivariate statistics* (6th ed.). Pearson Education.

Tonidandel, S., & LeBreton, J. M. (2011). Relative importance analysis: A useful supplement to regression analyses. *Journal of Business and Psychology, 26*(1), 1–9. doi:10.1007/s10869-010-9204-3

Weill, P. (1992). The relationship between investment in information technology and firm performance: A study of the valve manufacturing sector. *Information Systems Research, 3*(4), 307–333. doi:10.1287/isre.3.4.307

KEY TERMS AND DEFINITIONS

α: α (Y-intercept) is a constant that represents the intercept of the regression line with the Y-axis. That is, it is the value of the outcome (dependent) variable, Y_i, when the value of the independent (predictor) variable, X_i, is equal to zero.

Errors (e_i): e_i is the error or residual of the regression equation and represents the amount by which the observed value of the dependent variable (Y_i) deviates from its predicted value ($\hat{Y}_i$) for individual (case), i, in the estimated simple regression model.

Multiple Linear Regression: Multiple linear regression analysis is a predictive analytic method for explaining, analyzing and modeling the linear relationships between a quantitative dependent variable and two or more quantitative independent variables in the existing structured data set in efforts to build predictive models for making future predictions of organizational productivity and performance.

Organizational Performance: Organizational performance is a multidimensional construct that includes both financial and non-financial performance indicators that measure organizational outcomes for achieving organizational strategic and operational goals and objectives.

Predictive Analytics: Predictive analytics and modeling are statistical and analytical tools that explore and capture the hidden complex relationships and underlying patterns among the quantitative variables in the existing structured data in efforts to predict the future organizational outcomes such as productivity and performance.

R^2: Coefficient of Determination (R^2) is a measure of the proportion of the total variance in the dependent variable (Y) that is accounted for and explained by the linear combination of the independent (predictor) variables in the fitted regression model.

Regression Coefficient: A regression coefficient (B) represents the slope of the regression line, which is the amount of change in the dependent (outcome) variable (Y) for one unit change (e.g., one point, one year, one dollar) in the independent (predictor) variable (X).

Simple Linear Regression: Simple linear regression analysis is the simplest predictive analytics technique for explaining and modeling the linear relationship between a quantitative dependent variable and a single quantitative independent variable in a data set in efforts to build predictive models for making predictions of future organizational productivity and performance.

Chapter 15
Student Retention Performance Using Absorbing Markov Chains

Dennis M. Crossen
La Salle University, USA

ABSTRACT

Performance models are well established in the literature. More specifically, student performance has been of growing concern at all levels. To confront the challenges, researchers have collected data, monitored performance criterion, developed quantitative models, and analyzed patterns to formulate theories and adaptive measures. At the university level, many students' performance deficiencies are keenly noticed and actualized for a variety of reasons. Some reasons may include transition from a home-reporting educational environment to an autonomous setting; lack of a friendly support system; or a host of behavioral circumstances which exacerbate latent academic deficits. One such technique for reviewing student performance can be employed and analyzed using absorbing Markov chains. The use of Markov Chains can provide quantitative information such the characterization potential delays (latency points) within and throughout the system, prediction of probabilistic metrics which define transitions between each stage of a defined state, and adaptability options for enrollment outcomes for use by school administrators. Furthermore, Markov chains can be employed to determine the impact on system resources such as limitations in faculty schedules, classroom assignments, and technology availability. Managers, administrators and advisors may find this information useful when notified of such limitations. This paper is of value to a broad audience such as researchers, managers, and administrators since it augments standard approaches of the Markov model. The blend of stochastic mathematics, applications of stochastic methods and retention theory, as well as the inclusion of adaptive sensitivity analysis are effective performance measures. Therefore, applications in Markov chains and subsequent forecasting models are of contemporary values in educational performance. Each of these concepts and methods contribute to a broader consideration of Markov properties in a branch of mathematics known as Markov Decision Processes (MDP). These types of processes allow researchers the ability to adjust parameters based on rewards, sets of actions, and discount factors. The cases outlined in this paper may be helpful when considering reductions in recidivism rates, improving policies to diminish recidivism, and increasing enrollment options using Markov analysis.

DOI: 10.4018/978-1-5225-0654-6.ch015

INTRODUCTION

Performance models are conceptual constructions used to describe simple or complex systems using mathematical methods. These models are a corresponding form of a conceptual or originating abstraction which serve to simplify understanding or provision for differing viewpoints under study. Developing such models are cognitive activities (Lee & Wagenmakers, 2014) which are of practical consideration in many branches of science and research. Moreover, modeling can be realized using computer programs, drawings, physical structures, or structural formulations. Conceptual models are commonly applied in wide varieties of scientific research and are beneficial toward understanding the framework for adaptations for improving performance.

In geology, for example, laboratory and field observations are assembled in order to develop idealized performance models. Assembling a proper blend of variables can form the basis for understanding a phenomenon, ascertaining recurring patterns of behavior, or highlighting existing theories (Wolf, 1976). In the field of digital forensics, cloud deployment models have been used to differentiate public and private cloud activity to alter data collection processes, adapt identification protocols, and analyze results to determine potential criminal activities (Martini & Choo, 2012). These research efforts are assisting law enforcement agencies in their struggles to understand cyber-crime using ever-improving data mining strategies. Conceptual models are also used in Lean Six Sigma deployment. Hilton (2012) proposed a conceptual model which attempts to ascertain a relationship between technical and interpersonal skills, levels of influence in the organization, and organizational competencies (amongst others). In all cases, these models are designed to quantify phenomenon so that planned adaption or understanding is realized in order to improve performance.

Developing a conceptual model is typically one of the first initiatives of planned research activities. A researcher bears the responsibly for defining the most important characteristics and variables to be used in the study (Wolf, pp.14-15). In doing so, mathematical models are used to frame conditions such as behavior, interrelationships, and patterns. It is not surprising that mathematical models are used in research since the language of mathematics extends beyond culture and linguistics. This paper provides analysis of student retention conditions using absorbing Markov chains. This technique is used in an effort to understand the performance characteristics of students in a university environment. Two cases are proposed that ascertain useful statistics for:

1. Decreased recidivism of existing freshman; and
2. Increased enrollment of incoming freshman.

Organization of this Chapter

This paper provides analysis of performance metrics as they relate to:

1. Stochastic processes, discrete mathematical structures, and Markov models;
2. Student retention models; and
3. Forecasting metrics.

Two cases are outlined (decreased recidivism and increased enrollment). Concluding results are provided at the end of the paper which include long-term probabilities, expectation times at each classification, and time to absorption based on the implementation of absorbing Markov chains in a university setting.

MATHEMATICAL MODELS

The intrinsic relationships of a mathematical model are actualized using variables, parameters, and matrices (amongst other tools). Variables typically represents a value or number that can be used in other mathematical expressions or forms. For example, the equation of a line ($y = mx + b$) contains prediction, slope, observation, and intercept values, respectively. Each of these values relay certain information to a researcher such as rate of change over time and a baseline value when evaluated time at inception (that is, at zero time). Mathematical modeling can also use matrices and vectors to effectively determine solutions to complex problems. In fact, matrices are one of several methodologies used in solving Markov Chain type problems (Puterman, 2014; Nicholls, 2007; Al-Awadhi & Konsowa, 2007). Such problem determinations will be the focus of the direct application of absorbing Markov chains in this paper. In doing so, the framework of the conceptual and theoretical model will build a bridge to the realistic problems of student retention for decision making studies in management science.

Modeling, as it is used under the scientific method and management science, is expected to assist in the process of identifying issues in a real world environment compared with those on a conceptual world (Bair, 2012; Dym & Ivey, 1980). In a practical sense, problem identification and system experimental requirements utilize data to develop theoretical systems of equations. These mathematical equations are assembled using a particular series of simplistic or complex methods. The conduit between real world phenomena and conceptual predictive models provide an adaptive capability that is useful in research.

As shown in Figure 1, conceptual observations can form analytic models to establish predictions under a conceptual rubric. These models can be formed using the language of mathematics including linear equations and simulation strategies. In a more complex model, an iterative loop can be established which link phenomena with subsequent analysis having predictive feedback. Such models will not be considered in this paper.

Figure 1. Elementary scientific method
Adapted from Dym and Ivey (1980)

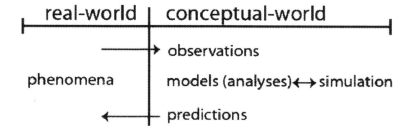

Stochastic Processes

A collection of random variables $\{X(t), t \geq 0\}$, as defined on a probability space, is called a stochastic process. This process is a function of two arguments: $X(\omega, t), \omega \in \Omega, t \in T$. The symbols $\omega \in \Omega, T$ correspond to any real-valued function, parameter space, and time parameter, respectively. Stochastic processes are quite flexible in application as more than one stochastic process can be created for one probability space (Bhat & Miller, 1972; Papoulis, 1991). This resilience is one of the major reasons for the popularity of applications of this principle.

Regarding classifications of stochastic processes, consider the parameter space $T : t \in T$ which can denote time, length, distance, or any other measurable quantity. For a family of random variables $X(.,t), t \in T$, a parameter space T is said to have three classifications:

1. Finite;
2. Countably infinite; and
3. Un-countably many (Puterman, 2014).

The first classification is the focus of this study, as it is applicable to the study of discrete-time Markov Chains. Other classifications will not be discussed.

To illustrate an example of this process, consider a two-dimensional random process $X(t) = [x_1(t), x_2(t)]$. We can denote $x_1(t)$ and $x_2(t)$ as two separate functions for determining the maximum temperature and minimum temperature at a specific location, respectively. This type of problem is similar to a linear optimization scenario. It also shows compatibility for other linear systems (linear regression, linear programming, and Markov Chains). This type of analysis can be expanded to include a broader sequence of functions where an n-dimensional array of random processes are required. Such a mathematical solution can be modeled as a series of functions: $X(t) = [x_1(t), x_2(t), ..., x_n(t)]$. This sequence of events can proceed as long as it meets the criterion.

Figure 2 shows the major delineates of the two major classifications of stochastic processes. The discrete-time stochastic process measures a sequence of integer states while the continuous-time stochastic process tracks the trajectory of real-valued functions.

To reiterate, the scope of this research is solely restricted to discrete-time random variables and discrete-time stochastic processes. Real-valued or continuous time applications implies that the trajectory

Figure 2. Stochastic process classifications

T	$\{X(t), t \in T\}$
(0, 1, 2, 3, ...)	integer-value or discrete-time
Real numbers	real-valued or continuous time

Student Retention Performance Using Absorbing Markov Chains

or path of a process has an infinite number of solutions. The research I am offering relates to countable events within a confined parameter space; therefore, continuous time processes will not be discussed in detail. I provide this information here only as a matter of clarity and differentiation.

Discrete Models

A stochastic process is a random variable that change its value randomly over time. The simplest type of stochastic process is a Markov process. More specifically, the focus of this research relates to discrete-time Markov processes where a countable set of states are defined in a stochastic environment using several properties which will be further analyzed and discussed.

Consider the following stochastic process: $\{X_t : t \in T\}$ where "t" is an element of a larger sample space (T) and the process is characterized by a conditional probability that is dependent on the prior state alone (Bolch, Greiner, de Meer & Trivedi, 1998):

$$\mathbb{P}\left(X_{t_{n+1}} < x_{n+1} \mid X_{t_n} = x_n, X_{t_{n-1}} = x_{n-1}, \ldots X_{t_0} = x_0\right) = \mathbb{P}\left(X_{t_{n+1}} < x_{n+1} \mid X_{t_n} = x_n\right)$$

Notice that all of the discrete states in the historical past are reduced to only to previous state. This is what characterizes the Markov state. Additionally, this process chain is considered a special case of the discrete-time stochastic process known as a Markov chain. A Markov chain is a stochastic process in which only the most recent point in the trajectory affects the next state alone (Haslett & Hayes, 1998). The expression X_{t+1} depends only upon X_t (the present state) but not on the past states $X_{t-1}, \ldots X_1, X_0$. In other words, the next state is "conditioned" on the current state. This is an important aspect of discrete-time Markov chains (Freedman, 1971). Additional properties and analyses of Markov Chains will be discussed in a subsequent section of this paper.

Illustrating the concepts of conditional probabilities relative to the state space and parameters as a sequence of time change, Figure 3 shows three states (s_0, s_1, s_2) over four time periods (T_0, T_1, T_2, T_3). Assuming that the process begins at the initial time slot (T_0) and the process initializes at state 0 (s_0), the state parameter migrates from state 0 to state 1 at time slot 1 (T_1). While in time slot 1, there are three possible conditions at T_1. From this time slot, the state path can proceed to states s_0, s_1, or s_2. The mathematical expressions for these "conditional" probabilities are noted in Figure 3. As an example, the

Figure 3. State-to-state transitions over time

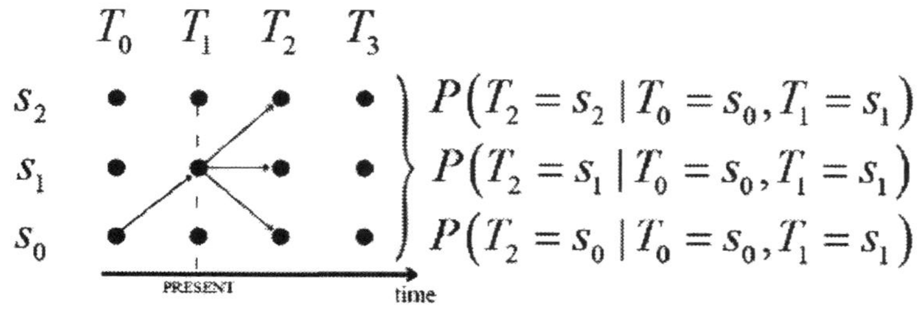

$$P(T_2 = s_2 \mid T_0 = s_0, T_1 = s_1)$$
$$P(T_2 = s_1 \mid T_0 = s_0, T_1 = s_1)$$
$$P(T_2 = s_0 \mid T_0 = s_0, T_1 = s_1)$$

particle that finally arrives at state s_2 at time T_2 in the future, is "conditionally" dependent on $T_0 = s_0$ and $T_1 = s_1$ occurring. The other probabilities follow a similar pattern.

This type of analysis and formulation is typical in any higher level textbooks on probability and statistics. An important distinction in referencing must be made when analyzes time dependent problems. That is, notations vary from source to source; therefore, it is incumbent on the researcher to define past, present, and future notations as these are the sequence of events that determine the process migration from state to state and from time slot to time slot.

To illustrate, consider a stochastic process X_t when time = t, depends on the prior time period (t-1) and not earlier sequences ($X_{t-2}, X_{t-3}, ... X_0$). The conditional probabilities of such a sequence can be formulated according to:

$$\mathbb{P}\left(X_t \mid \underbrace{X_{t-1}, X_{t-2}, ... X_0}_{\text{entire history of process}}\right) \Leftrightarrow \mathbb{P}\left(X_t \mid \underbrace{X_{t-1}}_{\text{single-step}}\right)$$

This mathematical formulation states that there is an equivalency between the conditional probabilities of an entire (historical) sequence of events (left side) and the single-step conditional probabilities with no consideration to items beyond the prior state. In other words, the memory from state to state is restricted to the previous time period alone. The entire history of the process (aside from the prior state process) has no contribution to the probable outcome. This is the memoryless property for Markov chains which will be utilized in subsequent sections of this paper.

Applying the Stochastic Model

A stochastic model can be analyzed in many ways. Stochastic models utilize random variables, prior probabilities from data, conditional probabilities, and joint probabilities. Stochastic models are also utilized when Bayesian inference is required in a study. These types of inferences use mathematical formation which revise the existing probabilities. Bayesian analysis is not within the scope of this research paper; however, it is important to note that the use of stochastic modelling is prevalent in many areas of scientific research. Regarding the current study, I wish to illustrate the use of a stochastic model as it relates to the applications of random variables and probabilities in the healthcare sector. The intent is to demonstrate how the previous discussions can be used in an aggregate framework relative to the decision making environment.

If we consider two random discrete (binary) variables, that is - having two states of existence, we can express the results using a stochastic process having a binomial distribution (two-states). For example, a two-state binary condition can be as simple as a switch turning on or off, an elevator going up or down, or whether a child is a boy or a girl. To illustrate the example, consider that the probability of a person having a rare disease is 3%. Moreover, it is shown that the probability that test results are positive, if the disease is present, turns out to be 90%. It has also been observed that if the patient does not have the disease, the probability that the test will yield a positive result is 2%. These phrases can be expressed mathematically, respectively as: $P(D) = 0.3; P(T \mid D) = 0.9; P(T \mid \bar{D}) = 0.02$.

The legend for the variables in this case are represented as D to indicate that the disease is present and T to represent that the test is positive. Assigning formal names to variables is a matter of preference and can be considered an arbitrary exercise. This is why it is imperative for a research to provide a legend of all variables so that there is alignment with the remaining analysis of the research. It is also imperative that the researcher understand the basic rules of probability. For instance, knowing the D represent that the "disease is present"; the notation for the "disease is not present" must be $\bar{D}$ (sometimes referred as "D-not"). Moreover, because the sum of all simple probabilities must equal one, the following expression must hold true:

$$P(D) = 0.3 \therefore P(\bar{D}) = P(D) - 0.3 = 0.7$$

Regarding the formulation of conditional probabilities, the information in the problem leads us to outline: $P(T \mid D) = 0.90$ and $P(T \mid \bar{D}) = 0.02$. These equations indicate that the probability of having a positive test result. The first equation is conditioned on the disease actually being present while the second equation is when the disease is not present. Again, these conditions are derived from patient observations from the past. Also, knowing that the sum of two conditional probabilities using random variables must equate to one, we therefore can calculate $1 - P(T \mid D) = P(\bar{T} \mid D) = 0.10$ and $1 - P(T \mid \bar{D}) = P(\bar{T} \mid \bar{D}) = 0.98$. This proof can be summarized using: $P(T \mid D) + P(\bar{T} \mid D) = 1$ and $P(T \mid \bar{D}) + P(\bar{T} \mid \bar{D}) = 1$. This pattern of analysis and sequencing of methodologies are consistent with well-established practices in the literature (Aczel & Sounderpandian, 2009; Berenson, Levine, Szabat & Krehbiel, 2012).

Completing all calculations for this stochastic problem, we must find the joint probabilities and marginal probabilities. Joint probabilities are outcomes of values that occur when two discrete random variables are common within a state space (Papoulis, 1991). The generic relationship between two discrete random variables and other probability conditions is $P(X,Y) = P(X \mid Y)P(Y)$. For this particular applications of the principle, the joint probabilities are calculated to be:

$$P(T,D) = P(T \mid D)P(D) = (0.9)(0.03) = 0.027 \text{; and}$$

$$P(T,\bar{D}) = P(T \mid \bar{D})P(\bar{D}) = (0.2)(0.97) = 0.0194 \text{; and}$$

$$P(\bar{T},D) = P(\bar{T} \mid D)P(D) = (0.1)(0.03) = 0.003 \text{; and}$$

$$P(\bar{T},\bar{D}) = P(\bar{T} \mid \bar{D})P(\bar{D}) = (0.98)(0.97) = 0.9506.$$

Finally, the marginal probabilities are calculated using the sum of all possible combinations of joint probabilities: $\sum_{all} P(T=t, D=d) = 1.0$, thereby deriving the following results:

$$P(T) = \sum_{T_i} P(d_i) = P(T,D) + P(T,\bar{D}) = 0.027 + 0.0194 = 0.0464;$$

$$P(\bar{T}) = \sum_{\bar{T}_i} P(d_i) = P(\bar{T},D) + P(\bar{T},\bar{D}) = 0.003 + 0.9506 = 0.9536;$$

$$\sum P(T_j) = \sum \left[P(T) + P(\bar{T})\right] = 0.0464 + 0.9536 = 1.0$$

It should be noted that the prior probabilities were calculated using a history of results that were observed and summarized by a researcher. The stochastic process utilized in this sequence of events were made possible by summarizing simple probabilities based on a single value that was averaged over time. This type of process is used to determine stochastic likelihoods and evidence in order to progress toward "a posterior" analysis (which is beyond the scope of the study). This procedure can be used; however, to model causality for future stochastic research. The next section will eliminate the need for summary aggregate of data since the "memoryless" property of a stochastic model will discussed used in a Markov chain.

Markov Models

Markov models employ stochastic processes that utilize random input variables in order to ascertain future forecasts based on current conditions. The memoryless property is a salient characteristic of Markov modelling since large tracts of historical data are unnecessary to perform substantive analysis (Puterman, 2014; Kleinrock, 1975; Norris, 1997). This provides enhanced flexibility in implementation of principles.

As previously outlined, the theoretical framework for a discrete-time stochastic process has significant support in the literature. More specifically, finite discrete-time Markov chains are paths of a trajectory of probabilities that adhere to an assembled number of finite states (Puterman, 2014). Two states of interest are transient states and recurrent states.

Transient states define a set of classifications which indicate that the path from state to state is ephemeral. A state is transient if the particular state can be quantifiable, that is, the transient state services the transportation flow of information from one state to another. Mathematically, this is written as $P\{t < \infty\} < 1$. Notice that the probability of the state-time is less than an infinitive period. In addition, the probability event must be less than 1 to account for the law of total probability. Since the inequality shows a "less-than" symbol, other states must be traversed in order to complete the cycle; thereby, necessitating the "less-than" inequality.

A recurrent state is defined as a state whose activities must return at some point (as the name implies). This guarantee of a return event assures that the law of total probability will be fulfilled ($P\{t < \infty\} = 1$).

In a practical sense, although the recurrent nature of the state is assured under some probabilistic value, the actual time of return could be very, very long. More precisely, the design of the system dictates whether the state is recurrent or not.

Markov Property

Earlier discussions of the memoryless property of Markov chains have been analyzed throughout this study. The details of this property requires additional mathematical rigor, analysis, and visualization to proceed. In doing so, an integrated discussion for how discrete random variables and the conditional probabilities interrelate to form a progressive chain of activities is offered.

Consider a sequence of discrete random variables: $\{X_0, X_1, X_2, ...\}$. This sequence forms the basis for a Markov chain if the random variables satisfy the memoryless characteristic of the Markov property. Recall that an historical probability sequence of random variables become a conditional probability equation using two time periods. In some of the literature, equations refer to the current and immediate (next) period; while others model events as last event and current event. What is to be learned from this activity is that the Markov property only relies on two time steps. The referencing is arbitrary. According to Haslett & Hayes (1998), this sequence becomes:

$$\mathbb{P}\left(X_{t+\delta} = s \mid X_t = s_t, X_{t-1} = s_{t-1}, X_{t-2} = s_{t-2}, ... X_0 = s_0\right) = \mathbb{P}\left(X_{t+\delta} = s \mid X_t = s_t\right)$$

Notice that the entire history on the conditional side (left-side) of the equation has been reduced to only a single step event (right-side). Moreover, in order to satisfy the conditions that Markov chains can be designed at any arbitrary time slot and across an entire suite of state parameters, the following constraints hold true: $\forall \ t = 1, 2, 3, ...$ & $\forall \ states \ s = s_0, s_1, s_t, s$. Further illustrating the distribution of the next state, the equation can be reduced to its simplest form:

$$\mathbb{P}\left(\underbrace{X_{t+1} = s}_{\text{distribution of } X_{t+1}} \mid \underbrace{X_t = s_t}_{\text{depends on } X_t}, \cancel{X_{t-1} = s_{t-1}, X_{t-2} = s_{t-2}, ... X_0 = s_0}\right)$$

This reduction shows that the probability distribution is simply the distribution of X_{t+1} conditioned on X_t. In other words, the random variable takes on the characteristics of the next step (X_{t+1}) given the prior step (X_t). Recall from a previous visual that the probabilities were conditioned based on several steps. The Markov property has simplified that condition. Figure 4 is a modification of that process with only the next state (T_2) conditioned on the present state (T_1). As referenced earlier, the current state (shown by a dashed-line) is arbitrarily chosen. Analysis of a Markov chain can begin at any point which the research deems of value.

Finite Markov Chains

To further the understanding for how the aforementioned mathematics and the Markov properties are integrated, an illustration is provided using a state-transition diagram (Figure 5). States are denoted using a series of random variables, A, B, and C. Each circle represents a single state. I have provided

Figure 4. State-to-state transition (memoryless)

$$P(T_2 = s_2 \mid T_1 = s_0)$$
$$P(T_2 = s_1 \mid T_1 = s_0)$$
$$P(T_2 = s_0 \mid T_1 = s_0)$$

Figure 5. State transition diagram

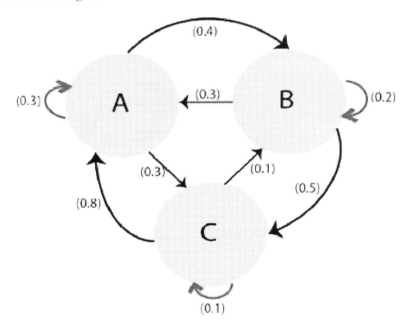

several arbitrary values to illustrate. For example, the circles contain the letters A, B, and C which represent the random variables. The corresponding states can be assumed to be s_a, s_b, s_c. The values on (or near) each arrow are the transition probabilities for each combination of possible movements between each state in a single step. The direction of each arrow is related to the trajectory flow.

Using the illustration of Figure 5, state-A is associated with five arrows. The top arrow represent the probability of migrating from state-A to state-B. That probability is 0.4. Subsequently, the probability from state-A to state-C is 0.3; state-C to state-B is 0.1, and so on. Of particular interest are the arrows that return back to the same states. These are the recurrent states discussed earlier. For example, there is a probability of 0.3 that state-A will remain in state-A. Similarly, state-C will remain in state-C 10% of the time. Notice that the sum of all activity of a state must equal 1. For state-B, 80% of the activity leaves the node (0.5 + 0.3) to other states while the remaining 20% is recurring within the same state. This again follows the rule of total probability where activities summing to 100% are mandated.

Student Retention Performance Using Absorbing Markov Chains

In mathematical terms, this visual activity is alternatively modeled using matrix algebra. The use of matrix algebra allows us to segregate the state conditions into various categories in order to determine probabilistic expectation and other parameters of interest (Caswell, 2013). This analysis cannot be easily obtained using a diagram. For example, using the information from Figure 5, a single-step probability transition matrix can be formed (Figure 6).

The present state and future state configurations are arbitrarily chosen. In many instances, the left-hand side of the matrix is the present state while the top end of the matrix is the future state. Using this convention, it is shown that the probability to move from state-A to state-B is 0.4. Correspondingly, the probability of state-C remaining in its current state is 0.1. Also, take note that the sum of all rows in the matrix must abide by the law of total probability and sum to a value of 1. In other words, $\sum_{i,j} s_{i,j}$, and is calculated below:

$$\sum s_a = 0.3 + 0.4 + 0.3 = 1$$
$$\sum s_b = 0.3 + 0.2 + 0.5 = 1$$
$$\sum s_c = 0.8 + 0.1 + 0.1 = 1$$

The process of modeling a Markov chains can begin using a transition diagram, probability matrix, or whatever means are convenient to the researcher. The information is consistent and holistic in all forms.

There is another conditional state in the study of Markov chains which is important to this study. A discrete-time absorbing Markov state is one in which it is impossible to leave the state once it is entered. In other words, the probability that a state, conditioned on itself, cannot be zero ($P(s \mid s) > 0$) and the probability of returning to another state or becoming a recurrent state is zero: $P(j \mid s) = 0$ or $j \neq s$ (Puterman, 2014; Kleinrock, 1975; Norris, 1997).

To visualize the concept of an absorbing state, I've revised several probabilities in the illustration (Figure 7). The figure depicts a Markov absorbing state scenario. The only means to enter state-C is through state-B. The probability of entering state-C through state-B is 0.5. Once state-C is entered, the probability of traversing to another state is zero since no directional arrow leaves the state. Moreover,

Figure 6. Single step probability matrix

$$P = \begin{pmatrix} & S_a & S_b & S_c \\ \hline S_a & 0.3 & 0.4 & 0.3 \\ S_b & 0.3 & 0.2 & 0.5 \\ S_c & 0.8 & 0.1 & 0.1 \end{pmatrix}$$

Figure 7. Absorbing state transition diagram

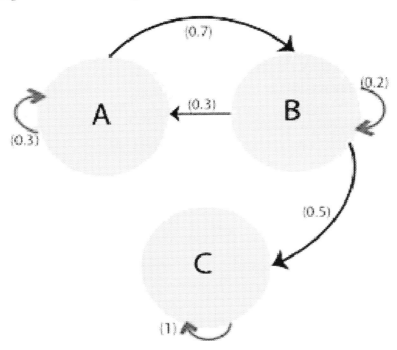

the seemingly recurring activity becomes an absorbing state since the probability of remaining in-state is 100%; therefore, there is no exit capability once the state is entered. As noted earlier, the state has zero probability of progression: $P(j \mid s) = 0$. This particular Markov property is useful in the analysis of customer, employee, and student retention problems (Igboanugo & Edokpia, 2014; Nyandwaki, Akelo, Samson & Fredrick, 2015; Al-Awadhi & Konsowa, 2007; Bessent & Bessent, 1980; Nicholls, 2008; Rahim, Ibrahim & Adnan, 2013; Rahim, 2015; Chen & Barnett, 2000; Kovačić, 2012). This will be the focus for the remainder of the paper.

Al-Awadhi & Konsowa (2007) meticulously designed a model that demonstrates the use of student flows within an academic setting. These results and associated analyses can be applied to many applications in industry and management science including those related to the "up and out" policies of consulting firms, performance in multinational organizations, organizational skill stagnation, or process policies that may be less applicable in a technology driven organization.

The process model for the analysis includes data acquisition, framing state transitions, and performing the mathematical analyses with the intent an objective of offering meaningful results (Al-Awadhi & Konsowa, 2007; Ekhosuehi & Osagiede, 2012; Ekhosuehi & Osagiede, 2013). Data can be acquired using a number of methods. Some options include acquisition from public records, administering a survey, or from archived records. Data can also be simulated in order to provide a suite of options for adaptive application. Moreover, data can be assembled and formulated from raw data counts, where the relative frequencies in each category can be calculated into probabilities.

In the Awadhi & Konsowa (2007) study, a random sample of 250 students were selected over a multi-year period to be used in the research project. Eight Markov states were selected as part of the design. States included freshman (F), sophomore (S_o), junior (J_R), and senior (S_R) status. Also, non-registered

(NR), graduated (G), drop-out (O), and transfer (T) student counts were provisioned. Using the data from 250 students, 1,237 state changes were recorded. The time period changes were by semester. The frequency matrix (Figure 8.) shows the recorded transition counts (per student).

As discussed and analyzed earlier, this matrix shows that 380 freshman remained as freshman during the next semester; 59 juniors were promoted to seniors; and 40 seniors graduated. Notice that the model has three absorbing states: graduated, dropped-out, or transferred. Once a student graduates, they do not return to the system under the same academic program or plan. The same condition holds for transfer and drop-out students. Interestingly, global dropout rates can be significant (Mustafa, Chowdhury & Kamal, 2012).

The next phase of the process is to convert the student counts to relative frequencies. The conversion process is necessary in order to structure the transition count matrix analysis into a probability transition matrix. This matrix is what is used for additional analysis using Markov chains. Converting student counts to relative frequencies are simplistic. For example, the individual values in each row is divided by the total row count. For the freshman to freshman probability, 380 is divided into 605 which yields: $380/605 = 0.628$. This value represents the probability that a freshman repeats the freshman year. Subsequently, 23.8% of freshman are promoted to the sophomore year.

To clarify the potential for using Markov chains, numerous insights, analyses, and metrics can be acquired from Figure 9. Notice again that the sum of each row-state equates to 100% so that the law of total probability remains validated and intact. Also notice in figure-9, that incoming freshman had 62.8% probability of remaining a freshman; there is a 5% probability of not registering for classes, there is 5.6% probability of dropping out of school, and there is a 23.8% probability to advance to the next state (sophomore). Also notice that senior students had a significantly high failure rate (72.7%). Further analysis shows that 57.8% of students (31.1 + 13.3 + 8.9 + 4.4) come back into the system after a period of non-registration, 20% of students remain non-registered, and 20% of the students drop out before completing the program.

Figure 8. Frequency matrix

$$freq(n=250) = \begin{pmatrix} & F & S_O & J_R & S_R & NR & G & O & T & Total \\ F & 380 & 144 & 0 & 0 & 30 & 0 & 34 & 17 & 605 \\ S_O & 0 & 152 & 82 & 0 & 9 & 0 & 17 & 29 & 289 \\ J_R & 0 & 0 & 72 & 59 & 1 & 0 & 2 & 3 & 137 \\ S_R & 0 & 0 & 0 & 117 & 2 & 40 & 2 & 0 & 161 \\ NR & 14 & 6 & 4 & 2 & 9 & 0 & 9 & 1 & 45 \\ G & 0 & 0 & 0 & 0 & 0 & 0 & 0 & 0 & 0 \\ O & 0 & 0 & 0 & 0 & 0 & 0 & 0 & 0 & 0 \\ T & 0 & 0 & 0 & 0 & 0 & 0 & 0 & 0 & 0 \end{pmatrix}$$

Figure 9. Probability transition matrix

$$P = \begin{pmatrix} & F & S_O & J_R & S_R & NR & G & O & T & \Sigma \\ F & 0.628 & 0.238 & 0 & 0 & 0.05 & 0 & 0.056 & 0.028 & 1 \\ S_O & 0 & 0.526 & 0.284 & 0 & 0.031 & 0 & 0.059 & 0.1 & 1 \\ J_R & 0 & 0 & 0.526 & 0.431 & 0.007 & 0 & 0.015 & 0.022 & 1 \\ S_R & 0 & 0 & 0 & 0.727 & 0.012 & 0.248 & 0.012 & 0 & 1 \\ NR & 0.311 & 0.133 & 0.089 & 0.044 & 0.2 & 0 & 0.2 & 0.022 & 1 \\ G & 0 & 0 & 0 & 0 & 0 & 1 & 0 & 0 & 1 \\ O & 0 & 0 & 0 & 0 & 0 & 0 & 1 & 0 & 1 \\ T & 0 & 0 & 0 & 0 & 0 & 0 & 0 & 1 & 1 \end{pmatrix}$$

RETENTION MODELS

This section describes and defines a Markov retention model that encompasses six Markov states; four transient and two absorbing states. Probabilities are associated with each states which are defined using an arbitrary set of relative frequencies. These frequencies are determined using standard provisions from customer/student counts. The categorization of each state are based on standard ranking provisions in a typical higher education setting. For example, freshman, sophomores, juniors, and seniors in college are typically assigned a ranking based on the number of credits they have completed. A typical categorization may be defined as having a range of credit hours according to:

$0 < F < 24;$

$24 \leq So < 54$

$54 \leq J < 84$

$84 \leq Sr < 120$

$120 \leq G$

This section provides details as to how students migrate through the system. Some metrics of interest determine the length of stay in each state, the probabilities of being retained in each state, and the likelihood that a student will reach an absorbing state (graduation or drop out) within a certain period of time. The period of interest is outlined in years. The model considers six years in the system with a four year retention rate as the normative time to complete.

Preliminary Review

A Markov chain of this paper can be modeled as a visualization of inter-related states having probabilities associated with each relationship. The visualization of the states are defined using arrows and circles to show how the system emerges. This visual component of the Markov chain is known as a state transition diagram. Figure 10 shows the state transition diagram that will be used throughout this analysis.

Student Retention Performance Using Absorbing Markov Chains

Figure 10. Markov state transition diagram

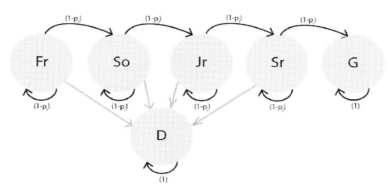

Students are categorized into typical classification rankings (s_3 = freshman; s_4 = sophomore; s_5 = junior; and s_6 = senior) while the absorbing states are defined as graduation and drop-out (s_1 = graduated; s_2 = dropout). The probabilities are arranged according to a canonical form of partitioned matrix:

$$P = \begin{bmatrix} S & | & 0 \\ \hline R & | & Q \end{bmatrix} \ldots \ldots P = \begin{bmatrix} ergodic & transient & | & \\ \hline S & 0 & | & ergodic \\ R & Q & | & transient \end{bmatrix}$$

The Q-matrix is concerned with processes for the state duration in the transient state. The R-matrix deals with transitions from transient states to ergodic states. An S-matrix is developed to ascertain the process after it has reached an ergodic state. For a Markov absorbing state, the S-matrix is known as the identity matrix (I) are is arranged as:

$$P = \begin{bmatrix} I & | & 0 \\ \hline R & | & Q \end{bmatrix}.$$

A typical outline for the partitioned is defined below:

$$P = \begin{pmatrix} s_1 & s_2 & s_3 & s_4 & s_5 & s_6 \\ 1 & 0 & 0 & 0 & 0 & 0 \\ 0 & 1 & 0 & 0 & 0 & 0 \\ \hline & & x & x & & \\ & & & x & x & \\ & & & & x & x \\ & & & & & x \end{pmatrix}$$

This paper defines two cases of interest. Case 1 models a six year retention system. The first year (year-1) is the baseline scenario which assigns an arbitrary freshman recidivism rate of 10%. This means that 10% of students who are classified as a freshman in the first year will repeat as a freshman while their colleagues migrate during the subsequent year. That is, the remainder will be promoted to the next classification ranking (sophomore). During subsequent years (ex: year-2, year-3, etc.), the recidivism rate is reduced by 0.5%. In other words, the second year freshman repeat rate is reduced to 9.5%, the third year rate is 9.0, and so on. This process continues until year 6 when the freshman recidivism rate is reduced to 7.5%.

In addition, the analysis sequences each year using a multi-step process which ultimately corresponds to a long term projection. The n-step analysis is a typical methodology used in Markov analysis to show a change in probabilities within the system over a defined set of periods. The process ultimately reaches a steady-state series of probabilities which are used to model adaptive behaviors or allow decision makers the ability to provide adjustments to the input variables of the design. Long term metrics are developed and obtained with matrix algebra using an N-matrix and M-vector. The N-matrix determines the years within each classification while the M-vector determines the years in the system before reaching an absorbing state (gradation or drop out). The B-matrix is also developed which provides long-term statistics on probabilistic transition in graduation and drop-out absorbing states.

The case 2 scenario uses a baseline recidivism rate with increase enrollment. The arbitrary enrollments are increased by 10%. Under this scenario, the raw counts of freshman entering the sophomore year was increase by 100 (n = 1100). For each state, a subsequent analysis was performed similarly to the process described earlier.

Lastly, several forecasting models will be used to consider several characteristics of the dataset. The outcomes of the Markov analysis will be described using a 3-period moving average to determine possible errors in the data alignment or regressed characteristic. A seasonality model using multiplicative decomposition will be considered to determine whether there is a pattern associated with the periodicity of the data. Also, the seasonality forecast model will consider the linearity of the ranked relationships.

Case 1: Freshman Remediation

As noted earlier, the student counts were chosen arbitrarily. In a real-world scenario, the data may be obtained from a university registrar or a generally available dataset from the research literature. Table 1 shows the dataset of 1,000 students within three typical classification is college. Freshman, sophomore, juniors, and seniors total 1,000. To further illustrate, the source and destination of the state transitions occur from left to right with the left axis being the "from" state (origin) and the top axis being the "to" state (destination). For example, 100 freshman in the first year must repeat as a freshman while 800 migrate to the sophomore state. Moreover, 100 freshman will drop out during the first year.

This data can be assembled in a transition probability matrix in canonical form as shown below.

Student Retention Performance Using Absorbing Markov Chains

Table 1. Registration data (10.0% freshman return rate)

	F	So	J	Sr	G	D	Total
F	100	800	0	0	0	100	1000
So	0	100	850	0	0	50	1000
J	0	0	500	900	0	50	1000
Sr	0	0	0	50	900	50	1000
G	0	0	0	0	0	0	0
D	0	0	0	0	0	0	0

Frequency Transitions (n = 1000)

$$P = \begin{pmatrix} & G & D & F & S_o & J & S_R \\ G & 1 & 0 & 0 & 0 & 0 & 0 \\ D & 0 & 1 & 0 & 0 & 0 & 0 \\ F & 0 & 0.1 & 0.1 & 0.8 & 0 & 0 \\ S_o & 0 & 0.05 & 0 & 0.1 & 0.85 & 0 \\ J & 0 & 0.05 & 0 & 0 & 0.05 & 0.9 \\ S_R & 0.9 & 0.05 & 0 & 0 & 0 & 0.05 \end{pmatrix}$$

The N-matrix (Figure 11.) values represent the number of years (expected value) spent at each classification level prior to entering the subsequent state or an absorbing state.

On average, a freshman will spend 1.1111 years classified as a freshman prior to entering an absorbing state. Why? Perhaps they may have to repeat a class. A freshman may dropout before reaching junior year; therefore, indicating that the average time a junior is classified as 0.8837. Someone already classified as a junior will never go back as a sophomore, therefore, the probability is 0. A freshman will spend approximately 1.1111, 0.9877, 0.8837, and 0.8372 years classified as a freshman, sophomore, junior, and senior, respectively. Sophomores will spend 1.1111, 0.9942, and 0.9418 years classified as a sophomore, junior, and senior, respectively. A junior will spend approximately 1.0526 and 0.9972 years classified as a junior and senior, respectively. Seniors spend 1.0526 years prior to entering an absorbing state.

Figure 11. N-matrix (year 1)

$$N_1 = (I-Q)^{-1} = \begin{pmatrix} & F & S_o & J & S_R \\ F & 1.1111 & 0.9877 & 0.8837 & 0.8372 \\ S_o & 0 & 1.1111 & 0.9942 & 0.9418 \\ J & 0 & 0 & 1.0526 & 0.9972 \\ S_R & 0 & 0 & 0 & 1.0526 \end{pmatrix}$$

The M-vector (Figure 12.) is the summation of the corresponding row values on the N-matrix. Each value corresponds to the absorption time for a state when reaching either the drop-out or graduation absorbing state. On average, freshman take 3.8196 years, sophomores take 3.0471 years, juniors take 2.0499 years, and seniors take 1.0526 years to reach absorption.

The values in matrix-B represent the long-term probabilities of transitioning from a non-absorbing state into absorbing states. There is a 75.35% chance that a freshman will eventually reach graduation. Also, the probability of dropping out as a freshman is 0.2465. There is a higher probability that upper-classmen will improve their chances of graduating (Figure 13).

For year 2, there is a decrease in freshman return rate. The baseline recidivism rate was initially 10% and now set to 9.5%. A 0.5% reduction is implemented year-over-year to correspond to a proactive process of assisting incoming freshman toward successfully completing all requirements for the transition to sophomore year. The transition probability matrix shows the recidivism metric. Recall that the baseline recidivism rate was set at 10% and reduced by 0.5% year over year. In this instance, the recidivism rate is 9.5% (Figure 14).

Figure 12. M-matrix (year 1)

$$M_1 = \begin{pmatrix} F & 3.8196 \\ S_o & 3.0471 \\ J & 2.0499 \\ S_R & 1.0526 \end{pmatrix}$$

Figure 13. Long-term probabilities

$$B_1 = \begin{pmatrix} & G & D \\ F & 0.7535 & 0.2465 \\ S_o & 0.8476 & 0.1524 \\ J & 0.8975 & 0.1025 \\ S_R & 0.9474 & 0.0526 \end{pmatrix} \text{(non-absorbing states)}$$

Student Retention Performance Using Absorbing Markov Chains

Figure 14. Transition probability matrix (P-canonical)

$$P = \begin{pmatrix} & G & D & F & S_o & J & S_R \\ \hline G & 1 & 0 & 0 & 0 & 0 & 0 \\ D & 0 & 1 & 0 & 0 & 0 & 0 \\ \hline F & 0 & 0.1 & 0.095 & 0.805 & 0 & 0 \\ S_o & 0 & 0.05 & 0 & 0.1 & 0.85 & 0 \\ J & 0 & 0.05 & 0 & 0 & 0.05 & 0.9 \\ S_R & 0.9 & 0.05 & 0 & 0 & 0 & 0.05 \end{pmatrix}$$

The N-matrix values represent the number of years (expected value) spent at each classification level prior to entering the subsequent state or an absorbing state. A freshman will spend approximately 1.1050, 0.9883, 0.98843, and 0.8378 years classified as a freshman, sophomore, junior, and senior, respectively. Sophomores will spend 1.1111, 0.9942, and 0.9418 years classified as a sophomore, junior, and senior, respectively. A junior will spend approximately 1.0526 and 0.9972 years classified as a junior and senior, respectively. Seniors spend 1.0526 years prior to entering an absorbing state.

The M-vector represents the summation of the corresponding row values on the N-matrix. Each value corresponds to the absorption time for a state when reaching either the drop-out or graduation absorbing state. On average, freshman take 3.8154 years, sophomores take 3.0471 years, juniors take 2.0499 years, and seniors take 1.0526 years to reach absorption.

The values in matrix-B represent the long-term probabilities of transitioning from a non-absorbing state into absorbing states. There is a 75.35% chance that a freshman will eventually reach graduation. Also, the probability of dropping out as a freshman is 0.2465. There is a higher probability that upper-classmen will improve their chances of graduating (Figure 15).

For year 3, the recidivism rate is now set to 9.0%. Recall that a 0.5% reduction is implemented year-over-year to correspond to a proactive process of assisting incoming freshman toward successfully

Figure 15. Long-term probabilities

$$B_2 = NR = \begin{pmatrix} & G & D \\ \hline F & 0.7535 & 0.2465 \\ S_o & 0.8476 & 0.1524 \\ J & 0.8975 & 0.1025 \\ S_R & 0.9474 & 0.0526 \end{pmatrix} \text{(non-absorbing states)}$$

completing all requirements for the transition to sophomore year. The transition probability matrix (in canonical form) is shown in Figure 16. The highlighted data (in red) shows the recidivism metric for this year. Recall that the baseline recidivism rate was set at 10% and reduced by 0.5% year over year. In this instance, the recidivism rate is 9.0%:

The N-matrix values represent the number of years (expected value) spent at each classification level prior to entering the subsequent state or an absorbing state. A freshman will spend approximately 1.0989, 0.9890, 0.8849, and 0.8383 years classified as a freshman, sophomore, junior, and senior, respectively. Sophomores will spend 1.1111, 0.9942, and 0.9418 years classified as a sophomore, junior, and senior, respectively. A junior will spend approximately 1.0526 and 0.9972 years classified as a junior and senior, respectively. Seniors spend 1.0526 years prior to entering an absorbing state.

The M-vector is the summation of the corresponding row values on the N-matrix. Each value corresponds to the absorption time for a state when reaching either the drop-out or graduation absorbing state. On average, freshman take 3.8111 years, sophomores take 3.0471 years, juniors take 2.0499 years, and seniors take 1.0526 years to reach absorption.

The values in matrix-B represent the long-term probabilities of transitioning from a non-absorbing state into absorbing states. There is a 75.35% chance that a freshman will eventually reach graduation. Also, the probability of dropping out as a freshman is 0.2465. There is a higher probability that upperclassmen will improve their chances of graduating (Figure 17).

The year 4 recidivism rate is now set to 8.5%. Recall that a 0.5% reduction is implemented year-over-year to correspond to a proactive process of assisting incoming freshman toward successfully completing all requirements for the transition to sophomore year. The transition probability matrix (in canonical form) is shown in Figure 18. The highlighted data (in red) shows the recidivism metric for this year. Recall that the baseline recidivism rate was set at 10% and reduced by 0.5% year over year. In this instance, the recidivism rate is 8.5%:

The N-matrix values represent the number of years (expected value) spent at each classification level prior to entering the subsequent state or an absorbing state. A freshman will spend approximately 1.0929,

Figure 16. Transition probability matrix (P-canonical)

$$P = \begin{pmatrix} & G & D & F & S_o & J & S_R \\ G & 1 & 0 & 0 & 0 & 0 & 0 \\ D & 0 & 1 & 0 & 0 & 0 & 0 \\ F & 0 & 0.1 & 0.09 & 0.81 & 0 & 0 \\ S_o & 0 & 0.05 & 0 & 0.1 & 0.85 & 0 \\ J & 0 & 0.05 & 0 & 0 & 0.05 & 0.9 \\ S_R & 0.9 & 0.05 & 0 & 0 & 0 & 0.05 \end{pmatrix}$$

Figure 17. Long-term probabilities

$$B_3 = NR = \begin{pmatrix} & G & D \\ \hline F & 0.7535 & 0.2465 \\ S_o & 0.8476 & 0.1524 \\ J & 0.8975 & 0.1025 \\ S_R & 0.9474 & 0.0526 \end{pmatrix} \text{(non-absorbing states)}$$

Figure 18. Transition probability matrix (P-canonical)

$$P = \begin{pmatrix} & G & D & F & S_o & J & S_R \\ \hline G & 1 & 0 & 0 & 0 & 0 & 0 \\ D & 0 & 1 & 0 & 0 & 0 & 0 \\ \hline F & 0 & 0.1 & 0.085 & 0.815 & 0 & 0 \\ S_o & 0 & 0.05 & 0 & 0.1 & 0.85 & 0 \\ J & 0 & 0.05 & 0 & 0 & 0.05 & 0.9 \\ S_R & 0.9 & 0.05 & 0 & 0 & 0 & 0.05 \end{pmatrix}$$

0.9897, 0.8855, and 0.8389 years classified as a freshman, sophomore, junior, and senior, respectively. Sophomores will spend 1.1111, 0.9942, and 0.9418 years classified as a sophomore, junior, and senior, respectively. A junior will spend approximately 1.0526 and 0.9972 years classified as a junior and senior, respectively. Seniors spend 1.0526 years prior to entering an absorbing state.

The M-vector is the summation of the corresponding row values on the N-matrix. Each value corresponds to the absorption time for a state when reaching either the drop-out or graduation absorbing state. On average, freshman take 3.8070 years, sophomores take 3.0471 years, juniors take 2.0499 years, and seniors take 1.0526 years to reach absorption.

The values in matrix-B represent the long-term probabilities of transitioning from a non-absorbing state into absorbing states. There is a 75.35% chance that a freshman will eventually reach graduation. Also, the probability of dropping out as a freshman is 0.2465. There is a higher probability that upperclassmen will improve their chances of graduating (Figure 19).

For year 5, the recidivism rate is now set to 8.0%. Recall that a 0.5% reduction is implemented year-over-year to correspond to a proactive process of assisting incoming freshman toward successfully completing all requirements for the transition to sophomore year. The transition probability matrix (in canonical form) is shown in Figure 20. The highlighted data (in red) shows the recidivism metric for

Figure 19. Long-term probabilities

$$B_4 = NR = \begin{pmatrix} & G & D \\ \hline F & 0.7535 & 0.2465 \\ S_o & 0.8476 & 0.1524 \\ J & 0.8975 & 0.1025 \\ S_R & 0.9474 & 0.0526 \end{pmatrix} \text{(non-absorbing states)}$$

Figure 20. Transition probability matrix

$$P = \begin{pmatrix} & G & D & F & S_o & J & S_R \\ \hline G & 1 & 0 & 0 & 0 & 0 & 0 \\ D & 0 & 1 & 0 & 0 & 0 & 0 \\ \hline F & 0 & 0.1 & 0.08 & 0.82 & 0 & 0 \\ S_o & 0 & 0.05 & 0 & 0.1 & 0.85 & 0 \\ J & 0 & 0.05 & 0 & 0 & 0.05 & 0.9 \\ S_R & 0.9 & 0.05 & 0 & 0 & 0 & 0.05 \end{pmatrix}$$

this year. Recall that the baseline recidivism rate was set at 10% and reduced by 0.5% year over year. In this instance, the recidivism rate is 8.0%:

The N-matrix values represent the number of years (expected value) spent at each classification level prior to entering the subsequent state or an absorbing state. A freshman will spend approximately 1.0870, 0.9903, 0.8861, and 0.8395 years classified as a freshman, sophomore, junior, and senior, respectively. Sophomores will spend 1.1111, 0.9942, and 0.9418 years classified as a sophomore, junior, and senior, respectively. A junior will spend approximately 1.0526 and 0.9972 years classified as a junior and senior, respectively. Seniors spend 1.0526 years prior to entering an absorbing state.

The M-vector is the summation of the corresponding row values on the N-matrix. Each value corresponds to the absorption time for a state when reaching either the drop-out or graduation absorbing state. On average, freshman take 3.8028 years, sophomores take 3.0471 years, juniors take 2.0499 years, and seniors take 1.0526 years to reach absorption.

The values in matrix-B represent the long-term probabilities of transitioning from a non-absorbing state into absorbing states. There is a 75.35% chance that a freshman will eventually reach graduation. Also, the probability of dropping out as a freshman is 0.2465. There is a higher probability that upperclassmen will improve their chances of graduating (Figure 21).

Student Retention Performance Using Absorbing Markov Chains

Figure 21. Long-term probabilities

$$B_5 = NR = \begin{pmatrix} & G & D \\ \hline F & 0.7535 & 0.2465 \\ S_o & 0.8476 & 0.1524 \\ J & 0.8975 & 0.1025 \\ S_R & 0.9474 & 0.0526 \end{pmatrix} \text{(non-absorbing states)}$$

For year 6, the recidivism rate is now set to 7.5%. Recall that a 0.5% reduction is implemented year-over-year to correspond to a proactive process of assisting incoming freshman toward successfully completing all requirements for the transition to sophomore year. The transition probability matrix (in canonical form) is shown in Figure 22. The highlighted data (in red) shows the recidivism metric for this year. Recall that the baseline recidivism rate was set at 10% and reduced by 0.5% year over year. In this instance, the recidivism rate is 7.5%:

The N-matrix values represent the number of years (expected value) spent at each classification level prior to entering the subsequent state or an absorbing state. A freshman will spend approximately 1.0811, 0.9910, 0.8867, and 0.84 years classified as a freshman, sophomore, junior, and senior, respectively. Sophomores will spend 1.1111, 0.9942, and 0.9418 years classified as a sophomore, junior, and senior, respectively. A junior will spend approximately 1.0526 and 0.9972 years classified as a junior and senior, respectively. Seniors spend 1.0526 years prior to entering an absorbing state.

The M-vector is the summation of the corresponding row values on the N-matrix. Each value corresponds to the absorption time for a state when reaching either the drop-out or graduation absorbing state. On average, freshman take 3.7988 years, sophomores take 3.0471 years, juniors take 2.0499 years, and seniors take 1.0526 years to reach absorption:

Figure 22. Transition probability matrix (canonical form)

$$P = \begin{pmatrix} & G & D & F & S_o & J & S_R \\ \hline G & 1 & 0 & 0 & 0 & 0 & 0 \\ D & 0 & 1 & 0 & 0 & 0 & 0 \\ \hline F & 0 & 0.1 & 0.075 & 0.825 & 0 & 0 \\ S_o & 0 & 0.05 & 0 & 0.1 & 0.85 & 0 \\ J & 0 & 0.05 & 0 & 0 & 0.05 & 0.9 \\ S_R & 0.9 & 0.05 & 0 & 0 & 0 & 0.05 \end{pmatrix}$$

The values in matrix-B represent the long-term probabilities of transitioning from a non-absorbing state into absorbing states. There is a 75.35% chance that a freshman will eventually reach graduation. Also, the probability of dropping out as a freshman is 0.2465. There is a higher probability that upper-classmen will improve their chances of graduating (Figure 23).

Case 2: Enrollment Increase

Table 2. corresponds to an increase in freshman enrollment. A 10% increase from the baseline of 1,000 students corresponds to a new analysis for 1,100 students. The additional 100 students successfully transitioned from freshman classification to sophomore status. The baseline recidivism rate of 10% is applied for the analysis.

The transition probability matrix (in canonical form) is shown in Figure 24. The highlighted data (in red) shows the recidivism metric for this year. Recall that the baseline enrollment rate was raised an additional 10%. Subsequent analysis for this case follow a similar pattern of the prior protocols for Markov chains.

The N-matrix values represent the number of years (expected value) spent at each classification level prior to entering the subsequent state or an absorbing state. A freshman will spend approximately 1.1, 0.99, 0.8957, and 0.8531 years classified as a freshman, sophomore, junior, and senior, respectively. Sophomores will spend 1.1, 0.9952, and 0.9478 years classified as a sophomore, junior, and senior, re-

Figure 23. Long-term probabilities

$$B_6 = NR = \begin{pmatrix} & G & D \\ \hline F & 0.7535 & 0.2465 \\ S_o & 0.8476 & 0.1524 \\ J & 0.8975 & 0.1025 \\ S_R & 0.9474 & 0.0526 \end{pmatrix} \text{(non-absorbing states)}$$

Table 2. Registration data (increased enrollment)

	F	So	J	Sr	G	D	Total
F	100	900	0	0	0	100	1100
So	0	100	950	0	0	50	1100
J	0	0	50	1000	0	50	1100
Sr	0	0	0	50	1000	50	1000
G	0	0	0	0	0	0	0
D	0	0	0	0	0	0	0

Frequency Transitions (n = 1100)

Figure 24. Transition probability matrix (canonical form)

$$P = \begin{pmatrix} & G & D & F & S_o & J & S_R \\ \hline G & 1 & 0 & 0 & 0 & 0 & 0 \\ D & 0 & 1 & 0 & 0 & 0 & 0 \\ \hline F & 0 & 0.0909 & 0.0909 & 0.8182 & 0 & 0 \\ S_o & 0 & 0.0455 & 0 & 0.0909 & 0.8636 & 0 \\ J & 0 & 0.0455 & 0 & 0 & 0.0455 & 0.9091 \\ S_R & 0.9091 & 0.0455 & 0 & 0 & 0 & 0.0455 \end{pmatrix}$$

spectively. A junior will spend approximately 1.0476 and 0.9977 years classified as a junior and senior, respectively. Seniors spend 1.0476 years prior to entering an absorbing state.

The M-vector is the summation of the corresponding row values on the N-matrix. Each value corresponds to the absorption time for a state when reaching either the drop-out or graduation absorbing state. On average, freshman take 3.8388 years, sophomores take 3.0431 years, juniors take 2.0454 years, and seniors take 1.0476 years to reach absorption.

The values in matrix-B represent the long-term probabilities of transitioning from a non-absorbing state into absorbing states. There is a 76.11% chance that a freshman will eventually reach graduation. Also, the probability of dropping out as a freshman is 0.2241. There is a higher probability that upperclassmen will improve their chances of graduating (Figure 25).

FORECASTS

Using the data from the prior analysis, I used several forecasting techniques to ascertain the potential validity of the Markov chain. Forecasting techniques are common provisions to validate models including the naïve approach, moving average, weighted moving average, exponential smoothing, linear trend analysis, and seasonality. Each have advantages and disadvantages. Some requires use of other metrics

Figure 25. Long-term probabilities

$$B_\uparrow = NR = \begin{pmatrix} & G & D \\ \hline F & 0.7611 & 0.2241 \\ S_o & 0.8562 & 0.1385 \\ J & 0.9066 & 0.0932 \\ S_R & 0.9569 & 0.0478 \end{pmatrix} \text{(non-absorbing states)}$$

such as alpha, specific weights, and optimization considerations. Each of these models utilize mean absolute deviation (MAD), mean squared error (MSE), and mean absolute percent error (MAPE). In many optimization models the MAPE metric is chosen to compare as the parameter has common error mitigation potential across all forecasting models.

For cyclic or periodic data, a seasonality model is used to determine whether the data has a seasonal component. This is an important matter as the error in seasonality models will indicate a lower MAPE value compared with others. The most common categories of seasonality models employ a multiplicative or additive decomposition technique. The trend, seasonal impact, and fluctuations components are either multiplied are added using the multiplicative or additive decomposition, respectively.

3-Period Moving Average

A three-period moving average forecasting model was implemented using the M-data. Recall that M-data determine the number of years a students is expected to transition from a transient state to an absorbing state. Of importance in this analysis is the substantial errors as calculate with the mean absolute percentage error (MAPE) and the other analytic metrics. A MAPE value of 75.62% indicates that the data residual values between the data points are substantially uncorrelated.

When a scatter plot and trend line is provided there is minimal relationship between the actual data points and the regression line. Using the M-data results, the regression trend line decreases due to the reduction of recidivism as time progresses through the system. The data trend is cyclical across time. The slight negative trend in the regression line ($\hat{y} = 2.795 - 0.0244X$) is most likely due to the increased effectiveness student obtain during the life cycle of their tenure in the system. As student remains in the system over time, the time spent prior to absorption decreases slightly. Although the MAPE value has little value to the validity of the model, the trend line has relevance in the long-term relationship between time in system and the time for reaching an absorbing state.

Similar analysis is performed on the B-data for the graduation absorbing state. As an outcome of this analysis, the mean absolute percentage error (MAPE) and the other analytic metrics appear to offer some reasonable accommodation for minimal error. A MAPE value of 75.62% indicates that the data residual values between the data points have some correlation between actual values and forecast projections. A scatter plot and trend line indicates a slight positive increase in chain progression. The slight increase in slope ($\hat{y} = 0.8409 + 0.0016X$) is relatively insignificant. The MAPE value (9.8%) is encouraging as a measure of validity as it suggest minimal error between actual and forecast values. Subsequent analysis is performed on the B-data for the drop-out absorbing state.

The model, as it is applied to the drop out data, had no significance or validity. Although the regression equation ($\hat{y} = 0.1591 - 0.0016X$) demonstrated a slight decrease over the life cycle, the MAPE value was substantially (90.17%) erroneous and insignificant.

Seasonality

A seasonality review of the M-data was performed. The low value of MAPE (0.06%) validates that the information derived using the Markov chain is cyclical and repetitive in nature. A scatter plot shows that the data has a cyclic characteristic. This validates that the Markov chain model over the long-period is predictive. The minimal slope of the regression ($\hat{y} = 2.4918 - 0.0002X$) is most likely due to the slight change in recidivism over the six year period.

Using the B-data graduation information, the forecast seasonality model was developed which demonstrated the periodicity of the data. Moreover, the outcomes of the model show that there is indeed a seasonal (or periodic) trend, as well as a relationship across the life cycle of the model. The scatter plot of this data has a linear trend with a cyclical pattern representing the linearity and repetitive nature of each rank in the classification system.

Finally, the calculations for MAPE, regression equation, and overall trend and fluctuations of the B-data (drop out state) were derived. The regression equation is $\hat{y} = 0.1385 + 0X$ while the MAPE is 0%. The MAPE indicates the pure cyclical nature of the information as it validated consistency over the life cycle.

CONCLUSION

Two cases were provided in this paper to show how retention metrics adapt over a six year period with subsequent years having diminished recidivism for freshman. A broader and deeper analysis may consider employing adaptation across all ranks (freshmen, sophomores, juniors, and seniors). In the second case, a model was developed to account for an increased enrollment option to determine how the increase impacted the long term projection within the system. To summarize, the two models had a baseline enrollment count while the second model included increased enrollment based on that baseline.

Comparing long-term probabilities for case 1 (Figure 26.), the probabilities for graduation increased as ranked students' progress through the system. A freshman has a 0.7535 probability of graduating but increased to a 0.9747 probability in the senior year. Similarly, there was a decrease in the probability of student's dropping out as they migrate from state to state.

Regarding the M-data over six years, there was a reduction of time to absorption as the various models were employed. Recall that the recidivism rate over the six year period (indicated as M1-M6 in Table 3.) diminished over time. The reduction of freshman repeats were selected to draw distinction between performance hypotheses. Such a demonstration provides a possibility for changes in policies which may have an impact in the life cycle of the system.

Furthermore, the N-data over the six year period in shown in Figure 27. Notice that there was a reduction of years in state for freshman over the six years analysis. Also, since the strategy was focused

Figure 26. Long-term probabilities (B-matrix)

$$B_{case1} = NR = \begin{pmatrix} & G & D \\ \hline F & 0.7535 & 0.2465 \\ S_o & 0.8476 & 0.1524 \\ J & 0.8975 & 0.1025 \\ S_R & 0.9474 & 0.0526 \end{pmatrix} \text{(non-absorbing states)}$$

Table 3. M-Data Comparison (Time to Absorption)

	M1	M2	M3	M4	M5	M6
Fr	3.8196	3.8155	3.8111	3.8070	3.8028	3.7988
So	3.0471	3.0471	3.0471	3.0471	3.0471	3.0471
Jr	2.0499	2.0499	2.0499	2.0499	2.0499	2.0499
Sr	1.0526	1.0526	1.0526	1.0526	1.0526	1.0526

Figure 27. Years within classification (N-matrix)

$$N_{1-6} = \begin{pmatrix} & F & S_o & J & S_r \\ F_1 & 1.1111 & 0.9877 & 0.8837 & 0.8372 \\ F_2 & 1.1050 & 0.9883 & 0.8843 & 0.8378 \\ F_3 & 1.0983 & 0.9890 & 0.8849 & 0.8383 \\ F_4 & 1.0929 & 0.9897 & 0.8855 & 0.8389 \\ F_5 & 1.0870 & 0.9903 & 0.8861 & 0.8395 \\ F_6 & 1.0811 & 0.9910 & 0.8867 & 0.8400 \end{pmatrix}$$

on freshman only for adaptation, the other ranked states (sophomore, junior, and senior) have no change over the six year period as hypothesized.

In case 2, the model considered a 10% increase in freshman to sophomore enrollment. Similar to the analysis and development provided in case 1, the graduation and drop out absorption diminished over time. This is most likely due to many factors (behavioral acclimation, high school transition conditions, etc.) which is beyond the scope of this paper. Of significance is the change in absorption between states over time (Figure 28).

The M-vector (Figure 29.) is the summation of the corresponding row values on the N-matrix. Each value corresponds to the absorption time for a state when reaching either the drop-out or graduation

Figure 28. Long-term probabilities

$$B_\uparrow = NR = \begin{pmatrix} & G & D \\ F & 0.7611 & 0.2241 \\ S_o & 0.8562 & 0.1385 \\ J & 0.9066 & 0.0932 \\ S_R & 0.9569 & 0.0478 \end{pmatrix} \text{(non-absorbing states)}$$

Figure 29. M-matrix (year 1, increased enrollment)

$$M = \begin{pmatrix} F & 3.8388 \\ S_o & 3.0431 \\ J & 2.0454 \\ S_R & 1.0476 \end{pmatrix}$$

absorbing state. On average, freshman take 3.8388 years, sophomores take 3.0431 years, juniors take 2.0454 years, and seniors take 1.0476 years to reach absorption.

The analysis demonstrated in this paper is unique as it analyzed the manipulation of one variable (ex: freshman increased enrollment) and its impact to overall probabilistic results of students in the system, time to absorption, and probabilities for reaching an absorbing state. Future research may consider changes across all states using actual data or formulating a simulation model using differing distribution patterns (uniform, normal, etc.). Further research may also account for statistical results for a model using transfer students, changes in enrollment across all rankings, and the possibility of a causal component.

ACKNOWLEDGMENT

The author would like to thank the anonymous reviewers and the editor for their insightful comments and suggestions.

REFERENCES

Aczel, A. D., & Sounderpandian, J. (2009). *Complete business statistics*. Boston, MA: McGraw-Hill/Irwin.

Al-Awadhi, S. A., & Konsowa, M. (2007). An application of absorbing Markov analysis to the student flow in an academic institution. *Kuwait Journal of Science and Engineering, 34*(2A), 77-89.

Bair, L. J., & Analytics, L. J. B. (2012). The Missing Link in Modeling and Simulation Validation. In *Proceedings of the 2012 Autumn AIAA Modeling and Simulation Technologies Conference*. doi:10.2514/mmst12

Berenson, M., Levine, D., Szabat, K. A., & Krehbiel, T. C. (2012). *Basic business statistics: Concepts and applications* (12th ed.). Englewood-Cliffs, NJ: Prentice Hall.

Bessent, E. W., & Bessent, A. M. (1980). Student flow in a university department: Results of a Markov analysis. *Interfaces*, *10*(2), 52–59. doi:10.1287/inte.10.2.52

Bolch, G., Greiner, S., de Meer, H., & Trivedi, K. S. (1998). *Queueing networks and Markov chains*. New York, NY: Wiley. doi:10.1002/0471200581

Caswell, H. (2013). Sensitivity analysis of discrete Markov chains via matrix calculus. *Linear Algebra and Its Applications*, *438*(4), 1727–1745. doi:10.1016/j.laa.2011.07.046

Chen, T. M., & Barnett, G. A. (2000). Research on international student flows from a macro perspective: A network analysis of 1985, 1989 and 1995. *Higher Education*, *39*(4), 435–453. doi:10.1023/A:1003961327009

Dym, C. L., & Ivey, E. S. (1980). *Principals of mathematical modeling*. New York, NY: Academic Press.

Ekhosuehi, V. U., & Osagiede, A. A. (2012). On the transition matrix of the flow mechanism in a multi-echelon educational system. *International Journal of Operations Research*, *9*(4), 209-219.

Ekhosuehi, V. U., & Osagiede, A. A. (2013). Benchmarking the enrolment structure of an educational system without exceeding the carrying capacity requirement. *Pakistan Journal of Statistics and Operation Research*, *9*(3), 265–276. doi:10.18187/pjsor.v9i3.459

Freedman, D. (1971). *Markov chains*. San Francisco, CA: Holden-Day.

Haslett, J., & Hayes, K. (1998). Residuals for the linear model with general covariance structure. *Journal of the Royal Statistical Society. Series B, Statistical Methodology*, *60*(1), 201–215. doi:10.1111/1467-9868.00119

Hilton, R. J., & Sohal, A. (2012). A conceptual model for the successful deployment of Lean Six Sigma. *International Journal of Quality & Reliability Management*, *29*(1), 54–70. doi:10.1108/02656711211190873

Igboanugo, A. C., & Edokpia, O. R. (2014). A Markovian study of manpower planning in the soft-drink industry in Nigeria. *Nigerian Journal of Technology*, *33*(4), 547–552. doi:10.4314/njt.v33i4.15

Kleinrock, L. (1975). Queueing systems: Vol. 1. *Theory*. New York, NY: John Wiley & Sons.

Kovačić, Z. J. (2012). Predicting student success by mining enrolment data. *Research in Higher Education Journal*, *15*.

Lee, M. D., & Wagenmakers, E. J. (2014). *Bayesian cognitive modeling: A practical course*. Boston, MA: Cambridge University Press.

Martini, B., & Choo, K. K. R. (2012). An integrated conceptual digital forensic framework for cloud computing. *Digital Investigation*, *9*(2), 71–80. doi:10.1016/j.diin.2012.07.001

Mustafa, M. N., Chowdhury, L., & Kamal, M. S. (2012, May). Students dropout prediction for intelligent system from tertiary level in developing country. In *Informatics, Electronics & Vision (ICIEV), 2012 International Conference on* (pp. 113-118). IEEE. doi:10.1109/ICIEV.2012.6317441

Nicholls, M. G. (2007). Assessing the progress and the underlying nature of the flows of doctoral and master degree candidates using absorbing Markov chains. *Higher Education*, *53*(6), 769–790. doi:10.1007/s10734-005-5275-x

Nicholls, M. G. (2008). The Use of Markov models as an aid to the evaluation, planning and benchmarking of doctoral programs. *The Journal of the Operational Research Society, 60*(9), 1183–1190. doi:10.1057/palgrave.jors.2602639

Norris, J. R. (1997). *Markov chains*. New York, NY: Cambridge University Press. doi:10.1017/CBO9780511810633

Nyandwaki, M. J., Akelo, O. E., Samson, O. O., & Fredrick, O. (2014). Application of Markov chain model in Studying progression Of Secondary School Students by Sex During The Free Secondary Education: A Case Study of Kisii Central District. *Mathematical Theory and Modeling, 4*(4). Available at: http://iiste.org/Journals/index.php/MTM/article/view/11744

Papoulis, A. (1991). *Probability, random variables, and stochastic processes* (3rd ed.). Boston, MA: McGraw-Hill.

Puterman, M. L. (2014). *Markov decision processes: discrete stochastic dynamic programming*. New York, NY: John Wiley & Sons.

Rahim, R., Ibrahim, H., & Adnan, F. A. (2013, April). Projection of postgraduate students flow with a smoothing matrix transition diagram of Markov chain. In *Proceedings of the 20th National Symposium On Mathematical Sciences: Research in Mathematical Sciences: A Catalyst for Creativity and Innovation* (Vol. 1522, No. 1, pp. 1385-1393). AIP Publishing. doi. doi:10.1063/1.4801291

Rahim, R. A. (2015). Analyzing Manpower Data of Higher Learning Institutions: A Markov Chain Approach. *International Journal of Human Resource Studies, 5*(3), 38–47. doi:10.5296/ijhrs.v5i3.7969

Wolf, K. H. (1976). Conceptual Models in Geology. *Classifications and Historical Studies, 11*, 11–78. doi:10.1016/B978-0-444-41401-4.50006-X

Chapter 16
An Analytical Employee Performance Evaluation Approach in Office Automation and Information Systems

Maryam Kalhori
University of Science and Culture, Iran

Mohammad Javad Kargar
University of Science and Culture, Iran

ABSTRACT

With the extension of information technology, human resource management has experienced fundamental changes. One of the most important issues in human resource management is performance evaluation. Unlike number of studies in employee performance evaluation, there is a lack for systematic and quantitative approaches. Issues such as incomplete information, subjective and qualitative metrics, and also the difficulty of evaluating the performance are the main problems of this field. Hence, the current study exploits the capabilities of information systems and presents an approach for quantitative and automatic evaluation of employee performance in office automation systems. The results reveal the automatic employee performance evaluation system is a discrete dimension for employee performance evaluation systems.

INTRODUCTION

Human resources are the key assets in assisting organizations to maintain their competitive advantage (Ahmed, Sultana, Paul, & Azeem, 2013). Generally, in the studies that have been done in the field of human resource management, employee performance evaluation is seen as one of the most critical tools in this area (Fukui, 2015; Manoharan, Muralidharan, & Deshmukh, 2011). Hence, using efficient tools with high accuracy in the process of employee performance evaluation is welcomed by the managers.

DOI: 10.4018/978-1-5225-0654-6.ch016

An Analytical Employee Performance Evaluation Approach

There are abundant studies in the field of evaluation employee performance. The main issue highlighted by these studies, is the accuracy of evaluation systems (Ahmed, et al., 2013; Manoharan, Muralidharan, & Deshmukh, 2012). Considering the fact that evaluation process is faced with problems such as subjective, incomplete Information, qualitative metrics, it leads to these systems are not readily accepted by users (Avazpour, Ebrahimi, & Fathi, 2013).

In recent years, with the advent of information technology, E-HRM (Yusliza & Ramayah, 2012) has become one of interesting subjects among researchers. In this regard, the computer systems that administer the evaluation are recently developed. However little attention has been paid to the relation between information systems and performance measurement systems (Dulebohn & Johnson, 2013; Garengo, Nudurupati, & Bititci, 2007; Nudurupati, Bititci, Kumar, & Chan, 2011). Generally evaluation systems are focused on recording the data, and there is no deep and meaningful outlook on data (Aqel & Vadera, 2010). While in web based office automatic systems, useful information is recorded automatically about individual's working procedure and they can be used for evaluating working performance.

Therefore, this chapter exploits the capabilities of information systems and proposes an appropriate approach for quantitative and automatic evaluation of employee performance in web base office automation systems. The chapter is organized as follows. In the next section, the review of the related literature is presented about assessment and ranking of employee performance. Then, in the next section the proposed approach is presented. In the last, we'll review the results of the system tests and will have the conclusion.

BACKGROUND

In general, recent researches attempt to remove the drawbacks of traditional evaluation methods (Deming, 1986; Manoharan, Muralidharan, & Deshmukh, 2009; Nudurupati, et al., 2011; Waldman, 1994) by implementing TOPSIS (Yue, 2014a), VIKOR (Park, Cho, & Kwun, 2013), non-parametric methods (Manoharan, et al., 2009), fuzzy neural network (Macwan & Sajja, 2013) and other ranking methods. Given that, evaluating and ranking performance evaluation systems are concerned with individual and personal factors, behavioral factors or the results; One of the difficulties of performance evaluation process is related to subjective judgment of the evaluators (Avazpour, et al., 2013) that is based on the past presuppositions. In this way some part of the data is always ignored either inadvertently or sometimes deliberately.

In this regard, present literatures can be classified into two groups: systematic and non-systematic methods. Non-systematic methods evaluate relying on evaluators' opinions and calculating individuals' absolute performance score (Espinilla, Andrés, Mart´ınez, & Mart´ınez, 2013) based on the mean of all opinions of evaluators or based on a proportion of input and output parameters (Manoharan, et al., 2009).Considering the role of evaluators in evaluation process in non-systematic methods, choosing who is going to do the evaluation process by itself has become a major challenge in evaluating individual's performance. Moon, Lee, and Lim (2010) believe in order for the evaluation to be fair, there should be no assumed segregation among evaluators. However, generally in ranking methods, the effect and importance of different evaluators' roles are considered differently (Andrés, Espinila, & Martínez, 2010; Espinilla, et al., 2013; Espinilla, Mart´ınez, & Mart´ınez, 2010; Park, et al., 2013) and (Xu, 2004). In such a way that in some studies like (Andrés, García-Lapresta, & González-Pachón, 2010; Espinilla, et al., 2010) and (Yue, 2014a) the opinion and effect of each evaluator on each criterion are not assumed equal. It should be noted that the segregation among evaluators can sometimes reinforce biased opinions. On the other hand, this hypothesis cannot be completely discarded, as each group of evaluators is different as to their knowledge and perspective.

Given the fact that a variety of qualitative and quantitative criteria can be considered for evaluation, it is very important to determine the scales that distinguish the view of the evaluators with appropriate level of accuracy. Espinilla et al. (2013) emphasizes this issue by proposing a framework in 3 inputs formats (numerical, linguistic and interval-valued information). In addition Ahmed, et al. (2013) propose an approach that it determines the performance indices of employees considering their respective performance in various qualitative and quantitative evaluation criteria. The appropriate input type defined based on the very nature of the criteria, would be more understandable and facilitated for evaluators, in addition to being more accurate. Consequently, the ranking methods are considerable as to whether the input data is homogeneous or heterogeneous.

On the other hand, since the linguistic expressions are close to the natural language, they are identified as useful and simple tools to show the evaluators' perspectives in comparison to subjective and imprecise criteria (Espinilla, et al., 2013); but it is not easy to determine the appropriate linguistic scale either. Some research apply a single set of linguistic labels for all evaluators (Beheshti & Lollar, 2008; Gürbüz, 2010); while Espinilla, et al. (2013) and Andrés, García-Lapresta, & Martínez, 2010) have introduced different Multi-granular linguistic expressions. They believe that as to the lack of equal understanding of the evaluator from those individuals being evaluated, fair evaluation would not be possible with a single scale.

In this case, the conventional method used for ranking is based on the total sum weight of evaluation elements and the weight of criteria which will lead to a different decision making considering evaluators sets, evaluators' weights and sort of the inputs. This process is known as the aggregation phase. Aggregation phase is one of the conventional steps in the group decision making process. But in aggregation process, some part of the data is usually inevitably lost (Yue, 2013) ; therefore the extended TOPSIS method has been provided by (Yue, 2014a). Unlike traditional TOPSIS method and other decision making techniques, the new method does not require aggregation phase.

But some other non-systematic methods are based on proportion of input and output parameters (Osman, Berbary, Sidani, Al-Ayoubi, & Emrouznejad, 2011). These types of studies, unlike the absolute methods, apply nonparametric technique - DEA, AHP and fuzzy neural network- and perform the evaluation procedure uni-dimensionally. These studies that have proposed a model for relative performance evaluation and measurement of employees have a numerical structure and framework. The DEA, which was able to classify employees into the efficient and inefficient ones, and also to identify benchmarks for inefficient units, is one of the methods used in evaluating employee performance. Since DEA sometimes erroneously identifies a DMU unit (an employee) efficient, Manoharan, et al. (2009) applies the method suggested by Doyle and Green (1994) (as cited in Manoharan, et al. (2009)) which is an effective way of measuring the false index of DMUs to overcome this problem. The significant feature of this method is the sensitivity to the number of input and output parameters. This problem limits the applicability of this method in different situations. On the other hand, the DMUs must have absolutely identical properties. In other words evaluated employees must be from the same department, i.e. it is not possible to compare the various departments.

Macwan and Sajja (2013) use soft computing in the process of evaluating employee performance. The advantage of this method is the ability to learn from input evaluation parameters, available data and experience to provide unbiased decision.

An Analytical Employee Performance Evaluation Approach

Additional, the problem of assigning weights to performance evaluation factors as an unstructured and multi-attributed issue (Golec & Kahya, 2007) is important. So some studies have applied scientific approaches like AHP (Lan and Li, 2010), FAHP (Manoharan et al, 2011, Sepehrirad, Azar, & Sadeghi, 2012) and FQFD (Manoharan et al., 2011). The striking point in applying FAHP and FQFD is the restriction of the main factors to seven ones as to the limitation in the size of the pairwise comparison matrix (Manoharan, et al., 2011) and the restriction of sub-factors to 30 criteria. Among all current studies, only three methods have considered dependence and interaction among the criteria in their framework.

Generally these authors believe their methods have adequately covered huge number of employees and indicators (Yue, 2014a). Due to the expansion and complexity of tasks, evaluators would not be able to have enough knowledge about all subjects assessed. Thus, it is essential to implement the methods and techniques which are capable of correctly analyzing individuals' working procedure and professional relationships among staff in daily activities.

On the contrary, systematic methods with considering the fact that conventional evaluation processes are costly and time-consuming for both evaluators and individual being evaluated, and lack of accurate, real and objective data about the working situation of individuals, have proposed methods relying on automatic data collection from working processes and professional relationships established by employees and recording routine activities. They attempted to provide evaluation results with a higher degree of accuracy by applying data warehouse techniques, data collection algorithms, and appropriate data analysis. In this type of research, human evaluators are almost deleted or used in a limited number of criteria and the work basis is the developed algorithms. Hence, Lan and Li (2010) have designed a web-based performance evaluation system for R&D staff in a medicine production factory using B/S pattern. By using analytical hierarchy process and combining assistant indicators, the researcher has overcome the default of the KPI analysis which sometimes neglects other fundamental criteria among key ones, also determined the weight value of system indicators, thus, providing a more comprehensive evaluation. Also, Rezaei, Çelik, and Baalousha (2011) have developed a web-based organizational automation system using data warehouse techniques to measure the performance factor of each employee as well as an activity performance factor in Civil projects. The key feature of this research is exploring the distinction between those individuals who have no subordinates, and those individuals who receive working reports from their subordinates. But it only relies on functional types of OBS operations and three indices of time, cost and quality.

In Table 1, an overview of the methods investigated in this chapter is provided.

Table 1. Recent studies in the field of employees' evaluation and measurement

Literature	Method	Research Focus	Decision Making	Data Collection	Heterogeneous
Ahmad (2013)	Fuzzy Approach	A fuzzy model for performance evaluation by using historical data of a company	by evaluator	Questionaries'	✓
Andres (2010)	Distance function mathematical model	Developing 360-degree appraisal model	by 360-degree	Questionaries'	-
Avazpour (2013)	Fuzzy AHP and TOPSIS	Developing a framework based on fuzzy hybrid multiple criteria decision making approach to identify the best person	by 360-degree	Questionaries'	-
Beheshti (2008)	Fuzzy logic	Developing a fuzzy logic framework to employee performance evaluation	by evaluator	Questionaries'	-

continued on next page

Table 1. Continued

Literature	Method	Research Focus	Decision Making	Data Collection	Heterogeneous
Espinila (2010)	Weighted average operator	Developing a Web based evaluation system	by 360-degree	Questionaries' on Web	-
Espinila (2013)	OWA/Weighted average operator/ Choquet integral	An integrated model for 360-degree performance evaluation	by 360-degree	Questionaries'	✓
Gürbüz (2010)	Choquet Integral/ MACBETH	To find the best employee	by DM	Questionaries'	-
Islama (2006)	AHP	Employee Performance Evaluation	by supervisors	Questionaries'	-
Javadein (2014)	Fuzzy TOPSIS	Developing an algorithm to assess and rank employees based on their protean and boundary less careers orientation	by evaluator	Questionaries'	-
Lan (2010)	Mathematics model	Performance assessment of R&D staff of the biological institute	-	Self-assessment	-
Macwan (2013)	Neural fuzzy	Modeling performance evaluation using soft computing techniques	by evaluator	Questionaries'/ Semi-Automatic	-
Manoharan (2009)	DEA	Evaluating of the performance of nurses in intensive care unit	by supervisors	Questionaries'/ Semi-Automatic	✓
Manoharan (2011)	FMADM	A model for employees' performance evaluation	by supervisors	Questionaries'/ Semi-Automatic	-
Moon (2010)	Fuzzy logic & Electronic nominal group technique	Developing a performance evaluation and promotion ranking system	by GDM	Questionaries' on Web	-
Osman (2011)	DEA	Aappraisal and relative performance evaluation of nurses	by evaluators	Questionaries'	-
Park (2013)	An extended VIKOR	To extend the VIKOR method to dynamic intuitionistic fuzzy environment	by evaluators	-	-
Rezaei (2011)	Data warehouse	Creating a decision tool for company managers to track employee performances	-	Automatic	-
Sepehrirad (2012)	Distance function mathematical model & SAW	Developing a hybrid mathematical model for 360-degree performance evaluation	by 360-degree	Questionaries'	-
Xu (2004)	ULHA/ ULOWA	Develop an uncertain linguistic approach to MAGDM	by GDM	Questionaries'	-
Yue (2014a)	IVIFN	aggregating interval data into interval-valued intuitionistic fuzzy information	by GDM	Questionaries'	-
Yue (2014b)	An extended TOPSIS method	Developing a new methodology for GDM problems in an intuitionistic fuzzy environment	by GDM	Questionaries'	-

THE PROPOSED APPROACH

As mentioned above, in most part of the literature, there is scant attention to the role of information systems (Garengo, et al., 2007). Besides, the employees of operational sectors are assessed, and no specific attention is paid to employees who are at a higher level in organization and indirectly play a role in some issues. Some authors like Aqel and Vadera (2010), Rezaei, et al. (2011), Wu and Hou (2010) show that considering the communication type in individuals' working activities in order to achieve better results is important in the evaluation process. Considering the actual operational data and business financial data, Wu and Hou (2010) presented a model for evaluating three levels of employees in a distribution center based on working hours and volume.

Accordingly, in this study, a new method is proposed for automatic quantitative assessment of employee performance in office automation system. This model is inspired by Wu model which is presented for industrial distribution center which is changed according to office automation system and Rezaei, et al. (2011) framework which is a model of evaluation in office automation systems in which individual performance is measured in two direct and indirect levels.

Furthermore, in order to follow up employee performance, some ideas are adopted from Xuan, Jiang, Ren and Zou (2012) method to solve developer prioritization in bug repositories. In this method, a graph is created out of the communications among the developers and the comments which are put in the system in order to remove bugs. A link is drawn among each two developers who write a comment on others' opinions, and the number of the comments is considered as the weight of the link. To make this method applicable for performance evaluation system, some changes are done. The proposed model is explained in the following.

Research Variable

According to the structure of office automation and the investigations done, performance variables can be divided into three general groups as Operational, Time-based, and Communication based which can be seen in Figure 1.

- **Operational Variables:** includes all activities done in automation system. Among the indices considered here are: the number of the letters received, the number of the letters sent/returned, the

Figure 1. Research variables

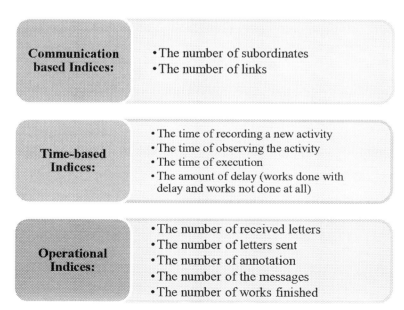

number of annotation, the number of accomplished works. It is worth mentioning about "the messages sent" is that we had to omit this evaluation factor as to the non-existence of this factor in the collected data set. The reason to choose this index as an evaluation index is that in this way, it is possible to follow up to which extent the individuals have spent their time to other works in their working hours. As mentioned above, this index is not considered in this study.

- **Time Variables:** by the three defined time points, and considering the time period that is allocated for each work, the time it takes to get the job done is calculated and in case of delay, the amount of delay is also calculated.
- **Communication based Variables:** as mentioned above, the research background was mainly focused on directed employees, and few studies have paid attention to evaluation factors and weight factors of indirect employee performance (Lan and Li, 2010). As the performance of indirect individuals can be influenced by employees at lower levels, this can be considered as one of the most important indices. Though, it must be considered that the low number of links does not indicate lower importance. The working volume can be of importance according to the level of position.

The Evaluation Method

In this study, we intend to present a new approach for quantitative evaluation of employee performance in office automation systems. Our proposed model is inspired by Wu model which is adjusted in proportion with office automation systems. Individual performance is measured in two direct and indirect levels. In this model, the levels of employees and organizational units are entered to the system as input. See the hierarchy of the proposed model in Figure 2, as you can see, METKA evaluation framework comprises three modules.

Module 1: Specifying the direct performance: actual performance, effective performance and the growth of each employee performance are utilized to measure the performance of those employees who don't have any lower level employee.

Module 2: Specifying indirect performance: in order to measure the performance of directors and those individuals who have subordinates, indirect performance should be measured.

Module 3: Final analysis of performance score: employee performance ranking based on the results of Module 1 and 2 and analysis, conclusion and preparing the reports.

Specifying Direct Performance

In order to measure the direct performance, the actual performance and effective performance should firstly be identified. To do so, the amount of the individual's activity in the system and the possible delays existing at work are extracted from the system.

- **Actual Performance:** For each employee who is in the primary level, the amount of actual performance of the individual is firstly calculated through Equation 1.

An Analytical Employee Performance Evaluation Approach

Figure 2. Employee performance evaluation procedure in METKA system

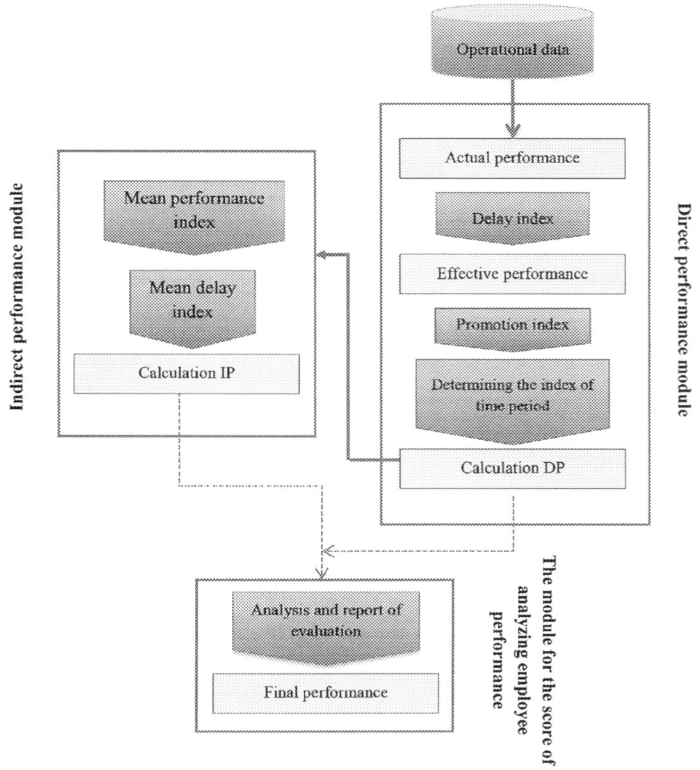

$$RP(W_{i,j,k}, T) = \frac{N(W_{i,j,k})}{TN} \tag{1}$$

In which $WR_{i,j,k}$ shows that employee k is in level i and department j. i=1 means that employee k doesn't have any lower level employee.

$N(W_{i,j,k})$= is the number of the individual activities in the system in time period T

TN= is the total activity done in system in time period T

- **Effective Performance:** As sometimes there is delay in executing the job, it can be considered as a negative coefficient in individual's performance. Also there might be some jobs that are left to others in that given time period that are delayed or are not done. Therefore, Negative Performance (NP) is calculated through Equation 4. Then accordingly, the effective performance is calculated.
- **Calculating the Number of Delays**

    $D1(W_{i,j,k})$: is the total number of jobs done with delay

    $D1(W_{i,j,k})$: is the total number of jobs that are not done and facing delay

$$D1(w_{i,j,k}, T) = \sum_{t=1}^{NUr_{tj}} Ur_t(w_{i,j,k}) + \sum_{t=1}^{NDe_{tj}} De_t(w_{i,j,k}) \tag{2}$$

An Analytical Employee Performance Evaluation Approach

$$D2(w_{i,j,k}, T) = \sum_{t=1}^{NUr_{tj}} Ur_t(w_{i,j,k}) + \sum_{t=1}^{NDe_{tj}} De_t(w_{i,j,k}) \tag{3}$$

- **Calculating the Amount of Delay**

It should be considered that the length of individuals' working line can be different; therefore, in order to calculate the rate of delay, the proportion of working volume should be considered to measure individual ranking more precisely.

$$NP(W_{i,j,k}, T) = D1(W_{i,j,k}, T) / N(W_{i,j,k}) \times TN + D2(W_{i,j,k}, T) / \text{number of recieved letters} \tag{4}$$

- **Determining Effective Performance**

Based on Wu's model (2010), effective performance is calculated through Equation 5.

$$EP = RP(w_{i,j,k}) \times (1 - NP(w_{i,j,k}, T)) \tag{5}$$

- **Final Performance (Direct Performance):** In order to calculate the direct performance, determining the time index and the amount of promotion index are two main elements. Time index is attained by the proportion of delay time to the time in which the job is done.
- **Determining the Confidence Interval in Performance**: In order to determine the promotion index, the existing historical data are used in system. By historical data, we mean the amount of effective performance attained in previous periods. To do so, the number of previous period should be determined. In Equation 6-8, n shows the number of previous periods.

In this way, the average and variance of effective performance of previous stages of evaluation are measured and confidence interval is determined for effective performance (Wu & Hou, 2010).

$$HEP(w_{i,j,k}, T) = \frac{\sum_{l=1}^{n} HEP_l}{n}, \quad HEPV(w_{i,j,k}, T) = \frac{\sum_{l=1}^{n} [HEP_l - \overline{HEP}]^2}{n-1} \tag{6}$$

$$C_1(w_{i,j,k}, T) = HEP(w_{i,j,k}, T) + Z_{\alpha/2} \sqrt{\frac{HEPV(w_{i,j,k}, T)}{n}} \tag{7}$$

An Analytical Employee Performance Evaluation Approach

$$C_2\left(w_{i,j,k}, T\right) = HEP\left(w_{i,j,k}, T\right) - Z_{\alpha/2}\sqrt{\frac{HEPV\left(w_{i,j,k}, T\right)}{n}} \tag{8}$$

If the effective performance attained from Equation 5 is in this range, it shows that the individual hasn't had any significant change in his/her performance. But if it is more than the upper limits of confidence interval, it means that the individual has improvements (Trl = 1). On the contrary, lower than lower limits of confidence interval reflects weakening the working performance of individuals (TrL = -1) (Wu & Hou, 2010).

- **The Total Delay Time:** To calculate the total delay time, both categories of jobs that are done and those that are not done and are delayed should be considered. Equation 9 calculates the total delay time.

$$TDWT\left(w_{i,j,k}\right) = \sum_{t=1}^{NUr_{tj}} DTUr_t\left(w_{i,j,k}\right) + \sum_{t=1}^{NDe_{tj}} DTDe_t\left(w_{i,j,k}\right) \tag{9}$$

- **Working Time Index:** Working time index can reflect the required time to get things done by the individuals (Wu & Hou, 2010). In other words, by working time index, the amount of working time value of each individual is meant. According to this, based on the total of working hours recorded in the system from the individual's working hour, the amount of the times in which the work is done with delay is subtracted, and the proportion of this number is assumed as time index. Equation 10 and 11 specify working time index.

$$TDI = 1 - \frac{TDWT\left(w_{i,j,k}\right)}{Total\ hours\ workd\ by\ individual} \tag{10}$$

$$WTI = 1 - TDI\ (w_{i,j,k}) \tag{11}$$

- **Calculating Performance:** As explained in part A, in order to specify the amount of working improvement of each individual, the average of individual effective performance in previous periods is calculated. In order to determine the weight of direct employee improvement index in a specific job, (Wu & Hou, 2010) utilize Equation 12. According to this, direct performance is calculated with regard to the effective performance and the working time index (Wu & Hou, 2010).

$$\beta = \begin{cases} \dfrac{EP(w_{i,j,k},T) - C_1(w_{i,j,k},T)}{C_1(w_{i,j,k},T) - HEP(w_{i,j,k},T)} & \text{if } TrI(w_{i,j,k},T) = 1 \\ 0 & \text{if } TrI(w_{i,j,k},T) = 0 \\ \dfrac{C_2(w_{i,j,k},T) - EP(w_{i,j,k},T)}{HEP(w_{i,j,k},T) - C_2(w_{i,j,k},T)} & \text{if } TrI(w_{i,j,k},T) = -1 \end{cases} \quad (12)$$

$$FP(w_{i,j,k},T) = EP \times WTI \times (1 + TrI \times \beta) \quad (13)$$

Specifying Indirect Performance

Determining the amount of manager/director performance cannot be specified merely based on their own performance as they should be responsive about the job of their subordinates too. The performance of their subordinates should be influential in their performance score. To do so, the α coefficient of each position should be specified.

To discover the effective nodes in a social network, (Kempe, Kleinberg, & Tardos, 2003) have proposed Equation 14.

$$\alpha_l = p_{v,u} = 1 - \left(1 - \frac{1}{\deg ree(u)}\right)^{weight(v,u)} \quad (14)$$

With regard to the fact that the amount and quality of relations are influential in returned works and consequently in the quality and the type of performance, they are assumed as a dimension in evaluation. On the one hand, the kind of individual relations can be assumed as a graph, and the individual who has more important and sensitive job can be considered a more important and more valuable node in the graph. As to this, in the current study, Equation 15 is used to calculate the effectiveness coefficient of each position which is the degree (u) of the total number of the letters that are sent and returned, also weight (v,u) is calculated from Equation 15.

$$weight(v,u) = \frac{number\ of\ work\ v\ to\ u}{Total\ Work\ v} \quad (15)$$

Now the performance of those individuals who have subordinates, the total of FP and an average of subordinates' FP is attained through Equation 16 (Rezaei, et al., 2011).

$$IP = 1/2 \left(FP(w_{i=2,j,k},T) + 1/n \sum_{l=1}^{n} \alpha \times FP_l \right) \quad (16)$$

An Analytical Employee Performance Evaluation Approach

In which n is the number of subordinates.

In addition, the average of the delays that are caused by the subordinates should be subtracted from the performance as a negative coefficient. Accordingly, the final score is attained from Equation 17.

$$FIP = IFP\left(w_{i=2,j,k}, T\right) \times (1 - 1/n \sum_{l=1}^{n} \alpha \times D\left(w_{i=1,j,k}, T\right)) \qquad (17)$$

The Implementation of the System

In order to administer and implement the proposed model for automatic and quantitative evaluation of employee performance, a basic automation system is required. But as to the fact that the assumed companies don't let us have access to theirs, we had to design and administer a basic organizational automation per force.

To design METKA basic automation system, PHP object-oriented language is chosen for implementation. Furthermore, in order to design the required database MySQL5.5.24 is utilized. Then by adding some modules which are explained in Section 3, the mention system is implemented for a period of about two months in a small company of installing telecommunication pylons.

In this system, the users can perform all organizational tasks by sending their written exchanges. All activities and users' entrance and exits are recorded in in the system.

Data Collection

In order to collect the required data and also to analyze the performance, the time that is allocated to performance in this study, Xuan structure is utilized (Xuan, et al., 2012). With defining n users in METKA system for evaluation, each employee d_i is assumed as a vertex in the graph. All vertexes are divided into k attributes based on the departments. The three elements (S_{ij}, R_{ij}, E_{ij}) show the number of letters sent, returned from employee i to employee j and the number of finished works of individual j that is depicted by a navigated link that is drawn from i to j. If there is no letter exchange between individual i and j, this value will be equal to zero. Each vertex saves values such as the allocated time for that given action, the time in which the work is done and the time and the number of delays. It is worth mentioning that there is no limitation on the type of the letters sent and the relations. In order to find a connective graph, an assumed employee d_0 is considered, and all individuals are connected to that. Then a bidirectional link is drawn between that employee and d_0.

This type of saving the individuals' activities in the system is advantageous because besides the data required for evaluation, other data like the volume of activities in each department and also the individuals who are more active as to the type of their position are firstly specified. In fact these vertexes can be considered as the separation points of the graph that by removing them, the graph would be disconnected. In this way, they key figures of the organizations are identified. Naturally, if this employee doesn't manifest pleasant performance, it brings about faults and weaknesses in other parts.

Evaluation in System

To evaluate, the director or the individual in charge of evaluation firstly chooses the allocated time range. After determining the range under evaluation and administering the evaluation algorithm, all information required for evaluation are extracted from the crude primary data which are saved in this period in the system.

For direct evaluation, Model 1 is implemented on the resulted data. In the next stage, Model 2 is applied for measuring the authorities' performance (indirect performance). See the data resulted from implementing the proposed approach in Table 2.

It is worth mentioning that comparison can be logical if the cases are similar and from the same classification. That's why here it is assumed that the working balance exists among the jobs. Moreover, as mentioned previously, for evaluation in each period, the results of the previous periods are required. Here, as there is only one period of background/history data to measure the performance in the second month of evaluation, instead of Equation 6, the EP of this period is contrasted with the last period, and the proportion of their difference is measured.

Result and Discussion

Factor analysis is a multivariate statistical method whose primarily purpose is to define the underlying structure in a data matrix. Therefore, in order to study the relationship between the variables, a correlation analysis has been conducted. Table 3 shows the corresponding results.

Table 2. Comparing evaluation outcomes

User	November	Rank	December	Rank	Expert	Rank
1	-	-	-	-	-	-
2	0.006328	11	0.00055	13	0.361667	10
3	0.003592	15	0.000666	12	0.331469	11
4	0.079078	1	0.110127	4	0.822819	5
5	0.048869	5	0.044615	7	0.913253	3
6	0.058655	2	0.13519	3	0.96631	2
7	0.051591	3	0.085604	5	0.672291	8
8	0.027931	7	0.159297	2	0.721249	6
9	0.009346	10	1.51E-07	15	0	14
10	0.050193	4	0.017688	9	0.060575	15
11	0.027513	8	0.045613	6	1	1
12	0.016557	9	0.178404	1	0.688717	7
13	0.006297	12	0	16	0.585348	9
14	0.02909	6	0.035264	8	0.898894	4
15	0.003105	16	1.26E-06	14	0.327371	12
16	0.006293	13	0.011143	10	0.229792	13
3	0.004505	14	0.009867	11	0.183506	16

An Analytical Employee Performance Evaluation Approach

Table 3. Results of variables analysis

	Sent	Received	Activity	Num_DD	Time_DD	Num_ND	Time_DN	Link	Subordinate
Sent		0.566*	0.783	-0.068	-0.192	0.616**	0.111	0.894**	0.655**
Received			0.818**	0.577**	0.004	0.519*	0.225	0.875**	0.540*
Activity				0.398	-.245	0.365	0.120	0.903**	0.422
Num_DD					-0.151	-0.050	0.122	0.271	0.126
Time_DD						0.96	-0.101	-0.112	-0.121
NumDN							0.329	0.651**	0.849**
Time_DN								0.183	0.064
Link									0.686**

*. Correlation is significant at the 0.05 level
**. Correlation is significant at the 0.01 level

As mentioned before, the communication type in individuals' working activities is important in the evaluation process. As seen in Table 3, 0.686 in level 0.01 reflects high positive correlation among the variable "link" (communication) and "the number of subordinates". Also, given that the variable "activity" is defined based on number of sent and receive letters, obviously there is significant correlation between "link" and "activity".

On the other hand, Correlation between the number of works that has been delayed (Num_DN) and "subordinates" and "link" is 0.849 and 0.651 respectively. When the number of links increases it can be attributed to the importance of the individual (occupation), and his performance affects other performance.

In Equation 4, the number of delays is considered as a negative factor on performance. Correlation, 0.577 shows that getting more works (received letters) can leads to more delay. But insignificant correlation between "activity" and "delayed works" partially reflect the relative nature of this relationship.

Accordingly, there are strong evidences that validate the results of this experiment; High correlation coefficients between many variables, justifiability and logicality of the high correlations show the validity of the results and the variables cover different aspects and results of employees' work.

In addition, in order to check the accuracy of the results achieved from the proposed evaluation model, a questionnaire is provided to assess individuals' efficiency and performance during these two months. To do so, a model named 360 degree model is applied. According to this model, each individual is assessed from four dimensions of supervisor, peer, subordinate employees and the customers/clients. Table 2 shows the results of professionals' assessment after the normalizing the data. As it can be seen in the table, user 3 is repeated two times in the table as that given individual occupies two positions for each of which the performance is assessed discretely.

SPSS is utilized to analyze the outcome of the proposed evaluation model. As seen in Table 4, 0.592 in level 0.01 reflects high positive correlation among the results by the system and professionals' assessment. On the other hand, the numbers are in such a way that it's not possible to put traditional evaluation absolutely aside. Table 5 also shows the mean and standard deviation of the results.

To have a better perspective of the results achieved, Figure 3-6 are presented. Figure 3 shows the comparison of the results in two month evaluation. Individual performance changes can be seen in this graph. Employees 8 and 12 have had significant improvement, while employee 5 and 14 haven't

Table 4. Analyzing the correlation of the results

	December	Expert
November	0.519*	0.537**
December		0.592**

*. Correlation is significant at the 0.05 level (1-tailed)
**. Correlation is significant at the 0.01 level (1-tailed)

Table 5. Mean and standard deviation of performance score

	Mean	Std. Deviation	N
November	0.0268	0.024	16
December	0.0521	0.0628	16
Expert	0.5477	0.3347	16

manifested any change. Figure 4 shows change in performance from another perspective. Based on the determined indices, user 1, as to being the admin, has approximately zero activity, which is reasonable.

In Figure 5, there is a comparison of individuals' ranking during the two month evaluation of the proposed method with the professional's opinions. As it can be seen, those individuals who are given higher scores by professionals, also have a higher rank in the system, that shows the correlation of the results. User 9 has a mean of approximately 0, as in the first and second month has acquired rank 10 and 15, and is given rank 14 based on the professionals' opinion.

For better comparison of the results of the system in Figure 6, the mean of individuals' rank during the two month is presented beside the professionals' opinion. As it is clarified in the graph, the values are so close to each other. This indicates the correlation of the results as previously mentioned. This Graph clearly shows that the results achieved by the system are acceptable and can be used as an evaluation system.

Figure 3. The comparison of November and December in METKA system

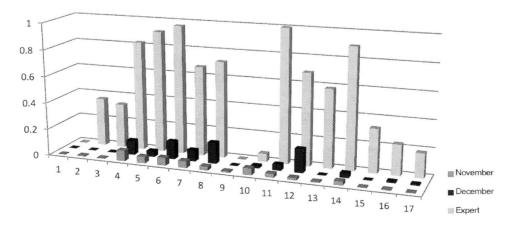

An Analytical Employee Performance Evaluation Approach

Figure 4. Individuals' performance changes during the two months

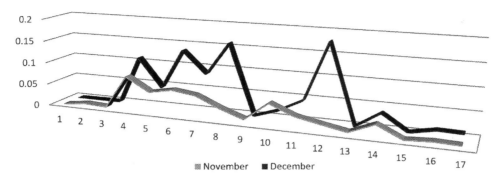

Figure 5. The comparison of the results of METKA system and the professionals

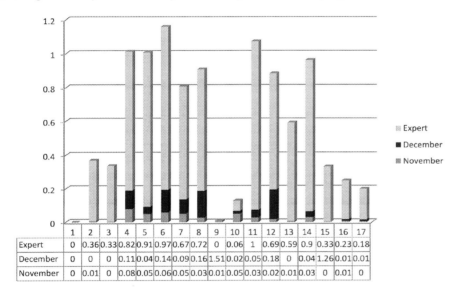

	1	2	3	4	5	6	7	8	9	10	11	12	13	14	15	16	17
Expert	0	0.36	0.33	0.82	0.91	0.97	0.67	0.72	0	0.06	1	0.69	0.59	0.9	0.33	0.23	0.18
December	0	0	0	0.11	0.04	0.14	0.09	0.16	1.51	0.02	0.05	0.18	0	0.04	1.26	0.01	0.01
November	0	0.01	0	0.08	0.05	0.06	0.05	0.03	0.01	0.05	0.03	0.02	0.01	0.03	0	0.01	0

Figure 6. The mean of the evaluation of the professionals and METKA system

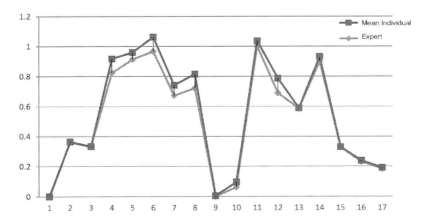

FUTURE RESEARCH DIRECTIONS

Based on this chapter, developing dynamic systems and produce tools based on computer techniques in order to apply human resources effectively in organizations and provide better decision making opportunities for managers and release a more accurate evaluation output to improve decision support systems are required. In order to continue the body of research in the scope of quantitative employee performance evaluation, investigating other types of existing data such as unstructured data can reflect more accurate results. By unstructured data, the reports that are provided in the stream of work are meant that need the web mining techniques. In this way, other indices such as working quality can also be measured. In addition, as to the possibility of sending useless letters in the system so that the individual pretends to be highly active, some information can be achieved by investigating the content of the letters as to whether they include formal words or not. Moreover, administering data mining methods on the data can be used to analyze and extract knowledge. Moreover, determining the working balance among different jobs can lead to a better assessment results.

CONCLUSION

Despite of various tools and methodologies proposed for evaluating employees' performance, still several studies still attest the fact that there is no complete and accurate data on the employee performance because performance indicators are usually not measurable. On the other hand according to these literatures, evaluation methods are often based on the opinions of the evaluators and their mindsets. Therefore, some problems such biases and lack of accuracy will follow. In addition while speaking of the employee performance evaluation, all attention is directed to performance evaluation in business sector and marketing, and the concentration is on the performance level of employees working in operational and physical departments of the organizations. In this regard, this study intends to eliminate the above problems by exploiting the capabilities of information systems. To do so, METKA system intended to evaluate individuals in two direct and indirect stages by using the relation. The results of evaluation showed that the achieved values based on the proposed approach are compatible with professionals' opinion and can be used as a discrete dimension for the evaluation of employee performance. Though, other evaluation methods cannot be set aside, as all indices cannot be measured quantitatively in the system, but can present a complete method together.

REFERENCES

Ahmed, I., Sultana, I., Paul, S. K., & Azeem, A. (2013). Employee performance evaluation: A fuzzy approach. *International Journal of Productivity and Performance Management*, *62*(7), 718–734. doi:10.1108/IJPPM-01-2013-0013

Andrés, R., Espinila, M., & Martínez, L. (2010). An Extended Hierarchical Linguistic Model for Managing Integral Evaluation. *International Journal of Computational Intelligence Systems*, *3*(4), 486–500. doi:10.1080/18756891.2010.9727716

Andrés, R., García-Lapresta, J., & Martínez, L. (2010). A multi-granular linguistic model for management decision-making in performance appraisal. *Soft Computing, 14*(1), 21–34. doi:10.1007/s00500-008-0387-8

Andrés, R., García-Lapresta, J. L., & González-Pachón, J. (2010). Performance appraisal based on distance function methods. *European Journal of Operational Research, 207*(3), 1599–1607. doi:10.1016/j.ejor.2010.06.012

Aqel, D., & Vadera, S. (2010). *A framework for employee appraisals based on sentiment analysis*. Paper presented at the 1st International Conference on Intelligent Semantic Web-Services and Applications, Amman, Jordan. doi:10.1145/1874590.1874598

Avazpour, R., Ebrahimi, E., & Fathi, M. R. (2013). A 360 Degree Feedback Model for Performance Appraisal Based on Fuzzy AHP and TOPSIS. *International Journal of Economy, Management and Social Sciences, 2*(11), 969–976.

Beheshti, H. M., & Lollar, J. G. (2008). Fuzzy logic and performance evaluation: Discussion and application. *International Journal of Productivity and Performance Management, 57*(3), 237–246. doi:10.1108/17410400810857248

Deming, W. E. (1986). Out of the Crisis. Cambridge, MA: Massachusetts Institute of Technology.

Dulebohn, J. H., & Johnson, R. D. (2013). Human resource metrics and decision support: A classification framework. *Human Resource Management Review, 23*(1), 71–83. doi:10.1016/j.hrmr.2012.06.005

Espinilla, M., Andrés, R., Mart'ınez, F. J., & Mart'ınez, L. (2013). A 360-degree performance appraisal model dealing with heterogeneous information and dependent criteria. *Information Sciences, 222*(0), 459–471. doi:10.1016/j.ins.2012.08.015

Espinilla, M., Mart'ınez, F. J. U., & Mart'ınez, L. (2010). *A Web based evaluation support system by integral performance appraisal*. Paper presented at the International Conference on Intelligent Systems and Knowledge Engineering (ISKE), Hangzhou. doi:10.1109/ISKE.2010.5680769

Fukui, N. (2015). Changes in Performance Appraisal in Japanese Companies. In N. Kambayashi (Ed.), *Japanese Management in Change* (pp. 141–157). Springer Japan. doi:10.1007/978-4-431-55096-9_10

Garengo, P., Nudurupati, S., & Bititci, U. (2007). Understanding the relationship between PMS and MIS in SMEs: An organizational life cycle perspective. *Computers in Industry, 58*(7), 677–686. doi:10.1016/j.compind.2007.05.006

Golec, A., & Kahya, E. (2007). A Fuzzy Model for Competency-Based Employee Evaluation and sSelection. *Computers & Industrial Engineering, 52*(1), 143–161. doi:10.1016/j.cie.2006.11.004

Gürbüz, T. (2010). Multiple Criteria Human Performance Evaluation Using Choquet Integral. *International Journal of Computational Intelligence Systems, 3*(3), 290–300. doi:10.1080/18756891.2010.9727700

Javadein, S. R. S., Ebrahimi, E., & Fathi, M. R. (2014). Ranking Employees based on their Career Orientation: Considering Protean and Boundaryless Career Attitudes. *Global Journal of Management Studies and Researches, 1*(3), 136–142.

Kempe, D., Kleinberg, J., & Tardos, E. (2003). *Maximizing the spread of influence through a social network*. Paper presented at the ninth ACM SIGKDD international conference on Knowledge discovery and data mining, Washington, DC. doi:10.1145/956750.956769

Lan, Y., & Li, S. (2010). *Design and realization of the research and development staff performance assessment system*. Paper presented at the Seventh International Conference on Fuzzy Systems and Knowledge Discovery (FSKD), Yantai, Shandong. doi:10.1109/FSKD.2010.5569414

Macwan, N., & Sajja, P. S. (2013). *Modeling performance appraisal using soft computing techniques: Designing neuro-fuzzy application*. Paper presented at the 2013 International Conference on Intelligent Systems and Signal Processing (ISSP), Gujarat doi:10.1109/ISSP.2013.6526943

Manoharan, T. R., Muralidharan, C., & Deshmukh, S. G. (2009). Employee Performance Appraisal Using Data Envelopment Analysis: A Case Study. *Research & Practice In Human Resource Management*, *17*, 17–34.

Manoharan, T. R., Muralidharan, C., & Deshmukh, S. G. (2011). An integrated fuzzy multi-attribute decision-making model for employees' performance appraisal. *International Journal of Human Resource Management*, *22*(3), 722–745. doi:10.1080/09585192.2011.543763

Manoharan, T. R., Muralidharan, C., & Deshmukh, S. G. (2012). A composite model for employees' performance appraisal and improvement. *European Journal of Training and Development*, *36*(4), 448–480. doi:10.1108/03090591211220366

Moon, C., Lee, J., & Lim, S. (2010). A performance appraisal and promotion ranking system based on fuzzy logic: An implementation case in military organizations. *Applied Soft Computing*, *10*(2), 512–519. doi:10.1016/j.asoc.2009.08.035

Nudurupati, S. S., Bititci, U. S., Kumar, V., & Chan, F. T. S. (2011). State of the art literature review on performance measurement. *Computers & Industrial Engineering*, *60*(2), 279–290. doi:10.1016/j.cie.2010.11.010

Osman, I., Berbary, L., Sidani, Y., Al-Ayoubi, B., & Emrouznejad, A. (2011). Data Envelopment Analysis Model for the Appraisal and Relative Performance Evaluation of Nurses at an Intensive Care Unit. *Journal of Medical Systems*, *35*(5), 1039–1062. doi:10.1007/s10916-010-9570-4 PMID:20734223

Park, J. H., Cho, H. J., & Kwun, Y. C. (2013). Extension of the VIKOR method to dynamic intuitionistic fuzzy multiple attribute decision making. *Computers & Mathematics with Applications (Oxford, England)*, *65*(4), 731–744. doi:10.1016/j.camwa.2012.12.008

Rezaei, A. R., Çelik, T., & Baalousha, Y. (2011). Performance measurement in a quality management system. *Scientia Iranica*, *18*(3), 742–752. doi:10.1016/j.scient.2011.05.021

Sepehrirad, R., Azar, A., & Sadeghi, A. (2012). *Developing a Hybrid Mathematical Model for 360-Degree Performance Appraisal: A Case Study*. Paper presented at the World Conference on Business, Economics and Management (BEM-2012), Antalya, Turkey. doi:10.1016/j.sbspro.2012.09.142

Waldman, D. A. (1994). The Contribution of Total Quality Management to a Theory of Work Performance. *Academy of Management Review*, *19*, 510–536.

Wu, Y.-J., & Hou, J.-L. (2010). An employee performance estimation model for the logistics industry. *Decision Support Systems*, *48*(4), 568–581. doi:10.1016/j.dss.2009.11.007

Xu, Z. (2004). Uncertain linguistic aggregation operators based approach to multiple attribute group decision making under uncertain linguistic environment. *Information Sciences*, *168*(1-4), 171–184. doi:10.1016/j.ins.2004.02.003

Xuan, J., Jiang, H., Ren, Z., & Zou, W. (2012). *Developer prioritization in bug repositories.* Paper presented at the Software Engineering (ICSE), 2012 34th International Conference on.

Yue, Z. (2013). An avoiding information loss approach to group decision making. *Applied Mathematical Modelling*, *37*(1–2), 112–126. doi:10.1016/j.apm.2012.02.008

Yue, Z. (2014a). TOPSIS-based group decision-making methodology in intuitionistic fuzzy setting. *Information Sciences*, *277*, 141–153. doi:10.1016/j.ins.2014.02.013

Yue, Z. (2014b). TOPSIS-based group decision-making methodology in intuitionistic fuzzy setting. *Information Sciences*.

Yusliza, M., & Ramayah, T. (2012). *Determinants of Attitude Towards E-HRM: an Empirical Study Among HR Professionals.* Paper presented at the International Conference on Asia Pacific Business Innovation and Technology Management. doi:10.1016/j.sbspro.2012.09.1191

KEY TERMS AND DEFINITIONS

Direct Performance: Determining the amount of performance individuals based on actual performance and effective performance.

Effective Performance: The performance that is calculated by the removal of the error and the delay of the actual performance.

Employees Ranking: A quantitative system to estimate contribution of each employee to achieve organizational goals and results during a period of time.

Indirect Performance: Determining the amount of manager performance based on their own performance and their subordinates as they are responsive about.

Information Systems: A complete system that is designed to produce, collection, organization, storage, retrieval and communication of information in an enterprise, organization or any other defined areas of society.

Non-Systematic Methods: Methods that evaluate relying on evaluators' opinions and calculating individuals' absolute performance score based on the mean of all opinions of evaluators or based on a proportion of input and output parameters.

Performance Measurement: A process that is used in organizations in order to evaluate employees' efficiency and productivity for planning Human Resource policies.

Systematic Methods: Web-based methods which, by using data warehouse and data collection algorithms, automatically collect detailed information on task completion, the portion of job content done, and professional inter-employee relationships in daily routine workplace activities through the designed systems.

Compilation of References

Abdullah, L., & Jamal, N. J. (2011). Determination of Weights for Health Related Quality of Life Indicators among Kidney Patients: A Fuzzy Decision Making Method. *Applied Research in Quality of Life*, *6*(4), 349–361. doi:10.1007/s11482-010-9133-3

Acar, A. Z., & Uzunlar, M. B. (2014). The Effects of Process Development and Information Technology on Time-based Supply Chain Performance. *Procedia: Social and Behavioral Sciences*, *150*, 744–753. doi:10.1016/j.sbspro.2014.09.044

Aczel, A. D., & Sounderpandian, J. (2009). *Complete business statistics*. Boston, MA: McGraw-Hill/Irwin.

Aeron, H., Kumar, A., & Janakiraman, M. (2010). Application of data mining techniques for customer lifetime value parameters: A review. *International Journal of Business Information Systems*, *6*(4), 530–546. doi:10.1504/IJBIS.2010.035744

Afshari, A. R., & Yusuff, R. M. (2012). Developing a structural method for eliciting criteria in project manager selection. *Proceedings of the 2012 International Conference on Industrial Engineering and Operations Management*.

Aghion, P., & Howitt, P. (1998). *Endogenous Economic Growth*. Cambridge, MA: The MIT Press.

Agilysys. (2015). *Stratton Warren System at Agilysys*. Retrieved February 12, 2016 from http://www.agilysys.com/solutions/by-products/inventory-procurement

Ahmed, F., Deb, K., & Jindal, A. (2013). Multi-objective optimization and decision making approaches to cricket team selection. *Journal of Applied Soft Computing*, *13*(201), 402-414.

Ahmed, I., Sultana, I., Paul, S. K., & Azeem, A. (2013). Employee performance evaluation: A fuzzy approach. *International Journal of Productivity and Performance Management*, *62*(7), 718–734. doi:10.1108/IJPPM-01-2013-0013

Al-Awadhi, S. A., & Konsowa, M. (2007). An application of absorbing Markov analysis to the student flow in an academic institution. *Kuwait Journal of Science and Engineering*, *34*(2A), 77-89.

Alchian, A. A., & Demsetz, H. (1972). Production, information costs and economic organization. *The American Economic Review*, *62*(5), 777–795.

Aldaihani, M. M., & Darwish, M. A. (2013). Optimal production and inventory decisions for supply chains with one producer and multiple newsvendors. *International Journal of Services and Operations Management.*, *15*(4), 430–448. doi:10.1504/IJSOM.2013.054884

Alfalla-Luque, R., Marin-Garcia, J. A., & Medina-Lopez, C. (2015). An analysis of the direct and mediated effects of employee commitment and supply chain integration on organisational performance. *International Journal of Production Economics*, *162*(0), 242–257. doi:10.1016/j.ijpe.2014.07.004

Altés, J. (2013). Papel de las tecnologías de la información y la comunicación en la medicina actual. *Seminarios de la Fundación Española de Reumatología*, *14*(2), 31–35. doi:10.1016/j.semreu.2013.01.005

Compilation of References

Amaratunga, D., Baldry, D., Sarshar, M., & Newton, R. (2002). Quantitative and Qualitative Research in the Built Environment: Application of "Mixed" Research Approach. *Work Study*, *51*(1), 17–31. doi:10.1108/00438020210415488

Anderson, J., & Gerbing, D. (1984). The Effect of Sampling Error on Convergence, Improper Solutions, and Goodness-of-Fit Indices for Maximum Likelihood Confirmatory Factor Analysis. *Psychometrika*, *49*(2), 155–173. doi:10.1007/BF02294170

Anderson, J., & Gerbing, D. (1988). Structural Equation Modeling in Practice: A Review and Recommended Two-Step Approach. *Psychological Bulletin*, *103*(3), 411–423. doi:10.1037/0033-2909.103.3.411

Andranovoch, G. (1995). *Developing community participation and consensus: The Delphi technique*. Los Angeles: Western Regional Extension.

Andrés, R., Espinila, M., & Martínez, L. (2010). An Extended Hierarchical Linguistic Model for Managing Integral Evaluation. *International Journal of Computational Intelligence Systems*, *3*(4), 486–500. doi:10.1080/18756891.2010.9727716

Andrés, R., García-Lapresta, J. L., & González-Pachón, J. (2010). Performance appraisal based on distance function methods. *European Journal of Operational Research*, *207*(3), 1599–1607. doi:10.1016/j.ejor.2010.06.012

Andrés, R., García-Lapresta, J., & Martínez, L. (2010). A multi-granular linguistic model for management decision-making in performance appraisal. *Soft Computing*, *14*(1), 21–34. doi:10.1007/s00500-008-0387-8

Andrienko, N., Andrienko, G., & Rinzivillo, S. (2015). Exploiting spatial abstraction in predictive analytics of vehicle traffic. *ISPRS International Journal of Geo-Information*, *4*(2), 591–606. doi:10.3390/ijgi4020591

Antonucci, Y. L., & Goeke, R. J. (2011). Identification of appropriate responsibilities and positions for business process management success: Seeking a valid and reliable framework. *Business Process Management Journal*, *17*(1), 127–146. doi:10.1108/14637151111105616

Aqel, D., & Vadera, S. (2010). *A framework for employee appraisals based on sentiment analysis*. Paper presented at the 1st International Conference on Intelligent Semantic Web-Services and Applications, Amman, Jordan. doi:10.1145/1874590.1874598

Armstrong, J. S., & Collopy, F. (1996). Competitor orientation: Effects of objectives and information on managerial decisions and profitability. *JMR, Journal of Marketing Research*, *33*(2), 188–199. doi:10.2307/3152146

Armstrong, M. (2006). *A handbook of human resource management practice*. London, UK: Kogan Page.

Arnott, D. (2004). Decision support systems evolution: Framework, case study and research agenda. *European Journal of Information Systems*, *13*(4), 247–259. doi:10.1057/palgrave.ejis.3000509

Arrow, K. (1969). Classificatory notes on the production and transmission of technical knowledge. *The American Economic Review*, *59*, 29–35.

Astrachan, C. B., Patel, V. K., & Wanzenried, G. (2014). A Comparative Study of Cb-Sem and Pls-Sem for Theory Development in Family Firm Research. *Journal of Family Business Strategy*, *5*(1), 116–128. doi:10.1016/j.jfbs.2013.12.002

Atlanta Regional Commission. (2010). Retrieved from: http://documents.atlantaregional.com/plan2040/docs/tp_PLAN2040RTP_072711.pdf

Atun, R. (2004). *What are the advantages and disadvantages of restructuring a health care system to be more focused on primary care services? Health Evidence Network (HEN)*. Copenhagen: Who Regional Office for Europe.

Austin, J., & Currie, B. (2003). Changing organisations for a knowledge economy: The theory and practice of change management. *Journal of Facilities Management*, *3*(2), 229–243. doi:10.1108/14725960410808221

Avazpour, R., Ebrahimi, E., & Fathi, M. R. (2013). A 360 Degree Feedback Model for Performance Appraisal Based on Fuzzy AHP and TOPSIS. *International Journal of Economy, Management and Social Sciences, 2*(11), 969–976.

Axelrod, R. (1984). *The Evolution of Cooperation.* Basic Books.

Ayton, P., Ferrel, W. R., & Stewart, T. R. (1999). Commentaries on 'The Delphi technique as a forecasting tool: Issues and analysis' by Rowe and Wright. *International Journal of Forecasting, 15*(4), 377–381. doi:10.1016/S0169-2070(99)00013-8

Azadeh, A., Gholizadeh, H., & Jeihoonian, M. (2013). A multi-objective optimisation model for university course timetabling problem using a mixed integer dynamic non-linear programming. *International Journal of Services and Operations Management., 15*(4), 467–481. doi:10.1504/IJSOM.2013.054886

Azvine, B., Cui, Z., Majeed, B., & Spott, M. (2007). Operational risk management with real-time business intelligence. *BT Technology Journal, 25*(1), 154–167. doi:10.1007/s10550-007-0017-5

Azvine, B., Cui, Z., & Nauck, D. D. (2005). Towards real-time business intelligence. *BT Technology Journal, 23*(3), 214–225. doi:10.1007/s10550-005-0043-0

Baars, H., Felden, C., Gluchowski, P., Hilbert, A., Kemper, H. G., & Olbrich, S. (2014). Shaping the next incarnation of business intelligence. *Business & Information Systems Engineering, 6*(1), 11–16. doi:10.1007/s12599-013-0307-z

Baars, H., & Kemper, H. (2008). Management support with structured and unstructured data: An integrated business intelligence framework. *Information Systems Management, 25*(2), 132–148. doi:10.1080/10580530801941058

Bagozzi, R. P., & Heatherton, T. F. (1994). A General Approach to Representingmultifaceted Personality Constructs: Application to State Self-Esteem. *Structural Equation Modeling, 1*(1), 35–67. doi:10.1080/10705519409539961

Bair, L. J., & Analytics, L. J. B. (2012). The Missing Link in Modeling and Simulation Validation. In *Proceedings of the 2012 Autumn AIAA Modeling and Simulation Technologies Conference.* doi:10.2514/mmst12

Ballou, R. H. (2004). Logistica Administracion de la Cadena de Suministro (E. Q. Duarte Ed. 5 ed.). Pearson Education

Bally Technologies. (2015). Retrieved February 9, 2016 from https://www.ballytech.com/Systems/Player-Tracking/CMS/CMP

Balogun, J., & Hope Hailey, V. (2003). *Exploring Strategic Change.* London: Prentice Hall.

Baltimore Metropolitan Council. (2011). *Plan It 2035.* Retrieved 5 October 2013 from: http://www.baltometro.org/plans/plan-it-2035>

Balzarova, M. A., Bamber, C. J., McCambridge, S., & Sharp, J. M. (2004). Key success factors in implementation of process-based management: A UK housing association experience. *Business Process Management Journal, 10*(4), 387–399. doi:10.1108/14637150410548065

Bansal, A. (2011). Trapezoidal fuzzy numbers (a, b, c, d): Arith-metic Behavior. *International Journal of Physical and Mathemat-ical Sciences, 2*(1), 39–44.

Baran, R., Zerres, C., & Zerres, M. (2008). Customer Relationship Management. *OSR Journal of Business and Management, 16*(1), 51-57. Retrieved February 9, 2016 from http://iosrjournals.org/iosr-jbm/papers/Vol16-issue1/Version-6/F016165157.pdf

Barker, B. (2014). *The News Leader.* Retrieved February 9, 2016 from http://the-news-leader.com/news%20local/2014/12/31/hard-rock-rocksino-northfield-park-celebrates-first-anniversary

Compilation of References

Barrett, D. J. (2002). Change communication: Using strategic employee communication to facilitate major change. *Corporate Communications*, *7*(4), 219–231. doi:10.1108/13563280210449804

Baumgartner, H., & Homburg, C. (1996). Applications of Structural Equation Modeling in Marketing and Consumer Research: A Review. *International Journal of Research in Marketing*, *13*(2), 139–161. doi:10.1016/0167-8116(95)00038-0

Bautista-Marín, M.-F., Rojo-Martín, M.-D., Pérez-Ruiz, M., Miranda-Casas, C., Martínez-Muñoz, P., & Navarro-Marí, J.-M. (2012). Implementation and monitoring of a quality management system based on the standard UNE-EN-ISO 15189 in a urine culture unit. *Clinical Biochemistry*, *45*(4), 374–377. doi:10.1016/j.clinbiochem.2011.12.016 PMID:22240066

Baxter, L. F., & Hirschhauser, C. (2004). Reification and representation in the implementation of quality improvement programmes. *International Journal of Operations & Production Management*, *24*(2), 207–224. doi:10.1108/01443570410514894

Baxter, P., & Jack, S. (2008). Qualitative case study methodology: Study design and implementation for novice researchers. *Qualitative Report*, *13*(4), 544–559.

Becker, J., Niehaves, B., Poppelbuß, J., & Simons, A. (2010). *Maturity models in IS research*. Paper presented at the European Conference on Information Systems (ECIS 2010), Pretoria, South Africa.

Becker, J., Knackstedt, R., & Poppelbuß, J. (2009). Developing maturity models for IT management: A procedure model and its application. *Business and Information Systems Engineering*, *1*(3), 213–222. doi:10.1007/s12599-009-0044-5

Becker, J., Kugeler, M., & Rosemann, M. (2003). *Process management: A guide for the design of business processes*. Berlin, Germany: Springer–Verlag. doi:10.1007/978-3-540-24798-2

Beheshti, H. M., & Lollar, J. G. (2008). Fuzzy logic and performance evaluation: Discussion and application. *International Journal of Productivity and Performance Management*, *57*(3), 237–246. doi:10.1108/17410400810857248

Beldona, S., & Tsatsoulis, C. (2010). Identifying buyers with similar seller rating models and using their opinions to choose sellers in electronic markets. *International Journal of Information and Decision Sciences*, *29*(1), 1–16. doi:10.1504/IJIDS.2010.029901

Bentler, P. M., & Chou, C. P. (1987). Practical Issues in Structural Modeling. *Sociological Methods & Research*, *16*(1), 78–117. doi:10.1177/0049124187016001004

Bentler, P. M., & Wu, E. (1995). *Eqs for Windows User's Guide*. Encino, CA: Multivariate Software.

Bentler, P. M., & Yuan, K.-H. (1999). Structural Equation Modeling with Small Samples: Test Statistics. *Multivariate Behavioral Research*, *34*(2), 181–197. doi:10.1207/S15327906Mb340203 PMID:26753935

Beran, T. N., & Violato, C. (2010). Structural Equation Modeling in Medical Research: A Primer. *BMC Research Notes*, *3*(1), 267. doi:10.1186/1756-0500-3-267 PMID:20969789

Berenson, M., Levine, D., Szabat, K. A., & Krehbiel, T. C. (2012). *Basic business statistics: Concepts and applications* (12th ed.). Englewood-Cliffs, NJ: Prentice Hall.

Berkman, T., Wagner, E. H., & Grumbach, K. (2002). Improving primary care for patients with chronic illness. *Journal of the American Medical Association*.

Bernard, A., & Jensen, J. (1999). Exceptional exporter performance: Cause, effect, or both? *Journal of International Economics*, *47*(1), 1–25. doi:10.1016/S0022-1996(98)00027-0

Berry, L. L., & Seiders, K. (2003). Innovations in access to care: A patient-centered approach. *Annals of Internal Medicine*, *139*(7), 568. doi:10.7326/0003-4819-139-7-200310070-00009 PMID:14530228

Berwick, D. M., & Nolan, T. W. (1998). Physicians as Leaders in Improving Health Care: A New Series in Annals of Internal Medicine. *Annals of Internal Medicine*, *128*(4), 289–292. doi:10.7326/0003-4819-128-4-199802150-00008 PMID:9471932

Beshtawi, M., & Jaaron, A. (2014). Change Management in Telecommunication Sector: A Managerial Framework. *Review of Contemporary Business Research*, *3*(1), 127–141.

Bessent, E. W., & Bessent, A. M. (1980). Student flow in a university department: Results of a Markov analysis. *Interfaces*, *10*(2), 52–59. doi:10.1287/inte.10.2.52

Bhamu, J., Khandelwal, A., & Sangwan, K. S. (2013). Lean manufacturing implementation in an automated production line: A case study. *International Journal of Services and Operations Management.*, *15*(4), 411–429. doi:10.1504/IJSOM.2013.054883

Bhat, S. (2008). The effect of ordering policies for a manufacturing cell changing to lean production. *Proceedings - Institution of Mechanical Engineers*, *222*(11), 1551–1560. doi:10.1243/09544054JEM1216

Bhatt, G. D., & Saad, G. H. (2005). Examining the relationship between business process improvement initiatives, information systems integration and customer focus: An empirical study. *Business Process Management Journal*, *11*(5), 532–558. doi:10.1108/14637150510619876

Bhuiyan, N. A. (2011). Framework for successful new product development. *Journal of Industrial Engineering and Management*, *4*(4), 746–770. doi:10.3926/jiem.334

Bi, H. H., & Zhao, J. L. (2004). Applying propositional logic to workflow verification. *Information Technology Management*, *5*(3/4), 293–318. doi:10.1023/B:ITEM.0000031583.16306.0f

Bilsel, R. U., Büyüközkan, G., & Ruan, D. (2006). A fuzzy preference-ranking model for a quality evaluation of hospital web sites. *International Journal of Intelligent Systems*, *21*(11), 1181–1197. doi:10.1002/int.20177

Biswas, P., & Sarker, B. R. (2008). Optimal batch quantity models for a lean production system with in-cycle rework and scrap. *International Journal of Production Research*, *46*(23), 6585–6610. doi:10.1080/00207540802230330

Bitkowska, A. (2015). The orientation of business process management toward the creation of knowledge in enterprises. *Human Factors and Ergonomics in Manufacturing & Service Industries*, *25*(1), 43–57. doi:10.1002/hfm.20533

Blair, J., & Presser, S. (1992). An Experimental Comparison of Alternative Pretest Techniques: A Note on Preliminary Findings'. *Journal of Advertising Research*, *32*, 2–5.

Blake, B. F., Neuendorf, K. A., & Valdiserri, C. M. (2005). Tailoring new websites to appeal to those most likely to shop online. *Technovation*, *25*(10), 1205–1215. doi:10.1016/j.technovation.2004.03.009

Bleistein, S. J., Cox, K., Verner, J., & Phalp, K. T. (2006). B-SCP: A requirements analysis framework for validating strategic alignment of organizational IT based on strategy, context, and process. *Information and Software Technology*, *48*(9), 846–868. doi:10.1016/j.infsof.2005.12.001

Blome, C., Schoenherr, T., & Eckstein, D. (2014). The impact of knowledge transfer and complexity on supply chain flexibility: A knowledge-based view. *International Journal of Production Economics*, *147*, 307-316. doi:10.1016/j.ijpe.2013.02.028

Blomström, M., Lipsey, R., & Zejan, M. (1996). Is fixed investment the key to economic growth? *The Quarterly Journal of Economics*, *111*(1), 269–276. doi:10.2307/2946665

Compilation of References

Böhm, C. A., Leone, H., & Henning, G. (2007). Industrial supply chains: Performance measures, metrics and benchmarks. In P. Valentin & A. Paul Şerban (Eds.), Computer Aided Chemical Engineering (Vol. 24, pp. 757-762). Elsevier.

Boje, D. M., Fedor, D. B., & Rowland, K. M. (1982). Myth making: A qualitative step in OD interventions. *The Journal of Applied Behavioral Science*, *18*(1), 17–28. doi:10.1177/002188638201800104

Bolch, G., Greiner, S., de Meer, H., & Trivedi, K. S. (1998). *Queueing networks and Markov chains*. New York, NY: Wiley. doi:10.1002/0471200581

Bollen, K. A. (2014). *Structural Equations with Latent Variables*. John Wiley & Sons.

Bonney, W. (2013). Applicability of business intelligence in electronic health record. *Procedia: Social and Behavioral Sciences*, *73*, 257–262. doi:10.1016/j.sbspro.2013.02.050

Boomsma, A. (1983). *On the Robustness of Lisrel (Maximum Likelihood Estimation) against Small Sample Size and Non-Normality*. Rijksuniversiteit Groningen.

Bosilj Vuksic, V., & Spremic, M. (2004). *Case study of PLIVA Pharmaceuticals Inc. – Aligning ERP system implementation with business process change*. Paper presented at the 26th International Conference on Information Technology Interfaces (ITI 2004), Cavtat, Croatia.

Bouhana, A., Abed, M., & Chabchoub, H. (2011). *An integrated Case_Based Reasoning and AHP method for personalized itinerary search*. LOGISTIQUA.

Bourlakis, M., Papagiannidis, P., & Fox, H. (2008). E-consumer behaviour: Past, present and future trajectories of an evolving retail revolution. *International Journal of E-Business Research*, *4*(3), 64–75. doi:10.4018/jebr.2008070104

Bradford DeLong, J., & Summers, L. (1991). Equipment Investment and Economic Growth. *The Quarterly Journal of Economics*, *106*(2), 445–502. doi:10.2307/2937944

Brailsford, S. C., Harper, P. R., Patel, B., & Pitt, M. (2009). An analysis of the academic literature on simulation and modelling in health care. *Journal of Simulation*, *3*(3), 130–140. doi:10.1057/jos.2009.10

Brannon, N. (2010). Business intelligence and E-discovery. *Intellectual Property & Technology Law Journal*, *22*(7), 1–5.

Bratton, J., & Gold, J. (1994). *Human Resource Management – Theory and Practice*. Houndmills, UK: The Macmillan Press Ltd.

Brent, A. C., Rogers, D. E., Ramabitsa-Siimane, T. S., & Rohwer, M. B. (2007). Application of the analytical hierarchy process to establish health care waste management systems that minimise infection risks in developing countries. *European Journal of Operational Research*, *181*(1), 403–424. doi:10.1016/j.ejor.2006.06.015

Briedenhann, J., & Butts, S. (2006). The application of the Delphi technique to rural tourism project evaluation. *Current Issues in Tourism*, *9*(2), 171–190. doi:10.1080/13683500608668246

Brockhaus, W. L., & Mickelsen, J. F. (1977). An analysis of prior Delphi applications and some observations on its future applicability. *Technological Forecasting and Social Change*, *10*(1), 103–110. doi:10.1016/0040-1625(77)90010-5

Brockhoff, K. (1975). The performance of forecasting groups in computer dialogue and face to face discussions. In H. Linstone & M. Turoff (Eds.), *The Delphi method: Techniques and applications*. London: Addison-Wesley.

Broersma, L., & van Dijk, J. (2005). Regional Differences in Labour Productivity in the Netherlands. *Tijdschrift voor Economische en Sociale Geografie*, *96*(3), 334–343. doi:10.1111/j.1467-9663.2005.00464.x

Browning, T. R., & Heath, R. D. (2009). Reconceptualizing the effects of lean on production costs with evidence from the F-22 program. *Journal of Operations Management*, *27*(1), 23–35. doi:10.1016/j.jom.2008.03.009

BRTF. (2005). *Regulation – Less is More. Reducing Burdens, Improving Outcomes. A BRTF Report to the Prime Minister*. London: Better Regulation Task Force.

Buchanan, L., & O'Connell, A. (2006). A brief history of decision making. *Harvard Business Review*, *84*(1), 32–40. PMID:16447367

Bucher, T., & Winter, R. (2006). Classification of business process management approaches: An exploratory analysis. *BIT – Banking and Information Technology*, *7*(3), 9–20.

Bucher, T., & Winter, R. (2009). Project types of business process management: Towards a scenario structure to enable situational method engineering for business process management. *Business Process Management Journal*, *15*(4), 548–568. doi:10.1108/14637150910975534

Buckingham, I. (2008). Communicating in a recession: Employee must engage with the brand during tough times. *Strategic Communication Management*, *12*(3), 7.

Bureau of Economic Analysis (BEA). (2006). *Gross domestic Product by State Estimation Methodology*. U.S. Dept. of Commerce. Retrieved 12 December 2013 from: http://www.bea.gov/regional/pdf/gsp/GDPState.pdf

Burt, D. N., Dobler, D. W., & Starling, S. L. (2003). World Class Supply Management (7th ed.). McGraw-Hill.

Büyüközkan, G., & Çifçi, G. (2012). A combined fuzzy AHP and fuzzy TOPSIS based strategic analysis of electronic service quality in healthcare industry. *Expert Systems with Applications*, *39*(3), 2341–2354. doi:10.1016/j.eswa.2011.08.061

Büyüközkan, G., Çifçi, G., & Güleryüz, S. (2011). Strategic analysis of healthcare service quality using fuzzy AHP methodology. *Expert Systems with Applications*, *38*(8), 9407–9424. doi:10.1016/j.eswa.2011.01.103

Byrne, B. (2006). *Structural Equation Modeling with Amos: Basic Concepts, Applications, and Programming* (2nd ed.). Lawrence Erlbaum.

Byrne, B. M. (2013). *Structural Equation Modeling with Lisrel, Prelis, and Simplis: Basic Concepts, Applications, and Programming*. Psychology Press.

Cabral, I. G. A., & Cruz-Machado, V. (2012). A decision-making model for Lean, Agile, Resilient and Green supply chain management. *International Journal of Production Research*, *50*(17), 4830–4845. doi:10.1080/00207543.2012.657970

Cabral, L. M. B. (2000). *Introduction to Industrial Organization*. Cambridge, MA: MIT Press.

Calabrese, A., Costa, R., & Menichini, T. (2013). Using Fuzzy AHP to manage Intellectual Capital assests: An application. *Journal of Expert Systems with Applications*, (40), 3747–3755.

Campbell, S. M., Roland, M. O., & Buetow, S. A. (2000). Defining quality of care. *Social Science & Medicine*, 51. PMID:11072882

Cantrill, J. A., Sibbald, B., & Buetow, S. (1996). The Delphi and nominal group techniques in health sciences research. *International Journal of Pharmacy Practice*, *4*(2), 67–74. doi:10.1111/j.2042-7174.1996.tb00844.x

Cao, J., Kambayashi, Y., Wang, H., & Zhang, Y. (2004). A global ticket-based access scheme for mobile users. *Information Systems Frontiers*, *6*(1), 35–46. doi:10.1023/B:ISFI.0000015873.35795.5e

Capaldo, A., & Giannoccaro, I. (2015). How does trust affect performance in the supply chain? The moderating role of interdependence. *International Journal of Production Economics*, *166*, 36–49. doi:10.1016/j.ijpe.2015.04.008

Carlberg, C. (2013). *Predictive analytics: Microsoft excel*. Pearson Education, Inc.

Carlsson, C., & Walden, P. (1995). AHP in political group decisions: A study in the art of possibilities. *Interfaces*, *25*(4), 14–29. doi:10.1287/inte.25.4.14

Carreira, C. (2006). *Firms' learning and selection and productivity growth over the economic cycle. Seminário GEMF*. Coimbra, Portugal: Grupo de Estudos Monetários e Financeiros. Facultade de Economia. Universidade de Coimbra.

Carroll, C., & Weil, D. (1994). Carnegie-Rochester Conference Series on Public Policy: Vol. 40. *Savings and growth: a reinterpretation* (pp. 133–192).

Carvalho, H., Cruz-Machado, V., & Tavares, J. G. (2012). A mapping framework for assessing supply chain resilience. *International Journal of Logistics Systems and Management*, *12*(3), 354–373. doi:10.1504/IJLSM.2012.047606

Castaneda, J. A., Rodriguez, M. A., & Luque, T. (2009). Attitudes' hierarchy of effects in online user behavior. *Online Information Review*, *33*(1), 7–21. doi:10.1108/14684520910944364

Caswell, H. (2013). Sensitivity analysis of discrete Markov chains via matrix calculus. *Linear Algebra and Its Applications*, *438*(4), 1727–1745. doi:10.1016/j.laa.2011.07.046

Cavaleri, S. A. (2008). Are learning organizations pragmatic? *The Learning Organization*, *15*(6), 474–481. doi:10.1108/09696470810907383

Cavana, R., Delahaye, B., & Sekaran, U. (2001). *Applied Business Research*. Wiley.

Chaffey, D., & Wood, S. (2005). *Business information management: Improving performance using information systems*. Englewood Cliffs, NJ: Prentice Hall.

Chan, A. P. C. (2002). Developing an expert system for project procurement. *Advances in Building Technology*, *2*, 1681–1688. doi:10.1016/B978-008044100-9/50207-2

Chan, F. T. S., & Kumar, V. (2009). Performance optimization of a legality inspired supply chain model: A CFGTSA algorithm based approach. *International Journal of Production Research*, *47*(3), 777–791. doi:10.1080/00207540600844068

Chang, C.-L., & Hsu, C.-H. (2009). Multi-criteria analysis via the VIKOR method for prioritizing land-use restraint strategies in the Tseng-Wen reservoir watershed. *Journal of Environmental Management*, *90*(11), 3226–3230. doi:10.1016/j.jenvman.2009.04.020 PMID:19482411

Chan, J. O. (2005). Toward a unified view of customer relationship management. *Journal of American Academy of Business*, *6*(1), 32–39.

Chaudhuri, S., Dayal, U., & Narasayya, V. (2011). An overview of business intelligence technology. *Communications of the ACM*, *54*(8), 88–98. doi:10.1145/1978542.1978562

Chen, X., & Siau, K. (2011). *Impact of business intelligence and IT infrastructure flexibility on competitive performance: An organizational agility perspective*. Paper presented at the International Conference on Information Systems (ICIS 2011), Shanghai, China.

Chen, C. C., Wu, J., Su, Y. S., & Yang, S. C. (2008). Key drivers for the continued use of RFID technology in the emergency room. *Management Research News*, *31*(4), 273–288. doi:10.1108/01409170810851348

Chen, H., Chiang, R., & Storey, V. (2012). Business intelligence and analytics: From big data to big impact. *Management Information Systems Quarterly*, *36*(4), 1165–1188.

Chen, I. J., & Paulraj, A. (2004). Towards a theory of supply chain management: The constructs and measurements. *Journal of Operations Management, 22*(2), 119–150. doi:10.1016/j.jom.2003.12.007

Chen, L., Gillenson, M. L., & Sherrell, D. L. (2002). Enticing online consumers: An extended technology acceptance perspective. *Information & Management, 39*(8), 705–719. doi:10.1016/S0378-7206(01)00127-6

Chen, S. H., & Hsieh, C. H. (1999). Graded mean integration representation of generalized fuzzy number. *Journal of Chinese Fuzzy Systems, 5*(2), 1–7.

Chen, S. J., & Lin, L. (2004). Modeling team member characteristics for the formation of multifunctional team in concurrent engineering. *IEEE Transactions on Engineering Management, 51*(2), 111–124. doi:10.1109/TEM.2004.826011

Chen, S.-H. (1985). Operations on fuzzy numbers with function principle. *Tamkang Journal of Management Sciences, 6*(1), 13–26.

Chen, T. M., & Barnett, G. A. (2000). Research on international student flows from a macro perspective: A network analysis of 1985, 1989 and 1995. *Higher Education, 39*(4), 435–453. doi:10.1023/A:1003961327009

Cheung, G. W. (2008). Testing Equivalence in the Structure, Means, and Variances of Higher-Order Constructs with Structural Equation Modeling. *Organizational Research Methods, 11*(3), 593–613. doi:10.1177/1094428106298973

Chou, D. C., Tripuramallu, H. B., & Chou, A. Y. (2005). BI and ERP integration. *Information Management & Computer Security, 13*(5), 340–349. doi:10.1108/09685220510627241

Chou, T. H., & Seng, J. L. (2012). Telecommunication e-services orchestration enabling business process management. *Transactions on Emerging Telecommunications Technologies, 23*(7), 646–659. doi:10.1002/ett.2520

Cho, V. (2006). A study of the roles of trusts and risks in information-oriented online legal services using an integrated model. *Information & Management, 43*(4), 502–520. doi:10.1016/j.im.2005.12.002

Christen, M., & Sarvary, M. (2007). Competitive pricing of information: A longitudinal experiment. *JMR, Journal of Marketing Research, 44*(February), 42–56. doi:10.1509/jmkr.44.1.42

Christie, C. A., & Barela, E. (2005). The Delphi technique as a method for increasing inclusion in the evaluation process. *The Canadian Journal of Program Evaluation, 20*(1), 105–122.

Ciccone, A. (2002). Agglomeration-Effects in Europe. *European Economic Review, 46*(2), 213–228. doi:10.1016/S0014-2921(00)00099-4

Ciccone, A., & Hall, R. (1996). Productivity and the Density of Economic Activity. *The American Economic Review, 86*(1), 54–70.

Cingano, F., & Schivardi, F. (2004). Identifying the Sources of Local Productivity Growth. *Journal of the European Economic Association, 2*(4), 720–742. doi:10.1162/1542476041423322

Ćirić, Z., & Raković, L. (2010). Change Management in Information System Development and Implementation Projects. *Management Information Systems, 5*(2), 23–28.

Clark, T. D., Jones, M. C., & Armstrong, C. P. (2007). The dynamic structure of management support systems: Theory development, research focus, and direction. *Management Information Systems Quarterly, 31*(3), 579–615.

Clayton, M. J. (1997). Delphi: A technique to harness expert opinion for critical decision-making tasks in education. *Educational Psychology: An International Journal of Experimental Educational Psychology, 17*(4), 373–386. doi:10.1080/0144341970170401

Clemens, B. (2006). Economic incentives and small firms: Does it pay to be green? *Journal of Business Research*, *59*(4), 492–500. doi:10.1016/j.jbusres.2005.08.006

Clibbens, N., Walters, S., & Baird, W. (2012). Delphi research: Issues raised by a pilot study. *Nurse Researcher*, *19*(2), 37–44. doi:10.7748/nr2012.01.19.2.37.c8907

Cohen, W., & Levinthal, D. (1990). Absorptive Capacity: A New Perspective on Learning and Innovation. Administrative Science Quarterly, 35(1), 128-152. doi:10.2307/2393553

E. Coiera, J. I. Westbrook, J. L. Callen, & J. Aarts (Eds.). (2007) Information Technology in Health Care 2007.*Proceedings of the 3rd International Conference on Information Technology in Health Care: Socio-technical Approaches*. IOS Press.

Contenti M., Mercurio G., Ricci F.L. & Serbanati L.D. (2010a). *Il processo di adozione del sistema LuMiR*. Deliverable progetto PreURT, n. PREURT31b_100.

Contenti, M., Mercurio, G., Ricci, F. L., & Serbanati, L. D. (2008). LuMIR: A Region-wide Virtual Longitudinal EHR. Proceedings of 9th International HL7 Interoperability Conference.

Contenti, M., Mercurio, G., Ricci, F. L., & Serbanati, L. D. (2010b). LuMiR: The Region-wide EHR-S in Basilicata. *Proceedings of 13th International Congress on Medical Informatics, Medinfo 2010*. IOS Press.

Cook, M. (2001). *Supply-Chain Survey*. Bain & Company. Retrieved from: http://www.bain.com/Images/BB_Supply-chain_survey.pdf

Côrte-Real, N., Ruivo, P., & Oliveira, T. (2014). The diffusion stages of business intelligence & analytics (BI&A): A systematic mapping study. *Procedia Technology*, *16*, 172–179. doi:10.1016/j.protcy.2014.10.080

Cramer, C. K., Klasser, K. D., Epstein, J. B., & Sheps, S. B. (2008). The Delphi process in dental research. *The Journal of Evidence-Based Dental Practice*, *8*(4), 211–220. doi:10.1016/j.jebdp.2008.09.002

Cronbach, L. (1951). Coefficient alpha and the internal structure of tests. *Psychometrika*, *16*(3), 297–334. doi:10.1007/BF02310555

Curran, J., & Blackburn, R. (2001). *Researching the Small Enterprise*. SAGE Publications Ltd.

Curtis, B., Kellner, M. I., & Over, J. (1992). Process modeling. *Communications of the ACM*, *35*(9), 75–90. doi:10.1145/130994.130998

D'Aprix, R. (2008). Providing a frame of references is key during times of change. In G. Ginsberg (Ed.), *Mecum's Top 50 Internal Communication Case Studies: An Anthology of Best-selling Research to Tackle Key Communication Issues* (pp. 123–127). London: Melcrum Publishing Limited.

Dajani, J. S., Sincoff, M. Z., & Talley, W. K. (1979). Stability and agreement criteria for the termination of Delphi studies. *Technological Forecasting and Social Change*, *13*(1), 83–90. doi:10.1016/0040-1625(79)90007-6

Dalkey, N. C., & Helmer, O. (1963). An experimental application of the Delphi method to the use of experts. *Management Science*, *9*(3), 458–467. doi:10.1287/mnsc.9.3.458

Dalkey, N. C., Rourke, D. L., Lewis, R., & Synder, D. (1972). *Studies in the quality of life: Delphi and decision making*. Lexington: Lexington Books.

Danaher, P. J., Bonfrer, A., & Dhar, S. (2008). The effect of competitive advertising interference on sales for packaged goods. *JMR, Journal of Marketing Research*, *45*(April), 211–225. doi:10.1509/jmkr.45.2.211

Davenport, T. H. (1993). *Process innovation*. Cambridge, MA: Harvard Business School Press.

Davenport, T. H. (2006). Competing on analytics. *Harvard Business Review, 84*(1), 99–107. PMID:16447373

Davenport, T. H., & Short, J. (1990). The new industrial engineering: Information technology and business process redesign. *MIT Sloan Management Review, 31*(4), 11–27.

Davis, D., & Cosenza, R. (2000). *Business Research for Decision Making*. Duxbury Press.

de Bruin, T., Rosemann, M., Freeze, R., & Kulkarni, U. (2005). *Understanding the main phases of developing a maturity assessment model*. Paper presented at the Australasian Conference on Information Systems (ACIS 2005), Sydney, Australia.

Debortoli, S., Muller, O., & vom Brocke, J. (2014). Comparing business intelligence and big data skills. *Business & Information Systems Engineering, 6*(5), 289–300. doi:10.1007/s12599-014-0344-2

Decreus, K., Poels, G., Kharbili, M. E., & Pulvermueller, E. (2010). Policy-enabled goal-oriented requirements engineering for semantic business process management. *International Journal of Intelligent Systems, 25*(8), 784–812. doi:10.1002/int.20431

Dehnad, K. (2012). *Quality control, robust design, and the Taguchi method*. Springer Science & Business Media.

Deighan, M., James, S. W., & Kinnear, T. C. (2006). *StratSim Marketing: The Marketing Strategy Simulation*. Charlottesville, VA: Interpretive Software, Inc.

Dekimpe, M. G., Franses, P. H., Hanssens, D. M., & Naik, P. A. (2007). Time series models in marketing. In Handbook of Marketing Decision Models. New York, NY: Springer Science + Business Media.

Delbecq, A. L., Gustafson, D. H., & de Ven, V. (1975). *Group techniques for program planning: A guide to nominal group and Delphi processes*. Glenview: Scott, Foresman and Company.

Deming, W. E. (1986). Out of the Crisis. Cambridge, MA: Massachusetts Institute of Technology.

den Hamer, P. (2005). *The organisation of business intelligence*. The Hague, The Netherlands: SDU Publishers.

Derian, J.-C., & Morize, F. (1973). Delphi in the assessment of research and development projects. *Futures, 5*(5), 469–483. doi:10.1016/0016-3287(73)90038-4

Dietz, T. (1987). Methods for analyzing data from Delphi panels: Some evidence from a forecasting study. *Technological Forecasting and Social Change, 31*(1), 79–85. doi:10.1016/0040-1625(87)90024-2

Disney, R., Haskel, J., & Heden, I. (2003). Restructuring and Productivity Growth in UK Manufacturing. *The Economic Journal, 113*(489), 666–694. doi:10.1111/1468-0297.t01-1-00145

Donohoe, H. M., & Needham, R. D. (2009). Moving best practice forward: Delphi characteristics, advantages, potential problems, and solutions. *International Journal of Tourism Research, 11*(5), 415–437. doi:10.1002/jtr.709

Dorfman, R., & Steiner, P. O. (1954). Optimal advertising and optimal quality. *The American Economic Review, 44*(5), 826–836.

Drejer, A., & Riis, J. O. (2000). New dimensions of competence development in industrial enterprises. *International Journal of Manufacturing Technology and Management, 2*(1/7), 660-882.

Dulebohn, J. H., & Johnson, R. D. (2013). Human resource metrics and decision support: A classification framework. *Human Resource Management Review, 23*(1), 71–83. doi:10.1016/j.hrmr.2012.06.005

Durham, D. R. (2002). Environmentally benign manufacturing: Current practice and future trends. *Journal of Operations and Manufacturing, 54*(5), 34–38.

Compilation of References

Dursun, M., Karsak, E. E., & Karadayi, M. A. (2010). Fuzzy Group Decision Making for the Assessment of Health-Care Waste Disposal Alternatives in Istanbul. World Academy of Science. *Engineering and Technology, 42*, 850–854.

Dursun, M., Karsak, E. E., & Karadayi, M. A. (2011). A Fuzzy MCDM Approach for Health-Care Waste Management. World Academy of Science. *Engineering and Technology, 49*, 720–726.

Dursun, M., Karsak, E. E., & Karadayi, M. A. (2011). A fuzzy multi-criteria group decision making framework for evaluating health-care waste disposal alternatives. *Expert Systems with Applications, 38*(9), 11453–11462. doi:10.1016/j.eswa.2011.03.019

Dursun, M., Karsak, E. E., & Karadayi, M. A. (2011). Assessment of health-care waste treatment alternatives using fuzzy multi-criteria decision making approaches. *Resources, Conservation and Recycling, 57*, 98–107. doi:10.1016/j.resconrec.2011.09.012

Dutta, A., Lee, H. L., & Whang, S. (2007). RFID and operations management: Technology, value and incentives. *Production and Operations Management, 16*(5), 646–655. doi:10.1111/j.1937-5956.2007.tb00286.x

Dutton, J. E., & Jackson, S. E. (1987). Categorizing strategic issues: Links to organizational action. *Academy of Management Review, 12*(1), 76–90.

Dym, C. L., & Ivey, E. S. (1980). *Principals of mathematical modeling*. New York, NY: Academic Press.

Earl, M. J., Sampler, J. L., & Short, J. E. (1995). Strategies for business process reengineering: Evidence from field studies. *Journal of Management Information Systems, 12*(1), 31–56. doi:10.1080/07421222.1995.11518069

Ebrahimnejad, S., Mousavi, S., Tavakkoli-Moghaddam, R., Hashemi, H., & Vahdani, B. (2012). A novel two-phase group decision making approach for construction project selection in a fuzzy environment. *Applied Mathematical Modelling, 36*(9), 4197–4217. doi:10.1016/j.apm.2011.11.050

Eckerson, W. W. (2006). *Performance dashboards: Measuring, monitoring, and managing your business*. Hoboken, NJ: John Wiley & Sons.

Economics, G. L. A. (2006). *Why distance doesn't die: Agglomeration and its benefits*. London: Greater London Authority.

Ekhosuehi, V. U., & Osagiede, A. A. (2012). On the transition matrix of the flow mechanism in a multi-echelon educational system. *International Journal of Operations Research, 9*(4), 209-219.

Ekhosuehi, V. U., & Osagiede, A. A. (2013). Benchmarking the enrolment structure of an educational system without exceeding the carrying capacity requirement. *Pakistan Journal of Statistics and Operation Research, 9*(3), 265–276. doi:10.18187/pjsor.v9i3.459

El Kadiri, S., Grabot, B., Thoben, K.-D., Hribernik, K., Emmanouilidis, C., von Cieminski, G., & Kiritsis, D. (2015). Current trends on ICT technologies for enterprise information systems. *Computers in Industry*. doi:10.1016/j.compind.2015.06.008

Elving, W. J. L. (2005). 'The role of communication in organisational change. *Corporate Communications, 10*(2), 129–138. doi:10.1108/13563280510596943

Engelbrecht, H. (2003). Human Capital and Economic Growth: Cross-Section Evidence for OECD Countries. *The Economic Record, 79*(Special Issue), S40–S51. doi:10.1111/1475-4932.00090

Eng, T. R. (2004). Population health technologies: Emerging innovations for the health of the public. *American Journal of Preventive Medicine, 26*(3), 237–242. doi:10.1016/j.amepre.2003.12.004 PMID:15026105

Espinilla, M., Mart'ınez, F. J. U., & Mart'ınez, L. (2010). *A Web based evaluation support system by integral performance appraisal.* Paper presented at the International Conference on Intelligent Systems and Knowledge Engineering (ISKE), Hangzhou. doi:10.1109/ISKE.2010.5680769

Espinilla, M., Andrés, R., Mart'ınez, F. J., & Mart'ınez, L. (2013). A 360-degree performance appraisal model dealing with heterogeneous information and dependent criteria. *Information Sciences*, *222*(0), 459–471. doi:10.1016/j.ins.2012.08.015

EU. (1995). *Green Paper on Innovation. Com (95) 688.* Brussels, Belgium: European Commission.

Felicio, J. A., Couto, E., & Caiado, J. (2014). Human capital, social capital and organizational performance. *Management Decision*, *52*(2), 350–364. doi:10.1108/MD-04-2013-0260

Field, A. (2009). *Discovering statistics using SPSS* (3rd ed.). Thousand Oaks, CA: Sage Publications.

Finch, B. J. (1999). Internet discussions as a source for consumer product involvement and quality information: An exploratory study. *Journal of Operations Management*, *17*(5), 535–556. doi:10.1016/S0272-6963(99)00005-4

Fisher, J. A., & Monahan, T. (2008). Tracking the social dimensions of RFID systems in hospitals. *International Journal of Medical Informatics*, *77*(3), 176–183. doi:10.1016/j.ijmedinf.2007.04.010 PMID:17544841

Fornell, C., & Larcker, D. (1981). Evaluating structural equation models with unobservable variables and measurement error. *JMR, Journal of Marketing Research*, *18*(1), 39–50. doi:10.2307/3151312

Foubister, V. (2000). Bench press: The technologist/technicians shortfall is putting the squeeze on laboratories nationwide. *CAP Today*, 84.

Frahm, J., & Brown, K. (2007). First steps: Linking change communication to change receptivity. *Journal of Organizational Change Management*, *20*(3), 370–387. doi:10.1108/09534810710740191

Frazer, L., & Lawley, M. (2000). *Questionnaire Design and Administration: A Practical Guide.* Wiley.

Freedman, D. (1971). *Markov chains.* San Francisco, CA: Holden-Day.

Friedman, T. (2006). *Gartner study on data quality shows that IT still bears the burden.* Stamford, CT: Gartner.

Fries, B. E. (1976). Bibliography of operations research in health-care systems. *Opns Res*, *24*(5), 801–814. doi:10.1287/opre.24.5.801

Fries, B. E. (1979). Bibliography of operations research in health-care systems: An update. *Opns Res*, *27*(2), 408–419. doi:10.1287/opre.27.2.408 PMID:10297447

Fuentes-Arderiu, X. (2006). Biological reference intervals and ISO 15189. *Clinica Chimica Acta*, *364*(1), 365–366. doi:10.1016/j.cca.2005.07.014 PMID:16139260

Fukui, N. (2015). Changes in Performance Appraisal in Japanese Companies. In N. Kambayashi (Ed.), *Japanese Management in Change* (pp. 141–157). Springer Japan. doi:10.1007/978-4-431-55096-9_10

Fumi, A., Scarabotti, L., & Schiraldi, M. M. (2013). The effect of slot-code optimisation on travel times in common unit-load warehouses. *International Journal of Services and Operations Management.*, *15*(4), 507–527. doi:10.1504/IJSOM.2013.054925

Garengo, P., Nudurupati, S., & Bititci, U. (2007). Understanding the relationship between PMS and MIS in SMEs: An organizational life cycle perspective. *Computers in Industry*, *58*(7), 677–686. doi:10.1016/j.compind.2007.05.006

Gebauer, J., & Schober, F. (2006). Information system flexibility and the cost efficiency of business processes. *Journal of the Association for Information Systems*, *7*(3), 122–145.

Compilation of References

Gefen, D., Straub, D., & Boudreau, M.-C. (2000). Structural Equation Modeling and Regression: Guidelines for Research Practice. *Communications of the Association for Information Systems*, *4*, 7.

Geissbauer, R., Roussel, J., Schrauf, S., & Strom, M. A. (2013). *Next Generation Supply Chains- Global Supply Chain Survey 2013*. Academic Press.

George, D., & Mallery, P. (2014). *IBM SPSS statistics 21 step by step: A simple guide and reference* (13th ed.). Boston, MA: Allyn and Bacon.

Geroski, P. A. (2000). Models of technology diffusion. *Research Policy*, *29*(4-5), 603–625. doi:10.1016/S0048-7333(99)00092-X

Gessner, G. H., & Volonino, L. (2005). Quick response improves returns on business intelligence investments. *Information Systems Management*, *22*(3), 66–74. doi:10.1201/1078/45317.22.3.20050601/88746.8

Gholizadeh, A.A., & Shekarian, E. (2012). A new approach on housing choice using fuzzy logic. *Tahghighat- E- Eghtesadi (University of Tehran)*, *47*(3), 65-84

Giannarou, L., & Zervas, E. (2014). Using Delphi technique to build consensus in practice. *International Journal of Business Science and Applied Management*, *9*(2), 1–18.

Giaquinta, M. (2009). *Mathematical analysis: An introduction to functions of several variables*. New York, NY: Springer. doi:10.1007/978-0-8176-4612-7

Gigerenzer, G. (2008). Why heuristics work. *Perspectives on Psychological Science*, *3*(: 1), 20–29. doi:10.1111/j.1745-6916.2008.00058.x PMID:26158666

Gilsdorf, J. W. (1998). Organizational rules on communicating: How employees are and are not learning the ropes. *Journal of Business Communication*, *35*(2), 173–201. doi:10.1177/002194369803500201

Girma, S. (2005). Absorptive Capacity and Productivity Spillovers from FDI: A Threshold Regression Analysis. *Oxford Bulletin of Economics and Statistics*, *67*(3), 281–306. doi:10.1111/j.1468-0084.2005.00120.x

Girma, S., Greenaway, D., & Kneller, R. (2004). Does Exporting Increase Productivity? A Microeconometric Analysis of Matched Firms. *Review of International Economics*, *12*(5), 855–866. doi:10.1111/j.1467-9396.2004.00486.x

Glaeser, E. L., Kallal, H. D., Scheinkman, J. A., & Shleifer, A. (1992). Growth in Cities. *Journal of Political Economy*, *66*, 1125–1152.

Gobakhloo, M. (2009). *It Adobtion in Manufacturing Smes*. University Putra Malaysia, Mechanical and Manufacturing Engineering.

Goldstein, D. G., & Gigerenzer, G. (2002). Models of ecological rationality: The recognition heuristic. *Psychological Review*, *109*(1), 75–90. doi:10.1037/0033-295X.109.1.75 PMID:11863042

Golec, A., & Kahya, E. (2007). A Fuzzy Model for Competency-Based Employee Evaluation and sSelection. *Computers & Industrial Engineering*, *52*(1), 143–161. doi:10.1016/j.cie.2006.11.004

González, J., De Boeck, P., & Tuerlinckx, F. (2008). A Double-Structure Structural Equation Model for Three-Mode Data. *Psychological Methods*, *13*(4), 337–353. doi:10.1037/a0013269 PMID:19071998

Goodman, C. M. (1987). The Delphi technique: A critique. *Journal of Advanced Nursing*, *12*(6), 729–734. doi:10.1111/j.1365-2648.1987.tb01376.x

Goodman, J., & Truss, C. (2004). The medium and the message: Communicating effectively during a major change initiative. *Journal of Change Management, 4*(3), 217–228. doi:10.1080/1469701042000255392

Gordon, T. J. (1994). *The Delphi method: Future research methodology*. Washington: AC/UNU Millennium Project.

Gottschalk, P. (2009). Maturity levels for interoperability in digital government. *Government Information Quarterly, 26*(1), 75–81. doi:10.1016/j.giq.2008.03.003

Gray, P. S., & Williamson. (2007). *The Research Imagination: An Introduction to Qualitative and Quantitative Methods*. Cambridge University Press.

Green Jr, K. W., Inman, R. A., Birou, L. M., & Whitten, D. (2014). Total JIT (T-JIT) and its impact on supply chain competency and organizational performance. *International Journal of Production Economics, 147*, 125-135. doi:10.1016/j.ijpe.2013.08.026

Greenaway, D., & Kneller, R. (2004). Exporting and Productivity in the United Kingdom. *Oxford Review of Economic Policy, 20*(3), 358–371. doi:10.1093/oxrep/grh021

Grefen, P., Mehandjiev, N., Kouvas, G., Weichhart, G., & Eshuis, R. (2009). Dynamic business network process management in instant virtual enterprises. *Computers in Industry, 60*(2), 86–103. doi:10.1016/j.compind.2008.06.006

Grewal, C. (2008). An initiative to implement lean manufacturing using value stream mapping in a small company. *International Journal of Manufacturing Technology and Management, 15*(3/4), 404–421. doi:10.1504/IJMTM.2008.020176

Griffith, R., Redding, S., & Van Reenen, J. (2003). R&D and absorptive capacity: From theory to data. *The Scandinavian Journal of Economics, 105*(1), 99–118. doi:10.1111/1467-9442.00007

Griliches, Z., & Regev, H. (1995). Firm Productivity in Israeli Industry: 1979-1988. *Journal of Econometrics, 65*(1), 175–203. doi:10.1016/0304-4076(94)01601-U

Grover, V., Jeong, S. R., Kettinger, W. J., & Teng, J. T. C. (1995). The implementation of business process reengineering. *Journal of Management Information Systems, 12*(1), 109–144. doi:10.1080/07421222.1995.11518072

Guibal, F., Iversen, L., Puig, L., Strohal, R., & Williams, P. (2009). Identifying the biologic closest to the ideal to treat chronic plaque psoriasis in different clinical scenarios: Using a pilot multi-attribute decision model as a decision-support aid. *Current Medical Research and Opinion, 25*(12), 2835–2843. doi:10.1185/03007990903320576 PMID:19916728

Gunasekaran, A., & Ngai, E. W. T. (2004). Information systems in supply chain integration and management. *European Journal of Operational Research, 159*(2), 269–295. doi:10.1016/j.ejor.2003.08.016

Gunasekaran, A., Patel, C., & McGaughey, R. E. (2004). A framework for supply chain performance measurement. *International Journal of Production Economics, 87*(3), 333–347. doi:10.1016/j.ijpe.2003.08.003

Gunhan, S., & Arditi, D. (2005). Factors affecting international construction. *Journal of Construction Engineering and Management, 131*(3), 273–282. doi:10.1061/(ASCE)0733-9364(2005)131:3(273)

Guo, P. (2010). One-shot decision approach and its application to duopoly market. *International Journal of Information and Decision Sciences, 2*(3), 213–232. doi:10.1504/IJIDS.2010.033449

Gupta, U. G., & Clarke, R. E. (1996). Theory and applications of the Delphi Technique: A bibliography (1975-1994). *Technological Forecasting and Social Change, 53*(2), 185–211. doi:10.1016/S0040-1625(96)00094-7

Gürbüz, T. (2010). Multiple Criteria Human Performance Evaluation Using Choquet Integral. *International Journal of Computational Intelligence Systems, 3*(3), 290–300. doi:10.1080/18756891.2010.9727700

Compilation of References

Guzel, O., & Guner, E. I. (2009). ISO 15189 Accreditation: Requirements for quality and competence of medical laboratories, experience of a laboratory I. *Clinical Biochemistry*, *42*(4), 274–278. doi:10.1016/j.clinbiochem.2008.09.011 PMID:19863920

Habul, A., & Pilav-Velic, A. (2010). *Business intelligence and customer relationship management*. Paper presented at the 32nd International Conference on Information Technology Interfaces (ITI 2010), Cavtat, Croatia.

Hair, B., Babin, Anderson, & Tabtam. (2006). Multivariate Data Analysis (6th ed.). Pearson International Edition.

Hair, J., Jr., Anderson, R., Tatham, R., & William, C. (1995). Multivariate Data Analysis. Englewood Cliffs, NJ: Prentice Hall.

Hair, J. F. Jr. (2007). Knowledge creation in marketing: The role of predictive analytics. *European Business Review*, *19*(4), 303–315. doi:10.1108/09555340710760134

Hair, J. F., Ringle, C. M., & Sarstedt, M. (2012). Editorial-Partial Least Squares: The Better Approach to Structural Equation Modeling? *Long Range Planning*, *45*(5-6), 312–319. doi:10.1016/j.lrp.2012.09.011

Hair, J., Anderson, R., & Tatham, R. (1987). *Multivariate data analysis*. New York, NY: Macmillan.

Hall, J. (2004). Business intelligence: The missing link in your CRM strategy. *DM REVIEW*, *14*, 36–40.

Hallowell, M. (2009). Techniques to minimize bias when using the Delphi method to quantify construction safety and health risks. *Proceedings of the Construction Research Congress 2009: Building a Sustainable Future*. doi:10.1061/41020(339)151

Hallowell, M., & Gambatese, J. (2010). Qualitative research: Application of the Delphi method to CEM research. *Journal of Construction Engineering and Management*, *136*, 99–107.

Hammer, M. (2007). The process audit. *Harvard Business Review*, *85*(4), 111–123. PMID:17432158

Hammer, M., & Champy, J. (2003). *Reengineering the corporation: A manifesto for business revolution*. New York, NY: Harper Business.

Hanafin, S., Brooks, A.-M., Carroll, E., Fitzgerald, E., Gabhainn, S. N., & Sixsmith, J. (2007). Achieving consensus in developing a national set of child well-being indicators. *Social Indicators Research*, *80*(1), 79–104. doi:10.1007/s11205-006-9022-1

Hanssens, D. M., Parsons, L. J., & Schultz, R. L. (2001). *Market Response Models and Econometric Time Series Analysis*. Boston, MA: Kluwer Academic Publishers.

Harding, W. (2003). BI crucial to making the right decision. *Financial Executive*, *19*(2), 49–50.

Harmon, P. (2007). *Business process change: A guide for business managers and BMP and Six Sigma professionals*. Amsterdam, The Netherlands: Elsevier/Morgan Kaufmann Publishers.

Harris, S. (2007). Supporting leaders through change. *Strategic Communication Management*, *11*(4), 12.

Hart, S. (1987). The Use of the Survey in Industrial Market Research. *Journal of Marketing Management*, *3*(1), 25–38. doi:10.1080/0267257X.1987.9964025

Haslett, J., & Hayes, K. (1998). Residuals for the linear model with general covariance structure. *Journal of the Royal Statistical Society. Series B, Statistical Methodology*, *60*(1), 201–215. doi:10.1111/1467-9868.00119

Hassini, E., Surti, C., & Searcy, C. (2012). A literature review and a case study of sustainable supply chains with a focus on metrics. *International Journal of Production Economics*, *140*(1), 69–82. doi:10.1016/j.ijpe.2012.01.042

Hasson, F., Keeney, S., & McKenna, H. (2000). Research guidelines for the Delphi survey technique. *Journal of Advanced Nursing*, *33*(4), 1008–1015.

Hattie, J., & Timperley, H. (2007). The Power of Feedback. *The Journal of Educational Research*, *77*(1), 81–112.

Helo, P., Anussornnitisarn, P., & Phusavat, K. (2008). Expectation and reality in ERP implementation: Consultant and solution provider perspective. *Industrial Management & Data Systems*, *108*(8), 1045–1158. doi:10.1108/02635570810904604

Hermida, J. M., Melia, S., Montoyo, A., & Gomez, J. (2013). Applying model-driven engineering to the development of rich Internet applications for business intelligence. *Information Systems Frontiers*, *15*(3), 411–431. doi:10.1007/s10796-012-9402-9

Herrmann, T., & Walter, T. (1998). *The relevance of showcases for the participative improvement of business processes and workflow management*. Paper presented at the Participatory Design Conference (PDC 1998), Seattle, WA.

Hervani, A. A., Helms, M. M., & Sarkis, J. (2005). Performance measurement for green supply chain management. *Benchmarking: An International Journal*, *12*(4), 330–353. doi:10.1108/14635770510609015

Hess, P. W., & Siciliano, J. (1996). *Management: Responsibility for performance*. New York: McGraw-Hill.

Hilmola, O.-P. (2010). Analysing global railway passenger transport through two-staged efficiency model. *International Journal of Information and Decision Sciences*, *2*(3), 273–284. doi:10.1504/IJIDS.2010.033451

Hilton, R. J., & Sohal, A. (2012). A conceptual model for the successful deployment of Lean Six Sigma. *International Journal of Quality & Reliability Management*, *29*(1), 54–70. doi:10.1108/02656711211190873

Hirschheim, R., Schwarz, A., & Todd, P. (2006). A marketing maturity model for IT: Building a customer-centric IT organization. *IBM Systems Journal*, *45*(1), 181–199. doi:10.1147/sj.451.0181

Hirshleifer, D., Low, A., & Teoh, S. H. (2012). Are overconfident CEOs better innovators? *The Journal of Finance*, *67*(4), 1457–1498. doi:10.1111/j.1540-6261.2012.01753.x

Hocevar, B., & Jaklic, J. (2010). Assessing benefits of business intelligence systems: A case study. *Management: Journal of Contemporary Management Issues*, *15*(1), 87–119.

Hoejmose, S., Brammer, S., & Millington, A. (2012). "Green" supply chain management: The role of trust and top management in B2B and B2C markets. *Industrial Marketing Management*, *41*(4), 609–620. doi:10.1016/j.indmarman.2012.04.008

Holey, A. H., Feeley, J. L., Dixon, J., & Whittaker, V. J. (2007). An exploration of the use of simple statistics to measure consensus and stability in Delphi studies. *BMC Medical Research Methodology*, *7*(1), 52. doi:10.1186/1471-2288-7-52

Hollander, M. C., Sage, J. M., Greenler, A. J., Pendl, J., Avcin, T., Espada, G., & Brunner, H. I. et al. (2013). International consensus for provisions of quality-driven care in childhood-onset systemic lupus erythematosus. *Arthritis Care and Research*, *65*(9), 1416–1423. doi:10.1002/acr.21998

Holtz, S. (2004). *Corporate Conversations: A Guide to Crafting Effective and Appropriate Internal Communications*. New York: AMACOM.

Holtz, S. (2005). The impact of new technologies on internal communications. *Strategic Communication Management*, *10*(1), 22–25.

Hopken, W., Fuchs, M., Keil, D., & Lexhagen, M. (2015). Business intelligence for cross-process knowledge extraction at tourism destinations. *Information Technology & Tourism*, *15*(2), 101–130. doi:10.1007/s40558-015-0023-2

Compilation of References

Houghton, R., El Sawy, O. A., Gray, P., Donegan, C., & Joshi, A. (2004). Vigilant information systems for managing enterprises in dynamic supply chains: Real-time dashboards at western digital. *MIS Quarterly Executive, 3*(1), 19–35.

Houy, C., Fettke, P., & Loos, P. (2010). Empirical research in business process management: Analysis of an emerging field of research. *Business Process Management Journal, 16*(4), 619–661. doi:10.1108/14637151011065946

Hsu, C.-C., & Sandford, A. B. (2007). Minimizing non-response in the Delphi process: How to respond to non-response. *Practical Assessment, Research & Evaluation, 12*(17), 62–78.

Hu, L. t., & Bentler, P. M. (1999). Cutoff Criteria for Fit Indexes in Covariance Structure Analysis: Conventional Criteria Versus New Alternatives. *Structural Equation Modeling: A Multidisciplinary Journal, 6*, 1-55.

Hu, G., Wang, L., Fetch, S., & Bidanda, B. (2008). A multi-objective model for project portfolio selection to implement lean and Six Sigma concepts. *International Journal of Production Research, 46*(23), 6611–6648. doi:10.1080/00207540802230363

Hughes, M., Price, R., & Marrs, D. (1986). Linking Theory Construction and Theory Testing: Models with Multiple Indicators of Latent Variables. *Academy of Management Review, 11*, 128–144.

Hu, L.-, & Bentler, P. M. (1998). Fit Indices in Covariance Structure Modeling: Sensitivity to Underparameterized Model Misspecification. *Psychological Methods, 3*(4), 424–453. doi:10.1037/1082-989X.3.4.424

Hung, H.-L., Altschuld, J. W., & Lee, Y.-F. (2008). Methodological and conceptual issues confronting a cross-country Delphi study of education program evaluation. *Evaluation and Program Planning, 31*(2), 191–198. doi:10.1016/j.evalprogplan.2008.02.005

Hung, R. Y. (2006). Business process management as competitive advantage: A review and empirical study. *Total Quality Management, 17*(1), 21–40. doi:10.1080/14783360500249836

Hurley, R. (1999). Qualitative Research and the Profound Grasp of the Obvious. *Health Services Research, 34*, 1119. PMID:10591276

Ifinedo, P., & Nahar, N. (2009). Interactions between contingency, organizational IT factors, and ERP success. *Industrial Management & Data Systems, 109*(1), 118–126. doi:10.1108/02635570910926627

Igboanugo, A. C., & Edokpia, O. R. (2014). A Markovian study of manpower planning in the soft-drink industry in Nigeria. *Nigerian Journal of Technology, 33*(4), 547–552. doi:10.4314/njt.v33i4.15

Il Progetto, L. U. M. I. R. (n.d.). Retrieved on 01/07/2015 at: http://www.sanitaelettronica.cnr.it/lumir/

Imran, R., Majeed, M., & Ayub, A. (2015). Impact of organizational justice, job security and job satisfaction on organizational productivity. *Journal of Economics. Business and Management, 3*(9), 840–845. doi:10.7763/JOEBM.2015.V3.295

Inmon, W. H., Imhoff, C., & Sousa, R. (2001). *Corporate information factory*. New York, NY: John Wiley & Sons.

Isik, Z. (2009). *A Conceptual Performance Measurment Framework for Construction Industry*. Middle East Technical University.

Isik, O., Jones, M. C., & Sidorova, A. (2011). Business intelligence (BI) success and the role of BI capabilities. *Intelligent Systems in Accounting, Finance & Management, 18*(4), 161–176. doi:10.1002/isaf.329

Isik, O., Jones, M. C., & Sidorova, A. (2013). Business intelligence success: The roles of BI capabilities and decision environments. *Information & Management, 50*(1), 13–23. doi:10.1016/j.im.2012.12.001

Iversen, J., Nielsen, P. A., & Norbjerg, J. (1999). Situated assessment of problems in software development. *The Data Base for Advances in Information Systems, 30*(2), 66–81. doi:10.1145/383371.383376

Jacobs, J. (1969). *The economy of cities*. New York: Random House.

Jannoo, Z., Yap, B., Auchoybur, N., & Lazim, M. (2014). The Effect of Nonnormality on Cb-Sem and Pls-Sem Path Estimates. *International Journal of Mathematical, Computational, Natural and Physical Engineering, 8*, 6.

Janz, B. D., Pitts, M. G., & Otondo, R. F. (2005). Information systems and health care II: Back to the future with RFID: Lessons learned–some old, some new. *Communications of the Association for Information Systems, 15*(1), 132–148.

Javadein, S. R. S., Ebrahimi, E., & Fathi, M. R. (2014). Ranking Employees based on their Career Orientation: Considering Protean and Boundaryless Career Attitudes. *Global Journal of Management Studies and Researches, 1*(3), 136–142.

Jensen, M. C. (1986). Agency costs of free cash flow, corporate finance, and takeovers. *The American Economic Review, 76*(2), 323–339.

Jensen, M. C., & Meckling, W. H. (1976). Theory of the firm: Managerial behavior, agency costs and ownership structure. *Journal of Financial Economics, 3*(4), 305–360. doi:10.1016/0304-405X(76)90026-X

Jerrard, R. N., Barnes, N., & Reid, A. (2008). Design, risk and new product development in five small creative companies. *International Journal of Design, 2*(1), 21–30.

Jerry Ho, W.-R., Tsai, C.-L., Tzeng, G.-H., & Fang, S.-K. (2011). Combined DEMATEL technique with a novel MCDM model for exploring portfolio selection based on CAPM. *Expert Systems with Applications, 38*(1), 16–25. doi:10.1016/j.eswa.2010.05.058

Jeston, J., & Nelis, J. (2008). *Business process management: Practical guidelines to successful Implementations*. Amsterdam, The Netherlands: Elsevier.

Johansson, B., & Sudzina, F. (2008). ERP systems and open source: An initial review and some implications for SMEs. *Journal of Enterprise Information Management, 21*(6), 649–659. doi:10.1108/17410390810911230

Jöreskog, K. G. (1982). The Lisrel Approach to Causal Model-Building in the Social Sciences. *Systems Under Indirect Observation, 1*, 81-100.

Jöreskog, K. G., & Sörbom, D. (1993). *Lisrel 8: Structural Equation Modeling with the Simplis Command Language*. Scientific Software International.

Jorgenson, D. (2005). Accounting for Growth in the Information Age. In P. Aghion & S. Durlauf (Eds.), *Handbook of Economic Growth* (vol. 1, pp. 743–815). Amsterdam: North-Holland. doi:10.1016/S1574-0684(05)01010-5

Joseph, K., & Richardson, V. J. (2002). Free cash flow, agency costs, and the affordability method of advertising budgeting. *Journal of Marketing, 66*(1), 94–107. doi:10.1509/jmkg.66.1.94.18453

Joshi, A., & Hanssens, D. M. (2010). The direct and indirect effects of advertising spending on firm value. *Journal of Marketing, 74*(January), 20–33. doi:10.1509/jmkg.74.1.20

Jourdan, Z., Rainer, R. K., & Marshall, T. E. (2008). Business intelligence: An analysis of the literature. *Information Systems Management, 25*(2), 121–131. doi:10.1080/10580530801941512

Jung, J., Choi, I., & Song, M. (2007). An integration architecture for knowledge management systems and business process management systems. *Computers in Industry, 58*(1), 21–34. doi:10.1016/j.compind.2006.03.001

Justinek, G., & Sedej, T. (2011). Knowledge sharing as a part of internal communication within internationalized companies. In *Knowledge as Business Opportunity: Proceedings of the Management, Knowledge and Learning International Conference 2011*. International School for Social and Business Studies.

Kagermann, H., Osterle, H., & Jordan, J. M. (2010). *IT-driven business models*. Hoboken, NJ: John Wiley & Sons.

Kaiser, H. (2010). *Mathematical programming for agricultural, environmental, and resource economics*. Hoboken, NJ: Wiley.

Kalaian, S. A., & Kasim, R. M. (2012). Terminating sequential Delphi survey data collection. *Practical Assessment, Research & Evaluation, 17*(5), 1–9.

Kalaian, S. A., & Kasim, R. M. (2015). Predictive analytics. In M. Tavana, S. B. Zhou, & S. K. Puranam (Eds.), *Handbook of research on organizational transformations through big data analytics* (pp. 12–29). Hershey, PA: IGI Global.

Kalaian, S. A., & Kasim, R. M. (2016). Analyzing quantitative data. In J. E. Jones & M. L. Baran (Eds.), *Mixed methods research for improved scientific study*. Hershey, PA: IGI Global. doi:10.4018/978-1-5225-0007-0.ch008

Kalla, H. (2005). *Integrated internal communications: a multidisciplinary perspective*. Corporate.

Kalra, A., & Soberman, D. A. (2008). The curse of competitiveness: How advice from experienced colleagues and training can hurt marketing. *Journal of Marketing, 72*(3), 32–47. doi:10.1509/jmkg.72.3.32

Kalra, J. (2004). Medical errors: Impact on clinical laboratories and other critical areas. *Clinical Biochemistry, 37*(12), 1052–1062. doi:10.1016/j.clinbiochem.2004.08.009 PMID:15589810

Kamakura, W., Mela, C. F., Ansari, A., Bodapati, A., Fader, P., Iyengar, R., & Wilcox, R. et al. (2005). Choice models and customer relationship management. *Marketing Letters, 16*(4), 279–291. doi:10.1007/s11002-005-5892-2

Kaplan, R. S., & Norton, D. P. (1996). *The balanced scorecard*. Boston, MA: Harvard Business School Press.

Karami, A. (2005). *Senior Managers and Strategic Management Process*. University of Bradford, Management School.

Karami, A. (2007). *Strategy Formulation in Entrepreneurial Firms*. Ashgate Pub Co.

Karim, J., Sommers, T. M., & Bhattacherjee, A. (2007). The impact of ERP implementation on business process outcomes: A factor-based study. *Journal of Management Information Systems, 24*(1), 101–134. doi:10.2753/MIS0742-1222240103

Kasemsap, K. (2015g). Implementing business intelligence in contemporary organizations. In A. Haider (Ed.), Business technologies in contemporary organizations: Adoption, assimilation, and institutionalization (pp. 177–192). Hershey, PA: IGI Global. doi:10.4018/978-1-4666-6623-8.ch008

Kasemsap, K. (2015a). The role of business process reengineering in the modern business world. In A. Singh (Ed.), *Achieving enterprise agility through innovative software development* (pp. 87–114). Hershey, PA: IGI Global. doi:10.4018/978-1-4666-8510-9.ch005

Kasemsap, K. (2015b). Implementing enterprise resource planning. In M. Khosrow-Pour (Ed.), *Encyclopedia of information science and technology* (3rd ed., pp. 798–807). Hershey, PA: IGI Global. doi:10.4018/978-1-4666-5888-2.ch076

Kasemsap, K. (2015c). The role of information system within enterprise architecture and their impact on business performance. In M. Wadhwa & A. Harper (Eds.), *Technology, innovation, and enterprise transformation* (pp. 262–284). Hershey, PA: IGI Global. doi:10.4018/978-1-4666-6473-9.ch012

Kasemsap, K. (2015d). The roles of information technology and knowledge management in project management metrics. In G. Jamil, S. Lopes, A. Malheiro da Silva, & F. Ribeiro (Eds.), *Handbook of research on effective project management through the integration of knowledge and innovation* (pp. 332–361). Hershey, PA: IGI Global. doi:10.4018/978-1-4666-7536-0.ch018

Kasemsap, K. (2015e). The role of radio frequency identification in modern libraries. In S. Thanuskodi (Ed.), *Handbook of research on inventive digital tools for collection management and development in modern libraries* (pp. 361–385). Hershey, PA: IGI Global. doi:10.4018/978-1-4666-8178-1.ch021

Kasemsap, K. (2015f). The role of business analytics in performance management. In M. Tavana & K. Puranam (Eds.), *Handbook of research on organizational transformations through big data analytics* (pp. 126–145). Hershey, PA: IGI Global. doi:10.4018/978-1-4666-7272-7.ch010

Kasemsap, K. (2015h). The role of data mining for business intelligence in knowledge management. In A. Azevedo & M. Santos (Eds.), *Integration of data mining in business intelligence systems* (pp. 12–33). Hershey, PA: IGI Global. doi:10.4018/978-1-4666-6477-7.ch002

Kasemsap, K. (2016a). The roles of business process modeling and business process reengineering in e-government. In J. Martins & A. Molnar (Eds.), *Handbook of research on innovations in information retrieval, analysis, and management* (pp. 401–430). Hershey, PA: IGI Global. doi:10.4018/978-1-4666-8833-9.ch015

Kasemsap, K. (2016b). The roles of lifelong learning and knowledge management in global higher education. In P. Ordóñez de Pablos & R. Tennyson (Eds.), *Impact of economic crisis on education and the next-generation workforce* (pp. 71–100). Hershey, PA: IGI Global. doi:10.4018/978-1-4666-9455-2.ch004

Kasemsap, K. (2016c). Advocating entrepreneurship education and knowledge management in global business. In N. Baporikar (Ed.), *Handbook of research on entrepreneurship in the contemporary knowledge-based global economy* (pp. 313–339). Hershey, PA: IGI Global. doi:10.4018/978-1-4666-8798-1.ch014

Kaynak, E., Bloom, J., & Leibold, M. (1994). Using the Delphi technique to predict future tourism potential. *Marketing Intelligence & Planning*, *12*(7), 18–29. doi:10.1108/02634509410065537

Keeney, S., Hasson, F., & McKenna, H. P. (2001). A critical review of the Delphi technique as a research methodology for nursing. *International Journal of Nursing Studies*, *38*(2), 195–200. doi:10.1016/S0020-7489(00)00044-4

Keil, S. K., Reibstein, D., & Wittink, D. R. (2001). The impact of business objectives and time horizon of performance evaluation on pricing behavior. *International Journal of Research in Marketing*, *18*(1-2), 67–81. doi:10.1016/S0167-8116(01)00027-1

Kelloway, E. (1998). *Using Lisrel for Structural Equation Modeling: A Researcher's Guide*. Sage Publications, Inc.

Kempe, D., Kleinberg, J., & Tardos, E. (2003). *Maximizing the spread of influence through a social network*. Paper presented at the ninth ACM SIGKDD international conference on Knowledge discovery and data mining, Washington, DC. doi:10.1145/956750.956769

Kerlinger, F. N. (1973). Foundations of behavioral research. Holt, Reinhart, and Winston.

Ketkar, M., & Vaidya, O. S. (2012). Study of Emerging Issues in Supply Risk Management in India. *Procedia: Social and Behavioral Sciences*, *37*(0), 57–66. doi:10.1016/j.sbspro.2012.03.275

Khalil, O. (1997). Implications for the role of information systems in a business process reengineering environment. *Information Resources Management Journal*, *10*(1), 36–43. doi:10.4018/irmj.1997010103

Khan, M. K., Sohail, M., Aamir, M., Chowdhry, B. S., & Hyder, S. I. (2014). Web support system for business intelligence in small and medium enterprises. *Wireless Personal Communications*, *76*(3), 535–548. doi:10.1007/s11277-014-1723-1

Khan, R. N. (2004). *Business process management: A practical guide*. Tampa, FL: Meghan–Kiffer Press.

Compilation of References

Kim, D., & Cavusgil, E. (2009). The impact of supply chain integration on brand equity. *Journal of Business and Industrial Marketing*, *24*(7), 496–505. doi:10.1108/08858620910986730

Kim, S. W. (2009). An investigation on the direct and indirect effect of supply chain integration on firm performance. *International Journal of Production Economics*, *119*(2), 328–346. doi:10.1016/j.ijpe.2009.03.007

Kirzner, I. (1973). *Competition and Entrepreneurship*. University of Chicago Press.

Kitchen, J. P., & Daly, F. (2002). Internal communication during the change management. *Corporate Communications:International Journal (Toronto, Ont.)*, *7*(1), 46–53.

Kleinrock, L. (1975). Queueing systems: Vol. 1. *Theory*. New York, NY: John Wiley & Sons.

Klein, S. M. (1996). A management strategic communication for change. *Journal of Organizational Change Management*, *9*(2), 32–46. doi:10.1108/09534819610113720

Kline, R. (2005). *Principles and Practice of Structural Equation Modeling* (2nd ed.). New York: The Guildford Press.

Kline, R. B. (2006). *Structural Equation Modeling*. Concordia University.

Kline, R. B. (2011). *Principles and Practice of Structural Equation Modelling* (3rd ed.). New York: The Guilford Press.

Kline, R. B., & Santor, D. A. (1999). Principles and Practice of Structural Equation Modelling. *Canadian Psychology*, *40*(4), 381–383. doi:10.1037/h0092500

Knack, S., & Keefer, P. (1997). Does Social Capital have an economic payoff? A cross-country Investigation. *The Quarterly Journal of Economics*, *112*(November), 1251–1288. doi:10.1162/003355300555475

Kneller, R., & Stevens, P. (2006). Frontier Technology and Absorptive Capacity: Evidence from OECD Manufacturing Industries. Oxford Bulletin of Economics and Statistics, 68(1). doi:10.1111/j.1468-0084.2006.00150.x

Knight, F. (1921). *Risk, Uncertainty and Profit*. New York: Houghton Mifflin.

Koch, T., & Rowell, M. (1999). The dream of consensus: Finding common ground in a bioethical context. *Theoretical Medicine and Bioethics*, *20*(3), 261–273. doi:10.1023/A:1009995919835 PMID:10474312

Kock, N. (2013). Using WarpPLS in e-collaboration studies: What if I have only one group and one condition. *International Journal of e-Collaboration*, *9*(3), 12. doi:10.4018/jec.2013070101

Kodogiannis, V. S. (2014). Point-of-care diagnosis of bacterial pathogens in vitro, utilising an electronic nose and wavelet neural networks. *Neural Computing & Applications*, *25*(2), 353–366. doi:10.1007/s00521-013-1494-8

Kohli, A. S., & Jensen, B. J. (2010). Assessing effectiveness of supply chain collaboration: an empirical study. *Supply Chain Forum*, *11*(2), 1-16.

Koivula, J. (2009). *Succeeding in Project Communication – Effective Tools for the Purposes of Change Management Case Company: VR Ltd. – Passenger Services*. Retrieved 18 October 2010 from: http://enable06.myenable.com/fusion/apps/doc/public/130/Productivity%20Study/2008%20Proudfoot%20Global%20Productivity%20Study.pdf

Koonce, R. (1991). The people side of organizational change. *Credit*, *17*(6), 22–25.

Kotter, J. P. (1996). *Leading Change*. Boston: Harvard Business School Press.

Kotter, J. P., & Cohen, D. S. (2003). *Srce spprememb: resnične zgodbe o tem, kako ljudje spreminjajo svoje organizacije*. Ljubljana: GV Založba.

Kovačić, Z. J. (2012). Predicting student success by mining enrolment data. *Research in Higher Education Journal, 15*.

Krantz, D. H., & Kunreuther, H. C. (2007). Goals and plans in decision making. *Judgment and Decision Making, 2*(3), 137–168.

Kreps, G. L. (1990). *Organizational Communication: Theory and Practice* (2nd ed.). New York: Longman.

Kuhns, M., & Johnson, K. (2013). *Applied predictive modeling.* New York: Springer. doi:10.1007/978-1-4614-6849-3

Kujansivu, P., & Lönnqvist, A. (2008). Business process management as a tool for intellectual capital management. *Knowledge and Process Management, 15*(3), 159–169. doi:10.1002/kpm.307

Kumar, S., & Parashar, N. (2009). Analytical Hierarchy Process Applied to Vendor Selection Problem, Small Scale, Me-dium Scale and Large Scale Industries. *Business Intelligence Journal, 2*(2), 245-257.

Kumar, A., & Zhao, J. L. (2002). Workflow support for electronic commerce applications. *Decision Support Systems, 32*(3), 265–278. doi:10.1016/S0167-9236(01)00114-2

Kuo, M.-S., & Liang, G.-S. (2011). Combining VIKOR with GRA techniques to evaluate service quality of airports under fuzzy environment. *Expert Systems with Applications, 38*(3), 1304–1312. doi:10.1016/j.eswa.2010.07.003

Kuznets, S. (1965). *Economic growth and structure.* London, UK: Heinemann Educational Books.

Kwan, M. M., & Balasubramanian, P. R. (1998). *Adding workflow analysis techniques to the IS development toolkit.* Paper presented at the 31st Hawaii International Conference on System Sciences (HICSS-31), Honolulu, HI. doi:10.1109/HICSS.1998.655287

Kwok, S., & Wu, K. W. (2009). RFID-based intra-supply chain in textile industry. *Industrial Management & Data Systems, 109*(9), 1166–1178. doi:10.1108/02635570911002252

Lago, P., Bizzarri, G., Scalzotto, F., Parpaiola, A., Amigoni, A., Putoto, G., & Perilongo, G. (2012). Use of FMEA analysis to reduce risk of errors in prescribing and administering drugs in pediatric wards: A quality improvement report. *BMJ Open, 2*(6), 1–31. doi:10.1136/bmjopen-2012-001249 PMID:23253870

Lambert, D. M., Cooper, M. C., & Pagh, J. D. (1998). Supply Chain Management: Implementation Issues and Research Opportunities. *The International Journal of Logistics Management, 9*(2), 1–20. doi:10.1108/09574099810805807

Lamont, J. (2006). Business intelligence: The text analysis strategy. *KM World, 15*(10), 8–10.

Lan, Y., & Li, S. (2010). *Design and realization of the research and development staff performance assessment system.* Paper presented at the Seventh International Conference on Fuzzy Systems and Knowledge Discovery (FSKD), Yantai, Shandong. doi:10.1109/FSKD.2010.5569414

Landeta, J. (2006). Current validity of the Delphi method in social sciences. *Technological Forecasting and Social Change, 73*(5), 467–482. doi:10.1016/j.techfore.2005.09.002

Lang, L. H. P., & Litzenberger, R. H. (1989). Dividend announcements: Cash flow signaling vs. free cash flow hypothesis. *Journal of Financial Economics, 24*(1), 181–191. doi:10.1016/0304-405X(89)90077-9

Larma, C., & Basil, V. R. (2003). Iterative and Incremental Development: A Brief. *History & Computing, 36*(6).

Lee, C. W., & Kwak, N. (2011). Strategic enterprise resource planning in a health-care system using a multicriteria decision-making model. *Journal of Medical Systems, 35*(2), 265–275. doi:10.1007/s10916-009-9362-x PMID:20703564

Leedy, D. P., & Ormrod, E. J. (2010). *Practical research: Planning and designing* (9th ed.). Pearson Education.

Compilation of References

Lee, H., Kim, M. S., & Kim, K. K. (2014). Interorganizational information systems visibility and supply chain performance. *International Journal of Information Management*, *34*(2), 285–295. doi:10.1016/j.ijinfomgt.2013.10.003

Lee, M. D., & Wagenmakers, E. J. (2014). *Bayesian cognitive modeling: A practical course*. Boston, MA: Cambridge University Press.

Lee, R. P., & Grewal, R. (2004). Strategic responses to new technologies and their impact on firm performance. *Journal of Marketing*, *68*(4), 157–171. doi:10.1509/jmkg.68.4.157.42730

Lei, P. W., & Wu, Q. (2007). Introduction to Structural Equation Modeling: Issues and Practical Considerations. *Educational Measurement: Issues and Practice*, *26*(3), 33–43. doi:10.1111/j.1745-3992.2007.00099.x

Lengel, R., & Daft, R. L. (1988). The selection of communication media as an executive skill. *The Academy of Management Executive*, *11*(3), 225–232. doi:10.5465/AME.1988.4277259

Lex team. (2012). Advertising: Valuations don't ad up. *Financial Times*. Retrieved 17 September 2013 from: http://www.ft.com/intl/cms/s/3/0d9b6450-66fe-11e1-9d4e-00144feabdc0.html#axzz2Vv5NhUM7

Li, Q., McNeil, S., Foulke, T.K., Calhoun, J., Oswald, M., Trimbath, S., Kreh, E., & Gallis, M. (2011). *Capturing Transportation Infrastructure Performance: Data Availability, Needs and Challenges*. Transportation Research Record: Journal of the Transportation Research Board, No. 2256. Transportation Research Board of the National Academies.

Liberatore, M. J., & Nydick, R. L. (2008). The analytic hierarchy process in medical and health care decision making: A literature review. *European Journal of Operational Research*, *189*(1), 194–207. doi:10.1016/j.ejor.2007.05.001

Li, G., Lin, Y., Wang, S., & Yan, H. (2006). Enhancing agility by timely sharing of supply information. *Supply Chain Management: An International Journal*, *11*(5), 425–435. doi:10.1108/13598540610682444

Lilien, G. L. (1979). Advisor 2: Modeling the marketing mix decision for industrial products. *Management Science*, *25*(2), 191–204. doi:10.1287/mnsc.25.2.191

Lilien, G. L. (2011). Bridging the academic-practitioner divide in marketing decision models. *Journal of Marketing*, *75*(July), 196–210. doi:10.1509/jmkg.75.4.196

Lin, C., Chow, W., Madu, C., Kuei, C., & Pei, Y. (2005). A structural equation model of supply chain quality management and organizational performance. *International Journal of Production Economics*, *96*(3), 355–365. doi:10.1016/j.ijpe.2004.05.009

Linstone, H. A. (1978). The Delphi technique. In J. Fowles (Ed.), *Handbook of future research*. London: Greenwood Press.

Linstone, H. A. (2002). Eight basic pitfalls: A checklist. In M. Turoff & H. A. Linstone (Eds.), *The Delphi approach: Techniques and applications*. Reading: Addison-Wesley.

Linstone, H. A., & Turoff, M. (1975). *The Delphi method: Techniques and applications*. London: Addison-Wesley.

Li, P., Wu, J., & Qian, H. (2012). Groundwater quality assessment based on rough sets attribute reduction and TOPSIS method in a semi-arid area, China. *Environmental Monitoring and Assessment*, *184*(8), 4841–4854. doi:10.1007/s10661-011-2306-1 PMID:21894505

Lippert, S. K., & Govindarajulu, C. (2006). Technological, organizational, and environmental antecedents to web services adoption. *Communications of the IIMA*, *6*(1), 146–158.

Little, J. D. (1970). Models and managers: The concept of a decision calculus. *Management Science*, *16*(4), B466–B486. doi:10.1287/mnsc.16.8.B466

Liu, H., Ke, W., Wei, K. K., & Hua, Z. (2013). The impact of IT capabilities on firm performance: The mediating roles of absorptive capacity and supply chain agility. *Decision Support Systems*, *54*(3), 1452–1462. doi:10.1016/j.dss.2012.12.016

Long, J. (2010). Do what yourself: Reevaluation of the value created by online and traditional intermediary. *International Journal of Information and Decision Sciences*, *2*(3), 304–317. doi:10.1504/IJIDS.2010.033453

Long, T., & Johnson, M. (2000). Rigour, reliability and validity research. *Clinical Effectiveness in Nursing*, *4*(1), 30–37. doi:10.1054/cein.2000.0106

Lucas, R. Jr. (1988). On the mechanics of economic development. *Journal of Monetary Economics*, *22*(1), 3–24. doi:10.1016/0304-3932(88)90168-7

Ludvigson, S. C. (2004). Consumer confidence and consumer pricing. *The Journal of Economic Perspectives*, *18*(2), 29–50. doi:10.1257/0895330041371222

Luecke, R. (2003). *Managing Change and Transition*. Boston: Harvard Business School Press.

Luftman, J., Kempaiah, R., & Nash, E. (2006). Key issues for IT executives 2005. *MIS Quarterly Executive*, *5*(2), 81–99.

Lydon, S. (2006). *Common Sense in a Changing world: Ipsos MORI Employee Relationship Management*. Retrieved 20 January 2009 from: http://www.ipsos-mori.com/_assets/erm/common-sense-in-a-changingworld.pdf

Maceratini, R., & Ricci, F. L. (2000). *Il medico on-line. Manuale di informatica medica*. Verduci, Editore.

Macwan, N., & Sajja, P. S. (2013). *Modeling performance appraisal using soft computing techniques: Designing neuro-fuzzy application*. Paper presented at the 2013 International Conference on Intelligent Systems and Signal Processing (ISSP), Gujarat doi:10.1109/ISSP.2013.6526943

Mahmood, M. A., & Mann, G. J. (2005). Information technology investments and organizational productivity and performance: An empirical investigation. *Journal of Organizational Computing and Electronic Commerce*, *15*(3), 185–202. doi:10.1207/s15327744joce1503_1

Mahmoodzadeh, E., Jalalinia, S., & Yazdi, F. N. (2009). A business process outsourcing framework based on business process management and knowledge management. *Business Process Management Journal*, *15*(6), 845–864. doi:10.1108/14637150911003748

Maisel, L. S., & Cokins, G. (2014). *Predictive business analytics: Forward looking capabilities to improve business performance*. Hoboken, NJ: John Wiley & Sons, Inc.

Malhotra, N. (2009). *Marketing Research: An Applied Orientation, 5/E*. Pearson Education India. doi:10.1108/S1548-6435(2009)5

Malmendier, U., & Tate, G. (2005). CEO overconfidence and corporate investment. *The Journal of Finance*, *60*(6), 2661–2700. doi:10.1111/j.1540-6261.2005.00813.x

Mamat, N. J. Z., & Danil, J. K. (2007). Statistical analyses on time complexity and rank consictency between singular value decomposition and the duality approach in AHP: A case study of faculty member selection. *Mathematical and Computer Modelling*, *46*(7-8), 1099–1106. doi:10.1016/j.mcm.2007.03.025

Management, B. (2015). Retrieved from: http://boundlessmanagement.com/

Manchanda, P., Xie, Y., & Youn, N. (2008). The role of targeted communication and contagion in product adoption. *Marketing Science*, *27*(6), 961–976. doi:10.1287/mksc.1070.0354

Compilation of References

Manglik, A., & Mehra, V. (2005). Extending enterprise BI capabilities: New patterns for data integration. *Business Intelligence Journal*, *10*(1), 10–17.

Mankiw, N., Romer, P., & Weil, D. (1992). A Contribution to the Empirics of Economic Growth. *The Quarterly Journal of Economics*, *107*(2), 407–437. doi:10.2307/2118477

Manoharan, T. R., Muralidharan, C., & Deshmukh, S. G. (2009). Employee Performance Appraisal Using Data Envelopment Analysis: A Case Study. *Research & Practice In Human Resource Management*, *17*, 17–34.

Manoharan, T. R., Muralidharan, C., & Deshmukh, S. G. (2011). An integrated fuzzy multi-attribute decision-making model for employees' performance appraisal. *International Journal of Human Resource Management*, *22*(3), 722–745. doi:10.1080/09585192.2011.543763

Manoharan, T. R., Muralidharan, C., & Deshmukh, S. G. (2012). A composite model for employees' performance appraisal and improvement. *European Journal of Training and Development*, *36*(4), 448–480. doi:10.1108/03090591211220366

Mansar, S. L., & Reijers, H. A. (2005). Best practices in business process redesign: Validation of a redesign framework. *Computers in Industry*, *56*(5), 457–471. doi:10.1016/j.compind.2005.01.001

Mansoornejad, B., Pistikopoulos, E. N., & Stuart, P. (2013). Metrics for evaluating the forest biorefinery supply chain performance. *Computers & Chemical Engineering*, *54*(0), 125–139. doi:10.1016/j.compchemeng.2013.03.031

Marinagi, C., Trivellas, P., & Reklitis, P. (2015). Information Quality and Supply Chain Performance: The Mediating Role of Information Sharing. *Procedia: Social and Behavioral Sciences*, *175*, 473–479. doi:10.1016/j.sbspro.2015.01.1225

Marinagi, C., Trivellas, P., & Sakas, D. P. (2014). The Impact of Information Technology on the Development of Supply Chain Competitive Advantage. *Procedia: Social and Behavioral Sciences*, *147*, 586–591. doi:10.1016/j.sbspro.2014.07.161

Marshall, A. (1890). *Principles of Economics*. London: Macmillan and Co., Ltd.

Martini, B., & Choo, K. K. R. (2012). An integrated conceptual digital forensic framework for cloud computing. *Digital Investigation*, *9*(2), 71–80. doi:10.1016/j.diin.2012.07.001

Maslow, A. (1954). *Motivation and personality*. New York, NY: Harper Business.

McDermott, C. M. (1999). Managing radical product development in large manufacturing firms: A longitudinal study. *Journal of Operations Management*, *17*(6), 631–644. doi:10.1016/S0272-6963(99)00018-2

McDonald, M. P. (2007). The enterprise capability organization: A future for IT. *MIS Quarterly Executive*, *6*(3), 179–192.

McKendrick, A. G. (1926). Applications of mathematics to medical problems. *Proceedings of the Edinburgh Mathematical Society*, *14*, 98–130.

McKinsey Global Institute. (2013). *Infrastructure Productivity: How to Save $1 Trillion a Year*. McKinsey Infrastructure Practice.

McNeil, S., Trimbath, S., Atique, F., & Burke, R. (n.d.). *TPI UPDATE 2013: Data for 2010,2011*. Final Report to the US Chamber of Commerce (unpublished).

McNeil, S., Atique, F., Burke, R., & Trimbath, S. (2014). Using the Transportation Performance Index to Understand the Impact of Regional Plans. *Proceedings of the ASCE TD&I Congress*. doi:10.1061/9780784413586.061

Mead, D., & Moseley, L. (2001). The use of Delphi as a research approach. *Nurse Researcher*, *8*(4), 4–23. doi:10.7748/nr2001.07.8.4.4.c6162

Medsker Larry, J., & Gina, J. (1994). A Review of Current Practices for Evaluating Causal Models in Organizational Behavior and Human Resources Management Research. *Journal of Management*, *20*(2), 439–464. doi:10.1177/014920639402000207

Mensah, P., Merkuryev, Y., & Longo, F. (2015). Using ICT in Developing a Resilient Supply Chain Strategy. *Procedia Computer Science*, *43*, 101–108. doi:10.1016/j.procs.2014.12.014

Merrell, P. (2012). Effective change management: The simple truth. *Management Services*, *56*(2), 20–23.

Merriam-Webster. (2005). *The Merriam-Webster Thesaurus*. Springfield: Merriam-Webster.

Merschmann, U., & Thonemann, U. W. (2011). Supply chain flexibility, uncertainty and firm performance: An empirical analysis of German manufacturing firms. *International Journal of Production Economics*, *130*(1), 43–53. doi:10.1016/j.ijpe.2010.10.013

Mertler, C. A., & Vannatta, R. A. (2013). *Advanced and multivariate statistical methods* (5th ed.). Glendale, CA: Pyrczak Publishing.

Meskell, P., Murphy, K., Shaw, D. G., & Casey, D. (2014). Insights into the used and complexities of the policy Delphi technique. *Nurse Researcher*, *21*(3), 32–39. doi:10.7748/nr2014.01.21.3.32.e342

Metts, G. (2004). *An Investigation of the Relationship between Strategy Making and Performance*. (PhD Dissertation). University of Toledo.

Michalisin, M. D., Kline, D. M., & Smith, R. F. (2000). Intangible strategic assets and firm performance: A multi-industry study of the resource-based view. *The Journal of Business Strategy*, *17*(2), 91–117.

Michalisin, M. D., Smith, R. F., & Kline, D. M. (1997). In search of strategic assets. *The International Journal of Organizational Analysis*, *5*(4), 360–387. doi:10.1108/eb028874

Miller, L. E. (2006). *Determining what could/should be: The Delphi technique and its application*. Paper presented at the meeting of the 2006 Annual Meeting of the Mid-Western Educational Research Association, Columbus, OH.

Minonne, C., & Turner, G. (2012). Business process management: Are you ready for the future? *Knowledge and Process Management*, *19*(3), 111–120. doi:10.1002/kpm.1388

Mintz, O. (2012). *What drives metric use? Evidence from 30 Countries*. Retrieved 25 Septebmer 2015 from: https://webfiles.uci.edu/omintz/www/MC%20Intl%20Metric%20Use.pdf

Mintz, O., & Currim, I. (2013). What drives the use of marketing and financial metrics and does metric use impact performance of marketing mix activities? *Journal of Marketing*, *77*(March), 17–40. doi:10.1509/jm.11.0463

Mishra, A., & Mishra, D. (2009). Customer relationship management: Implementation process perspective. *Acta Polytechnica Hungarica*, *6*(4), 83–99.

Mitchell, V. W. (1991). The Delphi technique: An exposition and application. *Technology Analysis and Strategic Management*, *3*(4), 333–358. doi:10.1080/09537329108524065

Mohammad, M. F., Shukor, A. S. A., Mahbub, R., & Halil, F. M. (2014). Challenges in the Integration of Supply Chains in IBS Project Environment in Malaysia. *Procedia: Social and Behavioral Sciences*, *153*, 44–54. doi:10.1016/j.sbspro.2014.10.039

Mohammed, M. F., Lim, C. P., & Quteishat, A. (2014). A novel trust measurement method based on certified belief in strength for a multi-agent classifier system. *Neural Computing & Applications*, *24*(2), 421–429. doi:10.1007/s00521-012-1245-2

Compilation of References

Mohanty, R., Ravi, V., & Patra, M. R. (2010). The application of intelligent and soft-computing techniques to software engineering problems: A review. *International Journal of Information and Decision Sciences*, *2*(3), 233–272. doi:10.1504/IJIDS.2010.033450

Monteagudo, J. L. (2006). *eHealth ERA. Priority Cluster Topic 2, focus on eHealth for Patient Empowerment*. Retrieved on 02/07/2015 at: http://www.ehealth-era.org/documents/

Monteagudo, J. L., & Moreno, O. (2007). *Report on Priority Topic Cluster two and recommendations - Patient Empowerment*. Deliverable D2.5, Project eHealth ERA - Towards the Establishment of a European Research Area. Retrieved on 01/07/2015 at: http://www.ehealth-era.org/documents/eH-ERA_D2.5_Patient_Empowerment_Final_31-03-2007_revised.pdf

Montgomery, C. A., & Wernerfelt, B. (1988). 'Diversification, Ricardian rents, and Tobin's q'. *The Rand Journal of Economics*, *19*(4), 623–632. doi:10.2307/2555461

Moon, C., Lee, J., & Lim, S. (2010). A performance appraisal and promotion ranking system based on fuzzy logic: An implementation case in military organizations. *Applied Soft Computing*, *10*(2), 512–519. doi:10.1016/j.asoc.2009.08.035

Moon, K. K.-L., Yi, C. Y., & Ngai, E. W. T. (2012). An instrument for measuring supply chain flexibility for the textile and clothing companies. *European Journal of Operational Research*, *222*(2), 191–203. doi:10.1016/j.ejor.2012.04.027

Moran, J. W., & Brightman, B. K. (2000). Leading organizational change. *Journal of Workplace Learning: Employee Counselling Today*, *12*(2), 66–74. doi:10.1108/13665620010316226

Morosini, P. (2004). *Indicatori in valutazione e miglioramento della qualità professionale*. Istituto Superiore di Sanità.

Morris, B. (2001, Summer). Can differences in industrial structure explain divergences in regional economic growth?. Bank of England Quarterly Bulletin, 195-202.

Morton-Clark, S. (2009). Peter Fader: How marketing works best with big messy maths. *Financial Times*. Retrieved 17 September 2013 from: http://www.ft.com/intl/cms/s/0/87fb6c82-e8de-11dd-a4d00000779fd2ac.html#axzz2Vv5NhUM7

Mouine, M. (2011). *Combinaison de deux d'analyse de sensibilité*. Mémoire à l'université Laval.

Mullen, P. M. (2003). Delphi myths and reality. *Journal of Health Organization and Management*, *17*(1), 37–52. doi:10.1108/14777260310469319

Mumel, D. (2008). *Komuniciranje v poslovnem okolju*. Maribor: De Vesta.

Munro, M. C., & Davis, G. B. (1977). Determining management information needs: A comparison of methods. *Management Information Systems Quarterly*, *1*(2), 55–67. doi:10.2307/249168

Mustafa, M. N., Chowdhury, L., & Kamal, M. S. (2012, May). Students dropout prediction for intelligent system from tertiary level in developing country. In *Informatics, Electronics & Vision (ICIEV), 2012 International Conference on* (pp. 113-118). IEEE. doi:10.1109/ICIEV.2012.6317441

Naik, P. A., & Raman, K. (2003). Understanding the impact of synergy in multimedia communications. *JMR, Journal of Marketing Research*, *40*(4), 375–388. doi:10.1509/jmkr.40.4.375.19385

Narayanan, A. (2012). A Review of Eight Software Packages for Structural Equation Modeling. *The American Statistician*, *66*(2), 129–138. doi:10.1080/00031305.2012.708641

Nathans, L. L., Oswald, F. L., & Nimon, K. (2012). Interpreting multiple linear regression: A guidebook of variable importance. *Practical Assessment, Research & Evaluation*, *17*(9). Available online http://pareonline.net/getvn.asp?v=17&n=9

Needham, R. D., & de Loë, R. (1990). The policy Delphi: Purpose, structure, and application. *The Canadian Geographer*, *34*(2), 133–142. doi:10.1111/j.1541-0064.1990.tb01258.x

Negash, S. (2004). Business intelligence. *Communications of the Association for Information Systems*, *13*(1), 177–195.

Nelson, R., & Phelps, E. (1966). Investment in humans, technological diffusion, and economic growth. *The American Economic Review*, *56*(1/2), 65–75.

Neslin, S. A., & Shankar, V. (2009). Key issues in multichannel customer management: Current knowledge and future directions. *Journal of Interactive Marketing*, *23*(1), 70–81. doi:10.1016/j.intmar.2008.10.005

Neubauer, T. (2009). An empirical study about the status of business process management. *Business Process Management Journal*, *15*(2), 166–183. doi:10.1108/14637150910949434

Neuman, W. (1997). *Social Research Methods*. Allyn and Bacon London.

Newton, R. (2007). *Managing Change Step by Step: All You Need to Build a Plan and Make It Happen*. Harlow: Pearson Prentice Hall Business.

Ngai, E. W. T., Chau, D. C. K., & Chan, T. L. A. (2011). Information technology, operational, and management competencies for supply chain agility: Findings from case studies. *The Journal of Strategic Information Systems*, *20*(3), 232–249. doi:10.1016/j.jsis.2010.11.002

Nicholls, M. G. (2007). Assessing the progress and the underlying nature of the flows of doctoral and master degree candidates using absorbing Markov chains. *Higher Education*, *53*(6), 769–790. doi:10.1007/s10734-005-5275-x

Nicholls, M. G. (2008). The Use of Markov models as an aid to the evaluation, planning and benchmarking of doctoral programs. *The Journal of the Operational Research Society*, *60*(9), 1183–1190. doi:10.1057/palgrave.jors.2602639

Nickell, S., Nicolitsas, D., & Dryden, N. (1997). What makes firms perform well?. European Economic Review, 41. doi:10.1016/S0014-2921(97)00037-8

Nickell, S. (1996). Competition and Corporate Performance. *Journal of Political Economy*, *104*(4), 724–746. doi:10.1086/262040

Niu, L., Lu, J., Zhang, G., & Wu, D. (2013). FACETS: A cognitive business intelligence system. *Information Systems*, *38*(6), 835–862. doi:10.1016/j.is.2013.02.002

Nobre, F. F., Trotta, L. T. F., & Gomes, L. F. A. M. (1999). Multi-criteria decision making– an approach to setting priorities in health care. *Statistics in Medicine*, *18*(23), 3345–3354. doi:10.1002/(SICI)1097-0258(19991215)18:23<3345::AID-SIM321>3.0.CO;2-7 PMID:10602156

Nofal, M. I., & Yusof, Z. M. (2013). Integration of business intelligence and enterprise resource planning within organizations. *Procedia Technology*, *11*, 658–665. doi:10.1016/j.protcy.2013.12.242

Nolan, R. L. (1979). Managing the crisis in data processing. *Harvard Business Review*, *57*(2), 115–126.

Nudurupati, S. S., Bititci, U. S., Kumar, V., & Chan, F. T. S. (2011). State of the art literature review on performance measurement. *Computers & Industrial Engineering*, *60*(2), 279–290. doi:10.1016/j.cie.2010.11.010

Nunnaly, J. (1978). *Psychometric theory*. New York, NY: Mc Graw Hill.

Nworie, J. (2011). Using the Delphi technique in educational technology research. *TechTrends: Linking Research and Practice to Improve Learning*, *55*(5), 24–30. doi:10.1007/s11528-011-0524-6

Compilation of References

Nyandwaki, M. J., Akelo, O. E., Samson, O. O., & Fredrick, O. (2014). Application of Markov chain model in Studying progression Of Secondary School Students by Sex During The Free Secondary Education: A Case Study of Kisii Central District. *Mathematical Theory and Modeling, 4*(4). Available at: http://iiste.org/Journals/index.php/MTM/article/view/11744

Nyu. (2011). *Guidelines for Writing a Proposal That Uses Sem and for Writing the Results Section of a Thesis*. Academic Press.

O'cass, A., & Fenech, T. (2003). Web retailing adoption: Exploring the nature of Internet users Web retailing behaviour. *Journal of Retailing and Consumer Services, 10*(2), 81–94. doi:10.1016/S0969-6989(02)00004-8

Obayashi, K., Teramoto, K., Yamamoto, K., Ikeda, K., & Ando, Y. (2009) Accreditation of ISO 15189 in the Department of Laboratory Medicine, Kumamoto University Hospital: successful cases. Rinsho Byori: The Japanese Journal of Clinical Pathology, 57(2), 156-160.

Oetega, B. H., Martinez, J. J., & Hoyos, M. J. M. (2006). Analysis of the moderating effect of industry on online behaviour. *Online Information Review, 30*(6), 681–698. doi:10.1108/14684520610716162

Ofner, M. H., Otto, B., & Osterle, H. (2012). Integrating a data quality perspective into business process management. *Business Process Management Journal, 18*(6), 1036–1067. doi:10.1108/14637151211283401

Okali, C., & Pawlowski, S. D. (2004). The Delphi method as a research tool: An example, design considerations and applications. *Information & Management, 42*(1), 15–29. doi:10.1016/j.im.2003.11.002

Okoye, P. V. C., & Ezejiofor, R. A. (2013). The effect of human resources development on organizational productivity. *International Journal of Academic Research in Business and Social Sciences, 3*(10), 250–268. doi:10.6007/IJARBSS/v3-i10/295

Olley, G., & Pakes, A. (1996). The Dynamics of Productivity in the Telecommunications Equipment Industry. *Econometrica, 64*(4), 1263–1297. doi:10.2307/2171831

Önüt, S., & Soner, S. (2008). Transshipment site selection using the AHP and TOPSIS approaches under fuzzy environment. *Waste Management (New York, N.Y.), 28*(9), 1552–1559. doi:10.1016/j.wasman.2007.05.019 PMID:17768038

Opricovic, S. (1998). *Multi-criteria optimization of civil engineering systems*. Belgrade: Faculty of Civil Engineering.

Opricovic, S., & Tzeng, G. H. (2002). Multicriteria Planning of Post-Earthquake Sustainable Reconstruction. *Computer-Aided Civil and Infrastructure Engineering, 17*(3), 211–220. doi:10.1111/1467-8667.00269

Opricovic, S., & Tzeng, G.-H. (2003). Fuzzy multicriteria model for post-earthquake land use planning. *Natural Hazards Review, 4*(2), 59–64. doi:10.1061/(ASCE)1527-6988(2003)4:2(59)

Opricovic, S., & Tzeng, G.-H. (2004). Compromise solution by MCDM methods: A comparative analysis of VIKOR and TOPSIS. *European Journal of Operational Research, 156*(2), 445–455. doi:10.1016/S0377-2217(03)00020-1

Opricovic, S., & Tzeng, G.-H. (2007). Extended VIKOR method in comparison with outranking methods. *European Journal of Operational Research, 178*(2), 514–529. doi:10.1016/j.ejor.2006.01.020

Osman, I., Berbary, L., Sidani, Y., Al-Ayoubi, B., & Emrouznejad, A. (2011). Data Envelopment Analysis Model for the Appraisal and Relative Performance Evaluation of Nurses at an Intensive Care Unit. *Journal of Medical Systems, 35*(5), 1039–1062. doi:10.1007/s10916-010-9570-4 PMID:20734223

Oswald, M., Li, Q., McNeil, S., & Trimbath, S. (2011). Measuring Infrastructure Performance: Development of a National Infrastructure Index. *Public Works Management & Policy, 16*(4), 373–394. doi:10.1177/1087724X11410071

Oswald, M., & McNeil, S. (2010). Rating Sustainability: Transportation Investments in Urban Corridors as a Case Study. *Journal of Urban Planning and Development, 136*(3), 177–185. doi:10.1061/(ASCE)UP.1943-5444.0000016

Ou Yang, Y.-P., Shieh, H.-M., & Tzeng, G.-H. (2011). A VIKOR technique based on DEMATEL and ANP for information security risk control assessment. *Information Sciences*.

Ozok, A. F. (2012). Fuzzy modelling and efficiency in health care systems. *Work (Reading, Mass.), 41*, 1797–1800. PMID:22316974

Pagliaro, L. (2007). Probabilistic and fuzzy logic in the clinical diagnosis. *Internal and Emergency Medicine, 2*(2), 75–75. doi:10.1007/s11739-007-0039-5 PMID:17622493

Pahlavani, A. (2010). A hybrid algorithm of improved case-based reasoning and multi-attribute decision making in fuzzy environment for investment loan evaluation. *International Journal of Information and Decision Sciences, 2*(1), 17–49. doi:10.1504/IJIDS.2010.029902

Paim, R., Cauliraux, H. M., & Cardoso, R. (2008). Process management tasks: A conceptual and practical view. *Business Process Management Journal, 14*(5), 694–723. doi:10.1108/14637150810903066

Paliwoda, S. J. (1983). Predicting the future using Delphi. *Management Decision, 21*(1), 31–38. doi:10.1108/eb001309

Pan, S. Q., Vega, M., Vella, A. J., Archer, B. H., & Parlett, G. R. (1995). Mini-Delphi approach: An improvement on single round technique. *Progress in Tourism and Hospitality Research, 2*(1), 27–39. doi:10.1002/(SICI)1099-1603(199603)2:1<27::AID-PTH29>3.0.CO;2-P

Papoulis, A. (1991). *Probability, random variables, and stochastic processes* (3rd ed.). Boston, MA: McGraw-Hill.

Parasuraman, A. (2000). Technology Readiness Index (TRI): A Multiple Item Scale to Measure Readiness to Embrace New Technologies. *Journal of Service Research, 2*(4), 307–320. doi:10.1177/109467050024001

Parera, B. A. K. S., Rameezdeen, R., Chileshe, N., & Hosseini, M. R. (2014). Enhancing the effectiveness of risk management practices in Sri Lankan road construction projects: A Delphi approach. *International Journal of Construction Management, 14*(1), 1–14. doi:10.1080/15623599.2013.875271

Park, B.-N., & Min, H. (2013). Global supply chain barriers of foreign subsidiaries: The case of Korean expatriate manufacturers in China. *International Journal of Services and Operations Management, 15*(1), 67–78. doi:10.1504/IJSOM.2013.050562

Parker, J. (2009). Using informal networks to encourage change at BP. *Strategic Communication Management, 13*(1), 24–27.

Park, J. H., Cho, H. J., & Kwun, Y. C. (2013). Extension of the VIKOR method to dynamic intuitionistic fuzzy multiple attribute decision making. *Computers & Mathematics with Applications (Oxford, England), 65*(4), 731–744. doi:10.1016/j.camwa.2012.12.008

Parsons, L. J. (1975). The product life cycle and time-varying advertising elasticities. *JMR, Journal of Marketing Research, 12*(4), 476–480. doi:10.2307/3151101

Patel, N. V., & Hackney, R. (2010). Designing information systems requirements in context: Insights from the theory of deferred action. *International Journal of Business Information Systems, 6*(1), 44–57. doi:10.1504/IJBIS.2010.034004

Patterson, M. G., Michael, A., West, M. A., Shackleton, V. J., Dawson, J. F., Lathom, R., & Wallace, A. M. et al. (2005). Validating the organizational climate measure: Links to managerial practices, productivity and innovation. *Journal of Organizational Behavior, 26*(4), 379–408. doi:10.1002/job.312

Compilation of References

Pearcy, D. H., & Giunipero, L. C. (2008). Using e-procurement applications to achieve integration: What role does firm size play? *Supply Chain Management: An International Journal*, *13*(1), 26–34. doi:10.1108/13598540810850292

Petroni, G. (2010). *Il trasferimento tecnologico*. Egea.

Phan, D. D., & Vogel, D. R. (2010). A model of customer relationship management and business intelligence systems for catalogue and online retailers. *Information & Management*, *47*(2), 69–77. doi:10.1016/j.im.2009.09.001

Pinna Pintor P. (2005). La qualità delle cure vista dal paziente. *QA, 16*(3).

Plebani, M. (2002). Continuing medical education: A challenge to the Italian Scientific Societies of Laboratory Medicine. *Clinica Chimica Acta*, *319*(2), 161–167. doi:10.1016/S0009-8981(02)00038-4 PMID:11955494

Podrecca, E., & Carmeci, G. (2001). Fixed investment and economic growth: New results on causality. *Applied Economics*, *33*(2), 177–182. doi:10.1080/00036840122890

Polit, D. F., & Hungler, B. P. (2013). *Essentials of nursing research: Methods, appraisal and utilisation*. New York: Lippincott Williams & Wilkins.

Popova, V., & Sharpanskykh, A. (2010). Modeling organizational performance indicators. *Information Systems*, *35*(4), 505–527. doi:10.1016/j.is.2009.12.001

Powell, C. (2003). The Delphi technique: Myths and realities. *Journal of Advanced Nursing*, *41*(4), 376–382. doi:10.1046/j.1365-2648.2003.02537.x

Prananto, A., Mckay, J., & Marshall, P. (2003). *A study of the progression of e-business maturity in Australian SMEs: Some evidence of the applicability of the stages of growth for e-business model*. Paper presented at Pacific Asia Conference on Information Systems (PACIS 2003), Adelaide, Australia.

Pratt, J. W. (1987). Dividing the indivisible: Using simple symmetry to partition variance explained. In T. Pukkila, & S. Puntanen (Eds.), *Proceedings of the second international Tampere conference in statistics* (pp. 245-260). Tampere, Finland: University of Tampere.

Prayag, G. (2009). *Visitors to Mauritius - Place Perceptions & Determinants of Repeat Visitation*. University of Waikato, Department of Tourism Management.

Price, R., & Shanks, G. G. (2005). A semiotic information quality framework: Development and comparative analysis. *Journal of Information Technology*, *20*(2), 88–102. doi:10.1057/palgrave.jit.2000038

Proctor, T., & Doukakis, I. (2003). Change management: The role of internal communication and employee development. *Corporate Communications:International Journal (Toronto, Ont.)*, *8*(4), 268–277.

Pruyn, A., & Riezebos, R. (2001). Effects of the awareness of social dilemmas on advertising budget-setting: A scenario setting. *Journal of Economic Psychology*, *22*(1), 43–60. doi:10.1016/S0167-4870(00)00036-2

Puterman, M. L. (2014). *Markov decision processes: discrete stochastic dynamic programming*. New York, NY: John Wiley & Sons.

Quinn, B., & Sulivan, S. J. (2000). The identification by physiotherapists of the physical problems resulting from a mild traumatic brain injury. *Brain Injury: [BI]*, *14*(12), 1063–1076. doi:10.1080/02699050050203568

Rahim, R., Ibrahim, H., & Adnan, F. A. (2013, April). Projection of postgraduate students flow with a smoothing matrix transition diagram of Markov chain. In *Proceedings of the 20th National Symposium On Mathematical Sciences: Research in Mathematical Sciences: A Catalyst for Creativity and Innovation* (Vol. 1522, No. 1, pp. 1385-1393). AIP Publishing. doi. doi:10.1063/1.4801291

Rahim, R. A. (2015). Analyzing Manpower Data of Higher Learning Institutions: A Markov Chain Approach. *International Journal of Human Resource Studies*, *5*(3), 38–47. doi:10.5296/ijhrs.v5i3.7969

Rais, A., & Viana, A. (2011). Operations Research in Healthcare: A survey. *International Transactions in Operational Research*, *18*(1), 1–31. doi:10.1111/j.1475-3995.2010.00767.x

Ramakrishnan, T., Jones, M. C., & Sidorova, A. (2012). Factors influencing business intelligence (BI) data collection strategies: An empirical investigation. *Decision Support Systems*, *52*(2), 486–496. doi:10.1016/j.dss.2011.10.009

Ramanathan, U., & Gunasekaran, A. (2014). Supply chain collaboration: Impact of success in long-term partnerships. *International Journal of Production Economics*, *147*, 252-259. doi:10.1016/j.ijpe.2012.06.002

Ranken, N. (2007). Communicating an IT system change: Eight tips for success. *Strategic Communication Management*, *11*(4), 16–19.

Rao, H., Raghav, S. A. F., & DosSantos, B. (1998). Marketing and the Internet. *Association for Computing Machinery. Communications of the ACM*, *41*(3), 32–34. doi:10.1145/272287.272294

Rapoport, A., & Chammah, A. M. (1965). *Prisoner's Dilemma: A Study in Conflict and Cooperation*. Ann Arbor, MI: Univ. of Michigan Press.

Ravesteyn, P. (2009). A context dependent implementation method for business process management systems. *Communications of the IIMA*, *9*(1), 31–45.

Raza, M., Hussain, O. K., Hussain, F. K., & Chang, E. (2011). Maturity, distance and density (MD^2) metrics for optimizing trust prediction for business intelligence. *Journal of Global Optimization*, *51*(2), 285–300. doi:10.1007/s10898-010-9598-5

Redman, T. C. (2004). Barriers to successful data quality management. *Studies in Communication Sciences*, *4*(2), 53–68.

Reich, B. H., & Nelson, K. M. (2003). In their own words: CIO visions about the future of in-house IT organizations. *ACM SIGMIS Database*, *34*(4), 28–44. doi:10.1145/957758.957763

Reid, A., & Catterall, M. (2005). Invisible data quality issues in a CRM implementation. *Journal of Database Marketing & Customer Strategy Management*, *12*(4), 305–314. doi:10.1057/palgrave.dbm.3240267

Reinschmidt, J., & Françoise, A. (2000). *Business intelligence certification guide*. San Jose, CA: IBM, International Technical Support Organization.

Remenyi, D., Williams, B., Money, A., & Swartz, E. (1998). *Doing Research in Business and Management*. Sage London.

Rexhausen, D., Pibernik, R., & Kaiser, G. (2012). Customer-facing supply chain practices—The impact of demand and distribution management on supply chain success. *Journal of Operations Management*, *30*(4), 269–281. doi:10.1016/j.jom.2012.02.001

Reynolds, N., & Diamantopoulos, A. (1998). The Effect of Pretest Method on Error Detection Rates: Experimental Evidence. *European Journal of Marketing*, *32*(5/6), 480–498. doi:10.1108/03090569810216091

Rezaei, A. R., Çelik, T., & Baalousha, Y. (2011). Performance measurement in a quality management system. *Scientia Iranica*, *18*(3), 742–752. doi:10.1016/j.scient.2011.05.021

Richard, P. J., Devinney, T. M., Yip, G. S., & Johnson, G. (2009). Measuring organizational performance: Towards methodological best practice. *Journal of Management*, *35*(3), 718–804. doi:10.1177/0149206308330560

Richardson, P., & Denton, K. (1996). Communicating change. *Human Resource Management*, *35*(2), 203–216. doi:10.1002/(SICI)1099-050X(199622)35:2<203::AID-HRM4>3.0.CO;2-1

Compilation of References

Rigby, D., & Ledingham, D. (2004). CRM done right. *Harvard Business Review, 82*(11), 119–129. PMID:15559450

Ringle, C. M., Sarstedt, M., & Straub, D. (2012). A Critical Look at the Use of Pls-Sem in Mis Quarterly. *Management Information Systems Quarterly, 36*.

Roglinger, M., Poppelbuß, J., & Becker, J. (2012). Maturity models in business process management. *Business Process Management Journal, 18*(2), 328–346. doi:10.1108/14637151211225225

Rohloff, M. (2011). Advances in business process management implementation based on a maturity assessment and best practice exchange. *Information Systems* and *e-Business Management, 9*(3), 383–403. doi:10.1007/s10257-010-0137-1

Romer, P. (1986). Increasing returns and long-run growth. *Journal of Political Economy, 94*(5), 1002–1037. doi:10.1086/261420

Romer, P. (1990). Endogenous technological change. *Journal of Political Economy, 98*(2), 71–102. doi:10.1086/261725

Roscoe, J. (1975). *Fundamental Research Statistics for the Behavioral Sciences*. CBLS.

Rosemann, M., & de Bruin, T. (2005). *Towards a business process management maturity model*. Paper presented at the European Conference on Information Systems (ECIS 2005), Regensburg, Germany.

Rosenthal, R., & Rosnow, R. (1991). *Essentials of behavioral research: Methods and data analysis*. Boston, MA: Mc Graw Hill.

Rossi Mori, A. (2010). La gestione elettronica della documentazione clinica. In F. Di Resta & B. Ferraris Di Celle (Eds.), *Il Fascicolo Sanitario Elettronico*. Roma: Edisef.

Ross, J. W., Beath, C. M., & Goodhue, D. L. (1996). Develop long-term competitiveness through IT assets. *MIT Sloan Management Review, 38*(1), 31–44.

Rowe, G., & Wright, G. (1999). The Delphi technique as a forecasting tool: Issues and analysis. *International Journal of Forecasting, 15*(4), 353–375. doi:10.1016/S0169-2070(99)00018-7

Rubin, E., & Rubin, A. (2013). The impact of business intelligence systems on stock return volatility. *Information & Management, 50*(2-3), 67–75. doi:10.1016/j.im.2013.01.002

Rusetski, A. (2012). Brand equity: Can there be too much of a good thing? *International Business & Economics Research Journal, 11*(3), 357–368.

Russ, T. L. (2007). Communication Strategies for Implementing Organizational Change. *Proceedings of the 2007 Association for Business Communication Annual Convention*.

Rust, R. T., Ambler, T., Carpanter, G. S., Kumar, V., & Srivastava, R. (2004). Measuring marketing productivity: Current knowledge and future directions. *Journal of Marketing, 68*(4), 76–89. doi:10.1509/jmkg.68.4.76.42721

Saaty, T. L. (1982). *Decision Making for Leaders*. Belmont, CA: Lifetime Learning Publications.

Saaty, T. L. (1982). *Decision making for leaders: The analytical hierarchy process for decisions in a complex world*. Belmont, CA: Lifetime Learning Publications.

Saaty, T. L. (1994). *The analytic hierarchy process*. New York: Mac Gray-Hill.

Sabet, P. G. P., Ansari, R., Fard, A. B., Aadal, H., & Raad, K. G. (2014). Necessary competencies of construction managers in Iran as a developing country. *Research Journal of Applied Sciences, Engineering and Technology, 7*(10), 2161–2171.

Sabherwal, R., & Becerra-Fernandez, I. (2010). *Business intelligence: Practices, technologies, and management*. Hoboken, NJ: John Wiley & Sons.

Sahay, B. S., & Ranjan, J. (2008). Real time business intelligence in supply chain analytics. *Information Management & Computer Security*, *16*(1), 28–48. doi:10.1108/09685220810862733

Sampson, S. E., & Spring, M. (2012). Customer Roles in Service Supply Chains and Opportunities for Innovation. *Journal of Supply Chain Management*, *48*(4), 30–50. doi:10.1111/j.1745-493X.2012.03282.x

Sanayei, A., Farid Mousavi, S., & Yazdankhah, A. (2010). Group decision making process for supplier selection with VIKOR under fuzzy environment. *Expert Systems with Applications*, *37*(1), 24–30. doi:10.1016/j.eswa.2009.04.063

Sande, T. (2009). Taking charge of change with confidence. *Strategic Communication Management*, *13*(1), 28–31.

Santos, J. R. A. (1999). Cronbach's alpha: A tool for assessing the reliability of scales. *Journal of Extension*, *37*(2), 1–5.

Sarkar, B. K., Sana, S. S., & Chaudhuri, K. (2010). Accuracy-based learning classification system. *International Journal of Information and Decision Sciences*, *2*(1), 68–86. doi:10.1504/IJIDS.2010.029904

Sarkis, J. (2006). The adoption of environmental and risk management practices: Relationships to environmental performance. *Annals of Operations Research*, *145*(1), 367–381. doi:10.1007/s10479-006-0040-9

Saunders, M., Lewis, P., & Thornhill, A. (2014). *Research methods for business students* (5th ed.). New Delhi: Dorling Kindersley.

Scheer, A. W. (1992). *Architecture of integrated information systems: Foundations of enterprise modelling*. Berlin, Germany: Springer–Verlag. doi:10.1007/978-3-642-97389-5

Scheer, A. W. (1999). *ARIS – business process frameworks*. Berlin, Germany: Springer–Verlag. doi:10.1007/978-3-642-58529-6

Schmidt, R. C. (1997). Managing Delphi surveys using nonparametric statistical techniques. *Decision Sciences*, *28*(3), 763–774. doi:10.1111/j.1540-5915.1997.tb01330.x

Schulte, S., Janiesch, C., Venugopa, S., Weber, I., & Hoenisch, P. (2015). Elastic business process management: State of the art and open challenges for BPM in the cloud. *Future Generation Computer Systems*, *46*, 36–50. doi:10.1016/j.future.2014.09.005

Schumacker, R., & Lomax, R. (2004). *A Beginner's Guide to Structural Equation Modeling*. Lawrence Erlbaum.

Schumpeter, J. (1934). Theory of Economic Development. Harvard University Press.

Scopus. (2016), Retrieved from: www.scopus.com

Scott, J. E. (2007). Mobility, business process management, software sourcing, and maturity model trends: Propositions for the IS organization of the future. *Information Systems Management*, *24*(2), 139–145. doi:10.1080/10580530701221031

Searcy, C., McCartney, D., & Karapetrovic, S. (2007). Sustainable development indicators for the transmission system of an electric utility. *Corporate Social Responsibility and Environmental Management*, *14*(3), 135–151. doi:10.1002/csr.124

Sedej, T. & Mumel, D. (2015). The optimal selection of internal communication tools during change in organisations. *International Journal of Globalisation and Small Business*, *7*(1), 6-25.

Sedej, T., & Mumel, D. (2013). How C-level views selection of internal communication tools in times of change. *Akademija MM. Slovenian Scientific Journal of Marketing*, *21*, 23–36.

Compilation of References

Sekaran, U. (2010). Research Methods for Business: A Skill Building Approach (5th ed.). New York: Wiley.

Sepehrirad, R., Azar, A., & Sadeghi, A. (2012). *Developing a Hybrid Mathematical Model for 360-Degree Performance Appraisal: A Case Study*. Paper presented at the World Conference on Business, Economics and Management (BEM-2012), Antalya, Turkey. doi:10.1016/j.sbspro.2012.09.142

Sethuraman, R., Tellis, G. J., & Briesch, R. (2011). How well does advertising work? Generalizations from a meta-analysis of brand advertising elasticity. *JMR, Journal of Marketing Research*, *48*(3), 457–471. doi:10.1509/jmkr.48.3.457

Shah, R., & Goldstein, S. M. (2006). Use of Structural Equation Modeling in Operations Management Research: Looking Back and Forward. *Journal of Operations Management*, *24*(2), 148–169. doi:10.1016/j.jom.2005.05.001

Shammout, A. (2007). *Evaluating an Extended Relationship Marketing Model for Arab Guests of Five-Star Hotels*. (Thesis). Victoria University, Australia. Retrieved from: http://vuir.vu.edu.au/1511/1/Shammout.pdf

Shankar, V. (2008). *Strategic allocation of marketing resources: Methods and managerial insights*. Marketing Science Institute Special Report, 08-207.

Shaw, D. R., Holland, C. P., Kawalek, P., Snowdon, B., & Warboys, B. (2007). Elements of a business process management system: Theory and practice. *Business Process Management Journal*, *13*(1), 91–107. doi:10.1108/14637150710721140

Shekarian, E. (2015). A novel application of the VIKOR method for investigating the effect of education on housing choice. *International Journal of Operational Research*, *24*(2), 161–183. doi:10.1504/IJOR.2015.071493

Shekarian, E., & Fallahpour, A. (2013). Predicting house price via gene expression programming. *International Journal of Housing Markets and Analysis*, *6*(3), 250–268. doi:10.1108/IJHMA-08-2012-0039

Shekarian, E., & Gholizadeh, A. A. (2013). Application of adaptive network based fuzzy inference system method in economic welfare. *Knowledge-Based Systems*, *39*, 151–158. doi:10.1016/j.knosys.2012.10.013

Shekarian, E., Olugu, E. U., Abdul-Rashid, S. H., & Kazemi, N. (2016). An economic order quantity model considering different holding costs for imperfect quality items subject to fuzziness and learning. *Journal of Intelligent & Fuzzy Systems*, *30*(5), 2985–2997. doi:10.3233/IFS-151907

Shieh, J.-I., Wu, H.-H., & Huang, K.-K. (2010). A DEMATEL method in identifying key success factors of hospital service quality. *Knowledge-Based Systems*, *23*(3), 277–282. doi:10.1016/j.knosys.2010.01.013

Shim, J. P., Varshney, U., & Dekleva, S. (2006). Wireless evolution 2006: Cellular TV, wearable computing, and RFID. *Communications of the Association for Information Systems*, *18*(1), 497–518.

Shipley, M. F., & Johnson, M. (2009). A fuzzy approach for selecting project membership to achieve. *European Journal of Operational Research*, (192), 918-928.

Siegel, E. (2014). *Predictive Analysis: The power to predict who will click, buy, lie, or die*. Indianapolis, IN: John Wiley & Sons, Inc.

Sierra-Amor, R. I. (2009). Mexican experience on laboratory accreditation according to ISO 15189: 2003. *Clinical Biochemistry*, *42*(4), 318. doi:10.1016/j.clinbiochem.2008.09.095 PMID:19863944

Simon, H. A. (1955). A behavioral model of rational choice. *The Quarterly Journal of Economics*, *69*(1), 99–118. doi:10.2307/1884852

Simon, H. A. (1979). Information processing models of cognition. *Annual Review of Psychology*, *30*(February), 363–396. doi:10.1146/annurev.ps.30.020179.002051 PMID:18331186

Simonton, D. K. (2014). Creative expertise: A lifespan developmental perspective. In K. A. Ericsson (Ed.), *The road to excellence: The acquisition of expert performance in the arts and sciences, sports and games.* East Sussex, UK: Psychology Press.

Singh, A., & Teng, J. T. C. (2016). Enhancing supply chain outcomes through Information Technology and Trust. *Computers in Human Behavior, 54*, 290–300. doi:10.1016/j.chb.2015.07.051

Skulmoski, J. G., Hartman, T. F., & Krahn, J. (2007). The Delphi method for graduate research. *Journal of Information Technology Education, 6*, 1–21.

Smith, A. A., & Smith, A. D. (2012). CRM and identity theft issues associated with e-ticketing of sports and entertainment. *Electronic Government: An International Journal, 9*(1), 1–26. doi:10.1504/EG.2012.044776

Smith, A. D. (2010). Balancing internal supply chain logistics: A comparative analysis of manufacturing and service firm operations. *International Journal of Logistics Systems and Supply Management, 3*(2), 145–166.

Smith, A. D. (2010). Customer relationships, information technology, and concerns for violence in videogaming materials. *International Journal of Management in Education, 4*(1-2), 233–250. doi:10.1504/IJMIE.2010.033460

Smith, A. D. (2011). Strategic leveraging total quality and CRM initiatives: Case study of service-orientated firms. *Services Marketing Quarterly, 32*(1), 1–16. doi:10.1080/15332969.2011.533088

Smith, A. D., & Clinton, S. R. (2015). E-commerce and its impact on expectations of customer service and quality control. In W. D. Nelson (Ed.), *Advances in Business and Management* (Vol. 7). Hauppauge, NY: NOVA Science Publishers, Inc.

Smith, A. D., & Motley, D. (2010). Operational and customer relationship management considerations of electronic prescribing among pharmacists. *International Journal of Electronic Healthcare, 5*(3), 245–272. doi:10.1504/IJEH.2010.034175 PMID:20643640

Smith, A. D., & Rupp, W. T. (2015). Supply chain integration and innovation in a global environment: Case studies of best business practices. *International Journal of Logistics Systems and Chain Management, 22*(8), 313–330. doi:10.1504/IJLSM.2015.072284

Smith, H., & Fingar, P. (2007). *Business process management: The third wave.* Tampa, FL: Meghan-Kiffer Press.

Smith, J. P., Miller, K., Christofferson, J., & Hutchings, M. (2011). Best practices for dealing with price volatility in Utah's residential construction market. *International Journal of Construction Education and Research, 7*(3), 210–225. doi:10.1080/15578771.2011.552935

Solomon, P., & Draine, J. (2009). An Overview of Quantitative Research Methods. In The Handbook of Social Work Research Methods. Academic Press.

Solow, R. (1956). A Contribution to the Theory of Economic Growth. *The Quarterly Journal of Economics, 70*(1), 65–94. doi:10.2307/1884513

Sorooshian, S., Teck, T. S., Salimi, M., & How, L. C. (2012). Develops in Latent Variable Methods of Analysis. *International Journal of Soft Computing, 7*(2).

Sorooshian, S., & Afshari, A. (2012). Structural Equation Modeling: Software Comparative Review. In *Proceedings of the 2012 International Conference on Industrial Engineering and Operations Management.*

Sprinthall, R. C. (2011). *Basic statistical analysis* (9th ed.). Boston, MA: Allyn & Bacon.

Srinivasan, R., Lilien, G. L., & Sridhar, S. (2011). Should firms spend more on research and development and advertising during recessions? *Journal of Marketing, 75*(3), 49–65. doi:10.1509/jmkg.75.3.49

Compilation of References

Stake, R. E. (1995). *The art of case study research*. Thousand Oaks, CA: Sage Publications.

Star L., & Moghadas S.M. (2010). *The Role of Mathematical Modelling in Public Health Planning and Decision Making*. Purple Paper. National Collaborative Center for Infectious Diseases. Issue n.22.

Steenkamp, J. B. E. M., Nijs, V. R., Hanssens, D. M., & Dekimpe, M. G. (2005). Competitive reactions to advertising and promotion attacks. *Marketing Science*, *24*(1), 35–54. doi:10.1287/mksc.1040.0069

Stevenson, M., & Spring, M. (2007). Flexibility from a supply chain perspective: Definition and review. *International Journal of Operations & Production Management*, *27*(7), 685–713. doi:10.1108/01443570710756956

Stohr, E. A., & Zhao, J. L. (2001). Workflow automation: Overview and research issues. *Information Systems Frontiers*, *3*(3), 281–296. doi:10.1023/A:1011457324641

Strnad, D., & Guid, N. (2010). A fuzzy-genetic decision support system for project team formation. *Applied Soft Computing*, *10*(10), 1178–1187. doi:10.1016/j.asoc.2009.08.032

Strnadl, C. F. (2006). Aligning business and it: The process-driven architecture model. *Information Systems Management*, *23*(4), 67–77. doi:10.1201/1078.10580530/46352.23.4.20060901/95115.9

Su, J.-P., Hung, M.-L., Chao, C.-W., & Ma, H.-. (2010). Applying multi-criteria decision-making to improve the waste reduction policy in Taiwan. *Waste Management & Research*, *28*(1), 20–28. doi:10.1177/0734242X09103839 PMID:19710114

Sukumaran, A., & Sureka, A. (2006). Integrating structured and unstructured using text tagging and annotation. *Business Intelligence Journal*, *11*(2), 8–17.

Swafford, P. M., Ghosh, S., & Murthy, N. (2008). Achieving supply chain agility through IT integration and flexibility. *International Journal of Production Economics*, *116*(2), 288–297. doi:10.1016/j.ijpe.2008.09.002

Świerczek, A. (2014). The impact of supply chain integration on the "snowball effect" in the transmission of disruptions: An empirical evaluation of the model. *International Journal of Production Economics*, *157*, 89–104. doi:10.1016/j.ijpe.2013.08.010

Swink, M. (1999). Threats to new product manufacturability and the effects of development team integration processes. *Journal of Operations Management*, *17*(6), 691–709. doi:10.1016/S0272-6963(99)00027-3

Swink, M. (2000). Technological innovativeness as a moderator of new product design integration and top management support. *Journal of Product Innovation Management*, *17*(3), 208–220. doi:10.1016/S0737-6782(00)00040-0

Tabachnick, B. G., & Fidell, L. S. (2012). *Using multivariate statistics* (6th ed.). Pearson Education.

Taguchi, G., & Clausing, D. (1990). Robust quality. *Harvard Business Review*, *68*(1), 65–75.

Tamburis, O., Ricci, F. L., & Pecoraro, F. (2014). A Mathematical Model to Plan the Adoption of EHR Systems. In J. Wang (Ed.), EBAO – Encyclopedia of Business Analytics and Optimization, (pp. 14-29). IGI-Global. doi:10.4018/978-1-4666-5202-6.ch002

Tamburis, O., Mangia, M., Contenti, M., Mercurio, G., & Rossi Mori, A. (2012). The LITIS Conceptual Framework: Measuring eHealth Readiness and Adoption Dynamics across the Healthcare Organizations.[Springer]. *Health Technology*, *2*(2), 97–112. doi:10.1007/s12553-012-0024-5

Tastle, W. J., & Wierman, M. J. (2007). Consensus and dissention: A measure of ordinal dispersion. *International Journal of Approximate Reasoning*, *45*(3), 531–545. doi:10.1016/j.ijar.2006.06.024

Taylor, F. W. (1911). *The principles of scientific management*. New York, NY: Harper Business.

Tellis, G. J. (2007). Advertising effectiveness in contemporary markets. In G. J. Tellis & T. Ambler (Eds.), *The SAGE Handbook of Advertising*. Thousand Oaks, CA: Sage Publications. doi:10.4135/9781848607897.n17

Tellis, G. J., & Fornell, C. (1988). The relationship between advertising and product quality over the product life cycle: A contingency approach. *JMR, Journal of Marketing Research, 25*(February), 64–71. doi:10.2307/3172925

The Ohio Lottery. (2015). *Ohio Lottery*. Retrieved February 9, 2016 from https://www.ohiolottery.com/About/Financial/VLT-Revenue

Theaker, A. (2004). *Priročnik za odnose z javnostmi*. Ljubljana: GV Založba.

Themistocleous, M., Irani, Z., & Love, P. E. D. (2004). Evaluating the integration of supply chain information systems: A case study. *European Journal of Operational Research, 159*(2), 393–405. doi:10.1016/j.ejor.2003.08.023

Theodorou, D. G., & Anastasakis, P. C. (2009). Management review checklist for ISO/IEC 17025 and ISO 15189 quality-management systems. *Accreditation and Quality Assurance, 14*(2), 107–110. doi:10.1007/s00769-008-0466-7

Thisse, J. F., & Vives, X. (1988). On the strategic choice of spatial price policy. *The American Economic Review, 78*(1), 122–137.

Thomé, A. M. T., Scavarda, L. F., Pires, S. R. I., Ceryno, P., & Klingebiel, K. (2014). A multi-tier study on supply chain flexibility in the automotive industry. *International Journal of Production Economics, 158*(0), 91–105. doi:10.1016/j.ijpe.2014.07.024

Thorelli, H. B., & Burnett, S. C. (1981). The nature of product life cycles for industrial goods businesses. *Journal of Marketing, 45*(4), 97–108. doi:10.2307/1251477

Tinbergen, J. (1942). On the Theory of Trend Movements. In Jan Tinbergen, Selected Papers. Amsterdam: North-Holland.

Tolentino, A. (2004). *New Concepts of Productivity and its Improvement*. Paper presented at the European Productivity Network Seminar, Budapest, Hungary.

Toma, M., Mihoreanu, L., & Ionescu, A. (2014). Innovation capability and customer relationship management: A review. *Economics, Management, and Financial Market, 9*(4), 323–331.

Tonidandel, S., & LeBreton, J. M. (2011). Relative importance analysis: A useful supplement to regression analyses. *Journal of Business and Psychology, 26*(1), 1–9. doi:10.1007/s10869-010-9204-3

Tran, D., Lester, H., & Sobin, N. 2014. Toward Statistics on Construction Engineering and Management Research. *Proceedings of the Construction Research Congress 2014: Construction in a Global Network*. doi:10.1061/9780784413517.117

Trimbath, S. (2010). *The Economic Importance of Transportation Infrastructure*. STP Advisors Working Paper STP2010_01.

Trimbath, S. (2013). *Calculating the Real Economic Payoff of Infrastructure*. STP Advisory Services Working Paper STP2013_02.

Trkman, P. (2010). The critical success factors of business process management. *International Journal of Information Management, 30*(2), 125–134. doi:10.1016/j.ijinfomgt.2009.07.003

Trochim, W. (2005). *Research Methods: The Concise Knowledge Base*. Cincinnati, OH: Atomic Dog Publishers.

Tsai, H. D., Huang, H. C., Jaw, Y. L., & Chen, W. K. (2006). Why on-line customers remain with a particular e-retailer: An integrative model and empirical evidence. *Psychology and Marketing, 23*(5), 447–464. doi:10.1002/mar.20121

Tsai, M.-C., & Lin, C.-T. (2012). Selecting an optimal region by fuzzy group decision making: Empirical evidence from medical investors. *Group Decision and Negotiation, 21*(3), 399–416. doi:10.1007/s10726-010-9214-6

Tsai, W.-H., Chou, W.-C., & Lai, C.-W. (2010). An effective evaluation model and improvement analysis for national park websites: A case study of Taiwan. *Tourism Management*, *31*(6), 936–952. doi:10.1016/j.tourman.2010.01.016

TSE, Tavolo di sanità Elettronica. (2006). *La strategia architetturale per l'eHealth*. Author.

TSE, Tavolo di sanità Elettronica. (2010). *Specifiche tecniche per la creazione del "Documento di Referto" secondo lo standard HL7-CDA*. Author.

Tversky, A., & Kahneman, D. (1974). Judgment under uncertainty: Heuristics and biases. *Science*, *185*(4157), 1124–1131. doi:10.1126/science.185.4157.1124 PMID:17835457

Tzeng, G. H., & Huang, J.-J. (2011). *Multiple attribute decision making: Methods and applications*. CRC Press.

U.S. Chamber of Commerce. (2010). Transportation Performance Index: Complete Technical Report. Washington, DC: McNeil, S., Li, Q., Oswald, M., Foulke, T.K., Calhoun, J. and Trimbath, S.

U.S. Chamber of Commerce. (2011). *Transportation Performance Index:2011Supplement*. McNeil, S., Li, Q., Oswald, M., Foulke, T.K., Calhoun, J. and Trimbath, S.

Umble, E. J., Haft, R. R., & Umble, M. M. (2003). Enterprise resource planning: Implementation procedures and critical success factors. *European Journal of Operational Research*, *146*(2), 241–257. doi:10.1016/S0377-2217(02)00547-7

Umble, E. J., & Umble, M. M. (2002). Avoiding ERP implementation failure. *Industrial Management (Des Plaines)*, *44*(1), 25–33.

Unsal, I., Fraterman, A., Kayihan, I., Akyar, I., & Serteser, M. (2009). ISO 15189 accreditation in medical laboratories: An institutional experience from Turkey. *Clinical Biochemistry*, *42*(4), 304–305. doi:10.1016/j.clinbiochem.2008.09.022 PMID:19863932

Urbanskienė, R., Žostautienė, D., & Chreptavičienė, V. (2008). The economic conditions of enterprise functioning: The model of creation of customer relationship management (CRM) system. *Engineering Economics*, *3*(58). Retrieved February 10, 2016 from http://faculty.mu.edu.sa/public/uploads/1361952698.7644customer%20relationship54.pdf

Uzoka, F.-M. E., Obot, O., Barker, K., & Osuji, J. (2011). An experimental comparison of fuzzy logic and analytic hierarchy process for medical decision support systems. *Computer Methods and Programs in Biomedicine*, *103*(1), 10–27. doi:10.1016/j.cmpb.2010.06.003 PMID:20633949

Vachon, S., & Klassen, R. D. (2008). Environmental management and manufacturing performance: The role of collaboration in the supply chain. *International Journal of Production Economics*, *111*(2), 299–315. doi:10.1016/j.ijpe.2006.11.030

Vachon, S., & Mao, Z. (2008). Linking supply chain strength to sustainable development: A country-level analysis. *Journal of Cleaner Production*, *16*(15), 1552–1560. doi:10.1016/j.jclepro.2008.04.012

Valdez, A. M. (2009). So much to learn, so little time: Educational priorities for the future of emergency nursing. *Advanced Emergency Nursing Journal*, *31*(4), 337–353. doi:10.1097/TME.0b013e3181bcb571

van der Aalst, W. M. P., Dumas, M., & ter Hofstede, A. H. (2003). *Web service composition languages: Old wine in new bottles?* Paper presented at the 29th Conference on EUROMICRO (EUROMICRO 2003), Washington, DC. doi:10.1109/EURMIC.2003.1231605

van der Aalst, W. M. P. (1998). The application of Petri nets to workflow management. *Journal of Circuits, Systems, and Computers*, *8*(1), 21–66. doi:10.1142/S0218126698000043

Vatalis, K. I., Manoliadis, O. G., & Charalampides, G. (2011). Assessment of the economic benefits from sustainable construction in Greece. *International Journal of Sustainable Development and World Ecology, 18*(5), 377–383. doi:10.1080/13504509.2011.561003

Vetschera, R. (1986). Sensitivity Analysis for the ELECTRE Multicriteria Method. *Z. Oper. Res.,* (30), 99-117.

Vick, S. G. (2002). *Degrees of belief – subjective probability and engineering judgement.* Danvers: ASCE Press.

Vidal, L.A., Sahin, E., Matelli, N., Berhoune, M., & Bonan, B. (2010). Applying AHP to select drugs to be produced by anticipation in a chemotherapy compounding unit. *Journal of Expert Systems with Applications,* (37), 1528-1534.

Vidgen, R., & Wang, X. (2006). From business process management to business process ecosystem. *Journal of Information Technology, 21*(4), 262–271. doi:10.1057/palgrave.jit.2000076

Vignali, C., Gomez, E., Vignali, M., & Vranesevic, T. (2001). The Influence of Consumer Behaviour within the Spanish Food Retail Industry. *British Food Journal, 103*(7), 460–478. doi:10.1108/00070700110401595

Violato, C., & Hecker, K. G. (2007). How to Use Structural Equation Modeling in Medical Education Research: A Brief Guide. *Teaching and Learning in Medicine, 19*(4), 362–371. doi:10.1080/10401330701542685 PMID:17935466

Viscusi, W. K. (1997). Alarmist decisions with divergent risk information. *The Economic Journal, 107*(445), 1657–1670. doi:10.1111/j.1468-0297.1997.tb00073.x

Vlachos, I. P. (2014). A hierarchical model of the impact of RFID practices on retail supply chain performance. *Expert Systems with Applications, 41*(1), 5–15. doi:10.1016/j.eswa.2013.07.006

Vogt, S. C. (1994). The cash flow/investment relationship: Evidence from U.S. manufacturing firms. *Financial Management, 23*(2), 3–20. doi:10.2307/3665735

Volz, K. G., & Gigerenzer, G. (2012). Cognitive processes in decisions under risk are not same as in decisions under uncertainty. *Frontiers in Neuroscience, 6*(July), 1–6. PMID:22807893

von Brocke, J., & Sinnl, T. (2011). Culture in business process management: A literature review. *Business Process Management Journal, 17*(2), 357–377. doi:10.1108/14637151111122383

von der Gracht, H. (2012). Consensus measurement in Delphi studies: Re-opinion and implications for future quality assurance. *Technological Forecasting and Social Change, 79*(8), 1525–1536. doi:10.1016/j.techfore.2012.04.013

Von der Heidt, T. (2008). *Developing and Testing a Model of Cooperative Interorganisational Relationships (Iors) in Product Innovation in an Australian Manufacturing Context: A Multi-Stakeholder Perspective.* Southern Cross University, School of Commerce and Management.

Wagner, E. H. (2004). Chronic disease care. *BMJ (Clinical Research Ed.), 328*. PMID:14739164

Waldman, D. A. (1994). The Contribution of Total Quality Management to a Theory of Work Performance. *Academy of Management Review, 19*, 510–536.

Wang, M., & Wang, H. (2006). From process logic to business logic: A cognitive approach to business process management. *Information & Management, 43*(2), 179–193. doi:10.1016/j.im.2005.06.001

Wang, T.-C., Lee, H.-D., & Cheng, P.-H. (2009). Applying fuzzy TOPSIS approach for evaluating RFID system suppliers in healthcare industry. In *New Advances in Intelligent Decision Technologies* (pp. 519–526). Springer. doi:10.1007/978-3-642-00909-9_49

Compilation of References

Wang, Y.-L., & Tzeng, G.-H. (2012). Brand marketing for creating brand value based on a MCDM model combining DEMATEL with ANP and VIKOR methods. *Expert Systems with Applications*, *39*(5), 5600–5615. doi:10.1016/j.eswa.2011.11.057

Warden, C. A., Wu, W. Y., & Tsai, D. (2006). Online shopping interface components: Relative importance as peripheral and central cues. *Cyberpsychology & Behavior*, *9*(3), 285–294. doi:10.1089/cpb.2006.9.285 PMID:16780396

Watson, H. J., & Wixom, B. H. (2007). Enterprise agility and mature BI capabilities. *Business Intelligence Journal*, *12*(3), 13–28.

Watson, H. J., Wixom, B. H., Hoffer, J. A., Anderson-Lehman, R., & Reynolds, A. M. (2006). Real-time business intelligence: Best practices at Continental Airlines. *Information Systems Management*, *23*(1), 7–18. doi:10.1201/1078.10580530/45769.23.1.20061201/91768.2

Wee, H.-M., Peng, S.-Y., & Wee, P. K. (2010). Modelling of outsourcing decisions in global supply chains: An empirical study on supplier management performance with different outsourcing strategies. *International Journal of Production Research*, *48*(7), 2081–2094. doi:10.1080/00207540802644852

WEF. (2004). *Global Competitiveness Report 2003/2004*. World Economic Forum, Geneva, Switzerland.

Weill, P. (1992). The relationship between investment in information technology and firm performance: A study of the valve manufacturing sector. *Information Systems Research*, *3*(4), 307–333. doi:10.1287/isre.3.4.307

Weske, M. (2007). *Business process management: Concepts, languages, architectures*. Berlin, Germany: Springer–Verlag.

Whitten, D. (2004). User Information satisfaction scale reduction: Application in an IT outsourcing environment. *Journal of Computer Information Systems*, *45*(2), 17–26.

WHO. (1978). *Alma-Ata 1978: primary health care*. Geneva: World Health Organisation.

Wiengarten, F., Humphreys, P., Gimenez, C., & McIvor, R. (2015). Risk, risk management practices, and the success of supply chain integration. *International Journal of Production Economics*. doi:10.1016/j.ijpe.2015.03.020

WIPRO Consulting Services. (2011). *WIPRO Consulting Services*. Retrieved February 9, 2016 from https://www.wipro.com/.../SupplyChainTransformations_Final.pdf

Wisner, J. D., Chan, K.-C., & Keong, L. G. (2012). *Principles of Supply Chain Management: A Balanced Approach* (3rd ed.). Mason, OH: Southwestern.

Wlendahl, H.-P., von Cleminskf, G., & Begemann, C. (2003). A Systematic Approach for Ensuring the Logistic Process Reliability of Supply Chains. *CIRP Annals - Manufacturing Technology*, *52*(1), 375-380. doi:10.1016/S0007-8506(07)60605-2

Wojtecki, J.G. & Peters, R.G. (2000). Communicating organizational change: information technology meets the carbon-based employee unit. *The 2000 Annual*, *2*, 1–16.

Wold, S., Trygg, J., Berglund, A., & Antti, H. (2001). Some recent developments in PLS modeling. *Chemometrics and Intelligent Laboratory Systems*, *58*(2), 131–150. doi:10.1016/S0169-7439(01)00156-3

Wolf, K. H. (1976). Conceptual Models in Geology. *Classifications and Historical Studies*, *11*, 11–78. doi:10.1016/B978-0-444-41401-4.50006-X

Wong, K. K.-K. (2013). Partial Least Squares Structural Equation Modeling (Pls-Sem) Techniques Using Smartpls. *Marketing Bulletin*, *24*, 1–32.

World Economic Forum. (2015). *Competitiveness Rankings*. Retreived 19 September 2015 from http://www3.weforum.org/docs/WEF_GlobalCompetitivenessReport_2014-15.pdf

Wright, S. (1920). The Relative Importance of Heredity and Environment in Determining the Piebald Pattern of Guinea-Pigs. *Proceedings of the National Academy of Sciences of the United States of America*, *6*(6), 320–332. doi:10.1073/pnas.6.6.320 PMID:16576506

Wright, T. S. A. (2006). Giving "teeth" to an environmental policy: A Delphi Study at Dalhousie University. *Journal of Cleaner Production*, *14*(9), 761–768. doi:10.1016/j.jclepro.2005.12.007

Wu, Y.-J., & Hou, J.-L. (2010). An employee performance estimation model for the logistics industry. *Decision Support Systems*, *48*(4), 568–581. doi:10.1016/j.dss.2009.11.007

Xu, C., & Jiang, Y. (2011). Analysis for susceptibility of breast cancer due to gene SMC4L1 based on a multi-criteria evaluation model. *Journal of Biomedical Engineering, 28*(3), 582.

Xuan, J., Jiang, H., Ren, Z., & Zou, W. (2012). *Developer prioritization in bug repositories*. Paper presented at the Software Engineering (ICSE), 2012 34th International Conference on.

Xu, Z. (2004). Uncertain linguistic aggregation operators based approach to multiple attribute group decision making under uncertain linguistic environment. *Information Sciences*, *168*(1-4), 171–184. doi:10.1016/j.ins.2004.02.003

Yalcin, N., Bayrakdaroglu, A., & Kahraman, C. (2012). Application of fuzzy multi-criteria decision making methods for financial performance evaluation of Turkish manufacturing industries. *Expert Systems with Applications*, *39*(1), 350–364. doi:10.1016/j.eswa.2011.07.024

Yang, S., Albert, R., & Carlo, T. A. (2013). Transience and constancy of interactions in a plant-frugivore network. *Ecosphere*, *4*(12), art147. doi:10.1890/ES13-00222.1

Yao, A., & Carlson, J. (1999). The impact of real-time data communication on inventory management. *International Journal of Production Economics*, *59*(1), 213–219. doi:10.1016/S0925-5273(98)00234-5

Yin, R. K. (2003). *Case study research: Design and methods* (3rd ed.). Thousand Oaks, CA: Sage Publications.

Young, M., & Post, J. E. (1993). Managing to communicate, communicating to manage: How leading companies communicate with employees. *Organizational Dynamics*, *22*(1), 31–43. doi:10.1016/0090-2616(93)90080-K

Yucel, G., Cebi, S., Hoege, B., & Ozok, A. F. (2012). A fuzzy risk assessment model for hospital information system implementation. *Expert Systems with Applications*, *39*(1), 1211–1218. doi:10.1016/j.eswa.2011.07.129

Yücenur, G. N., & Demirel, N. Ç. (2012). Group decision making process for insurance company selection problem with extended VIKOR method under fuzzy environment. *Expert Systems with Applications*, *39*(3), 3702–3707. doi:10.1016/j.eswa.2011.09.065

Yue, Z. (2014b). TOPSIS-based group decision-making methodology in intuitionistic fuzzy setting. *Information Sciences*.

Yue, Z. (2013). An avoiding information loss approach to group decision making. *Applied Mathematical Modelling*, *37*(1–2), 112–126. doi:10.1016/j.apm.2012.02.008

Yue, Z. (2014a). TOPSIS-based group decision-making methodology in intuitionistic fuzzy setting. *Information Sciences*, *277*, 141–153. doi:10.1016/j.ins.2014.02.013

Yu, L., Suojapelto, K., Hallikas, J., & Tang, O. (2008). Chinese ICT industry from supply chain perspective—A case study of the major Chinese ICT players. *International Journal of Production Economics*, *115*(2), 374–387. doi:10.1016/j.ijpe.2008.03.011

Compilation of References

Yusliza, M., & Ramayah, T. (2012). *Determinants of Attitude Towards E-HRM: an Empirical Study Among HR Professionals*. Paper presented at the International Conference on Asia Pacific Business Innovation and Technology Management. doi:10.1016/j.sbspro.2012.09.1191

Zabjek, D., Kovacic, A., & Stemberger, M. I. (2009). The influence of business process management and some other CSFs on successful ERP implementation. *Business Process Management Journal*, *15*(4), 588–608. doi:10.1108/14637150910975552

Zack, M. H. (2007). The role of decision support systems in an indeterminate world. *Decision Support Systems*, *43*(4), 1664–1674. doi:10.1016/j.dss.2006.09.003

Zadeh, L. A. (1965). Fuzzy sets. *Information and Control*, *8*(3), 338–353. doi:10.1016/S0019-9958(65)90241-X

Zadeh, L. A. (1975). The concept of a linguistic variable and its application to approximate reasoning—I. *Information Sciences*, *8*(3), 199–249. doi:10.1016/0020-0255(75)90036-5

Zailani, S., Jeyaraman, K., Vengadasan, G., & Premkumar, R. (2012). Sustainable supply chain management (SSCM) in Malaysia: A survey. *International Journal of Production Economics*, *140*(1), 330–340. doi:10.1016/j.ijpe.2012.02.008

Zang, C., & Fan, Y. (2007). Complex event processing in enterprise information systems based on RFID. *Enterprise Information Systems*, *1*(1), 3–23. doi:10.1080/17517570601092127

Zeng, L., Li, L., & Duan, L. (2012). Business intelligence in enterprise computing environment. *Information Technology Management*, *13*(4), 297–310. doi:10.1007/s10799-012-0123-z

Zeng, Q.-L., Li, D.-D., & Yang, Y.-B. (2013). VIKOR Method with Enhanced Accuracy for Multiple Criteria Decision Making in Healthcare Management. *Journal of Medical Systems*, *37*(2), 1–9. doi:10.1007/s10916-012-9908-1 PMID:23377778

Zhang, M., & Tansuhaj, P. (2007). Organizational culture, information technology capability, and performance: The case of born global firms. *Multinational Business Review*, *15*(3), 43–77. doi:10.1108/1525383X200700012

Zhao, G., Feng, T., & Wang, D. (2015). Is more supply chain integration always beneficial to financial performance? *Industrial Marketing Management*, *45*, 162–172. doi:10.1016/j.indmarman.2015.02.015

Zhu, Q., & Sarkis, J. (2004). Relationships between operational practices and performance among early adopters of green supply chain management practices in Chinese manufacturing enterprises. *Journal of Operations Management*, *22*(3), 265–289. doi:10.1016/j.jom.2004.01.005

Zikmund, W., Carr, B., Griffin, M., Babin, B., & Carr, J. (2003). Business Research Methods (Vol. 8). Dryden Press.

Zikmund, W., Carr, B., Griffin, M., Babin, B., & Carr, J. (2000). *Business Research Methods* (Vol. 6). Dryden Press Fort Worth.

Zimmermann, H. J. (2001). *Fuzzy set theory-and its applications* (4th ed.). Springer. doi:10.1007/978-94-010-0646-0

Zou, X., & Moon, S. (2014). Hierarchical evaluation of on-site environmental performance to enhance a green construction operation. *Civil Engineering and Environmental Systems*, *31*(1), 5–23. doi:10.1080/10286608.2012.749871

Zulnaidi, Y. (2008). *A Structural Relationship between Total Quality Management, Strategic Control Systems and Performance of Malaysian Local Governments*. (Thesis). Universiti Utara Malaysia. Retrieved from: http://etd.uum.edu.my/53/2/Zulnaidi_Yaacob(PHD_GRADUATE_SCHOOL_GRADUATE_SCHOOL.pdf

Zupan, J. M. (2013). *Upgrading to World Class: The Future of the New York Region's Airports (An Update)*. OECD International Transport Forum, Discussion Paper No. 2013-1.

About the Contributors

Madjid Tavana is Professor and Lindback Distinguished Chair of Business Analytics at La Salle University, where he serves as Chairman of the Business Systems and Analytics Department. He also holds an Honorary Professorship in Business Information Systems at the University of Paderborn in Germany. Dr. Tavana is Distinguished Research Fellow at the Kennedy Space Center, the Johnson Space Center, the Naval Research Laboratory at Stennis Space Center, and the Air Force Research Laboratory. He was recently honored with the prestigious Space Act Award by NASA. He holds an MBA, PMIS, and PhD in Management Information Systems and received his Post-Doctoral Diploma in Strategic Information Systems from the Wharton School at the University of Pennsylvania. He has published 10 books and over 200 research papers in international scholarly academic journals. He is the Editor-in-Chief of Decision Analytics, International Journal of Applied Decision Sciences, International Journal of Management and Decision Making, International Journal of Knowledge Engineering and Data Mining, International Journal of Strategic Decision Sciences, and International Journal of Enterprise Information Systems.

Kathryn A. Szabat is Associate Professor in the Business Systems and Analytics Department at La Salle University. Her instructional responsibilities include teaching of business statistics and management science to undergraduate and MBA students. Her current interests include promoting the inclusion of business analytics in business school curriculums and the development of analytical capabilities of business students. She is actively involved in several academic and professional associations. She received her PhD in Statistics, with cognate field in Operations Research, from the Wharton School of University of Pennsylvania.

Kartikeya Puranam is an Assistant Professor of Business Systems and Analytics at La Salle University's School of Business. He received his M.S. degree in Mechanical Engineering from the Indian Institute of Technology - Bombay and his Ph.D. in Supply Chain Management from Rutgers University. He was awarded the Lindback emerging scholar award for his outstanding research. He has done consulting work with the University of Vermont Medical Center's blood bank that has helped the blood bank streamline their inventory practices. His research interests include bidding strategies in auctions, learning in sequential auctions, inventory management, marketing and operations interface, Markov chains and Markov decision processes and supply chain management. He has published in various journal's including Operations Research Letters and European Journal of Operational Research.

***

About the Contributors

Giner Alor-Hernández is a full-time researcher of the Division of Research and Postgraduate Studies in Orizaba's technological institute: Tecnológico de Orizaba. He received a MSc and a PhD in Computer Science from the Center for Research and Advanced Studies of the National Polytechnic Institute (CINVESTAV), Mexico. He has led 10 Mexican research projects granted by CONACYT, DGEST, and PROMEP. He is author/coauthor of around 130 journal and conference papers on computer science. Also, he has been a committee program member of around 30 international conferences sponsored by IEEE, ACM, and Springer. He also holds the position of editorial board member of eight indexed journals; he has been guest editor of JCR-indexed journals such as Journal of Universal Computer Science, Pervasive and Mobile Computing, Journal of Educational Technology & Society, Science of Computer Programming Journal, International Journal of Software Engineering and Knowledge Engineering, Computational and Mathematical Methods in Medicine, Journal of Medical Systems, Journal of Industrial and Management Optimization. He is the main author of the book entitled Frameworks, Methodologies, and Tools for Developing Rich Internet Applications, published by IGI Global Publishing. His research interests include Web services, e-commerce, Semantic Web, Web 2.0, service-oriented and event-driven architectures, and enterprise application integration. He is an IEEE and ACM Member. He is a National Researcher recognized by the National Council of Science & Technology of Mexico (CONACYT).

Farzana Atique is a Ph.D. candidate at University of Delaware and a Highway Engineer at Mc-Cormick Taylor. She received her M.Sc. in Civil Engineering from University of Delaware (2004) and B.Sc. in Civil Engineering from Bangladesh University of Engineering and Technology (1999). Her research interest is in asset management of infrastructure, data analysis using statistical methods and copula modeling. She has published in the journal *Construction & Building Materials*.

Noor Azlinna Azizan is a Professor of Finance and Director of Entrepreneurship at Universiti Malaysia Pahang. She received her Ph.D. in Finance from University of Liverpool, England, M.Sc. in International Banking and Financial Studies from University of Southampton, England, and BBA in Finance from Western Michigan University, Kalamazoo, USA. Her specialization is in Derivatives Market, Investment Analysis, and Entrepreneurship. She also obtained a Postgraduate Diploma in Entrepreneurship from University of Cambridge, England in 2013. Her research interest includes investment analysis, derivatives market, risk management, and entrepreneurship. She has published in international and national journals including ISI and Scopus Journals.

Younes Boujelbene is a Professor at the University Sfax- Tunisia. He works currently on business, economics, Multi Criteria Decision Making, and data analysis. He is interested particularly on health insurance reform, management resources, parametric method and data envelopment analysis. He has published in journals such as Journal of Transportation Systems Engineering and Information Technology, International Journal of Productivity and Quality Management, Journal of Policy Modeling, among others.

Ryan Burke is an Assistant Professor in the Department of Military & Strategic Studies (MSS) at the United States Air Force Academy. Prior to his appointment at the Academy, Dr. Burke earned his Ph.D. from the University of Delaware where his research emphasized applying process improvement methodologies to complex military operations. Before academia, Dr. Burke was a captain and logistics officer in the U.S. Marine Corps, specializing in transportation logistics operations. Following his military career and before completing his Ph.D., he worked as a Senior Consultant and Logistics Analyst in the Pentagon performing long-range forecast analysis on military transportation and base infrastructure requirements. Dr. Burke has authored or co-authored research in a variety of fields and mediums including military and defense, disaster studies, public policy, and transportation engineering.

Miguel Ángel Canela is Visiting Professor at IESE Business School, University of Navarra. He holds a Ph.D. in mathematics from the Universitat de Barcelona and has been a professor in the Faculty of Mathematics of this university for the last thirty years, as well as a senior consultant and director of the Master in Quality Management at the Institut Català de Tecnologia. After some years devoted to research in mathematical analysis, Prof. Canela's interest was driven towards interdisciplinary research. His research experience covers a wide spectrum of applications, from statistics and mathematical modeling to diverse fields such as biochemistry, botany, nutrition and medicine. His main concern, however, is management science. He is the author of several papers on pure mathematics and has coauthored three books and a number of papers in various other fields.

Dennis Crossen is an instructor in the Business Systems and Analytics Department at La Salle University, where he teaches courses in Operations Management, Project Management, and Quantitative Models (Statistics), Mathematical Methods, Analytics, and Optimization. He also served as LaSalle's faculty advisor for the Business Systems and Analytics (BS&A) Club. Dennis has taught and practiced in industry for over 35 years. He is the former Program Manager at the NASA Kennedy Space Center (KICS contract) and has participated within corporate, governmental, and commercial sectors having diverse levels of responsibilities. During his career, Dennis has developed complex technological solutions for numerous organizations including the United Nations, Department of Defense, Department of Health & Human Services, National Institute of Health, the Pentagon, RCA, Lockheed-Martin, Siemens, Verizon, and others. He has been a Guest on Comcast's' CN8 "Money Matters Today" and "Comcast Newsmakers" television programs speaking on technology issues. Dennis is a 2010 recipient of the Robert Noyce Teacher Scholarship from the National Science Foundation (U.S.) in Education. He holds MSc, MBA, and Electrical Engineering degrees from Drexel University. While in industry, he has completed academic programs at Oxford University (Computing) and Georgetown (International Business), as well as professional development coursework at Harvard (Information Systems), MIT (Computing), and Columbia University (Optics). He is currently completing his doctoral dissertation in Applied Management and Decision Sciences.

Amber A. Ditizio is presently a doctoral student in the Department of Kinesiology from Texas Woman's University in Sports Administration. While acquiring strong analytical and professional skills after completing MS in Sport Management, BSBA and MBA from Robert Morris University, with BS from Kent State University in athletic training and related studies, she also holds various personal certifications in the sports performance and athletic areas. She is the author of several academic articles in the sports performance and athletic fields and plans to pursue an academic teaching/research career upon graduation.

About the Contributors

Abderrahman El Mhamedi is a Professor in the Production and Engineering Department of University Paris8-France. He is the Director of the QUARTZ-MGSI laboratory. His research interests include Multi-State Systems; Markov Graph, Interoperability, Dynamic Manufacturing Network, PLM. He has published in journals such as Journal of Decision Systems, International Journal of Revenue Management, Journal of Intelligent Manufacturing, among others.

Jorge Luis García Alcaraz is a full time researcher of the Department of Industrial Engineering at the Autonomous University of Ciudad Juarez. He received a MSc in Industrial Engineering from the Colima Technology Institute (Mexico), a PhD in Industrial Engineering from Ciudad Juarez Technology Institute (Mexico) and a Postdoc from University of La Rioja (Spain). His main research areas are related to Multicriteria decision making applied to manufacturing, production process modeling and statistical inference. He is founding member of the Mexican Society of Operation Research and active member in the Mexican Academy of Industrial Engineering. Currently, Dr. Garcia is a National Researcher recognized by the National Council of Science & Technology of Mexico (CONACYT) and is working with group research from Colombia, Spain and Dominican Republic. Actually, Dr. Garcia is author/coauthor in around 120 journals, international conferences and congress.

Burçin Güçlü is Assistant Professor of Management in BES La Salle, Universitat Ramon Llull. Previously, she earned BA degrees in Business Administration and Economics from Koç University, and a Master of Research in Management (MRM) and PhD in Management from IESE Business School, University of Navarra. She also held teaching positions in EADA Business School, Toulouse Business School and Universitat Internacional de Catalunya. Regarding her research, she is interested in quantitative methods in marketing, working on the applications of behavioral decision theory to managerial issues in marketing.

Juan L. Hernández-Arellano is full time teacher and researcher of the Design Department at the Autonomous University of Ciudad Juárez, Mexico. Dr. Hernandez´ research topics are industrial ergonomics, product design, structural equation modeling and biomechanics.

Sema Kalaian (Professor of Statistics and Research Methods) in the College of Technology at Eastern Michigan University. Professor Kalaian was a recipient of the (1) "Best Paper" award from the American Educational Research Association (AERA), and (2) "Distinguished Paper Award" from the Society for the Advancement of Information Systems (SAIS). Over the years, Dr. Kalaian taught introductory and advanced statistical courses such as Research Methods, Research Design, Multivariate Statistics, Survey Research, Multilevel Modeling, Structural Equation Modeling, Meta-Analysis, and Program Evaluation. Professor Kalaian's research interests focus on the development of new statistical methods and its applications. Much of her methodological developments and applications have focused on the (a) development of the multivariate meta-analytic techniques for combining evidence from multiple primary studies; (b) applications of the meta-analysis methods to various projects in different fields of study; and (c) developments of statistical methods for analyzing Delphi survey data.

Maryam Kalhori is a graduated student at the Department of Computer Engineering at University of Science and Culture, Tehran, Iran in M.Sc. degree in Software Engineering. She received her Bachelor in Applied Mathematics from Tehran University. Her research interest is information systems and information quality.

Mohammad Javad Kargar is an Assistant Professor at the Department of Computer Engineering at University of Science and Culture, Tehran, Iran. He received his Bachelor in Software Engineering, M.Sc. in Computer Architecture from University of Sciences and Researches, and Ph.D. in Information Technology and Multimedia System from University Putra Malaysia (UPM). He has published several articles in the science –research journals and IEEE and ACM conferences. Dr. Kargar has also been serving on the Editorial Review Board for the International Journal of Advancements in Computing Technology and International Journal of Science and Advanced Technology. His research interest is Web applications and mining, distributed systems and applications.

Kijpokin Kasemsap received his BEng degree in Mechanical Engineering from King Mongkut's University of Technology Thonburi, his MBA degree from Ramkhamhaeng University, and his DBA degree in Human Resource Management from Suan Sunandha Rajabhat University. He is a Special Lecturer at Faculty of Management Sciences, Suan Sunandha Rajabhat University based in Bangkok, Thailand. He is a Member of International Association of Engineers (IAENG), International Association of Engineers and Scientists (IAEST), International Economics Development and Research Center (IEDRC), International Association of Computer Science and Information Technology (IACSIT), International Foundation for Research and Development (IFRD), and International Innovative Scientific and Research Organization (IISRO). He also serves on the International Advisory Committee (IAC) for International Association of Academicians and Researchers (INAAR). He has numerous original research articles in top international journals, conference proceedings, and book chapters on business management, human resource management, and knowledge management published internationally.

Nabeel R. Kasim is a Master's degree candidate at the College of Engineering in the Industrial and Operations Engineering department at the University of Michigan in USA. He holds a Bachelor's of Science degree also in Industrial and Operations Engineering from the University of Michigan in USA. His academic interests are aimed at operations research and engineering management.

Rafa M. Kasim served as a professor of statistics and research design in the College of Education at Kent State University prior to his joining the private sector as a statistician and research consultant and the faculty of Indiana Tech University. Previously he was a senior statistician at the Evaluation, Management & Training Associates Inc. (EMT). His research focused on the application of multilevel analysis to study the effects of educational and social contexts on educational outcomes and human development in large-scale longitudinal data sets. Some of Dr. Kasim work has also addressed the issues of selection and attrition bias in multi-site large studies. He has collaborated on numerous studies in fields such as adult literacy, education, and substance abuse treatments. Some of his work appears in Application of Multilevel Models (book chapter), Journal of Educational and Behavioral Statistics, Harvard Educational Review and Advances in Health Sciences Education.

About the Contributors

Lyes Kermad is an Assistant Professor at the University of Paris 8-France. He works currently on risk management. He is interested particularly on risk management in the implementation of project, risk management in supply chain hospital and human resource management. He has published in journals such as Complex Systems Design & Management, International Journal of Behavioural and Healthcare Research and International Journal of Economics & Strategic Management of Business Process.

Ikram Khatrouch is a PhD in Industrial Engineering science and quantitative methods from the university of Paris8-France and university of sfax-Tunisia. His research interests are in human resource management, hospital logistics and risk management, Operations Research, Multi Criteria Decision Making and artificial intelligence. Ikram Khatrouch has published in journals such as European Journal of Industrial Engineering, International Journal of Behavioural and Healthcare Research, International Journal of Economics & Strategic Management of Business Process and Interdisciplinary Environmental Review.

Manoj Kumar received B.Tech in Production Engineering from Bihar Institute of Technology Sindri, India, M.Tech in Mechanical Engineering from Regional Institute of Technology Jamshedpur, India and Ph.D in Mechanical Engineering from Indian Institute of Technology Delhi, India. He is presently working as Director, Nalanda International Engineering Services, H. No.- 87A, RZI – Block, West Sagarpur, New Delhi – 110046, India. He has authored or coauthored over 55 research papers in Journals and Conferences. His research work appeared in International Journal of Physical Distribution and Logistics Management, International Journal of Production Economics, Computers & Industrial Engineering, International Journal of Integrated Supply Chain Management, and Advances in Industrial Engineering etc.

Aide A. Maldonado-Macías completed her bachelor degree, M. Sc. degree and Ph. D. studies at the Technological Institute of Ciudad Juarez Mexico. She is actually a professor investigator for the Autonomous University of Ciudad Juarez. She is a professional ergonomist and a member of the Mexican Society of Ergonomists and the Mexican Society of Lean Manufacturing. Her main research interests are applied ergonomics, work systems evaluation and design, cognitive ergonomics, work stress related studies, axiomatic design applications, structural equations and optimization of production systems. She has participated in multiple conferences and symposiums. She has published in the International Journal of Advanced Manufacturing Technology, Expert Systems with applications, International Journal of Industrial Engineering, Work: a Journal of Evaluation, prevention and rehabilitation among others. She has recognition of the National Council of Investigation.

Sue McNeil is Professor of Civil and Environmental Engineering and Professor of Urban Affairs and Public Policy at University of Delaware. A native of Australia, she earned her bachelor's degrees at the University of Newcastle in New South Wales and went on to earn master's and doctoral degrees in Civil Engineering at Carnegie-Mellon University. McNeil was formerly the Director of the Urban Transportation Center and Professor in the College of Urban Planning and Public Affairs and the Department of Civil and Materials Engineering at University of Illinois at Chicago; and Professor of Civil & Environmental Engineering and Engineering & Public Policy at Carnegie Mellon University. Her research and teaching interests focus on transportation infrastructure management with emphasis on the application of advanced technologies, economic analysis, analytical methods, and computer applications.

McNeil is founding Editor-in-Chief for the ASCE Journal of Infrastructure Systems. She is a registered professional engineer.

Ezutah Udoncy Olugu is currently working as Senior Lecturer at the Faculty of Engineering, Technology and Built Environment, UCSI University, Malaysia. He obtained his B.Eng in Mechanical and Production Engineering from Nnamdi Azikiwe. University, Nigeria, M.Eng in Advanced Manufacturing Technology and PhD in Industrial and Manufacturing Engineering at the Universiti Teknologi Malaysia. He was involved in teaching, research and consultancy services at the Center for Product Development and Manufacture, University of Malaya, Malaysia. Dr. Olugu's current research interest includes Green Manufacturing, Sustainable Production, Green Supply Chain management, Reverse Logistics, Total Quality Management, Inventory management, Industrial Ergonomics and Maintenance Engineering.

Salwa Hanim Abdul Rashid is a Senior Lecturer in the Department of Mechanical Engineering, Faculty of Engineering, University of Malaya. She obtained her Doctorate Degree in Sustainable Manufacturing Management from Cranfield University, United Kingdom. She also holds both Masters and Bachelor degrees in Manufacturing Management from Loughborough and Salford University, United Kingdom, respectively. She is an active researcher interested in understanding issues in the implementation and management of the green strategies, with respect to design and manufacturing process in order for companies to achieve industrial sustainability. Her current research is focused on factors that drives, inhibits and enables manufacturing companies to implement sustainable design and manufacturing strategies. She has published more than 40 reputable academic journals, articles and conference papers.

Fabrizio L. Ricci is an Electronic Engineer. He is Research Director of the Italian National Research Council (CNR), and currently works at the Institute for System Analysis and Computer Science. He is also member of the LAVSE, Laboratory of Virtual Health Informatics of the CNR. His research activities mainly concern public and private information modeling (i.e. Electronic Healthcare Records Systems, protocols, clinical trials, tacit knowledge, among the others) for clinical, management and epidemiological purposes. He also deals with topics related to knowledge transfer and scientific communication in the fields of electronic health, connected health, and telemedicine.

Cuauhtemoc Sánchez-Ramírez is a full-time researcher of the Division of Research and Postgraduate Studies of the Orizaba Technology Institute. He received a PhD in Industrial Engineering from COMIMSA, center of research of National Council of Science & Technology of Mexico (CONACYT). His research projects have been granted by CONACYT, TNM and PRODEP. Dr. Sanchez is member founding of the Mexican Logistics and Supply Chain Association (AML) and member of the National Researcher System by CONACYT. His research interests are modeling and simulation of logistics process and supply chain from a system dynamics approach. He is author/coauthor around 20 journal and conference papers in logistics and supply chain management.

Tanja Sedej obtained her doctorate in business and economic science from the Faculty of Business and Economics of the University of Maribor in Slovenia. She is the founder and director of Raziskave in raziskave d.o.o., and has over ten years of practical experience in the areas of marketing and communication. She is also the author and co-author of several scientific and expert papers on marketing, corporate communications and entrepreneurship.

About the Contributors

Ehsan Shekarian is currently a PhD candidate at the University of Malaya in Manufacturing Management. He received his BSc in Statistics in 2006 at the University of Allameh Tabataba'i in Tehran, Iran. He holds an MSc in Industrial Engineering from the Alghadir Higher Education Institution, Tabriz, Iran in 2009. His research interests are in the area of supply chain management, inventory systems, fuzzy set theory, multi-criteria decision making and heuristic applications of artificial intelligence methods. He has published various research papers in national and international journals such as Knowledge-Based Systems, European Journal of Industrial Engineering, Journal of Intelligent and Fuzzy Systems, Computers & Industrial Engineering, International Journal of Operational Research, International Journal of Housing Markets and Analysis, International Journal of Fuzzy Systems, and International Journal of Production Research. He is the editorial board member of some journals such as International Journal of Supply Chain and Inventory Management, International Journal of Multivariate Data Analysis.

Jyoti Singh is presently working as Research Analyst, International Engineering Services, H.No.-87A, RZI – Block, West Sagarpur, New Delhi – 110046, India. She has authored or coauthored over 5 research papers in Journals and Conferences. Her research work appeared in Advances in Industrial Engineering, IUP Journal of Mechanical Engineering, etc.

Priya Singh is presently working as Research Analyst, International Engineering Services, H.No.-87A, RZI – Block, West Sagarpur, New Delhi – 110046, India. She has authored or coauthored over 5 research papers in Journals and Conferences. His research work appeared in Advances in Industrial Engineering, IUP Journal of Mechanical Engineering, etc.

Alan D. Smith is presently University Professor of Operations Management in the Department of Marketing at Robert Morris University, Pittsburgh, PA. Previously, he was Chair of the Department of Quantitative and Natural Sciences and Coordinator of Engineering Programs at the same institution, as well as Associate Professor of Business Administration and Director of Coal Mining Administration at Eastern Kentucky University. He holds concurrent PhDs in Engineering Systems/Education from The University of Akron and in Business Administration (OM and MIS) from Kent State University, as well as author of numerous articles and book chapters.

Shahryar Sorooshian is lecturer of Faculty of Industrial management, Universiti Malaysia Pahang. He completed his B.Sc., M.Sc., and Ph.D. in Industrial Engineering. He is a member of the editorial board in some scientific journals and conferences. His research interest includes operational management, engineering management, and business modelling. He has served as the editorial and scientific committee member of some international journals and conferences in the area of engineering and management. He has published books, journals and conference papers.

Carlos Alberto Talamantes Padilla is a Masters student at the Autonomous University of Ciudad Juarez, Mexico. He received his bachelor's degree in industrial engineering from Durango Institute of Technology. Besides studying, Ing. Talamantes enjoys traveling and reading, his favorite author is Alexandre Dumas.

Oscar Tamburis is a Manufacturing Engineer, with a PhD in Health Organization Management and a Post-Doc in eHealth Dynamics. He is a Lecturer of 'Strategies of Healthcare Informatics' at the University of Naples Federico II, Italy. His main research interests concern innovation and strategic management for performance improvement in the public health field, with a particular emphasis on two main topics: the assessment and institutionalisation of emerging technologies in healthcare organisations, and the design and implementation of strategies for promoting knowledge-sharing behaviours among healthcare professionals.

Susanne Trimbath received her Ph.D. in Economics from New York University and holds an MBA in Management from Golden Gate University. Her research focuses on mergers and acquisitions, global economics and capital market regulation. Prior to forming STP Advisory Services in 2004, Dr. Trimbath was Senior Research Economist in Capital Studies at the Milken Institute and Senior Advisor on the Russian Capital Markets Project (USAID-funded) with KPMG/Peat-Marwick. She previously served as a manager in operations at Depository Trust Company in New York and the Pacific Clearing Corporation in San Francisco. Dr. Trimbath authored, edited and contributed chapters to six books, including *Mergers and Efficiency* (2002), and *Methodological Issues in Accounting Research* (2006). Her media credits include appearances in the Emmy® Award-nominated Bloomberg report Phantom Shares and *Radio Wars: The Secret History of Sirius-XM Satellite Radio* (2012), nominated for Best Documentary by the New York City International Film Festival.

Abd Hamid Zahidy is a Professional Engineer and the founder of an engineering consulting firm and a construction company. He is also a member of the Institution of Engineers, Malaysia. He obtained his B.Eng. (Hons) in Civil Engineering from Universiti Teknologi Malaysia, MBA from Universiti Utara Malaysia, and Eng.D. from Universiti Teknologi Malaysia. Currently, he enrolled his second doctoral program at the Faculty of Industrial Management, Universiti Malaysia Pahang. He has more than thirty years experience in the construction industry. His research interest includes construction engineering management, project management, quality management, and performance management. He has published several papers in international journals and conference proceedings.

Index

A

absorbing Markov chains 290-292
alignment 3-4, 82, 87, 89, 296, 305
analysis 1-11, 13-16, 18-23, 25-26, 28-33, 40, 64, 67-68, 70, 81, 83-84, 88, 95, 98-99, 104-105, 116, 123-127, 259, 265, 269, 290-293, 295-298, 300-303, 305, 313-318
Analytic Hierarchy Process (AHP) 4, 16, 120, 127
analytics 1-5, 13, 16, 18, 20, 22-23, 35, 40, 80, 84-85, 87, 96-98, 101, 103, 106
and Competition 233, 235, 242, 252
Automatic Identification and Data Capture Technologies (AIDC) 81, 94, 99, 113
automation 1-7, 10, 12, 103, 114

B

business 1-11, 16-18, 20-24, 29, 35, 40, 82-83, 87, 95-99, 101-102, 104-107, 114-116, 237, 245, 249, 251, 255, 259-261, 263, 269-270
business analytics 4-5, 18, 20, 23, 35, 40
Business Intelligence 1-3, 5, 8, 21
Business Process Management 1, 3-4, 6, 21

C

capabilities 1-2, 5-6, 8-9, 17, 81, 83, 86-87, 89, 95, 106
change management 4, 259-260, 264, 273
competition 2-3, 14-15, 24, 107, 233, 235, 238, 241-242, 244-245, 247, 249, 251-252, 255, 259
consensus 9, 13-14, 20, 63-65, 69-70, 72, 74, 258
criteria 1-4, 7, 10, 15-16, 22, 28, 31, 66, 68, 71-72, 74, 116-118, 120-122, 126
customer 1-3, 7-11, 13, 22, 80-89, 94-100, 102-106, 113-114, 301, 303
Customer Relationship Management (CRM) 82, 86, 94, 96, 114

D

data 1-14, 16-23, 25-31, 33, 35, 64, 66, 68, 70, 80-82, 84, 87-88, 94-95, 97-99, 101, 104, 113, 115-116, 121, 124, 126, 233-236, 244-245, 247, 250-252, 257-258, 264, 269-270, 290-292, 295, 297, 301-302, 305, 309-310, 312-316, 318
data collection 4-5, 8, 12, 19-20, 25-28, 35, 68, 80, 87, 94, 113, 291
data mining 2-3, 5-6, 17, 21, 84, 98, 291
Data Reliability 68, 80
decision making 1-11, 16-18, 20-24, 63, 65, 80, 99, 116, 292, 295
decisions 1-6, 8-11, 14, 19-20, 22-23, 25, 28-29, 31, 35, 68, 82, 87, 89, 95, 101, 116, 127
Delphi 63-74, 80
Delphi study 63-64, 66-74
Direct Performance 7, 20
Distributor 22, 114

E

effective performance 7, 9-10, 20, 290
ELECTRE I 115-117, 119-120, 123-124, 126-127
employees 3-7, 14, 17, 20, 84, 88-89, 97, 99-100, 102, 104-105, 124, 245, 251, 258-264, 270, 273
Employees Ranking 20
enterprise resource planning 2, 4, 21
Entrepreneurship 7, 72, 233-235, 239-240, 242, 247, 251-252, 255
Errors (ei) 10, 16
evaluation 1-9, 11-17, 33-34, 66, 68, 72, 81, 88, 95, 115-116
expert panellists 68
experts 3-5, 15, 27, 63-66, 68-72, 74, 80, 264-267, 270

F

factor analysis 13, 21, 23, 26, 40
Feedback in internal communications 263, 273
field experiment 24, 28
fuzzy set theory 1-3, 5, 15-16, 21

H

human resource management 1

I

ICT 1-3, 5-6, 9, 11, 14-17, 31
improvement 1-7, 12-14, 16, 31, 34, 82, 89, 96-98, 100, 102, 104-106, 126
indicator 4-5, 8, 10, 12-13, 16, 21, 25, 31, 236, 241-242, 244-245, 247, 251
Indirect Performance 11, 13, 20
information overload 1-2, 9, 24, 28
Information Systems 1-7, 17, 20-21, 82, 88
information technology 1-3, 21, 98-99
infrastructure 1-9, 13-14, 16, 21-22, 31, 235, 256
innovation 32, 80-81, 83, 86-87, 89, 95, 100, 106, 233-235, 237-239, 241-242, 244, 251-252, 255
integration 1-4, 6, 10-11, 14-17, 22, 31, 80-83, 85-87, 89, 96, 101-102, 105, 107
internal communication tools 258-270, 273
internal communications 258-265, 269-270, 273
investment 2, 4-9, 13-14, 22, 97, 104, 106, 233, 235-238, 245, 247, 249-250, 252, 256
ISO 15189 1, 3, 9, 15-16, 22

L

latent variable 5-6, 8-9, 11, 13-15, 21-22, 26, 31
Lean management 95-96, 105, 114
logistics 4-5, 13, 95, 104, 114
LuMiR project 1, 25

M

Manufacturer 22, 114
marketing strategy 2, 6, 28-29
Markov 290-295, 297-298, 300-305, 313-315
Mathematical modeling 1, 292
MCDM 2-5, 7, 15-16, 22, 116
medical laboratory 1-3, 9, 11-12, 15, 22
methodology 1-5, 8, 11-13, 18, 20, 23, 31, 34, 68, 83, 116, 305
Metropolitan Statistical Area (MSA) 16

modeling 1-7, 10, 13-14, 16, 18-22, 31, 34-35, 40, 80, 95, 291-292, 300
multiple linear regression 9-13, 16
multiple regression analysis 11

N

network 1-4, 11, 14, 16, 22
New Product Development (NPD) 80-84, 86, 88-89, 95, 100
New Product Manufacturing (NPM) 86, 95
non-systematic methods 2-3, 20

O

office automation 1-2, 6-7
Operating Theatre 124, 127
Operations Efficiency 80, 95
Organisational Change 273
organizational change 258-260, 264-265, 269
organizational performance 1-7, 9-11, 16, 89
overspending 1-5, 8, 11, 14, 22-25, 29

P

path analysis 21, 23
performance 1-17, 20, 22, 72, 81-84, 86-87, 89, 95-96, 101, 107, 114-115, 118, 120-122, 124, 235, 241, 244, 250-251, 255, 259, 263, 290-291, 301, 316
Performance Management 1
Performance Measurement 2, 4, 7, 16, 20, 87, 290
practical flowchart 23, 35
predictive analytics 1-3, 13, 16, 84-85
Predictive Modeling 1
purchasing management 80

Q

qualitative research 19-20, 25-26, 35, 64, 80
quantitative methods 19-21

R

R2 9, 12-13, 16-17, 236, 239-241
regression analysis 1-5, 8-11, 13-14, 16, 18, 21
regression coefficient 4-5, 7-9, 11-12, 16
regression modeling 3
research method 2, 40
Result Validity 80
Retailer 22, 114
RFID-Embedded Technologies 95

Index

Risk behavior 23, 29

S

Selection Teams 115, 127
SEM Application Algorithm 40
simple linear regression 3-4, 7-10, 12-13, 16
Simple regression analysis 3, 11
simulation game 2, 6-7, 11, 14, 22-25, 29
Skills 3-4, 6, 13, 17, 69, 106, 233-239, 243, 247, 251-252, 256, 291
software 3, 5-10, 13-14, 16, 21, 30-31, 33, 82, 97-99, 103, 107, 114
Stratton Warren System (SWS) 103, 114
Structural Equation Modeling (SEM) 1, 9, 13, 233, 252
student retention 290-292, 301
supplier 3, 22, 80, 82-89, 95-96, 101, 106, 114
Supply Chain Integration 1, 3
supply chain management 2-3, 7-9, 86, 95-96, 114
Supply Chain Management (SCM) 86, 95-96
Surgical Team 115, 127
Systematic Methods 4, 20

T

technology 1-6, 8-10, 21, 32, 80-81, 84, 86, 89, 95, 98-99, 102, 238-239, 243, 261, 263, 290, 301
tools 1-3, 5-13, 16-17, 19-25, 27-28, 35, 81, 83, 258-270, 273, 292
transportation 1-10, 13-14, 16, 22, 84, 235, 241, 297
transportation infrastructure 1-3, 5-7, 13-14, 16
Transportation Performance Index 1-3, 6-7, 16
trapezoidal fuzzy number 5-7, 22

V

variable 3-16, 20-23, 25-26, 31, 40, 86, 245, 247, 251, 294, 298, 318
Vendor-Managed Inventory Systems (VMI) 101, 114
VIKOR 1-3, 5, 7-9, 14-16, 22

W

workflow 3, 7-8

Become an IRMA Member

Members of the **Information Resources Management Association (IRMA)** understand the importance of community within their field of study. The Information Resources Management Association is an ideal venue through which professionals, students, and academicians can convene and share the latest industry innovations and scholarly research that is changing the field of information science and technology. Become a member today and enjoy the benefits of membership as well as the opportunity to collaborate and network with fellow experts in the field.

IRMA Membership Benefits:

- **One FREE Journal Subscription**
- **30% Off Additional Journal Subscriptions**
- **20% Off Book Purchases**
- Updates on the latest events and research on Information Resources Management through the IRMA-L listserv.
- Updates on new open access and downloadable content added to Research IRM.
- A copy of the Information Technology Management Newsletter twice a year.
- A certificate of membership.

IRMA Membership $195

Scan code to visit irma-international.org and begin by selecting your free journal subscription.

Membership is good for one full year.

www.irma-international.org